LEEDS
UNITED A.F.C

THE ONLY PLACE FOR US

Pitch Publishing Ltd
A2 Yeoman Gate
Yeoman Way
Durrington
BN13 3QZ

Email: info@pitchpublishing.co.uk
Web: www.pitchpublishing.co.uk

First published by Pitch Publishing 2015
Text © 2020 Jon Howe

2

A CIP catalogue record for this book is available from the British Library.

13-digit ISBN: 9781785310089
Design and typesetting by Olner Pro Sport Media.
Printed and bound in India by Replika Press Pvt. Ltd.

THE ONLY PLACE FOR US

AN A-Z HISTORY OF

ELLAND ROAD

HOME OF LEEDS UNITED

JON HOWE

FOREWORD BY DAVID BATTY

On 21st November 1987, Elland Road was the whole world to me, just as it was for the 15,457 loyal supporters in the crowd to see Leeds United take on Swindon Town.

The difference for me was that, finally, I had taken the step from standing among the fans, craning to see with the help of a crate on the Lowfields terrace, to standing among the players, on the famous old pitch that has been graced by so many great players before and since.

Just over two years earlier I had started my apprenticeship at Elland Road, so I already knew the place well. You see it differently when you work there every day, as we did when the training pitches were on the old Fullerton Park behind the West Stand.

We came to know as much about the area around Elland Road as about the stadium itself. On my second day as a 16-year-old lad at Leeds, standing five feet four and weighing eight stone, I was sent with the other apprentices on the first of many long runs through the streets around the ground. Some of the runs were much shorter: the first job of the morning for us young players was to sprint across the road to get bacon-and-egg and sausage sandwiches for the seniors. Young footballers might not do that sort of thing today, but to me it was an honour to bring a great player like John Sheridan his breakfast!

Another honour bestowed on me was to be 'gofer' for the manager who influenced me so much, Billy Bremner. Every afternoon he'd find me and shout, "Batty, go and get me 20 cigs." Fetching those cigarettes for Billy was a privilege, as it was for me and the other starry eyed apprentices to find ourselves playing football with the gaffer, Billy Bremner himself in his suit and patent leather shoes, when he'd finish up his work for the day and join us for a game.

By the time I was established in the first team Howard Wilkinson was manager, and my knowledge of the stadium layout was an advantage when my dad negotiated my new contract with Howard and the money man at the time, Bill Fotherby. Unknown to Howard and Bill, we'd found out from Vinnie Jones what he was earning; and unknown to my dad, I took advantage of building work in the offices to sneak inside a temporary partition wall next to Fotherby's office so I could listen in. My dad was magnificent in there, staying cool under pressure as he sorted my first major deal;

and Vinnie's reaction was magnificent too, when he found out I was going to be making more than him!

When I left for Blackburn in 1993, I didn't think I'd ever be back. But that feeling of being Leeds never left me while I was away. As a player who had come through the ranks, and a local lad into the bargain, Leeds fans really took me to their hearts and I can't deny that I revelled in it. Fans are never afraid to let players know their feelings after a bad piece of play, but while the supporters always focused on me, it was always to give encouragement.

In the weeks before I re-signed from Newcastle our team coach would often pass Elland Road on the motorway, and there would be a chorus from the lads at the back of the bus: "You'll soon be back there, Batts." Although injuries meant my return didn't start as planned, my comeback from the bench against Sunderland in December 2000 was just as memorable as my debut in 1987. I was given an incredible reception by the sell-out 40,000 crowd, and the thrill of that will live with me forever.

I'm fortunate to have many great memories of the years I spent at Elland Road. Reading Jon's book is a great way to relive them, whether you know Elland Road as a player, as a fan, or like me, as both.

David Batty

FOREWORD

THE RHUBARB FIELDS OF ISLINGTON

Elland Road is in the bones, like it or not. It seeps through the senses. The sights, the noise, the taste and the distaste, all magnified. The wonderment of growing up when everything is a thrill, a life yet to be embittered, the adventure of youth, the smell of adulthood: beer, fags, obscene bodily odours, cigars, working men, disgruntled, shouting, violent men. The sizzle of the burger vans outside and the stench of fat and fried onions, sidestepping the horse manure on Lowfields Road as mounted police control the baying crowds. The awe-inspiring floodlights like pathways to the stars, the stunning patch of endless green and the looming sense of theatre that draws us in, language and noise you've never heard and is only heard here, heart-in-mouth suspense you might never experience again. The godforsaken, the unholy, but the wouldn't-change-it-for-the-world.

With time comes attachment beyond all rationality. There is sadness at the demise of a series of derelict haulage buildings which anywhere else would be a Thatcherite blemish on the landscape. We mourn the dismantling of a set of four wounded towers, simple and functional yet illuminating more than can merely be measured, and the electronic scoreboard that glowed on a sodden and cheerless February afternoon. A concrete underpass takes on Elysian significance as it conveys us onwards. Or you can stand at the top of Beeston Hill, feeling supreme powers as you look down on your own heaven, unquestionably taller than you were.

There is both a history and a mystery to Elland Road; the only constant throughout Leeds United's existence, once residing in the unfolded, featureless pastures of Beeston, Leeds, but now in a geographical bubble all of its own. Once a football ground, now a stadium; shiny blue plastic and sinuous aesthetics might have replaced

the mud, the cold concrete, the crumbling brickwork, the grass banks, the pre-fab misconstruction, the wire fences and the scattered crash barriers, but it is shrouded in, marked by, and reeking of the traditional still.

The literary world of books, magazines, websites, chat forums, football programmes and newspapers is awash with photographs, stories and potted histories of Elland Road. Some purely cover the basics, some tell part of the story and miss the key details but none do it justice. Never, to the best of my knowledge, has the full yarn been put together in one place. Leeds United histories are numerous, and nobody need try too hard to have all the details of the players, games, managers and personalities at their fingertips. Detailing the history of Elland Road, therefore, is the final piece in the jigsaw: full circle. Bringing the unknowns, the forgotten and the miscellaneous together to complete the picture of a tangled history almost as ragged and traumatic, and as resilient and restorative as the football club and its banished predecessor that it has hosted since 1904.

Had football never taken root in LS11 we may still refer to the area as the 'rhubarb fields of Islington', for no more convoluted reason than that's exactly what they were. Rhubarb might remain attainable today, but the borough of Islington is gone forever, replaced by a bounteous tapestry of widespread resolution, sullied success, endeavour, mismanagement, criminality, malaise, natural disaster, vision, fortitude, ineptitude and rank misfortune.

But the mystery remains, and not just in why so many development plans for the stadium and surrounding area have come to nought. Mystique and charm is also in the solitary facets that combine to give Elland Road standout characteristics, shared by no other. Throughout its 117-year history as a football venue only

seven head groundsmen have been employed to tend to the pitch, and only four building companies have been responsible for the complete mutation from a barren field surrounded by unaccommodating mud banks to a celebrated all-seater stadium witness to the highest sporting drama on an international stage.

In attempting to document the drama, quirks, endurance and stock occurrences that have combined to build the history of this theatre of endless intrigue, I have utilised my own memories and experiences but also those from many literary sources and an assortment of people I have spoken to: fans, ex-managers, ex-directors, associates, staff and local residents. Clearly, with over 100 years of history to chronicle, it is impossible to cover everything and doubtless there are details missing where living memory and documented evidence offer little help. I am told, for example, that the Harlem Globetrotters American basketball team played an exhibition game on the Elland Road turf in June 1959, but can find no evidence of this actually taking place. Other such oddities, of which there are many, can be substantiated. Similarly I have had to make calculated assumptions where clarity and specific confirmation are vague or non-existent. Furthermore, when listening to stories and anecdotes it is lamentable that at some point you have to stop because every Leeds fan everywhere has their own. Elland Road memories are a very personal thing; some are shared by the thousands that were there, some are unique and solitary, but all are worthy. They all combine to tell a compelling story, and each one here will trigger a thousand more, but time alone dictates that at some point a snapshot has to be taken; and here it is.

To paint a picture that does justice to this stage of brutally fluctuating fortunes you need to look far beyond what is visible, or even used to be visible. At times I have diverted to nearby stadia of other sporting pursuits or extra-curricular activities. I have also dallied in seemingly tenuous aspects of the match day ritual that matter to Leeds fans, or if they don't this explains why they should, things we walk past every week and take for granted, and I make no apology for it, because the Elland Road experience is not just about Elland Road, everybody has their own journey. I have documented the good times, the bad times and the ugly times. I talk about hooliganism and racism not to glamorise, but because they are inescapable components of a chequered past. It would be wrong to ignore them, and they are part of what makes Elland Road what it is: esoteric in its beauty, dripping in magnetism warts and all and always, always there.

In essence I have tried to cover the full spectrum, and to anyone or anything I have missed, I acknowledge it here. So doffing the cap to the persistence of standing in the rain on the old Gelderd End, to the pre-match buzz of the pubs and pie queues, to the impatient wait for the Football Specials, to the incoherent din of the underpass, to the surging masses on Lowfields Road and especially to the winning goals when we are seeing stars; this is the story of the only eternal refuge in Leeds United's history, the only place we return to on our never-ending travels; the only place for us.

Jon Howe

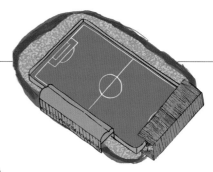

(1904–05)

1800s	The area surrounding Elland Road is used for coal and clay mining and extensive rhubarb cultivation. The land upon which Elland Road is later built is used as a pumping station for several nearby pits.
1826	The Old Peacock pub opens, originally called the 'Peacock Inn'.
1830	A turnpike road opened in 1785 is formally named as 'Elland Road'.
1842	The New Peacock pub opens.
1878	A patch of land is bought by Bentley's Brewery and made into a sports ground. It is also adopted as home by Leeds Athletic Rugby Football Club, who later become Yorkshire Wanderers. Although they leave to use Royal Park Ground, they return to what is now known as the Old Peacock Ground until 1882.
1883	The Old Peacock Ground is run by Bentley's Brewery as a company sports ground.
1897	Holbeck Rugby Club move from the nearby Recreation Ground onto the Old Peacock Ground. They build a small terraced stand along Elland Road and later erect a temporary wooden stand along the north touchline.

The first game of association football takes place on the extended ground when Hunslet (technically the forerunners of Leeds City) beat Harrogate 1-0 in the West Yorkshire Cup Final.

1901	Holbeck Cricket Club, who shared the Recreation Ground with the rugby club, move to the cricket ground on Lowfields Road, opposite the football ground.
1902	Amateur football club Leeds Woodville become tenants of Holbeck Rugby Club and share what has by now become known as 'Elland Road' for the 1902/03 season.
1904	Holbeck Rugby Club resign from the Northern Union and fold. Leeds Woodville, as tenants of the rugby club, also leave Elland Road.

Leeds City Football Club is formed from the remnants of Hunslet AFC.

Leeds City buy Elland Road from Holbeck Rugby Club for £4,500.

1905	With Leeds City successfully elected to the Football League, a 'grandstand' is built on Elland Road at a cost of £1,050 to accommodate dressing rooms, press and 4,000 seated spectators. They also demolish the temporary wooden stand on the north side.

The pitch runs from east to west and the remainder of the ground is just small, banked terraces. Capacity is estimated at 22,000.

(1906–1920)

1906	Leeds City buy land on the west side of the ground from Monk's Bridge Iron Company and build a 4,000-seater West Stand with a barrelled roof.

The pitch is moved 90 degrees in orientation and the terraced banking on the north and east sides is built up. Capacity is estimated at 45,000.

1912	Leeds City go into receivership, and the Leeds Cricket & Athletic Club offer to move the club to Headingley, but City survive.
1914	A syndicate of Leeds sportsmen offer to run the financially beleaguered City, and guarantee to put down £1,000 and pay £250 annually to keep City at Elland Road. The offer was accepted by receiver Tom Coombes.
1914	During World War I, Elland Road is used for army drilling and shooting practice. Regional leagues and friendlies replace the Football League games during the war, in which 'guest' players are used.
1919	After being tipped off by a disgruntled ex-player the Football League expel Leeds City for paying guest players during the war. It is thought many other clubs did exactly the same thing, but only Leeds' dealings were uncovered.

All of Leeds City's assets are sold at auction.

Yorkshire Amateur FC briefly take on the Elland Road tenancy from the receiver and play a series of friendlies.

Plans are formulated to turn the ground into a brickyard to make use of the rich clay deposits beneath the surface.

Leeds United FC are formed and after a dispute with Hilton Crowther, chairman of Huddersfield Town, in which he attempted to merge the two clubs, Crowther becomes Leeds United's first chairman and purchases Elland Road for Leeds United.

1920	Leeds United are elected to the Football League.

Stadium development graphics by Joe Gamble

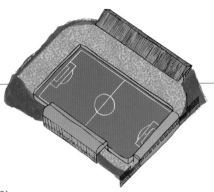

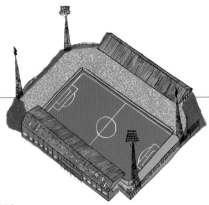

■ (1921–1956)

1920s The grandstand built by Leeds City in 1905 is demolished and replaced with a small terrace with a barrelled roof, which becomes known as the Scratching Shed.

The north terrace and east/popular terrace are each built up in size over a number of years, and become around three times their original size with both remaining un-roofed. Capacity is estimated at around 50,000.

1923 The opening of the thoroughfare known as Lowfields Road in 1923 links Elland Road with Gelderd Road and also means the pitch orientation has to be settled permanently as north to south.

1927 Elland Road Greyhound Stadium opens.

Fullerton Park Speedway Stadium opens, initially as a rival greyhound track, before concentrating solely on speedway from 1928.

1928 The Lowfields Road terrace is roofed in three stages, partly financed by the Leeds United Supporters' Club.

1930s Elland Road hosts three FA Cup Semi-Finals. Crowds range between 43,000 and 49,000.

1938 The Rugby League Championship Final between Hunslet and Leeds RL is staged at Elland Road. Becoming known as the 'All Leeds Final' the game attracts a record rugby league crowd of 54,112.

Fullerton Park Speedway Stadium closes.

1941 Foreign Secretary Anthony Eden visits Elland Road to make a public address to 10,000 people during World War II.

1950 Huddersfield Town play two 'home' games at Elland Road following a fire at their Leeds Road ground.

1951 Leeds United purchase the derelict land on Fullerton Park and create two training pitches.

1953 Floodlights are erected and used for the first time for a friendly against Hibernian.

1956 Following promotion to the First Division, seats are put under the roofed section of the Lowfields Road terrace, funded by the Leeds United Supporters' Club.

A fire destroys the 1906-built West Stand. The team temporarily uses dressing rooms on nearby Whitehall Printeries Sports Ground for first team matches.

■ (1957–1967)

1957 A new West Stand is built at a cost of £180,000, partly funded by the sale of John Charles to Juventus for a world record £65,000 fee, and a public appeal. The stand can accommodate 4,000 seats and 6,000 standing, and has modern facilities and a regal façade.

1962 Holbeck Cricket Club is wound up, but the ground remains until 1974, becoming local league football pitches.

1967 Elland Road holds its record attendance, officially recorded as 57,892, for an FA Cup Fifth Round Replay against Sunderland. In the ensuing chaos, the game is stopped for 17 minutes as 32 injured fans are taken to hospital.

The northern section of the West Stand paddock (from the Kop to the tunnel) is seated.

ELLAND ROAD TIMELINE
EARLY 1800s TO PRESENT DAY

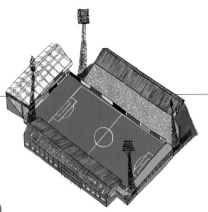

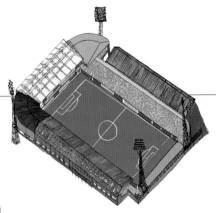

(1968–1969)

1968 On-field success under Don Revie allows the club to commence a masterplan to completely redevelop Elland Road. The first development is to excavate tonnes of earth in demolishing the open Spion Kop, and build a new propped cantilever stand behind it at a cost of £250,000: the new 17,000-capacity Kop.

An area spanning 18 metres is created behind the Kop-end goal and in front of the new stand.

Huge gaps are left in the north east and north west corners, where temporary floodlights are erected.

(1970–1973)

1970 The north end of the Lowfields Road terracing is chopped away, almost up to the roofed section, in readiness for building the North East Corner Stand. This also creates the first grass bank.

The North West Corner Stand is opened in February 1970, holding 1,779 seats with terracing below, at a cost of £200,000.

To link the West Stand to the North West Corner Stand, an extended straight section is built onto the West Stand at the same time.

The pitch is moved nine metres northwards at the end of the 1969/70 season.

1971 Work starts on the North East Corner Stand, with terracing built into the corner linking the Lowfields and the Kop.

Both the temporary floodlights at the north end are now located outside the ground.

A wall is built along the back of this new terrace section which extends all the way along the rear of the Lowfields Road terrace section. Part of this, along the seated section of the Lowfields Road Stand, creates what becomes known as the 'shelf'.

Undersoil heating is installed beneath the pitch for the first time.

1972 The Sports & Souvenir Shop on Elland Road opens.

1973 The upper seated section of the North East Corner is completed.

The pitch is moved a further nine metres towards the Kop at the end of the 1972/73 season, now leaving a gap of 18 metres behind the goal at the Scratching Shed end.

Three new floodlights are installed. The fourth, in the south east corner, is not installed as the area awaits development.

Stadium development graphics by Joe Gamble

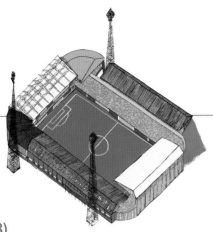

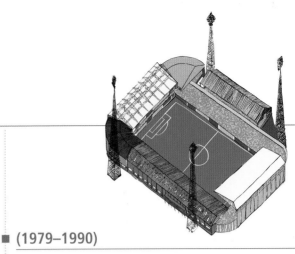

■ (1974–1978)

1974 After approximately 50 years, the Scratching Shed is demolished and the South Stand is built on Elland Road, a propped cantilever stand holding 4,500 standing and 3,000 seated above. The stand costs £500,000 to build.

The southern section of the West Stand paddock is seated.

1975 The section of the M621 which passes Elland Road is opened. This and the network of new roads which feed off it necessitate the closing of Petty's Field Sports Ground, Holbeck Cricket Ground and the New Peacock pub, not to mention the demolishing of several hundred local houses. Lowfields Road is bisected into two parts and the underpass which takes fans beneath the M621 is created.

1977 The Queen visits Elland Road as part of her Silver Jubilee celebrations. 40,000 people attend.

Seats are installed in the lower section of the South Stand.

1978 At the end of the 1977/78 season the south end of the Lowfields Road upper section is demolished and foundations are put in to construct the South East Corner Stand. This preparation alone costs £1 million.

It is decided to install the fourth floodlight pylon in the south east corner, mainly for aesthetic reasons as the lights are so bright that, technically, the fourth one isn't needed.

The Leeds United board decide not to go ahead with the South East Corner Stand and East Stand development due to financial constraints.

Following various outbreaks of crowd trouble fences are erected in front of the Kop and surround all four sides of the ground by the end of the decade.

■ (1979–1990)

1979 An electronic scoreboard is installed underneath the Kop roof.

1982 Elland Road Greyhound Stadium closes.

Hunslet RL take up a lease to play home games at Elland Road.

Queen play a concert on the Elland Road pitch.

1983 16 executive boxes are installed in the South Stand in readiness for the 1983/84 season.

1985 Elland Road and the Fullerton Park training pitches are sold to Leeds City Council for £2.5 million.

Bradford City play four 'home' games at Elland Road during the 1985/86 season after a fire at their Valley Parade ground.

1986 Leeds Cougars American Football team play a number of games at Elland Road.

1987 U2 play a concert on the Elland Road pitch.

Seven more executive boxes are installed in the South Stand, but these only utilise half of a second row of boxes, leaving an irregular feature of the ground.

Seats are taken out of the South Stand lower section again, and it reverts to terracing for three seasons.

1989 Following the Hillsborough Disaster, dramatic terracing restrictions are enforced and the overall Elland Road capacity is cut to just under 33,000.

1990 Following promotion back to the First Division, the remaining nine executive boxes are installed in the South Stand.

Seats are put back into the South Stand and it is renamed the Family Stand.

A new two-tier ticket office is built at the south end of the West Stand car park.

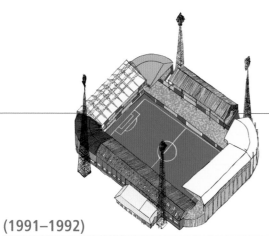

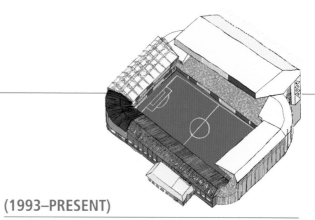

■ (1991–1992)

1991 The Happy Mondays play a concert on the Elland Road pitch.

Finally, the South East Corner Stand is constructed.

A £150,000 police control box is built in the North West Corner Stand.

1992 The Banqueting Suite is built on the back of the West Stand. This results in the loss of the famous façade, and also changes the layout of the reception and office areas and the upstairs boardroom and function rooms.

Within days of Leeds being crowned the last Football League Division One champions, the Lowfields Road Stand is demolished after nearly 70 years. The lower terraced section remains whilst the East Stand is built above it.

The two diamond floodlights on the eastern side of the ground are removed whilst the East Stand is constructed. Temporary lights are installed behind builders' hoardings at the back of the Lowfields terracing.

■ (1993–PRESENT)

1993 In February a section of the lower tier of the new East Stand is opened to away fans for some fixtures.

At the end of the 1992/93 season the two remaining western floodlights are removed, leaving all floodlighting roof-mounted.

The £5.5 million, 17,000-capacity East Stand is fully opened for the West Ham fixture in August.

1994 At a cost of £1.1 million, 7,000 seats are installed in the Kop making Elland Road an all-seater stadium for the first time.

A big screen scoreboard is erected in the south west corner.

1995 The Kop's electronic scoreboard is removed.

England draw 3-3 with Sweden in a friendly held at Elland Road before 32,008 fans.

1996 Leeds United move into the Thorp Arch training complex near Wetherby, leaving the Fullerton Park training pitches to be turned into council-owned car parks.

Leeds United Supporters' Club are moved out of their headquarters and social club on Elland Road.

The dressing room area and dugouts are completely re-designed and refurbished in readiness for Euro 96.

Elland Road hosts three group games in Euro 96.

The megastore in the south east corner is built.

1997 Leeds United, now owned by the Caspian Group, buy back Elland Road from Leeds City Council for £11.3 million. They immediately announce plans for an arena and sporting complex.

1999 Two years after his death, the Billy Bremner statue is officially revealed in the south east corner outside the megastore.

2004 Elland Road is sold to Manchester businessman Jacob Adler for £8.5 million. It is later sold on to a company known as Teak Trading Limited.

2017 Weeks after taking 100% controlling interest in the club, Andrea Radrizzani buys back Elland Road from the company now known as Teak Commercial Limited in the British Virgin Islands through Greenfield Investment Pte Ltd, the Aser Group Holding company and parent company of Leeds United Football Club.

2019 Leeds United celebrates its centenary year still at Elland Road and unveils a revamped Centenary Square in celebration.

Stadium development graphics by Joe Gamble

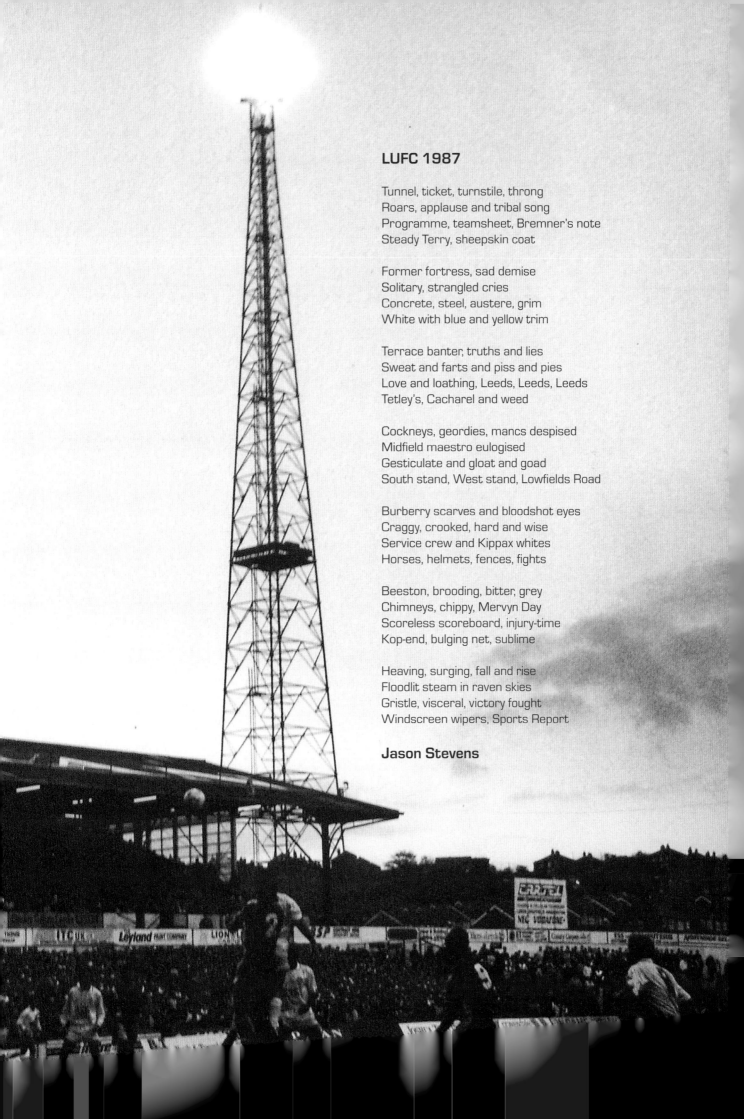

LUFC 1987

Tunnel, ticket, turnstile, throng
Roars, applause and tribal song
Programme, teamsheet, Bremner's note
Steady Terry, sheepskin coat

Former fortress, sad demise
Solitary, strangled cries
Concrete, steel, austere, grim
White with blue and yellow trim

Terrace banter, truths and lies
Sweat and farts and piss and pies
Love and loathing, Leeds, Leeds, Leeds
Tetley's, Cacharel and weed

Cockneys, geordies, mancs despised
Midfield maestro eulogised
Gesticulate and gloat and goad
South stand, West stand, Lowfields Road

Burberry scarves and bloodshot eyes
Craggy, crooked, hard and wise
Service crew and Kippax whites
Horses, helmets, fences, fights

Beeston, brooding, bitter, grey
Chimneys, chippy, Mervyn Day
Scoreless scoreboard, injury-time
Kop-end, bulging net, sublime

Heaving, surging, fall and rise
Floodlit steam in raven skies
Gristle, visceral, victory fought
Windscreen wipers, Sports Report

Jason Stevens

A

ABNORMAL PROMOTION

Leeds United wore the Championship like a ball and chain; a crippling encumbrance. Promotion back to the Premier League had become an exhausting and all-consuming problem; not so much a monkey on the back but an entire tribe of African elephants. Or something like that. Elland Road had echoed to the strained anguish of entire seasons merging into one indistinguishable fat-ball of mediocrity. The Leeds United shirt weighed heavy, the name energised the opposition like the circus coming to town, and pressing reset on ambitions and expectation became an annual ritual around February time, sometimes earlier.

No-one of sound mind or rational judgement could have foreseen the chain of events that took Leeds United to promotion in 2020, but when you've tried every conventional route available, it sometimes takes extraordinary things to make extraordinary things happen. At the end of the 2017/18 season, when Leeds United had finished their sixth campaign out of the last seven with a negative goal difference and were marooned and lonely in mid-table like a stranded fisherman's boat in a deserted harbour, it is difficult to assess what would have been the more unlikely scenario for any Leeds fan predicting what would unfold from this point: one of the greatest coaches in world football will become your manager, or you will get promoted, but a global pandemic will paralyse the entire world and amongst many other things, will rid you of the opportunity to see it.

It is true that if you think about something for too long it can become a fixation, but also it can become abnormal, exaggerated and almost something that is too huge to accurately contemplate any more. That had become the case with promotion to the Premier League for Leeds United; a step change in status that had become more than an obsession. Most Leeds fans had run through in their minds how they would one day celebrate it, but it was a fantasy that was so divine and other-worldly that no one could imagine how it would really feel. And so it is perhaps no surprise that Leeds United fans didn't ever get the chance to experience how it really feels.

Marcelo Bielsa made an immediate impact on Leeds United like a wrecking ball to the terminally mediocre, and the 2018/19 season continued apace with all the hallmarks of ending in promotion, until the very shuddering moment, or moments, when it didn't. So if that wasn't a promotion season, we didn't know what the hell one looked like. Except that another one came along straight away that was almost identical.

In the early months of 2020 news of a deadly respiratory virus originating from China and now sweeping the world became too credible and enduring to ignore. It was coming closer to home in every sense. Leeds United meanwhile were racking up five consecutive wins with five consecutive clean sheets and showing convincing signs of actually finishing the job. Before a crowd of 36,514, Leeds steamrollered

Leeds United's Jack Harrison acknowledges the 'crowdies' in the empty stands of Elland Road after putting Leeds 3-0 up in the crucial defeat of Fulham in June 2020.

The Leeds United squad celebrate promotion and the league title on the Elland Road pitch after the 4-0 win over Charlton Athletic with the legend 'Vamos Leeds Carajo' depicted in the empty seats above.

over local rivals Huddersfield Town, and Elland Road was in raptures. Fans swapped jocular gestures mocking pre-match advice to avoid hugging and high-fiving whilst celebrating goals, for fear of transmitting the virus.

But life came around fast and a week later the laughter had stopped. Elland Road was silent. And shut down. Football and the world was on hold. Social media banter about the footballing gods incredulously denying Leeds the promotion they craved through a global pandemic, was a stark reality.

"When everything got cancelled because of Covid," Kaiser Chiefs bassist and lifelong Leeds fan Simon Rix explains, "obviously it was awful on many levels, but on a football level, at first I actually enjoyed the break. There's constantly been something going on at Leeds, good or bad, for 20 years. And especially in the last couple of years the pressure has been massive. When the break happened we were top, we might get promoted without playing again, and if the season continued then actually maybe the break was good for our lads to recharge their batteries? I was pretty confident we were going up."

Of course, somehow, after months of agonising uncertainty, football started again, but in a surreal atmosphere of social distancing, thrice-weekly COVID

testing, bio-secure match day bubbles and empty stadiums. The haunting prospect of the season being voided completely was quickly dismissed, and by the end of June Leeds United were playing out their final nine games behind closed doors and the stands at Elland Road were filled only with crowdies – cardboard cut-outs of fan likenesses of which Leeds sold a record 22,000 – and officials sterilising the ball when it went out of play. In the meantime, football had lost Norman Hunter, Trevor Cherry and Jack Charlton; all of whom sadly passed during lockdown and the period dubbed as 'project re-start'. Undoubtedly this focused minds and ensured Leeds got the job done; Norman's chilling and enduring words that he would love to see Leeds United back in the Premier League in his lifetime, were all the spur anyone needed.

"Once football finally started," Simon continues, "I found it pretty difficult. Sitting on my own in my house on WhatsApp or Face-time with friends and family really didn't cut it. I don't think the result of the first game helped much to be honest (a 2-0 defeat away at Cardiff City) but I needed to be with some people."

The mind-blowing heft of how Elland Road would have looked and sounded in those final five home games is something the world was robbed of. Theatre, drama, spectacle and art, all wrapped up in one convenient package. Alas, it still feels too huge to even comprehend. We did our best. We watched on TV and celebrated in a socially distant manner with friends where we could. On the Friday evening that promotion was achieved via a Huddersfield Town win over West Bromwich Albion, of all things, fans were helplessly and magnetically drawn to Elland Road with an impulse it was hard to resist. Joyous scenes ensued over the next week, as legitimate reasons to open the champagne arrived in an unrelenting convoy like buses. But it wasn't the same. Or was it? We'll never know, because we still can't compare it to anything. We still don't know, and while maybe it was easier to watch on TV knowing the players felt less pressure in an empty stadium, we would much rather have had the chance to find out, and to live it. Leeds United fans were robbed of their moment, and so too were the players.

"I ended up going to the pub for a few of the games," adds Simon, "and had a small party in my garden for the Derby game. It was something that I needed to share with other people, particularly the ones I've sat with through the 16 years of the EFL. I do feel disappointed that we didn't get that moment of joy inside Elland Road. I think we had all dreamt of that moment for years and it definitely involved mass celebrations, a bus parade around the city, being on the pitch at Elland Road, rather than watching players celebrate through a fence or lifting the trophy to an empty stadium. Equally I'm just so glad it happened and because of the way it happened it meant the celebrations lasted a week; every day brought another dose of happiness. A socially distant version of happiness, but it was great and something that we'll (hopefully) never experience again."

Street artist and Leeds fan Andy McVeigh felt much the same: "Promotion was bittersweet; incredible and emotional, but something was missing. I tried to put it out of my head what the celebrations would have been like in the stadium, in the city centre, etc. It was too painful to think about. I wanted it for the players too. They deserved the full glory. I was genuinely proud of them. But I just kept thinking about the NHS staff, the people who lost their lives, etc. It sounds cheesy but it gave you perspective and you just accepted it for what it was."

A very different perspective was that of Adam Pope, BBC Radio Leeds commentator, not only because he was actually there, but because he is used to having to make himself heard above the incessant din of the Elland Road crowd:

"A soulless mausoleum I'm afraid," Adam solemnly responds when I ask him to describe the 'behind-closed-doors' Elland Road 'experience.' "When commentating you ride the crowd's emotion and it helps you to perform. I also feel that if we had been all together it would have helped everyone grieve for the loss of loved ones and club legends who had passed. It will always be a deep regret that we can never share that huge communal moment of joy when Liam Cooper lifted the Championship trophy to announce United's return to the top flight. I felt it was vital that we were always mindful that our coverage reflected we were privileged to be there when thousands could not. It was important to me that I captured a very emotional and poignant event for all those listening as vividly as I could. Seeing silverware glint in the Beeston sky was special."

Oh man. Somehow Adam's words exacerbate the sense of loss, and I'm writing this several months after the event. And while promotion was still certainly vindication for the Leeds fans, despite the unusual circumstances, it also felt very satisfying after quite a journey for 'Popey' too: "There was a certain vindication for following the club through its worst period. The nadir was administration and relegation to League One. So to have commentated upon a historic success watching the purest of football feels like redemption of sorts. I think I will always be grateful to be able to say I saw first-hand a side managed and coached by a genius in Marcelo Bielsa. Plus, I've always said I would appreciate every moment of even just one campaign with Leeds in the Premier League."

Former *Yorkshire Evening Post* chief Leeds United writer, now writing for *The Athletic*, Phil Hay insists he was just a neutral observer, but his words can't hide a sense of personal satisfaction at Leeds being promoted, in large part for the arduous voyage he has shared with many Leeds fans over the years. "The feeling when it happened was fabulous," Phil admits. "I was so pleased for Bielsa and the players because the work behind promotion was exceptional, but I'm probably more happy for the people I've seen year after year away at Histon, Gillingham, Sutton, Newport. Sometimes I wondered how and why they stuck with it. This is why."

And the regret at this happening in front of an empty stadium still hangs heavy: "Were it not for Covid, we'd be talking about guaranteed sell-outs. When I think of the bad times, I think of 16,000 turning up for Leeds v Wolves in 2006. It's been a long slog. But an empty Elland Road is incomparable to a full Elland Road. It was my one big regret about promotion – that it came at a time when there were no supporters inside the ground. It should have been their moment and I know the players felt that too."

Leeds fan and writer Andy Peterson is one of those that has seen it all, and his thoughts upon missing out on witnessing promotion in the flesh were as much for those who had lived through the bad times and hadn't seen the resurgence under Marcelo Bielsa at all, as they were for himself. Promotion was a form of absolution, and a cleansing experience after what had come before, and whilst Elland Road might have been empty, there was still a presence and we were still

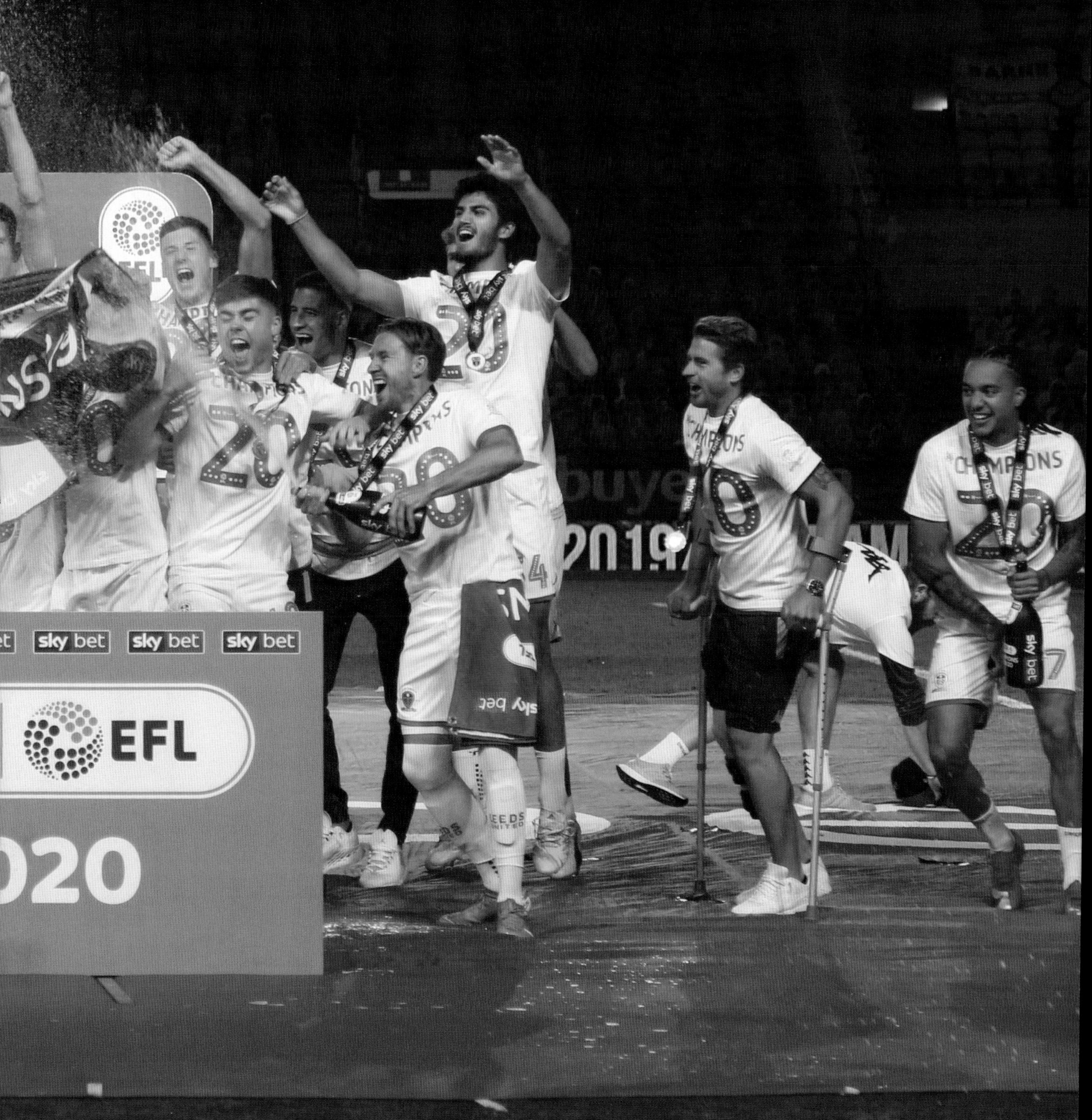
sky bet
sky bet
sky bet
EFL

represented. "If the old ground's walls could've talked that fateful night," Andy begins when asked to describe his feelings when Liam Cooper lifted the Championship trophy after the 4-0 demolition of Charlton Athletic, "they'd have said a lot about the bitter words and recriminations spat out like daggers which had hit them, the peeling Dulux stripped off in anger or the profanity of the resigned and the those in despair. They'd ring with the speeches of ghosts, echoes of people no longer walking up and down it's sharpened steps, of bums no longer in seats for whom god's waiting room snapped them up at some hour, day or minute of the 16 years without a top flight goal, pass or save to witness."

"No solace for them, but these spirits of mams and dads and sons and daughters and the bloke who you once sat next to who just stopped coming one year, were all there in a row that July night; roaring amongst the silence and players' shouts, as dreams – if you have them, when you can't wake up from them – were finally answered with balls in the net and champagne and fireworks and the righteous howl of victory that's eternal. Elland Road was full when we went up. Just not with us."

It's a poignant reminder that promotion brought deliverance to many different people in many different ways, and perhaps being remote from it allowed us to cherish it as much for Norman, Trevor and Jack, and all those we once knew ourselves, as we did for the mental acquittal it allowed us personally. Our day will surely still come, when we feel the visceral thunder of Elland Road once again rise from the soles of our feet, and ready to consume us whole.

When or if Elland Road witnesses such scenes again, when or if full capacity stadiums are permitted, what will the atmosphere be like? Will we remember what songs we used to sing? Will those cherished but already-fading chants be forgotten forever? The world has changed, Elland Road has changed, we have changed. We're not in a hurry to undergo a promotion charge again, but we long for the rush, the adrenalin, the momentary loss of control and the iron-clad emotional bond of communal love for Leeds United. We long for the healing and the belonging that only Elland Road can bring to our lives. And while that separation persists and aggrieves us, thank God we were healed by promotion.

Leeds-born talisman Kalvin Phillips greets the crowds gathered on Lowfields Road in the minutes after promotion back to the Premier League was confirmed on the evening of Friday 17th July 2020.

ALCOHOL

Whether it's a complimentary benefit, a welcome diversion or an absolute necessity, for many die-hard fans who attend Elland Road on auto-pilot once a fortnight, the match day experience is as much a social occasion as an expected feast of sporting endeavour, and alcohol inevitably is absolutely central to that.

There has been a licence held at Elland Road to sell intoxicating liquor since 1st April 1959 when four bars in the West Stand were permitted to sell alcohol for one hour before and one hour after each game. Prior to the mid-1980s alcohol had gradually become available in most of the public refreshment bars in the ground; underneath the Kop, in the West Stand, behind the Lowfields Road Stand and in the concourse below the South Stand. Alcohol sales were, however, temporarily suspended on the Kop following crowd trouble at the infamous FA Cup Third Round game with Manchester City in 1978. The availability of alcohol had not necessarily been blamed for triggering any direct disruption, but the rise in hooliganism and obscene chanting was very much seen as a social ill, and it was naive to suggest the two didn't go hand in hand.

Prior to 1989, when nationwide restrictions were put in place, you could drink beer on the terraces. As Leeds fan and author Gary Edwards recalls: "A lot of fans in those days tended to drink in the ground as opposed to the pubs – there were a few bars downstairs in the Kop. Of course they were plastic glasses, but you could take them up onto the terrace – I can't remember when this stopped – possibly towards the end of the '70s. But I can remember coming back on to the Kop with three or four pints; there wasn't that much by the time you arrived back at your place though. Also I can remember being sat on the terrace drinking Tetley's maybe two hours before kick-off."

Another Leeds fan, Stephen Talbot, also remembers drinking in the Lowfields Road terrace: "We went in the Lowfields a lot in the early 1980s, and you had the seats with steps going up and wing-walls, big wing-walls for another little tier that they used to stand in as well (the shelf), so you had your Lowfields terrace, some steps going up to that shelf thing, and from the shelf you went up under the seating area into a tunnel and you had a bar on your right and a café on your left, and we used to drink at that bar there. There was only one bar, it was very busy. I think you could take a drink down on to the terrace but we never did. We used to just drink there and you could walk outside to the back and basically look out on to Lowfields Road, and there were the big steps all the way down. I can't remember anybody being told they couldn't take a beer on to the terraces, but we never did."

Inevitably, the temporary ban after the Manchester City game in 1978 was a forlorn action from the Leeds board, who were increasingly embarrassed by the spiralling descent in the behaviour of their fans. By the mid-1980s stronger action was required after the board closed the Kop on two different occasions following crowd disorder, and so a permanent alcohol ban was self-enforced at Elland Road. This was aided a few years later by the implementation of the 'Alcohol Act 1985', which affected sporting events nationwide.

To give it its full title, The Sporting Events (Control of Alcohol etc.) Act 1985, which, incongruously, only applied to football matches, made drunken entry into a football ground an arrestable offence, and banned the consumption of alcohol at games completely, although this was later relaxed to "within view of the playing area". The act, which is still in place today, also had wider-reaching effects, banning the consumption of alcohol on certain coaches, trains and motor vehicles travelling to a designated football match.

This is where the legislation went further than the ban enforced specifically by Leeds United at Elland Road. Former Leeds United Supporters' Club (LUSC) secretary Ray Fell remembers the government-enforced alcohol ban vividly, as it meant that the rules had to change for LUSC members taking alcohol on coaches for away games. But with regards to the ban at Elland Road he recalls the stark contrast between how football fans and fans of other sports were treated: "What always struck me," says Ray, "was when Hunslet played at Elland Road. You would come on a Saturday to watch Leeds United and there was a drinking ban, then you would come the next day on a Sunday to watch Hunslet and you could drink a pint on the terraces."

Primarily as a result of the Hillsborough Disaster, but also aided by the Alcohol Act 1985, alcohol was banned from the public bars of all sporting grounds in the UK between 1989 and 1994. Bill Fotherby – speaking in 2014 and who sadly died in 2019 – was a beleaguered and hard-working commercial director when the club, which was already struggling to make money, first prevented itself from profiting from a vital income source in the bleak mid-1980s, and was later prevented by legislation: "Not being able to sell alcohol at Elland Road was a killer for me," says Bill with trademark vehemence, "and it was stopping people coming to Elland Road; sponsors, supporters. I was fighting like hell with the bodies in charge of renewing the certificates for selling alcohol. But some of our supporters were terrible, they were. I went to every away game of Leeds United for 16 years, abroad, reserve team games, etc. I did everything, and some of the supporters were nasty. But they're nasty at every club, there's a nastiness at every club. But it was a big problem to me as commercial director, a tremendous problem and I had to get over that."

Leeds United invested £1 million in the Banqueting Suite in 1992 so they could accommodate the demand from hundreds of pre-match guests, but they couldn't serve alcohol, only at functions on a non-match day. This was a dramatic loss of income in addition to the

ALL SEATER

same restriction in all the public bars in the ground for general fans. On the eve of the 1989/90 season Leeds did win a legal battle with the police and magistrates to sell low-alcohol Swan Lager in bars at Elland Road, as a licence wasn't required to sell that product, but needless to say low-alcohol lager cut little ice with the majority.

By the mid-1990s sufficient measures were in place to control crowd trouble, and clubs were again at liberty to sell alcohol before games when the nationwide restrictions were lifted. The effect of the Taylor Report and the move to all-seater stadia had meant disorder within football grounds was almost non-existent, and coupled with the advent of CCTV security systems within the ground's concourses, it was also felt that Elland Road was a safe environment in which to re-introduce alcohol sales to fans. Leeds, as well as most other league clubs, have since exploited this economically as a welcome revenue source on match days.

Following the re-introduction of alcohol sales, the club installed two specific bar areas in function rooms at the back of the Kop to tap into the sizeable market of ever-thirsty Leeds fans that like to make a day out of attending a game. Soon enough, pretty much all food and refreshment bars underneath all the stands were again serving alcohol, and it had returned to being a staple ingredient of the pre-match routine in and around the ground. The Centenary Pavilion and Billy's Bar opened as specific pre-match drinking establishments and they were joined in 2017 by the Fosters Fan Zone, an outdoor drinking area outside the North East Corner Stand; a location famously accommodating to al fresco refreshment at all times of year......

We came, we saw, we sat down, or at least some of us did. Elland Road officially became an all-seater stadium in the close season of 1994, when the capacity of the Kop was reduced from an already-downsized 9,000 to 7,000, by the installation of seats at a cost of £1.1 million, £400,000 of which was paid by the Football Trust. Essentially the move to all-seater stadia was a directive of the Taylor Report, a documented inquiry into the Hillsborough Disaster of 1989. The report was published in January 1990, although its key findings were well-known before that, and it recommended, amongst other things, that all English and Scottish football league clubs in the top divisions have all-seater stadia.

With the completion of the East Stand in 1993, Elland Road had lost its once-formidable Lowfields Road terrace and the Kop was the only standing section left in the ground. Prior to this all four sides of the ground had at one point housed terracing for spectators, and before the early 1970s sitting was considered a rare luxury solely for the elite.

The first game at Elland Road as an all-seater stadium was on Tuesday 23rd August 1994, when 34,218 saw Leeds beat Arsenal 1-0. It was generally recognised that whilst the health and safety of the supporters was undoubtedly enhanced, which was rightly uppermost in the original objective, the end of terracing brought a doleful conclusion to a memorable era for football fans of a certain vintage, which today's more antiseptic experience routinely fails to replicate.

Having said that, although Leeds eventually succumbed to an all-seater stadium out of necessity, it was a very different story back in 1973 when the club

The Kop is stripped of all its bare essentials in readiness for becoming an all-seater stand in the summer of 1994.

had altogether more ambitious, and at the time, quite unconventional designs. Following the completion of the North East Corner Stand in the spring of 1973, the club were looking at the next phase of their piecemeal redevelopment which involved the east side of the ground.

Of course the redevelopment was put on hold for 20 years, but back in 1973 chairman Manny Cussins was suggesting that the club's plans to turn Elland Road into one of the most modern stadiums in the country did not just extend to building stands, saying: "We may have total seating in three years' time. We are ambitious people, though if we do not have success on the field then major improvements are impossible." Creating an all-seater stadium in 1973 was certainly a distant prospect, as the seated capacity of Elland Road upon completion of the North East Corner Stand was still only 13,445, just over a quarter of the ground's capacity. In contrast, by 1989, when the club was forced to reduce terracing capacity drastically after the Hillsborough Disaster, seating capacity was over 56%, with 18,000 out of the then 32,000 total ground capacity.

Whilst the concept of sitting down at a football match is an accepted form of the modern game, in 1973 the suggestion that the club may get rid of all terracing from the ground was quite radical, and to say the least, would not have been wholeheartedly welcomed even at a club and with a board who were enjoying unprecedented success. Doubtless the cries of derision would have been immediate from an inflexible fanbase; famously iron-willed and sufficiently opposed to 'change' that some grumbled at the pampered luxury of a roof on the Kop to stop them getting wet.

There is no doubt that modern social behaviour, on-pitch misfortune and off-pitch stewardship are as much to blame for the loss of atmosphere at Elland Road, and in fairness most other British football grounds, as all-seater stadia is. However, the eradication of terrace culture along with the freedom of choice, the bouncing, shoving, grappling and surging entertainment of the Elland Road terraces, and the ability for like-minded souls to gather together to make themselves heard, appears to be central to why Elland Road has lost its intimidation and vibrancy. Thom Kirwin, a Leeds fan and now Head of LUTV, mourns the loss of the vibrant atmosphere at the all-seater-era Elland Road, but admits that other people he comes across don't always see it the same way: "Sometimes when I talk or think about Leeds United I wonder 'am I just thinking that because I'm a fan and I love the club and I'm looking at it through biased eyes?' and one of those things is always the atmosphere. Doing the job I do, and when you speak to people who are coming here they all go 'well Elland Road's amazing' you know, the wall of noise and when it gets going it's fantastic.

I think it's quite the opposite when it isn't going well, I think it can feel like a really desolate place sometimes. I think that's partly why we've struggled in recent years. It's not the fans' fault of course, but when things aren't going well and there isn't a 'feel good' factor I think Elland Road becomes very cavernous and it's really hard for players to perform in it. I don't know how much is down to the buildings and the stadiums, but people say in all the new stadiums the atmosphere has fallen a little bit but that's down to the fans really and the type of support you have."

All-seater stadia and the promotion of families has changed the experience, but it had to happen as society changes, as Thom illustrates: "The families thing is great really, because I look back at my early teens going in the Family Stand with my mum, and think 'would my mum have been able to take me if it had been the Kop and the Lowfields?' and I don't think she would have really, it was a different environment, and then we had a family-orientated environment and I definitely wouldn't have been able to get to as many games.

"The atmosphere here is reinforced to me a lot," Thom continues, "when other people who don't watch Leeds every week, other journalists, other reporters, ex-players and they go 'bloody hell, that was some atmosphere today', and I don't think there are many grounds like that. The Bristol Rovers game (where Leeds clinched promotion in May 2010) summed up everything that was great about Elland Road. There is no doubt, and everyone said it, it was the crowd as much as anything that won it, those Bristol players just did not know what hit them. But that was like desperate times, it was do or die, so even people in the Kop who would never normally sing will have been shouting and screaming because they were thinking 'the whole season's going to go down the swanny here'. If you think of all the big games at Elland Road in our lifetime, that we've won, the crowd has always played a part."

Thom is clearly a student of the philosophy that the atmosphere at every ground is different now, and football has moved on, but Elland Road remains one of the few grounds where the acoustics can blend to create a fearsome backdrop, ie. when it's good, it's very good. "I think Leeds fans are quite smart though," Thom notes. "It's a bit of a cliché but like Liverpool fans, I think they understand the game. The biggest factor for me at Elland Road, and of course there are times when the crowd has got on the players' backs probably for the right reasons, and booed or whatever, but you can always tell when things aren't going too well because it's quiet. At some grounds you'll see the home team not playing very well for 20 minutes and they'll get booed straight away. That doesn't really happen at Leeds, but if the team isn't playing well, Eddie (Gray) will nudge me and go 'listen, listen' and that tells you everything you need to know, that there

isn't any noise. I think Leeds fans probably follow the saying 'if you haven't got anything nice to say, just say nothing'. But that's what I mean when I say the silence is almost worse, I'm not saying booing would be better but the silence does create an uneasy atmosphere. But I speak to a lot of the players, going back a few years now, and there are some players who probably can't believe they ever played for Leeds United, but they're not just trotting it out. To play at Elland Road is very special and I know it's been a deciding factor, or one of the main factors, in a lot of players who have signed."

ATTENDANCE RECORD

The night of 15th March 1967 is enduringly significant in the history of Leeds United and Elland Road itself, and is likely to remain so for the foreseeable future, not just for events on the pitch during an intense FA Cup Fifth Round Replay, but primarily for what happened off it.

Relations between Leeds United and Sunderland Football Clubs had grown fraught in the years leading up to what was an epic FA Cup trilogy, in which Leeds eventually prevailed after a second replay. The mutual animosity was largely triggered by the traditional boiling pot of regional rivalry, but was also inflamed by the head-to-head Second Division promotion chase between the two clubs in 1963/64, when Leeds eventually triumphed as champions. However, what happened after that was an objectionable twist in the tail that left Leeds fans and officials bristling uncomfortably for some time, and stoked further what were already raging flames prior to this enticing FA Cup tie. In the months following Leeds' promotion in 1964, Sunderland openly courted Don Revie as the preferred occupant of their newly vacant manager's seat. Given Revie's past association with the club prior to joining Leeds as a player in 1958, there was genuine concern amongst Leeds fans, albeit thankfully it came to nothing and Revie remained in situ to oversee his masterplan at Leeds United.

Though Leeds navigated few games in the mid- to late 1960s without some form of physical on-pitch altercation, and at the very least, an undercurrent of potential hostility, games between Leeds and Sunderland, in particular, had by then become unnaturally heated affairs. A series of personal vendettas had been established all over the park, and an above-average awarding of free-kicks and bookings inevitably spilled over into aggression and confrontation off the field too.

The pairing of the two in the FA Cup in March 1967 was therefore seen as a powder-keg duel between two evenly-matched but brusquely unaccommodating clubs. Four days after Leeds and Sunderland had fought out a bruising 1-1 draw at Roker Park in front of 55,763 fans, the replay was arranged for Elland Road.

In 1967, capacity for all-ticket games at Elland Road was officially set at 52,000, but given the short turnaround in the games there was no possibility of making the second encounter all-ticket, which was not necessarily standard practice for big cup games at the time anyway. Indeed Leeds' secretary at the time, Cyril Williamson, acknowledged in the aftermath that there had simply been "insufficient time" to make the game all-ticket. Nor, in hindsight, were Leeds able to prepare for an unprecedented swarm of eager fans descending on the ground. But the club were not unaccustomed to huge crowds in the mid-1960s, despite having yet to hit the heights Revie envisioned. In the previous season, 1965/66, Leeds had drawn crowds exceeding 49,000 on two occasions, and previous home ties in the 1966/67 FA Cup run had attracted 37,768 and 41,329 respectively, higher than the average league gate. A Leeds fan of the time, Howard Mais, remarks: "These were higher figures than would have attended league matches against the same teams and so a decent crowd would have been expected for the replay against Sunderland."

This was a time, of course, when the FA Cup was one of the world's premier sporting competitions, and winning it was every player's dream, long before Sky, ITV and the Premier League combined to vacuum any life or appeal from it. The allure of the competition and the holy grail of reaching Wembley was immediately intoxicating to everyone connected with the game, much more so than the relentless, humdrum slog of the league.

Therefore, the FA Cup's seductive attraction, the lack of any other midweek distractions in mid-1960s Britain, archaic health and safety laws, the dispassionate policy of the police and football club towards spectator safety and the quick turnaround in games, were circumstances which conspired against Leeds United. This series of contributing factors meant interest in actually attending the game was exceptional, which it appeared, even taking into account those previous crowd figures, neither Leeds nor the police had anticipated. Near-disaster would result, and the next day the newspapers reported not the absorbing detail of another gripping contest between the two duelling clubs, but instead carried photos of fans in tears and the mangled wreckage of the disfigured crash barriers afterwards.

Amid chaotic scenes, the official attendance was recorded as 57,892, earning receipts of £15,147, which unlike the physical attendance was not a record for the ground. Still, there were thousands locked outside when the thorny decision was taken to close the gates at 7.07pm, 23 minutes before kick-off.

Howard Mais described the scenes outside the ground, as enthusiastic and impatient fans flocked upon the stadium in extraordinary numbers: "Back then I tended to watch from the Lowfields Road terraces and as I was only 13 I joined a long queue for the juniors and old age pensioners turnstile at some time within

Gary Sprake eyes the massed throng in the Gelderd End while an apprehensive-looking policeman supervises the overspilling fans during the Sunderland FA Cup tie in 1967.

the hour before the match. All the queues were long but I had seen long queues before and so had been expecting them anyway.

"In those days," Howard continues, "the layout of the turnstiles was different to now with the perimeter wall containing bays within which the turnstiles were sited. As I recall there were at least four turnstiles, or perhaps six, in the bay that my turnstile was in and this led to the queues snaking around each other.

"The first real inkling I had of the size of the crowd was when the turnstiles began to close around 20 minutes before kick-off, as that was something I had not experienced before. They did not all close together but one by one, with the result that fans in the queue for a turnstile that closed simply then intermingled with the fans queuing for other turnstiles that remained open. Some fans, with the help of their mates, got into the ground by clambering over the walls near the turnstiles.

"It was not too long before all the turnstiles had closed on Lowfields Road except the one for juniors and old age pensioners. This turnstile remained open until well after the match kicked off and as I remember it was about 25 minutes after kick-off time when I got into the ground, long after all the other turnstiles had shut. Although it was the turnstile for juniors and old age pensioners there were some from the other queues that did intermingle with the queue to try to get in that way."

With the 7.30pm kick-off time long since passed and still huge crowds outside, amid scenes of mayhem, many fans scrambled on to the roof of the Scratching Shed and the Old Peacock pub to see the game. Given this, coupled with the desperate jostle for admittance prior to the turnstiles being shut and the illegal entry taken by many afterwards, the unofficial figure of

people actually able to watch the game may have more realistically approached, and possibly surpassed, 60,000.

In the event, the stadium was evidently not capable of coping with the enormous volume of people compressed within it, and after just ten minutes the game had to be stopped when a crash barrier in the corner of Lowfields Road and the Scratching Shed collapsed, and an estimated 1,000 fans spilled out on to the pitch.

Another Leeds United fan, Alan Ryan, was at the game, standing on the Elland Road end of the Lowfields Road terrace, exactly where the main problems occurred. He recalls the evening as a confusion of exhilarating action quickly giving way to danger at the almost wilful neglect of the crowd's safety: "The problem occurred after the gates were closed, but this didn't prevent many, many fans climbing over the walls to gain access. As a result the crowd were so tightly wedged together it was practically impossible to move. Some that managed to free themselves were actually running down towards the pitch on the heads of the crowd to escape the crush. The barriers eventually collapsed and the crowd spilled onto the pitch, holding up the game for quite a while."

The referee on the night was a certain Ray Tinkler, who was to face another troublesome encounter at Elland Road four years later in an infamous match against West Brom, but in 1967 he made a somewhat more appreciated decision to halt the game for 17 minutes after a lone police officer ran on to the field of play to ask him to do so. In this time, amid cries of panic, people were being pulled out of the crowd. Dozens of fans were tended to for injuries and 32 were taken to Leeds General Infirmary for further

treatment, three of those remaining in hospital overnight.

In the *Yorkshire Evening Post* the next day reporter Jim Brady, who had been stood in the ground as a fan, wrote: "The stricken corner of the ground looked as though an avalanche had engulfed it. The crowd behind on the terraces swayed dangerously, the dazed fans forced over the wall were standing and lying in a ragged semi-circle, a dark mass against the floodlit green baize of the turf."

Elsewhere in the ground, where the concentration of fans was at full capacity but still relatively trouble-free, frustrations grew over the delay. Leeds chairman Harry Reynolds took to the stadium PA to appeal for calm, as bewildered and meandering fans in the south east corner of the ground were simply herded off the pitch to enable the game to continue.

"Whilst it wouldn't be allowed now," Alan Ryan continued, "after the game was re-started the crowd were left to view the match amidst huge metal stanchions that had been uprooted. Whenever play came over to the Lowfields Road side of the pitch it was terrifying, as the crowd surged forward from the back, and the noise was like a rumbling sound, and you were fearful of being spiked on one of the stanchions."

Hundreds of fans squatted along the touchlines on all sides of the ground as Leeds, curiously wearing blue shirts while Sunderland wore all red, fell behind to a 37th minute goal from John O'Hare, who was later to join Leeds under Brian Clough, but equalised a minute later through Johnny Giles. Defences remained on top and extra time couldn't separate the teams, with a second replay meaning Leeds faced the punishing prospect of six games in ten days, as they chased glory on three fronts.

But Alan Ryan recalls that fans had more immediately pressing concerns than Leeds' fate in the FA Cup: "At half-time and full-time people were wandering around looking for all sorts of possessions that had gone missing, like shoes, scarves, etc. I lost a complete set of buttons from my overcoat. The following day, suffering from pains in my chest and arms, my employer sent me to Dewsbury General Hospital for x-rays, which diagnosed me with nothing more than severe bruising."

Jim Brady of the [YEP] also described the almost fatal scenes as play continued in maximum discomfort: "Packed so tightly that it was impossible to move, arms imprisoned in a vice of solid humanity, the crowd on the popular side (Lowfields) staggered forward as the play

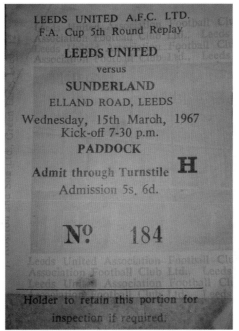

One of the few advance tickets sold for the FA Cup tie against Sunderland in 1967; the sheer size of the crowd was unforeseeable with the game too hastily arranged to be all-ticket.

reached a corner and everybody strained to see.

"Down they lurched on the backs of those in front, frightened screams came from women, curses from the men. Then back they came again pushed from those in front, staggering and gasping and yelping as toes were pounded by scores of feet."

Gary Edwards was also there that night, as he remembers: "We watched a few games through the dusty glass panels on the Elland Road end of the Lowfields terrace. We were stood there for the first replay against Sunderland in the fifth round of the FA Cup. Thousands of fans came over the perimeter walls on all sides of the ground making the attendance much nearer 60,000. Only quick thinking and sterling efforts by police, ambulance crew, stewards and the faithful St John's Ambulance Brigade prevented a certain tragedy, when a crush barrier gave way under the strain, injuring hundreds of spectators. I was really grateful that we hadn't found our usual spot near the front wall – the barrier that gave way was only about ten yards behind where we usually stood."

Another Leeds fan of many years, Dougie Wales, queued up for the Scratching Shed but didn't get in that night. He ended up watching a quarter of the pitch through the gap between the Scratching Shed and the West Stand, stood outside the newsagents along from United Fisheries. He adds: "I think it took them by surprise, and they weren't prepared for it. You didn't get ten days to prepare like you do now, the replay was hastily arranged. They never expected that crowd to turn up and of course there were no tickets, it was just turn up and pay on the turnstiles. It was a free-for-all, you just turned up and it was pot luck whether you got in or not. It was chaos."

Some of the injured fans nursed their bruises the next day and commented on their horrific experience: "I don't want to experience anything like that again," said Albert Gavins, and Brian Burnell added: "Suddenly the ground underneath me moved upwards as the barrier came out of its concrete supports. People were screaming, the crush was terrific. I've never been as frightened in my life. Grown men around me were crying, and people struck them in the face to pull them together."

The third game and second replay was arranged for Hull's Boothferry Park five days later on a Monday evening, and two days before Leeds played Bologna away in the Inter-Cities Fairs Cup on the Wednesday. Indeed the team had to delay their flight out to Italy by 24 hours as a result of having to fit the game in.

A beleagured policeman carries a shoeless woman to safety as fans who have escaped the crush mill about the south east corner of the pitch during the 17-minute stoppage.

The second replay versus Sunderland was won 2-1 by Leeds, but back at Elland Road a probe into the events of the first replay led to replacement crash barriers on the Lowfields Road terrace, but little other change; a typical laissez-faire response of the time to what was seen as simply a big crowd. Nobody, at Leeds or elsewhere within the game, anticipated that this could quite easily evolve into tragedy, never mind considering the fundamental human right to partake of an enjoyable pastime in relative comfort.

Dougie Wales is emphatic in his conclusion: "They got away with it that night, Leeds United, as a club. It was no Hillsborough by any means, but they got away with it. It could have been a lot worse than it was. It didn't get out of hand, but it could have and they were lucky."

Dave Cocker, son of Don Revie's right-hand man Les Cocker, was in and around the ground on a daily basis as a youngster in the 1960s and he remembers the aftermath of the Sunderland game vividly: "That was dangerous, we were lucky nobody got killed there. I went in the following day and to see the barriers crushed and mangled like that, and it was people that did that? You think 'how the fuck has nobody died here?'"

Two years later and it seemed that not much had been learnt from the near-disaster at the Sunderland game. On 8th January

1969, 40 fans needed treatment after spilling out of the Lowfields Road terracing onto the cinder track during the FA Cup Third Round Replay defeat to Sheffield Wednesday. This occurred in the exact same location as the injuries in 1967, the south east corner. With a 48,234 gate the overcrowding issue was less severe, but clearly Elland Road was still not well-prepared for big crowds.

The Sunderland game was obviously one of many huge, high-profile encounters for Revie's men during that era, and the fact that many of the most eagerly anticipated contests were midweek did not help matters in terms of what passed as 'organisation'. As people tend to arrive later for midweek games, chaotic melees outside the turnstiles in the pitch darkness, with people undoubtedly more anxious about getting in than their own safety, were commonplace. Dougie Wales also remembers when Leeds played Arsenal in 1971 on a Monday night, when the two clubs were competing for the league title, and although 'only' 48,350 were present, he recalls the act of queuing outside the new Kop on the narrow, dark access road behind the stand as being "horrendous". "It was a nightmare trying to get in that night," Dougie recalls. "They

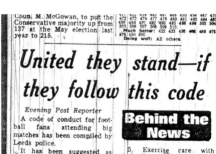

Evening Post Reporter

A code of conduct introduced at Elland Road following the near-fatal crushing during the Sunderland FA Cup tie in 1967. Leeds fans from the 1970s and '80s will chuckle wryly when considering how closely most of this was observed.

THE LEEDS MERCURY, WEDNESDAY, DECEMBER 28, 1932.

Leeds United Draw Record Gate : Sutcliffe's Test Escape.

A sprawling canvas of people, hats, suits and overcoats on the northern end of the 'Popular Side' as a then record crowd gathers for the game against Arsenal on December 27th 1932, a record that stood for nearly 35 years.

were neck and neck at the top of the league, Leeds and Arsenal. I was in the Kop, but you queued a long time to get in. It's more organised now, you've got to have a ticket no matter what game it is, but you just paid on the turnstiles then, and there was no crowd control outside, there was no orderly queue it was just a mass of folk, and it was simply pot luck whether you got in or not."

Prior to 15th March 1967, Leeds' highest crowd had stood for 35 years, this being the 56,988 that watched a 0-0 draw against Arsenal in a post-Christmas encounter on 27th December 1932. At this time, Leeds were flirting with the top end of Division One for the first time in their existence, and having beaten Herbert Chapman's all-conquering Arsenal 2-1 at Highbury 24 hours earlier on Boxing Day, that astonishing result had prompted overnight, city-wide interest in the return fixture. A fervent crowd with none of today's festive distractions descended on the ground, and the *Yorkshire Evening Post* reported: "The crowd overflowed onto the roof of the newly covered part of the popular side (Lowfields) ... scores were seen watching from the roof of an inn (the Old Peacock) ... so great was the crush that gates had to be opened to relieve some of the pressure." On this occasion Leeds' season faded out, and so did the crowds. Following this goalless draw and a 5-1 defeat at Derby on New Year's Eve, the next home game against Blackburn on 7th January 1933 attracted just 14,043 fans, an astonishing loss of 42,753 people in just over a week.

In the all-seater era Leeds United's biggest crowd remains the 40,287 who attended on 22nd December 2001 for a highly-charged affair with Newcastle United. Prior to that, the biggest crowd of the modern 'Premier League' era was in the one season where the 17,000 capacity East Stand was fully open and the Kop was also still standing. This was on 27th April 1994, when 41,127 packed into the ground for a midweek game against Manchester United, in which Leeds lost 2-0.

A week later on 3rd May, the 'Kop's last stand' was celebrated in a game against Sheffield Wednesday, before seats were installed and the ground capacity cut accordingly.

But certainly, until the club enjoys a dramatic change in fortunes and extends Elland Road with the unlikely addition of an extra 20,000 seats, the Sunderland attendance record will stand. Even if Elland Road had the capacity, you wonder whether something similar to the set of circumstances that night would ever combine to produce such an attendance again?

AWAY FANS

Like charging blindly into no-man's land on the Western Front in World War 1, the 'away end' at Elland Road has been considered a place only for the truly valiant and lion-hearted for much of the period of football's rampant evolution since the 1970s; an area of jeopardy and discomfort reserved solely for the stout-hearted and foolhardy. But it was not always so. Until the 1960s, and like any other football ground, visiting fans were usually present but rarely conspicuous within Elland Road, and even when they were visible, the more hospitable nature of football and life in general in that era ensured there was scarcely more than some hearty banter over an exchange of mints and a shared Bovril.

Reg French attended his first game at Elland Road in the 1934/35 season and was still attending in his late eighties. Safe to say he has pretty much seen it all, and he recalls the post-war years as a friendly era where fans of opposing sides attended football simply for the love of the game: "There was no segregation, and of course there was no trouble either. Everyone got on with each other. I've talked to away fans because there was no reason not to. They were just there. Fans got on rather better than as the years rolled on. People could go anywhere they wanted in the ground, whether they were supporting Leeds or they were from Liverpool or wherever."

Alan Roberts, a former general manager of the club, was a Leeds United fan long before he was employed by them, and he can remember away fans in the West Stand. He said: "I can remember my first visit to Elland Road for a match against Tottenham Hotspur, when I stood on the old open-ended Kop. I always remember the Tottenham fans housed in what is now the upper tier of the West Stand having cardboard or plywood cut-outs of cockerels mounted on three or four foot high sticks."

For many years away fans actually congregated in their greatest numbers in the original Spion Kop. It seems baffling to the point of incongruity now, but this was fairly normal and accepted protocol up to the late 1960s, particularly given Leeds' more vocal contingent were situated in the Scratching Shed, and the gradual change of ends prompted by the building of the new Kop in 1968 had yet to begin. However, when it did, many away fans were slow on the uptake and with Leeds fans' confrontational reputation steadily growing in the early 1970s this led to some uncomfortable afternoons for visiting fans seeking a safe haven.

Gary Edwards recalls a number of games where away fans either consciously or unconsciously found themselves behind the increasingly more prominent enemy lines: "I remember that Wolves were one of the first teams to come to the new Kop (post-1968) and they got a good hiding as they queued at the turnstiles. A lot of away fans didn't cotton on and loads were in the Kop at the same time as Leeds – Liverpool were right up in the right hand corner as you look at the Kop from the pitch, Man City and Newcastle were gathered down around the front entrances that are still there today."

The early 1970s saw gatherings of away fans in the Scratching Shed growing more noticeable as the following of all teams was done increasingly as a collective, due largely to the safety factor of numbers. As a more prominent target it was inevitable that a more structured dichotomy between home and away fans would evolve and security measures would have to be put in place accordingly, though it was some time before Leeds United, and other clubs, would acknowledge this need.

Dougie Wales recalls an unfortunate encounter with an Everton fan whilst stood shoulder-to-shoulder with intimate proximity in the Scratching Shed: "I think it was about 1969, and a very young Joe Royle had scored for Everton, but Leeds won. It was jam-packed in there, and there were a few Everton lads in, and true as I'm sat here, the Everton lad started peeing down the side of my leg, because he couldn't get out to get to the toilet. I felt this trickle going down my leg..........."

An Elland Road-attending Leeds fan from the 1950s until his sad passing in 2015, John Cave recalled those first rumblings of tribalism and social rancour that

quickly evolved into a more serious issue: "The first time that I can recall fan 'trouble' as such at Elland Road was against Everton in around 1965 or 1966 when a lot of vehicles were damaged in the West Stand car park by the simple expedient of the Everton fans using their roofs and bonnets as a footpath out onto Elland Road." This was at a time when cars were simply shoehorned into the West Stand car park with little pre-planning for how difficult it would be to get them out again.

As times changed, trouble between rival fans increased both inside and outside the ground. My Dad, Alan Howe, recalls an incident in the late 1960s on Lowfields Road with Liverpool fans as he queued outside the turnstiles to get in: "There was loads of argy-bargy, pushing and shoving and the police separated the Leeds and Liverpool fans, and chucked this single Liverpool fan into the same police van as the Leeds fans, and the van was literally rocking all over the place. And after about five minutes they opened the door and said 'oh sorry, have we put you in the wrong van?' and took him out. They just stood there laughing, the police."

Gary Edwards remembers the somewhat chaotic arrangements that used to take place when the growing number of away fans used to travel to Elland Road "...we were forced to seek refuge near the glass panels (in the Lowfields Road Stand) when Glasgow Rangers and seemingly half of Glasgow rolled into Elland Road for the quarter final of the Inter-Cities Fairs Cup (in April 1968). Rangers' fans, most of them drunk, were everywhere and a pile of empty beer bottles retrieved by the police stood by the goalpost in front of the Scratching Shed throughout the match. The pile of bottles was so high it almost came up to the waist of Leeds' keeper David Harvey." That Rangers game is particularly memorable as the occasion when the Scottish fans took over the city of Leeds, not just Elland Road. With an estimated 20,000 Rangers fans in the stadium even making the old Kop their home as well as most other parts of the ground, it was a particularly 'jovial' evening, though the police may have viewed it differently. The game was stopped on several occasions for the retrieval of whisky bottles from the pitch, as fans recall shot glasses being filled and the empty bottles slung casually goalwards. Incidentally, a certain A. Ferguson was playing up front for Rangers, though there are no confirmed reports that he touched a drop of whisky. Television pictures also show the Scratching Shed as a heaving mass of Celtic fans during the 1970 European Cup Semi-Final First Leg, and it was clear that the era of opposing fans mixing convivially was drawing to an end.

It was an era of confusion and the authorities could do little to predict where away fans would pop up. Gary Edwards continues: "When the away fans started using the Shed, I remember Arsenal coming on a Monday

night, I think it was in 1971 – it was a crucial title game and some of them were stood on the roof of the Shed and one of them fell off the back. I'm not sure if it was the first season of the 'new' Kop but Man Utd were in the Shed and they came across the pitch and got into the Kop – but they weren't there long! Loads of Leeds fans were downstairs in the bars and a lot of fans were sat on the terraces drinking and sent us young fans downstairs for 'reinforcements'. Leeds came at them from all angles, including the entrances that used to be at the back of the Kop." This is the game on 11th January 1969 which many fans cite as the day the Kop became the generally accepted home of Leeds' hardcore support, and the Scratching Shed became the unofficial away end. Manchester United had thousands of highly visible and vocal fans in the Kop but they were charged out by Leeds fans and resided back in the Scratching Shed. From that match on, which Leeds won 2-1 before a crowd of 48,145, the majority of away fans did the same and slowly the Shed became the domain of the away fan and segregation of rival fans had begun, though it still wasn't formal.

Slightly after this, however, a famous attempt to claim the Elland Road Kop was made by Newcastle United fans. Leeds fan David Kirby recalls: "The date would have been 26/12/70. I was nine at the time and went to the game with my parents and younger brother. We arrived as the gates opened so we could get at the front with the buffets we had to stand on to watch the game. As we took our place on the wall the Newcastle fans were already coming into the Kop. At least two or three hundred of them made their way to the back centre of the Kop and started singing. The occasional Leeds fan came up the vomitories but went straight back down. David Harvey came out of the tunnel to see what was going on. It must have been like this for around 30 minutes before the Leeds fans came up from underneath the stand in large numbers. I don't remember any fighting, just the Newcastle fans making a hasty exit from the stand and being pelted with snowballs as they left. The Leeds fans must have gathered underneath the stand building up their numbers and been passing word to those outside the ground who must have entered armed with the snowballs. By the time the players came out to play the game the Kop had been cleared of all the Newcastle fans. There were 60 arrests, 21 in the ground and the newspapers reported pitched battles in Elland Road after the game and further trouble in the city centre that evening with 15 shop windows broken."

So it was that a distinct police presence began to separate the away fans as they routinely gathered in the corner of the Lowfields terrace and the Scratching Shed, but it was not until the South Stand was built in 1974 that there was a definitive 'away

end'. "Before that they (away fans) could go anywhere," says Stephen Talbot, a Leeds fan from the early 1970s onwards, "they could go in the Scratching Shed, in the Lowfields, in the Lowfields seats, there was always a lot in the Lowfields seats. There was a single fence in the corner between the Scratching Shed and the Lowfields but that was it, and they were always at it in that corner."

A match day programme from early in the 1974/75 season details the policing operation at Elland Road, in the wake of widespread problems elsewhere in the country. Of Elland Road, the writer proudly declares "…it is fair to say that Leeds United do not have a particular hooliganism problem…suffice to say that Elland Road is not a haven for hooliganism". Doubtless those words were retracted several times over the course of the next ten years when the club had to take increasingly severe action over a problem that they very quickly couldn't ignore.

The match against Luton Town in September 1974 saw the first direct segregation within a stand at Elland Road, and despite their previous disregard of the perceived problem, it appears Leeds United were one of the first clubs to champion 'partitioning' fans. That alone was considered a draconian measure at the time, as the match day programme for the Luton game explains: "Today marks a further development in our crowd control measures. A barrier fence has been erected in the new South Stand to assist in this segregation."

But in explaining the new stringent police measures, the local chief superintendent of the time, when communicating with the visiting club prior to the game, explains how he would "give them a plan of the ground and suggest that visiting supporters use the South Stand". It would not take long for that 'suggestion' to become a little less convivial.

Since 1974 the away fan at Elland Road has led a nomadic existence. As soon as the South Stand was built half of this would be given to away fans if volumes demanded it, hence the segregation mentioned above. But as attendances dwindled towards the end of the 1970s the corner terrace between the South Stand and the 'home' areas of the Lowfields terrace was where the away fans would traditionally be housed, and for larger numbers, more pens of the Lowfields terrace could be opened as necessary. Nevertheless, incidents of one sort or another were frequent. "I always remember playing Cardiff in the FA Cup (January 1975)," comments Stephen Talbot, "that kicked off, and two of those Cardiff fans ran onto the pitch at half-time with a Welsh flag, put the flag on the centre spot and started bowing to it, and this Leeds fan just ran on to the pitch and booted one in the head and started brawling with the other, the police ran on and there were three of them at it in the centre circle."

Of course at this time there were just as many incidents outside the ground as inside it, as railway stations, housing estates and parks like Holbeck Moor leading up to Elland Road, became open battle grounds, whoever happened to be visiting, as Stephen Talbot adds: "They just used to let them out in those days, the police, they'd let them straight out of the ground. Leeds wasn't a nice place to go to, you speak to fans of other clubs, especially some that I know. I know a Tottenham fan and they used to call it 'Suicide Corner' round the back of the South Stand and Lowfields, they didn't like coming to Leeds at all. People go on about the atmosphere now, but it's not a patch on what it was like in the '70s, that was an evil ground.

"I always remember when it kicked off with Newcastle on the motorway (M621) before it was built," continues Stephen. "The Geordies always used to bring thousands, and it was always feisty. But one year they got chased on to the motorway when they were still building it."

By this time, in the mid-1970s, the Lowfields was segregated by specific caged pens, providing the quarantining that was now an absolute necessity. On occasions, such as the infamous FA Cup tie against Manchester City in 1978, away fans would come in huge numbers and take up the Lowfields pens normally reserved for home fans. On this afternoon City brought nearly 10,000 fans, who were housed in the South Stand, which by now was seated, and in the Lowfields Road Stand almost up to the halfway line. Events on this afternoon are chronicled elsewhere, but a visiting fan's account again highlights what a difficult place to come to Elland Road was for visiting fans. Stephen Talbot again takes up the tale: "I was working in Leeds quite recently and there were builders working with us who were from Manchester. They were a similar age to us and they supported City, and one said 'I'll never forget your place, after the game (in 1978) we got hammered and we got chased all the way down and down into Leeds and I ended up jumping into the river. I didn't know where I was but I jumped in the river to get to the other side and away from it all.' When he described where it was it was actually near the old *Yorkshire Evening Post* buildings (adjacent to the Inner Ring Road at the end of Wellington Street, but now demolished) so I don't know whether it was the canal or the river, but that road connected all the way up to Elland Road and he'd been chased all the way down and ended up jumping in the river. He said it was 'the worst night of my life'."

Back at Elland Road itself, away fans were generally penned in a bleak and solitary environment in the corner, with the menacing venom of snarling Leeds fans visible and audible from both sides. This remained the case throughout the 1980s when attendances only rarely required Leeds to give up any of the South Stand capacity to away fans. However, as Leeds' fortunes changed in the early 1990s, so the attendances grew. In the promotion season of 1989/90 Leeds were criticised for the paltry allocations offered to clubs such as Sunderland and Sheffield United, though Leeds, hamstrung by the terracing capacity cuts insisted upon by the Taylor Report, argued they were within their rights to primarily look after the demand of their own fans. These rules soon changed, and home clubs were obliged to offer a certain percentage of tickets to away fans in the first instance. In 1991 Leeds built the 1,700-capacity South East Corner Stand to ease this situation, though it would have been built regardless.

Since 1993 away fans have drifted around and have only recently been given a permanent home. They were the first people to use the new East Stand when it was partly finished, they have predominantly used the South East Corner Stand, and when demand requires they have also used half or all of the South Stand. From 1993, the lower section of the East Stand was separated from the away end in the south east corner by a short wall and little else, not even a line of stewards on most occasions. Thom Kirwin remembers the unsettling but compelling proximity of the rival fans: "Me and my brother enjoyed that for many years, because you could really hear what they were saying and you felt like you were on the border of a warzone really. I remember these two Chelsea fans once, I can't remember which year it was, but I think we'd gone in front or something and we were cheering. We were literally eight seats away from the wall and they're leaning over, they were right there. So we were cheering and my brother caught the eye of one of these Chelsea fans and my brother's smiling obviously, and one of these Chelsea fans goes 'here son, come over here' so my brother goes over and I'm saying 'what are you doing?' and these two guys whipped out rolls of notes, there must have been about four grand in notes, and they said 'you'll never see money like this in your life son' and just put the money away. My brother just walked away laughing going '1-0' with his fingers. I thought we were going to get thrown out."

In 2011 the club spent close to £300,000 renovating the south section of the West Stand to accommodate away fans in a new, permanent home which is felt to have been largely detrimental to the overall atmosphere. With unprecedented hospitality, away fans have now even been provided with a dedicated bar directly adjacent to their turnstiles. Although the organisation and security of football matches has changed significantly, as has the demographics of those attending, it is clear that segregation between home and away fans will always be required. Although the Elland Road atmosphere and unofficial 'welcome' is much-diluted from previous eras, clearly it has not quite gone full circle.

THE ONLY PLACE FOR US

B

BILLY BREMNER

1942 - 1997

LEEDS UNITED

1959 - 1976

771 APPEARANCES; 115 GOALS

BALL BOYS

Like the referee or the bar staff in the Kop, the role of the ball boy at Elland Road is something of an unforgiving one. For the large part you are doing nothing; usually sat on the perimeter track of the pitch being either rained on or just gripped by the ferocious cold. The only time anyone really notices you is when Leeds are losing and you can't get the ball back to the throw-in taker quick enough, or when the keeper scowls at you because your undeveloped ten-year-old legs can only kick the ball a distance that necessitates him having to walk ten

Over the years ball boys have been selected from local junior football teams and also from the club's various youth teams, and many famous faces have told tales in the match day programme of their brief stints patrolling the perimeter of the pitch, such as Alan Smith, Jonathan Woodgate and Noel Whelan, and in bygone years Revie-era youngsters Chris Galvin, Glan Letheren and Gwyn Thomas were all regular ball boys.

Going back a few years, Leeds fan Karl Skirrow recalls his own ball boy duties during reserves games at Elland Road. One day Karl's youthful giddiness to impress ended rather painfully: "It was about 1978/79ish," Karl recalls, "and my Dad was mates with Pete Gunby who had a lot to do with the youth set up with Leeds. Pete used to tell me to come down to Elland Road to ball boy the reserve games on a Tuesday or a Wednesday night. There'd be about ten of us waiting outside the West Stand, then this bloke would come out to meet us. He was like Brian Glover in Kes, he'd tell us our duties then walk us up the tunnel and out onto the pitch.

Not only did fans at Elland Road have fences obstructing their view in the 1980s, there was also a bored-looking ball boy and a quite often rotund policeman.

"My area one particular week was the South Stand. Leeds were playing Aston Villa, the game was about ten to fifteen minutes in when the ball flew over my head and into the stand behind me. I remember John Burridge (Aston Villa keeper) shouting for the ball back, so as I quickly turned round to retrieve the ball, bang, I'd only ran straight into one of the standing barriers and knocked myself out. Next thing I'm being carried across the pitch by John Burridge into the physio's room and onto the bed where I received treatment for my head wound. After my treatment I was OK to carry on my ball boy duties. I came out onto the pitch to loud applause from the 200-strong West Stand crowd."

inconvenient yards to retrieve it. On other occasions the ball is hit into the empty rows of West Stand seats and gathering it as it bounces erratically around is like trying to catch a butterfly that's eaten a Jumping Jack.

At this point you become the focus for the fans' ire and as such, not much sympathy is doled out to the unfortunate souls, and in many cases future club starlets, whose primary purpose is to keep the pace of the game flowing.

Even in the 1950s ball boys were not necessarily held in high esteem, although not without some fondness, as John Cave recalls: "Felix the diminutive ball boy was a regular feature at each match. Now I don't know if his name was 'Felix' – I suspect not – and we probably nicknamed him that because of the way he dementedly ran around like his cartoon namesake Felix the Cat. In addition to collecting in the kick-about balls, which was an entertainment all on its own, he had the job of scurrying down the tunnel and outside the ground to retrieve the match ball when it had been lofted over the stands during play."

However many stories you hear about first year professionals having flash cars and too much money to spend, one thing that is unlikely to change is that the ball boys surrounding the Elland Road pitch will be unpaid awestruck youngsters simply experiencing a first shot of the limelight. Whether their career at Elland Road progresses and they fancy another brush with fame might just be down to how grumpy and impatient we fans are on a Saturday afternoon.

BANQUETING SUITE

When it was built and officially opened in April 1992, as the club homed in on the last ever First Division championship, the Banqueting Suite was far from a popular extension to Elland Road; indeed it was a symbol to many of how the club was worryingly moving away from its core business. Twenty-nine years later and corporate entertainment is an accepted entity within football, almost as much a part of the furniture as coloured boots, undisclosed transfer fees and season ticket renewal forms in January.

Despite supporters' misgivings about the importance of the income derived from corporate activities, the main issue with the Banqueting Suite back in 1992 was the fact that it caused, without ceremony, the removal of the famous West Stand façade. Stuck plainly on the back of the West Stand like a toddler would apply a sticking plaster, the ground floor entrance to the Banqueting Suite became the new home of the club's main reception areas. Hence, the iconic blue facia with the golden lettering and Leeds United emblem, so shrouded in a famous past, was suddenly gone forever, to be replaced by a soulless, obtrusive, square brick construction and a symbol of the modern game that few supporters could relate to.

Today, the Banqueting Suite is a vital cog in the club's omni-present corporate activities, and an annex to the West Stand that we barely even notice any more. Essentially, it is the toy left on the landing that you have bypassed for so long you no longer even trip up on it.

The upstairs suite itself is now officially called the Norman Hunter Suite following an extensive and stylish refurbishment in 2017. This, the main suite, still combines its uses between hosting corporate fans on match days, and conferences, weddings and awards dinners. Upon its opening the suite was a symbol of the club's ambition to tap into new markets, although the décor and styling quickly dated. Standing at over 5,000 square feet the capacity of the suite gives it great versatility and it even forms part of the Stadium Tours as it houses many framed photographs, and is entered via the main staircase at the top of which, until recently, were many of the trophies and pieces of memorabilia the club has collected over the years.

When it was built in 1992, the Banqueting Suite was originally on stilts, with only an upstairs operation, and the reception area on ground floor level remained the same as previously. At first, it was still possible for fans on match days to walk under the building along the whole length of the West Stand. Gradually, over the next two years the remainder of the Banqueting Suite took shape, with a suite added on the ground

The Banqueting Suite shortly after it was built in 1992; standing to the left of it is the old glass Centre Line tower which caused Bill Fotherby some mirth with the council.

floor (what is now the Bremner Lounge) backing on to what is left of the car park, initially using a white, plastic marquee-type construction, but eventually bricked up, and then sliding doors were added to the sides and a new reception area constructed.

In all, the Banqueting Suite has done little to improve the aesthetics of the Elland Road ground. However, it is something of a hub to club activities which largely excludes the common fan, and hence will forever be tarnished with an image of opulence that most fans care little for. This is not helped by the hard-nosed masking of the iconic West Stand facade, although former director and chairman Bill Fotherby could see only the bigger picture, and when asked whether he was aware of any fans' opposition at the time he replied "none whatsoever". He was more forthcoming with the philosophy behind the Banqueting Suite, for which he puts forward quite a strong case:

"The idea was to make money for Leeds United. The only way to make money for Leeds United was to copy Manchester United, was to go to Arsenal and see the hospitality and the money that was coming in from hospitality, and so I built that Banqueting Suite."

Half of the cost of building the Banqueting Suite, £500,000, came from a deal with Joshua Tetley's, but only after Bill had played hard-ball by opening rival negotiations with John Smith's at Tadcaster. Upon realising that Tetley's executive management would lose their privileges of attending the big matches at Elland Road, of which there were many at the time, a franchise agreement was swiftly reached for Tetley's to supply the Banqueting Suite and half the cost of building it was covered.

"Full steam ahead with the Banqueting Suite," cheers Bill, "and I had to negotiate the rest of the money when it was completed. We got a top man in charge of the catering, we went to sale houses and got second hand fridges and everything. What a success that was that Banqueting Suite, I can't tell you, oh my god, absolutely unbelievable. We had shows there during the week, motor shows, companies represented, bringing money in. In our own little way the money was going out again on players and transfers to keep us up there, but I knew that was what we needed."

A telling story of how close to the wind Leeds United sailed during their second most successful period, but also an indication of how important the Banqueting Suite was at a crucial time in funding the ongoing business; a gamble that probably paid off.

BENTLEY'S BREWERY

If Tetley's is the most recent name synonymous with the city of Leeds and its traditional brewing of local beer to bite the dust following its closure in 2011, then Bentley's Yorkshire Brewery was the previous much-missed symbol of an almost-forgotten past.

In terms of the Elland Road ground itself, Bentley's Brewery is most notable as being the owner of the land, according to several different sources, when Holbeck Rugby Club bought it in 1897. Prior to that, it is believed that Bentley's purchased the land in 1878 and as well as using it themselves during the intervening 19 years, also leased the ground to Leeds Athletic Rugby Football Club, Elland Road's first tenants. Though in many Ordnance Survey maps in the late 1890s, the site shows nothing other than open land and a pumping station left over from the now defunct coal mines.

Back in 1897, 'Elland Road' was a large plot of land known as the 'Old Peacock Ground' and was acquired by the rugby club for the princely sum of £1,100. This was on the proviso that the ground remained a 'football' ground for at least seven years and Bentley's retained the catering rights; 'football' being an all-encompassing name referring not so much to what we now know as association football, but more to the oval-ball game that had only just been split into two codes.

Quite what Bentley's were doing with the land is open to debate as there is certainly no record of an actual brewery being on the site, and it is well known that Bentley's main brewery was in Woodlesford, near Rothwell, south east Leeds, and had been since 1828. Therefore, it can be presumed that the ground was just used as the company's private recreation ground, and a useful source of income when rented out; hence, it was not a major amendment to the business plan when an opportunity came up to sell the land in 1897. Nevertheless, the brewery's original decision to buy the land and at some point mark it out as a playing field, unwittingly kick-started a period of rich sporting history, played out on what otherwise would have been an anonymous and neglected expanse of grassland.

Bentley's Yorkshire Bitter was very popular in the Leeds area in the 1940s and, 50s despite being something of an acquired taste. Indeed it was popularly known as 'Baby's Yellow Baba' to those of

an unaccommodating palate, such was its colour and distinctive taste. Bentley's, as a local brewery, owned a number of pubs across Leeds in the 1900s, most notably the Old and New Peacock on Elland Road. The left hand external wall of the New Peacock pub, which overlooked the boundary edge of the Holbeck cricket pitch, carried a huge advert for the brewery for many years as a prominent feature of the landscape, which proclaimed "There's No Better BEER than BYB".

Bentley's main brewery at Woodlesford closed in 1973 about ten years after Bentley's had been bought out by Sheffield brewery Whitbreads. The New Peacock became a Whitbread pub, therefore, for about ten years prior to its closure in 1974, and the Old Peacock was a Whitbread pub well into the 1980s.

BIG SCREEN

It was a sore point amongst the crowd at Elland Road, and deeply endemic of the times, that there was no functioning big screen at the ground during the first two years of the club's enlightening tenure in League One between 2007 and 2009. It was almost symbolic that as soon as the club was relegated to the third tier for the first time in its history, the existing screen packed up and was deemed too expensive to repair. Indeed, in his programme notes chairman Ken Bates declared that the screen had been on its last legs for a few years and in the summer had "given up the ghost"; much like the team and the fragile hope of most fans.

Hence, the likes of Leon Constantine and Felipe Da Costa charged around the sacred turf to the backdrop of a blank screen between the West and South Stands, as if the crowd were being spared the visual 'spectacle' of highlighting the club's plight any more than was absolutely necessary.

It was therefore with great fanfare that the Philips 'Vidiwall' was installed during the summer of 2009, appropriately in readiness for the season where Leeds gained a long-awaited promotion back to the Championship. It was considered to be representative of a turning of the tide for Leeds United when the procurement of the Vidiwall was finally announced, however reluctant the curmudgeonly Bates was to part with precious cash, although tellingly, the screen was second hand, and partly funded for the first year by local car showroom Ringways, who have had a family association with the club since the late 1950s. Ringways sponsored the big screen for 12 months, rightly taking an excellent advertising opportunity from gifting a scoreboard back to the fans of the club.

The screen itself measures 5.6 metres x 8.8 metres, giving an overall coverage of 49.28 square metres. It has a resolution of 352 x 224 pixels, albeit that is designed to offer perfect viewing only from a distance of the halfway line, anywhere further away or closer is not as good. And this was 'state of the art' over a decade

ago of course. Perhaps surprisingly, the screen hasn't been updated since. However, certainly it has greatly enhanced the match day experience at Elland Road, and with it being linked directly to the LUTV studios the screen is capable of broadcasting all team news, pre-match build-up, match time elapsed, half-time scores, half-time highlights and live replays during the match of key moments. With the pitch-side LED advertising boards now appeasing sponsors requiring constantly rolling advertising space, it seems unlikely the screen will be updated any time soon.

In 1995, the sorely-missed Kop scoreboard was taken down, having shared the duties for one season with a much smaller screen than the present one, installed in the south west corner in the summer of 1994. This was effectively just a square scoreboard and held none of the maladroit charm of its much-cherished predecessor. The 1994 screen looks fairly basic and unexceptional now but at the time it was heralded as the biggest colour scoreboard of its type in the UK, and given it was a considerable step up from the 'dancing men' scoreboard it certainly caused quite a flutter in our more impressionable youth. Two people were required to operate the screen on a match day, and one person had to spend a somewhat labour-intensive four hours programming the board for each use.

Instant action replays shown during games weren't permitted by the Premier League until the late 1990s, and so as Leeds' fortunes picked up, the beginning of the 1998/99 season saw the scoreboard become accompanied by a similar sized screen showing replays of match action and an hour of build-up material prior to every game. This new screen was a 35-metre-square LED television.

For four years the two screens existed side by side until an upgrade to a single, dual-purpose screen in 2003 which acted as a replay screen and scoreboard. The screen did undertake an upgrade in the summer of 2004 which meant it was out of action for the first four home games of the 2004/05 season – ironically, also the first games in a new, lower division. But it remained in place until the lights, quite literally, went out upon relegation in 2007.

In addition to its match day duties, the current Vidiwall was used in May 2010 to relay live action back to fans at Elland Road from Charlton Athletic, in a key away game that could have resulted in promotion out of League One. Going back many years this has been an infrequent exercise adopted by the club with various different justifications. Special screens were erected during the 1989/90 promotion season when small ticket allocations were offered for crucial games at Middlesbrough and Sunderland. Despite 6,000 fans watching the Sunderland game on screens at Elland Road, the club usually ran these operations at a loss, hence they weren't a regular occurrence.

The white projector screens erected for the closed-circuit screening of the Rangers game in April 1968; note also the crush barriers painted red in the Kop and Lowfields stands.

When the second screen was installed in the south west corner in 1998, the club ran a number of beambacks of major Premier League away games, as Leeds enjoyed sold out allocations all over the country. Another short-lived venture was to show away games on a big screen in the East Stand concourse. The West Ham away game in 1993/94 was the first time this was tried, at a time when the club was desperate for any excuse to utilise the 'magnificent, new' facilities the East Stand had to offer. The game attracted a 1,800 sell-out of standing-room-only fans, and was repeated a number of times that season.

Closed-circuit beambacks were not a modern phenomenon, however, and there were several during the Revie era when away travel wasn't such a regular thing. The first such venture was for an away tie versus Glasgow Rangers at Ibrox, in the first leg of the Inter-Cities Fairs Cup Quarter-Final on 28th March 1968, when 22,000 sat or stood in the Kop, Lowfields and West Stand to watch a, presumably grainy, broadcast of the action. The event was billed in the local press as the "Big Night Out" and as a result of attempting the venture Leeds returned 2,000 of their 3,000 ticket allocation for what was a 60,000 "sell-out" tie. Such was the scale of the exercise, which was being replicated by Rangers for the return leg at Elland Road, that the kick-off was specially arranged for 8.30pm to ensure the perfect viewing conditions of darkness back at Elland Road. Five giant screens measuring 30 feet by 40 feet were erected on the pitch, two each in front of the Lowfields Road and West Stands, and one in front of the Kop. In earlier years, Leeds had attempted similar closed-circuit television ventures, most notably the previous season when they had beaten Valencia away 2-0. On that occasion technical difficulties prevented a broadcast; however, the relatively short distance between Leeds and Glasgow meant there were no snags in 1968.

Although 22,000 turned up to watch the tie on the big screens, a 38,000 crowd limit had been set and the resultant crowd was well below the club's break-even figure for the exercise. As a result the big screen beambacks weren't often repeated in the Revie years, but they have made a comeback in the new Millennium, with the Centenary Pavilion, Billy's Bar and the Norman Hunter Suite regularly packing in fans for big screen transmission of several Leeds United away fixtures.

BILLY BREMNER STATUE

As a monument to past glories and a cornerstone for the spirit of the club, few images have become more symbolic of Elland Road in recent years than the Billy Bremner statue that stands behind the South East Corner Stand, overlooking Elland Road itself. Whilst maybe the West Stand façade or the diamond floodlights were the iconic emblems of the 1950s to the 1990s, the modern era of Elland Road is best represented by the solid bronze sculpture of the 'Red-Headed Tiger known as Billy'. It is the perennial backdrop to so many TV reports and images that it is hard now to imagine the Elland Road landscape without it, and after a torrid few years Leeds fans are finally enjoying the media using Billy's backdrop for the reporting of something positive.

Following Bremner's death on 7th December 1997 there was an immediate public clamour for a permanent memorial to Leeds United's greatest ever captain. The club were not slow to react and posted an article in the *Yorkshire Evening Post* requesting artists to submit a proposal for what had been decided would be a sculpture.

The club finally commissioned sculptor Frances Segelman to create the statue that we see today.

The Billy Bremner statue reimagined in its bright new surroundings of Bremner Square.

Frances, who had previously enjoyed the dubious pleasure of sculpting Terry Venables amongst many others, and has since done the Duke of Edinburgh, had previously lived in Roundhay, Leeds but had relocated to London by the time the work was commissioned.

Sculpted from bronze, the statue took a year and a half to complete and measures nine feet from the top of Bremner's outstretched hands, raised in clench-fisted celebration, to the tip of his boot. Frances describes the cautious process she undertook by way of preparation for the project: "I was given many very famous photos of Billy Bremner, with his arms up in the air as I depicted him, and I visited Billy's wife at her home before I made the sculpture and chatted to her about him. The *Yorkshire Post* gave me lots of photos from the archive of Billy playing football also. I put these up all over the walls in my studio, which was on the top floor in my home in Wapping, This was the best room with a high ceiling. We reinforced the floor boards, as the sculpture is very heavy.

"I began with a steel frame," Frances continues, "which was welded together and I used tons of clay, as this was my first very large commission. As I am a self-taught artist it was a huge learning curve and a few clay legs ended up in the bin. I also interviewed some of Billy's friends at the club, so that I could understand his character. I studied video footage and went to a few football games at Elland Road, whilst I was sculpting."

Frances worked with the club to decide where she thought the statue would look best and also chose the design of the surrounding steps with the architect. The final wording agreed for the plaque beneath the statue reads:

"Billy Bremner, 1942–1997, Leeds United 1959–1976, 771 appearances 115 goals, Inspirational Captain of the Great Revie Team"

The statue was officially unveiled at midday on 7th August 1999 prior to Leeds' first game of the season against Derby County, and the occasion was preceded by Bremner's widow Vicky scattering the famous skipper's ashes on the pitch at the Kop end in a private family ceremony, something Bremner himself had requested in the event of his death. Many of Bremner's colleagues from the Revie era attended the ceremony, plus ex-players from prior to that, such as Harold Williams and John Charles, as well as players that Bremner had inspired as a manager, such as Glynn Snodin.

At a time when the incumbent young team were sweeping all before them, it was a fitting point at which to create a permanent reminder of the past. Since then the statue has become a hub and the nucleus of the ground. It is the point at which many people meet friends and colleagues pre-match, it is where almost everyone visiting the ground during the week will have a photo taken, and perhaps most

significantly it is where all tributes and memorials surrounding Leeds United begin; almost a homing beacon in troubled times.

Shortly after the unveiling, the murder of two Leeds fans in Turkey in April 2000 saw the statue become a shrine to Kevin Speight and Christopher Loftus as floral tributes were paid by fans of Leeds and many other clubs. Since then, most notably, the deaths of John Charles, Gary Speed, Norman Hunter, Trevor Cherry and Jack Charlton have been recognised with memorials centred around the statue. This was also the case when Leeds entered administration following relegation to League One in 2007, and amid uncertainty and confusion surrounding the complex financial position, many feared the club itself was about to draw its terminal breath. Flowers, scarves and tributes were laid accordingly. That mournful event was soon followed by the statue being vandalised by Huddersfield Town fans on the eve of the first Yorkshire derby between the two clubs in many years. Leeds won the game 4-0 to add to the moral victory, with the cowardly fans that daubed "HTFC" on the plinth under cover of darkness being roundly condemned by followers of both clubs. Fortunately the paint cleaned off.

In April 2010 the statue was cordoned off for two days whilst maintenance was carried out, including a lick of paint which gave Billy a somewhat different appearance for a few weeks before the weather again aged the colours. This prompted many fans, including myself, to query whether the original sculpture had been painted, as nobody could remember the colours being quite that pronounced. Frances explains: "On the original sculpture, the colours were there. By using heated flame the waxes and colours were put onto the bronze before the unveiling, not paint. They were more subdued but the colours were there."

In 2018 the steps and the area around the statue were extensively refurbished to make a feature renamed as 'Bremner Square'. The statue remained the same but was joined by squares depicting ten Leeds legends, voted for by fans, and hundreds of paving stones bought and inscribed by fans with their own unique messages. It has freshened up the area and provided a striking feature which continues to act as a focal point to the external area of the ground and an obvious meeting point pre- and post-match. Frances is not a regular visitor to Elland Road but whenever she visits family in Leeds she always drives past to check it, which must be an odd sensation given the intimate work that went into creating it over such a long period.

And whilst older fans stand and stare, children jump and play on the steps and hang on to Bremner's leg for photos. Maybe they don't fully understand exactly what he did for the club, but they recognise that they are in the presence of greatness.

BOARDROOM

It is true that many of the conversations, deals, agreements and disagreements that shaped Leeds United's destiny over the 20th century took place in the boardroom at Elland Road. Today, they are just as likely to take place in a hotel or on a yacht or even via Zoom in two non-descript locations of little significance, and with the protagonists not necessarily more than half-dressed.

The image of the 'boardroom' evokes memories of wooden panelling, long tables, a decanter of Scotch and seven or eight stout, balding men we largely don't recognise chewing the fat in a room thick with cigar smoke. Certainly in any period up to the mid-1990s this was a fairly accurate description, as local businessmen made up the Leeds board and meetings were frequent and well-attended.

In 1996 the Caspian Group bought Leeds at a time when English football was spreading its influence far and wide, and the club became a PLC. Since such time the business activities of most major football clubs in England are rarely discussed on a local basis. The explosion of possibilities in terms of communications and internet conferencing means that the traditional image of a boardroom as the central hub of a club's operations rarely exists today, certainly not in the main stand of the club itself.

Until the building of the Banqueting Suite in 1992 changed the operational layout of the first floor nucleus to Leeds United as a business, the club's chairmen down the years had discussed signings, wages, coaches, ticket policies and what colour to paint the Lowfields crash barriers in pretty much the same self-contained suite housed in the myriad of tight corridors underneath the West Stand, albeit this was re-built following the fire in 1956.

Therefore, it is with some sadness to discover that if you look up the 'boardroom' at Elland Road today you will be directed to a plush executive suite that is set up for conferences, weddings and parties. The room itself that carries the title 'boardroom' is actually themed on the boardroom of the Revie era, and when not in use the trophy cabinets it houses also form part of the popular Stadium Tours. In other words, it is essentially a gimmick. Former chairman Ken Bates created his own suite within the West Stand where he sat pre-match and fed and watered his guests for the day. After the 2011/12 season he moved this to the refurbished East Stand and this room temporarily became the press lounge. However, this is as close as we will get to a modern day 'boardroom' and while it may be privy to business decisions surrounding sponsors and corporate income, the key decisions that shape the club's future will often take place far away from Elland Road, and will rarely involve democratic decisions chewed over by 'the board'.

Back in the 1960s, the boardroom was integral to the club, and Dave Cocker recalls its location vividly: "It was right above the dressing rooms basically. As you went to the top of the stairs, on the right hand side, as you looked from outside, was the 100 Club with a bar area and the trophies were all in a cabinet which was like the dividing wall between the 100 Club and the foyer, then as you walked round the corner that was the entrance up into the directors' box, and on the right was the entrance to the directors' lounge and that overlooked the façade. On the left hand side as you looked at the façade, where it said 'LEEDS' you have the balcony outside. Part of the balcony is in front of the 100 Club, part of it was this big wide foyer with a big fancy staircase coming up, and then it led out onto the balcony under the façade. They only went out there to raise the flags on the flagpoles, that's all it was there for really. Then as you walked down the foyer inside on the left hand side, next to the directors' lounge was the boardroom."

The 100 Club was an important part of the club's make-up over the latter half of the 20th century, and along with its occupants was as central to the club's structure and management as the boardroom itself. As a room, technically the 100 Club still exists, also as a corporate entertainment room on match days, the Revie Room Suite, but for many years it was the only function room the club had. However, the 100 Club itself, as an organisation, existed for nearly 50 years right up until Ken Bates' tenure when their annual donations to the club were stopped because Bates wanted to control all income streams himself. Now, confusion surrounds whether the lifetime guarantee that came with membership can still be honoured. The 100 Club was a self-regulating private members club, the main reason for Bates' disapproval, and was started in 1957 by F.G. Morehouse, who owned Morehouse Jam factory in nearby Holbeck. As Ray Fell explains, "I used to work at the jam factory between 15 and 18, but F.G. Morehouse was the managing director, and I think he was also a director at Leeds United in the 1950s, I think he also acted as treasurer for a time. But if you were a member of the 100 Club you had your own room, you got parking facilities and a seat in the West Stand."

The first meeting was held on 17th June 1957 at the Queens Hotel in Leeds, and the first members paid 50 guineas each, the money going directly to Leeds United. Quite soon, the 100 Club expanded to accept more members, and moved into a purposely created room along from the boardroom at Elland Road. Other prime movers in the initial formation were Norman Watson, owner of Waddingtons Games, and Norman Wilkinson. By this time, 200 lifetime season tickets were available for 100 guineas each, so each member was effectively next in line to royalty in terms of their status at the club. The private funding was quite unique in football and the members were made aware that they were expected to remain a loyal, fully paid-up and committed member for many years; indeed, membership became subject to a ten-year agreement. Founding member Eddie Binks became president in the 1967/68 season,

and was still a member in 2004; his son Nigel Binks is among the group who still attend games together in a West Stand suite today, even though the official 100 Club no longer exists.

Membership of the 100 Club over the years has included some of the most prominent businessmen and women across Yorkshire. Several businessmen that went on to become Leeds United directors, including former chairmen Leslie Silver and Professor John McKenzie, have also been fully paid-up members.

Bill Fotherby endured an arduous route to 100 Club membership and beyond as he famously made his way up the ladder to the very top at Leeds United over a 17-year period. Bill started as a regular businessman and simply a Leeds United fan and his story shows how far support, commitment, knowing the right people and sheer brass neck can take you: "There was an article in the *Yorkshire Evening Post* in the late 1970s," starts Bill, "giving the name of every shareholder at Leeds United. So I said to my secretary 'write to every shareholder' and the shares were 1p shares, so I said 'offer them £1 a share'. She did that and I got the answers back and I purchased some shares. Then you have to go through the procedure of trying to get on the board. So I did that and the secretary at the time, Keith Archer, wrote back and said the board had turned me down. They didn't want anybody buying shares and attempting a takeover or something, and that's how it went for years. I used to stand outside the West Stand on match days and see them in the 100 Club, they had one private club, the 100 Club. You couldn't get in, couldn't get in. The membership was always full and you have to know somebody if you're not making any headway. I got to know a couple of gentlemen, a Howard Levenson, who was the chairman of the 100 Club, and another gentleman who helped me get on the waiting list. But I used to see them roll up in their Bentleys and Rolls Royces, and get out and get their blankets and their girlfriends or wives out and go in the 100 Club. And I'd park at Harold Williams' house, an ex-Leeds United player, at the top of Beeston Hill and walk down with my colleagues.

"Eventually I got in the 100 Club," Bill continues, "and Manny Cussins used to come in and with the directors they'd all make fun going 'Oh Bill wants to be a director, don't forget Bill'. I got to know Leslie Silver and we got very, very friendly. It was during the Arab/Israeli war and I was a clothier in Leeds. Leslie used to come round and we'd have a drink together on a Sunday morning after the game, and one day he said to me 'I've been invited to join the Leeds United board'. Oh, my heart sunk. 'Oh Leslie,' I said. 'I know how you feel Bill.' Leslie wasn't really fanatical about Leeds United, like I was. But I said 'take it Leslie, take it' after I'd got over the disappointment. I said 'take it Leslie, then try and get me in for god's sake'. I tried everything, I'm courting directors, I'm taking them to boxing events, I'm taking

them out for dinner, I'm trying to court them, to get me on the board. A few weeks later, due to (Leeds United directors) Rayner Barker and Jack Marjason, one Sunday morning the wife says 'Manny Cussins is on the phone for you'. So I took the call and said 'Yes, Manny what is it?' He'd been trying to do a business deal with me over my business, which I wouldn't agree to. So he said 'are you still interested in being a director of Leeds United?' 'Oh,' I said, 'you must be joking, of course I am', he said 'well be down on Tuesday, but I must tell you, I'm against it because I think you're a trouble-causer.'"

Bill laughs at the memory. It escalated pretty rapidly for him from there and he can recall many, shall we say, 'interesting' discussions and meetings taking place in the boardroom over the years, at a time when it was the hub of the club on a very localised basis. One of these involved a very high profile transfer that Leeds United were involved in back in 1995, and when it fell through Bill himself took much of the flak for it, but a fly on the wall in the boardroom would have been able to save him two decades of mirth from Leeds fans. At the time, the team had suffered a hangover from their league title success of 1992 and although they were established as a top five Premier League club, manager Howard Wilkinson was under pressure to sign the high-profile players that various other clubs were now buying, via Sky's millions. Until now, the truth behind what prevented Leeds signing Czech striker Tomas Skuhravy from Genoa has never come out.

"He was built like Attila the Hun," says Bill of his first meeting with Skuhravy. "I said to Howard (Wilkinson) 'if I can get him to Leeds United, my god they'll go crazy'. I went over to Italy and I take over one of the biggest agents in the country, Gianni Paladini, an Italian agent, and we want this Skuhravy. So we arrange everything, we go over there and we're picked up at the airport and taken to Genoa's ground. We get in this big boardroom there and we're waiting for the president to come, he walks in through the door and he's got his overcoat on his shoulders like they all do. They don't speak English, by the way, only when they need to. He says (adopts Italian accent) 'Fotherby, I cannot sell you Skuhravy', 'oh, what are we doing here then? I've come over here to negotiate a deal for this Skuhravy. Your agent tells me and your head coach tells me that this deal we can do?' He replies: 'I would never be forgiven if we sell Skuhravy, the supporters would kill me.' So he's going through all this business, anyway eventually, that's all an act, all a big act and yes, he'll agree to do it, but he'll make a decision the following day. So I say 'well, I've got to fly back tonight, I must have a decision now,' but he can't do it. He says, 'I have to go, I have an appointment, but my boys will take you out and give you a meal and you can get the late flight back.' So his coaches take me out for dinner and there's Gianni Paladini and a lot of small talk and they're going to come to Elland Road the following day, and they're going to bring the player.

"So, the following day comes," continues Bill. "We pick them up from Leeds Bradford Airport and go to Elland Road. Ooh, he looked like a mountain this fella, long flowing hair, tremendous. You look at videos, but videos can be deceiving because they just pick out the best bits. Anyway, we're in the boardroom at Elland Road and we're discussing, and we're all agreed, and I'm wanting Skuhravy to go for his medical and for some reason the president is always delaying it 'no, momento, momento'. We had to finalise his salary with him, so I finalised the salary with the agent of the player and he goes for the medical.

"We're in the boardroom and we're having a drink and we're all congratulating each other, the television cameras are outside, radio is outside all waiting for the result. There's a knock on the boardroom door; it's Alan Sutton the physio, 'Mr Chairman can I have a word with you please?', 'yes, yes', so I go outside and say 'what is it Alan?' He says 'you're not going to like what I have to show you'. He takes out the x-rays of Skuhravy's knee. Well, when you're involved in football, and as closely as I was with the players and the physios and injuries, it didn't take me long to see that, well, there was hardly any knee left. So I said 'what are we gonna do?' So these Italians, well, they're like the mafia, and I said 'I've got to go back in to see that president and I've got to tell him there's going to be no deal, we're not going to buy this boy'. The agent's saying 'well, you can't do that', I said 'I can't do it? We're gonna do it!' I said 'everybody's waiting outside'. But the thing was, how do you go about it? What do you say? Well, it went crazy. If he'd had a gun (the president) he'd have shot me. So then he comes back and says, 'You must not dare say that he has got this bad injury. You must not do that. We would never be able to sell this boy.' So I had to make this story up that we couldn't agree and the supporters thought it was Leeds United that couldn't get the money and stuff, but that was the truth. But we dare not say, because first of all, these people you're dealing with, well, afterwards you can get shot somewhere or whatever. You're dealing with villains. You're dealing with top people that are talking about money and if you say that he had a bad knee they would never sell him. So we had to say they wouldn't pay the money he was entitled to, to leave Genoa, which didn't go down well with the Leeds United supporters; 'Bill Fotherby promises, he doesn't get', but you've to live with that."

Alan Sutton, a Leeds United physio since 1986, has a slight tangent to the story of his rare and certainly most fearful appearance in the Elland Road boardroom and he takes up the story from the same afternoon. "Wilko (Howard Wilkinson) was away on holiday somewhere. We had a press conference booked, 'our new signing', but we hadn't even done a medical. So I went to the hospital with Skuhravy and this interpreter. They had a private plane stood at Leeds Bradford Airport at something like £5,000 an hour, true story. According to Bill this was like the Italian mafia that were over. So

"Brian Clough; manager of Leeds United?" Manny Cussins finds something amusing in the Elland Road boardroom.

we go to the hospital to see John Lawton the off-peak surgeon and when we're there, the player Skuhravy, you could tell, was really, really nervous. He kept on going out, having a fag, coming back in. John's said to him, 'right I need an x-ray on this knee, an MRI scan'. So we got it sorted out straight away. This interpreter then rings up somebody back down at Elland Road in the boardroom. We were in that MRI scan no more than 10 minutes, maybe five. The interpreter comes back in saying 'we're wanted back down at Elland Road, they want us back there now' because John said, 'I'm not happy about this knee'. The girls that did the MRI, even before we left said 'by the way, looking at that you know his knee is not very good at all'.

"So we've gone back down to Elland Road," continues Alan, "and I've gone 'Mr Fotherby, can I have a word with you?' He said 'what is it Alan?' All the press are there and everything, I said 'listen, we can't sign him, there's a massive problem with his right knee and we can't possibly pass his medical at the moment.' So Fotherby is like 'WHAT? Listen, listen, I can't tell them, I can't possibly tell them. If I tell their directors they'll bloody shoot me. YOU'VE got to tell them.' This is Bill Fotherby telling me. So I go in there to all the Italians and say 'erm sorry, we've had our medical people look at the player and we're not right happy with the right knee, it might need surgery and this and that and that.' So Bill's stood behind me and then he comes out and says 'right, what we're going to do is tell the press there's been a last minute problem, and we cannot come to an agreement over his financial demands.' So I had to ring Wilkinson up too. But normally you're in the MRI scan for 30 minutes but they dragged him out after 10 minutes. They knew, they knew. They thought

they'd pulled one on us, and you could tell how nervous they were."

Alan Sutton adds that his only other appearance in the Elland Road boardroom was in October 1988, the day after the sacking of Billy Bremner as Leeds manager. "Leslie Silver called me in," begins Alan. "He wanted to explain the reasoning behind sacking Billy. That just shows the class of the man and that board. Can you imagine now, the chairman calling the physio in personally to explain why the manager was sacked?"

Doubtless the boardroom has reverberated to the sound of many heated discussions such as that of the failed Skuhravy transfer over the years, deals that happened, and as many deals that didn't. That original room, situated off the first floor landing, was first used in 1959, and some fans may like to note that the building of the Banqueting Suite in 1992 refurbished the West Stand operations to such an extent that the location of the original boardroom from 1959 to 1992 is now a back kitchen for the catering facility that serves the various corporate suites in the West Stand on match days. Amid the construction, the league game against Notts County in February 1992 marked the last time that the original boardroom was used, for either meetings or entertaining the visiting club's directors. A new boardroom was created across the landing, but that quickly became a corporate suite. What the likes of Hilton Crowther, Ernest Pullan and Harry Reynolds would think, we can only guess. Today, a boardroom in the East Stand does exist by name, and is seen most often by fans when new signings smile stiffly for the camera, and as a plush, glass-walled and largely informal-looking open-plan office it is a far cry from the secretive, smoke-stained and wood-panelled boardroom of yesteryear.

BOXING

Boxing may not immediately trip off the tongue when listing the sports that have taken place on a serious level at Elland Road, but the ground has a history of staging significant bouts including charity exhibitions that have been well-supported in the Centenary Pavilion and previously the Banqueting Suite, and genuine title fights on the Elland Road pitch itself.

The first high profile boxing to take place at Elland Road was the bill that included British title fights for both Henry Wharton, from York but a Leeds fan, and Herol 'Bomber' Graham from Sheffield. On a Wednesday night, 23rd September 1992 to be precise, a ring was set up in the corner of the ground in front of the West Stand and South Stand and a bill of six title fights took place.

Second on the bill was the British middleweight title fight between the unorthodox Graham and Frank Grant from Bradford. Given Henry Wharton's following were predominantly Leeds fans, the presence of a following from Bradford for such an event inevitably led to tensions amongst the crowd on the evening, particularly when Grant knocked out Graham in the ninth round to take the title amid jubilant scenes.

Next up and top of the bill was Henry Wharton's British and Commonwealth super-middleweight title fight against Sheffield's Fidel 'Castro' Smith. Wharton was considered something of a brutish fighter, rather than a skilful boxer, though he approached the fight undefeated, and in his career would only lose three fights to illustrious opposition in Nigel Benn, Chris Eubank and Robin Reid.

At Elland Road, Wharton won the middle of the fight but was unanimously out-boxed at the beginning and the end, and it was in controversial circumstances that the fight was awarded to Wharton when most observers expected Smith to comfortably win the points decision.

The fight was quite an event and many of the Leeds United first team squad were in attendance, including Gary Speed and Eric Cantona, and as reigning league champions at the time it was another high profile occasion for the club to profit from.

Boxing returned to Elland Road on a more regular basis when the Pavilion was built in 1999. Leeds-residing but Irish-born Derek Roche, a British Welterweight Champion, defended his title there in May 2000, and particularly since its expansion to the Centenary Pavilion in 2011, there have been numerous boxing functions of varying description held in the venue. However, a mass brawl, described as "sickening" by

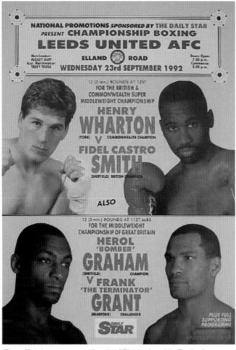

The official programme for the "Championship Boxing" event held at Elland Road in September 1992.

terrified onlookers, erupted at a White Collar Boxing event in the Pavilion in February 2017, which culminated in eight of the men involved being sentenced to a total of 16 years in prison. Since then, Leeds United have not hosted an amateur boxing event.

Prior to that, on 27th September 2013, Leeds fan Josh Warrington defended his English Featherweight title with a unanimous points victory over Ian Bailey, held in the Pavilion. This led to a series of bouts at the Leeds Arena, which built up to Warrington being given the chance to challenge for the IBF World Featherweight title, versus Lee Selby of Wales in June 2018 and on the Elland Road pitch. In a pivotal moment of his career, Warrington lapped up the atmosphere of a ravenous home crowd, and with Lucas Radebe accompanying him on his ring walk as the Kaiser Chiefs played 'I Predict A Riot', he drew confidence from an emphatically 'Leeds' occasion. Warrington defeated Selby by a split decision, with the Welshman badly misjudging the hostility of the Elland Road crowd.

BOYS' PEN

The Boys' Pen; safe and secure, far from warm and dry, but nevertheless a playground on that confusing cusp of adulthood. Long before Family Stands and the relative safety of all-seater stadiums most clubs did still encourage children to attend football matches by creating a half admission charge for juniors. Leeds United, like many, also quite quickly adopted what was known as a 'Boys' Pen'.

Initially, this was situated in the bottom left hand corner of the vast, open Gelderd Road Spion Kop, as you looked at it, and was a rectangular enclosure with around ten steps that stretched almost to the centre of the pitch by the goal, and was segregated from the Kop by a simple timber fence attached to the crush barriers. Photos show evidence of this as far back as the mid-1920s, ie. effectively from when the old Spion Kop was first built up to its eventual size, and the same picket fenced area is visible in aerial photos right until it was demolished in 1968.

The Boys' Pen, of course, was the ready-made alternative to the difficulty most youngsters faced in watching games among adults on swaying and dangerously packed terraces. It was designed so that the younger generation could have an unrestricted view of the pitch in a safe zone away from the rest of the crowd, and offered a kind of Enid Blyton cocoon of innocence away from the cruel and crude realities of life. The name itself does prompt memories of the somewhat backwards nature of life at a time when 'political correctness' was just some remote Marxist theory, and presumably the invitation to use the enclosure was also open to females. But it does remind you that football was a strictly male domain at the time and nobody will have thought twice about the name being inappropriate. That said, a name for the enclosure sometimes used by the more learned supporters, but not routinely how it is now remembered, was the "Children's Paddock".

In addition to general admission at discounted prices, free tickets for the Boys' Pen were regularly distributed around Leeds schools for players in the various football teams. Gary Edwards remembers some of his very early sojourns to Elland Road involving life in the Boys' Pen, before he got the irresistible urge, like many others before and since, to join the adults in the Kop. "Looking back," Gary recalls, "the ground in the early to mid-sixties was, to be fair, a bit of an eyesore – but no-one seemed to care, least of all the hundreds of 11 and 12 year olds like me. On occasion I went in the Boys' Pen in my younger days, but I always preferred to stand with my Dad and the blokes smoking pipes and Woodbines and swearing at the referee. Not much has changed there, apart from the smoking."

Gary himself was an early exponent in the art of the shorter person seeking a more prominent position amongst the crowd, adding: "Most of the boys, including myself, would stand on a wooden stool or buffet as they were called. It was commonplace to see them all walking down Elland Road or Lowfields Road with the wooden stool/buffet or a crate tucked under their arm with a rattle in the other hand. Health and Safety would have a field day these days."

Youngsters standing on a crate was an accepted and common practice for decades, and surprisingly wasn't banned from Elland Road until 1992, as a result of safety measures implemented via the Taylor Report. Then general manager Alan Roberts used a famous David Batty goal against Manchester City to validate the regrettable move, saying: "When David Batty scored one of his rare goals, the jubilation in the Kop was such that three mature supporters received broken ankles in all the excitement that followed. The club's concerns with regards to crates, or youngsters sitting on barriers or walls, is that, in the excitement of celebrating a goal, any crowd surge could result in youngsters being pushed off the crates or barriers and walls."

As with the Kop itself and the rest of the ground generally, the Boys' Pen was bereft of what you would call 'facilities', and refreshments came via a more traditional route, as Gary Edwards recalls: "Vendors would constantly walk around the pitch selling soft drinks, Bovril, nuts, crisps and chocolate. People not near the front would throw the money down to the vendor shouting what they wanted. It was nearly always coins that were thrown forward; paper money such as ten bob notes (50p) and £1 notes belonged to people sitting in the middle of the West Stand. Nuts, crisps and chocolate would be thrown back to the owners while drinks were passed back by the helpful spectators.

"If any of the young ones fainted," Gary recalls, "which happened sometimes, or if they just wanted to go to the front and stand near the wall, they would be hoisted above the crowd and passed down over everybody's heads. The injured were treated by the mostly small and overweight men and women of St John's Ambulance, who were all volunteers."

John Cave also goes misty-eyed at cherished childhood memories of his first adventures into 'independent' football-watching at Elland Road via the Boys' Pen: "I was soon allowed to go to matches with school mates from Lower Wortley when we would stand en masse in the open-to-the-elements Boys' Pen behind the Gelderd Road end goal. I would have been about seven when this first occurred in about 1951, but still too young to take advantage of the free pass that all kids got if they played for their school team. Later when these free passes were about we would pull the old 'one pass gets all in' trick by simply slipping the free pass back out through a convenient gap in the corrugated iron perimeter fence to your waiting mates, repeated then until all the kids from our Kirkdales estate were all in the ground.

"It normally cost 6d, 2.5p in 'new' money, to go to games," John continues, "and I do not think this ever changed for as long as I was in the Pen – perhaps five or six seasons. There was a single policeman – it was the same bobby for years – stood at the entrance to the pen and he became well known to us all. I am unable to recall there ever being any reason for him to intervene in any disturbance throughout my time in the Pen."

A common sight at full-time of a given match was to see adults vaulting over the fence from the Kop into the Boys' Pen, with little regard for its occupants, in a rush to get out of the ground. With the North West Corner Stand not built until 1970, it was possible to exit the ground via a daredevil slide down the banking at the side of the old Kop, the severity of which was lessened if you approached it through the Boys' Pen at the bottom of the stand, but still, clearly a practice that would not be allowed today. The Boys' Pen was also frequented for a time by bus and tram drivers of the 'Football Specials', given free tickets until '3/4 time' when they had to return to their vehicles to transport the masses home.

In April 1968 the original Kop was re-developed and the current "North/Revie/Gelderd/Kop" stand replaced it. The North East Corner Stand was not completed until 1973 and it was to here that the Boys' Pen was moved, occupying the terracing in the corner below the seats above.

A photo taken by my Dad on the Kop during the England v West Germany charity match for the Bradford Fire Disaster in 1985; visible in the photo are number 5 Jack Charlton, number 6 Bobby Moore and number 4 Nobby Stiles.

For almost all of the 1970s and most of the 1980s, admission to the Boys' Pen was a mere inflation-retardant 50p. It was a practice as common as John Cave's one-pass-for-all trick for children of a certain age to pay to get in the Boys' Pen and, attracted by the menacing allure of the Kop or Lowfields terraces, to vault the fences when the stewards weren't looking and disappear into the throng for an adventurous afternoon of growing up fast. Indeed, the promotion of a fan from the Boys' Pen to the Kop or Lowfields was seen as a rite of passage in being a Leeds fan, and the day when you started to legitimately pay to enter other stands was the day you had truly graduated. Leeds fan Chris Mabbott recalls many an afternoon spent trying to dodge the stewards: "The usual routine was to go into the Boys' Pen entrance (50p at the time) and try and sneak past the stewards at the bottom of the stairs which lead into the Lowfields Road standing area. If we failed to get past them we would go into the Boys' Pen and try to get under the fence between the said area and the Kop. We used to ask anybody in the Kop to watch out for the stewards and there was one specific 'step', if you were thin enough, where you could squeeze under and gain access to the Kop. We had many happy hours trying to outwit the stewards/police. We used to get our 50p for the games by selling programmes at the greyhound stadium. If I remember rightly we used to get 2p for every programme sold."

However, most teenagers have that awkward period where they don't feel like they quite belong in the adult world, but they still feel occasional urges to escape the smothering confines of childhood. With the obvious gulf between the safety of the Boys' Pen and the tempting playground of the Kop and Lowfields, there was very little middle ground for a teenager resisting those nervous fumblings through a crippling confidence crisis. Reserves games were one such accommodating outlet and often gave youngsters licence to experience the freedom of Elland Road, albeit in a fat-free and almost entirely synthetic light. John Cave was one such youngster: "Reserve team games were not always the most exciting events so we often entertained ourselves by either playing football at the back of the Lowfields stand between the turnstile blocks, only climbing up the steep steps at half-time to get an update on scores; or alternatively scrounging about at the back of the Kop where they always dumped the litter collected from previous home games, thus giving us the opportunity to look for discarded old programmes and cigarette cards."

By the late 1980s the Boys' Pen disappeared, as the club's success and the restrictions of the Taylor Report demanded more terrace capacity for those paying adult prices. Integral also to this was the implementation of the first Family Stand in the North West Corner Stand in 1985. Gone was the opportunity to make-believe you were 'at-the-match' on your own, gone was the buffer zone where mates grew up together, gone was the possibility of enterprise and entrepreneurship. Here, for now, was the family experience and those cursed apron strings.

BRADFORD CITY

The afternoon of 11th May 1985 was enduringly significant for football in West Yorkshire and was to have lasting repercussions. Whilst Leeds United's slim play-off hopes were ended by a 1-0 defeat at Birmingham City on an afternoon ravaged by repeated pitch invasions and frequent chaos that resulted in one young Leeds fan dying when a perimeter wall collapsed, Bradford City were entertaining Lincoln City in the final game of the season, having just been crowned Division Three champions.

As everyone knows, the distasteful events involving both Leeds and Birmingham fans at St Andrew's were overshadowed by the 56 deaths that occurred when Valley Parade's main stand caught fire; a further 265 Bradford fans were treated for injuries.

From the first sighting, it took just four minutes for the antiquated wooden stand to be engulfed in a fireball, and a celebratory occasion was turned into a horrific nightmare that scarred the club, the local community and the football world. As a result Bradford spent 19 months on the road whilst Valley Parade was re-developed, playing mainly at Odsal, the neighbouring home of the city's rugby league and speedway clubs. Bradford also played at Leeds Road, Huddersfield, and staged four games at Elland Road.

In circumstances identical to Huddersfield Town in 1950 when their main stand caught fire, Bradford were grateful for the assistance of their neighbours and the four games played at Elland Road were:

- **a 3-1 win versus Stoke City on 1st September 1985 before 6,999 fans**
- **a 4-1 defeat to Sheffield United on 26th October before 7,448**
- **a 1-0 defeat to Grimsby Town on 1st March 1986 before 5,185**
- **a 1-0 win over Oldham on 4th March before 3,964**

It should also be noted that the game at Elland Road between Leeds United and Bradford City on 21st September 1985, which Leeds won 2-1, was originally scheduled to be an away game for Leeds. The scheduled home and away games with Bradford were swapped on the fixture list, due to the availability of Odsal and the resulting folly of Leeds potentially playing an 'away' fixture at Elland Road.

As a result, Leeds had the rare convenience of home fixtures on three consecutive Saturdays.

Adding to the link with Leeds United was the fact that Bradford's manager at the time was Trevor Cherry, a former Leeds captain with 477 appearances to his name from a 10-year career at Elland Road. His assistant was another former Leeds man, Terry Yorath.

Following the Bradford Fire Disaster, a national appeal raised more than £3.5 million, a £46,000 portion of which was from a match staged before 20,000 fans at Elland Road in July 1985 between the surviving members of the 1966 England and West Germany (as it still was then) World Cup Final teams. In what was a somewhat bizarre spectacle, in hindsight, as some players were in their fifties, and yes I was present, the game was a half-hearted affair bordering on pantomime played out in torrential rain, which England won 6-4. Trevor Cherry, fittingly, was one of the many England substitutes.

BRS HAULAGE

Images and clips from yesteryear of Leeds United players training on Fullerton Park or signing autographs in the West Stand car park, or of managers rushing to their car pursued by a horde of photographers and reporters; all have one common feature in the background. It's not Alan Sutton with his leather physio bag, it's not Jack 'the Rottweiler' Williamson, the former head of security, attempting to maintain order, it's not even long-standing groundsman John Reynolds chasing crows away from his grass seed. No, it's the BRS Haulage buildings.

A series of docile brick warehouses lined up from the corner of Lowfields Road all the way along to the outer edge of the Fullerton Park pitches/car park, the BRS Haulage buildings provided a dark and industrial backdrop to many famous images from the point of their construction in the early 1960s, which preceded the building of the M621.

To this day, with the buildings now gone, the access road behind the Kop is separated from the land by a wire fence, but previously the walk along this road provided a good view of activities at BRS and the shadowy, almost clandestine buildings cast a menacing shadow over the pre- and post-match journey, not to mention the iconic and contrasting landscape they provided for hundreds of pen pictures featuring Leeds United's most famous players. For nearly 50 years, the buildings added to the compelling mixture of muck and glamour that made Elland Road such a fascinating sector of discovery.

The arrival of the M621 was seven years after the Kop had been re-developed in 1968, but the expanse of land between the Kop and the motorway had already become occupied, in the early 1960s, by a company then called Castle Brothers Haulage, who owned the freehold of the land. Prior to the M621 construction the area behind the original Kop was open marshland including the notorious 'Wortley Beck', which snaked around the area and caused frequent flooding issues. Given the proximity of their business to the ground, it is likely that Castle Brothers knew of the imminent plans for the M621 and the accessibility it would afford them, but the haulage buildings were certainly amongst the first industrial units to take occupancy in the area that is saturated with them today.

As a business, Castle Brothers consisted of three brothers, Sid, Jack and Joe, who had previously owned the United Garage on Elland Road, now a branch of Subway, above which they also lived. They sold that garage in 1960 and bought a section of the marshy wasteland behind the Kop shortly after. Prior to this, in the 1940s and '50s, the land had been used for match day car parking, which would appear to have been a perilous enterprise given the frequent occasions that the beck flooded. However, having established their haulage business on the developing land, Sid Castle offered the land to Leeds United, with whom they had a close relationship, in 1968 when he heard they were looking to build a new Kop. As Dave Cocker recalls, Don Revie was the main motivator behind expanding the ground but, although most shared his vision, he ultimately didn't get the board's full financial support: "Don really wanted them to buy the land behind the Kop, but they never bought it. Don always wanted a bigger Kop, he wanted a far bigger stadium and more fans, he was always dissatisfied with the attendances." The Don's argument is supported by many who feel the re-built 1968 Kop could and should have been much bigger than it was.

Content that they had enough land already on which to reconstruct the ground as planned, the club turned down the Castles' £1 million offer. As a result, Sid Castle rented the land and buildings to BRS Haulage, which stood for British Road Services and was owned by British Rail. From there and for many years, the buildings and the famous backdrop remained the same, with the land listed officially on planning documentation as being owned by the "Castle Family Trust". Sid Castle remained close to the club, and was a big friend of Revie's and Les Cocker's. Also, all the brothers were members of the '100 Club'.

Eventually, having become a major player in the UK haulage industry and requiring bigger premises, BRS, then owned by the Exel Group, vacated the site and the lease was taken on by Leeds United in the early 2000s. The open land that was available on the perimeter up to the motorway was occasionally used for car parking, but in essence the club did very little with it.

In 2004 Stanley Leisure paid £5 million to secure the rights and first option to buy the Castle Brothers site, plus additional land, for five years, with the intention of it forming part of a 'super casino' in the event that the government passed certain gaming laws in the UK. Eventually they did pass the laws, but the plans to build the casino on that land never materialised and Stanley Leisure subsequently gave up the rights to the seven acres of land. As the casino development proposal covered sections of land at that time owned by the Castle family, Leeds City Council and Leeds United, the £5 million was shared between those three parties. In 2004, it came as a considerable boost to Leeds United's severely ravaged finances, although with no

positive end in sight, the club of course sold Elland Road in its entirety later the same year.

Having stood empty and derelict for nearly a decade, in 2009 the original Castle Brothers and BRS buildings were demolished and the whole site was flattened, allowing clear views of the back of the Kop for the passing traffic on the M621 and providing a brighter thoroughfare for fans walking to and from the ground behind the Kop. Unofficially, demolition had started a year earlier as the famous backdrop to so many iconic photos began to be dismantled by fans queuing

An aerial photo from 1964 showing a good view of the BRS Haulage buildings when they were still owned by Castle Brothers. Note also the greyhound stadium in the distance, the cricket ground and Petty's Field sports ground at the bottom of the picture and the fleet of buses parked on Lowfields Road.

overnight for Play-Off Final tickets in 2008. In a bid to find fire wood to keep warm, fans stormed the derelict site and ripped down 20 foot high wooden doors to burn through the night.

In 2011, with the Stanley Leisure option having expired, Leeds City Council secured the land from the Castle Family Trust, meaning the council owned almost all the land surrounding Elland Road other than the shops and houses on Elland Road itself. Leeds United again use the land on match days for supporter car parking, and over the summer of 2020 the council's

successful Park & Ride scheme was expanded to take in some of that land, and the area was neatly landscaped, whilst a relief road was also built leading out on to Lowfields Road. This will come into its own on match days when fans can use the Park & Ride spaces and drive away safely afterwards, rather than through a rubble and pot-hole strewn former industrial wasteland, as previously. Intriguingly, enough of the former BRS Haulage land has been left vacant and untouched, should Leeds United wish to expand the Kop in the future.

The extended Park & Ride facilities and relief road constructed in the summer of 2020; note in the top right corner the Police HQ on the old greyhound stadium site and the Ice Rink, and also note the land where the BRS Haulage buildings stood has been left vacant for possible future development.

C

CAPACITY

Ground capacity; the 'my Dad's bigger than your Dad' of sporting stadia. Sources differ as to what is currently the official capacity of Elland Road, and it is difficult to get a definitive answer. This is largely due to the East Stand extension work which reduced the capacity of the East Stand upper tier during the summer of 2011, by removing five rows of seats to make room for more executive boxes. Three available sources put the figure at 39,460 but it is likely to be nearer the 37,890 quoted on the official club website and in the book *Leeds United: The Complete Record*, with those seats recently being lost.

Certainly there is often a difference between the official physical capacity and the maximum capacity available for a given match, due to the variable methods required for crowd segregation, and in the case of the East Stand upper, the number of seats that are set aside for corporate use only rather than for the general fan, and therefore are sometimes left unused. The Brighton & Hove Albion game which kicked off the 2013/14 season was declared a sell-out to 'general' supporters just prior to kick-off, and yet the attendance was only 33,432, largely due to a meagre away following from Brighton, but also due to unused corporate seats in the East Stand upper tier. Many of the 'sold out' home fixtures during Marcelo Bielsa's reign at Elland Road have seen no match day tickets available well in advance of the game, but the biggest crowd, and therefore the generally accepted 'capacity', has been around 36,500.

There can be few grounds that have had their capacity increased and then reduced as frequently as Elland Road has over the years. Quite apart from the simple building of stands at different stages, which has fundamentally changed the size of the ground, we have had seats put on terracing (Lowfields Road upper, West Stand Paddock, North East Corner lower, South Stand lower, South East Corner lower and Kop), seats taken out and terracing restored (South Stand), executive boxes installed in three stages (South Stand), existing stands part-demolished (Lowfields Road Stand upper tier), and standing capacities reduced (Kop and Lowfields Road terrace).

Therefore, to quote a figure as an official capacity is something of a moving target; however, in simple terms, it has been around the 40,000 mark since the East Stand was built in 1993. Indeed, for one season (1993/94) when the East Stand was completed but before the Kop was seated, the capacity was nearer 43,000. Prior to that, the restrictions on standing capacity following the Hillsborough Disaster in 1989 meant that in the club's most successful recent seasons, the promotion in 1989/90 and the league championship win in 1991/92, the Elland Road capacity was just under 33,000.

Of course in days gone by, little regard was given to a ground's 'capacity' and rather than it being an elementary part of the safety certificate and match

"Mind if I put my umbrella up?" "Yes, we can't see" "But it says 'Leeds United' on it" "We don't care" "And it's raining" "Wear a hat then" "I don't have one" "EVERYBODY has one" – a 42,694 gate for the FA Cup tie versus Bolton in 1927.

day operations, the capacity was merely a vague parameter often overlooked until a situation became perilous. In the Leeds City years there was no 'official' capacity initially, but stung by a growing appetite for the game in Leeds it was eventually listed as 22,000. Yet there were several attendances of over 30,000, amid, presumably, anarchic scenes of chaotic crowd control. The 1910 FA Cup Semi-Final at Elland Road between Barnsley and Everton had to be stopped several times due to crowd encroachment on to the pitch, and this was a 36,000 crowd in what the club claimed was a ground by then somehow capable of holding 45,000, despite it being far from fully developed.

That same capacity was in place just two years later when Elland Road staged a hastily arranged FA Cup Fourth Round replay between Bradford City and Barnsley. No lessons had been learned and confirmation was emphatically established that the ground was simply not set up for large crowds, and also the club's officials were equally incapable of implementing the correct procedures. Mounted police spent all afternoon clearing the pitch and with the tie in extra time, the referee ended the game early as it was impossible to continue. The FA, however, were keen to build crowds in a region still known more as a rugby league stronghold and actively wanted Elland Road to stage big games. Clearly, the ground had to evolve, however, and the capacity edged up to 50,000 when the Kop, Scratching Shed and Lowfields were completed in the 1920s. A number of FA Cup Semi-Finals were subsequently staged at the ground in the 1930s, '40s and '50s which drew attendances of between 43,572 and 54,066, thankfully without incident.

The colour and carnival of Elland Road's Kop during the 1970s, when the officially stated 'capacity' was still a rough aim rather than a strict limit.

After the main ground development was complete by the late 1950s, the physical capacity was around 58,000 depending on how stringently the standing capacities were controlled, which in those days could be described variously as 'hit and miss' or 'borderline illegal', though Elland Road was no different to any other ground in that respect. Certainly the occasion of the record 57,892 attendance in 1967 showed that near-fatalities would occur when capacity was approached, and the 'official' all-ticket capacity at the time was set at a more measured, prudent and controllable 52,000. The capacity gradually reduced as more seats were introduced, segregation put in place and restrictions on standing capacities implemented. These safety measures saw the capacity set at 48,000 in April 1969.

As with any mainly terraced stadium, of course, the capacity was at the mercy of where people chose to stand and how well 'packed' the stadium was. My Dad recalls a game on Boxing Day 1964 against Blackburn, the one and only time my Mum has ever been to Elland Road, when a crowd of 45,341 saw a 1-1 draw, or at least some of them did. "We were walking up the big stone steps (at the back of the Lowfields/North East Corner), great big high steps with handrails coming down, and we never got to the top, it was just a mass of people, we didn't get to the top to even see the pitch until half-time. I can't remember any serious problems as a result of overcrowding, just occasions where you couldn't even see the pitch, because everyone is coming in and there weren't sufficient entrances."

By the 1969/70 season when Leeds United were league champions and after the new Kop but prior to the North West and North East Corner Stands being built, capacity was officially still 48,000. This gradually reduced even when the corner stands appeared, as the huge terraced corner on the Lowfields Road side was chopped away. But by the time the South Stand was completed during the 1974/75 season, the capacity was officially increased to 50,000. This was reduced by the shortening of the Lowfields Road upper tier and the installation of stairways and pens in the terracing below, which meant by 1978, when all plans to develop the ground stood dormant for 13 years, the capacity stood at a strangely precise 43,900, and remained so for a number of years. Through the stagnant 1980s the capacity was reduced by the installation of executive boxes in the South Stand, the increasing need for segregation and more officious regulations on standing capacities, which is how we arrive at the 33,000 figure that witnessed Leeds' most recent triumphs.

The restrictions imposed weeks before the start of the infamous 1989/90 season saw nearly 9,000 cut from the capacity, and the resulting restrictions on away fans (in order to accommodate as many home fans as possible) meant Leeds estimated they would lose between £250,000 and £300,000 in revenue that season. The Kop capacity was reduced from 12,563 to 7,866 (37% reduction) and the Lowfields terracing was cut from 8,189 to 4,426 (46%). For Leeds United, it couldn't have come at a worse time after years of struggling to attract fans. The club were frantic to find extra capacity to satiate the frenzied desire of Leeds fans that had been reawakened by the smell of success. Mid-season, 1,300 spaces were found by putting seats back in the shelf on the Lowfields, utilising the first row in the West Stand now that the fences had been removed and moving barriers to create some precious standing spaces. They were well-received.

Following promotion back to the First Division the club were quick to finally look at expanding Elland Road. In September 1990 a scheme was proudly announced, in partnership of course with Leeds City Council, to lift the capacity back up to 40,000. This involved a less ambitious East Stand than was actually built in 1993 and included the South East Corner Stand exactly as it later appeared, but also included a second tier on the West Stand and a corner stand in the south west area. The development didn't quite happen like that, and the 40,000 landmark was reached simply by pushing the boat out a little further with the 17,000 East Stand.

Bill Fotherby remembers the club making plans to really go to town on Elland Road and maximise all potential after the league title win in 1992, and when Leeds were established as a top five Premier League club in 1994. Maximising potential was something that the club had never really been able to accomplish during periods of success, but at that time the East Stand, the Banqueting Suite and possibly new stands would allow that:

"I would sketch out plans," Bill begins, "and then they would go to architects to do it properly, but I did plans for the capacity to go to 60,000, and the chairman would say 'Bill, you're exaggerating, 60,000?' I said 'listen, you get Manchester United coming, you get Arsenal coming, you get Liverpool, Newcastle, and you know what happens? We can only give them 3,000 tickets'. I said in a board meeting 'we had the FA Cup match when we could have sold 15,000 to Barnsley! So if you take the seven or eight times a year that you can fill that 60,000, it's worth doing, because that's the way it's going' and it was. We'd gone up from our 11, 13, 15,000 in the mid-80s up to 42,000 people and leads were coming in commercially from London. Money was coming in, it was marvellous." Clearly buoyed by the option of offering substantial allocations to the big clubs that would be almost guaranteed to take them, and also the supplementary takings from the thriving corporate business side of the club, Bill was clearly excited by that visionary word that he often repeats: 'potential'.

"People say now that Leeds' gates are fantastic. Leeds' gates? They're losing money, what did they do? So people say 'ooh, great crowds at Leeds, 30,000', they're nothing to what they should be, we should be talking 50,000 every week."

Another factor that has influenced the Elland Road capacity is the officious governing of UEFA relating to European ties. The famous game against Stuttgart in 1992 had a low attendance of 20,457 due partly to many fans giving up after the 3-0 deficit incurred after the first leg, but also due to UEFA designating the game a 'Category A' status, ie. a high risk of crowd trouble, and the capacity in certain areas was restricted accordingly. Also, in the Champions League season of 2000/01, the increased regulation height of UEFA's advertising boards dictated the ludicrous situation of the first five rows of all stands being empty because the spectators could not see over them, thus UEFA's showpiece occasions had a crowd 4,000 lower than normal league games of the time.

CENTENARY

Leeds United's imminent centenary was a welcome distraction for a number of years, particularly if you wanted something nice to think about instead of Leeds being shipwrecked in the Championship until the end of time. Alas, as the date and year grew closer there was well-founded concern amongst the fanbase over whether the incumbent guardians of the club fully understood its heritage and importance, and had a grasp on the creative processes available to suitably celebrate its 100th birthday. Fortunately a change in ownership at exactly the right time dispelled many of those fears, and in a situation where every fan will have their own individual ideas as to how something like this should be recognised, in general the club did a good job in being faithful to the history and symbolism Leeds United's 100 years have evoked. In short, you can't please everyone.

While the centenary was very much about the club itself, Elland Road was of course central to the celebrations and stands as a physical legacy of the achievement as the only ground Leeds United have called home on a permanent basis, and quite literally, the only place for us. However, 17th October 2019 was marked first, and appropriately, at the point where it all started, at Salem Chapel in Hunslet where a public meeting of a different sort was held 100 years on from Leeds United's formation. Fans who shared the club's birthdate were invited along for a shindig they will never forget, whilst author and Leeds fan Daniel Chapman addressed the attending crowd by reading a passage from his epic *100 Years of Leeds United* tome, released to mark the occasion.

BBC Radio Leeds commentator Adam Pope remembers the poignant occasion well: "The event at Salem Chapel was particularly memorable as I was allowed in and heard Daniel Chapman deliver an excellent speech about how the club had been born out of strife thanks to the will of the fans a century before. As well as owner Andrea Radrizzani being present alongside (current captain) Liam Cooper, club legend the late Norman Hunter was there, whilst ex Supporters' Club chairman Ray Fell and current co-chairman Phil Beeton joined us on air on BBC Radio Leeds. The club invited fans who shared their birthday to attend, which was a nice touch. All done in the shadow of the old Tetley's Brewery, it showed how durable an institution Leeds United has been to survive when others have not."

A truly unique and pinch-yourself-if-you-were-there moment as a dazzling array of Leeds United legends congregate in the Banqueting Suite prior to the Centenary Gala Dinner on 17th October 2019.

For once the fixture list was kind to Leeds United, and two days later a home game against Birmingham City saw many of the legends paraded again, whilst fireworks and a party atmosphere surrounded a 1-0 win secured by Leeds-born Kalvin Phillips.

In addition to the events surrounding the date itself, the club commissioned a 'Dream Scene' painting produced by celebrated Australian artist Jamie Cooper, a photo history book, a DVD, tonnes of merchandise and wore a unique kit for the Birmingham game, albeit this met with a mixed response by not directly mimicking any specific kit Leeds had worn before and being quite prohibitively priced.

After a humble and suitably respectful ceremony, it was off for a quick civic reception in which the Revie legends were awarded the freedom of the city, before the congregation headed off to get their glad rags on for the evening. Fans were thrown a free party in Millennium Square whilst over 50 legendary ex-players including Tony Yeboah, Vinnie Jones, Lucas Radebe, Gordon Strachan and Gary McAllister joined the Revie legends and current squad in a night of glitz and glamour in the appropriately titled Centenary Pavilion. The players had congregated prior to the event in the Banqueting Suite and reacquainted themselves with former colleagues amidst exceptional scenes that will never be repeated, before posing for a unique group picture to mark the occasion – a team photo to make any Leeds fan of any era go weak at the knees – ahead of a night of celebration over the road.

The centenary was the culmination of several years' work and several months of drip-feeding projects and announcements in the build-up to the 17th October date. The Kaiser Chiefs gig in June 2019 kicked off the 'centenary season' in effect, and Leeds had planned a 'centenary friendly' against Bayern Munich (if any game against this opposition could ever be described as friendly) but this was cancelled in the wake of the biggest sweep of Coronavirus disruption. Any such regret was bittersweet, however, because if the centenary had been 12 month later the entire project would have been completely kyboshed.

The 2019/20 vintage recreate the Leeds United wave prior to the Centenary fixture versus Birmingham City on 19th October 2019

The newly created Centenary Square outside the Pavilion on Lowfields Road.

"In the main I think the club did well," Adam adds when asked about the centenary celebrations, "CEO Angus Kinnear made the right call based on his experience at Arsenal not to drag them out for a protracted period of time. I look back at October 2019 as an extremely busy period but one I believe the club, the local media and supporters' groups like the Trust and Supporters' Club used well to remind and educate young and old of the Whites' rich history, whilst a new chapter was unfurling on the pitch under Marcelo."

Phil Hay adds his thoughts on how the club generally did well in difficult circumstances: "A lot of it was very good. There was a proper effort made to acknowledge 100 years. It would have been nice if the special centenary shirt had been more affordable, but in terms of the tone, I thought it was mostly spot on."

As it was, the lasting, physical legacy of the centenary that the club wanted to create was completed but never revealed with any ceremony. Centenary Square was created outside the Pavilion on Lowfields Road and took the form of a roll of honour of every player who had played for the club (excluding, to my personal chagrin, players from the Midland League season in 1919/20 and who had represented the club during the Second World War) and four granite benches depicting club captains, the Revie era, European nights and, of course, Elland Road. On the left-hand side another phase is being added celebrating the achievements of the 2019/20 'centenary season'. The square was created around a base of personalised stones purchased by fans in much the same way that Bremner Square was finished. And just like Bremner Square, the work

has further stamped an identity on the surrounding area around Elland Road whilst also providing a visual spectacle and celebrating the club's indomitable 100 years in a humble and dignified way.

Whilst celebrating the Centenary as a Premier League club felt like it would have been perfect, Leeds United always likes a plot twist and a playful swipe of non-conformity, and as it happens, getting promoted at the end of the centenary season was, in fact, the fitting finale we didn't realise we all wanted.

CENTRE CIRCLE

Cast your mind back to the array of Leeds United legends that have approached the centre circle pre-match, tossed a coin, posed for photos and shaken the officials' hands. Liam Cooper, Billy Bremner, Lucas Radebe, Gordon Strachan, Trevor Cherry, Bobby Collins, Wilber Cush, John Charles, Wilf Copping, erm.... Kevin Nichols, Paul Butler, Lee Peltier, OK, OK that's enough.

Add to that the crunching tackles that have taken place within that famous circle over the years. Kalvin Phillips, Shaun Derry, David Batty, Vinnie Jones, Ian Snodin, Brian Flynn and Johnny Giles have all steamed into a meaty challenge in the heat of the battle for midfield domination, causing some fans to wince, others to feel a rush of adrenalin and most opponents to retrieve scattered body parts.

The centre circle of any football ground is a focal point of many memories and Elland Road is no different. Mainly, however, the centre circle of the Elland Road pitch is notable for three things, and one of them is the

Billy Bremner leads his troops in the orchestrated wave to the crowd from the centre circle in November 1974.

fact that the actual position of the centre circle has changed many times. Firstly, Holbeck Rugby Club played with a pitch orientation of east to west until Leeds City took occupancy of the ground in 1904, and it is believed this was tampered with on at least one other occasion before the ground development accelerated in the 1920s, and the pitch orientation was settled on a permanent basis.

Add to this the fact that the building of the new Kop in 1968 created in total 18 metres of additional space at that end of the pitch, and so between 1968 and 1973 the pitch was moved northwards on two occasions. After the Kop was built it wasn't until the end of the 1969/70 season that the pitch was moved northwards by nine metres, meaning for the first two years of its existence, the inhabitants of the Kop had a strained view of proceedings. A nine metre gap existed behind both goals for three years until the end of the 1972/73 season. In readiness for the building of the South Stand at the end of the following season the pitch position was moved again in the summer of 1973, and finally settled upon, including the position of the centre circle. Therefore, the league championship season of 1973/74 was the first season played with the pitch position as it is now. As an aside, Elland Road's pitch dimensions have remained a

UEFA-standard 105 metres by 68 metres for as long as anyone can remember, bar Howard Wilkinson and George Graham each reducing the width for tactical reasons at certain points of their tenures.

The second point of interest with regards to the centre circle was the decorative lining up of the players for many years as they ran on to the pitch prior to kick-off. As part of Don Revie and Paul 'The Beaver' Trevillion's masterplan to improve the club's public image, the players were instructed to run on to the pitch via the tunnel and head straight to the centre circle where they would all line up, and in a choreographed fashion, turn 360 degrees and wave to all four corners of the ground before heading off to warm up.

This was a far cry from the casual ambling on to the pitch in no particular order before embarking on what passed for a 'warm-up', which had been deemed sufficient since time began. In the days of Revie's illustrious team this was showmanship of almost arrogant proportions, and supplemented the aloof aura of the team that never warmed other fans to them. Conversely, it also added an intimidatory feel and did create a superior belief among the players. By the mid-1980s, however, the likes of Kevin Hird and Ronnie Robinson attempting the same thing before the

COAL AND CLAY MINING

concrete expanses of a half-empty ground bordered on the ridiculous and Howard Wilkinson swiftly put a halt to the practice when he took over in 1988. Brian McDermott made a vain and short-lived attempt to re-introduce the wave in 2013, but again, the quality of the personnel somewhat diluted the message, whilst Marcelo Bielsa's team made a more genuine re-enactment of the wave on the day of the club's centenary game in October 2019. In addition to the ceremony of the occasion, the table-topping and suitably track-suited team being on their way to promotion made this a more faithful homage to greatness.

Third and finally, the centre circle at Elland Road was supposedly the location of buried treasure in 1975, according to the characters Norman Stanley Fletcher (Ronnie Barker) and Blanco Webb (David Jason) in an episode from series two of BBC comedy series *Porridge*, named 'Happy Release'. The two characters fooled another soon-to-be-released inmate, Norris, into believing there was treasure under the pitch at Leeds United's football ground. The end of the episode saw the 'Elland Road' floodlights being turned on to expose Norris in the act of digging up the centre circle, although the BBC actually filmed the scene at QPR's nearby ground Loftus Road.

Our much-cherished patch of LS11 might be most famous for occasional sporting triumph and plentiful occurrences at the other end of the scale, but in the big scheme of the universe and its interminable evolution the area has, believe it or not, been the scene of other activities of a much less emotionally draining nature. Whilst other regions of Yorkshire may be more famous for their coal industries, Leeds and its surrounding expanses supported a network of thriving pits for the best part of three centuries, until the last colliery in Leeds, Allerton Bywater, closed in March 1992.

Within the boundaries of Leeds there were several mining communities built up in Middleton, Rothwell, Morley, Haigh Moor, West Ardsley, Garforth, Kippax, Wortley and of course Beeston. At its height in 1880 there were 111 collieries in Leeds, but most were mined to only 300 feet and average output, at around 500 tonnes per day, was low compared to other areas of the country. Still, coal mining had an enormous influence on the economy and social life of the city in the 18th and 19th centuries, but now the collieries are silent and in most cases levelling and landscaping have combined to eradicate any evidence of the mines ever existing.

This is particularly true in the area around Elland Road football ground, which in the 19th century was a

The four towering chimneys of the disused Leeds (Wortley) Fireclay Company remain in this aerial photo from 1964; note also the excavated 'Quarry' area on the opposite side of Elland Road and the whitewashed wall of the New Peacock pub on the boundary edge of the old cricket pitch.

landscape rich in clay and coal outcrops. Whilst coal had always been mined to varying degrees right from the 13th century, the industry had routinely suffered through the lack of transportation for the bulky commodity, which restricted it to local markets. By the 18th century the Aire and Calder Navigation Canal and the Leeds and Liverpool Canal had opened up the possibility of bigger export markets and with the advent of the railways the industry began to thrive.

It was in the 1800s that a number of small mines were built in the Beeston area as the local population began to grow accordingly. In 1817 only 894 people were listed as residing in Beeston (from a Leeds total of 62,534), but by 1894, when most of the local pits existed and were owned under manorial rights by the Low Moor Iron Company, the population was a more healthy 2,952. To put that into context, in 2018 the population of Beeston and Holbeck was around 26,000.

Still, various pits were scattered around the area surrounding what is now the football ground. 'Lee Pit' was situated a few yards along from the original site of the Drysalters pub at the foot of Elland Road, which now forms part of the A6110 Beeston Ring Road. 'Hall Pit' was on the steep land just above the site of the old greyhound stadium before you reach Crow Nest Lane. 'Beggars Hill Colliery' was behind the streets known as the Cannonburys and Hoxtons, but in modern day terms was just behind where McDonalds is now situated.

The two pits that were closest to the football ground were the 'Garden Pit', which was about 300 yards from the ground, past the Wortley Beck and approximately where the Latchmore Road Industrial Estate is now, off Lowfields Road, and finally the 'Peacock Pit', which was behind the huge works of the Leeds (Wortley) Fireclay

Company in the area then known as Islington, but in the middle of what is now the M621.

The Leeds (Wortley) Fireclay Company produced glazed pottery pipes and gullies for the water industry and both glazed and unglazed fireclay bricks. It actually operated four small pits in the area between Gelderd Road and Elland Road, which was locally known as the 'low fields' area. These pits worked out all the reserves of coal and fireclay from under the surrounding ground and having opened in 1873, the Fireclay Company became a dominant business in the area in the 1890s, with its towering chimneys taking over much of the landscape and dwarfing the small pits around it. For the fire bricks, the main mine of the Fireclay Company was in New Farnley, from where the materials were transported to the Elland Road works to be made into fire bricks.

Despite the plentiful coal seams in the area, many of which almost reached the surface, mining on such a small scale was not profitable, and all the five pits around the football ground site became disused between 1890 and 1910. This was long before the national coal industry commenced its decline in the 1920s, as a result of export markets lost during World War 1. In 1910 all the pits were still visible, but this gradually changed over the next few years. The Leeds (Wortley) Fireclay Company also closed in the 1920s, possibly as a knock-on effect of the pits closing, although the huge chimneys are visible in photos from as late as the mid-1960s.

Of course, in 1897 Holbeck Rugby Club took ownership of the plot of land on Elland Road and began to build a stadium. Prior to that Bentley's Brewery had used the site as a recreation ground and adjacent to

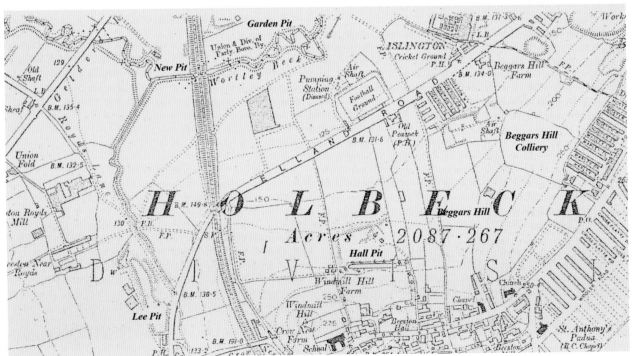

An Ordnance Survey map from 1905 shows the location of the already disused Lee, Hall and Garden Pits and the Beggars Hill Colliery. The only working pit at this time appears to be the New Pit between the railway line and Gelderd Road.

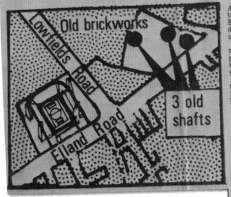

Old mine shaft find kicks off big alert

Almost within "throw-in" distance of Leeds United's Elland Road ground, three disused mine shafts have been uncovered.

Leeds Corporation workmen, demolishing the former premises of Leeds Fireclay Company, stumbled on the shafts this week.

Immediate precautions were taken, including fencing round the old shaft tops. Notices warning of possible danger were put up.

NEAR PITCH

Although all three disused mine workings are close to Elland Road, and to the United pitch, a spokesman for the Corporation said that he could not see the shafts being dangerous.

"They will be tested and if, as we think, the shafts are only capped off, they will be properly filled in," he said.

He added that the shafts were right in the path of the new South West Urban Motorway which sweeps across Elland Road.

A newspaper report from 1973 details the disused mine shafts found during preparatory work for the M621.

their land was an unused pumping station and an accompanying air shaft that had previously served the nearby pits as a welcome water source.

During the very short period between Leeds City's demise and the official formation of Leeds United, in 1919, there was brief talk of turning the Elland Road football ground site into a brickworks, and using the fertile clay deposits that were accessible beneath the top soil of the pitch. Given the healthy array of brickworks in the local area, not only at the time but for many years prior to 1919, it is something of a curiosity that this had never happened previously. Several clay works on Elland Road diversified from just manufacturing clay pipe to also producing bricks and chimney pots for the rapidly expanding housing industry. Indeed, Samuel Barker's Executors Works on Elland Road had a famous brick-making machine. Thankfully for all of us, however, the scheme to use the clay deposits beneath the Elland Road pitch never gathered pace and Yorkshire Amateur AFC and then Leeds United briskly took over the site, and never looked back.

Elsewhere, as soon as the land surrounding the football ground was made available when the mines began to shut in the late 19th century, it was snapped up for housing and other building development and the district of Beeston, which had previously been an area of mostly fields surrounding a small village, began to grow into a substantial suburb of Leeds. In 1973, three of the unused mine shafts from the previous Leeds Fireclay Company were uncovered during preparatory work for the feeder roads leading off the M621 motorway.

Living memory of the coal and clay mining industries in Beeston is now effectively gone forever, and it is sad but not unusual to see such a significant cultural shift. Amid the changing landscape of the locality it is hard to believe that there will ever be a similar obliteration of evidence that a football club once existed in the same area.

THE CRACKED EGG (SHEILA'S CAFÉ)

Insignificant though it may be in the illustrious history of Leeds United Football Club, the Cracked Egg Café will have seen several hundred of the club's employees wander in and out of its doors over the years, and if walls could talk, doubtless they would have many stories to tell us.

I know this site as 'The Cracked Egg' because it was so-named from around 1990 right through the club's heady Premier League days. Previously it was known for many years as 'Sheila's Café' from when it opened in 1965. By 2006 it was known as the inspiringly titled 'Elland Road Café & Sandwich Bar', but with a nod to its pioneering predecessor it carried an 'established 1965' note underneath on the signage, then 'The Café @ 259', based on its precise address on Elland Road, and today it is simply the 'Elland Road Sandwich & Café Bar', perhaps taking inspiration from the Yorkshire Radio/Radio Yorkshire approach to fooling people into thinking something had changed.

The café is situated on the parade which houses the 'United Newsagents' on the corner of Heath Grove. The café itself is next door to 'Graveley's Fish & Chips' which, of course, was famously known as 'United Fisheries' for many years. The Cracked Egg is not renowned necessarily for its service to fans as an essential part of the match day experience, more for its feeding of players and staff during the week. Long before Thorp Arch was a coveted hankering in Howard Wilkinson's long term vision for Leeds United, the players used to train daily on Fullerton Park and once finished would retire to the café across the road with the drifting smell of bacon enticing them into a brisk trot from the West Stand car park.

Prior to the Cracked Egg days, Sheila Kaye ruled the roost of café-dom around Elland Road for a generation or more. 'Sheila' of Sheila's Café fame also happened to be Terry Yorath's mother-in-law, the mother of his wife, Christine, who Yorath met at a local youth club when he was lodging in Beeston and on the club's ground staff. They married in 1971. Before Sheila had the café, the unit was a bookmakers run by her husband Fred Kaye from the point at which bookmakers became legal in the UK in 1961, and before this it is believed it was a TV repair shop.

Certainly the café became central to everyday life at the club, particularly in the Revie era. The wider football world might picture the best group of footballers in the country carrying themselves like film stars or visiting VIPs, arriving at elegant baroque restaurants in the best part of town, sliding with effortless cool out of a sleek sports car with a model on their arm and nodding to a uniformed doorman. Not in Yorkshire; that sort of stuff was for Chelsea. At Elland Road in the 1970s, the players preferred a place that to them was every bit as good, but had no

The match day throng around Sheila's Café and the adjacent United Fisheries.

alluring frontage, no waiters, and even no tablecloths, except when Sheila spotted the Don through the window striding up and they got out "some clean linen", because "after all, he's a bit special isn't he?"

A classic photo exists of Revie's great side resplendent in cheesecloth shirts, tank tops and collars that would poke your eye out, sat in the back room of the café surrounding the radio as they await the FA Cup Fifth Round draw in 1973. It is not hard to imagine this scene was common in that era. Indeed right up until the mid-1990s, when the building of Thorp Arch rid the area of the players' presence on a day-to-day basis, the café was a frequent meeting point for the players after training, before they headed off to fill the gaping vacuum that was the rest of their day.

Sheila admits that the Revie players' presence was good for trade as fans would often come in, knowing there was a fair likelihood that a good chunk of the most formidable team in Europe would be finishing

off a plate of home-cooked wonderment. That said, it wasn't all fry-ups and cakes. Sheila did play an integral part in maintaining the players' fitness during the 1960s and 1970s, and sits as an example of how Revie had absolute control over his 'family' and ensured every little detail was covered. Dave Cocker remembers the role Sheila played: "My Dad was into diets and energy drinks before anybody else, England were on Gatorade in 1970 and Dextrosol, through my Dad, and before anybody else had heard of it. So what they'd do, they had players on diets and they had an account at Sheila's so the players would go in and Sheila knew exactly what each player was allowed to eat. So if they walked in and asked for a full breakfast 'No, sorry.' But they would go in after training most days."

Commenting in a match day programme from 1974, Sheila herself said: "Eddie Gray and Mick Bates always order double portions of our home made steak pie and go without potatoes. All the players love our roast beef, and of course, Norman Hunter always has his special…"

Norman Hunter's "special" evokes wonderful fantasies of the infamous hard man devouring half a cow every lunch time, or gnawing on the remains of a chicken he killed and plucked himself just minutes earlier or maybe a lovingly prepared stew that had been slow-cooked for hours in honour of the great man? "No, actually it's a salad sandwich," Sheila confirms with myth-shattering understatement, "even in the middle of winter Norman always asks for them. We've never known him have anything else."

Sheila opened her café in 1965, and much of its business must have come from the football club on its doorstep, as Dave Cocker continues: "The club would send out there. They'd send one of the juniors up there and he'd come back with lunch for me Dad and Don because although Don had his office, he would always be in the coaches' room with me Dad and Syd (Owen)."

Certainly the lonely trudge up to the café, whether it was Sheila's or the Cracked Egg that followed afterwards some time in the early 1990s, was a well-trodden path for the junior player trying to earn his stripes. David Batty articulated the situation of bygone days when he was "simply a lackey" and when it was "an honour" to fetch bacon butties for certain senior pros.

Clearly, this was when the strict regime of Revie, and indeed Sheila, had long gone. But today the 'café opposite Elland Road' steadfastly remains a going concern, perhaps oblivious to the faithful and meticulous contribution it made to Leeds United's most famous legacy.

CRICKET

With a perfectly respected and established cricket ground on its doorstep between 1901 and 1962, the sport of cricket was never likely to feature strongly at Elland Road itself. When the Holbeck Cricket Club was disbanded in 1962 their New Peacock Ground pitch was soon taken over by local football teams, but still Elland Road never echoed lustily to the sound of leather on willow. That was until cricket made a brief, and as far as I am aware one-off, visit to Elland Road on Saturday 30th August 1986.

Leeds United had just lost 1-0 at home to Sheffield United in the early stages of the epic 1986/87 season when the pitch was very quickly transformed to stage the 'Ringways Floodlit Test' between a Yorkshire XI and a Barbados XI. The 25-overs-per-side game started at 8.30pm and featured the likes of Malcolm Marshall, Geoff Boycott, Joel Garner, David Bairstow, Gordon Greenidge, Martyn Moxon, Desmond Haynes and Viv Richards.

The game was one of the many diverse fruits of the relationship with then stadium owners Leeds City Council. But football grounds have never leant themselves well to the game of cricket, with the inevitability of short boundaries rendering the game somewhat farcical, not to mention the fact that the pitch had hosted a professional football game just hours earlier. As Ian Baird slid in studs-first on an opposition defender, I dare say he cared little for ensuring Joel Garner's run-up was left divot-free. Stephen Reynolds recalls the game which his dad, long-standing groundsman John Reynolds, will have adopted new techniques to prepare for: "I think Viv Richards put a ball through the South Stand roof when he hit a six" was his overriding and quite predictable memory.

Some 23 years later a Twenty20 friendly exhibition game was scheduled for Elland Road on 31st July 2009, a Friday night, and was billed as a warm-up event for the Ashes Test Match at Headingley the following week. This was to be between a Leeds United XI and a Lashings World XI. However, just two weeks before the event when, naturally, ticket sales had already commenced, Leeds United had to cancel the game as they couldn't secure a suitable artificial playing surface to create the wicket. The club said they rejected alternative options which would have reduced the quality of the cricket on show.

The Lashings World XI were a famous international touring team, and were due to include ex-international players Alvin Kallicharan, John Emburey, Devon Malcolm, Graeme Hick, Phil DeFreitas, Ian Harvey and Jason Gillespie. Leeds United, meanwhile, had roped in then manager Simon Grayson and his brother Paul, a professional at Essex and formerly Yorkshire, plus Pakistan internationals Rashid Latif, Saqlain Mushtaq and Mohammad Akram, Courtney Walsh and Richie Richardson of the West Indies, and Paul Jarvis and Nick Knight of England.

At a time when Leeds' playing fortunes had reached a nadir (they had just lost a Play-Off Semi-Final to Millwall, thus securing a third consecutive season in League One) it was seen as yet another PR disaster for the rudderless club where simply nothing appeared to be going right.

THE DAMNED UNITED

Published in August 2006, the novel by David Peace entitled *The Damned Utd* (note: strictly 'Utd' not 'United'; it's a '70s thing) was a fascinating and innovative account of a turbulent yet absorbing period in Leeds United's history; the 44-day reign of Brian Clough as manager in 1974. The book has been put on a pedestal as a groundbreaking venture in sports writing, was in the bestseller lists for a number of years and has provoked heated debate on the merits of its fictional depiction of Clough's reign and the construction of his antipathy towards Don Revie and Leeds United.

On the back of the book's unbridled success a film adaptation was made in 2008 (directed by Tom Hooper) entitled *The Damned United*, already losing its faithfulness to the book by changing its title. With many scenes shot at Elland Road, and amid much fuss, the film opened up the debate again regarding the depiction of Clough and the story itself, but in truth, anyone who had read the book first was likely to view the film as a much inferior work, though it remains an enjoyable watch.

David Peace's novel is written as a first-person stream-of-consciousness through Clough himself and portrays him as a paranoid, muddled and confused character who frequently seeks solace in alcohol.

Period motors line the car park for the filming of *The Damned United* in 2008.

Fullerton Park back as a training ground; but only temporarily as the set for *The Damned United* film is created in 2008. The West Stand façade is also recreated, in rather less imposing fashion than the original, on the back of the North West Corner Stand.

With brilliant wordplay and tense characterisation, slowly Clough works himself into a frenzy of regret over taking the position at Leeds and doubts his own merits as a football manager. The film, on the other hand, was a far simpler version of events and bears little resemblance to the ingenious craft of the book. Rather than representing the dexterous fictional elements of Peace's novel, the film was just a story of the story; a straightforward account of Clough's rise as Derby manager, his dislike of Revie and Leeds and his controversial and ultimately disastrous 44-day reign.

Riddled with factual inaccuracies relating to games, scorelines and key incidents (for example Revie's walk through the crowds from the team bus and subsequent snub of Clough never happened), the film panders to a series of clumsy stereotypes of Leeds United in that era, including actors' portrayals of the likes of Johnny Giles and Billy Bremner which stretch artistic licence to its credible limits. The film perpetuated the popular anti-Leeds agenda and was a stark contrast to the premise of the original book, and you left the cinema thinking rather than the Clough family being upset about the adaptation (as they perhaps rightly were with the novel), probably the Revie family should be.

Elland Road staged several film scenes for *The Damned United* between May and July 2008. The famous blue West Stand façade was re-created for the film, but for obvious reasons could only be placed on the north end of the West Stand where it curves round to the Kop and, therefore, lacked the stature and size of the original. The mysteriously vanishing gold 'LEEDS UNITED A.F.C.' letters were recreated specially for the filming. Tunnel scenes were actually shot in the police tunnel between the Kop and West Stand, from where a cack-handed glimpse of the 1993-built East Stand can be seen in some shots. Vintage cars from the 1970s were liberally parked around the West Stand car park to add authenticity to scenes where Clough arrived on his first day with his two sons in tow, though the Banqueting Suite prevented the same main entrance being used. Finally, grass was temporarily re-laid on Fullerton Park for the training scenes, including the famous "throw your medals in the bin" speech. The one scene that could be shot on the actual location it happened.

DANCERS

Harmless, superfluous and a mild distraction it might be, but pre-match entertainment at Elland Road has always been something of a hit and miss affair, although it was many years into the club's existence before any efforts were made to get crowds in early and offer them something to watch in the often painfully slow crawl towards kick-off time.

Pre-match and half-time entertainment can be dated back to the 1950s and many fans will recall a brass band playing on the pitch prior to games right up until the mid-1960s.

We also endured police dogs leaping around assault courses during the interval and the dubious spectacle of voracious and highly trained Alsatians attacking the padded arm of a pantomime villain.

Cheerleaders became commonplace on the Elland Road pitch in the 1990s when Sky's initial influence on the game involved the squalid Americanisation of almost everything we had ever known. However, Elland Road had been graced by such delights before. At the beginning of the 1985/86 season the club launched a plea within the match day programme for fans to arrive early to avoid the frantic rush at the turnstiles around kick-off time. "For your comfort and convenience we have organized a full programme of pre-match entertainment which starts half an hour before kick-off right through the season," stated the programme for the Wimbledon game on 21st August 1985. First up were the Thornhill Lees Militaires, an award-winning military band from Dewsbury, who over the next few months became almost as regular a feature of afternoons at Elland Road as Neil Aspin shinning a cross into the Kop, and your Dad shaking his head in solemn remembrance of better days.

One of the first more visual attempts to entice fans in early was the never-to-be-forgotten Leeds Blue Cats, a cheerleading troupe affiliated to the Leeds Cougars American Football team. The Cougars played at Elland Road for a short time in 1986 and it was around this time, amid the UK's first wave of interest in American Football, that the Leeds Blue Cats were asked to perform pre-match at Elland Road.

Sensibly sporting colours of white, blue and gold the Leeds Blue Cats didn't quite match the glamour and celebrity of the Dallas Cowboys cheerleaders from the NFL, but they were a dedicated bunch. Through wind and rain and faced with a somewhat mystified and apathetic crowd at Elland Road they 'carried on regardless', though sadly only lasted a few months. After that, pre-match entertainment on the heaving Lowfields Road terraces reverted to trying to prevent yourself being pushed face-first into the pie of the gentleman stood in front of you.

Quite possibly the first example of dancing on the Elland Road pitch came under the first team management of the famously eccentric Major Frank Buckley. Buckley was a pioneer of youth development programmes and scouting networks, indeed he discovered John Charles in 1948, but at the time his methods were not universally embraced. In training he adopted a mechanical kicking device and also insisted on the players taking extract of monkey glands through injection and in tablet form, supposedly to boost their mental and physical powers. Sadly, the league tables didn't offer a huge amount of support for his techniques. However, during his period at Elland Road from 1948 to 1953, Buckley also introduced 'dancing' into the training regime. With music blaring out of the stadium's PA

system to the befuddlement of passers-by outside, the players were forced into dance routines on the pitch to enhance their balance and co-ordinate the movement of their feet.

It can only be imagined what footballers of that generation, including a very young and famously brusque Jack Charlton, thought of the Major's techniques.

A second example of Leeds players 'dancing' on the pitch was perhaps even more unlikely. In 1972 maverick artist and innovator Paul Trevillion approached his boyhood club Tottenham Hotspur with a view to them adopting his various PR tactics to engage with the fans prior to kick-off. Then Spurs manager Bill Nicholson laughed off the suggestion, but being close friends with Don Revie suggested Trevillion try his luck at Elland Road, as Leeds in Nicholson's words "needed some brightening up". Certainly this was true, and Revie immediately took to Trevillion and his visionary ideas, which extended to the design of the Smiley badge; the iconic emblem of Leeds United's style and swagger in that era, emblazoned on the kit, individually named tracksuits and even the corner flags. The players, on the other hand, took some convincing. Already hugely unpopular with opposing fans and media, the Leeds players risked large-scale ridicule for 'prancing about' on the pitch in formation patterns with a full and expectant crowd looking on. But that is what they did; skipping, jumping and stretching in a tight formation, rigidly focused and oblivious to the disbelieving crowds watching them.

Les Cocker's 'military' pre-match drills were perfected in training and at 2.45pm the Leeds players would enter Elland Road and away grounds like gladiators. Albeit, gladiators wearing blue numbered sock tags, and carrying target footballs which they kicked into the crowd having waved in regimented fashion to all four corners of the ground. The very first game in which this practice was carried out was the FA Cup Sixth Round tie at Elland Road against Tottenham Hotspur in March 1972. Ironically, the club which dismissed Trevillion's inventiveness were put to the sword and admitted they were beaten before they even set foot on the pitch, with the 2-1 scoreline not telling the full story of a ruthless, yet bejewelled victory.

Dave Cocker, again, remembers this period vividly: "They were shitting themselves were Spurs because of all this stuff going on outside. But my old man didn't want any part of it at first. He was in agreement though, he'd always wanted to take the players out but it was banned at the time. The FA wouldn't allow it. You were allowed to go out two minutes before kick–off; quick kick about and then kick-off. But eventually Leeds just thought 'well, we'll do it'. They did other things obviously as well. I mean Trevillion also wanted to change the name of the club, to Leeds Crusaders, with a big cross on the front of the shirts. But it started with the Smiley badge and the sock tags, but they did the pre-match drills until they (Revie and Cocker) left in 1974. It brought the crowds in, because you would go away and the grounds were full 30 minutes before kick-off, because everybody wanted to watch it. Everyone hated us, but they all wanted to go and watch Leeds. So my Dad was reluctant at first but it was the thought that he could get them out and get them warmed up as he wanted to, you can't do that in the dressing room. The players just did what they were told, because before that they'd be in the dressing room just running on the spot, knocking the fuck out of Herbert Warner (Revie's friend, confidante and dressing room court jester) and just generally messing around and getting psyched up. Then all of a sudden the buzzer goes and until that referee pressed the buzzer you couldn't leave the dressing room. Two minutes later you're kicking off.

"But my Dad was Trevillion's contact at Leeds," continues Dave, "because Billy Nicholson had wanted my Dad to become manager at Spurs around the same time Trevillion appeared. But my old man thought Trevillion was a fucking lunatic. I remember in the new players' lounge (in the North West Corner Stand) when Trevillion came in and was introduced to the team, and he had this little golf putter with him. He'd invented this little putter that weighed an absolute tonne. Before the game, what the players did was have a putting competition and there'd be money on it. They had bingo and whatever, and it was all for relaxation. They'd go in at two o'clock and Don would go through the team and how they were going to play, and then they had like 30 minutes before they went to the dressing rooms. So they had a game of bingo and then a little putting competition. Some would take part and some would watch the wrestling on ITV. Anyway, Trevillion brought this putter out and he never missed, and that's how he got the players' confidence, with this little fucking putter. They all bought into it after that, the names on the back of the tracksuits and all that, it was his idea, and then everybody else started doing it."

DAVID 'SOLDIER' WILSON

Players become synonymous with the most famous occasions at Elland Road through events on the field; Eddie Gray, Mark Viduka, Paul Rachubka – we can all recall their defining moments. Whilst the name David Wilson may not trip off the tongue as one of the most distinguished players to have graced the Elland Road turf, he remains unique in a very significant way. In October 1906 Leeds City were less than two months into their second season in professional football. The club were struggling financially and in the first season of their existence had failed to set the world alight, although they finished an encouraging sixth in Division Two. The new season had started badly, though three consecutive wins had lifted City from 16th to eighth in the table. Inconsistency was rife, however, and football

wasn't catching on with the local public as the club and the Football Association, desperate to establish 'the kicking game' in a predominantly rugby-orientated area, had hoped. Indeed, continuation with the association football experiment in West Yorkshire seemingly hung by a thread.

The despondency and uncertainty surrounding Leeds City hit a devastating low on 27th October 1906 during a 1-0 defeat to Burnley in front of 15,000 fans, when striker David Wilson tragically died in the dressing rooms during the final minutes of the game.

Wilson, 23 and a former soldier in the Boer War, hence his nickname 'Soldier', hailed from Hebburn in the north east, and had been a £150 signing from Hull City the previous December. He had finished his first half-season with the club with a very productive 13 goals from 15 games. He was a dependable, hard-working striker who lacked pace but was adept and skilful. The financially stricken club could have turned around a quick profit on the striker, having received offers of £500 for him in the summer, but they recognised his worth to the team. Manager Gilbert Gillies was fiercely protective of him and leapt to his defence in the wake of the tragedy when fans and reporters, searching for signs to explain his untimely demise, noted he had lost form in the opening exchanges of the new season, failing to score a goal.

On the day of the game Wilson had declared himself fit, and showed no signs of ill-health. He left his home at 8 Catherine Grove at the top of Beeston Hill at 2pm, as normal for a home game, and along with his wife walked down to the ground carrying his ten-month-old daughter in his arms. They parted at the players' entrance and would never speak to each other again.

Despite the contest with Burnley being a typically Yorkshire–Lancashire, rough and tumble affair, Wilson's only complaint at half-time was of a couple of goals he should have scored, having skimmed the bar from distance on two occasions. Observers later noted, however, that he had been winded in a first half challenge that saw him sandwiched between two Burnley defenders. In the inquest later, it was this incident that a Dr Taylor believed was the main cause of death.

The *Leeds Mercury* takes up the story of the second half: "...about a quarter of an hour after the game had been restarted Wilson was seen to leave the field, and in answer to the club trainer, he said he felt a heavy pain in his chest. He was unable to account for it, as he had not met with any injury while the game was in progress."

Wilson had though shown visible discomfort when heading a ball goalwards in those first 15 minutes of the second half. As he left the field, he was followed by a policeman, PC John Byrom, who was concerned at his outward appearance. When Byrom got to the dressing room he found Wilson "writhing in evident pain and suffering intense pain in his chest, neck and left arm". He was helped onto a bench in the dressing room

whilst medical assistance was called. The *Leeds Mercury* continued:

"Doctors Fawcett and Taylor, who were on the stand, at once went to Wilson's assistance, and subsequently Dr Whittaker, who had travelled with the Burnley team, also lent his aid. Wilson was carried into the directors' room, and the medicals were of the opinion that he had had a heart attack. He was brought round, and a cab was telephoned for to take him home. Meanwhile word was brought into the room that two of the Leeds City players had been injured, and when Wilson heard this he pluckily offered to go back to the field."

John Lavery and Harry Singleton had taken blows out on the field, and although Lavery was soldiering on he was clearly a passenger, whilst Singleton had to leave the pitch and was not fit to resume; City were effectively down to eight men. The *Yorkshire Evening Post* reported: "Though his chest was very sore, Wilson said he could not remain there while the Leeds City team were in such straits. So, although many of those in the room endeavoured to dissuade him from his purpose he went out to resume play, his reappearance being greeted by a storm of cheers."

The *Leeds Mercury* also reported on Wilson's ill-advised resurrection: "The doctors and the club officials present advised him against this step, he walked out of the room and returned to the field... but it was very evident that he was too ill to play. He himself recognised the hopelessness of continuing, and again (after just three minutes and not a single touch of the ball) he left the field. He was escorted into the dressing room, and volunteered to have a warm bath, believing it would revive him."

PC Byrom recounted what happened next: "I assisted him to the dressing room, and helped him to undress. He said he would have a hot bath, but all at once after getting into the bath he laid down and started kicking his legs violently. I took hold of him and held his head out of the water, but he seemed to lose consciousness, and never spoke again. I called for assistance, and we lifted him out of the bath and on to a table. The doctor came and saw him on the table, but he died right away."

The *Leeds Mercury* continued their story of events: "Hardly had he got into the water when he seemed to have a stroke. His agony was pitiful to witness, and he was immediately lifted out of the bath and placed on a table, but he expired in a few seconds. His death occurred just before the game ended, and it can be imagined what a shock it was to the players when they returned from the field and found their old colleague stretched out in death."

Leeds had fought heroically with just eight fit men, and were homing in on a valiant goalless draw when Burnley snatched a winner in the final seconds. The Leeds players' dismay at the loss of points was to be immeasurably compounded by the devastating scene that awaited them in the dressing room.

As supporters filed out of the ground, shaking their heads at another home defeat for their fragile and embryonic team, news began to filter out regarding the tragedy that had occurred. Wilson's wife had abruptly left at the final whistle, concerned at the nature of her husband's second half dramatics, and chose to await his return at home. Leeds City manager Gilbert Gillies ran up the steep lane that later became Wesley Street to find her and before she got home she was intercepted and asked to return to the ground. As she entered the dressing room, the full extent of the tragedy was clear.

Wilson's body was taken by ambulance to his home in Beeston and with relatives hastily rushed down from Scotland, a funeral was arranged for the following Wednesday, which Leeds City both paid for and attended.

The official reason for death given at the inquest was "over-exertion" or more generally, according to official records, it was "over eagerness to be of service to his club that was Wilson's undoing. The doctor who was in attendance upon him at the last expressed the emphatic opinion that the fact of going on to the field a second time caused Wilson's death – that, in a word, if he had remained in the directors' room he would have had a good chance of getting better. The actual cause of death was angina pectoris, a medical term which signifies what is more commonly known as heart anguish; and the jury at today's inquest certified that Wilson had died from 'heart failure, from over exertion in a football match'."

In other words, he met his death due to the misguided belief that he should get back on the field and help his under-manned team. At a mere 23 years of age Wilson's death devastated the club and the game. His widow and ten-month-old daughter benefited from a fund-raising match staged against Hull City a few weeks later, but with a crowd of 3,000 producing receipts of £96 to watch a 3-3 draw it was meagre, albeit welcome compensation.

To overcome the loss of Wilson in football terms, Leeds bought striker Billy McLeod from Lincoln City for £350, who scored 16 goals in 24 games in the remainder of that season and over the next 14 years became Leeds City's biggest club legend with an incredible 178 goals in 301 appearances. Out of the club's most devastating tragedy came their most celebrated son, but Elland Road was shaken to the core by the harrowing events, and the unsettling aura of doom was something the troubled and ill-fated Leeds City never truly shook off.

Another mysterious fatality would occur at Elland Road 14 years later, this time during the embryonic existence of Leeds United. "Tragedy on a football ground" was the headline to a remarkably understated and matter-of-fact article in the Saturday 9th October 1920 edition of the *Yorkshire Evening Post*, with just four lines of text explaining an apparent murder of a local man from Holbeck, found with his throat cut. An inquest into the death offered more detail a few days later, concluding that the man's death was in fact "suicide whilst of unsound mind". The body had been found on the land between the football ground and the cricket ground – then just a dirt track in the years before Lowfields Road was built – with an inquest statement recording that "his head was practically severed and a razor was in his hands". The man's wife explained at the inquest that work troubles had triggered depression, and he had left the house on a Friday evening to go for a walk, but never returned. His body was found on Saturday morning.

DIRECTORS' BOX

Pictures paint a thousand words, and many telling portraits of life in the pressure cooker atmosphere of Elland Road have been focused on figures of prominence in the directors' box. There is the doomed face of manager Jimmy Adamson with the looming presence of his predecessor Don Revie stood up behind him. There is Jimmy Armfield sat alone, deep in thought as the legacy he inherited slips further from his grasp. There is Revie himself, flushed with success and signing programmes for spectators as he sits, contented and relaxed. And there is Victor Orta stretching the boundaries of acceptable etiquette whilst Leeds show signs of blowing promotion again.

Certainly, in times of trouble, the camera lens has zoomed in sharply on this area as the men making the decisions try to avoid telling a story through their facial expressions, and in days of yore they would hope the haze of cigar smoke obscured their obvious discomfort. There is no doubt that a seat close to the directors' box will afford you a good sense of the mood in and around Leeds United, as even the more restrained surroundings of the West Stand are known for being infiltrated by forthright opinions when things aren't going well. In good times, the cameras point only pitchwards and yet the directors' box will always be the central focus to the inner workings and the greatest influence over the club, and as BBC Radio Reporter Stuart Hall famously quipped after the 1987 Fifth Round FA Cup win over Queens Park Rangers "the fur coats and Rolls Royces are back at Elland Road".

In 2012 Ken Bates briefly moved his 'suite' to the controversially refurbished boxes in the East Stand, but the directors' box has since returned to its spiritual home and indeed where it has been situated in the upper section of the West Stand for all of Leeds United's existence, even prior to the current West Stand being built in 1957. Whilst the pitch has been moved northwards, the directors' box generally hasn't, and therefore, the view has not always been as central to the action as it once was, remaining above the tunnel. That was until Ken Bates arrived on the scene in 2005 and promptly up-rooted the main section of the directors' box and moved it Kop-wards towards the halfway line, upsetting and up-seating many established West Stand season ticket holders in the process.

The directors' box in the West Stand is also used for guests, sponsors and visiting officials, and is really just a section of padded seats which is not segregated to any great degree from the rest of the stand, with only the presence of a steward and a length of transparent Perspex separating the men in power from the many vocal detractors in close proximity.

All inhabitants of the directors' box are essentially guests of the Leeds United chairman and over the years there have been occasions where that invitation was not forthcoming to the visiting side, most notably in recent years. In 2006 Peter Ridsdale, as new chairman of Cardiff City, was denied a return to Elland Road by his

Leeds United counterpart Ken Bates. It was Bates again who denied Derby County manager Nigel Clough a seat in the directors' box in August 2010, because he was wearing a tracksuit. Rumour has it that the former Leeds chairman and owner also took great exception to ties that were too short and anyone wearing brown shoes. Which seems perfectly fair.

Wooden seats in the directors' box in 1989? It wouldn't be long before P. Ridsdale ensured such hardship was a thing of the past for the Elland Road powerbrokers.

DON REVIE

The typically pensive and committed demeanour of Don Revie in the Elland Road dugout.

What would Elland Road look like without the success of the decade between 1964 and 1974? An under-developed relic of a mediocre past? Like many other under-achieving clubs with few happy memories and no great, treasurable history to tie us to it, Leeds United may have even left the eyesore behind by now and moved to a flat-pack Meccano stadium in a retail park. So whilst many individuals have shaped the course of Leeds United's history and the development of Elland Road itself, few can claim to have influenced the landscape of the modern day stadium as strongly as Don Revie.

To say Revie revolutionised the club is something of an understatement, although he needed the guidance, faith and business acumen of chairmen Harry Reynolds, Albert Morris, Percy Woodward and Manny Cussins also. But Revie made the club what it is today, at least in terms of its spirit, philosophy and expectation, which apart from Elland Road itself and the name 'Leeds United' are the only remaining constants where the fans are concerned. From the early 1960s Revie instilled a discipline and a winning mentality into the club that took it further than anyone in humble LS11

had ever dreamed of, and this was created from an influence that reached far beyond what the job description of first team manager should have.

In addition, Revie created a warm family atmosphere that harnessed a siege mentality and a fierce will to win, but also meant players were rarely unhappy, and peripheral squad members such as Mick Bates, Terry Yorath and for a long time David Harvey, were happy to remain as such, just to be a part of it. Revie looked after and took an interest in his players' families because it was one less worry for his players, allowing a better focus on the job in hand. The players themselves were no less attended to. Revie and physio Bob English religiously gave each one a full, soapy body massage every Thursday, and on a Monday before a Wednesday game. Hands-on management techniques it is hard to imagine Jose Mourinho getting too involved in.

When Revie became manager in 1961 the West Stand was only four years old, and a still-impressive addition to the Elland Road ground. On the south side stood the homely but unimpressive Scratching Shed and the rest of the ground was one long terrace which stretched from the north end of the West Stand, uninterrupted, all the way round to the south end of what was then known as the 'Popular Side'. Three quarters of the ground was unaltered since the 1920s, bar the installation of seats under the Lowfields Stand's roof in 1956.

Before any changes to the ground were made under Revie's management, Elland Road staged its record attendance of 57,892 in 1967, but just a year later the ground began to change radically. Revie's long term masterplan for the club, fashioned with the guidance of Harry Reynolds, involved not only success on the pitch but also the provision of a top class, aesthetic, modern stadium for his adopted city, and this work began in earnest when the original Spion Kop was replaced by the current Kop in 1968.

The partnership of Revie and Harry Reynolds was particularly significant in terms of forging a club-wide belief that anything could be achieved, and to widen the ambition of people who had never had any reason to look much further than their own front door. Reynolds spoke in January 1967 when the details of the estimated £1 million 'Elland Road grand plan' were announced: "The ground badly needs to be re-developed, we know, and my board's intention is to make it worthy of the club and the city with all modern amenities and attractions. We want it to be a great social and recreational centre, with people feeling they belong to it, as well as a fine modern football ground."

Shortly after the Kop was built, as Leeds began to celebrate the first tangible success of their existence with domestic and European trophies, the two corner stands were built on the north side to connect the Kop with the adjacent stands. In 1974 following Revie's last trophy win, the South Stand was built and the basis for the current footprint of the ground was largely complete. With Revie now gone to manage England it is no coincidence that the ground development then abruptly stopped, but Revie's long term plan, devised well before the club had won anything, had clearly been that he would create a modern stadium to match the quality of his side; extraordinary vision, not to mention intrepidity and belief.

Dave Cocker does, however, slightly underplay Revie's involvement in the ground re-design saying: "Don was involved in it, because Don was the manager. Don wanted total control of the club. That was really his downfall because one guy wouldn't accept that from Don and that was (director) Bob Roberts. Bob Roberts owned Ringways (Ford car dealership based in Wortley, Leeds, and associated with the club for many years) and a building firm. He built the West Stand, the North Stand, the South Stand, the corners, everything. But the relationship with him was absolutely shocking, because me Dad and Don used to go in board meetings and they (the board) would be going 'we're not happy that you've booked a flight down to Southampton, you could have gone by road'. Don's answer to everything

The Don Revie statue unveiled in 2012 and flanked by two of the flair players from that great side: Eddie Gray and Johnny Giles.

was 'well Mr Roberts if you don't agree with the flight you drive and we'll fly; next question'. Businessmen don't like being spoken to like that. It was Bob Roberts that appointed Brian Clough, even though he wasn't the chairman, Manny Cussins didn't want him. But Bob had a say because Bob was owed money for the North Stand and the South Stand, he had them over a barrel. So when you get someone in that situation it's very difficult to manage them because they'll just say 'well I want my money then.'

So the development of the ground was as much the brainchild of Harry Reynolds and later Manny Cussins, mostly with Revie's agreement, as Dave continues: "It was done piecemeal really wasn't it? It was like 'OK, let's get rid of the mound (the Kop)' and it all went from there. But with the North Stand, it was like a pile of shit on one side and a pile of shit on the other with a new stand in the middle, rather than doing it all in one go."

Dave refers to the unfinished nature of the ground whilst the club saved enough money from their European expeditions to add the two corner stands, and this prudent approach was evident throughout the whole ground's development. Until the momentum stopped.

Foundations were put in place in the south east corner to connect the South Stand with the Lowfields in 1978, but the club thought better of it from a financial point of view, and the foundations lay untouched for 13 years until the South East Corner Stand was built in 1991. Photos that show action on the pitch post-Revie combine with a good view of the houses and open

fields of Beeston Hill and Holbeck Cemetery in the background, and are a stark reminder of a dark, fallow period in the club's history following the end of Revie's golden tenure.

But while financial decisions were largely out of Revie's hands, Dave Cocker emphatically states: "What Don wanted, Don got. Don managed the entire club, Don decided if we were flying, everything. I remember flying down to Southampton in about 1967. The alternative then was driving for eight or nine hours. It just made sense." But while that influence extended to travel plans, undersoil heating, new badges and new kit manufacturers, he didn't perhaps get the board support he wanted in terms of expanding the ground to match his ambitions for the club.

As mentioned elsewhere, Revie wanted the club to buy the land behind the original Kop from Sid Castle to build a much bigger North Stand, and he also wanted to relocate the club when they had an opportunity to tap into other, potentially larger, sections of the Leeds population. But board opposition ultimately frustrated him and perhaps led to a number of dalliances with other clubs, notably Sunderland and Everton, during his Leeds tenure, before he eventually took the ultimate job in English football with the national team.

The following years saw Leeds United in rapid decline, hamstrung by a succession of managers trying to replicate Revie's success but finding it a sizeable millstone round their neck. The team gradually broke up and were replaced by lesser players and before long the club was relegation fodder; likewise Elland Road also degenerated in appearance. This was when an energetic, bullish and visionary businessman called Bill Fotherby joined the board. He didn't have sufficient influence to halt the decline, and didn't exert his authority for nearly ten years, but when he first entered the boardroom and spent time in the ground as the 'Ground Chairman' he could sense the ghost of Revie in the empty stands, the echoing corridors and underneath the peeling paintwork: "It was all over," Bill begins. "Don Revie was in that boardroom, he was there. He was everywhere at that club Don Revie. It wasn't a problem to me, but you could smell it. There was nothing wrong with it, it was good. But Don had gone. The job I had to do (in later years when Fotherby became managing director) was find a replacement that was like him."

Journalist and Leeds fan Eddie Taylor could also sense Revie's spectre in every corner of Elland Road, and unlike many, felt that the comfort of nostalgia was not necessarily a positive thing. It seemed as if a team that many of us never saw dominated the atmosphere at Elland Road even in the mid-1980s. "Like most stadia pre-Taylor Report," begins Eddie, "Elland Road was a ramshackle combination of its own history. At 2pm on a mid-winter Saturday it was a familiar footballing landscape of corrugated iron, barbed wire, chain-link fencing, weeds protruding from rusting drainpipes, pre-fab souvenir shops, cracked paint, turnstiles buried in red-brick walls and a fair amount of cement. But the Revie era was still the dominant influence, not just the South Stand and its Trusthouse Forte flagpoles but also the covered Kop opposite, whose whitewashed entrances first spat out fans in 1968 and which, even in the 1980s, was usually home to a Glory Days-sized crowd.

"The reminders weren't just in the architecture," Eddie continues. "On one of my first trips to a match alone as an adolescent, an Easter encounter at the end of another unfulfilling campaign, the fan beside me on Lowfields Road wore a 1974-vintage Admiral silk scarf carrying pictures of Smiley-badged Scotland internationals. Another sported a faded denim jacket with 'Super Leeds' cloth patches by Coffer sewed onto the back. The programme contained a feature on Mick Jones, and 'Marching on Together' and its A-side, 'Leeds United', were given frequent airings by those around me. No one was moving on. No one had any reason to.

"It's perhaps why I stayed on the Lowfields. Not only was the worst part of the stadium rendered invisible by the fact you were in it, but whenever a goal did go in you could squint up to your right and pretend the tumult on the Kop meant something more than a tepid victory over Notts County. Don Revie once made a gypsy urinate on the pitch to remove spirits from Elland Road. Little did he realise the power of the ghosts he was to leave behind."

Following the onset of the crippling motor neurone disease that eventually led to his death, Revie made two emotional returns to Elland Road within the last 18 months of his life. In September 1987 before a 2-0 win over Manchester City, Revie was able to walk on to the turf with the aid of a walking stick; he waved to the crowd and looked cheerful. He was at the ground to perform the opening of the Centreline Club in the West Stand, but having done so was not strong enough to climb the steps to even have a look inside it. Revie's final appearance at Elland Road was in May 1988, less than a year later, when a charity match was held in his honour. With Revie having this time taken to the field in a wheelchair and barely able to raise a hand to wave at the fans, a visibly moved Kevin Keegan, representing an All-Star XI, spoke of Revie's legacy to local TV pre-match: "...I look around this great stadium, and this is Revie's stadium, he built this...". Sad to say, as Keegan's eyes surveyed the ground from the pitch, the stadium looked tired, abandoned and dispirited, but we took his well-meaning point nonetheless.

Shortly after Revie's final appearance at Elland Road, although that obviously wasn't known then, Howard Wilkinson left First Division Sheffield Wednesday and took on the reins at Leeds United and set about changing the focus and ambition of the once proud club that he felt was stuck in a rut of its own making. Wilkinson famously removed the photos of the Revie era from the reception area, foyer and executive suites in and around the West Stand, demonstrating extraordinary perception and a long-term vision reminiscent of Revie himself.

"It didn't happen straight away," explains Howard, "but it happened nearly straight away. I just felt after a very short period there that the whole Revie thing had become a hindrance, people were sort of taking comfort from it, it was too much of a crutch. It was like people would go home and think about the good old days, but the good old days don't help you when you're in the bad old days. I just felt that when we've got a club that reflects all the qualities that all those players and that manager reflected, we'll put them back up. When we've got a club worthy of them, we'll put them back up. Did I believe it? Yeah. Was there a sense in which I thought 'I need to change things here and I need to change them quickly, and I need to do things that send a signal out'? Yeah."

Howard spoke directly to the staff and the players about his reasoning for the action, which clearly will have ruffled a few feathers, that being entirely the intention. "I explained and made sure people understood," Howard continues. "Whether they agreed or not was a different matter. Yeah it upset a few people, but it was a price I was willing to pay at the time, because I thought it was in the best interests of the club to make people aware that 'look, we mean business here, we're going to change'. We needed to put the past into perspective. The past is fantastic, particularly when it's a fantastic past. But your fantastic past will not change the situation you're in at the moment, that is the future, and the future is the people here."

With progress made very quickly, Howard was true to his word and quick to dispel any lingering doubts that he was disrespectful to Revie's legacy. "The pictures went back up fairly quickly, I think fairly soon after we got promoted. We started to do things internally, and again, you have to deal with the reality and the present, and when we got promoted there was a feel-good factor around the place, we tried to tart the place up. The builders were still in the night before the season started, and you've got to go with that, you've got to make hay while the sun shines."

Revie's pictures depicting his glorious past are rightly still on display today, almost omnipresent in the club's visible external façade. Less than a year after Howard Wilkinson's appointment Revie died, but his legacy is not only in the size, stature and honour of the club we still support, but in the very seats and surroundings that we watch them in. What Leeds United and Elland Road would be without Don Revie is difficult to imagine, and is perhaps a redundant discussion given the absolute influence he had. Suitably, and many argue belatedly, a statue was erected behind the East Stand in May 2012 to commemorate this, and to ensure that the Don will watch over Leeds United forever more.

DRESSING ROOMS

Whether it's fights, celebrations, motivation, psychological warfare, massages or supreme buffoonery, it all goes on within four sacred walls that we will never be party to. Elland Road is not unlike any other football ground in the world, in that the dressing rooms are the hub of much activity on a match day and a strictly out of bounds area that is central to the outcome of the day's proceedings. Footballers are on show far more than is strictly necessary; the dressing room is their only sanctum and so it should be.

Currently the home dressing room at Elland Road is on the right hand side of the corridor as you turn into the concourse which leads from the tunnel. Smartly appointed and neatly refurbished prior to the 2017/18 season, and with plenty of tools to help with the manager's last-minute and half-time instructions, the room is not especially big but, pleasingly, is larger than the away dressing room across the corridor.

In the Revie era the home dressing room was infamous for the 'Keep Fighting' sign that was hung above Jack Charlton's peg, a simple message which embodied the close-knit unit that never lay down, and the dressing room was their lair, the sanctuary where plots were laid. More recently by way of inspiration, there was an impassioned plea written by a fan, a Falklands veteran, which was sent to the club as it stared the delights of League One in the face. Then manager Dennis Wise took a particular liking to it – despite the fact that it patently didn't work – and had it enlarged and fixed to the wall. It has since been removed.

The approximate location of the dressing rooms has always been the same since the current West Stand was re-built in 1957, and they have been refurbished a number of times, but most radically in 1996 in preparation for the stadium hosting three matches in the European Championships, when the layout of all the rooms in the block was changed.

Dave Cocker spent half of his life in those hallowed corridors in his youth, and recalls the layout vividly: "In the early 1960s there were two ways in (to the dressing room block), one was under the old Leeds United façade where you went in through the directors' entrance and you ended up on the right hand side of the dressing room area near the old snooker room, and there was also a players' entrance which is not there now. It was just a door with 'players' entrance' above it, and it brought you into the left hand side of the dressing room area.

"The home dressing room was the first door on the right (if you entered through the players' entrance)," Dave continues, "so if you look at the old picture of the blue 'LEEDS UNITED' façade, there's a balcony and if you look down to the left there's some big frosted glass windows, above head height. They were in four sections all together in a row. You had the home dressing room on the far left, then the home bathroom, there were no showers just a huge bath, then the away bathroom and

The 1991/92 league champions celebrate in what is now part of the away dressing rooms following the re-design for Euro 96.

then the away dressing room. The baths then were like half a room, absolutely massive and I used to go and play in there. They had floating soap, because the bath would be about three foot deep like a swimming pool, and you'd need scuba equipment to find the bloody soap."

Dave goes on to explain the daily routines and the other operations that went on in the homely atmosphere that Revie famously and crucially created: "Of course in those days they used those dressing rooms day in day out. So the reserves used the away dressing room and the first team used the home dressing room and the juniors used the dressing rooms on Fullerton Park, which are still there. Opposite the away dressing room, directly before you turned left to go down the tunnel, was the referee's room and behind that the referee's bathroom. Next to that was the away toilet, then the laundry room which had huge washing machines for washing the kit and was run by two women. That had a door into a drying room, where they would dry the kit, it was very hot because I used to go in there at half time to get warm. Then at the end, opposite the home dressing room was the home toilet. Every room looked the same, it was just painted brick, even the dressing rooms."

The laundry room remained the same right up until 1996 when the first team moved to Thorp Arch and the dressing room area was completely re-designed. But the primitive laundry situation was a clear example of how the Elland Road operations were being outgrown by the modern game, where match strips, track suits

and training kits were required for all levels. Back in the mid-1960s it was just as hectic, and the laundry operation was absolutely critical to the running of the club, as Dave Cocker explains: "At that time we bought the strips from Jimmy Frew's shop (on Roundhay Road) and one strip had to last the whole year. Bobby Collins always went out and his socks looked yellow. Bobby always played in the same socks, he kept them for years and he would only wear wool. They were his lucky socks, and if you see any photographs of Bobby Collins he would only wear these woollen socks and they used to darn them in the laundry to keep them going for him. So look at any old photos, and his socks are totally different to the rest of his kit.

"But the laundry room was huge," Dave continues. "The washing machines were on big concrete blocks but the girls used to do everything. They used to repair the shirts, if they got ripped they would stitch them up. When they bought the strips they were plain strips and the girls in the laundry, Kath and I can't remember the name of the other one, they used to sew the numbers and the badges on. They didn't get them made up from Umbro, that all came later."

With a precious and pretty much unique insight, which any youngster of a similar age stood on the terraces would probably faint at the prospect of, Dave Cocker also recalls the basic nature of the dressing room layout in Revie's day: "There was just a big table in the middle, a big wooden gloss-painted table, 8 or 9 foot long, with a tea urn on it, packets of Dextrosol (an energy supplement), chewing gum and all the tie-ups and medical kit. As you walked into the home dressing room, the first door on the left led into the bathroom, next to that they had an old-fashioned mirror hanging on a chain and next to that was the 'Keep Fighting' sign, which was just resting on two coat pegs, it wasn't even fixed up. Big Jack (Charlton) used to get changed under that. Billy, Gilesy and Big Jack were the senior players, they were who they all looked up to, and Bobby Collins of course at first. In the dressing room there was also a little room which I think got knocked out in the end. It was like a little cubby hole where they kept all the medicine balls and eventually in about 1966/67 that got turned into a little sauna."

Physio Alan Sutton also recalls the sauna room as an annex to the home dressing room, which evidently survived quite a number of years: "They had a sauna and a sunbed in there, and when Wilkinson came he soon got rid of all that lot. It had a flat roof like an extension. The story was that a lot of players used to spend about half an hour in the sauna every Friday before they got weighed. I also remember massaging Michel Platini in there before the John Charles testimonial (in 1988), Kenny Dalglish was there too and Ian Rush. I was massaging Michel Platini whilst he was smoking a fag! That back room had all the kit in it too, there were loads of cupboards and that's where they kept the kit."

Dave Cocker also recalls a classic example of Revie's mental approach to gaining advantages wherever he could, and this extended to the dressing rooms: "The windows were quite high, about seven foot high and

they were often open and you could just hear everything going on outside, the fans were all just outside. In fact just outside those windows in the car park were three parking spaces marked prominently with 'Referee', 'Linesman' and 'Linesman'. That was Don's psychology, so the ref knew that if they had a bad'un, everyone knew where their cars were......didn't do us any good though did it?"

I took Dave on a nostalgic trip down to the modern day dressing room area so he could talk me through how it had changed, and I was amazed at how little generally hadn't. The fixtures and fittings were much more plush of course, the décor had moved on from exposed, painted brick, and a few walls had been knocked down and doors blocked up, but the general layout was similar. One thing that had most definitely gone, however, was the simpler and more earthy feel to football back in the 1960s and 1970s, when Elland Road was quite literally 'home' and the game was less partisan for all concerned. The feeling of friendship and mutual respect between teams and rivals was something Dave Cocker witnessed first-hand, and he was almost choked as he relived, from nearly 50 years ago as it was at the time, his unique and supremely privileged childhood spent among Revie's infamous inner circle.

"Behind the toilet was the boot room," Dave recalls. "I used to love it in there, because that's where my Dad and Don used to go with the likes of Billy Nich and Shanks (Spurs manager Bill Nicholson and Liverpool manager Bill Shankly) and Matt Busby and sit and have a drink and a chat after the game, not in the office. I

The home dressing room as it currently appears in the 2020/21 season.

The white construction to the left of the façade was the annex to the home dressing room that included a sauna. The other three sets of windows to the right were the home bathroom, away bathroom and away dressing room. All this changed post Banqueting Suite build and Euro 96 re-design.

used to go in and brush all the boots off after a game, and it's one thing I miss more than anything, to be in there with people like Shanks or Bob Paisley and Joe Fagan, we all got on great with them.

"People go on about Manchester United," Dave continues, "but Matt Busby did us so many favours, you know with Johnny Giles; that was a real snip. Nobody else could have got it (the deal). Matt said 'how much can you afford?' and Don said 'well, £30 grand' 'oh, OK then'. That was it, they were mates. My Dad was mates with him because he'd been on a course with him and played with him at Stockport County. On a Saturday night or Sunday morning after games, when the newspapers arrived Matt would be on the phone to Don and then Shanks would ring, then Don would phone Billy Nich, just to have a chat. Bob Paisley used to phone my Dad for a chat after the game. Even when we won the Cup, Matt Busby was a guest at the banquet." A lost and much cherished world, and a time that makes you think that maybe football has now grown too big?

Today, the old home dressing room is one end of a much larger away dressing room, switched round during the extensive refurbishment for Euro 96. The switching of the home and away dressing rooms didn't happen straight away though. After the Euro 96 upgrade the 'home' dressing room stayed where it was for the first two games of the season against Sheffield Wednesday and Wimbledon. But then, eyeing the larger and more accommodating spaces in the 'away' dressing room across the corridor, it

was decided to switch to the locations that remain today, with the scene of many of Leeds' most famous celebrations now for visitors only.

The away dressing room now incorporates showers (which were actually converted from the old communal baths in 1989), toilets, individual baths, changing facilities and treatment facilities. Indeed the scene of the famous celebrations from the 1971 Inter-Cities Fairs Cup win against Juventus and 21 years later when Wilkinson's unlikely heroes sprayed champagne from the dressing room floor to hail the 1992 league championship win, is now unrecognisable. The exact location is partly the away treatment room and partly the away changing room, with a wall in between. Most poignantly, the exact location of the 'Keep Fighting' sign, from which Leeds United's most golden generation gleaned immeasurable inspiration, is a space in the middle of the away dressing room because the wall against which it rested has been knocked down.

Continuing the theme of the refurbishment, the old drying room, boot room and laundry all form part of the new, extended home dressing room. What was the away dressing room is now the referee's room, and what was the referee's room is now the 'coaches' room'. Alan Sutton recalls a time in the late 1980s when the players from both teams used the same toilet, as there was only one, and you can imagine some of the conversations that went on in there pre- and post-match, and perhaps most intriguingly, at half-time.

What was perhaps most eerie for Dave Cocker as he revisited his lost childhood was that the central corridor that links all the rooms and even the strange diagonal angle to the double doors at the far end of the corridor, were exactly the same in 1960. What were the laundry and home toilet doors have now been blocked off as the new home dressing rooms are significantly bigger, but other than that Dave could still have been stood there greeting an immaculately coiffured Sniffer as he sauntered in before a match, or listening to Billy having a heated discussion with the ref at half time or to Big Jack chatting with his brother Bobby on their way to the players' lounge.

The West Stand fire of 1956 was significant in terms of the dressing rooms and indeed most of the kit being completely destroyed. For the next match against Aston Villa and for many others in subsequent months, the players used dressing rooms at the nearby Whitehall Printeries Sports Ground whilst the stand was re-built. They also used the dressing room block erected on Fullerton Park. The first West Stand, built in 1906 by Leeds City, was heralded as a 'state-of-the-art' grandstand at the time and amongst the innovatory facilities it trumpeted were 'dressing rooms', suggesting that previous facilities were somewhat more primitive.

As a savoured feature of the daily stadium tours around Elland Road, it is impossible to sit in the dressing room and sufficiently soak in the history, as you try to visualise the sheer number of legends and not-so-legends that have sat in the same seats. A few minutes' solitude is required to concentrate on the ghostly echoes of Leeds United's past, as there you sit, insignificant and awestruck, in the very place where countless battles have been won and lost.

DRYSALTERS ARMS

Many away fans visiting Elland Road on a match day will advise that the area is quite poorly served by pubs. This is mainly based on the fact that the ground is away from the city centre, and also on the, to be fair quite accurate, belief that the majority of pubs around the ground would not be the recommended habitat for an away fan, given Leeds fans' deep-rooted, hostile reputation. One such pub that prides itself on an open acceptance and invitation to away fans, however, is the Drysalters. And as such it should be applauded for at least attempting to break down the barriers of the sometimes tiresome inter-club rivalries, and also in venturing to modernise the perception of Leeds United, its fans and the city itself.

The Drysalters Arms is situated on the Beeston Ring Road a few yards from the bottom of Elland Road. Whilst the Drysalters' away-friendly nature is widely known through the network of fans' guides and websites, it is still likely that many away fans never actually make it there. The pub is set back from the main carriageway and not easily viewable from the road, particularly as it is situated after the long bend from the bottom of Elland Road. Hence, if you didn't know it was there, heading away from the ground as kick-off approaches will doubtless result in many a hasty about-turn when time is tight.

Nevertheless, the five-to-ten-minute walk up to the ground from that direction is a visually arresting one as the East Stand looms into the panorama, and you are afforded a good distant view of the thousands of fans milling around Elland Road itself as you approach.

The Drysalters has only been in its current location since around 1960. Prior to that the pub was a few yards further along the corner nearer to the ground; indeed, on Elland Road itself. This is perhaps a reason why the pub still bears an Elland Road address, when technically it's now on the A6110 Ring Road. This original pub, which was across the road from the Lee Pit, is known to have existed as far back as 1834.

Behind the original pub, which was much smaller than the current one and opened out directly onto the pavement, was a tannery factory that later became part of the 'Sausage Factory of English & Continental Casings', also known at one stage as 'Kraft and Hornings' and as a tripeworks. Many believe the 'Drysalters' name originated from the meat-preserving operations that were undertaken in the sausage factory behind and adjacent to the pub. Another theory is that there used to be a leatherworks nearby in Millshaw, and the curing of leather may have been a reference to 'drysalting'. But the name is just as likely to be the more direct fact that a 'drysalter' actually traded in the premises behind the pub for many years.

In the 1834 Leeds Directory a Joseph Lee is listed as a "Drysalter, oil dealer, preparer of peachwood, camwood, cotton manufacturer and victualer of the Drysalters Arms", and therefore is likely to have lent the name of his main trade to the name of the pub he also ran. It is also likely that his family name had a connection to the nearby 'Lee Pit'.

The original Drysalters was demolished and moved in the early 1960s due to the construction of the next phase of the Beeston Ring Road. The stretch of the Ring Road that the current pub sits on was constructed in 1927, at least 30 years before the pub was moved, but the next section from the bottom of Elland Road, past the now-closed Wheatsheaf pub and up towards Farnley and Wortley, was constructed much later. This work involved shaving a small section off the bottom of Elland Road to provide a wider junction and this included the corner that housed the original Drysalters.

To this day the Drysalters remains a habitual aspect of many Leeds fans' match day schedule, prior to the short stroll to the ground, and if away fans can make it too, all the better.

DUGOUTS

Don Revie and his right-hand man Les Cocker. Basically, in a dugout that size you had to get on pretty well.

Stop for a minute and look at the enormous padded car seats that most Premier League clubs adopt today to form their dugouts. They symbolise such outrageous and senseless opulence that they might as well recline and produce grapes and Veuve Clicquot from a flap for Jürgen Klopp to devour, whilst we watch from ten yards away shivering on a plastic tea tray and with not enough leg room to kick a passing cat when we concede. With so much money to spend on inconsequential features of the game, it can't be long before wheeled chariots transport Premier League footballers on to the pitch before kick-off to avoid potential wear and tear. Compare today's dugouts to Revie and Cocker huddled intimately and peering out from an Anderson shelter constructed from plywood and corrugated iron half an hour before the season started, whilst outside the sub sits on a wooden stool in a woolly jumper being rained on. As the money, facilities and personnel involved in football continue to expand at a rate defying all logic and social awareness, this can be relatively demonstrated by the scale of the dugouts seen in grounds across the country where it is not uncommon to see over 20 personnel lined up and bored rigid in matching snowsuits. Alas, we will soon need to get used to this at Elland Road ourselves.

At Elland Road the dugouts currently remain fairly modest in size and comfort, but are still a far cry from the glorified chicken shacks of yesteryear. Of course

until the mid-1960s the only personnel within a dugout were the manager and his right-hand man, maybe occasionally a physio. So accordingly, the dugouts at Elland Road used to be quite moderate affairs situated closer to the tunnel than they are now as a result of the pitch being moved. None of the spectators behind the dugouts had their views obscured, indeed they actually had a better view than anybody sat in the dugouts, as, bizarrely, the team management were seated below pitch-level with their eyes literally on the same level as a forest of ankles on the pitch, hence the name 'dugout'.

Probably the only physical improvement made was a hotline telephone system that was installed into the dugouts in 1975, linking the management in the dugout to other personnel, as required, in the directors' box above. It was used for the first time against Wimbledon in the FA Cup. Other modifications have been scarce, however, given this is a facility, below Premier League level at least, that is merely a pretty basic and unpretentious area to sit or stand and watch a game of football within shouting distance of the pitch.

Prior to the 1989/90 promotion season the dugouts were extended from accommodating four people to seven, and the home dugout was swapped in position with the away to be nearer the tunnel. The 1990s saw a minor concession to health and safety

Something tells me we're not winning this game. Peter Reid and his assembled team in the Elland Road dugout in 2003 and how the dugouts still remain today.

with the provision of a padded cushion on the lip of the dugout ceiling, for when Howard Wilkinson saw a misplaced Nigel Worthington backpass and quite literally hit the roof. But as the match day entourage grew so the dugout grew in size as a consequence, and again it was Euro 96 that led to the dugouts being expanded to their current size. Today, the dugout is like a huge bicycle shed, with curved plastic protecting the staff from the crowd behind, and the height of the dugout now ensures the first five rows of seats directly behind are rarely sold. Staff can now stand up in the dugout, though most managers now tend to stand pitch-side in the grassed 'technical area'.

Bar the tinkering-with of formations and countless inspired substitutions, not many significant events have occurred in the dugouts. Don Revie famously felt the need to pick up his picnic blanket and leave the dugout to approach referee Ray Tinkler on the pitch following the controversial 'offside' goal conceded against West Brom in 1971. BBC commentator Barry Davies perfectly captured the gravity of the decision as he described Revie looking up to the heavens with cynical incredulity as another cruel twist of fate befell his cursed team. In recent years, loanee defender Michael Gray was sent off for fighting with Gillingham striker Darius Henderson on the lip of the dugouts in 2005, when staff from both dugouts promptly joined in to form a 20-strong melee. Two years later Leeds

manager and protector-of-the-peace, Dennis Wise, held a very strongly worded exchange with Luton boss, and his Leeds predecessor, Kevin Blackwell in front of the dugouts at the final whistle of a game in the '-15' League One campaign. Most recently, moral guardian John Terry prowled the dugouts and was particularly vocal over the need for Marcelo Bielsa's Leeds to concede a goal to balance up the controversial opener scored by Mateusz Klich in the 1-1 draw with Aston Villa in April 2019. Following the ensuing melee, Leeds duly did and picked up a FIFA Fair Play Award for their trouble.

Again, like most grounds, the dugouts at Elland Road are no hiding place for the manager from the abuse and 'helpful advice' from supporters in very close proximity, and likewise, fans sat nearby are afforded a front row seat of occasional tantrums and misdemeanours. And whilst the current West Stand endures as a compact and dated facility free from much-needed re-development, that is likely to remain the case. Upon promotion to the Premier League in 2020, Leeds were given special dispensation to delay the upgrading of the dugouts to 'Premier League standards' because they intend to carry out this work at the same time as re-laying the pitch and upgrading the undersoil heating, which is long overdue. So drink in the relative poverty of the current dugouts whilst you can, because the age of the enormous padded car seats will soon be upon us.

E

EAST STAND

Everybody knew a kid at school who grew up quicker, towered above the rest in the playground and was just better than everyone at everything. There was a respect, a sense of awe, but then gradually over the years, that kid just blended in.

Completed in 1993, the East Stand was unveiled as the final instalment in the current stadium that is Elland Road. Whilst it dwarfs the other stands it is connected to, we are kind of used to that now. At the time of completion it was the biggest cantilever stand in the world, though it was soon overtaken by constructions at Celtic's Parkhead, Old Trafford and St James' Park, and since then by many others. Nevertheless, the rear steel pillars that provide the 'cantilever' support to the roof structure remain an arresting and distinguishable sight.

The East Stand linked the ground together and mirrored the ambition the club had at the time of its completion, as that of a club that stood squarely together with the best in English football. The East Stand was the towering bastion of that new prosperity and was a conscious and conspicuous gentrification of Elland Road at a significant time; a step change on to new pastures, much as the South Stand had been when replacing the Scratching Shed after the 1974 league title win. Built at a cost of £5.5 million, and also existing to a great extent to ensure Elland Road was selected as a Euro 96 venue, for the first five years of its existence reference to the stand was almost constantly prefixed by the words 'magnificent' and 'new', and such reference was frequent.

Regardless, the club were right to boast about the stand which succeeded the diamond floodlights as the dramatic and imposing landmark on the skyline of south west Leeds. Almost as soon as the celebrations died down from the First Division league championship win, the bulldozers moved in during the summer of 1992 and the East Stand began to take shape. The much-trumpeted arrival of the Premier League and Sky Sports coverage began with the unfortunate sight of many grounds bearing the empty stands, exposed steelwork and structural confusion of enforced redevelopment. Stung by the demands of the Taylor Report, several clubs were taking the opportunity to build new stands and Elland Road was no different.

The East Stand project was one of the most tangible benefits of the club's relationship with Leeds City Council, who owned the stadium at the time. However, plans for building 'an' East Stand had been in place since the mid-1970s, as the final piece in making Elland Road a modern 'bowled' complex. It didn't happen then of course, but as soon as Howard Wilkinson was in the managerial hot seat the board of directors adopted more long-term thinking and at the start of the 1989/90 season managing director Bill Fotherby was already proclaiming the imminent arrival of the new East Stand, which at that time was scheduled to be completed for the beginning of the 1991/92 season.

Planning approval and financing arrangements for the complex were expedited through the convivial relationship between the club and the council, but still delayed the construction until 1992. Finance for the development came from a number of sources, not least the 'Leeds United Bond' and a substantial £2 million grant from the Football Trust. Also, while the council made it very clear there was to be no burden to the local poll tax payers, they provided £1.5 million of what was mysteriously described as savings ploughed back as a result of "surplus on the rent the council receives from the club".

The Lowfields terrace is finally reduced to virtually nothing as the shell of the East Stand rises above it, and the less said about those red builders' hoardings the better.

A pre-megastore side view of the emerging East Stand; note also the line of temporary floodlights along the back of the Lowfields terrace.

The Leeds United Bond was heralded with much fuss in February 1992, including an unprecedented TV commercial featuring Howard Wilkinson himself. For the price of £500 fans were entitled to a £100 discount on the cost of their season ticket for the next seven seasons after 1992/93. In addition, the season ticket price that bondholders paid would be fixed at 1992/93 prices. The deal allowed for the fact that season ticket holders on the Kop and Lowfields in 1992 would be seated by the end of the bond period in 1999/00, which meant that those fans could sit for the price of standing, as well as enjoying a £100 discount. Overall it was a deal of stand-back-and-gasp generosity. That said, the take up wasn't quite what the club had hoped for, and while a sizeable chunk of upfront cash was produced, it fell short of the £2 million required. The fanfare of the launch soon subsided and after a few months the only reminder of the Leeds United Bond was seeing the additional perk of the bondholder's name etched onto their seats, some of which can still be seen around the stadium today.

Nevertheless, the club had taken the decision to proceed with the East Stand and were understandably keen to take advantage of the position the club were steadily reaching. In reality there was little choice as the necessity to make Elland Road all-seater by 1994 was looming, and the prospect of doing that with the existing Lowfields Road Stand would result in a much-reduced capacity, and hence was a non-starter. Chairman Leslie Silver, speaking in February 1992 as the bond was launched, also suggested that "building costs will never be as low again as they are now", perhaps unwittingly

revealing the more believable reason for the haste. He added the deadly postscript that if the £2 million wasn't raised, the 'East Stand' would have to stay as it is; a loaded threat indeed.

The speed with which the club needed to cash in on its status was accelerated by the league title win of 1992, immediately after which the ground capacity had to be slashed as the East Stand was built. Howard Wilkinson remembers the general line of thinking at the time: "As far as I can remember it wasn't a long term thing, it was a case of 'let's go ahead, let's get it done, let's increase our capacity to generate revenue, to drive things forward'."

Eddie Taylor well remembers the magnitude of the East Stand project and how it overtook almost everything Leeds United-related at the time: "Excitement over the 'magnificent, new' East Stand almost overshadowed the build-up to what would be our title-winning campaign. Season ticket books for 1991/92 and advertisements for the newly launched Leeds United bond scheme all carried an artist's impression of the new structure, which unlike earlier, less ambitious plans showed the lower tier climbing to the height of the Kop and North East Corner, while somehow managing to underestimate the sheer scale of the upper. With work to start in the summer of 1992, I probably wasn't the only Leeds fan mentally fast-forwarding a year."

With the title secured in stunning circumstances, it was clear the club was moving apace to another level and Eddie was in the thick of it watching on: "In the summer after the title had been secured I took at least two mini-pilgrimages to Elland Road to measure the progress of the new stand. The first on a weekday to gape at the hole left by the removed earth banking and that crow's nest stand that sat atop it, the second to buy tickets for the Makita tournament and study the emerging skeleton of burgundy piles and gun-metal grey joists. After the impermanent, almost anti-climactic joy of winning the league, this was the concrete-and-steel evidence of what Leeds had achieved under Wilkinson: a permanent return to England's top table."

As Leeds kicked off the first ever Premier League campaign in August 1992 against Wimbledon, the setting was the unusual and somewhat disorderly sight of the Lowfields terrace backed by red construction hoardings, and the towering steel framework of the cantilever stand above it. Visual evidence of the stand's forthcoming stature did leave many fans aghast, however, and for once in a good way. Gradually over the proceeding months the work progressed with the Lowfields terrace untouched, until some of the upper section of what would become the East Stand lower tier was made available for use by away fans on 30th January when Middlesbrough were the visitors. At the end of the 1992/93 season seats were put on the Lowfields terrace and this section was joined with the existing seats above to form the 10,000 capacity East Stand Lower. Above it, work was finalised on the 7,000 capacity East Stand Upper.

"Upper", "lower" and "tiers" were new words in the Leeds fans' lexicon as the season 1993/94 began, and the first home game against West Ham on 17th August saw the stand's grand opening. It was not until

the following February that a 40,000 plus crowd was achieved when Liverpool visited, but clearly the ground capacity had now been raised, and fans were able to strut with a more self-satisfied smugness that at last the next base camp had been reached.

"It was a tremendous complex the East Stand," says Bill Fotherby. "They came from Arsenal, David Dein and his colleagues, and they said 'Bill, my god, we're planning to build a stand at Arsenal, how much did you pay for this Bill?' I said 'the basic was £5.5 million and £1 million on the infrastructure', ie. the fridges, and everything that went into the restaurant, because if you build something you need to have the backing of a restaurant and all the facilities. Fortunately I got on to the board of directors a man called Peter Gilman from GMI Builders. I tell you, that man never got the credit he deserved. He was fantastic, his company built everything at Leeds (at that time), he got the business, but my god, did he deliver on time. And did he deliver at a price? He built that whole complex and when Arsenal came and saw it and they said what they were going to pay..... They were going to pay for something that wasn't even half the size of Leeds United's. 17,000 seats was the East Stand, 17,000 seats! Arsenal's was going to cost them £13–14 million and it was something like 5,000 extra seats. They were amazed at what we'd done at Leeds, amazed.

"But Peter Gilman did a magnificent job with GMI," Bill continues. "I can't stress what a job he did. 17,000 seats; everybody in football admired it. We had jazz bands playing, and I filled it with shops all the way down. The first ones were the Flying Pizza doing pizzas on a match day, I had all different shops in there, I had it full

A more recognisable look to the East Stand mid-construction during the 1992/93 season.

The updated players' mural created by Robert Endeacott and friends in the East Stand stairwell.

in there, packed. People were saying 'oh, what a magnificent job Mr Fotherby, it's a wonderful job you've done here'. I can't tell you, I was the King."

The stand, in terms of management and administration, became almost a stadium in itself, and indeed the club employed an 'East Stand manager'. The 'shopping mall' underneath the stand was open six days a week at first, and was pre-eminently fitted with match day drinks, food, betting and merchandise facilities. This was Leeds United moving to another level and embracing modern football. Gone was the standard football cuisine rigidly centred on Bovril, Wagon Wheels, 'Fish and Chip' crisps, Kwenchy Kups orange juice and Clix chewing gum, and in came the unmistakable aroma, detectable at over 100 feet, of the Chicken Balti Pie. But the biggest difference was felt initially by the players who suddenly were emerging from the tunnel not to the dilapidated Lowfields, but to be confronted by a wall of faces and noise; an epic canvas of people and a towering panorama that in itself could have accommodated the average attendance of six Premier League clubs in the previous 1992/93 season.

Many fans in the upper tier cite the view of south west Leeds and the green hills between Bradford and Halifax to be as good as it is of the dots on the pitch, and certainly a new perspective was put on football for those with a Row Z vantage point. Suddenly the lofty environs of the upper tier were offering regular top flight football served with a choice of food and smiling stewards, all a far cry and several hundred feet from the decades of history, revelry and rancour of the concrete steps below.

Adding a touch of colour to an otherwise bland interior below the stand, is a mural painted by author, Leeds fan and local resident Robert Endeacott in the early 2000s, which depicts a collection of Leeds United players from various eras in a team group with the old West Stand façade as a backdrop. It is still displayed today on the wall of the stairwell nearest to the Kop, but Robert was able to re-design the mural in 2018, along with vital help from friends Johnny and Paul Kent, to improve some likenesses, replace certain players whose inclusion had always irked him and flank the team group with the cerebral presence of Howard Wilkinson and Don Revie either side.

Some fans see the East Stand as the main physical legacy of Howard Wilkinson's tenure as manager, although the Thorp Arch complex has perhaps been more influential. But the East Stand only became necessary and possible through the performance of Wilkinson's teams, and this was brought home to Eddie Taylor on a significant later date: "The point was made most forcibly the day he left the club in September 1996. I was a cub journalist, not long into my first full-time job with the company that produced the official Leeds United magazine, when Howard Wilkinson was given the sack, a decision announced

The East Stand during the controversial 'in-fill' refurbishment in 2011.

on the Monday following a crushing 4-0 home defeat by Manchester United.

"I sprinted down to Elland Road for the lunchtime press conference," recalls Eddie, "which Wilkinson himself attended, and once the various forms of 'this is in the best interests of the club' had been committed to tape, I walked around the ground to capture the thoughts of any Leeds fans in the vicinity. The response in the West Stand car park, on Lowfields Road and in the queue at United Fisheries was one of resignation. He had to go, the thoughts ran; time for a change. Things had got stale. The exception was a woman in her late twenties emerging from the East Stand concourse. 'I can't believe it. It's outrageous,' she said when asked for her response, her intensity catching me off guard amid the general shoulder shrugging. 'Look up, look around you. He built this. Have we forgotten what Leeds United was like before he came? Have we forgotten what he did for us? He changed it all. And they do this to him?' It remains a compelling argument."

Indeed recurring, if slightly muted, calls have been made for the stand to bear Wilkinson's name, as nowhere else at Elland Road, firmly excluding a failed restaurant project, is there a permanent recognition for Leeds' second greatest manager.

A sad but inevitable side issue to the East Stand's construction was the requirement for sponsorship. From the beginning of the 2001/02 season the stand was re-named the 'Lurpak Stand', then for just the 2005/06 season it was the 'ADT East Stand'. From 2006/07 it was the 'LSS Waste Management East Stand' and in 2010 it became the 'Hesco Bastion East Stand'. The unavoidable visual assault of the sponsors' branding on the end and roof fascias changed from Clipper Logistics into 'HiSense' in November 2020, and at the same time Leeds United officially renamed it the 'Jack Charlton Stand' in honour of their record appearance-maker, who had died earlier in the summer shortly before the club were promoted back to the Premier League. It was a fitting tribute, widely welcomed by the club's fanbase, and means Howard Wilkinson must now await suitable recognition elsewhere.

While the lower concourse was hailed for its facilities in 1993 (which haven't been updated since, we should add) the upper tier was cheaply finished and afforded very poor facilities, which perhaps explains the highly competitive 'price' that Bill Fotherby referred to. It was closed on a semi-permanent basis by Ken Bates after the 2004/05 season, and over the next decade was only opened on a match-by-match basis where demand required it, which as the club's fortunes dwindled, wasn't often.

It was no surprise in 2010 when Bates announced plans for the East Stand 'in-fill' that would eventually double the executive box capacity, afford much better facilities in the upper tier and provide more office and conferencing facilities during the week. There were also plans for a Leeds United museum, a nightclub, hotels and a bigger superstore, but none of this has materialised. Work on the first stage was completed in 2012 and although corporate seating is most of what occupies the upper tier, seats are back on sale to regular fans for each game.

The East Stand continues to be the focal point of most commercial and administrative activity at the club, and has prompted a gradual shift from the West Stand of day-to-day offices and, for a brief period, the directors on a match day. Even the façade on the back of the stand is now the 'money-shot' for local news reports. With the Bremner statue helping to provide the visual identity to the club in modern times, whether the West Stand will ever regain its former glory and its status as the centre of Leeds United is doubtful.

ENGLAND

It is well known that Elland Road is one of the easiest grounds to access from all areas of the country, and as such has a good history of hosting FA Cup Semi-Finals and high profile rugby league games. In football terms, what is more recent, however, is the use of Elland Road for England home international matches.

It was with a combination of surprise and nervous, gushing pride that the ground was selected to host an England international against Sweden on 8th June 1995, 12 months prior to the start of the proper Euro 96 tournament. The Umbro Cup International Challenge Tournament was staged as an end-of-season friendly event, but effectively also as a dummy run for a selection of grounds primed for action a year down the line. The tournament involved four teams, England, Brazil, Japan and Sweden, and matches were staged at five different grounds: Wembley Stadium, Elland Road, Goodison Park, Villa Park and the City Ground. England, however, played two games at Wembley and one at Elland Road. Yes, Elland Road.

It was to be the first full England home international staged away from Wembley Stadium for 29 years, since a friendly match staged in similar circumstances, at Goodison Park against Poland in January 1966. So the Elland Road game was a prestigious event, and from a logistical point of view a crowd of 32,008 attending with no issues of note ensured the evening was a great success. Football-wise though, you can always rely on England to bulldoze the revelry out of any occasion. It wasn't going too well, with Terry Venables gaining precious early experience of helplessly struggling at Elland Road, as his team trailed 3-1 to Sweden in the second half and the ground rapidly emptied, before goals from David Platt and Darren Anderton in the 89th and 90th minutes, respectively, rescued the affair.

Whilst it somehow took the FA six years to re-build Wembley Stadium, England gave provincial fans a rare opportunity to sample the dubious delights of watching them in the flesh, touring 14 grounds between 2001 and 2007. On 27th March 2002 it was the turn of Elland Road to host a friendly against Italy as England geared up towards the World Cup in Japan and South Korea. Before a crowd of 36,635 England lost 2-1 to a last minute penalty, with then Leeds striker Robbie Fowler netting the England goal. Fowler was one of nine half-time substitutions made by manager Sven Goran Eriksson, though Leeds United were at least represented from the start by goalkeeper Nigel Martyn and right back Danny Mills.

In June 2018, Elland Road was again a somewhat surprising choice to host the national team as Gareth Southgate chose a then Championship ground to stage his team's final friendly before the World Cup in Russia. Local fans in the 36,104 crowd were cheered by the presence of ex-Leeds midfielder Fabian Delph playing a full 90 minutes in a much-changed side, whilst England triumphed 2-0 against Costa Rica with goals from Marcus Rashford and Danny Welbeck.

The first recorded use of Elland Road as an international venue was on 20th November 1909, when an amateur international between England and Ireland was staged before a crowd of 8,000. The meagre crowd saw an entertaining 4-4 draw. Various other amateur, under-23 and under-21 internationals have been staged at Elland Road over the years mainly up to the mid-1960s, though an under-21 international was staged at Elland Road in 2005 (see Neutral Games).

EURO 96

Gazza's goal versus Scotland, Poborsky's chip at Hillsborough, the Dutch humiliation at Wembley? Despite an array of 0-0 draws, a few too many penalty shoot-outs and David Seaman's frankly unspeakable moustache, the first major tournament on English soil since the World Cup 30 years previously was an unqualified success. On the pitch England surpassed all expectations, and whilst the scintillating attacking play was inevitably mixed with pre-tournament scandal, anti-climactic draws and a fortunate win on penalties, the route to the semi-final defeat to Germany created mass hysteria across the country. Off the pitch, Euro 96 was a big test of the new and/or improved stadia constructed following the Taylor Report and the influx of money from the Sky TV deal. But more significantly it was a huge test of the security resources and the 'new', improved football fan in the face of the widespread hooligan issues of the 1970s and '80s. Amid much pre-tournament fear, the abiding memory now is of a rare summer of sunshine, an atmosphere of convivial hospitality and a celebration of all that is good in football.

Elland Road was chosen to host three matches in Group B all of which involved Spain, whilst Newcastle's St James' Park was to host the other three games in a group consisting of Spain, France, Bulgaria and Romania. UEFA delegations had visited Elland Road several times over the preceding three or four years prior to selecting it as a tournament venue. To the club's credit, the Banqueting Suite, the East Stand, and the move to an all-seater stadium were all done with Euro 96 in mind, albeit all were an inclusive business necessity at the same time too.

The key plus points in Elland Road's favour as a major tournament venue were features that many fans maybe didn't appreciate. These were the substantial VIP and refreshment areas, the media facilities, police and security facilities, the ample car parking and bus facilities within the immediate vicinity of the stadium and the proximity to both the railway and motorway network. The awarding of three games to Elland Road was felt to be a "fair return for the enormous amount of effort that a lot of people have put in at Elland Road" according to the then chairman, Leslie Silver. He added that the club did not expect to make any money out of the venture but would end up with a better stadium with better facilities, and it would be the city of Leeds that would benefit the most through restaurant and hotel trade.

Leeds United's general manager Alan Roberts was appointed as centre director for the North East, and the infrastructure of the ground underwent significant improvements in the lead up to June 1996. During the tournament itself the outside of the ground was also overhauled with banners, flags and additional, temporary signage erected to assist the thousands of visiting fans, who were also issued with 'Supporters' Guides' for each hosting city, published by the Football Supporters' Association.

This embracing of the visiting fans was mirrored in the centre of Leeds where Euro 96 was a ubiquitous presence. Banners were attached to lampposts throughout the city, giant footballs sat outside the Town Hall and the flags of the four competing nations flew outside the Queen's Hotel. Street music festivals were organised, as well as five-a-side tournaments for visiting fans. There was also a camping village for up to 3,000 fans set up in the grounds of Temple Newsam and the licensing hours of pubs and clubs were extended, which brought a reminder of how far behind our European cousins we truly were.

Back at Elland Road, the crowds attracted for Spain's three games were very respectable and certainly better than those attending the other games in Group B at St James' Park, although the numbers of visiting fans from Romania and Bulgaria were sparse. The healthy gates, however, were despite extortionate ticket prices, set by UEFA: £45 in the East Stand Upper, in 1996, for example. There was very little segregation other than for the high profile Spain/France game, as pockets of fans from all countries were littered around the ground,

Spain and France enter the field before their Euro 96 encounter at an Elland Road ground sporting themed Euro 96 facias on all stands.

mingling with the Yorkshire locals who largely claimed an 'underdog' attachment to Bulgaria.

On 9th June 1996 Spain drew 1-1 with Bulgaria in front of 24,006. On 15th June France drew the big game with Spain also 1-1, which attracted 35,626 on a day that Leeds Bradford Airport reported record flights and passengers, including a visit from Concorde. Finally, on 18th June Spain beat Romania 2-1 in front of 32,719 to finish second in a group that, in truth, had failed to inspire. Without doubt though, the atmosphere in the city and around Elland Road on match days was truly unique and is remembered fondly.

For the tournament, Leeds United's head groundsman John Reynolds was appointed by the FA as a consultant for all the training pitches and grounds in the northern area. His widow, Maureen, recalls: "All the pitches had to be the same size, cut the same way, with the grass the same length. It was that era when they started having fancy patterns with circles and zig-zags, and UEFA wanted a uniform tartan design on every pitch. So they made the training grounds and the stadium pitches all the same. It was very warm that summer in 1996 and we had a hosepipe ban. All the teams wanted sprinklers to water the pitch but John had to say 'sorry, we can't'.

John's son Stephen Reynolds also recalls: "That was the year that Elland Road got the square goals. I always used to badger my Dad because we used to watch Italian football and I always thought the square goals looked great but he never put them up, because apparently they were a pain in the arse to put up with different footings. But for Euro 96 they had to put them up, and we've had them ever since." The move was not

without its implications though, as Stephen adds: "The concrete underneath them (the Euro 96 goals) for the sockets is about a tonne in weight, they've put that much of a concrete footing in you can't extend the length of the pitch. If we had to change the length we would need some new goalposts. These are the only posts in the whole of the Football League and Premier League that are five inch thick. They came from Germany. Every goalpost in every other club is four inch in diameter, ours are five inch and you can only go up to five inch (hence the extra concrete required)." Another curious and rather random victory for a feature of Elland Road.

Leeds United received glowing praise from UEFA delegates and visiting fans for the standard of hospitality, transportation and organisation, and the two years' work spent building up to the tournament was considered to be justified. The fallout from the tournament inevitably brought a sense of anti-climax, although at Elland Road during the summer of 1996, the club was in the middle of a protracted takeover. But then, seemingly, when isn't it?

As the Caspian Group made inroads into the Leeds United boardroom and the PLC-era loomed on the horizon, at floor level Alan Roberts worked to amend the ground regulations to allow flags back in to Elland Road in order to replicate the colour and carnival of the Euro 96 tournament. It was difficult to recreate that on a wet Tuesday night in February, but nevertheless his intentions were honourable. Not so his public call for a 'Leeds United oompah band' to help create and maintain atmosphere, much as the Dutch one famously did during Euro 96. A group of six Leeds College of Music students did briefly have a stab at

Spain fans make the South Stand their home during the match against Bulgaria at Euro 96.

this, starting at the Liverpool game in November 1996. With predestined inevitability they were hounded down mercilessly by Kopites fiercely loyal to traditional methods, and having failed to lift the spirits during a particularly dank period in terms of on-pitch fortunes, they only lasted a few games.

EXECUTIVE BOXES

Snaffling prawn sandwiches and peering down on the great unwashed from their ivory towers; a lazy generalisation perhaps but the executive box holder has an indelible image in modern day football, and particularly at Elland Road since their arrival in the austere times of the mid-1980s, despite their income being critical to the lifeblood of the club then and since. The era of the executive box has seen football clubs uncover new revenue streams and build lucrative business partnerships through a hitherto untapped tangent of the football world, and it hit Elland Road with an unheralded bump in 1983, with the installation of 16 boxes underneath the roof of the South Stand.

With crowds dwindling, the loss of five rows of seats at the time was insignificant in the scheme of things. Leeds have been particularly ravenous in embracing the hospitality sector ever since, yet the 'executive box' will forever be viewed by the average fan as a distant world that they are not party to, and hence there remains an attitude largely of detachment and disdain towards this area of the club's activities.

Bill Fotherby takes up the story of how the move into the corporate world came about under his stewardship as commercial director, with the club desperate to increase revenue: "We had to go after business people, accountants, they were the people that I went for commercially. These are the people that can afford to pay £1,000 membership and that was the beginning for Leeds United. I started building, building. Well, I went down to West Brom, I had two days at West Brom

because they were one of the first clubs to put boxes in and I went to see how it was done. And what I did was, there was a man who I got for sponsorship at Leeds and he started Televista Studios, and I always hang a carrot for these people that it was possible for them to become directors of Leeds United. So this man was a very good sponsor and he invited me down to the opening of his studios in Leeds. I can see it now, and I went down there and he had a member of the royal family opening it for him. So he said 'I want to show you something Bill' and he took me out into the yard and there was what you would call a Portakabin, what I called a 'mobile building'. He opened the door and we went in and I've never seen anything like it, it was like *Doctor Who*. My god, there was chandeliers, velvet wallpaper, magnificent regency furniture and the toilet! 'My god,' I said, 'you can't believe this is a portakabin.' He said, 'well this is the royal restroom' and I was like 'oh, this is a marvellous idea'.

"Now I had been quoted £400,000-odd for 16 boxes in the South Stand," Bill continues, "and I couldn't raise that money. I asked him where he had got it (the box) from and he said it was from the chairman of Scunthorpe United. It was him that built these boxes and then you've got to add furniture. So I went to see him and I asked him 'how much were these boxes?' and he said 'I can do you a box for £4,000'. I thought 'ooh £4,000?' Now, I'd spent two days down at West Brom, saw what they were doing with stone and brick boxes that cost money, and then I arranged for a 'cheese and wine evening' at Elland Road and I had a sample box there. I got any business from Yellow Pages, I took any good business and invited them down, 100 Club members, invited them down. To have your own private box to seat eight or ten, to have your own drinks cabinet, your own television, you can watch the match, do a bit of business. On that night I sold four boxes, and I was charging £5,000 a season, if you signed for three seasons I reduced it to £12,000. I finished up and I sold the whole 16 boxes there, fronted them up with a cement fascia on and looking lovely, and nobody knew they were just Portakabins with an interior copied from West Brom."

Whilst Bill Fotherby undoubtedly looked after the average Leeds United supporter in difficult times, he also knew that the businessmen were where the real money was. "I built a suite upstairs right next to the boardroom which was for judges, QCs, lawyers, £2,500 they were paying. You know they have the money, they can afford these things. You look at clubs and you think 'for god's sake get a strong commercial side' because it's out there."

The first match day programme of the 1983/84 season for the visit of Newcastle United shows an artist's impression of the view from the new boxes in the South Stand, which after fittings and the costs of the adjoining restaurant were said to have cost the club around £200,000 in total. The programme proudly boasts the 'facilities' contained within: a television, a telephone, a fridge and 'luxury seating'; quite clearly, another world. The boxes were linked to the Goal Line restaurant and lounge area below the stand which was accessed via an exit that had transparent panelling to form a tunnel, hence separating the 'executives' from the average South Stand Leeds fan of the mid-1980s.

Four years later, presumably flushed with the success of their first serious moves into the commercial sector, the club installed a second layer of boxes below the original ones. This was done in stages with seven boxes installed for the beginning of the 1987/88 season, prompting the untidy sight of one and a half rows of boxes for three years before the remaining nine boxes were installed for the beginning of the 1990/91 season, following the club's promotion.

Bill Fotherby didn't stop at providing private boxes for his wealthy guests either, he even provided a car-washing service in the West Stand car park in 1988, albeit this was short-lived. A power-jet car wash was installed in the far corner of the car park, where the two-tiered main ticket office would soon replace it. Fotherby used his nous and intuitive nose for a deal to spot that there was no other public car wash facility in the area, and corporate guests using the Goal Line restaurant during the week could get their car cleaned whilst Fotherby squeezed more money out of them for sponsorship and other commercial deals.

The capacity of the upper section of the South Stand has remained the same ever since 1990, with just nine rows of seats available. It has long been thought that the club could remove these boxes should the corporate requirements be satisfied elsewhere in the ground (ie, in the East Stand and/or through a re-developed West Stand) and hence increase the capacity of the South Stand, but so far this has never happened, nor looked likely to. The South Stand boxes were described as "out-dated" compared to the East Stand ones, but they are currently being used. Although the lower level boxes were taken out altogether for the beginning of the 2010/11 season and replaced with a 'Family Viewing Deck', effectively an open plan seating section behind glass, with ticket deals for parents and children. The South Stand boxes have also been used by various TV stations during live coverage of games at Elland Road, but it appears they are basic and much smaller compared to the second wave of executive box hysteria that hit the club following the title win of 1992.

By this time, Elland Road was a flurry of corporate activity with affluent fans plying associates with cheap wine in the executive boxes, but also in the various suites built in the West Stand: the Banqueting Suite, the 100 Club, the Centre Line club, the Captains' Lounge and the Executive Club, which later became the Premier Lounge.

In 1993 the East Stand opened, complete with 20 executive boxes spanning the whole length of the stand. By now, facilities had improved including the option to watch the game from seats in front of the boxes, effectively with the rest of the crowd. In 2011 the club re-developed the East Stand, installing a further 20 boxes and suites to double the capacity of the available executive hospitality. This was a controversial move in the eyes of many fans, who saw money being spent on the corporate community but not on the team itself. The West Stand still hasn't escaped the corporate touch with various executive suites remaining contained within its skeletal framework, including the Radebe Suite, the Revie Room Suite, the Presidents' Suite, the Norman Hunter Suite and the Bremner Suite.

It's a far cry from those first tentative steps in 1983 when having a fridge with cold beers in at Elland Road was like some kind of Utopian otherworld, but now, undeniably, the executive boxes and the hospitality throughout the ground is an imperative income source for the club.

A great photo of the pitch invasion at the end of the Leicester game that brought promotion a step nearer in 1989/90, but of course we are not looking at the feast of denim and wedge cuts but at the one and a half rows of executive boxes that stood awaiting completion.

F

FA CUP SEMI-FINALS

Neutral fans generally dislike Elland Road, mostly by default; simply because it's Leeds United's ground. Therefore the frequently recurring boast citing the ground's ease of access via the motorway network, with the M621 that connects to both the M1 and the M62, running within yards of the ground, is unlikely to cut much ice when it is selected as an FA Cup Semi-Final venue. Nine FA Cup Semi-Finals have been staged at Elland Road over the years, and the oft-mentioned motorways argument is rendered somewhat irrelevant when you consider that seven of those nine games were staged before the M621 was even an urban planner's dream. So you have to assume it is the general position of Leeds being located roughly equidistant of the two competing teams that has seen it allocated as the chosen venue on each occasion.

That said, the first Semi-Final to be staged at Elland Road was actually as a 'thank you' from the FA for the efforts Leeds City had made in establishing professional football, in response to the FA's palpable encouragement, in a staunchly rugby-orientated area. It was a gracious gesture to the fledgling club that the FA would live to regret.

On 26th March 1910 the FA Cup Semi-Final between Barnsley and Everton was watched by an estimated crowd of 36,000, paying gate receipts totalling £2,478. Sadly the day ended in acute embarrassment. The vast crowds arriving could not be accommodated and thousands of those who were inside were unable to see the game. The gates were shut 30 minutes before kick-off with thousands of disgruntled fans locked outside and scurrying for vantage points on the Peacock roof and further up Beeston Hill. Indeed, some official supporters' coaches from Merseyside, with tickets, had not even arrived in Leeds by the time the gates were shut. Initial and seemingly spurious estimates as to the ground's capacity by the Leeds board had fallen woefully short, and a chaotic day did not sit well with the FA.

However, two years later in 1912 the FA gave Leeds a chance to redeem themselves via the staging of a Fourth Round Replay between Barnsley and Bradford. Astoundingly the occasion met with the exact same results: over-crowding from an estimated 45,000 crowd, locked gates, and turnstiles being rushed and looted.

After 1912 it would be over a decade before the ground was fully developed. This wasn't acknowledged until 1930 when the FA again trusted Elland Road with the staging of a contest between Arsenal and Hull City, which thankfully passed without incident.

The full list of FA Cup Semi-Finals staged at Elland Road is as follows:

26th March 1910
Barnsley 0 Everton 0
(Attendance 36,000)

22nd March 1930
Arsenal 2 Hull City 2
(47,549)

14th March 1931
Birmingham City 2 Sunderland 0
(43,572)

16th March 1935
West Bromwich Albion 1 Bolton Wanderers 1
(49,605)

29th March 1947
Charlton Athletic 4 Newcastle United 0
(47,978)

The souvenir programme for the FA Cup Semi-Final between Charlton and Newcastle held at Elland Road in March 1947.

2nd April 1952
Newcastle United 2 Blackburn Rovers 1 (Replay)
(54,066)

18th March 1961
Leicester City 0 Sheffield United 0
(52,095)

16th April 1980
West Ham United 2 Everton 1 (After Extra Time) (Replay) (40,720)

9th April 1995
Everton 4 Tottenham Hotspur 1
(38,226)

In more recent years the West Ham victory in 1980 was famous for the celebration of Frank Lampard Snr after he headed the Hammers' winner two minutes from the end of extra time. He ran to the south east corner of the ground where the West Ham fans stood on the open terracing and did a circuit of the corner flag running backwards. Seventeen years later Lampard's son Frank Lampard Jnr repeated the celebration following his goal for West Ham at the same end. Though the goal put the Hammers 1-0 in front, Leeds hit back to win 3-1 and hence that particular goal celebration does not merit quite as many YouTube views. That Semi-Final in 1980 held the record for Elland Road's highest gate receipts for many years, with £146,483 being taken at the turnstiles. The 1995 Semi-Final inevitably blew that out of the water though, as the Everton v Tottenham game still holds the ground's receipts record at £1,006,000.

A near-miss occurred when the all-Sheffield FA Cup Semi-Final clash between United and Wednesday was initially scheduled to take place at Elland Road in April 1993. The decision prompted immediate outrage from both competing clubs, who didn't see Elland Road as fit to host what was seen as a historic occasion. Whilst the argument barely hid the bitterness that has always been directed 30 miles northwards from Sheffield, it was in fairness hard to disagree with it. Elland Road at the time was still a building site, with the East Stand under construction and only partially open. Indeed the capacity was little over 32,000 and in the event Wembley was the chosen venue, as it was for the other Semi-Final, the all-London affair between Arsenal and Tottenham. A 75,364 crowd watched Wednesday triumph 2-1 at Wembley and the event was very much a Sheffield love-in, untarnished by the spectre of 'dirty Leeds'.

For the 1995 clash, Tottenham Hotspur were allocated 18,478 tickets, which included the whole East Stand and corporate seats in the West Stand, whilst Everton received 17,609 tickets; effectively the rest of the ground. Since then, Wembley Stadium in both its original and re-built forms has largely been used to stage Semi-Finals, much to the chagrin of the rest of English football.

FAÇADE

Like the diamond floodlights and the electronic scoreboard, one of the most enduring and endearing images of the Elland Road of yesteryear is the West Stand façade, or more accurately, the West Stand façade with the addition of an array of club legends lined up in front of it. Added to the final construction of the 'new' West Stand in 1957, the blue, rectangular signage that sat proud of the red brick walls and the windows running the length of the stand, is an emblem of the first successful age in the club's history. It was a modern façade for the 1950s and created a styled

entrance to the stand which was rare among post-war stadia. Football grounds connoisseur and critic Simon Inglis considers that only Villa Park and the exterior leading into the marble halls of Highbury rivalled the West Stand façade, at the time, for the sense of prominence and architectural dignity it afforded the club's main entrance. It was an enlightening example of someone, somewhere within Leeds United AFC having forethought and vision at a club that had no history, at that juncture, beyond the mediocre.

During the period that the club trained on Fullerton Park most team photos were taken specifically with the West Stand façade proudly in the background. The façade had a ridged surface and was mid-blue with a bold, concrete, white outline and golden capital lettering spelling out 'LEEDS UNITED A.F.C.'. Beneath the lettering was the coat of arms for the city of Leeds, which was adopted by both Leeds City and Leeds United as the club crest between 1908 and 1961.

Underneath the crest there were three sets of double doors from the West Stand interior which opened out onto a small balcony. Onto this balcony in the early 1980s was added the brass engine name plate from a locomotive named 'Leeds United', originally built in 1936. One rail enthusiast valued the 'Leeds United' nameplate that hung below the façade at between £2,000 and £4,000, and a plate from a similar class of steam train was sold in 2005 for a staggering £60,000. The valuation of the 'Leeds United' plate was printed in a match day programme in 1991, a little liberally you might think given the several thousand people reading who could do a lot with £2,000 and were well aware of the nameplate's accessible location. When the Banqueting Suite was built in 1992 the locomotive nameplate was put into storage, where it remains today.

The balcony below the façade led from what was the '100 Club' lounge and the main foyer area and was directly above the main reception area, next to which was the original hexagonal ticket office and then, post-1973, the base of the huge floodlight pylon. In front of the façade were three flagpoles attached to the balcony. The largely superfluous balcony was used only to raise and lower flags on the flagpoles, which added a regal nature to the club's main frontage.

Throughout much change at the club the façade stood unaffected, including the retention of the Leeds city arms despite the club crest changing numerous times in that period. The façade itself and the yardage around the main reception areas of the West Stand were given a facelift during the summer of 1983, in readiness for the new season. This included the blue colouring being touched up, but other than that the façade remained largely untouched for the 35 years it existed on the back of the stand. Robert Endeacott remembers the vivid colour of the façade: "I don't know what material it was made out of but the glorious 'oceanic' blue always seemed to stay brilliantly strong, which just added to the whole appeal.

The magnificent and stately West Stand façade pictured in 1979; note the flagpoles, balcony and reception area and the location of the hexagonal ticket office.

It was a beautiful blue that just preserved itself, I don't know anything about architecture or construction but the number of shop fronts or department store fronts that just fade over time, this never seemed to fade; the blue just stayed blue and the Leeds United name just stayed high in the sky and in reputation. I absolutely loved that whole aspect of the stadium."

It was with some considerable regret that the West Stand façade was removed and unceremoniously covered over by the construction of the Banqueting Suite in 1992. To the dismay of many supporters it appeared that the club's history was being wiped from the record books under the new, admittedly successful regime.

Robert Endeacott comments on the lack of public outcry at the time: "Don't forget there was less media about then, no internet or mobile phones so it just happened with practically no one even knowing about it. My Dad was still working at Elland Road then and I think there was a bit of an uneasy atmosphere around the club even though we were on the up. It was a very successful period but the manager and the board of directors were very much about 'getting a job done', which was fair enough, but they won't have considered much about employees' feelings and in a way the façade and the lettering and the whole reception area, that was possibly too much of a 'Revie memory' for some, I

don't know. It's absolutely stupid that nobody seemed to care about those brilliant letters or that fantastic insignia, it's in so many kids' childhood memories. In the end the directors were doing a job, but Don Revie brought the club up to fame and fortune and a lot of that was down to the family atmosphere that he encouraged. Anybody who worked there will tell you that, from the lowest level of workmen right up to possibly even the directors. Don Revie was a bloody good guy, full stop. Everybody loved him. After he left, obviously that faded, as did the club itself, and that was the stupid directors' making.

"There is nothing nasty in what Howard Wilkinson did in removing the photos and everything," continues Robert, "but it's possible that his relatively cold attitude rubbed off on the directors, and it was proven right because it got us back to glory, so you can't fault him for that. But his (Howard Wilkinson's) influence over the directors maybe led them to get rid of the façade as well. I believe it was in a skip for ages, the coat of arms and all the blue insignia. I wish I'd had more nous about me at the time because I would have loved to have nicked some of that gold lettering for the back garden."

In response, Howard Wilkinson himself puts the decision to build the Banqueting Suite and in so doing,

The construction of the façade in the summer of 1957 and before the brilliant and regal blue sheen that enriched our lives for 35 years was added.

covering up the façade, down to necessity at the time: "If you change things you've got to expect that people will have a different opinion, and you've got to be prepared to deal with that opinion. You can't resent it, you can't feel slighted by it; it's natural. But at the same time you've got to keep your eye on the horizon, and the horizon was for me, particularly after the Sky deal looked as if it was starting to become a reality, was that salaries had begun to increase and the inexorable road was that your position in football would be determined by how much you paid, and to try and ignore that? It wasn't going to happen. It's not a democratic activity spectator sport, it is what it is, and that's the reality. So you might want to change the world but if you're focusing on what's real you're saying 'how do I deal with the world I'm in?' And the world that a one-eyed man could see was that salaries were going to go up, your ability to attract players was affected. It had already started, I was having problems, not problems I resented, but with the Battys of the world, the McAllisters of the world, the Gary Speeds of the world, all these things, but that's the reality. So you have to try to, where possible, meet people's reservations but try and also at the same time convince them that it's for a better future."

So with progress came the covering up of the past and a commercial, money-making future. Standing by the left side of the Banqueting Suite today you can see the six or seven metres of brickwork that was added on to the West Stand frontage to completely obliterate the iconic visage of old, before the Banqueting Suite itself sweeps out across the car park. However, standing on the right hand side in front of the new away ticket office and entrances, if you look towards the top corner of the Banqueting Suite as it runs away from the back of the West Stand, amid the myriad of air conditioning units, pipework and cabling, romantics might like to note that one very small corner of the concrete plinth that supported the old façade, with its white-painted border, is still just visible.

The original Leeds city coat of arms did sit on the Banqueting Suite walls for some time, but was eventually removed. Sadly the blue façade sat in skips for several weeks during the construction of the Banqueting Suite before being disposed of, and many believe the gold lettering went with it. Today, golden 'LEEDS UNITED A.F.C.' lettering can be viewed by visitors to the Hope Inn pub on York Road, Leeds, but confusion surrounds its authenticity, ie. whether it is the original lettering that sat resplendent on the West

OK, it's not much and it's got some aircon units disrespectfully sat on top of it but you can still see a tiny corner of the old white painted plinth that the façade sat on. So get straight down to Elland Road now and bow down before it!

Stand from 1957 to 1992, or whether the letters were a reconstruction made for the filming of *The Damned United*. The general consensus is that they are not the original letters, but they look fantastic all the same. Others think they might be genuine.

Gary Barrass runs the pub and is branch secretary of what is also an official Leeds United regional members' club, and he takes up the story: "I am led to believe that the letters were in storage down at Elland Road and that when they were making the film *The Damned United* the producers asked someone down at Elland Road if there was anything at the ground that they could use to make a reconstruction of the old West Stand for the film set, with regards to the scene of the day that Brian Clough came to Leeds to sign as the new manager. One of our members, a guy called Martin

Parker, was working on the film set and he called me up one day to ask me if I was interested in the sign, which also had the Leeds city coat of arms with it, exactly how it used to be when it was on the side of the West Stand façade. Originally I told him that I was interested in just having the letters 'L U F C' so that I could put them on the wall at the front of my pub that faces onto the main road. He said 'what about the car park wall?' You could have the full sign on there and he said he would put it up for me for the price of a few pints. So I agreed, and that is where it is today. The Leeds coat of arms? Well someone else who was working on the film location claimed that, so I just ended up with the letters. Martin told me that if nobody wanted the letters they were just going to scrap them, so I'm glad I said 'yes'!"

Today, it is clear that the old West Stand façade would have looked rather dated had it still existed without a radical overhaul, something that would have perhaps ruined the effect. Clearly the club are making strides to ensure the East Stand is now the façade that is the main focal point of the stadium, with the contemporary brick and glass fascia depicting the famous mantra "Side Before Self Every Time" providing a stately and magnetising presence. Add to this the stadium 'dressing' on the East Stand side with the huge player banners either side of the central façade. In comparison, the West Stand exterior now is an understated clutter of different entrances and operations. But still, the original West Stand façade remains an image that dazzles and immediately whisks you back to a post-war Leeds United Football Club that was very different: unsophisticated, honest, naïve, stoically provincial, steeled to make a point and with a fierce hunger to succeed.

The golden 'LEEDS UNITED' letters retrieved from *The Damned United* film set in 2008 and adorning the car park wall at the Hope Inn pub on York Road.

FAMILY STAND

Football was no place for children in the late 1970s and 1980s. I am glad my Dad took me to games back then and I was delirious at the time, but looking back it was far removed from what would pass as family entertainment today. Attendances had diminished and the often poisonous mood at games was such that it was almost inconceivable that a parent would take his or her children to a game as a 'family experience'.

Football was a working class obsession, a ritualistic escape, and most of society and the media thought of it that way – some still do. Football fans of the 1970s and '80s were tarred pretty much with the same brush, and it was only when the Heysel Disaster, the most high-profile of a litany of major incidents, brought things to a head, that the government and football clubs drew a line in the sand and established plans to clean up football's image. That said, the Hillsborough Disaster of 1989 triggered the Taylor Report which, though not a response to hooligan issues, ultimately did the most to control them.

Children had of course been encouraged to attend Elland Road previously, through the 'Boys' Pen', which was mostly a case of children being seen but not heard, out of harm's way and with little consideration as to whether the environment was actually suitable for them. So it was that the first 'Family Stand' was created in 1985 in the North West Corner Stand. The seats were exclusively allocated to members of the Family Stand and seating and refreshment facilities were made available in the concourse behind the stand. This was quite a departure for 1985 and the stand also boasted a crèche facility, upon demand, and was clearly seen as the club making strides to change the image and demographic of their typical supporters.

This first Family Stand was an initiative instigated by Bill Fotherby and membership was strictly by season ticket holder only, albeit with generous discounts for family members. In essence it was one of Fotherby's many ventures into 'members only' clubs and suites, partly to improve the club's image, but reading between the lines it was also to get as much money 'upfront' as possible, standard practice for most football clubs. Fotherby remembers the venture very well: "It was very, very successful and an idea that we copied from Manchester United. I made committees in different parts of the ground and a gentleman called Wilfred Webb and his wife were in charge of that Family Stand in the North West Corner. He looked after it and got memberships."

However, it was really the partnership with the sticker collection company Panini, that bastion of youthful obsession and pocket money vacuum system, a couple of years later that made the Family Stand a major success. Panini sponsored a number of Family Stands in other grounds in the country at the time, and did a lot of work in breaking down the barriers of cross-club rivalries; a brave and unprecedented exercise.

In 1990, with Leeds having gained promotion to the old First Division, the Family Stand had outgrown the North West Corner Stand and with seats newly re-installed in the bottom tier of the South Stand, was re-located there. New, bigger facilities were available underneath the stand and it became a huge success. For the title-winning season of 1991/92 the stand was famously named after and funded by the club's shirt sponsors *Yorkshire Evening Post*.

Upon opening the East Stand in 1993, the Family Stand grew larger again as their home now became a section of the 10,000 capacity lower tier, sponsored by McDonalds, again with improved facilities in the impressive concourse behind the new stand. Today the Family Stand is effectively the entirety of the East Stand lower tier, bar one central section that is open for general sale. The experiment to encourage families back to the game has undoubtedly worked and the football experience has benefited from it in terms of being a more courteous and civilised event. However, in contrast, many feel that the general atmosphere at games throughout the country and particularly at Elland Road has suffered as a consequence, and will never hold the fearsome and exhilarating reputation it once had and that many thrived on. Whether that is more of a reflection on society in general or footballing fortunes is difficult to judge, but perhaps at Elland Road the difference is more contrasting.

By definition the Family Stand contains some of the youngest fans in the ground, many of whom are experiencing their first tentative steps in being a Leeds fan. Most fans can remember if not their first game then certainly many early experiences. Those first games are often a strange adventure where there is too much to take in and, therefore, are not always enjoyable regardless of the result. The crux is whether you keep on going.

Thom Kirwin recalls his first game: "It was on my birthday in 1990, the 2-2 draw with West Brom, 24th February. That was the first time I went, but I didn't really enjoy it that much. I was only six, there was a lot of swearing, it was cold and I didn't really get it. It was the following year when it really hit me and I was hooked, but it was a very strange place to come for the first time. Swearing was the big thing, because I'd never heard some of the words coming out at Elland Road, but the noise and the shouting, I'd watched football on TV but when you're sat behind a goal it's such a different perspective and I couldn't work out what was going on. I didn't really understand it, and the smells, a bit of stale beer, that waft of beefburgers..... But it's impressive when you're that young and you see so many people in one place. I was showing off at school telling people I was going to the match at the weekend and people were so jealous, but I just felt it was a let-down, I was too young to fully appreciate it. What it is, is it's an assault on your senses, there's way too much going on at first and it's only when you get used to the language or the smells, the sounds, the sights that you get into it."

David Kirby also recalls an early game he attended alone: "The first time I went to a match on my own without my parents or friends Leeds were playing Nottingham Forest, 27th March 1972. I believed my friends would be on the Lowfields either at the wall at the front or on the shelf. I searched both but could not find them. I found out later they'd gone on the Kop. By this time all the spaces on the wall had been taken. I noticed someone climbing a little way up a floodlight that stood in the ground near the front of the north east corner (prior to the corner stand being built). I decided to do likewise otherwise I'd have a limited view of the game. By half time I needed the loo but I knew if I went I'd never get back to a position where I'd be able to see the game. With Leeds 4-1 up and just a couple of minutes remaining I could wait for the loo no longer and decided to leave early. As I arrived at the toilets located where the Lowfields ticket office is now, Leeds scored. As I then made my way to the Football Specials Leeds scored again. Two goals scored in injury time taught me never to leave early."

Andy Peterson has an early memory that highlights the perils of a certain generation who grew up in the 1970s and 1980s. Football was a very different beast and your reaction to certain events could have scarred you forever, and depending on how you look at it, could have spared you a lifetime of heartache and considerable expense, or conversely could have prevented you experiencing some of your most exhilarating moments. Andy comments: "My earliest memory of Elland Road is of a missile. Not your Cruise type, but still something fired in anger. The projectile in question was a piece of tarmac, thrown by a never-identified Chelsea fan after my first ever game, a 3-3 draw in February 1983. Despite the sentiment, and unlike Elvis Costello, the proto-hooligan's aim wasn't true, and the rock broke up on the ground at the end of my shoe just like my heart at the end of the 2008 play-off final. I often think about whether there would've ever been a second game for me had I ended up wearing it, and if so the alternative path my life would've taken."

Another damaging early memory is that of Karl Skirrow, who recalls the pitfalls of taking youngsters to football games when they are really too young to take a full interest in the game, or the people or the experience, and therefore find other things to do: "My Mum and Dad had a season ticket for the West Stand in the early 1970s. Before and after every game I'd have a tennis ball and would play football in the bar area as my Mum and Dad would have a drink. I used to dribble my ball past all the half-cut people who liked a drink after the game, me thinking I'm either Giles or Eddie Gray. I'd nutmeg and sprint past people who'd encourage me to shoot and score the winning goal, etc. I remember flipping the tennis ball up one day and

catching it plum in the middle and bang; goal. Well not really, the ball flew past my Dad's head and smashed straight through the window. The whole area went quiet, and the next thing a steward arrived and had a quiet word with my Dad. Then two weeks later my Dad got a bill for £200 for the window and I was banned from playing football at Elland Road."

Personally, my first experiences of Elland Road from 28th October 1978 and a 4-0 win over Derby County onwards, were dominated by not understanding why there was no commentary for people to follow. The transition from watching football on telly to watching it live was a difficult one, because I needed someone to tell me who the players were and why the ref kept stopping the game. In addition to the prolific and virtuoso swearing I was now party to, I also smelt cigar smoke for the first time, and even today there is a specific brand of cigar smoke that I can all-too-rarely smell and it transports me immediately back to winter afternoons in the West Stand, grown men shouting abuse at John Hawley and a flask of coffee at half-time. I would genuinely bottle that smell if I knew which brand it was. If future technology offers us anything, I would urge millions to be invested in a means of recreating the magic of those early football-attending years and the hypnotic enchantment of seeing the expanse of grass and the goalposts and the mass of people for the first time. I'm sure I am not alone in wishing the drudgery, routine and sense of reluctant duty that sometimes encompasses an afternoon at Elland Road in your forties, or at least did until recently, could be replaced by the sheer virginal wonder of that first time.

FARSLEY CELTIC

Let's face it, some of the most prominent FA Cup memories for Leeds fans are when we haven't been in it, which is most of the time. As a magnet for giant-killing humiliations we often adopt a dark, schadenfreude attachment to the underdog in the hope that some other wretched soul can walk in our shoes for a few days, weeks or in most cases, decades. Hence, attentions turned with salivating anticipation to Farsley Celtic one afternoon in 1974.

As a small village to the north west of Leeds, almost bordering Bradford, a football club in Farsley was only ever likely to have ambitions within the confines of non-league football. However, from being founded in 1908 Farsley Celtic gradually negotiated the Yorkshire League and the Northern Counties East and Northern Premier Leagues on its ascent up the non-league ladder. They also enjoyed maybe their finest hour on the Elland Road turf.

In 1974 Farsley Celtic, then a Yorkshire League side, won through the preliminary rounds and earned a place in the First Round proper of the FA Cup, causing much fuss and publicity in the area. They were awarded

with a 'home' tie against Tranmere Rovers of the old Third Division, then managed by ex-Liverpool stalwarts Ron Yeats and Tommy Lawrence, and advised by one Bill Shankly.

After careful consideration Farsley elected to move the game to Elland Road, home of the current league champions who shared their city but dwarfed them in size. On 23rd November 1974, therefore, Farsley, playing in borrowed Leeds United shorts because they had forgotten theirs, and in front of 10,337 rain-saturated fans, lost the game 2-0 to a Tranmere side that featured a 19-year-old Steve Coppell. It was the soon-to-be-Manchester United ace who scored the first goal in the early stages. Farsley then kept it respectable until the closing minutes when Bobby Tynan added a second.

In truth Farsley were overawed by the occasion and didn't make much of an impression. Indeed, a player at the time and future Farsley manager, Denis Metcalf, recalled that: "The trouble was we were all just happy being there and being part of it...I think we only got into their half about four times."

Farsley's leisurely rise up the football pyramid continued and in the season 2006/07 they were promoted for the first time from the Conference North Division into the Conference Premier. This combined with Leeds United's undignified and calamitous descent into League One and meant that for the 2007/08 season there were just two leagues separating the wayward behemoth of Leeds United and the cocksure minnows from the village of Farsley. However, sadly Farsley were relegated in their first season in the Conference Premier and then endured a torrid period of financial uncertainty and were formally disbanded in March 2010. A new club, Farsley AFC, was immediately formed and, albeit much lower down the league ladder, they are still enjoying life at Throstle Nest today.

FENCES

Combining steel and militant antipathy, the fences that were erected in front of the stands on all four sides of Elland Road in the late 1970s were a symbol of a very forgettable period in the club's history. The Elland Road ambience had very quickly degenerated from a bubbling vibrancy promoting togetherness and success to a decaying emblem of coldness and undesirable austerity, like a deserted concentration camp.

Examples of trouble at Elland Road had steadily escalated in frequency since the late 1960s and gained increasingly withering media attention in the mid-1970s. But the main trigger for the fences being installed was the FA Cup tie against Manchester City in 1978 when a fan entered the pitch from the Kop, with no fences to stop him, and confronted City keeper Joe Corrigan. The Kop therefore became the first stand to have fences erected immediately after the City game. £30,000 was spent making the barrier from the floor to the top of the fence ten feet high in time for the next home game. Before the decade was out all four sides of Elland Road had perimeter fences erected, even the traditionally more genteel surroundings of the West Stand. Images of the time show the ugly steel enclosures as a backdrop of empty seats or terracing, and certainly this was an unpleasant period for the game, not just at Elland Road, but across the country as attending football became an unfashionable, tyrannised and cynical experience. Steel fences had first been discussed at Elland Road in 1974, as other grounds in the country had adopted the measure in the face of the growing problem in the game. At that time the FA and Football League wanted clubs to build moats around the pitch as many continental clubs had done. At Leeds, they simply hoped the problem would go away.

As the outbreaks of trouble continued into Leeds' eight-year residence in the old Second Division during the 1980s, so the authorities' zero tolerance attitude towards crowd control was intensified. On top of the already erected fences were installed a series of brutal 18 inch spikes in August 1984, which pointed inwards at an angle; further adding to the prison camp aesthetic where comfort and safety for attending spectators were way down the list of priorities. The club also considered using anti-vandal paint as a further measure but feared it would get on the players' shirts if the ball hit the fences during play.

The staging of a football match in the 1980s was routinely an exercise in preventing 'serious' crowd trouble; football was policed as a necessary evil rather than a form of entertainment. Football fans were treated like caged animals mainly because a huge percentage of the dwindling crowds behaved like one, or so the theory went. The very existence today of the Football Supporters' Federation and Supporters' Trusts suggests that mentality still exists to some extent, although no one who attended Elland Road in the 1980s could possibly say the venomous atmosphere and overwhelming sense of imminent threat that was present then is in any way evident today.

Incongruously, the fences were party to some positive experiences during the 1980s with famous goal celebrations by Brendan Ormsby, Mel Sterland and Vinnie Jones ensuring that the fences added to the explosive theatre of manic revelry. Despite few examples of supporter unrest at Elland Road in the latter part of the 1980s, even with crowd levels increasing under Billy Bremner and then Howard Wilkinson, the fences remained in place until the Hillsborough Tragedy of 15th April 1989. In physical terms it was clear that the perimeter fences at Hillsborough had been the main obstacle to supporters attempting to escape the crush in the Leppings Lane terrace, and almost overnight the authorities woke up to the concept that perimeter fencing was quite literally a death trap. However, although Leeds United

The Leeds United fan of the 1980s: Bleached denim? Check. Beanie hat? Check. Looking pretty hacked off? Check. Peering through a huge wire fence without any complaint? BINGO!

tried to get the Elland Road fences taken down before the end of the 1988/89 season, ie. immediately after Hillsborough, a legal row between the club, the police and the council prevented it. Initially the terracing capacities were cut as an alternative measure, and gates in the fences were left open.

On the eve of the 1989/90 season at Elland Road, the Kop and Lowfields terraces lost nearly 9,000 spaces at a stroke. The club also installed a tannoy system to communicate with fans outside the ground, as a measure to allay potential overcrowding in the queues that were steadily building with the club's long-awaited success, and which had been a feature of the panic witnessed at Hillsborough. But finally, the fences started to come down.

Before 1989, younger fans like myself who liked to stand at the front will have never watched a football game without the obstruction of an ugly blue mesh fence, until Howard Wilkinson lifted the gloom and provided a clearer view of prosperity in much more than a metaphorical sense. Although the Hillsborough Disaster prompted a relaxation of the dogmatic approach to crowd control the mood change did coincide, at least at Elland Road with a more positive vibe generally. Howard Wilkinson's team had created a buoyant, natural vibrancy to match days and a fan base stung by years of mediocrity saw very clear signs of a return to greatness. Finally there was no reason to lash out, less of a chip on the shoulder and there was something encouraging and a collective energy to rally around. As well as Wilkinson's team, which

contained several players fighting for cult hero and fans' favourite status, many people cite the emerging dance scene in Leeds and its associated Ecstasy culture as contributing to a softening of past attitudes amongst fans. Suddenly, altruistic young fans who would previously be arriving at the match looking for confrontation, were on the R2 buses still coming down from the night before and arrived looking for kinship and communion. There was plenty of that at Elland Road in 1989/90 and the hordes of beatific youths in bleached denim, flares, parallels, dungarees and beanie hats were feeding off blissful nights out and a football club they could be proud of again. The holy triumvirate of juvenescent wellbeing – football, music and socialising – combined perfectly and it was an unforgettable time to be a Leeds United fan.

The West Stand fences were removed in time for the 1989/90 promotion season. And with Leeds United ushering in a new era of trust and general, positive inclusiveness which was heading for warp-speed, the South Stand fences were also removed in time for the 1990/91 season when it was transformed into a fully seated family stand. But the Kop fences remained in place (though minus the spikes so that escape was marginally easier) until the start of the 1991/92 title-winning season. These were removed following a 12-month period of consultation and monitoring involving safety teams, emergency services and the police. The move was finally granted based on the good conduct of the fans in the Kop during the 1990/91 campaign. At the same time that this was announced, the club also

Even the genteel folk in the West Stand couldn't be trusted to refrain from storming the pitch.

Brendan Ormsby scores the late winner versus QPR in the FA Cup Fifth Round in February 1987, thus creating an earthquake in LS11. The fences added to the theatre and the ball boys threw protocol and impartiality to one side in a joyously unrestrained moment.

informed fans in the Lowfields that their conduct could result in those fences coming down. However, ground development work intervened and the Lowfields fences weren't fully removed until the East Stand began to take shape during the 1992/93 season.

Today, images of fencing at football grounds represent the barbaric conditions which football fans had to simply accept. They were one of a number of all-encompassing measures through which every fan was uniformly judged and sentenced. Looking back at how widespread violence was at Elland Road and how dramatically different the football-watching experience was for 'normal' fans, it is difficult to see how panic-ridden and despairing authorities could have acted any differently, however extreme the fences seem now. In this sense, the fences were a perfect metaphor for how life was in the political minefield of the late 1970s and 1980s, and their absence since also, perhaps, mirrors how society and attitudes have evolved?

FIRE

Asked to name one event that changed the face of the modern day Elland Road and most might say the signing or appointment of Don Revie; others might identify Howard Wilkinson becoming manager. How many would mention a fire in 1956? It is perhaps in unusual circumstances, but the event that signalled the first construction of the 'modern' Elland Road occurred in the early hours of Tuesday 18th September 1956.

Leeds United had just secured promotion after nine seasons in the Second Division, and under manager Raich Carter had made a promising start to life back in the top flight. Progress was undone though when a raging fire was discovered in the original West Stand

and like a dramatic and costly onset of amnesia, virtually all of the club's history up to that point was lost. The alarm was raised by Arthur Price, owner of the fish 'n chip shop opposite the main gates on Elland Road, and father-in-law of Leeds right back Jimmy Dunn. Price ran out of his premises barefoot and in his pyjamas, but the fire had already begun to take over the stand and the roof had collapsed into the seating below before the fire brigade even arrived. Ten minutes after the fire engines had begun tackling the fire the stand was ablaze from end to end, but within an hour it was under control.

Despite the fire brigade's best efforts the morning light brought the solemn vision of a smouldering wreck, a shell of twisted iron and steel, with all the contents destroyed. This included all the records from the admin offices, the dressing rooms, the kit, the boots, nets, goalposts, trophies and silverware won in friendly competitions, and all the medical equipment. The fire is the main reason why there is such little memorabilia around today from the pre-1956 era.

Stephen Reynolds recalls his dad John's reactions as he arrived at work the next day on the ground staff: "He said he was coming down the hill on the tram, and he thought 'something looks different'. He said he got off the tram and thought 'ah yes, that's what it is; the West Stand's gone! No training today then....' He lived at Cross Flatts, which is pretty close to the ground and he said he never heard, smelt or saw a thing."

The damage, which included a scorched ten yard area of the pitch along the touchline, was estimated at £100,000 and the club's insurance was found to be woefully inadequate. It was clear that the stand could

not be salvaged and whilst the players helped to clear up the rubble, an emergency board meeting agreed to ask for council assistance with a public appeal for funds.

Both the general public and Leeds United fan base were deeply shocked by the events. John Cave, who was 12 years old at the time, remembers the sense of loss that quickly became apparent: "The fire came as a great shock to me, I could not believe that my revered second home had been so severely damaged, but with a corrugated iron and wooden superstructure built over a metal frame, little was left of the old stand by the time the fire brigade had it under control. Much was lost in the fire and it was not until much later in my life, when I had an interest in the club history, did I realise how much a loss of all the club's playing records would become."

Reg French was 30 years old when the fire devastated the burgeoning football community of Leeds and he also remembers the impact: "It was a major event obviously, everybody I spoke to was upset about it and wondered what the implications would be for the club."

The fire and the upset in circumstances affected Leeds' form, although the first home game after the fire, a mere four days later against Aston Villa, was won 1-0 with a John Charles goal in front of a 35,388 crowd that was actually 320 people higher than the previous home gate. The game was played with a few thousand intrepid fans nonchalantly packed onto the remaining terraces, and effectively standing amid the ruins of a relatively perilous construction.

It was a monumental effort to get a game staged at all, particularly to the backdrop of a smouldering and crumbling wreckage, as Reg French recalls: "The

A clear view of the complete devastation caused by the fire of September 1956; the dark stain on the pitch is where the heat of the fire scorched the grass.

With the exterior wall of the original West Stand still to be demolished, footings are prepared for the construction of the new West Stand post-fire in 1956; note also the goalposts of Fullerton Park in the background.

amazing part, when you consider the extensive damage from the fire, was that they were able to get a game on. If you thought about the same thing happening today it would be impossible with the safety regulations. Until there had been a thorough investigation and they had reached conclusions they wouldn't have been allowed to play a game within a couple of days. The safety situation was quite different to what it is now."

Leeds fan and Supporters' Club secretary Ray Fell also remembers the days after the fire: "I have a photo on my wall of John Charles running down the wing in that game against Aston Villa, in the background there's people in the ruins watching the match. They must have cleared it enough to accommodate people actually in the ruins. But one of our Supporters' Club members, Eric Mahon, was looking around the stand after the fire and he picked up a number 5 shirt, which was John Charles's, and years later he gave it to me and I passed it on to the club, who should still have it." This tale is slightly different to that printed in a match day programme from 9th February 2009, against Millwall, which tells the same story, but claims it was the number 8 shirt that Charles wore that season and that was recovered from the wreckage. This is correct when studying the stats, as Charles wore both the number 8 and number 9 shirts during the 1956/57 season. The programme shows a picture of the badge which was taken from the shirt and later handed to the club. It claims that even 53 years later, as it was then, you could still smell smoke on the badge.

Raich Carter had ordered 40 pairs of new boots for the Aston Villa game, with strict instructions for the players to wear them at home to break them in. The order was to remove the studs so that the players could wear them in the house, and only screw the studs back

In the aftermath of the fire, fences are erected to 'make good' the stand in readiness for the Aston Villa game.

in on match day. On the day of the Aston Villa game the players got changed in the nearby Whitehall Printeries Sports Ground on Lowfields Road and after a short coach journey walked gingerly through the empty skeleton of the stand onto the charred pitch. For a time afterwards the hastily built changing room block on Fullerton Park was also used by the first team during the week, as well as the juniors. With the loss of all medical equipment and facilities former trainer Arthur Campey opened his nearby private practice up to the club to treat injured players. The hospitality of the local populace did not end there: nearly 400 cushions from the more exclusive West Stand seats had been lost in the fire and a local company replaced them, without prompting, free of charge.

Another concern for the club amid the insurance wrangling and replacing kit and equipment, was the disappearance of the 'Leeds United cat' around the time of the fire. 'Blackie' lived in the West Stand and

John Charles on the attack during the 1-0 defeat of Aston Villa four days after the fire; note the fans packed onto the concrete terrace of the charred stand and the coat pegs conveniently provided by the fences erected at the back of the stand to 'make it safe'.

hadn't been seen on the night of the fire when security had locked up as normal before going home. Staff at the ground commented in the grisly aftermath of the fire that Blackie "can't have been in the stand" and that "when he gets back he'll see things have changed". It remained unspoken but most staff at the club expected that Blackie had indeed perished in the fire, but miraculously the feline friend of Leeds United turned up right as rain the following Monday, exactly a week after the fire. The very fact that a cat had been adopted by the club and lived in the main stand in the full knowledge of all, perfectly encapsulates the monochrome nature of post-war life, and serves as a sharp contrast to the dispassionate departmental titan that Leeds United is today.

By the time of the second home game after the fire, against Birmingham City on 13th October, the whole lower section of the West Stand had been cleared and a very sizeable crowd, around the same size as what became the West Stand Paddock in the soon-to-be-built stand, were able to teeter on some form of terracing to watch the game, albeit there was no shelter from the elements as there was no roof. Behind them, the charred wreckage of the upper section of the 1906 stand remained. Over 2,000 season ticket holders from those West Stand seats had by then been relocated to the new seats installed in the Lowfields Road Stand only a few weeks prior to the new season. A public appeal raised an impressive but unfortunately inadequate £60,000, and as the club had always operated within tight financial constraints they were left in a perilous state. John Charles held a fearsome reputation at the time and had almost single-handedly gained Leeds promotion the previous year. There were doubts that he could transfer his form into the top division but he

proved all his critics wrong by amassing an astonishing 38 goals in 40 league games in that first season. By the summer, however, with the new £180,000 West Stand almost finished, the board bowed to the inevitable and accepted a world record fee of £65,000 for Charles from Juventus; the shortfall necessary to pay for the new construction. The fire, which had far-reaching effects on the ground, the club and the team, was believed to have been started by an electrical fault, though with no legal obligation to establish a cause this was never confirmed and arson was never suspected.

Incredibly, three years later there was very nearly a repeat during a midweek reserves game against Preston North End. Following the game some fans spotted a burning glow in the new West Stand through a window as they walked home. Club Secretary Cyril Williamson and other directors successfully fought the fire, which was thought to have been started this time by a discarded cigarette in the concourse under the stands, and no significant damage was done.

The most recent fire incident at Elland Road happened outside the ground. Many fans will recall seeing an R2 Football Special bus on fire near Lowfields Road when Liverpool visited on 15th September 1979. Dave Kirby is one such fan: "As we approached from Holbeck we could see thick black smoke coming from at or close to the ground. Initially I thought the ground itself could be on fire. As we got closer we could see flames coming from a Football Special on Elland Road close to the junction with Lowfields Road. The bus was totally gutted and I heard afterwards it had been caused by someone pushing newspaper down the back of the seats and setting it alight. There were pictures of it in the *YEP* the next day and I remember people were threatening to stop running Football Specials."

FLOODLIGHTS

"Lights, Tony Currie, action!" It is hard
to explain, but one thing that is sure
to get Leeds United fans of a certain
generation in a nostalgic lather is a
photo of the old diamond floodlights
that shone over Elland Road and most
of south west Leeds for only 20 years.
Show me a grainy but evocative image
of the 260 feet of lamp-laden tubular
steelwork and I am overcome by a
maudlin state of dewy-eyed regret
that they no longer exist, this despite
their looming presence bookmarking a
period of stony-hearted poverty. And
while it may seem that they shone on
our lives for an eternity, it's a sobering
reality that they have now been down
for much longer than they were up.

A triumphant return, albeit less awe-inspiring, for the diamond floodlights in 2020.

For any away fan, or any Leeds fan new to Elland
Road, the day the East Stand was opened in 1993
was the day that finding the ground involved actually
asking someone. Since 1973 the diamond floodlights
had dominated the skyline for miles around, being
considerably taller than the city's tallest block of flats
when they were first erected, and they were a guiding
light to what felt like home. In 1993 they were cruelly
ripped down without ceremony and it is no coincidence
that satnavs were invented shortly after.

But while 40-something Leeds fans have fond
memories of the time they grew up with pure unsullied
souls, before adulthood and the pollution of home
defeats to Wigan corrupted us, they see only the
ethereal diamonds piercing the night air. Though as
we hurried home and looked back in wonder as we
held our parent's hand to see how brightly they shone

and how far we had travelled, away fans would turn
round to check if they had evaded the baying mob and
catch a glimpse of their four-pronged, evil, taunting
glare. Furthermore, older Leeds fans just saw them
illuminating mediocrity, laying bare Leeds United's
decline with unnecessary intensity. So opinion is split;
yes, they were iconic, but what they represented is open
to interpretation.

The first floodlit match at Elland Road was on 9th
November 1953, when a friendly match against
Scottish league side Hibernian heralded the installation
of floodlights for the first time; these lights being much
smaller and more modest than the epic diamond lights
but also the most expensive in the country at the time
at £7,000.

Leeds fan John Cave recalls well the lead up to the
decision for the club to install floodlights: "In the core

A classic view depicting the formidable scale of the diamond floodlights; an unmistakable image across the skyline of Leeds.

winter months football matches had to kick off at 2pm on a Saturday in order to get games finished before it became too dark. However, a more reliable technology now allowed that certain games could be played under floodlights, although the Football League would not allow league games to be played under lights until 1956. Showing quite remarkable foresight, the Leeds United board installed floodlights at Elland Road in 1953, probably in the first batch of league clubs to do so."

The game against Hibernian was something of a glamour occasion in south west Leeds, as John Cave continues: "In 1953 this was a real coup as Hibs were THE premier side in Scotland in the late 1940s and early 1950s. In between 1949 and 1953 they were champions twice and runners-up twice and their attack known as the 'Famous Five' was probably the best known in these islands."

In the friendly game, second division Leeds beat the 'mighty' Hibernian 4-1 with two goals apiece from John Charles and then manager Raich Carter, and 31,500 came along to bask in the glow of the new concept of night time football, and it wasn't just the eye-catching nature of the result that sparked a jubilant mood. John Cave vividly recalls the collectively open-mouthed awe of the 'Close Encounters' experience: "For a Leeds-based football mad ten-year-old, used to the second division delights that regular fixtures against the likes of Bury and Lincoln City provided, this fixture was exciting enough without the added allure of a first floodlit game. It is difficult to describe how grown up one felt being allowed to go to the match, on a Leeds November night, along with your mates, to stand behind the goal in the Boys' Pen.

"It was a very strange experience walking to Elland Road (I lived in Lower Wortley) in the pitch black of night. As we approached the ground all of the normal Saturday afternoon sensations were multiplied a thousand-fold by the darkness. From outside, the floodlights themselves did not seem particularly spectacular and indeed once inside we could see well enough but frankly it was a bit of a let-down. However, as the teams came up the tunnel the floodlights were all turned on full power and it was amazing, the 31,500 crowd gasped as night time was turned into day. The pitch was greener, the white lines stood out like chapel hat pegs, our blue and old gold kit was bloody magnificent and those famous green Hibs shirts with

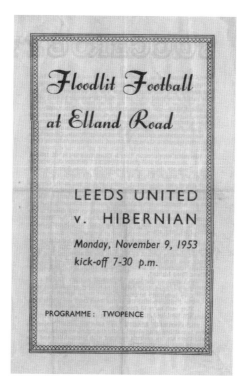

Floodlit Football at Elland Road

LEEDS UNITED v. HIBERNIAN

Monday, November 9, 1953
kick-off 7-30 p.m.

PROGRAMME: TWOPENCE

The official programme from the friendly game with Hibernian which heralded the switching on of the first floodlights at Elland Road in 1953.

white sleeves made the occasion so memorable. And we played with a whitewashed ball of all things." The inherent drama and intrigue of floodlit football had begun and a ripple of excitement warmed through the game as floodlit league games became commonplace, although maybe Big Jack was not able to get away with a crafty fag during the second half of quiet games any more...

Elland Road, and indeed every football ground in the country, was affected by political change in the grim austerity of the early 1970s. The three-day week would have a distinct knock-on effect in many areas of normal life, and there was nothing more normal than going to a football match. What became a very different experience to 'normal' in 1972, however, were the power cuts brought on by the miners' strike, which prompted a number of midweek games to be played in the afternoon rather than at night when under lights. These became a quite surreal experience where the magic of watching Revie's 'Super Leeds' was transported to an otherworldly juxtaposition amid what was in every other sense the mundanity of a routine Wednesday afternoon.

One such notable game was the FA Cup Fourth Round Replay against Liverpool on 9th February 1972. Despite the inconvenience of the 2.30pm kick-off time, Elland Road bulged to capacity with hundreds locked out and watching from the roof of the Old Peacock, as 45,821 dodged school or work to watch an epic contest which Leeds won 2-0 on their way to their only Wembley

The price of progress: another floodlight is dismantled in the West Stand car park.

triumph. Some Saturday games around the same time also kicked off at 2.00pm rather than 3.00pm to ensure the game finished in daylight hours.

The rapid re-development of the various stands at Elland Road in the 1960s and 1970s meant that the original 1953 floodlights were quite rapidly not tall enough and had a reduced effect. Indeed, the very fact that the two at the north end were sunk into the earth on which the original Spion Kop was constructed meant that they had to go when the new Kop was built in 1968. In their place were two slightly taller lights with a different, more rectangular-shaped head. These sat in the gap of excavated earth either side of the new Kop, effectively inside the ground, for two years until the corner stands were built. At this point they were each moved a few yards back behind the new stands, though it should be added they were not tall enough to be used effectively in this way. The temporary lights were taller and brighter than the two 1953 lights that remained in situ at the other end because the club were under pressure from UEFA to improve the lighting generally. This would ensure that the quality of lighting was suitable for colour television, which had started broadcasting some European games in the early 1970s. In similar circumstances, history has gone full circle in 2020, and Leeds are required to re-fit floodlights on the West Stand side in order to satisfy requirements for Ultra HD 4K TV in the Premier League. With the disparity in viewing levels between the West Stand and current East Stand, it wasn't possible for Leeds to merely upgrade the lights on the lip of the West Stand roof upon gaining promotion to the Premier League. Lighting demands in the top division are nearly three times those in the Championship (2000 Lux compared to 700 Lux) because of the requirements for TV coverage. This would dazzle fans sat in the East Stand lower, and hence Leeds had to invest in two new floodlights on the West Stand side.

In a wonderful nod to 1970s nostalgia these were designed as diamond-shaped, but sadly were much less awe-inspiring in terms of their sky-scraping height. Deep pits were dug in the West Stand car park for the footings – much further back than for the original lights – because the bent, angular design of the lighting towers needed a counterbalanced structure to accommodate the angle, as they would eventually peer just over the roof of the West Stand, but sufficiently high not to risk permanent blindness for those sat opposite. Stand-mounted lights were also upgraded in the summer of 2020 in the East Stand and installed in the North and South Stands, to create a rather brilliant balance of light. Alas, this welcome reincarnation of the fallen diamond lights will likely only be temporary, with Leeds planning to re-build the West Stand within the next decade, which will enable them to resort to neat and efficient, but far less romantic, roof-mounted lights.

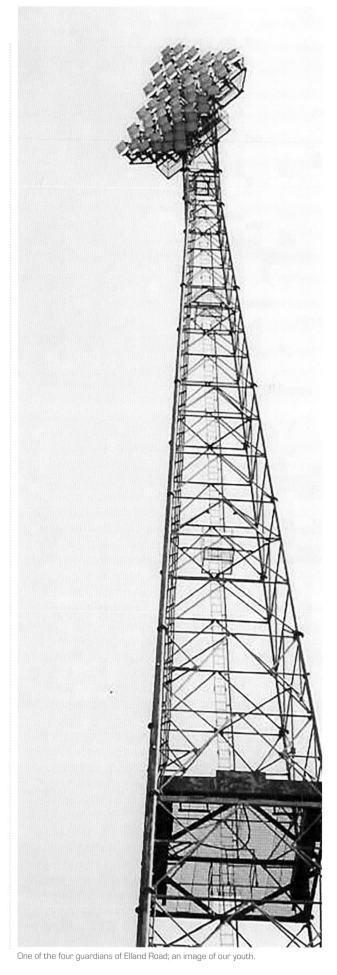

One of the four guardians of Elland Road; an image of our youth.

The past stares out the future: a rare photo of the diamond floodlights and the East Stand existing together during the 1992/93 season when the lights on the west side remained for one season.

When planning began for the 1974 South Stand construction, it was decided to install the famous diamond floodlights, and also due to the design of the corner stands, to build them outside the ground, hence the reason they had to be so tall. At Elland Road, it was decided that the footings of the giant floodlights would not be too much of an obstruction to pedestrians in the West Stand car park, where one stood virtually right outside the old hexagonal ticket office. Many grounds at the time built the floodlights in a corner stand or attached to the roof of the stand. Whether the lights had to be quite as tall as they were is not known, but praise be to the engineer that decided to bung an extra 40 feet on to create the superstructure that was, in reality, a concept upon a concept.

At 260 feet (79.2 metres) the floodlights were installed at a cost of £50,000, and were the tallest in Europe at the time, and for those first couple of seasons at least they were a homing beacon for Europe's elite. They were the best, we were the best and maybe that's why they were always thus. Each tower weighed 20 tonnes and held 55 100-kilowatt triple halidine lamps, which sound fantastic whatever they were. The collection of lamps alone weighed two tonnes, and not surprisingly they were three times brighter than the previous versions. According to a *Yorkshire Evening Post* (*YEP*) article from 1973, when the floodlights were erected each bulb pushed out as much heat as "...a normal two bar electric fire", which is something you might have to ask your Grandma about.

Although the lights were officially turned on for the Wolves game on 5th September 1973, when 39,946 had their retinas fried by the dazzling luminance of the 'space age' pylons, the lights were actually first used for a West Riding County Senior Cup Final on 21st August 1973, when Leeds beat Halifax Town 2-1 and just 4,650 were able to validate the old adage of never looking at the sun.

With plans for the development of the South East Corner Stand ongoing, only three floodlights were initially installed in 1973; two either side of the Kop and a third in the south west corner. For four years there were a series of smaller temporary lights erected on and behind the Lowfields roof to cover the light emissions required in the south east corner of the pitch, and also some lights were slung under the West Stand roof. The diamond lights' brilliance now far surpassed the required standards for colour television broadcasting at the time, and the match day programme article for the Wolves game also informed that the floodlights were installed "...to bring the club in line with the stringent new floodlighting specifications recently stipulated by UEFA. Indeed, so bright are the lights that the fourth pylon will not be erected until redevelopment of the Lowfields Road side of the ground is complete."

In the event, the fourth pylon was installed nearly five years later in the summer of 1978 when the club admitted defeat with further re-development plans, to complete the iconic image that is indelible in the minds of anyone who saw them, although it was more of an aesthetic measure in the end as the brilliance of the other three lights meant the fourth wasn't really needed.

Robert Endeacott recalls: "Looking back, I know now that we only had three for about four years, but it's like my mind insists on remembering all FOUR being there throughout that era, as a quartet of miracles! But they were quite a revolutionary thing at the time. They were famous weren't they? World famous I mean, and they looked bloody great as well. As a kid I just remember standing at the foot and holding on to them because if you didn't and you looked up you would fall over. There were some Royal Mail first day covers, the stamps, during the 1974/75 European Cup run, they showed the floodlights and they were just drawings but they were still fantastic. I was always proud of them

floodlights, absolutely brimming with pride. I have felt plenty of resentment against the club over the years, especially in recent years of course, but the dismantling of those fantastic floodlights was one of my earliest and most severe gripes."

Like Robert, I can personally recall as a young boy standing at the foot of the floodlights and looking up into what felt like outer space, to see the diamond just about visible at the top. This would repeatedly induce dizziness and neck pain and the very real possibility of toppling backwards, yet I was transfixed, such was their imposing majesty. From that angle and at that age it was hard to imagine anything in the world being higher. For evening matches the glow from the lights lit up the sky like a hovering UFO was about to rise into view. Even now I can cast a glance in the direction of the ground from anywhere in Leeds and almost expect to see the lights towering above anything else in the panorama. And yet they've been gone now for 28 years, and it still fries my brain to think there are diehard Leeds fans with no knowledge or recollection that they even existed.

Back in 1973 it would take the local electrician Howard Whitaker, from Kippax, ten minutes to climb each light, and he would make good use of the rest platforms that were situated at 40 foot intervals. He told the *YEP*: "It is a fairly strenuous climb...but the first time I climbed up I got a real sense of achievement. I can see Kippax, Ferrybridge Power Station and beyond from the top – it's a pity I can't signal the wife to let her know if I'm going to be late home for tea."

Guy Roberts of the Ringways Group also recalls: "I remember the floodlight towers being built, and my father (Leeds United board member Brian Roberts) decided he was going to go up one, one day. I think he got to the first platform and thought 'I'm not going any higher!'"

Cleaning and maintenance was undertaken twice yearly by Howard the electrician, who would have to ascend the mighty lights. Any of the lamps might need to have been replaced at any time of course, though it was wise to pick and choose the day, as Howard remarked: "There has been a bit of a breeze up there, and the towers have a sway at the top." Indeed John Reynolds had to climb up the towers on occasions, and his wife Maureen was told there was a quite alarming six foot sway in the floodlights on a windy day.

With re-development comes progress and the construction of the 17,000 cantilever East Stand in 1993 with its huge, angled roof rendered it impossible to retain the diamond floodlights. So spotlights, bereft of charm, architectural splendour or supplementary navigation uses, were installed on the roof edge of the East and West Stands to compensate; just as bright, but not so exhilarating to replicate in a colouring book. During the East Stand's construction three temporary lights were installed behind the Lowfields terrace which remained in situ as the mammoth construction rose

above it. The two diamond floodlights on the west side of the ground did remain for the 1992/93 season, but eventually with the full opening of the East Stand and the re-aligning of lighting along the lip of this and the West Stand roofs, they too succumbed on 28th July 1993 and by the start of the 1993/94 season there were no diamonds shining over Elland Road. That was until the autumn of 2020 of course.

Back in 1993, however, the harrowing sight of the floodlights being removed and burnt into pieces with gas torches was like walking in on the faithful family pet being put down at the vet's. Like watching Ali being beaten by Leon Spinks; a symbol of eminence, distinction and splendour reduced to a spectacle of indignity that nobody should ever see. With graphic finality it signalled the end of an era between 1973 and 1993 that many fans hold dear. Despite the wretched football often on offer and the diminishing fortunes of the club in general it was a period of metamorphosis that swept the innocent along. The unique diamond floodlights were a portrait of a more innocent time, when football-watching was a simple pleasure and rather than an iPad or an XBox, we were grateful just for an Arthur Graham sew-on patch for a birthday present; before Sky Sports, foreign investors, all-seater stadia and extortionate replica shirts. For some it was an era that will forever resonate, for some there is a light that never goes out.

FUNERAL

An empty football stadium on a non-match day is often a place for reflection and solemnity, a vivid and almost overpowering contrast to its natural purpose. The death of Leeds United legend John Charles on the morning of Saturday 21st February 2004 shook the club and most of the football world, such was the status that he unanimously held. Fierce club rivalries were put aside later that day at Old Trafford, as 67,000 Leeds United and Manchester United fans held a poignant minute's silence. Charles had been taken ill in Italy and was treated and flown back to the UK at the expense of Juventus FC, where he had recently been voted their best ever foreign player. He died at Pinderfields Hospital, Wakefield, within days.

A week later Leeds' then chief executive Trevor Birch held an on-pitch presentation to Charles' widow Glenda before the 2-2 draw with Liverpool at Elland Road. During it Birch announced the club were re-naming the West Stand the 'John Charles Stand' with immediate effect.

The next day, Monday 1st March, appropriately St David's Day, Charles' funeral was held at Leeds Parish Church and was attended by an impressive wealth of football names: Sir Alex Ferguson, Denis Law, John Toshack, Gary Speed, Mark Hughes, Jack and Bobby Charlton, Argentine Omar Sivori, his strike partner at Juventus, and many of Revie's and Wilkinson's Leeds

Attendees applaud as a hearse leads John Charles' body away from Elland Road for the very last time in March 2004, following the memorial service to commemorate his death.

United heroes. Over 1,000 people attended the church for the funeral, for which Paul Reaney, Norman Hunter, Peter Lorimer and Allan Clarke were pall bearers, but in an effort to maintain it as a private observance, a memorial service was also arranged at Elland Road for all to attend.

At 12.30pm on a brilliantly sunny afternoon, a hearse carrying Charles' coffin entered Elland Road through the police tunnel in the north west corner; it drove around the perimeter of the pitch and stopped at the halfway line before a crowd of people in the East Stand, estimated at between two and three thousand and including all the famous names that had attended the church service earlier. Prior to the service the big screen had shown a montage of the few existing clips of John Charles in action, reminding the crowd, as if they needed it, of the iconic status he held as a phenomenal footballer in an age where there were no stars. Indeed, Charles was arguably the greatest individual player to ever grace the Elland Road turf.

Eddie Gray, at that time the caretaker manager of the club, read a moving speech where he attempted the impossible task of summarising Charles' effect on football. Then following a 20 minute service the hearse drove out of Elland Road as 'Marching On Together' was played on the speakers. The mourning crowd stood up and burst into spontaneous applause as Charles left the Elland Road arena for the very last time.

Outside Elland Road, Billy Bremner's statue had become a shrine of flowers, scarves and shirts in John Charles' memory. In a stark reminder of the singular influence Charles had on the Leeds team of the 1950s, and also bringing into sharp focus the abysmal predicament the club, at that time, found themselves in as they careered out of control towards relegation from

the Premier League, one shirt bore a very touching tribute to Charles' greatness and potential inspiration. It read: "King John, send us goals from heaven, and save us from this hell."

During the 2020 Coronavirus pandemic Leeds United lost three of its treasured former players within a few weeks of each other, and whilst Trevor Cherry and Jack Charlton had private funerals outside of Leeds, Norman Hunter's family and the entire Leeds United fanbase were moved by the sight of Norman being given one last trip onto the Elland Road turf that had been the stage for his talents over 14 years and 726 appearances. With the nation firmly in lockdown Leeds United's social media channels published a deeply poignant video showing Norman's coffin being carried past the dressing rooms, down the tunnel and onto the sacred pitch one last time.

FULLERTON PARK

"I don't see Jack Charlton, Dad, I see gravel, overgrown shrubbery, potholes and wind-strewn debris." A young Leeds fan looking at the decidedly underwhelming area known as Fullerton Park today will have no idea as to how much history that desolate patch of land holds, but from the 1920s right up to 1996 it was an area of varying and not insignificant activity.

Ordnance Survey maps of 1910 show the expanse that became Fullerton Park as simply open fields bordered by the railway track that still operates today. Prior to this the area was acres of arable land upon which a huge rhubarb forcing shed once stood, and was owned by the Monk's Bridge Iron Company. However, in 1927 plans were in place to build a greyhound track on the site and a competition in the local paper was run

Anyone who says players didn't take training seriously in the 1960s, feel free to discuss this with Jack Charlton. PS: This was actually just a break in a pre-season photo shoot on Fullerton Park.

to find a name for the track. The winner was 'Fullerton Park', named after a famous and frequently triumphant greyhound from the late 1800s called 'Fullerton'. Sadly, greyhound racing only survived on this site for one year as it couldn't compete with a rival and ultimately much more well-known track already operating opposite on the south side of Elland Road.

Back on Fullerton Park, the dirt track created initially for greyhound racing soon became adapted for speedway and for four years between 1928 and 1932 held several meetings involving the 'Leeds Lions' team (see Speedway). After an unsuccessful attempt to resurrect speedway in 1938 the site was then left derelict for nearly a decade, including during World War II, except for a brief stint as an Army Training Camp during the hostilities. The site was first, unsuccessfully, put up for sale in 1939, but somehow, through all this the 'Fullerton Park' name prevailed.

By 1946, the 'Leeds Belle Vue-to-be' had been flattened and became a car park. Leeds United had briefly used the middle grassed area of the derelict

speedway stadium for training purposes, with designs to purchase the land for themselves. But this wasn't formally completed until 1951, when they bought the land off Totalisator Ltd, the parent company of the Leeds Greyhound Association.

Leeds United bought the land initially just for the use of their junior sides, who until then had been playing home games at Farsley and – bizarrely – Harrogate. But they subsequently used the land as their training pitches. It turned out to be a wise investment which the pioneering and somewhat eccentric then manager, Major Frank Buckley, was instrumental in, as few other clubs had such space and training facilities at the time, and certainly not adjacent to their stadium.

The club had wanted to purchase all the land extending up to the railway line on the far west side but could only afford sufficient space to build two football pitches. This land adjacent to the training pitches, which had previously housed part of the speedway stadium, eventually became the site of Jackson Boilers. They later became T.I. Catering and traded on the site

Leeds players training on Fullerton Park in 1978 with a nice view of Wortley in the background.

until the 1980s, when a company called 'Grimstons' took over the premises. Indeed the buildings were a backdrop to the Fullerton Park training pitches until the early 1990s. In 2014 this land became a Park & Ride facility, which has expanded twice since due to its success, and much-delayed plans for an ice rink also finally came to fruition in 2019.

Long-standing Leeds fan Reg French also recalls that the area opposite the old greyhound stadium, between the Jackson Boilers site and right up to the rail track on the boundary of the land, was used as a coach park at least into the 1980s. "We used to travel with Abbey Coachways from Selby where we lived in the 1960s," comments Reg, "when there were sufficient supporters to run a coach, and they parked on Fullerton Park opposite the greyhound stadium. The coach park was used for both home and away fans in the 1950s and 1960s, and there was never any trouble."

However, for many years after the land's acquisition the Fullerton Park training pitches were surrounded by literally nothing but fields. Images exist of John Charles limbering up before training in the 1950s, and in the background is simply a ghostly, foggy void. Even the Castle Brothers Haulage buildings had yet to appear, and the grey, empty marshland that extended all the way up to Gelderd Road and beyond painted a very different picture to the busy, industrial landscape of today, bisected of course by the M621.

Fullerton Park became the base for the first team, reserves and juniors until 1996; home in every sense. Training took place there every day and on Saturday mornings the juniors would play Northern Intermediate

League games on one of the two pitches, meaning that Fullerton Park was not only the first public platform for all Leeds United's famous home grown youngsters from the 1950s onwards, but also the production line of starlets from many other clubs. The pitches were also the scene of many official squad photos of the time, with the iconic blue façade in the background.

The father of Robert Endeacott was employed on the ground staff in the 1960s and had Fullerton Park within his remit, but that didn't extend to tending to the pitch necessarily: "To be honest I don't think anyone tended to the Fullerton ground," Robert muses. "The playing surface I believe was pretty rank, it was a notoriously bad surface because they didn't really tend to it and of course it was used so much. They didn't really pay much attention to the proper Elland Road pitch until the early 1970s either. It was a groundbreaking decision to buy the land and set up Fullerton Park, and it was strange for the club to come up with anything groundbreaking in the 1950s."

Stephen Reynolds, son of head groundsman John, agrees that the Fullerton Park pitches weren't the best: "They were good for the time," he explains, "but they weren't the same dimensions as Elland Road, or as good."

There were two full-size pitches side by side on Fullerton Park, with just a wire fence at the near end separating the pitches from the West Stand car park. This therefore allowed any passing fans, vagrants or disorientated lorry drivers priceless accessibility to stand and watch the team training, something that would involve several security checks and a damn

A great aerial view from 1980 of not just the Fullerton Park training pitches, but the LUSC Social Club on the left, the asphalt five-a-side pitch adjacent to it, the greyhound stadium in the distance and the Jackson Boilers industrial site that bordered Fullerton Park.

good justification today at Thorp Arch. However, Fullerton Park is endearingly special in that it was the scene where plans were formulated and rehearsed in painstaking detail, which then led to all of the club's major triumphs in the Revie and Wilkinson eras.

Dave Cocker was one of those star-struck youngsters who would spend hours watching Revie's heroes train on Fullerton Park. Dave of course had more access than most, with a practically daily interaction with almost every player at the club: "They were up and down those steps all day long, every single day. Every player that went through that club from the 1950s right until 1996 used those steps every single day." Despite so much history, and the ability for fans to walk in the footsteps of their past heroes, no protection was afforded to the steps that led from the players' entrance in the West Stand on to the Fullerton Park training pitches, and in the autumn of 2020 they were removed to make way for a bigger, dedicated outside broadcast compound on part of the Fullerton Park land, to suit Premier League TV requirements.

The two full-size pitches on Fullerton Park were complemented by a small pre-fab dressing room block which was built in 1956 as temporary dressing rooms after the West Stand fire. Next to this was the Leeds United Supporters' Club (LUSC) building, built in 1960 and finally demolished in 1998, and next to that and adjacent to the passing traffic on Elland Road, was eventually built a small concrete five-a-side pitch where Sniffer Clarke and co would practise while we were all at school or work or not even born. You can't visualise it now.

LUSC's headquarters was effectively a long, narrow wooden building which faced onto Elland Road, but was built by the members themselves. Ray Fell recalls: "I don't think I'd get the members to do that now! John Reynolds was chairman at the time and it was before I was involved with the committee. The club said 'look there's a piece of land there, go and build yourself a hut on it and it's yours'. Of course we could never prove that and when the council owned the ground in later years we had nothing to prove we had been given it, so it got a bit awkward for a while."

The building became known as the 'Leeds United Supporters' Social Club' for most of its existence and was later extended to provide a lounge area and a concert room. In 1988 it was completely refurbished with new carpets, furnishings and a full-sized snooker table to provide what Leeds United called "some of the best social facilities in the city". The facelift was masterminded by Bill Fotherby who always ensured through his many schemes, relocations and refurbishments that LUSC were looked after. The Social Club remained a well-used building by both LUSC and the club itself. When Elland Road hosted Euro 96 matches the LUSC HQ and Social Club was used as a temporary exhibition centre for a project called 'More Than A Game' which ran throughout the tournament. After the tournament had finished LUSC never settled back into the buildings. Ray Fell explains, "The council owned the ground at the time and the Social Club needed attention, there's no doubt about that, but the council had plans to build on Fullerton Park with an arena, nightclubs, a skating rink, various other things, restaurants and a cinema I think, it sounded wonderful. Caspian bought the club and it sounded like Leeds United was taking off, but the plans never materialised. But these plans were in hand to build and develop the area so we had to move out. We had about six months' warning prior to Euro 96. The club were going to build us some premises under the Captains' Lounge but that never happened either. But we always had a good relationship with the club, they always found us somewhere to hold meetings and for social drinking, and an area on match days." Note the past tense.

By 1998 the LUSC buildings were demolished despite no immediate prospect of the grand plan for the arena and other facilities actually going ahead. Finding themselves homeless, LUSC then used various premises for meetings such as the Goal Line restaurant in the South Stand, the Captains' Lounge and the Banqueting Suite, before they were removed completely from the public face of Leeds United Football Club by Ken Bates. At least until he sold the club and they were swiftly welcomed back.

Somewhat curiously, considering there is no use for it and it is now something of an eyesore, the dressing room block that the Social Club was built next to still stands on Fullerton Park today. Bearing in mind that Leeds United youngsters from the early 1960s onwards used to change in there daily, and looking at it today, overgrown by weeds and with the majority of its paint having peeled away, you can't help but think it's another example of the club's glorious past just allowed to wither and deteriorate without an afterthought to the history within its walls.

Although the Fullerton Park facilities may look fairly basic compared to what Thorp Arch offers now, back in Revie's day they were the envy of the league. With many professional clubs still training on municipal park pitches, it was rare for a club not only to have its own

facilities but also to have them on their own doorstep. Dave Cocker recalls what else was available to the players: "There was quite a big gap in the middle of the two football pitches, and they eventually put a few big white boards up, like cricket sight screens, for hitting balls against, shooting practice. They had a big fence at one end to stop the balls going over on to Jackson Boilers' land, but the boards were strutted at the back and players just used to practise free-kicks; Peter Lorimer would be hitting shots at it all the time. The other boards backed on to the car park."

On occasions the team would train on the 'Leeds Industrial Co-operative Society' (LICS) pitches on Lowfields Road, and sometimes the Whitehall Printeries Sports Ground also known as the Petty's Field Sports Ground. As Dave recalls: "It was football fields and cricket pitches, a huge sports ground. What they'd do is if they were playing at Wembley they needed lush turf, so they used to train at Farnley Park to get used to the lush grass, because at Fullerton Park it was a bit nasty; short and bare. Other times they'd train at LICS because it had better grass that mirrored a few other grounds."

Though few significant single events have occurred on the Fullerton Park training pitches, bar the masterminding of tactics, countless dressing downs and doubtless some fisticuffs, one memorable event that did was the infamous first team talk of one Brian Clough. Here he addressed his purple-tracksuited squad and utterly stunned the reigning league champions by instructing them to chuck their medals into a dustbin because they had cheated to win them. Present that day as a school-dodging 11-year-old was Leeds fan Stephen Talbot, who recalls: "I went down when Cloughie

The derelict dressing room block on Fullerton Park: built after the 1956 fire, it proudly accommodated some of Leeds United's most famous names but has been ripe for demolition for over 20 years.

The steps leading from the car park and the old players' entrance in the West Stand on to the Fullerton Park training pitches. There was perhaps more history in this set of concrete steps than in anything still standing at Elland Road, but sadly they were removed in the autumn of 2020.

did his first training session on Fullerton Park, I watched it. It's crazy. I remember he split them up and half went one way and half the other. Jimmy Gordon (Clough's coach) put David Harvey in net and started kicking the ball to him and he kicked the ball over the fence and I went into the car park, got the ball and kicked it back. You could just stand and watch them, and I remember Cloughie talking to them in a big group, he had his shorts on, he always wore shorts. You didn't know what was going on, you were just watching and they were all there just talking, but it's weird how you see it now and you think 'yeah, I was there then. I was there that day'."

Stephen Reynolds recalls how Howard Wilkinson used to play golf on Fullerton Park after training, creating numerous divots in the turf. "It used to drive my Dad nuts, but he (Wilkinson) asked me to play once. I'm left-handed but he had a right-handed club and you don't say anything to the manager do you? 'You'll learn son,' he used to say to me. But he just hit shots from one corner to the other."

Howard Wilkinson himself has few fond memories of Fullerton Park, at least in terms of its part in his grand plan. When asked if it was fair to say the Fullerton Park pitches were not always in the best condition, he replied: "No, despite the best efforts of John (Reynolds) bless him, they weren't even that good. They were rubbish, it was a constant battle. It was a daily battle, I would talk to John every day about what we were doing the next day. At times I imagine it resembled the Somme. Not the best surfaces to train on, everything was poor."

Alan Sutton concurs on that point and raises the running theme of golf practice as an example: "Yeah, he's right, but there were that many games played on there it's hardly surprising. The funny thing was, when I took up golf in 1995 I used to practise on there with a nine iron and I'd go on the second pitch to the right as you walked up the steps, and you'd have to search around for a blade of grass to put the ball on to hit it. It was just completely bare."

When Thorp Arch was built in 1996 the Fullerton Park training ground became redundant and by the end of the millennium the pitches had been tarmacked over. Having never actually changed ownership as part of the sale of Elland Road from the council back to Leeds United in December 1997, it was quite straightforward for Leeds City Council to then operate the land as car parks on match days. On two separate occasions plans were drawn up to build a Leeds Arena on the site, but these never came to fruition and still we await concrete plans to bring life to land that has remained, frankly, a developer's dream for nearly 20 years.

The section of Fullerton Park that formerly housed the training pitches (currently a car park) has combined with the section that runs to the railway track to host the annual Valentine's Fair in the February half-term holidays for several years from 2002 onwards. Part of the section towards where the derelict dressing room block is has also been sectioned off as a coach park for the away fans, when they were moved into the West Stand in 2011.

Tellingly, the history of the old training ground is not lost on many fans who question the wisdom of moving to Thorp Arch, a section of prime real estate which the club were forced to sell in 2004 and appear unlikely to ever buy back. For a long time the luxurious qualities of Thorp Arch felt like they were pampering mediocre players, whilst a succession of Leeds teams struggled with home form and a sense of detachment from Elland Road; their actual home. It's a view shared by Dave Cocker, who offers his take on it: "I still believe that if they had stayed there it remains Fortress Elland Road, because right now none of those players visit or spend time there, it doesn't mean anything to them, when they had Fullerton Park they were living there, it was like being there every day of their lives, they grew up there. That's why it was such a fortress."

Howard Wilkinson not surprisingly sees the move and its benefits very differently: "Times were changing, football was changing, plus it was next to the ground. I always felt you want the ground to be a special place. If you go into the ground every day it's where you work, it shouldn't be where you 'work'. You don't rehearse a show for three months on the Palladium stage. The Palladium stage is for the dress rehearsal and 'we're on!' It's a magical place and you want the ground to be like that. That was just part of the move to Thorp Arch. That was a bigger idea given the game was changing, we needed to get in there now and put our marker down in terms of youth development and producing our own players, and if they don't play for us, let's sell them and let them play for somebody else. But let's get a training ground that says 'excellence', let's get facilities that say 'excellence', so that when people walk into them to 'work', the standards you require of the individuals are met by the standards in the environment."

Wilkinson is persuasive in his argument that players were no longer attracted to the club because of the Fullerton Park facilities, which had been such a feather

in the club's cap 30 or 40 years previously, saying with heavy understatement: "There was no attraction to Fullerton. We used to take them training on cricket pitches that let us use their outfield, we used to go all over the place searching for surfaces, training up at Horsforth in pre-season. All over the place just looking for somewhere different, somewhere where they wouldn't walk up them steps like they did at Fullerton and look at it and mutter 'oh what a shit heap!'. Also it's difficult when you're in the dressing room Friday morning, the floors covered in muddy shirts and boots and everything else, and then you're back in there Saturday morning. I just felt it was far better to come in to a dressing room that looks as if it's been waiting for you for a week."

It would seem a succession of Leeds United managers would agree with that sentiment, but while the land remains undeveloped and screams out "come home", the opportunity is there to recreate history. In 2017 it was announced that Leeds United did finally accept that they were missing out on recruiting Leeds-based talent with their remote Thorp Arch base, and wanted to create a more Leeds-centric identity with an Academy based near Elland Road, and to have every strand of their business within a much smaller radius. This was part of the comprehensive 'Elland Road 2020' scheme announced shortly after Andrea Radrizzani gained majority ownership of the club, and which would involve a new training academy, new facilities on Fullerton Park and eventually a new West Stand. Several factors have combined to suggest '2020' was a touch ambitious; nevertheless, the plans are still going ahead.

A 'Parklife' facility would be built on Fullerton Park, on the land currently used as car parking. This would be a 'community sports hub' partly funded by Leeds City Council and the Football Foundation, and would involve five 3G artificial pitches, covered and uncovered, a community café, meeting rooms, fitness gym and studio, medical facilities (GP surgery and pharmacy) and changing rooms. Car parking could also be linked to Elland Road to create away coach parking on match days and safe access to the stadium for away fans via a covered tunnel to their turnstiles.

It was an exciting announcement and was originally made in conjunction with plans for the Leeds United first team Academy to be moved to the former Matthew Murray School site in Holbeck, with chief executive Angus Kinnear proclaiming the arrival of "elite facilities with community access". Whilst the 'Parklife' scheme was a community project, it is believed part of the development would be used by Leeds United to contribute to their Academy facilities. Planning approval was granted for the 'Parklife' scheme in July 2020 and as it stands, all systems are go for construction to commence in the summer of 2021. However, with regards Leeds United's daily training base moving back to LS11, and at least within a casual five minute stroll of Elland Road, plans appear to be only moving forward very slowly at present.

G

GAELIC FOOTBALL

Amongst the many sports that have been played on the Elland Road turf perhaps the most fleeting is Gaelic football. One game was played on 2nd October 1988 between Dublin and Mayo, organised by the Yorkshire County Board of the Gaelic Athletic Association (GAA).

Leeds has a strong Irish community, particularly originating from Mayo, and actually hosted five Gaelic football teams at one time. These were formed as a result of the Yorkshire County Board becoming a division of the GAA in 1948, with the premise that the teams would help to forge a community spirit amongst the Irish in Leeds.

There have also been strong links between the Irish community and Leeds United, particularly helped by the success of players like Johnny Giles, John Sheridan, Denis Irwin, Gary Kelly, Ian Harte, Robbie Keane and, indirectly, Jack Charlton. Indeed it was Sheridan's hero status at the time in both Leeds and Ireland, where he had recently made his first international appearance, which prompted the GAA to attempt to promote the game to a new audience by arranging the one-off game at Elland Road between the two leading clubs. The game ended in a 16-16 draw.

GANTRY

When the current West Stand was constructed in 1957 it included a number of facilities which were labelled as 'state-of-the-art' at the time. Not least amongst these was the television gantry perched underneath the roof of the stand, and even today it is apparently the envy of many clubs. In an era when televised football had yet to spring into the nation's consciousness, it is likely that the gantry was initially provided just as much for the purposes of radio commentators and newspaper journalists and indeed it was a little smaller than it is now, but today it is admired throughout the football media world.

Currently the gantry spans around two thirds of the length of the pitch, with its centre point naturally being on the halfway line. The gantry was re-built for the start of the 1973/74 season when the pitch was finally moved right up to the Kop in readiness for the demolition of the Scratching Shed at the end of that season. With the pitch position finally concreted, the fixed halfway line point allowed for the final location of the television cameras.

In the 1960s, '70s and '80s the gantry was used for radio broadcasts and the occasional visit from *The Big Match* or *Match of the Day* cameras. But also, in the 1980/81 season manager Allan Clarke employed a local company called Televista to film every game on a wide-angle camera for the players to study individual performances, set pieces and overall patterns of play afterwards. It was a novel concept at the time which Clarke and his assistant manager Martin Wilkinson had employed at previous club Barnsley.

The first ever *Match of the Day* broadcast from Elland Road for the match against Everton on 20th March 1965, a 4-1 win for Leeds, actually had the main cameras positioned on a platform behind the goal in the original uncovered Kop. But, apart from the two games against VFB Stuttgart and Sampdoria in the pre-season Makita tournament in 1992, when TV cameras recorded from the shell of the emerging East Stand, live action and recorded highlights have always been filmed from the West Stand gantry. The first live game ever broadcast from Elland Road was also against Everton, when Eddie Gray's fledgling Second Division team lost 2-0 to the then cup holders on a Friday night in January 1985.

The gantry was extended prior to Euro 96, by which time media saturation of football ensured that every game was filmed in some form. The facilities on the gantry were also more heavily utilised during Leeds' one season in the Champions League in 2000/01. For this purpose you can see the need for the vast expanse of accommodating 'stations' available on the gantry for the various media personnel involved in the high profile tournaments. However, for the 99% of Leeds United's existence where such media coverage has not been necessary, it is clear that the vast majority of the gantry has simply never been used. That has changed now for the Premier League, and the gantry has been re-fitted with new flooring, new seating and smart new workbenches.

I have been fortunate enough to watch a first team match from the gantry and there is no doubt that it provides a view of the game that simply cannot be bettered. Not only are you sat on the halfway line, but you are also further forward towards the pitch and more elevated than it is possible to be in any regular seat in the entire stadium. Looking over the lip of the gantry you are almost directly above the touchline and so the gantry affords you a unique view of proceedings.

Various sockets and cables are available at each station underneath the desk, and along the front of the gantry is a convenient construction of safety netting should your pen roll off the 'desk' and threaten to land on an unsuspecting West Stander below.

Upon the occasion that I was on the gantry, there were LUTV and local radio commentators present along with cameras for BBC/Sky coverage, a BBC Five Live reporter, Dean Windass reporting for Sky Soccer Saturday and a local radio reporter for the opposition. Whilst this sounds like quite an array of personnel it still only represented probably a 10% utilisation of the spaces available on the gantry.

Head of LUTV and former commentator Thom Kirwin could at one stage class the gantry as his second home, and it is clear he has formed an unlikely bond with it, warts and all: "I don't think much has been done to it over the years," begins Thom. "I think they just patch it up. It still feels a bit, I don't know, I've been going up there for a few years now and it still feels as if it's going to fall down. I don't look at the structure of it too much because

you'd think 'this is really old' but of all the grounds I've been to covering Leeds games, the Elland Road gantry is probably the best. Most people that come to Elland Road, visiting press and stuff, they love it because the view is incredible, you feel close but you can see the whole pitch. There's also a lot of space up there, they haven't just thrown the press into a little corner where they're all squashed. At some grounds, once you're in you're in, and you ain't getting out."

The comment that "not much has been done" could equally be read as "not much has been removed": "When you look at it closely you can see years and years of history," Thom continues, "just based on the fact that stuff is just piled on top of other stuff. Wires everywhere, you see the same at other grounds and stuff isn't taken out. If there is an ISDN line that is used for radio commentary they don't just take it out if it's dead or it's old or it's knackered, they just put a new one on top. So you go up to the gantry and there's so many wires, it's just 'oh, we'll whack that on top of that' and you can actually see stuff that goes back years hidden up there. But it serves its purpose and its appearance isn't all that important. The gantry gives everyone a clear view of the game and they can report on it, and ultimately that's what it's about. There won't be many clubs in the country that have a full-length-of-the-pitch gantry that size and able to accommodate that many people. I'd be stunned if there was."

Phil Hay confirms the sense that inspecting the nooks and crannies of Elland Road is much like peeling away the layers of history, sometimes literally. "Generally speaking," he begins, "the facilities at Elland Road have been behind the times for a while. Up until this summer when the press box was re-built, there was still a 1990s telephone kicking around there. I like that though. The stadium's old and rough and ready and I think it fuels the atmosphere. And ultimately, if you have a desk, electricity and internet connection then you've got what you need."

Although the age and appearance of the gantry might not be too important it is always on your mind when you are up there, and it would be for me if I was sat below in the relative and unwitting comfort of the West Stand. "It does fluctuate from game to game how busy it is up there," says Thom. "You can always tell when Leeds are doing well, or are of interest, because it's a lot, lot busier up there. At the Bristol Rovers game (8th May 2010), I thought the whole thing was going to collapse; just because I've never known any noise like that. I thought when Beckford's goal went in the place was shaking. We've always joked about it, it's always been a running joke, the creaky floorboards and bits of wood patching up holes, stuff like that. I'm sure it's absolutely sound, it just looks dodgy and it's just appearances really.

"You're not allowed hot drinks up there," Thom adds with a wry chuckle. "In the winter that is hard going up there. That gantry is always cold. In pre-season it's cold.

All that iron and metal, I don't know what it's made of but when the weather's hot it just shields it and keeps it cool and when it is cold there's no warmth whatsoever. It's got to be the coldest place on the ground. I can't complain though because it's great."

Over the years managers and players not in the first team squad have been known to watch games from the gantry, and it certainly holds as much history as any other part of the ground. When stood on it you can appreciate the true seniority of the West Stand as you are head-bangingly close to the aging steel rafters and the corrugated roofing, but you can also appreciate the range of personalities that have commentated from the vantage point and the vast array of famous games they have presided over from that very spot. Thom continues: "There has been so many times where the game will start or five minutes before when I'm chatting with Eddie, and I'll look to my left and see somebody. You get the Sky Sports reporters up there, they're at the far side so you always see them. You might see Iain Dowie come and do a game, but for me, I'm not really interested in that. I'm more interested in the fact that Mark Viduka, Alan Smith, quite a few of those guys have been up there because if they come back to a game – Alan Smith's been back a couple of times, I don't know how he got into the ground, if he was disguised or whatever – they get there and the gantry is like a sanctuary really, because you're not going to be bothered by any fans, everyone's working up there, so a lot of them come up there to watch. Mark Viduka came up there, he came back for a game and he kept it quiet. So obviously they all want to come and see Eddie, don't they? So that was a big thrill for me seeing Mark Viduka."

The gantry was also 'home' to Norman Hunter in his later years, as he would take a break from entertaining corporate guests to take in the serious business of the game. Everyone who saw Norman up there will testify that he was still kicking and heading every ball well into his seventies, and he still felt every emotion with Leeds United; win, lose or draw.

Of other visitors to the gantry, Thom is a little more puzzled: "When we played Derby County, first game of the season when Nigel Clough stopped the bus (outside the ground, to make his players walk through the crowds in August 2010) and all the build up to the game was 'I haven't watched *The Damned United*, it was disrespectful, I haven't watched it, I haven't watched it' and then he does something that was only in the film and never really happened. Then, you know in the film where Brian Clough has always got his two sons with him, well Nigel Clough had his two sons with him (on the gantry as Ken Bates had banned him from the directors' box for wearing a tracksuit). I turned around in the second half because I could hear this movement. Obviously nobody's moving around up there during the game, but Nigel Clough's walking around with his two kids, not even watching the game, just walking up and down the gantry. It was weird because I was thinking 'he's just trying to be his dad walking around with his two kids' because that's what was in the film. I don't know any manager who's brought his kids with him...... whilst the game is going on."

Another frequent 'host' on the gantry is BBC Radio Leeds commentator Adam Pope, who claims as a vantage point the gantry is "unrivalled". Adam also reflects on the media facilities at Elland Road, the privilege of being a regular visitor and the hardship of when he was denied that privilege: "The match day staff are very welcoming," Adam begins, "and many are also supporters, which helps. There is something very comforting about seeing the same faces as the seasons roll by. I love working there. I've been to nearly all the newer Premier League grounds and whilst Manchester City and Arsenal are incredible, nowhere has the brilliant mix of a stadium like Elland Road. It still has that visceral feel of the 1970s when I started watching football, combined with an increasing corporate modernism required for the club to progress."

"The sense of wonderment walking into the stadium never fades. I nearly always take a photo just to say I'm here, knowing that it's pretty much the same image each time. I always recall the first time I made the climb up the stairs in the West Stand to the gantry to commentate with Eddie Gray for the opening game of the 2005/06 season against Millwall. The theatre of Elland Road laid out before me below. What a sight. I can still feel the nerves and excitement. Promotion to the Premier League has meant my summariser Noel Whelan and I are currently off the gantry to allow for the TV broadcasters, so we are at the back of the stand below. But wherever we are is better than not being there at all, which appeared to have been the wish of the club when former chairman Ken Bates was in charge. During that time I and another ex-player Andy Ritchie presented our pre-match, half-time and post-match show from The Old Peacock over the road, whilst only being able to provide a few short reports during the game from inside the ground. Elland Road when United are strong on the pitch is unique. I have been blessed to have worked there so often."

Although the gantry may be a feature of the ground that many fans have never even noticed, it is another fixture of Elland Road that has been witness to almost every major event that has impacted upon the club. Thom concludes: "The gantry was so busy on the Bristol Rovers game, every ticket was wanted so all the academy staff, the players that weren't involved all had to go up there to watch it because the complimentary tickets they'd usually get were at the back of the West Stand, but the club wanted to sell them. So the only other place to sit is on the gantry."

In moments of incomparable jubilation, such as when Jermaine Beckford struck the winning goal to signal promotion from League One, it is sometimes difficult to control your movements. But Thom confirms that even then the occupants of the gantry had one eye on the miraculous events taking place before them, and one on the ageing construction bolted onto another ageing construction: "Nobody wanted to jump around too much up there because 300 people standing up and jumping around at the same time would be interesting."

GELDERD ROAD

"Gelderd, Gelderd give us a song", "Gelderd Aggro", "Gelderd Boot Boys", "I was born under the Gelderd End". The word 'Gelderd' is barely used today in the parlance of the modern fan, but it was a stock feature of the Leeds United vocabulary at any point during Elland Road's mass, swaying popularity up to the 1990s. But whilst the Kop is still known by a small minority of fans as the 'Gelderd End', Gelderd Road itself is no longer even the nearest road to run parallel to the back of the Kop, standing, as it always has of course, a good quarter of a mile away from the ground. Having sprung up in the 1970s, Latchmore Road is the nearest road to the Kop and further up Lowfields Road is Benyon Park Way, which houses Jump Inc. But somehow the 'Latchmore Road End' or 'Benyon Park Boot Boys' just don't quite cut it.

It is safe to say, nevertheless, that the term 'Gelderd End' pre-dates the industrial estates and even Lowfields Road itself, and historically was the name used for the huge end on the north side of the ground roughly from when the original Spion Kop was built in the mid-1920s. At this time, of course, little but empty marshland stood between the somewhat marooned Elland Road football ground and the civilisation of Gelderd Road.

Still, the section of road now known as Gelderd Road was built in the mid-19th century and tithe maps from 1851 show the road in place but referred to as the 'Birstall Turnpike Road'. In a local directory from 1866 the road is listed but spelt as 'Geldard Road', though by 1890 Ordnance Survey maps showed it clearly and forever more as Gelderd Road.

The official origin of the name 'Gelderd' is unknown, though there are a number of theories. There is no place called 'Gelderd' in West Yorkshire or over the Pennines, as the name implies, and as expressly illustrated in the name 'Elland Road'. A simplistic explanation could be that Gelderd is a derivative of the word 'Gildersome', as the road passes through there and changes name shortly after. A more likely explanation comes from local speculation that the road was a 'drove track' in previous years, which was basically a route used to 'drove' or transport livestock, and hence the phrases 'Gelded Herd' or 'Gildersome Herd Road' may have been informal names that became commonplace via a derivative. A 'Gelderd' is also an occupational name for a tender of oxen and gelded horses, which is a more direct version of that theory.

The functional thoroughfares surrounding Elland Road are a haven for graffiti and this fine art from the Holbeck area survived at least until this photo was taken in 1996.

Prior to the construction of Lowfields Road in 1923, the section of Gelderd Road that passes the football ground was a route through open fields and the frequently over-flowing banks of the Wortley Beck, whilst also bisecting the railway line that ran nearest to the football ground. Since then the area has become gradually more developed, and today houses many thriving and long-established major businesses, including those housed in the industrial estates of 'John Charles Way'.

Gelderd Road is similar to Elland Road in that it is the name attached to a relatively small section of a major 'A' road. Indeed, both Gelderd Road (A62) and Elland Road (A643) start at the same location: the Armley Gyratory to the south west of the city centre. The A62 is 41 miles in length and was the major road linking Leeds and Manchester prior to the M62, which largely runs parallel to it.

To Leeds United fans, Gelderd Road is where many people park their cars on match days. It is also where many arrive having walked down the ginnel linked to Whitehall Road if approaching from Wortley, as Leeds fan Chris Miller used to: "The best games were midweek games," begins Chris. "As my Dad worked in Lower Wortley until 6.30 each evening, Mum would take me by bus to meet him on Whitehall Road. We'd meet at Search and walk down the ginnel, which still to this day links Whitehall Road with Gelderd Road. The walk down the ginnel was usually in the dark, but we didn't need street lights, as the glow of those floodlights beckoned. Every time I see that ginnel these days, usually from the Gelderd Road end where I park, bottle necked with people trying to get home post-match, my memories are straight back to the midweek days of being drawn to Elland Road, moth like, by the tallest floodlights in the universe."

Gelderd Road is also a route via which you could walk to the ground, maybe in the past from the Packhorse or Wheatsheaf pubs, passing by the old Wallace Arnold depot and the YEB buildings. Today neither pub exists, nor does Wallace Arnold, and the section of Gelderd Road from the ring road takes in mainly new office blocks, a Premier Inn complex and Porsche and Mercedes car showrooms.

On the other side of Lowfields Road, heading towards Leeds city centre, Gelderd Road is a pedestrian route back into town for Leeds fans which previously would have taken in the Smyths Arms pub, also no longer there, before joining Whitehall Road just before the inner ring road. The Smyths Arms was another small and unremarkable pub, an oddity in a distinctly non-residential area, and a drab establishment which definitely wouldn't exist today, even if it had somehow survived the mid-1990s. Andy Peterson has less-than-fond memories of it from ritualistic approaches to Elland Road on match days: "Demographic change, the smoking ban and rising prices have forced many well-loved pubs out of business in the last ten years. The Smyths Arms was not one of those. Its strength – being near to Elland Road – couldn't quite outweigh its deficiencies, which were enough to see it cease serving pints well before the new millennium. My warmest memory of the place was being served chicken drumsticks – god's finger food – by a man sporting a plaster which looked like it had last been changed by Florence Nightingale. The site at the bottom of Copley Hill now plays host to an Enterprise Rent-A-Car office, which trust me, is for the best all round."

Eventually, it seems likely that Gelderd Road will lose its association with Elland Road football ground purely through its lack of proximity, and it will remain simply a major road out of the city centre and most prominently, and lamentably, a convenient back route to Ikea. For now, the 'Gelderd End' is a term to cherish and amongst a certain generation of fans will always be the name for the place where many fond memories have been formed and childhoods spent.

GOAL LINE RESTAURANT

In 1983 Leeds United made their first tangible connection with fans from the corporate sector, an area that would become an integral part of their business plan over the next 30 years, with the installation of the first executive boxes in the South Stand.

With the desire to house corporate fans and invoice them with the appropriate financial cargo for the privilege, came the need to wine and dine them as part of the package. From that came the proposal to have a permanent restaurant on site for the use of the box holders on match days, and to occasionally have open to the public during the week. It was a long way from the fine-dining experience that Howard's Restaurant was marketed as, and by no means was it pitched as a stand-alone operation in its own right, but it was the first move in attempting to diversify and realise the potential income that could be gained from fans and the business sector on non-match days.

"I had to have a service behind (the boxes), a restaurant," explains then commercial director Bill Fotherby. "You must be able to service your boxes with sandwiches, food, crisps, drink. I had a good relationship with the bank. One of the things that I learnt very quickly was that banks don't like to be surprised. You've got to be honest with them and I was telling them 'I need the money to put a restaurant in here, it's going to cost me x thousand pounds, can I have it?' 'OK', the money was there, and we filled every one of those executive boxes."

For most of the restaurant's existence it was known as the Goal Line Restaurant, a literal reference to its location behind the goal at the back of the South Stand. But one of its early guises was as the 'United Executive Restaurant'. Later on at the end of the 1984/85 season it was re-launched as the 'Lunch Box Restaurant', which was especially for the summer closed season when the 'Executive' reference didn't

apply and the ready cash of the 'normal' fan became just as sought after.

A match day programme from the 1985/86 season shows an unassuming advert for the restaurant displaying the teeth-grindingly impassive style of advertising synonymous with the 1980s. There were no artistic photos of the elegant surroundings or tempting images from the presumably 'sumptuous' menu; there was simply a staged photo of two vacant and desperately uncomfortable waitresses, shrouded in darkness and looking more wooden than The Wicker Man's shed, accompanied by the underwhelming promise of a "Cold Buffet" for £2.50 or a "Hot Buffet" for £3.50. Above it was the 'snappy' by-line informing us that the restaurant was available for "Business Lunches or just Snacks or for Weddings or other events"; a triumph of marketing patter. We can only wonder what "just Snacks" may have entailed, and we can only speculate as to how successful this venture was, but it is true that the restaurant became the Goal Line Restaurant for the beginning of the 1986/87 season, and existed with varying success for some years after. In 1988 it was known as the 'Goal-Line Bistro', but future uses also included a midweek meeting place and social club for the Leeds United Supporters' Club after they lost their premises on Fullerton Park in 1996.

In September 2006 the restaurant was substantially re-structured and re-branded as Billy's Bar, and for the first time proper windows were fitted to face outwards, lifting the veil and revealing the fact that a venture open to the public did actually exist. At this point the restaurant went from being a little-known enterprise effectively just serving the executive boxes and club functions to a well-marketed concern that at first opened throughout the week, but now concentrates on match day trade.

An advertising budget for the new restaurant or sign a midfielder? "Welcome to Leeds: John Donnelly".

THE UNITED LUNCHTIME RESTAURANT
Open Mondays to Fridays — Fully Licensed

For Business Lunches or just Snacks or for Weddings or other events

EASY ACCESS — FREE PARKING

Telephone Leeds 706560
*for details and reservations
or just call in you will be very welcome*

Cold Buffet £2.50 — Hot Buffet £3.50

GRASS BANKS

Lush green grass at the back of the Lowfields Road Stand promotes a skewed view of prosperity as Leeds celebrate the league title win in May 1992.

A resplendent carpet of lush, green grass is a given in football grounds of any era; not so much the extraneous sight of grass above floor level....amid the stands. During matches played at Elland Road between 1971 and 1992 a vision of the ground that will forever offer sentimental thoughts are the one, then two grass banks that lay either side of the Lowfields Road upper stand.

Any such sight at a top flight ground today would appear inconceivable in an era of brand new, aesthetically pleasing stadia with multi-million pound sponsorship deals. But at a time when artistic attention wasn't largely paid to the outward style and refinement of a football stadium, the grass banks were there through necessity. They were simply clumsy and incidental deposits resulting from excavation work in re-developing the ground and were never meant to become a fixture. Alas, they became a curiosity that added a touch of inelegant character to Elland Road, but far more than that, while some fans may hold a romantic attachment to the grass banks as a backdrop to their teenage years, in reality they came to symbolise a situation of abrupt decline. For the entirety of their visible existence they were the physical embodiment of plans gone wrong, a fallow period, a situation changed and a development quite literally left in unfinished situ.

The grass bank on the left hand side nearest the Kop appeared first, and rose from the top of the terraced stand on Lowfields Road up to the glass partition on the side of the seated stand. This first appeared in 1971, three years after the current Kop had been built, when the high banking in the north east corner of the ground was heavily excavated, right up to the point where the Lowfields roof started. Prior to this the original Kop and the Lowfields were a huge, continuous terrace that stretched around a full half of the ground. But the building of the new Kop and the excavation of the north east corner was paving the way for the 're-developed' and modern Elland Road that Revie had dreamed of.

Building the new Kop allowed the pitch to be moved northwards and meant that the start of the Lowfields roof that was originally in line with the goal line, was now level with the edge of the penalty area. When the North East Corner Stand was built in 1972/73 a gap of about ten yards remained between the new stand and the Lowfields Road upper stand, separated of course by the grass bank. There were plans in place then for the Lowfields Road Stand to make way for another stand to link between the North East and South East Corner Stands and complete the bowled arena of Elland Road, but this didn't happen for another 20 years. And so the grass bank remained, like a boil that couldn't be lanced.

The twin grass bank on the southern extremity of the Lowfields Road Stand didn't appear until 1978 when the upper seated section of the stand was almost chopped in half in readiness for the, eventually shelved, plans for the development of the south east corner. By this time Leeds United were hurtling uncontrollably towards strangulating mediocrity and relegation. Again, the grass bank rose diagonally from the top of the terrace to the glass partition above, and added a perfect, if graceless and ham-fisted, symmetry to the Lowfields Road Stand when viewed from the West Stand opposite. Little did we know it then but Leeds United was retiring into a deep and profound post-Revie slumber, during which time appeared to stand still and slow, festering decay was the only visible movement.

"I used to stand under that West Stand," recounts Bill Fotherby of the depressing late-1970s period before he became a board member and was just a normal fan. "January, February, you couldn't get a cup of coffee, you could get a pint of beer and it would freeze in your hands under there. It was terrible, and I'm saying to colleagues there 'if I ever get the opportunity I'll make this so you can come in comfort and sit down and have a bag of crisps and a sandwich and a hot drink'." Hardly blue sky thinking, but such was the archaic level of customer service at Elland Road, and to be fair most grounds, at that time.

Plans for the development of the stadium had hit an abrupt financial wall and it became a fetid and tumbledown relic with little charm to those without an iron-willed emotional attachment. The club itself

was faring no better. Leeds United was not so much a sleeping giant but a gravely ill and decomposing one, with sharp and dispassionate minds discussing the very real prospect of cutting off the life support machine.

Eddie Taylor remembers well the grim austerity of the late 1970s and early 1980s when Elland Road resembled a threadbare playing field the week after the circus had gone, and the period of stasis appeared to also affect a wilderness era for the surrounding vicinity in the city of Leeds too. "The 1980s was a cruel decade for Leeds fans," Eddie begins. "Relegation just seven years after appearing in a European Cup Final was the first of several humiliations as crowds fell below 10,000 for the first time since 1962. It was an eight-year wilderness marked by defeats to Chester and Scunthorpe in the League Cup, finishing below Bradford City twice and Ronnie Robinson inheriting the number 3 shirt from Frank Gray; grim times. Even Elland Road itself recoiled in horror, with part of the Lowfields Road stripped away to leave a truncated chicken coop perched over a newly fenced and segmented terrace. Council-owned and by now shared with Hunslet Rugby League Club, it was a million miles from the compact, well-appointed fortress envisaged by Don Revie as his side attracted record crowds to LS11.

"But it did have nostalgia," continues Eddie. "Ingrained into every trip to Elland Road in the 1980s, especially

A few weeks later and while the floodlights remain the excavators finally rip away tonnes of earth and nearly two decades of stagnation.

for those who never experienced the glories of the Revie era, were ghosts of Christmases past. For out-of-towners coming from the West, as I did, the first of them were glimpsed from the train as it crossed the A58 by Armley: the enormous diamond-topped floodlights, almost Soviet in their scale and statement as they rose out of the South Leeds gloom, seemed to encapsulate the continental confidence of that all-conquering side. Indeed, the reek of the 1970s, a decade in which post-war, town-planned urban possibility had given way to grey, grafittied regret, continued right up to the ground. The modernist flats on Holbeck Moor, the tiled subway under the new M621, the spiralling tarmac footbridge over it and the purpose-built halts behind the Lowfields Road Stand for the match day buses from Sovereign Street and Morley, all offered clues as to what Leeds-coloured optimism might have once looked like. So too did the concrete pillars of the South Stand, erected as the club marched all the way to their Parisian date with Bayern Munich and still barely ten years old when the heirs to Billy, Norman and Allan were preparing to face Shrewsbury and Walsall in Division Two."

This was the situation, stifled by nostalgia and neglect, which Howard Wilkinson inherited in 1988. He took the very brave and somewhat illogical move of giving up life at Sheffield Wednesday, an established top five First Division club, for the poisoned and thankless hot seat at Elland Road, which always had a ghostly sense of Don Revie peering over the shoulder of subsequent managers, as tumbleweed rolled by unnoticed. When he arrived Wilkinson saw the situation for what it was. He said: "I think I described it, and it seemed to stick, as a Rolls Royce body with a Mini engine." Wilkinson was talking about the club as a whole, but integral to that, and visible to the outside world, was Elland Road; the ruined remains of former and distant glories. "The club as a whole was, well..." he pauses, "as long as you were a long way from it, it looked OK. It looked as if it was a real big football club, but once you got close up, it needed a lot doing to it."

Clearly, however much Leslie Silver had sold the concept of 'Leeds United' to Howard Wilkinson, once he got on the inside the job looked much different. That's not to say he thought any less of the challenge, but the size and scale of the obstacles came into sharp focus. "On my very first day," recalls Howard, "a lady who was actually in the canteen, a cook called Barbara, she seemed to be a spokesman for everybody, including sometimes the players, she came to see me. She said 'we need a new washing machine', I asked why, 'because the one we've got is broken'. Not one of the ones we've got is broken, the 'one' we've got is broken. So the club was not at its best at that time."

The floodlights have gone and so too the grass banks. Fast forward.

A fisheye view of Elland Road in 1989: the green of the pitch still matched by green among the stands.

Despite the ground being council-owned in the late 1980s and the benefit of little love and attention never mind finance, Wilkinson, as he was so adept at doing, saw a deeper reason for the decay: "The trouble with having a benevolent dictator like Don Revie, is that when they go nobody knows how it happened, who does what, so it started to unravel pretty quickly, and it was just a good job that Leslie Silver was there really. He just stepped in and kept it afloat."

Bill Fotherby also remembers well the dormant scene he inherited at Elland Road and the very delicate state of the finances, particularly in the early 1980s prior to Wilkinson's arrival: "I never spent a penny unless I knew there was something coming back from it. If I was spending something in the ground or if I was taking an area and making it a club, I knew that I would be making a profit from that for Leeds United." Basically he had to, there was very little to play with, and for many years very little ambition. "It was dead," continues Bill. "There was no atmosphere, it was dead. Well that was marvellous for me, because I knew I'd bring life to it. God gave me a personality and a charisma and I had everybody believing 'we're going to have success'. Every improvement in that ground I was responsible for, I would sketch them out."

While life for Leeds United had at best stood still and in some cases gone backwards, to many, Leeds United and Elland Road still retained an outwardly behemoth-like status, perhaps the "Rolls Royce body" that Wilkinson spoke of. Physio Alan Sutton saw great improvement when he joined Leeds United in

1986, and in relative terms his working life improved immeasurably: "The average gate when I joined Leeds was only about 10 or 12,000 but we got to the FA Cup Semi-Final in my first season, and the Play-Off Final and I remember thinking 'well, this is alright'. We haven't been in a semi-final since then. I came from Halifax Town and Halifax Rugby League and going to Leeds United was like living the dream. We used to have packed sandwiches at Halifax Town and at Leeds we were eating steak and chips, and gateaux to finish with, and we had coaches with televisions, it was like coming from the back streets of Bradford, where I'm from, to Hollywood."

The ten-year masterplan that convinced both Wilkinson and chairman Leslie Silver that between them they could achieve great things was formulated over a three-week period, and involved far more than simply the 11 players on the pitch, as Wilkinson describes: "It was the whole thing, it was me having been at Boston United, having been at Notts County, having been at Sheffield Wednesday, so I'd had plenty of experience across the whole gamut of football and I just knew and felt that the thing you had to aspire to were the Arsenals, were the Liverpools, were the Aston Villas. You know, the clubs that were more than just a name; that stood for something, that had history and had an infrastructure and were institutions, and that doesn't happen just by having a good team, it's everything underneath it. So it was that sort of picture that struck a chord with Leslie. Having been the son of immigrants, having started off with nothing and built a business of his own, I think it resonated with him. He bought into it

and I don't just mean he bought into it as something nice to do, he bought into it as something he himself wanted to have a part in. It's more than just talking about the football or players, it's about looking ahead and having a dream or a view of the future you wanted to create. It's like life, you have to adapt or die and football's changed on and off the field and with it has come a change in aspiration, in terms of 'what kind of club would we like to be?'"

For once, what the club wanted, or felt was achievable, was in line with what the fans wanted. For Wilkinson that future vision involved a lot of work on the finer details to make a small but significant difference, and that very quickly snowballed into making a much bigger difference. "I always wanted the playing surface to be as good as possible," he explains. "I immediately set about trying to make the dressing rooms better and effect improvements there. I immediately set about making the laundry situation, the kit situation and the food situation better. You're just looking for quick wins, you're looking for little things that say to people 'Christ they mean business, if you stand still here the carpet's changed'. We changed the music we ran out to, we changed to not being too rigid with training times, just to keep people on their toes. There's got to be a reason for it, it has to be justified, you can't be a lunatic, but to keep people more alive and thinking 'what can we do better now?'"

Certainly Howard Wilkinson triggered that change in mind-set which focused the board, the management, the players and the fans, and the club naturally and very quickly became a resurgent and powerful force again. "It was almost all happening too quick to keep pace with. We actually thought that at the time. It was like, the first season up when we finished fourth, well I'd said we'd get promoted in the first or second season, that was the plan and then maybe five years on we'd be genuine contenders for the championship, but there we were. But we still had this history of the council owning the ground, overdrafts, money owing and so on. It became a real job of keeping a lot of balls in the air. You're trying to look smart in your new suit and not reveal that there wasn't too much underneath it. It's important with the players as well because you can't go 'oooh, hang on lads, just slow down here, we're doing too well'."

To expand the analogy, the club may have appeared ready to cover up the grass banks with a spanking new stand, as if embarrassed by its recent past, but could it genuinely afford to? Were the grass banks still more attuned to the club's actual status than a cheaply built, if more aesthetically pleasing stand?

Nevertheless, soon enough success on the pitch effected change off it, with the first positive physical changes to the Elland Road landscape since Don Revie's resignation had prompted a 15-year period of decline. In September 1990, with promotion to the First Division finally achieved, Leeds City Council leader Jon Trickett announced a five-year plan to increase Elland Road's capacity, severely hampered by the recent Taylor Report, by 8,000 to 40,200. This was through the building of the East Stand replacing the Lowfields but first, the completion of the South East Corner Stand. At the time the council, and indeed Bill Fotherby, also intended to add another tier to the West Stand, though that became a fanciful notion given the age of the stand and the complexity of the operations that continued beneath it.

Most significantly, the grass banks that had bookended both the Lowfields Road Stand and the period of false comfort in Revie's disappearing legacy, were finally built over, as if the wheels of progress had been unblocked from 1978 and the rush of built-up and suppressed energy couldn't wait to catch up with itself.

To anyone who hadn't visited Elland Road and only saw the ground on television, the grass banks appeared to be a peculiar oddity, but from outside the ground it made more sense as the steps from the turnstiles up to the top of the Lowfields Road Stand were cut into the very same grass banks which, indeed, were the untended remnants of the dirt, brick and colliery waste that the entire stand was built on. It was only when the East Stand was constructed in 1993 that the built-up mounds of earth deposited in the 1920s were finally dug away.

Arguably Elland Road is in the midst of another period of slumber and stasis at the moment; and the club is again, somehow, a Rolls Royce body with a Mini engine. Despite Peter Ridsdale's maniacal over-spending around the turn of the millennium, very little was done to Elland Road other than cosmetic decoration. Financial meltdown soon followed and amid overhead cuts, stadium maintenance was right up there amongst the disposable costs. Whilst Elland Road didn't visibly fall into disrepair there were certainly no improvements. Somewhat surprisingly, Ken Bates took immediate action upon taking on the ownership and chairmanship of the club in January 2005, when he described Elland Road as "shabby, decrepit and almost seedy". Bates professed to spending £3 million in his first six months in charge on improving the infrastructure of Elland Road, ie. the toilets, fast food bars, circulation areas, and hospitality areas. He later spent an estimated £7 million on the East Stand 'in-fill'.

In the middle of the 2010s it felt like maybe we would envisage the cream-clad East Stand extension in much the same way we remember the grass banks now; as a symbol of frugal mismanagement that defined a dormant era and as something we would secretly wish to be eradicated from the landscape. At that point the only movement was the furious treading of water, much like in the late 1970s. Yet, as they did in 1990, Leeds have hit fast-forward since then, but unlike the grass banks, the East Stand extension fulfils its purpose, and is very much here to stay.

GREYHOUND STADIUM

Greyhounds, football or both? It was a choice once mulled over by the Leeds public, as for many years during the middle of the 20th century the greyhound stadium on Elland Road was as thriving a sporting arena as the neighbouring football ground. The thirst for greyhound racing in Leeds was raging and this was boom time for the sport.

The greyhound stadium on Elland Road was built in 1927 and held its first race meeting, attended by 7,000 people, on 16th July 1927, at which point the sport was actually more commonly known as 'electro-hare racing'. The Elland Road track was operated by the Leeds Greyhound Association, a rival racing association to the Fullerton Park track which opened a couple of months later (4th October 1927) and quickly gave up the battle and concentrated solely on speedway.

From that point onwards the Elland Road greyhound stadium grew to become a staple ingredient of the area's rich and varied sporting culture and hosted race meetings for 55 years. The track itself was famous for having only five lanes, presumably due to the tight constraints of the space available, and therefore held

a notoriety for unpredictable results via fancied dogs that couldn't adapt to the unusual conditions. There was no lane 3 at the idiosyncratic track and with traps being numbered 1, 2, 4, 5 and 6, sage advice that was frequent and actually went without saying suggested you, "nivver back t'3 dog".

The stadium had three small stands and a short stretch of open terracing around the track and the main stand housed a bar and restaurant that at one stage was called 'Bar 7'. Whilst this acted as a source of refreshment for the punters at the twice-weekly greyhound meetings, it also opened on Saturday lunchtimes to serve football fans watching Leeds United, as an alternative to the nearby Drysalters and the New and Old Peacocks.

Throughout its lifespan though, the stadium led a variable existence. In the late 1930s the stadium enjoyed a brief spell staging baseball matches when the Leeds Oaks resided there for two seasons. In 1936 the Leeds Oaks, as a professional outfit, were founder members of the Yorkshire League, but after two very successful seasons at the Elland Road greyhound stadium the Yorkshire and Lancashire Leagues merged, and subsequently restricted each club to just two professional players. A knock-on effect to the league merger was that Leeds Oaks moved their home ground to the more-affordable Headingley Rugby Ground.

Adaptability was the name of the game again in early 1963 when the country was wrapped in an 'ice age' which brought the sporting calendar and much of the nation to a standstill for weeks. Elland Road, like most grounds in the country, was deemed unplayable and no competitive games were staged in January or February. However, somehow the grass in the centre of the greyhound track was playable and was able to stage a much-needed practice game for Leeds United despite itself also being snow-covered. Don Revie took his team the short distance down the road

An aerial view of the greyhound stadium taken in 1948. On the other side of Elland Road is acres of completely undeveloped fields, including the remains of the recently demolished speedway stadium on the Fullerton Park land that Leeds United would soon buy, and the snaking Wortley Beck.

to play Bradford Park Avenue in a friendly which ended 2-2. Furthermore, in December 1965 the greyhound stadium once again demonstrated its versatility and accommodated a private training session for SC Leipzig as they prepared for a Fairs Cup second-leg tie with Leeds United at a snow-covered Elland Road.

A new stand costing £67,000 was built and opened in July 1968 as the track still operated profitably, and in 1973 the stadium began to host rugby league. Through vandals, Hunslet RL had suffered a devastating fire at their Parkside Ground two years previously and endured severe financial difficulties as a result, so much so that the club folded in 1973. Almost immediately a new club was formed, initially called 'New Hunslet', and terms were negotiated to lease the greyhound stadium for home games.

Typically, the stadium was never ideally suited to rugby league; at first it didn't even have dressing rooms and the players used Leeds United's facilities at Elland Road. But it provided a home for Hunslet when mere survival was the main priority, though naturally, loyal fans recall the period with little fondness. The highest crowd Hunslet ever attracted (the 'New' was dropped quite quickly) at the greyhound stadium was 5,859 for a Challenge Cup tie with Warrington in 1975. The pitch was uneven and the narrowest in the league, and by then the stadium had only a few rows of seats on the Elland Road side and a bank of terracing on the opposite side underneath a social club. The best views of the pitch were from behind glass in the main stand with its multi-span roof, where bars and restaurants, which were usually busy, accommodated fans but afforded no atmosphere whatsoever for the players and hardy souls stood outside. To add to the unorthodox nature of the ground the stadium also adopted curious 'tuning fork' style goalposts often seen in American Football, but never in rugby league.

By the 1980s the stadium was looking rundown, and in the words of local resident Robert Endeacott it was no longer a focal point of the area, like it had been when greyhound racing was thriving in the post-war years: "I don't think it was a big part of the community then, I went to a race once and there weren't many people there. In terms of rugby league, Hunslet had been a truly brilliant team in the past, but Elland Road isn't 'Hunslet' for one thing and the club was in decline for a long time; I don't know if not being in Hunslet had any bearing on attendances. The stadium always looked a bit ramshackle to me and uncared for."

Ray Fell remembers the Leeds United Supporters' Club using the greyhound stadium for some functions and meetings in the 1970s and early 1980s: "There had been some kind of silly Supporters' Club/ Social Club fallout and we had some meetings at the greyhound stadium for a while. It didn't last long, maybe 12 months or so, then it was resolved and we moved back to the Social Club (next to the Souvenir Shop on Elland Road)." But Ray also remembers a far more interesting use of the greyhound stadium: "When Leeds United got to Wembley they had a couple of 'It's A Knockout' competitions at the greyhound stadium with Eddie Waring and everything. It was Chelsea and Leeds and Arsenal and Leeds. They were televised and there's a *Radio Times* front page with Eric Carlisle, our then secretary, and the Chelsea equivalent on it."

In terms of rugby league, Hunslet enjoyed some success at the stadium but had to leave in 1982 when the then owners, Ladbrokes, sold the stadium and demolished it almost immediately. The Leeds Greyhound Association had sold the stadium to the Totalisators and Greyhound Holdings (TGH) many years previously, and these were bought out by Ladbrokes in 1974. The track kennels were closed first in 1979, followed three years later by the track itself. There was brief talk of moving greyhound racing to the Elland Road football stadium, but this was quickly dismissed on the grounds of the costs involved, not to mention the practicalities. It is true that by this time greyhound racing was a dying spectacle, and there was no way Hunslet alone could afford to stay at the stadium. They then encountered a nomadic existence playing at Mount Pleasant Batley, at Elland Road football ground, and on to Bramley before settling at South Leeds Stadium in 1995.

However, for a significant period the greyhound stadium at Elland Road was a major part of the entertainment landscape of the city. Meetings were generally on Monday and Saturday nights, and on post-war Saturdays some of the trams taking fans to the football would also be carrying passengers with early designs on attending the greyhound racing one stop further down the line. The last race meeting was on 15th March 1982 and the stadium was officially closed for business a few weeks later on 3rd April. This brought a golden period of sporting variety for the area to a close, as the cricket and speedway tracks that also shared Elland Road with the football ground had already long since gone. Demolition of the stadium started on 25th October 1982.

For most of the following years the site was earmarked for development but nothing gathered momentum and it lay empty. Eventually the site acted as the match day Car Park C for the football ground, but due to the smaller crowds attracted it was rarely used after the club's Premier League era. The site was sold to West Yorkshire Police in 2011 and building work started the following year on an impressive Divisional Police Headquarters, which opened in 2014. There remain two sturdy stone gateposts further down Elland Road which were part of the original main entrance to the stadium and these may forever stand in place in remembrance, but other than that you would be hard pushed to find a reminder of a rich sporting past.

GRIDIRON

Fledgling TV station Channel 4's decision to broadcast American Football direct from the NFL in 1982 triggered a tidal wave of interest in the UK, as if the game had never existed before. Within months the crazed obsession with the sport peaked with fully-fledged teams sprouting up around the country to form a UK League.

The city of Leeds didn't escape the entrancing phenomenon that surrounded this most overly complex of sports, and inevitably a team was formed in 1984 called the Leeds Cougars. The Cougars didn't start competitive action in the AFL-UK until 1985 when they were based at McLaren Field, Bramley, also playing some games in Roundhay Park. But due to an influx of sponsorship money from Budweiser in preparation for the 1986 season, the club sought more professional facilities. This was their story at least; officials at Bramley also claimed they didn't renew the agreement with the Cougars due to the damage being caused to their pitch.

In 1986 Elland Road was owned by Leeds City Council, and financially stricken Leeds United were struggling to maintain anything vaguely resembling a promotion challenge in the old Division Two. On the Leeds United board at the time was a council representative named Malcolm Bedford who was also chairman of the Sports Council in Leeds. He was keen to promote family-orientated entertainment at Elland Road and championed a move to welcome the Leeds Cougars and American Football to the ground.

Stung by the need to find additional income streams, which meant the pitch condition was pretty much a non-issue, the council offered Elland Road to Leeds Cougars for the 1986 season, although fixture clashes with Leeds United led to only five games actually being played on the sacred but already threadbare turf. These were all post-May after the football season had finished and moreover were at a time when the pitch was also being used by Hunslet RL, albeit their season still followed the same winter pattern as Leeds United's.

Before the Cougars kicked off their own campaign, council bosses made a bold attempt to hijack the country's growing fascination with the NFL. A pre-season game between Chicago Bears and Dallas Cowboys was staged at Wembley Stadium in August 1986 and enquiries were made to stage a second game between the two at Elland Road, but predictably that came to nothing.

The first Cougars game at Elland Road was against the Tyneside Trojans, which Leeds won 40-6, but head groundsman John Reynolds faced yet another challenge to his adaptable skills in preparing the markings and posts for American Football. John's son Stephen recalls the gridiron experiment: "We went down to watch it and it was horrible. The most boring afternoon I've ever known. I think one of the board of directors was big into it, thought it was the 'future'. I was only young and it didn't interest me one little bit."

A match day programme from one of the five American Football games played by Leeds Cougars at Elland Road in 1986.

Not surprisingly with hordes of heavily armoured men shuffling in formation on the bare pitch for sometimes upwards of three hours, the move didn't win many friends among the overall hierarchy of Leeds United, and whilst they were powerless to stop it, they made their feelings known. It was planned to stage a further five games in the 1987 season, but council bosses relented and agreed that American Football wasn't helping Leeds United's cause in playing attractive football on an already stricken and rutted, grassless plot of a pitch. The Leeds Cougars' first game of the 1987 season was swiftly switched to Throstle Nest, home of Farsley Celtic. At the time the Leeds Cougars' chairman still intended to return to Elland Road, but this never happened.

One off-shoot of the Leeds Cougars' brief tenure at Elland Road was the frequent appearances of the Leeds Blue Cats, the Cougars cheerleaders, who also appeared before and at half-time of Leeds United games around the 1986/87 season. The Leeds Cougars went on to play 'home' games back at Bramley, but also at Odsal, Bradford, Throstle Nest and West Park, the home of Brayhope RUFC, before finally folding in 1995 amid dwindling interest in the game.

GROUND STAFF

Barry Endeacott (left) and a sadly unnamed colleague enjoy some brief respite from their heavy toil at Elland Road as they stand on the Kop in the 1970s.

Throughout its 117-year history as a football venue, just seven different men have had full responsibility for ensuring the condition and playability of the Elland Road pitch. This is mainly due to three specific head groundsmen serving for exceptionally long periods, and is an astonishing fact made all the more remarkable when you consider three of those seven employees have come into the job since 1996.

Since 1904 when Leeds City inherited Elland Road, the list of head groundsmen reads:

Albert Stead 1904-1945
Cec Burroughs 1945-1966
Ray Hardy 1966-1974
John Reynolds 1974-1996
Bill Butterworth 1996-1998
Norman Southernwood 1998-2012
Kiel Barrett 2012-present

Albert Stead is actually known to have been on the ground staff when rugby league was played at Elland Road, before Leeds City took over the ground from Holbeck Rugby Club. But certainly he was head groundsman through those difficult early years when the pitch condition threatened to close the club down, hampered as they were by flooding from the Wortley Beck. Stead also doubled up as a 'trainer', though it is not known if that was to coach the team or to simply keep them fit.

Cec Burroughs was on the ground staff during World War II and gradually took on more responsibilities, eventually taking over the head groundsman duties when Albert Stead retired in 1945. Burroughs had many of the famous Revie youngsters under his wing as apprentices working as ground staff in and around Elland Road. He retired in 1966 and died aged 81, in March 1983.

Head groundsman between 1966 and 1974 was Ray Hardy, who eventually left to run a village store in Cleethorpes. Hardy, as with his predecessor, was responsible for the three pitches at Elland Road: the main pitch and the two on Fullerton Park. John Reynolds began working on the ground staff under Cec Burroughs, and found increased responsibility under Ray Hardy. In 1974 when Hardy left the job, the club at that point would spend £500 on grass seed each summer and the crush barriers, toilets, turnstiles, exit gates, railings and refreshment bars were all re-painted annually. That was the extent of the stadium maintenance budget.

Football grounds are notoriously bad from an agricultural point of view. The stands which hem in the carpet of grass keep drying winds from blowing, and in sunlight cause patching where shadows are thrown across the pitch. Ray Hardy spoke in a match day programme of how advanced the club were in 1974 when Revie ensured no expense was spared. Hardy explains: "We were one of the first clubs in the country to have a line marking machine which paints a five inch line, most other clubs are still on a three inch model." Impressive stuff. It's difficult to say how much difference those extra two inches would make to results on the pitch, but famously, Revie's mentality was that every little improvement mattered. If someone at the club wanted something and it improved their job and could be justified, they got it.

Robert Endeacott spent a lot of time at Elland Road around this time as his father was employed at the club: "My Dad, Barry Endeacott, joined the ground staff in about 1971," Robert begins. "There's a difference between being on the ground staff and being the groundsman, that was one of my early lessons in life! Being the groundsman is quite an honorary position, obviously it means a lot of marked responsibility and hard work, and you were in charge of a fair few workers too. Dad joined in the Revie era and that's where my support for the club stems from, because he had always been absolutely potty over Leeds and got possibly a dream job down at Elland Road as one of the ground staff. Although, basically, they got all the shitty jobs, literally: cleaning toilets, all the litter at matches, etc. is for them to sort out, all the terraces all around the stadium, maintaining the facilities, tending to the pitch whatever the weather. It was a full-time job and he really worked hard, very, very hard, and it wasn't good pay either, in fact notoriously poor pay, but he had the bonus of being a Leeds fan and being in and around the club at the best possible time. He enjoyed it but he was dog tired virtually every time I saw him, I sometimes felt I didn't really have that great a relationship with him in a way because he was virtually always working, including over Christmas, because Christmas holidays never applied to professional football clubs. He left in 1998, and in all honesty, he had lost much of the love for it all, it hadn't been the same ever since Don Revie left in 1974." Robert's father actually retired in February 1998, at the age of 63 and largely through ill health, and having served the club for 26 years. Sadly, Barry Endeacott died in August 2013.

"I helped my Dad out a few times off-season really," Robert continues. "Whenever the season ended they always needed a new paint job on the barriers on the Kop and Lowfields, which were all red for years by the way, but there was always tons and tons of work to be done. You were never allowed anywhere near the pitch, you'd get a right bollocking for going even within inches of it. When I was old enough, in summer holidays my Dad would just ask if I wanted to go down and help out. I also came down after certain big games like in 1982 when Newcastle had been in the seats in the Lowfields Road Stand. They were wooden seats and it was pretty horrible, pretty antiquated, but they trashed all the seats anyway, which must have taken some doing. The damage must have been considerable as I remember my Dad's request was more an order, that they needed help. I went with my old mate Chris Archer that day, Keith's son (former general secretary at Leeds United, Keith Archer). We were just clearing up broken seats and seeing if any were repairable. Them bloody Geordie heathens! I remember coming down in the summer when Don Howe was here as coach, so that must have been around the Jimmy Armfield time, 1975 or 1976, and we got lots of photos with Don Howe, and we tried to get lots of autographs. Don Howe was a real gent that day too. I must have knocked off school which was pretty stupid of me seeing as my Dad was there too. I was pretty lucky because we got a bit more access than normal lads, but it didn't really mean much because my Dad often had to work Sundays. So I would come down on a Sunday and it was deserted, so you hardly ever saw any players or officials really, not even other members of the ground staff. Dad used to let my brother and his band rehearse there on Sundays too."

Naturally, Robert has intimate knowledge of the inner workings of the ground and the club itself, those little details that fans don't see but which make the club tick and make match days possible: "There was a groundsman's store underneath the West Stand," he recalls, "where they kept all the equipment, which was quite an eerie thing to see because there was no light when you first went in. It possibly stretched all the way from the Kop to the halfway line and all the pitch and ground equipment was kept there, and it had a slanted roof, obviously, as it was under the West Stand." The storage is still there in the same position today, and actually extends under the stand as far as the halfway line.

Through researching his book *Dirty Leeds* and speaking with his father, Robert's knowledge of the staff at Elland Road extends beyond the period of Barry Endeacott's employment: "The old groundsman at Elland Road was a guy called Cec Burroughs, long gone now unfortunately, but he basically trained John Reynolds as well; this was all in the 1950s. John Reynolds had been a very promising player apparently but he got a bad knee injury and had to retire and he became the groundsman after Cec retired. I got to know John very well, and he was my Dad's boss. But Cec was a very hard-working man, reputedly a bit of a grouch but a lovable fella. I was too young to know him very well really, but John Reynolds told me that Cec used to swear like a trooper. Most of the players from that era will remember Cec fondly, and no doubt with a bit of a twinkle and a grin. Some of the players were notoriously lazy when they worked on the ground staff, especially certain Scottish lads I believe. They used to have a peephole in the white boards on Fullerton Park so they could see when Cec was approaching. It's amazing to think that all these world famous footballers started on the ground staff, Eddie Gray, Peter Lorimer, Norman Hunter, Paul Reaney, but Cec Burroughs was the man in charge of them all, so probably no doubt he was often swearing and with good reason, I've read Peter and Eddie's books!"

Eddie Gray confirms, in his autobiography *Marching On Together: My Life with Leeds United*, these attempts to skive off his ground staff duties with Mick Bates by finding a hiding place in the back of the West Stand. Eddie admits that he was brought before manager Don Revie on more than one occasion for shirking his duties, when the rebukes that followed were more of the tongue-in-cheek variety.

The junior players' role on the ground staff was nevertheless an important one, involving sweeping down the terraces, painting or wiping the seats, weeding the pitches, helping with the laundry, running and cleaning the baths in the Elland Road dressing rooms before and after training, and cleaning boots. Eddie Gray also recalls having to spend hours putting straw on the pitch after training on a Friday during the winter months, to protect the pitch overnight. The future stars would spend the night in the players' lounge where the club provided them with bowls of hot soup and bacon sandwiches, before getting up at the crack of dawn to remove the straw from the pitch. It was hard work but it helped form a bond between young players and the club, which in Eddie's case has never been broken. However, he also admits that the day he was relieved of his ground staff duties must have been one of the happiest in Cec Burroughs' life.

John Reynolds' son Stephen recalls a story from Cec Burroughs' days that captures perfectly the unique atmosphere around the club in the 1960s that Don Revie had worked so hard to foster: "All the ground staff were in a syndicate for the pools and they won just short of £1,000 each, which was a lot of money in those days. My Dad went up to Don Revie and said 'look Gaffer, I haven't told them they've won it, could you present them with it?' Revie said 'yeah, just tell them I want to see them later on'. So Dad went in and told them all and they all thought they were in trouble for something. So Revie was good enough to play along with it. He came in and everyone's sat there quietly but Revie explains he's got this cheque for them. They gave my Dad a right doing. But apparently they all hit every bar in the ground before staggering home. When Cec got home he fell in to the mantelpiece and knocked over a clock and smashed it. His wife started shouting at him but he said 'don't worry love I'll buy you a thousand clocks!'"

Stephen Reynolds also recounts the story behind the red crash barriers that surrounded three sides of the ground for many years in the mid-1960s and would simply not be tolerated today: "One pre-season the juniors all came in and they were given a paint brush to paint all the terraces, fences and barriers red. Red! It was the only colour paint they had, so everything was red. I suppose they didn't have the same rivalry with Manchester United back then, so it didn't matter so much."

John Reynolds' widow, Maureen, also recalls the many and varied things that her beleaguered husband had to contend with as the often public face of Leeds United on non-match days: "When they had to get straw and prepare for really bad weather they used to get, not vagrants, but people who didn't work, shall we say, they were regulars but they would just turn up at the ground and say 'have you got anything for us to do?' John said he used to have his regulars who he knew would turn up and who would work, and they used to give them a match ticket afterwards. Some came who didn't really want to work, so they'd just give them a couple of quid and say 'sorry, we haven't got any work for you'."

As for the pitch itself, it was never in great condition in those days, and Stephen claims John Reynolds' long-standing mantra was simply 'let's roll it flat and get on with it!' After 45 years serving Leeds United at Elland Road, John Reynolds was moved to Thorp Arch in 1996 in readiness for that opening as the new training ground, and Bill Butterworth took over as the head groundsman at Elland Road. Butterworth had previously been stadium manager at Halifax Town, though he lasted only until April 1998 at Leeds when Norman Southernwood took over the reins. Southernwood had looked after the rugby pitch at Headingley for many years, which by then was being used all year round with summer rugby league and two teams (Leeds RU and Bramley) playing winter rugby union. Leeds brought

Southernwood in as soon as the purchase of the ground back from Leeds City Council had been ratified, and after much criticism of the pitch under the stewardship of Bill Butterworth, Southernwood soon set about transforming the quality of it.

In the modern era, the term 'ground staff' really just refers to the permanent employees that tend to the Elland Road pitch, of which there are just two. The rest is taken care of by temporary employees on a match day and contracted cleaning companies, with the club's academy staff many miles away and spared the daily chores that toughened up some of the club's greatest ever players. Kiel Barrett is the current head groundsman, a 32-year-old recruited from Headingley Carnegie in 2012. Kiel explains: "On match days we get staff coming down from Thorp Arch to help out, to divot the pitch after the game, to roll it after or maybe use the rotary mowers to pick up the debris."

Looking at the Elland Road pitch in modern times, it is hard to believe any player could have a complaint about what is essentially a carpet, but Kiel admits he has received a few passing comments when a result has not gone the way it should have... "They like a moan, they'll say it's bobbley if they lose, they still use that excuse. Or it needs more water, it's never their fault. I remember a lot of complaints over Christmas 2012, but it's pressure isn't it? They're looking at getting three points out of twelve instead of nine, or whatever. Different managers have different opinions and it's not just the Leeds players that like to moan, the opposition do too."

A modern phenomenon that affects Kiel's job a lot more than the likes of John Reynolds, is that the pitch is assessed after every game: "The pitch gets marked by the referee and the away team manager," Kiel explains. "They mark it one to five, and you get two readings, one at Christmas time and another at the end of the season, and if your average is under three you have to report to the Football League and explain why it's like that. It's been in place for a few years and that's how they judge the Groundsman of the Year award." The mind immediately switches to Cec Burroughs and his rudimentary pitch maintenance techniques, and you wonder quite how he would have reacted to being hauled before the Football League to explain the state of his pitch. One can only wish it was Lord Mawhinney asking the questions.

Modern techniques and knowledge are clearly far more advanced than even ten years ago, as are the demands of the modern players and managers. As a result Kiel carries out a lot of research and has close contacts in particular at Arsenal's Emirates Stadium. "A few years ago Arsene Wenger said to the Arsenal ground staff 'outside, that's our office and it needs to be the best'." It is the office, and Elland Road is possibly the best office in the world; tired, worn and maybe patched-up in places, but tended to by generations of love.

GYMNASIUM

The often-referenced facilities at Leeds United's current Thorp Arch headquarters are lauded with such gushing relish that it is easy to forget that Elland Road was once the team's base. A little-known feature of the 1957-built West Stand was a small gymnasium in the centre for the use of the players for pre-season conditioning, fitness tests, training in bad weather and youth team training.

Dave Cocker, as a youngster who trained with the Leeds United junior teams and as an observer on the periphery of Don Revie's great side in the 1960s, explains the rough location and the role the gymnasium played: "If you came out of the home dressing room door and turned left there was a pair of double doors there. Those doors took you straight into the West Stand Paddock, which was before they built the walkway for the players' entrance. But through the two doors took you straight into the concourse underneath the West Stand. All you did then was walk 15 yards, I think there was a bit of a bar area for the fans, which is probably still exactly the same, and there was just a single door there. So you went in and the gym was about half the size of a basketball pitch, with basketball nets in. It was marked out as a basketball court, and in there they had benches and whatever, and they used to do all the circuit training in there. My old man never believed in players doing any running on hard surfaces because it's muscle-jarring, so it was mostly circuit work."

It was a strange and perhaps unique feature of the ground where the two contrasting worlds of the fan and the player would almost collide, and most fans would be oblivious to the fact that during the week Revie's all-stars would regularly pass where they stood and enter the unassuming locked room that most people largely ignored.

"Then what they did in the winter for the academy, because I was in that from being about 12 or 13," Dave continues, "on a Tuesday and Thursday night the kids would go down and use the dressing rooms, it was great. You would get changed, go to the gym and it was held by either Syd (Owen), my Dad, Cyril (Partridge), depending on who was there; sometimes Bob English, but Bob not so often. And we'd spend a couple of hours in winter in that gym, working on ball skills or whatever. That's where a lot of the Leeds greats came through at that time. There were between a dozen and 18 of us, just kids between 13 and 15. At 15 you left school and signed on, or some obviously signed a professional contract then at 17 years of age. The first team went in there as well, mainly in pre-season because they'd come back with a bit of weight on, to do some conditioning. There was nothing much in there really, just pull-up bars on the wall and benches, just what you would have at school basically. It wasn't even really required. It was there when we arrived at the club in 1960 and it was still there in the mid-1970s when we left."

It appears that the gymnasium, as it was, lasted until the late 1970s or early 1980s, because by the time physio Alan Sutton had joined the club in 1986, this area was all open-plan except it had been bricked up to separate it from the fans' concourses in the West Stand. The area still housed a gymnasium of sorts, and the first door on the left as you entered from the players' entrance in the West Stand car park was also the players' lounge for many years. So the walls of the original gymnasium from the 1957-build must have been knocked through, and while part of it became the players' lounge, the area was still generally used for the same fitness purposes.

"When you came in through the players' entrance you were into that big area there, just a big open space," Alan Sutton explains. "When I first moved there they had one of those big multi-gyms, it was metal and had all these apparatus on it, one for bench presses, one for pull-ups, one for dips. That area (the gymnasium) was that big, and if you look at it now you can't even imagine it, but on the back wall was a cupboard with the underside of the steps from the West Stand in it. It was so cold in that cupboard that everyone used to put their cold drinks in there to stay cool (unbelievably this cupboard is still there, and now forms part of the physio room extension to the home dressing room). But it was so open and big that area that Billy Bremner, when he was manager, at about four o'clock on an afternoon he used to get people like Gary Speed and David Batty and Simon Grayson all playing 'piggy' for hours with a ball. It used to be hilarious. Eventually they got rid of the multi-gym and had all the apparatus on the walls, sometime in the early 1990s. I always remember David O'Leary spending a lot of time in there doing rehab when he was still a player. We always had these competitions between the injured players and I remember Chris Kamara doing loads of challenges, and Mel Sterland and David O'Leary had these Irish against the English competitions."

The big open space that Alan talks about has subsequently been filled with a myriad of small corridors and box rooms for various purposes. In 2008 it became the LUTV studios, but in the summer of 2020 was knocked through to form the new Premier League-standard media suite for post-match press conferences. And it is hard to imagine that this rabbit run of varying activities was once the home-from-home to the 1991/92 championship-winning squad, amongst many other players from various eras. There is also no concept that you are just a brick wall away from the rank and file fans on a match day. Conversely, doubtless fans queuing for a cup of tea on a Saturday afternoon in the title-winning season, were blissfully unaware that the famous camaraderie built up among Howard Wilkinson's troops was fostered just a few yards away from where they contemplated how the day's events would unfold.

GYPSY CURSE

The media never needed much of a stick with which to beat Don Revie's unpopular team, and much collective derision was brought upon the club by the players' own actions. One more direct aspect of Revie's management that the media used to undermine him, however, was his perceived obsession with rituals and superstition. This was brought into the most high-profile focus in 1971 when the famously exhaustive and meticulous manager attempted to lift a curse believed to have been left on Elland Road by gypsies.

Looking back at Elland Road's potted history up to that point, indeed there had been the death of David Wilson, the extinction of Leeds City through wartime mis-payments, FA Cup Semi-Final chaos, numerous fines and perceived mistreatment by the Football League and officialdom, and a fire destroying the main stand and all the club's records and equipment, not to mention little success on the pitch, much of which was deemed to be the result of sheer bad luck. Whether that list equates to the vague ramifications of a gypsy's curse is open to question, but certainly Revie was of a belief that his team deserved way more than they were actually achieving, and looking at football results and trophies alone, it was hard to argue with that.

One person who knew the Don's character very well was Dave Cocker: "Don wasn't really that superstitious in a way. People are, everybody goes to a game and they'll wear their lucky shoes or lucky coat. A lot of people do don't they? But we were in a situation where there were a lot of things that had happened that weren't good. If you look at what happened at the FA Cup Semi-Final (versus Chelsea in 1967 when Peter Lorimer had a last minute free-kick disallowed in bizarre circumstances, for alleged encroachment) at Villa Park, we knew straight after the game what that was through, with the referee Ken Burns. The police were then trailing the Kray twins (who incongruously were West Ham fans) and they were speaking to Ken Burns outside the ground before the game. Then you had other refs, Tinkler and everybody else. If you look at what happened in Greece, I went to that game in Salonika (the European Cup Winners' Cup Final versus AC Milan in 1973), I was there, and we knew, we all knew that that game had been fixed at one o'clock that afternoon. It all just got to Don really. He never discussed it with my Dad, it's just something he did himself."

So whilst Dave believes much of what can be termed as 'bad luck' occurred simply through officials' mistakes or the alleged intervention of third parties, and in other words they were explainable occurrences beyond the players' or Revie's control, Revie himself still felt tortured by what he believed was more than just the acceptable kind of misfortune that will and does occur on a football field.

Revie spoke in a television interview in the late 1970s about his ritualistic practices and how he was approached with a potential solution to the continuing ills that were befalling his team: "Gypsies used to live on Elland Road before it was a football ground," said Revie, "and I got this letter one day saying that there had been a curse put on the ground by the gypsies when they were moved off for it to become a football ground, and the only way I could get the curse removed was to get a practising gypsy to come to the ground. So to cut a long story short, I sent a car to Blackpool to bring Gypsy Rose Lee to the ground. She shifted everybody from the ground except me, the office staff, the groundsman and the cleaning women. She went into the ground and stood in the middle of the pitch, scratched the grass and threw some seeds down, then went to each corner flag and did the same. Then she came to my office for a cup of tea and said 'now you'll start winning things', and we did from that year on."

That year was 1971, when Leeds won the Inter-Cities Fairs Cup in a two-legged final with Juventus having, admittedly, suffered some shocking bad fortune during a fallow period since winning the league championship in 1969. It should also be noted, however, that despite winning the FA Cup in 1972, Leeds were not exactly devout in their belief that karma had been restored after the twin catastrophes of 1973. Though maybe simply lifting the curse on Elland Road didn't necessarily change the club's fortunes away from home?

There is no record of gypsies inhabiting Elland Road prior to its 1897 full-time occupation by Holbeck Rugby Club or before that by Bentley's Brewery. It is known though that travelling communities have and still do frequent the area around LS11. The derelict site of the old Wallace Arnold depot adjacent to Gelderd Road saw gypsy communities temporarily decamp there in the early 2010s, before the site was built on by car showrooms, and a site further up Gelderd Road past Churwell Cemetery has also been well used. Whether that practice was the same in the late 1800s is difficult to prove and unlikely to be found on any official records. It is possible the story was a complete fabrication and the fruits of the creative mind of an opportunist preying on Don Revie's famous paranoia. Nevertheless, keen to leave no stone unturned in providing his players with every possible opportunity to perform to their utmost, evidently the Don went 'what the hell!'

"I'm a superstitious man," Revie explains in a different TV interview. "I have the same routine that I've had since the first day of the season, the same lucky tie, one or two lucky charms in my pocket. I walk to the traffic lights every morning, turn round and walk back to the hotel." The accompanying film shows him doing exactly that. It is clear that Revie's obsession with the preparation for games extended to his own rituals, which became a mild form of the common obsessive-compulsive disorder, and while he was a slave to routine and the rituals were seen as eccentric, they were really just his way of ensuring his players were exorcised of all elements of bad luck that might adversely influence their performance.

Don Revie leads out his team for the 1970 FA Cup Final v Chelsea at Wembley wearing his threadbare 'lucky' Blue suit. Leeds lost after a replay.

Revie's observance of rituals and practices was by no means a secret, and his players were well aware of what he did and why he did it. All-time Leeds United leading goalscorer and Revie disciple, Peter Lorimer, also spoke in a television interview: "The (lucky) suit he wore was blue mohair, and you could see his underpants through it, it was so worn on the backside, but he wouldn't change it. It was quite embarrassing and I think he had to wear his coat even in summer to cover it up, but obviously in the dressing room when he took his coat off and turned round it was threadbare, but he wouldn't change that suit."

Terry Yorath also speaks of a number of Revie's superstitions in his autobiography *Hard Man, Hard Knocks*. These included a fear of ornamental elephants and the well-known bird phobia which led to Revie changing the club's badge from the owl to the 'LUFC' script, also in 1971. As Yorath was a habitual substitute during his Elland Road career he was well-placed to see many of Revie's superstitions and rituals first hand, such as taking only three puffs on a cigar before sucking on a mint for one minute, then swapping it for gum, which he chewed for ten minutes.

This apparently continued throughout the game in a strict cigar, mint, gum order. Yorath also speaks of having to go with Revie back to the manager's home from the team hotel in Leeds when he forgot one of his dossiers. Yorath was brought along because Revie wouldn't go back into his own home himself, as "you should never go back in the house once you've left it".

Yorath also had to stand outside the away dressing room at Derby County and count to ten, before going inside to retrieve a player's spare pair of boots upon Revie's instruction. Other rituals included rubbing Terry Cooper's back with liniment before every game.

It is fair to say that while Revie's ways may have appeared irregular, his influence was such that the whole club got caught up in it, and many critics believe Revie's psychosis and his almost neurotic preoccupation with the opposition began to affect his players, particularly on the big occasions. Jack Charlton insisted on being the last player to run out of the tunnel before games. Charlton and his centre-back partner Norman Hunter had to head the ball back and forth to each other 20 times before leaving the dressing room. If the team won a game, the entire squad had to wear the same suit and tie to the next game. On the face of it, these are harmless practices common throughout the game, but they can very quickly fester into all-consuming anxieties when things are going wrong.

What is for sure is that when Leeds were good under Revie they were very good, which was more often than not, even prior to 1971, and hence throws doubt on the consistency of any gypsy's curse that was thrust upon Elland Road, whether you believe in such things or not. Meanwhile the club's bad fortune since the league title win of 1992 is attributed by many to the move to Thorp Arch from Elland Road in 1996, or perhaps the lifting of the curse in 1971 was only actually on a temporary basis?

H

HAPPY MONDAYS

The aggressively probing phrase "Are you Man U, you?" has been uttered countless times round the back of the South Stand, or in the dark and sinister underpasses surrounding Holbeck Moor or even around the train station in central Leeds, as the search goes out for travelling Manchester United fans seeking anonymity. Only once has it been bellowed in jocular fashion by a zoned-out wind-up merchant of a rock star to 30,000 fans from a stage in the middle of the Elland Road pitch. The Happy Mondays concert held at Elland Road on 1st June 1991 is considered a legendary event, not only in terms of the gig itself, but also as a document of its time with the 'Madchester' scene in full swing; a potent cocktail of indie and dance music but also a proudly northern youth fashion movement.

Elland Road as a venue was an interesting choice from the outset, with the band being synonymous with the Manchester musical movement of the time, and also as several band members were sworn Manchester United fans. The legions of fans that would travel over from Manchester for the event considered this to be a seminal day, in keeping with the special one-off mega-gigs or 'occasions' that fellow Manchester band The Stone Roses occasionally held, in preference to the relentless slog of touring. To hold such a reverential occasion at the home of Manchester United's bitter rivals, and quite apart from the football rivalry, to hold it in one of the nearest comparable cities to where the scene was centred upon, was curious to say the least. No strangers to confrontation, the Happy Mondays were notoriously lacking in the pretentions that many comparable groups picked up and they never evolved from their working class roots. Whilst the drug culture they embraced had a positive and welcoming ethos at its core, at least musically, inevitably that frequently spilled over into hostilities and there must have been fears of that in staging a milestone 'Manchester' occasion at the most visible of Leeds landmarks.

Nevertheless, it was a trouble-free and baking hot Saturday as 30,000 'baggy' revellers descended on Elland Road for this unprecedented event, which was billed as the "Match of the Day" on posters and programmes. Given the combination of terrace and fashion cultures that surrounded football at the time, local residents may have noticed no difference on the surrounding streets to a normal Saturday afternoon, that is until the music started, utilising what was claimed to be the biggest PA system of its kind at the time.

The gig's line-up included some of the biggest names of the baggy movement – The High, Northside, The La's and The Farm – in addition to the Happy Mondays, who were at the height of their powers and conquering all before them in their inimitably shambolic fashion.

Andy Peterson was there that day and has fond memories of what he also recalls as being a brilliant event at a peculiar venue: "It was an event which still even now merits a straight ten on the Scally-ometer,

A ticket for the "Match of the Day" event: the Happy Mondays at Elland Road in June 1991.

one widely regarded as one of the Madchester era's definitive moments – and it happened at Elland Road. Not long after United had signed off on a remarkable, renaissance-affirming season back in the old First Division, the ground which had proved so truculent and impermeable between August and May opened itself up for the gig of the year, an all-day bill of baggy heaven, topped off by none other than the uber-Mancunian Happy Mondays.

"Up until the summer of 1989," Andy continues, "a concert at the stadium which guaranteed to draw sons and daughters from every village between Carlisle and Coventry would've seemed like a very bad idea, but the second summer of love had, supposedly, blissed out the football hooligans' souls, turning Saturday nights in the provinces into one big peace-out. OK, so the reality on the ground wasn't quite that but even so the roster of bands – despite lacking Leeds' own Bridewell Taxis – made attendance compulsory. Whilst The High were largely forgettable and Northside were well...Northside, anticipation built as first The La's and then The Farm stoked up the atmosphere, with the latter's front man (and professional Scouser) Peter Hooton quipping 'I bet this is the biggest crowd youse lot have seen here in years'. Oh, how we laughed."

The gig was a resounding success and several tales exist of ticketless fans adopting physically challenging techniques to gain entry. 'Elland Road' is still considered an "I was there" moment of the Madchester scene, with front man Shaun Ryder, notably not a huge fan of football, famously heckling the crowd from the stage with playful taunts of the sneering goad: "Are you Man U, you?"

Andy Peterson also recalls the gig itself: "The Mondays themselves were on the crest of the wave which had

taken their third release *Pills 'n' Thrills and Bellyaches* to the top of the album charts, and although on closer inspection some of it sounded like echoes of its far superior predecessor *Bummed*, their pixelated take on indie rock, funk and '60s day-glo had entranced the nation. This was their night. And yet their thunder was nearly stolen by an anonymous punter who, clearly deciding that his vantage point wasn't good enough, climbed one of the ground's famous floodlight pylons to catch the likes of 'Loose Fit', 'Hallelujah', 'Step On' and 'WFL' from a dizzy and dangerous height. My own favourite memory is having retired to the Lowfields seats to watch the show, then inhaling the strong whiff of jazz cigarettes coming up from the throng before watching them suddenly burst into a life-affirming, pogo-tastic melee during 'Donovan'. It was a 24 hour party during which all our petty quarrels were put to one side. Away fans have probably never been so welcome, before or since."

The event went so well that the Happy Mondays eventually released an official album recording of it via Factory Records, entitled simply *Live*, to counter the plethora of bootleg recordings that were circulating afterwards, one of which was a sly money-making side project by Shaun Ryder himself. The official version is now considered amongst the best live albums ever released, a proud boast from rock music's sweaty, exhausting and wondrous heritage that I don't think Old Trafford can claim.

HOLBECK CRICKET CLUB

A proud cricket heritage in LS11 that pre-dates Headingley cricket ground? The Yorkshire County Cricket Club (CCC) purists might not like it, but it is true. Holbeck Recreation Ground at the very eastern end of Elland Road, and adjacent to the park land that is now known as Holbeck Moor, was the original home of Holbeck Cricket Club, and was held in high esteem as a cricket venue in the late 19th century. It played host to a number of England representative games from 1856 onwards and despite being an unremarkable but homely ground it was still known as the 'best sporting arena in Leeds' for many years. It also featured the curiosity of a grandstand at one side that had been transported lock, stock and barrel from the former Leeds Racecourse on Pontefract Road.

In addition to its local cricket legacy, the ground was also involved in several early attempts to establish association football in Leeds. The Holbeck Recreation Ground was the location for the first known association football game in Leeds, when on Boxing Day 1877 two representative sides travelled up from the pioneering football city of Sheffield, in an attempt to rouse some interest in the sport in the West Riding. It largely fell on deaf ears.

However, it was as a cricket ground that the venue truly made a name for itself. Yorkshire CCC played

three first class games on the ground, winning all three, including a famous Roses match in 1868 when Lancashire were destroyed by an innings and 186 runs, one of the biggest ever winning margins for Yorkshire in this fixture. Yorkshire's last recorded fixture on the ground, which was also known informally as 'Top Moorside', was in 1886 against Derbyshire. With superior facilities, Headingley was opened shortly after in 1890, and it quickly became Yorkshire CCC's Leeds base and meant the Holbeck venue was left behind.

Holbeck Cricket Club was a well-run and well-established local league club and shared the Recreation Ground with Holbeck Rugby Club, but with both clubs thriving, bigger facilities were required. These necessities led to a move from the Recreation Ground to two new sites further up Elland Road, which the cricket club undertook slightly later than their rugby associates, in 1901. Holbeck Cricket Club became a permanent resident on their site in the area then known as Islington. Meanwhile back at the original cricket ground, new housing was already being built and a series of terraced streets known as the 'Recreations' very quickly took over the land and still exist on the site today.

The new cricket ground on Elland Road was adjacent to the site inherited by Holbeck Rugby Club in 1897 (ie. the site of the football ground today), although with Lowfields Road yet to be built, just a dirt track and a few yards of land separated the two sporting venues. The new Holbeck Cricket Ground had good facilities, including a pavilion and a separate building housing the scoreboard. There was also of course the New Peacock pub on the boundary edge. The ground became known equally as 'Holbeck Cricket Ground' and 'The New Peacock Ground', and the team grew into one of the best local sides in the Leeds leagues.

With the neighbouring rugby club having ceased to be in 1904, association football had finally prospered in the area via Leeds City, and often in later years Leeds United players would 'guest' for the cricket team during the summer. Also, Leeds United would regularly field a team of their own during the summer months for charity matches, with most of the players living locally and keen to keep fit.

The boom years for Holbeck Cricket Club were between 1952 and 1961 when they won the Blackburn Trophy (Leeds' premier cricket league) nine times out of ten. Unfortunately, rather than consolidating their position as a major local club, Holbeck found that boom was soon followed by bust. At the 1961 club AGM no officials could be found to run the administration of the reigning league champions, and unbelievably a club with so much talent and tradition was left to expire; it immediately ceased to field a team and the club was wound up in 1962.

On the Elland Road side, the cricket ground was bordered by a combination of housing and the New Peacock pub, whose stone back wall was regularly

While the Holbeck team roll their pitch flat, they care little for the sloping grass bank of Elland Road's Lowfields Road Stand behind them.

peppered by batsmen scoring sixes. On the north side, the ground bordered the Petty's Field Sports Ground, also known in earlier years as the Whitehall Printeries Recreation Ground, which ran along Lowfields Road, until the building of the M621 in 1975. Also, part of the tram siding for the football matches bordered the cricket ground, which later would become the Tram Knackers' Yard.

Following the cricket club's demise the ground was used for amateur football for several years by many different teams, including Monk's Bridge Iron Company who played in the Leeds Combination League. This continued until the early 1970s when the land was acquired as part of the M621 project. Some of the land was lost to the access roads for the motorway, but in 1980 the majority of the area was still available and Leeds United made an unsuccessful attempt to develop it. They put forward a proposal to the council to build a sports centre on the land for community use, and to be shared with the club as a winter training centre. Like many ideas to develop land around Elland Road, the scheme never got off the ground.

The site is now completely unrecognisable as Leeds United's growth, local businesses and the M621 feeder road network has taken over. The actual site of the cricket pitch is now a combination of the Centenary Pavilion and Leeds United Foundation offices, the council-owned bus depot (used only on match days) and the adjacent car parks and neighbouring businesses of Eyre & Elliston and Brandon Lifting Hire. As Elland Road turns into the A643 travelling eastwards, the carriageway popularly known as Stadium Way bisects what would have been the eastern boundary of the cricket pitch. As with the similarly blanket expunging of the greyhound and speedway stadiums, a significant part of the area's history is in danger of being lost in the mists of time, and that's 'just not cricket'.

HOLBECK RUGBY CLUB

In 1897 association football had little or no presence in the city of Leeds or the West Riding of Yorkshire in general. Various attempts had been made by local amateur sides to build an interest in an area that was staunchly loyal to rugby and cricket, and only two years earlier in 1895 rugby had been divided into two codes by the formation of the 'Northern Union'.

One established club in the Leeds area was Holbeck Rugby Club who played at Holbeck Recreation Ground, which they shared with Holbeck Cricket Club. The rugby arm of the Holbeck club had opted to join the Northern Union as a rugby league club. Since the beginning of the 1890s the club had faced a conundrum concerning the growing interest in rugby and cricket and how they could accommodate both sports on the same pitch, and it was felt they needed to expand. Following various meetings with the owners of the estate, the club were unable to acquire extra land at the Recreation Ground and in 1897 the decision was made to move the rugby club to the 'Old Peacock Ground', half a mile along Elland Road. Some of the Holbeck Recreation Ground still stands today as the grassed area that borders the eastbound carriageway of the M621.

Holbeck Rugby Club bought the Old Peacock Ground off Bentley's Brewery for £1,100 and the rugby league side therefore became the first club to become permanent residents and owners of the site, and were able to use their own staff as labour to build a new stand almost immediately. This ran along Elland Road, as the pitch prior to Leeds City's existence ran from east to west rather than the current north to south. The club also built a small wooden terrace on the north side of the pitch in readiness for the first season at their new home.

Like the neighbouring cricket club, Holbeck Rugby Club blossomed on their new site and by 1904 they faced a play-off game with St Helens to join Division One of the Northern Union. By this time Holbeck were sharing 'Elland Road', as the Old Peacock Ground had very quickly become generally known, with local association football team Leeds Woodville, who were tenants of the rugby club. Football had found some acceptance in the area and it was clear there was a growing appetite for the game.

The play-off game against St Helens ended in defeat, which was a crippling blow to the club as they attempted to make their name in the flourishing rugby league domain of the West Riding. As they faced fierce competition from other local clubs Hunslet, Bramley and Leeds RL, the St Helens defeat led to the Holbeck club folding and putting the Elland Road ground on the market. Within a matter of weeks interested parties from the rugby club and former association football club Hunslet FC had voted, along with supporters and local businessmen, to form an association football club, Leeds City, who took on the rent of Elland Road and life went on from there.

A Play-Off Final actually benefiting Leeds United? Now there's a thing. Had Holbeck beaten St Helens in that Play-Off Final in 1904 the immediate future of the club would have been secured, and most likely the club would have progressed in the then top division of the game. Whilst an association football club of some sort would inevitably have been formed in the city, this would not have been the Leeds City and subsequently Leeds United we know today, and most significantly, it is unlikely they would have been playing at Elland Road. Another venue in Leeds would have staged all our hopes, dreams and nightmares, and maybe one without a gypsy's curse on it...

HORSE.....PANTOMIME HORSE

"Leeds and Liverpool are still deadlocked at 0-0 here at a packed Elland Road. Clarke to Jones. Jones shimmies past Tommy Smith and lays the ball off to Giles. Giles in characteristic fashion gazes round the field for options and passes squarely to Bremner. A challenge comes in from Emlyn Hughes which Bremner rides, before passing the ball to...oh my goodness...it's a pantomime horse."

Of all the unruly events that have held up play at Elland Road over the years, certainly the most bizarre, and the most covertly planned and expertly executed, occurred on 20th October 1973 in a Division One match against Liverpool. During Leeds' 1-0 victory through a Mick Jones effort in front of 44,911 on their way to winning the title, the pitch was invaded by a pantomime horse. With comic brilliance the horse trotted nonchalantly on to the pitch and was pursued by two policemen, helmets dislodged to add to the Benny Hill artistry, prior to an unceremonious detainment amid a tangle of arms and legs, and before the confused gaze of some of the country's most expensive footballers.

Some pitch invasions are a spontaneous reaction to certain on-field events but this was an orchestrated encroachment many weeks in the making; a furtive and strategic intrusion that required a level of underground design not seen since 'The Great Escape'.

One of the group involved in the famous incident was Nick Hammond, a season ticket holder of many years until 2013, who has recently moved to Cornwall. "At the age of ten," Nick begins, "my best friend's father, a season ticket holding Scot, encouraged two football playing youngsters to accompany him in his car to Elland Road. He left us outside the 'boys' pen' with strict instructions to watch the game from its relative safety in the bottom corner of the old Kop. After passing the vast sum of two bob, ten of your shiny new pence, to the turnstile man I entered Elland Road for the first time. Exiting some two hours later, but five minutes before the end of the game to 'miss the traffic', after a 6-1 home win. Life couldn't get any better. I was hooked.

"Fast forward eight years of trial, tribulation, a championship, FA Cup and League Cup," Nick continues, "I gained a place at Sheffield University and quickly started to see a very different world. Almost immediately I became embroiled in the Rag Week events. Mainly drinking, which I wasn't good at, and the vague promise of interaction with the opposite sex. Each year there was an attempt to attract publicity to the Rag Week by creating some unusual stunt which might make the local press. Over beers one evening with about a dozen others, a plan was formulated to kidnap a pantomime horse from the foyer of the local theatre. After several more beers this had exploded into a much bigger idea relating to the horse and any sporting event that would be televised. We looked at the football fixtures and the nearest match that was bound to be televised was The Mighty Whites versus Liverpool at Elland Road. I was therefore put in charge of the strategy for the stunt. We abandoned the kidnapping as one member of the group was involved in the Uni Dramatic Society and he was certain that they had a pantomime horse costume which could be borrowed.

"We decided that the best place to attempt to enter the pitch was opposite the TV cameras, which then, as now, were in the West Stand. We obviously needed to be right at the front of the terracing and midway between where the stewards sat. In those days there were far fewer stewards and they sat facing the pitch so that they could watch the game, there was never any trouble in the Lowfields Road terracing, that came much later! But we needed to be there early in order to claim the front row. The other major issue was how to get the horse into the ground without attracting suspicion. Some bright spark came up with the idea of bedecking the head of the horse in blue, yellow and white and stating that it was our mascot for the day, people did bring bizarre things into the ground such as wooden rattles and banners on lethal sticks, so a horse's head wouldn't look too outlandish? I should add it was before *The Godfather* hit the cinema screens!"

In the stark sobriety of an autumn morning, it was decided that the plan would still go ahead, and all those last-minute details that make the vital difference between success and failure were ironed out to the backdrop of what is becoming a common theme in this tale.......more beer. Nick takes us through the final preparations: "The next day, Friday, we reconvened over lunchtime beers, the horse costume had been procured and I brought in all my LUFC paraphernalia: rosettes, scarves, a wooden rattle.... A minibus was hired from the University and a time of 9.30 for setting off was agreed. There were about eight of us in the main party, but the Rag committee had agreed to pay for our petrol and admission to the ground, so as it was a free trip we were certain to fill the minibus! Eventually we left the Union Bar to rehearse the entry onto the pitch. This was achieved using a four foot high brick wall

As Leeds United and Liverpool lock horns in a top-of-the-table clash, a sniggering Lowfields Road Stand and a lone policeman are distracted by an escapee pantomime horse in October 1973.

outside. It appeared easier for the two halves to go over separately and join once over; however, we realised that the stewards could interrupt the half horses' progress before they had become one. It was therefore planned that two of the group would go to both the nearest stewards and distract them by some means or other, so their attention was diverted from the area between them. The rest of the afternoon was taken up with increasingly less humour as the two occupants of the horse attempted to get some natural movement in a forward direction without the horse becoming two halves and falling over.

"We set off from Sheffield the next morning," continues Nick. "Saturday October 20th 1973. The minibus was full, a total of 15 people. We had all the necessary equipment, the horse costume bedecked in LUFC colours and a banner saying 'Sheffield Rag Week 1973', and arrived at Elland Road about 11.00. We immediately joined a queue at the turnstile on Lowfields Road for the main terracing. We weren't first in the queue and tactics were discussed. I said that we wouldn't try to get on the halfway line but would get nearer the Kop, then if we didn't manage to get onto the pitch, the two bodies, horse costume and banner should be taken round the pitch to the north west corner to be interviewed, arrested or whatever, which might give further opportunity to proclaim the 'cause'. It was all for charity folks. The gates opened about 12.30, the man behind the turnstile enquired as to why we were carrying a horse's head, but was reassured that it was simply a mascot to be placed on the wall at the front of the

terracing, 'Fine, but don't throw it at anyone, those teeth look nasty!' After entering the ground we legged it as fast as possible up the banking and down the terracing and got to the front. We stood in two rows to ensure that no urchins got in front of us because they couldn't see over our heads. Standing in the ground for two and a half hours before kick-off was not unknown to me, but it was still a very long time, particularly with the constant enquiries from newcomers about our 'mascot'."

As kick-off approached and the ground filled up tensions were growing; amongst the 40,000 fans anticipating a classic battle between old enemies, and amongst a group of 15 students about to invade the pitch in a pantomime horse costume. Nick describes the main event: "We'd decided that we'd wait until about 15 minutes into the game and then stage the invasion. Three o'clock arrived, as usual Billy won the toss and chose to play towards the Scratching Shed. There was a good crowd of over 40,000, we were leading the division and Liverpool were mid-table, but both teamsheets read like the stars that they were, Harvey, McQueen, Hunter, Lorimer, Clarke, Jones vs Clemence, Smith, Lloyd, Hughes, Keegan, Heighway, Toshack. It was Match of the Day! As 3.15 approached we created a semicircle round the two starring lads, they donned the back half and the front half, we removed the head from the terrace wall. The two distracters started shouting to their stewards some rubbish or other and we lifted the two halves over the wall. We'd started doing this when the play was very close to us; however, in the 30 seconds that elapsed to

get them over the wall and the head in place the play had moved to the other end of the pitch. It was too late to abandon the attempt, so the horse ploughed onto the field. It got about ten yards on and started to run around in circles before anyone in authority noticed. Then the stewards realised there was an equine invasion and about four of them ran onto the field and apprehended the horse. It seemed to be over almost before it had begun, the linesman signalled to the referee and the game was briefly brought to a halt whilst the horse was removed to the side of the pitch. I don't think any of the players actually saw what had happened, there was certainly no reaction from them.

"As we'd expected," Nick recalls, "the two incumbents and the head were marched round in front of the Kop towards the north west corner. When they were about a third of the way round there started a murmur from the back of the Kop that became louder and louder, 'My Horse, My Horse, I Was Saying Goodbye to my Horse, and as I was saying Goodbye to my Horse I was Saying Goodbye to my Horse.' Repeated ad nauseam for the rest of the afternoon.

"The remainder of us then watched the rest of the game, 1-0 win with M.I., M.I.C., M.I.C.K, Mick Jones! scoring the only goal of the game. After the game we went round to the outside of the north west corner and enquired as to the whereabouts of the 'two' hooligans that had invaded the pitch. The police told us that they had been released, but were being interviewed by national news reporters. We asked that a message be passed onto them that we'd be waiting in the Peacock. About six o'clock they turned up in the bar, still with the horse. We had a couple more beers and heard that they'd been treated very well. The stewards told them off with smiles on their faces, police warned them not to try it again, with smiles on their faces' and then they'd been held until after the game so that the reporters could interview them. Mission accomplished we headed back to Sheffield. Unfortunately, as it's nearly 50 years ago I can't remember any of the names of the people involved. I know we made it into the *YEP*, the *Sheffield Star* and I think one or two national papers. It was certainly classed as one of the more successful Rag Week stunts."

The Kop's spontaneous rendition of the traditional navy song of the time 'Saying Goodbye to My Horse' (to the tune of 'Bless Them All'), as the four-legged captive was forlornly led away, remained a staple ingredient of the Leeds fans' repertoire for some time afterwards, often sung to the backdrop of bemused fans who had no idea of the relevance or origins of the song. Even considering some of the strikers Leeds United employed in their recent three-year League One tenure, whether this episode in Elland Road's history will ever be bettered for sheer slapstick genius is open to question.

HOUSING

What is currently and unromantically known as the A643 began life as a turnpike road built in 1785. It didn't become known as 'Elland Road' until sometime between 1830 and 1834 according to local directories. It is easy to forget that Elland Road is a very busy road seven days a week, a major route for journeys from Leeds to the outer-lying towns of West Yorkshire and really just a functional part of the nation's road network. Indeed, rumour has it that some drivers pass Elland Road in their vehicles and do not once cast their eyes right to gaze lovingly into the megastore windows, nor do they drift into melancholic reflection over the old flagposts that stood regally on the back of the South Stand.

Elland Road also used to be a densely populated area. Imagine half the Leeds United first team squad, bright-eyed academy youngsters and coaching staff living yards from the ground. Imagine the area around Elland Road as a bustling community keeping several pubs and corner shops afloat. Around the turn of the 20th century Elland Road was surrounded by a heavily occupied area of housing, industry and thriving local businesses, and prior to this was the site of a number of collieries. Whilst the business community is still largely evident today, albeit on a different scale, the industry and the most immediate housing aren't. Indeed, in view of the stadium itself the only housing directly on Elland Road are the four houses forming part of the 'Heath Estate' which leads onto Elland Road bang opposite Fullerton Park. The Heath Estate, a sizeable network of streets off Elland Road, is famous for once having housed both John Charles and Jack Charlton, amongst others, during their playing days, as the club forged a sense of community far removed from the football world we encounter today.

Whilst the area to the south of Elland Road is still almost completely housing, Elland Road itself is now emerging from a once lifeless and unsightly mixture of empty land, car parks, nondescript businesses and the intertwining motorway network, which is largely the reason why the housing originally disappeared. The area has seen some life restored to it in the last decade by the building of the new police headquarters on the site of the old greyhound stadium, plus a successful Park & Ride scheme and an ice rink on Fullerton Park. There are other plans for Fullerton Park still to come also.

Travelling past the site of the stadium eastwards towards the centre of Leeds, this stretch of Elland Road was mainly housing right until the late 1960s, and whilst populated was known as the district of 'Islington', though there is virtually no evidence of this name today. Incorporated in this area on the left hand side of the road was the Holbeck Cricket Ground and the New Peacock pub, along with a short stretch of housing that comprised a small myriad of streets including Knowles Yard. This area housed a small community that mostly worked at the Leeds Fireclay Company which stood behind the houses.

The angle that Elland Road takes from the football ground carried on in a straight line over what is now the M621 towards the Waggon & Horses pub, and was an area saturated by houses until the 1950s.

The main section of housing was on the opposite side of Elland Road. Several streets ran off Elland Road to the right including Perseverance Street, Dobson Street and Hartley Street which stood where the Volkswagen showroom is now situated, and these were demolished around 1969. The streets that ran directly off Elland Road, and stood right up to the corner opposite Lowfields Road, were known as the 'Hoxtons' and 'Canonburys'. These survived until the late 1970s when they were demolished and are now the huge match day car parks, although Hoxton Mount still survives today. The houses were evacuated long before they needed to be and lay empty for years, inevitably becoming the target for missiles as wars raged outside Elland Road after games in the 1970s. Indeed many away fans were glad to see the dark streets and shadowy Victorian houses disappear, as they provided further obstacles and shuddering dead-ends in the avoidance of stalking Leeds fans.

Robert Endeacott, as a local resident of Beeston, particularly remembers these streets: "The Hoxtons were there right until the late 1970s but they were mostly derelict by then. I started high school at Matthew Murray in Holbeck in 1978, and we used to walk through the Hoxtons every morning to get to school. There was a corner shop we used to go in on the junction of Elland Road and one of the Hoxton streets, and I met (former Leeds coach) Maurice Lindley in there once."

The general grocers' shops appeared on several corners in the 1950s and survived nearly into the 1980s amongst the many terraced houses, which helped to garner the community feel that has been lost

as Leeds United and the motorway network has taken over. "I suppose they used the shops as a business but didn't actually live there," Robert continues, "but most of the houses were empty from what I remember. I always hated those houses anyway, they just made Elland Road look like any other old '60s football ground. Old Trafford, Anfield and Everton, just terraced houses everywhere, and those places could become real death traps if you got chased by away fans."

Canonbury Terrace does still exist today, running parallel to Elland Road along the back of the vast Car Park A, and is effectively just a dirt track. Before Wesley Street was built in the 1920s, 'Canonbury Avenue' was the one vertical road at the foot of the hill that many fans march down today. This was a short street that separated the horizontal Canonburys from the vertical Hoxtons and was re-named Wesley Street when this was built and extended up to Beeston Town Street.

Demolition of most of the housing along and around Elland Road was prompted by plans to build the M621, which actually started work in 1971 but wasn't completed until 1975. Prior to that, an extensive 'slum clearance' demolished a lot of housing in the Beeston area off Elland Road around 1959 and wiped out communities in its wake. But as the road network that feeds the M621 developed, further housing was demolished, including the Hoxtons, to quite savagely change the very nature of the area from largely residential to a vital transport hub.

Today Wesley Street also has housing very close to the ground itself, separated from Elland Road by the A and B car parks. But as recently as the 1960s these houses didn't exist. In 1910 Wesley Street appears on

This photo from a clash with Liverpool in 1979 shows housing in the distance right up to the crossroads of Elland Road, Wesley Street and Lowfields Road.

Ordnance Survey maps only as a small pedestrian lane following the same winding path, and as such didn't appear as the main road it is today until the 1920s. Even up to the 1960s there were no houses on the majority of the road and on the left hand side, as you walked down from Beeston Town Street towards Elland Road, it was open fields and a vast expanse of allotments which stretched down to directly behind the Old Peacock pub.

Towards the top of Wesley Street a road branches off to the left called Sunnyview Gardens. This is a regular side street often used to 'nip through' from Town Street onto Wesley Street. At the top of Sunnyview Gardens is a building company called JP Pullans, who are referenced elsewhere as building the original Spion Kop and Lowfields Road Stands at Elland Road, although they deal only in property management today. The company has existed on this site since 1885 and were responsible for building all the houses on the street itself in the 1930s, which all cost £500 to buy when they were built. Pullans also built the houses on Wesley Street and the streets known as the Nosters and Marleys which provide the iconic and distinctly 'northern' backdrop to many panoramic photos of Elland Road, even today.

Walking down Wesley Street pre-game you finally become 'one of the crowd' and you almost run to the ground with giddy haste, even though it's only about 1.30pm. After the game, when you're often exhausted by the drama, Wesley Street is a steep never-ending

incline that provides no respite. It twists deceptively around another corner, then another corner. Hunched shoulders, head down, it is a steadfast ascent requiring the kind of single-minded persistence of the foreign legion. And that is when we win.

Wesley Street existed as part of the extended Leeds United community in its early years, and was also a vital conduit to the centre of Beeston. Ray Fell recalls the 'local' connection that the surrounding area used to have with Leeds United as a football club in years gone by, particularly at the top of Beeston Hill on the busy Town Street: "There was a house on the corner, opposite the White Hart pub, they used to take the shirts up for a lady to wash them every week. And on the corner of what used to be Webster's Fold on Town Street, where the Co-operative is now, there used to be a cobblers there, and just after the war the manager used to take all the boots up there himself to be mended."

Certainly it can be summarised that a combination of the motorway network, the absence of significant housing and the disappearance of the New Peacock, the cricket ground and the greyhound stadium all in the space of just over 40 years, means that a weekday stroll around Elland Road sees significantly less pedestrian activity than it did around the beginning of the 1970s. As a result Elland Road now resembles what it is, an essential link road that joins far away towns rather than joining the almost extinct community once on its doorstep.

HUDDERSFIELD TOWN

Despite no serious rivalry ever existing, there is an undeniable antipathy towards Leeds United from the Huddersfield Town side, and two notable incidents in the Terriers' past may therefore be conveniently ignored when assessing the contribution Leeds United has made to Huddersfield's ongoing survival. One of these helped it function in a time of need, and prior to that certain other events conspired to ensure Huddersfield survived a real threat to its very existence.

As a result of a fire at their Leeds Road ground on 3rd April 1950, Huddersfield Town, then riding high in the top division, played their last two 'home' games of the season at Elland Road. The two games were against Derby County on Easter Saturday 11th April 1950, a 2-0 win before 30,167, and three days later on Easter Tuesday against Newcastle United which was also well attended by the Huddersfield faithful with a crowd of 37,765 seeing a 2-1 defeat. The fire at Leeds Road began in the schoolboys' enclosure and spread to the West Stand, destroying its roof and upper tier. The stand had been designed by the famous architect Archibald Leitch with ornate gables and was re-built to a similar design after the fire.

This was not, however, Huddersfield's first involvement in attempting to 'take over' Elland Road. At the time of Leeds City's demise in 1919, then Huddersfield Town chairman Hilton Crowther and two other directors were owed £40,000 for their own personal investment in the Terriers. Frustrated by this not being re-paid and by a lack of interest in football generally in Huddersfield, Crowther threatened to move Huddersfield "lock, stock and barrel" to Elland Road to amalgamate with the newly formed Leeds United and therefore fulfil 'Huddersfield's' last games of the season at Elland Road as 'Leeds United'.

The move had the blessing of the newly elected United board and Huddersfield's players, and because of the unpaid debt, amazingly even the

Football League board endorsed it. Those protagonists had underestimated, though, the strength of feeling among the Town supporters. Dismissed as apathetic towards their team, the fans rallied round in the face of a public outcry and raised the money to repay the debt, and Crowther's plans therefore came to nothing.

Crucially by this time, Crowther had seen the potential across the West Riding and had set his heart on building a successful football club in Leeds. He subsequently became the first chairman of Leeds United and was instrumental in obtaining ownership of Elland Road for Leeds United in the sale of Leeds City's assets. A Mr W.H. Platts took up the liabilities of Leeds City and upon their demise he leased Elland Road to local football club Yorkshire Amateur, with the initial lease being until August 1921 including the option for renewal for another five years. This was never taken up as Yorkshire Amateur conveniently moved aside for Leeds United, and in 1920 Crowther had secured the option of buying Elland Road for £5,500. This was to be exercised co-jointly with the floating of a company with £25,000 nominal capital. Crowther immediately invested £2,400 to put the ground and its stands in a "thorough state of repair" with the plan being to create a "scheme of extension to give the ground a holding capacity of 60,000". Between them, Crowther and Platts negotiated the purchase of both the ground and an adjoining strip of land, which would allow for this ground expansion.

Huddersfield Town survived and indeed prospered. In a bizarre twist Crowther immediately appointed Huddersfield's Arthur Fairclough as Leeds United's first manager, and Huddersfield subsequently appointed the last Leeds City boss, Herbert Chapman, as their next manager. Chapman then guided Huddersfield to prolific success in the 1920s, including three successive league titles.

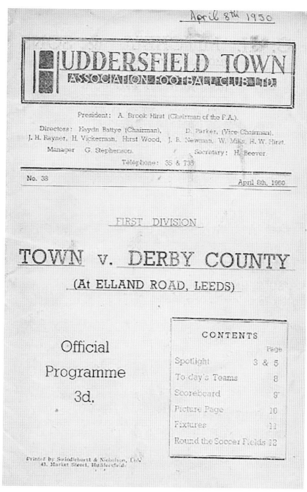

A match day programme from one of Huddersfield's two 'home' games at Elland Road in April 1950.

THE ONLY PLACE FOR US

ISLINGTON

ISLINGTON

Like marbled halls, Charlie Nicholas and tedious offside traps, to most Leeds United fans the name 'Islington' means only one thing: Arsenal, and more specifically, the borough of London that housed previously Highbury and now the Emirates Stadium. However, it may surprise some to know that right up until the early 1960s the area immediately around Elland Road was also known as 'Islington'.

As the Industrial Revolution gathered pace in the late 1700s, significant numbers of migrating workers from London were settling in other towns in the country on the promise of work in the mills, mines and factories rapidly being developed. The inner city district of Leeds known as 'Little London', just north of the city centre, got its name in this way as migrants from London settled there, and Islington is believed to have informally found its name in the same circumstances.

Generally speaking, the area known as Islington only covered the square mile that now encompasses Lowfields Road and Brown Lane West to the east of the ground, and from the foot of Wesley Street along Elland Road and up to Holbeck (over the M621) to the point where the Holbeck Moor now begins. That said, the area hosting the football ground has been variously referred to as Holbeck, Islington, Hunslet and Beeston over the years, so this boundary is naturally somewhat fluid.

The locality around Elland Road was known for its brick and clay pipe making in the early 19th century and Islington, specifically, also housed a coal mine called the 'Peacock Pit' that supplied fuel to these brick works. Houses were built to accommodate the workers and hence the hamlet of Islington, which was listed in the 1854 Leeds Directory as being a borough of Hunslet, was created. Knowles Yard was the most populated of the tight back-to-back cobbled streets that ran directly off Elland Road and even a pub was built to refresh the workers: the New Peacock. In the mid-19th century a huge brick works was built on the area to the north side of Elland Road called the 'Leeds (Wortley) Fireclay Company', which had four towering chimneys that dominated the skyline long before Leeds United's diamond floodlights. This brick works survived well into the 20th century, by which time it bordered the cricket pitch and serviced another annex site further up Elland Road using a small cable railway, where the bricks were fired in kilns.

Islington and Holbeck were also areas famous for the production of vinegars and pickles. The huge, sprawling Cambrian Vinegar Brewery stood on Elland Road between 1875 and 1958, on a spot now in the middle of the M621 yards after Junction 2a which peels off to feed Holbeck and Beeston. The brewery is remembered

A letterhead depicting its Elland Road premises used by the Cambrian Vinegar Brewery in 1900.

An Ordnance Survey map from 1952 showing the area still referred to as Islington. In the top right corner are the 'Recreation' streets, named after the Recreation Ground, home to Holbeck Cricket and Rugby Clubs, which stood on this site.

by street names such as Cambrian Road and the smaller Cambrian Street, which still exists today. A pub called 'The Cambrian' also operated on the corner of Ninevah Road and Marshall Street in Holbeck until 1990, in the distinctive red brick building which was originally a public library built in 1901 and is now offices.

Inevitably, the often-mentioned 'slum clearance' of 1959 started to make sweeping changes to the landscape and eventually, in the mid-1960s, took all the streets in Islington with it. By this time the Leeds Fireclay Company had long been closed and only the cricket pitch, the other recreation ground behind it (Petty's Field Sports Ground) and Matthew Murray School remained. It was deemed that the need for

A road sign from July 2013 for signalling work on the road network outside Elland Road shows that the name 'Islington' is still used for planning purposes.

certainly there are very few living people who have any recollection of it. The name is still listed in the Leeds Directory of 1894 but not after that. It is possible, therefore, that the name was officially withdrawn in the early 1900s and simply carried on through local hearsay, although it does appear on Ordnance Survey maps into the 1950s.

Today there is virtually no reference to the area of Islington ever existing. A building called 'Islington House' stands as a unit on Brown Lane West, part of the Gelderd Trading Estate, and is probably the only existing permanent reminder of the name. A former resident of Beeston, Graham Schofield, recalls a red iron post box set in to the wall near the New Peacock pub with the word 'Islington' cast into it, but obviously this has long since disappeared. In more recent times a council road sign informing of roadworks at junction 2 of the M621 leading away from Elland Road, also referenced the district of Islington, and what it named 'Islington Roundabout'. So it is possible that for council land and planning purposes the name Islington still exists, but not in a publicly known or used sense.

While the name Islington appears on several old Ordnance Survey maps it would otherwise seem to have been erased from everyday use, even before the houses were demolished and the subsequent brutal dehumanisation of the locality eradicated the sense of place and community that once thrived there. Nevertheless, search engines may well direct confused Arsenal fans to this book via the frequent references to their homeland contained within it, and for that small victory it is perhaps worth a spirited attempt to keep the name alive.

housing in the locality was greatly reduced, and coupled with the plans for the M621 meant the demolition of the Islington district was inevitable.

Among the wide-scale destruction of the area all traces of the Islington name were obliterated and only folklore appears to keep it alive. It is difficult to identify exactly when the name 'Islington' disappeared and

J

JACK CHARLTON SOUVENIRS

Jack Charlton's brash and outspoken exterior and his self-assertive and cocksure side often landed him in hot water in his early days at Elland Road. Under Don Revie he grew into a trusted leader of men, but he retained an entrepreneurial spirit that was not uncommon among professional footballers in an age prior to today's unpalatable wealth. This was a time, even after the maximum wage was abolished in 1961, where footballers were nowhere near the untouchable, millionaire, borderline-royalty they are today, and professional players regularly sought additional income to supplement their contracted earnings. Charlton became a World Cup winner but was equally renowned for running menswear shops called 'His', one of which was on Roundhay Road in north east Leeds, and my Dad remembers buying suit lengths and having bespoke trousers made in Jack's shops, as many people did then. But with his wife, Pat, Jack Charlton also ran a souvenir kiosk outside Elland Road on match days.

Jack Charlton serving customers from his souvenir kiosk outside Elland Road in December 1970.

The small wooden kiosk was parked outside the main gates to Elland Road on the site where the Sports & Souvenir Shop was subsequently built in 1972. The kiosk was effectively like a garden shed on wheels, with an opening at the front that became a counter and serving hatch when propped open, much like a small version of the many burger vans that line up outside the ground today. Charlton would sell pennants, books, scarves, photos and programmes and it was not long before the club, although fully sanctioning Charlton's enterprise, cashed in themselves and built their own official souvenir shop.

Charlton would regularly ask his team-mates to sign photos and other souvenirs to add value to his stock. Indeed a famous photo exists of a number of players from Revie's illustrious team lined up in their respective international jerseys and caps for a unique team photo on the Elland Road pitch. The story goes that this was arranged by Jack himself, with a view to printing and stocking the photos in his shops; a team full of internationals. As Giles donned his green Ireland jersey, Yorath and Sprake put on their Wales shirts, Bremner, Gray and Lorimer waited patiently in the royal blue of their Scotland shirts and Reaney, Jones, Madeley and Clarke changed into their white England shirts ready for the photo, it transpired that Charlton himself had forgotten to bring his own shirt to training on the day. The mirth and condemnation Charlton will have received at this gaffe doesn't take much to imagine, but the evidence is in the photo itself, showing ten of the international all-stars grinning mischievously, but not Charlton, whose idea it was in the first place.

Nonetheless, it does demonstrate the ingenuity and dynamism that Charlton possessed and was required to inject into his extra-curricular business activities in order to make them succeed, and the kiosk became a familiar sight outside Elland Road from the mid-1960s until the club's own shop appeared. Jack Charlton spanned generations at Elland Road as he saw the almost resigned mediocrity of the early 1950s and the rise under Revie in the mid 1960s, and he retired in 1973 with the great Leeds side at the very peak of their domestic and European assertiveness.

When Charlton left Leeds to become manager of Middlesbrough in 1973, he clearly carried this business sense with him. Dave Cocker recalls: "When Jack went to Middlesbrough, part of the deal was that he wanted to open and run their souvenir shop. I speak to one of their directors at the time every week, a guy called Neil Phillips, who was the England team doctor from 1960 to 1974, and he was a director at Middlesbrough back then. So Jack went up there, and him and Pat ran the souvenir shop at Middlesbrough."

Most of the players can't hide a smirk as they pose in their international kits and caps while Jack Charlton forgot his.

Charlton's enterprise added to his character and standing in the game, and showed a kind of *Only Fools and Horses* spirit of durability and perseverance that was entirely self-motivated and far removed from the team of advisors, associates and agents that would be required to simply tempt a modern footballer away from the X-Box after training. It was one of the reasons why he was much loved throughout the game, and why his sad passing in 2020 resonated with so many football fans around the globe.

JEHOVAH'S WITNESSES

As a youngster I would consider a match day at Elland Road to be akin to visiting Mecca or a church of all things good; the enlightening hope, the vision in white, the gospel according to John Sheridan. Indeed I and many others showed a devotion to the club that was almost spiritual, but that kind of subsided when I grew up and the second coming of Lee Chapman turned out to be something of an anti-climax. In the cold reality, the only bona fide religious congregations to have taken place at Elland Road are the regular conventions of the fundamentalist Christian sect, the Jehovah's Witnesses.

First started in 1987 when 15,000 attendees came together for a three-day convention, two weeks after the famous U2 concert in what must have been a traumatic summer for John Reynolds and his ground staff, the denomination have since held near-annual assemblies at Elland Road that became something of a tradition. There has been no visit from the summer of 2013 onwards though, and it would appear the conventions have now moved on to a new home.

Delegates typically travelled from all over Yorkshire and Lincolnshire to attend and the events passed with very little hassle or upheaval to the club or notable incident, although in 1999 the West Stand had to be evacuated when there was a hoax bomb scare. The conventions were officially called the 'District Assembly' and prior to settling at Elland Road there was a long-standing tradition of holding the gatherings at football grounds, with Hillsborough, the City Ground and the Baseball Ground, Derby, all previously used.

Usually a stage was erected on the pitch for the main speaker and the remainder of the pitch and all surrounding stands were used for the attendees. Whilst it would seem this was an inconvenience to the club at a busy time of pre-season pitch preparation during the summer, Ken Bates was known to express delight in the fact that the Jehovah's Witnesses gave the whole stadium a spring clean from top to bottom prior to the convention. Indeed, I'm told they even re-painted some walls in the South Stand one year, and they would also return the stadium to the club in pristine condition afterwards. Furthermore they paid for the privilege, so it is not hard to see why Bates welcomed the assembly. It was the kind of passive

revenue that the often truculent chairman was prone to embracing, but sadly now, with the absence of the Assembly, the reverence of divinity at Elland Road must focus solely on Marcelo Bielsa.

JOHN CHARLES

Sir Bobby Robson on John Charles: "Where was he in the world's pecking order? He was right up there with the very, very best. Pele, Maradona, Cruyff, Di Stefano, Best. But how many of them were world class in two positions? The answer to that is easy: none of them."

Much of the credit for the shaping of the modern Elland Road rightly goes to Don Revie. It was the money that Revie's team brought in that allowed the stadium to be modernised and developed, in line with the masterplan the manager and board designed for every level of the unexceptional club. However, undoubtedly Revie's task would have been considered a foolhardy vision without palpable foundation had it not been for the part John Charles played in re-shaping the outlook of the club, and effectively putting it on the map.

Leeds United, it is fair to say, had yet to make a notable impression on the football world when Charles made his debut in April 1949, and whilst trophy success still eluded them during the reign of King John, by the time he left it was clear that they were making strides towards becoming the footballing name we know today. The very fact that the modest club had bred one of the greatest footballers in the European game was a not-so-subtle hint at what could be achieved from very little, with the right guidance and philosophy.

It is not inconceivable that without John Charles opening people's eyes to what was possible, Don Revie might not have found the support for his all-encompassing dream. Elland Road might have deteriorated into a perished, concrete relic to faded post-war optimism and the club itself might never have found an ambition beyond competing with Leeds RL for local support. That it looked far beyond that is partly down to John Charles and his abilities, though Ray Fell tells the story of how close Leeds were to losing the "best thing that ever happened to the club" shortly after his arrival on trial from Swansea in South Wales: "He arrived at the club with his brother Mel," states Ray, "but his mother wanted one of them back, so we lost Mel for that reason. It could have been either of them."

Charles played a talismanic part in Leeds' promotion campaign of 1955/56, although his greatest goalscoring exploits came in the 1953/54 season when he amassed a record 42 goals that still stands today. But what was clear among the 157 goals scored in 327 appearances, many of which were made as a centre-half, was that Charles had become by far the biggest personality to be attached to Leeds United in its existence, literally carrying the club with his presence. It is difficult to convey his stature in the game at a time

John Charles picks up a perished shirt from the embers of the West Stand following the fire in 1956 which expedited his inevitable sale to Juventus in 1957.

a series of record transfer fees and mastermind of the famous 'Revie Plan', a tactical tour de force employed at previous club Manchester City, and hailed throughout the game.

The rest is history, albeit not before a second ill-fated and perhaps ill-advised stint at Leeds when Revie brought Charles back from Italy amid much publicity. Ray Fell remembers paying "7 and 6, which was an awful lot in them days" to stand on the Lowfields terrace to watch the first game of Charles much-anticipated return, as

when football was less global and not open to worldwide media saturation and debate, but trusted opinions held him amongst the world's greatest players of the time. To have such a lauded figure at downtrodden and uncultivated Elland Road brought a purpose to the club, and it is not hard to see why the local population would flock to see him and why youngsters would revere him like a Greek God against the backdrop of the largely graceless and pedestrian mortals that had trodden the uninspiring mud patch thus far. Charles' abilities ensured Leeds United were talked about, and such were his talents that it was no surprise when clubs of the ilk of Juventus became interested in his signature; when two worlds collide.

The timing of Charles' transfer to Juventus in the summer of 1957 is thought by many to be directly attributable to the money Leeds needed to fund the building of the new West Stand at Elland Road, which had been burnt down the previous September, just a month into the club's return to the top flight. There is no doubt the money was crucial to the club but there was an air of inevitability about the transfer, and sooner or later the club were going to receive an offer for Charles that they couldn't refuse. He held an awesome and imperious stature that dwarfed the remainder of the humble club, and the West Stand fire was more accurately a timely circumstance that contrived to make the transfer the common sense development for all concerned.

What Charles had done, in addition to getting Leeds promoted, was raise the profile of the club and trigger the dormant ambitions of the board. Leeds was still a football backwater struggling to attract consistently good crowds, and the club were a run-of-the-mill operation with little or no tangible achievement in the game, yet they could produce a quality player capable of alerting a club like Juventus? Twelve months after Charles' departure Leeds were able to attract Don Revie to the club; an England international involved in

the club had to quite brazenly up the ticket prices to fund his transfer.

While Revie raised the bar completely of course, it is fair to say that Charles played his part in bringing life to Elland Road and offering a glimpse of what any unassuming football club could achieve with the identification, nurturing and management of raw talent. The success of Leeds' further investment in youth just a couple of years later speaks for itself, but acts as an intangible effect of John Charles' stunning emergence. In plain materialistic terms the money Leeds received for Charles, £65,000, did allow the club to fund the shortfall required to complete the West Stand. As a result, Charles' legacy remains today in the ageing but functional structure that has stood as a constant in the footprint of Elland Road, whilst all around it changes. It was therefore fitting when Leeds United re-named the stand in John Charles' honour the day before the funeral service also held at the ground, following his death in 2004. It might be the only remaining structure from John Charles' playing days, but the rest of Elland Road is as much a reason to celebrate his life and what is truly achievable.

JOHN REYNOLDS

Few individuals can claim to have had an influence over the fortunes of Leeds United for more than 20 years or so. But one man that directly impacted upon the team and the club itself across five decades, just short of 60 years, and via 15 different first team managers, was John Reynolds; a name that runs through the bricks and mortar, the paintwork, the plumbing and the lush, green turf of Elland Road like a stick of rock. What John Reynolds didn't know about the day-to-day functioning of Elland Road frankly wasn't worth knowing. But despite his impact on the ground extending from the barren mud of Fullerton Park to the undersoil heating, his long

association with the club could have been brief and insignificant, and as a case of good fortune emerging from bad fortune, came about quite literally by accident.

A 15-year-old John Reynolds arrived at Elland Road for the very first time as a Welsh Junior international footballer, and a highly rated defender, in the 1951/52 season when Major Frank Buckley was the Leeds manager. He hailed from Swansea in South Wales and had been spotted by Jack Pickard, the same scout that recommended John Charles (and in later years Gary Sprake, Terry Yorath and Carl Harris), and indeed Pickard was once quoted in a newspaper clipping in the 1950s, which John treasured for many years, as having classed Reynolds as a potentially better player than Charles. John Reynolds' widow, Maureen, explains: "John's mum and dad wanted him to go to Swansea, as they lived just six miles from Swansea, but he came up and liked Leeds and never went back really."

John was a full back originally but was converted to a striker at Leeds. He had the honour of playing in a West Riding Cup game alongside the great John Charles while he was a junior, but sadly, John's playing career was ended abruptly, during a season in which he had already scored 38 goals for Leeds' junior side, by the kind of career-ending injury that would be treatable today.

His son Stephen takes up the story: "My Dad was playing a Youth Cup game at West Brom and he got injured. Back then they didn't have subs, so he stayed on for nuisance value to 'run it off'. He had a couple of come-backs after that but he never recovered. He'd done his cruciate ligaments and you would never come back on nowadays, but back then they said he'd never play again. He used to say: 'To this day I don't know where the hell that lad came from, I was about to look up and shoot for goal and the lad just came across me.' All he did was block the shot."

Sadly an injury that can now be operated on and fully recovered from in six months was then a life-changing bombshell. John partially recovered but the injury gave him a lot of trouble over the next 12 to 18 months until he eventually broke down in a training match, and at the age of only 18½ had to pack the game in completely. Speaking in 1996, John was typically philosophical and grounded about the injury and how things turned out for him, saying: "In a way having to pack in playing because of that knee injury was a blessing in disguise because if I'd carried on playing I could have been out of work when I eventually retired, with no other career to fall back on."

Stephen describes the process through which John did eventually make a career for himself, albeit one featuring a lot less glamour: "He used to travel up from South Wales with John Charles and a couple of other Welsh lads, and I think he wanted to stay with his mates, so they offered him a job on the ground staff. So he ended up staying at Elland Road not necessarily thinking 'I'm going to make a career out of this'."

By 1954 John Charles was an established first team player but he still travelled back and forth to South Wales when time off allowed, and John Reynolds would travel with him. Maureen explains: "When they went back home for the weekend they used to catch the night mail train and they used to toss up to see who was sleeping on the long seats, and who was sleeping on the luggage rack. I think John lost more than he won." The train journey would often take up to eight or nine hours, plenty of time to forge bonds with players and indeed the club you were doing the travelling for.

Reynolds was only 17 when he first sustained the injury in 1954 but it was halfway through the 1955/56 season when he reluctantly called

John Reynolds during testing of the water for the well in the Elland Road pitch.

time on his football career, though he had started work on the ground staff even before he had officially given up playing, just to "make himself useful" to the club. Having officially retired from playing, Reynolds progressed in the role and was therefore offered the job as assistant to head groundsman Cec Burroughs by then manager Raich Carter. He worked mainly on the pitches back then primarily because it was harder work, as Stephen explains: "The pitches needed straw in the winter and things like that and there was much more manual labour involved, but there was only a couple of them involved, just him and Cec."

Naturally the ground staff utilised quite primitive methods in those days. In 1962/63 Leeds went 13 weeks without a home game as a result of freezing conditions. Having used braziers and other methods to thaw out the pitch, John recalls how they used to use straw: "I would turn up at dawn to remove the straw on match days and then stay until 1.00am putting it back after the game."

Although Ray Hardy was brought in between 1966 and 1974 as head groundsman when Cec Burroughs retired, John Reynolds was promoted to head groundsman and stadium manager in 1974 when Ray Hardy retired. John became a permanent, visible fixture at Elland Road to all the many visitors on non-match days and was central to many unseen and unofficial things that the club did, such as spreading the ashes of deceased fans on the pitch, as he once explained in a match day programme: "We dig a little part out of the pitch, the relatives or whoever put the ashes inside and we put the turf back. People are so grateful. They treat the ground as a kind of shrine."

Reynolds was in the position of head groundsman until he was moved up to Thorp Arch in 1996 when that facility was opened. Speaking at the time, John said: "At first it was a shock to the system when I left Elland Road for Thorp Arch, because I had gone through those gates every day of my working life, but my life revolves around the football side, and with the players training at Thorp Arch most days, I'm pleased to be working there," a reminder that the job of head groundsman at Elland Road in modern times is a somewhat lonely and solitary one.

Back in 1974 the dual role of head groundsman and stadium manager that Reynolds was given was also something of a thankless task, and a position with an almost endless scope, as Stephen explains: "The stadium manager now would have nothing to do with the pitch, it's more of a security and safety job. The role of head groundsman and stadium manager is two different roles." Maureen agrees, adding: "John had to sign off that the stadium was fit to use, every game, but I think it was after the Bradford fire in 1985 that they thought they should have a proper safety officer."

Stephen recalls the inexhaustible range of jobs that John would often get involved in during the average of 50 to 60 hours a week he would spend at Elland Road:

"I remember him getting radio calls ten minutes before kick-off saying something like 'south-east corner ladies toilets blocked', and he'd have to head off with a plunger to unblock it, or a turnstile won't go round somewhere and somebody can't get through. Someone would come up and say 'have you got a black plastic bag?' The answer would always be 'see John'. Very strange, at the time we didn't think anything of it, that's just what he did, but it's not what you'd expect of a stadium manager today."

Maureen also explains the strain John's dedication to an unenviable job sometimes put on their relationship: "I didn't always know when John was coming home. I was warned when I married him. It was normally 7pm when he would come home after an afternoon match. He liked to repair the pitch straight away. Also the club used to have two nightwatchmen, who used to ring John at all hours when things went off. There was an old boy called 'Taffy' (Taff West) who would always ring John. Many a time he had to go down on a night when they've heard something and something's banged, and it would just be a fox or a cat."

The cold and eerie nature of an empty football ground at night doesn't change, regardless of the success of the team or the vibrancy that resonates from it during the day. "I used to go down with him sometimes and just follow him about," Stephen adds, "or I'd sit at reception and wait for him. But I didn't like it, you used to walk down long, dark corridors in eerie silence and I wasn't happy about it."

John's dedication to duty extended way beyond what most people would be expected to do. He was even persuaded to open up the ground at 7.30am one morning after an inebriated Eddie Gray and Peter Lorimer called him up the previous evening. The star duo had encountered former show jumper Harvey Smith in a Leeds restaurant and over several drinks had somehow agreed to a crackpot handicap race on the Elland Road pitch. In it, Lorimer would run the full length of the pitch while Harvey Smith would start on the halfway line carrying Eddie Gray on his back. Lorimer won the race, just, and each of the players won a £50 bet. Whether the somewhat exploited John Reynolds got anything out of opening the ground first thing especially to stage this momentous event is not known.

Christmas was another period when John took his duty far beyond what others would expect: "If Leeds were at home on Boxing Day", says Stephen, "then they would want to train on Christmas Day. So my Dad wouldn't have a drink until he'd gone down, set it all up and made sure everything was alright, let 'em in, watch 'em train, come back and then he'd have a drink at night. Nine times out of ten though, if they were drawn away on Boxing Day they would want to train on Christmas Day at home anyway, before they travelled. So most Christmas Days he was working. Same with New Year's Eve, New Year's Day, all Bank Holidays, always the same."

John Reynolds at his second home: the Elland Road pitch. Note also the vertical fence running up the middle of the Kop in the background, which served to instigate much 'left side', 'right side' merriment among Leeds fans for many years.

Such devotion and commitment to whatever was perceived as 'duty' was born out of a tremendous love for the club, which such lengthy service naturally forms. John was a Leeds fan as much as anything else and existed as a key member of the 'Elland Road family' that Revie was so keen to foster, and which meant every individual was as important as the next. Physio Alan Sutton became a great friend of John's, recalling: "He used to stand at the end of the tunnel and shake hands with the players, after a game and before it. Mick Jones and Allan Clarke have told me the same from before I was there. John would always stand at the end of the tunnel and shake the players' hands."

Although John Reynolds was integral to the match day operation in terms of preparing a pitch that the Leeds United manager, in particular, was happy with, this didn't necessarily happen seamlessly. Stephen explains how John Reynolds and Howard Wilkinson didn't always see eye-to-eye on how the training pitches and the Elland Road pitch could or should have been prepared in often difficult circumstances.

"He (Wilkinson) and my Dad clashed," Stephen recalls, "because maybe my Dad answered back, and he wasn't used to that. Howard used to moan about the pitch and my Dad used to say 'but you're winning aren't you? You've just won the league on this pitch!' I think ultimately Howard respected people that stood up to him, but he didn't like to show he was backing down."

Howard Wilkinson himself, however, doesn't recall having a particularly strained relationship with John Reynolds. "If we did, John never told me," Howard explains. "If John had a problem it was probably the fact that he was being asked to do far, far, far more than probably you had a right to ask him, both in terms of his time and in terms of what his salary was. All I knew is that we needed to be able to train every day on an acceptable surface. I don't know, maybe he did go home and moan about me, but then so did the players, so did the kitchen staff (adopts moaning female voice): 'oh bloody hell we can't fry it anymore, it's got to be grilled'..."

The Wilkinson era was a fruitful one for John Reynolds, however, because success on the pitch brought a new outlook to the club where every facet was looked after in a bid to ensure the success continued. Then managing director Bill Fotherby remembers that even the ground staff became part of the investment in infrastructure: "That time was amazing," recalls Bill. "Everybody was coming to work happy. John Reynolds and his staff, they were getting the backing. You know, if you were the groundsman you've got to make sure that you've got at least two good mowers, never mind just one, and then the ground was looked after."

John's widow, Maureen, also recalls the more personable side of Howard Wilkinson that the wider world didn't often see, and also confirms that any day-to-day disagreement was merely in the pursuit of professional goals: "When John passed away (in 2012) we received a lovely letter from Howard. We were shocked, but he said he'd liked to have come to the funeral but he was working away with the FA. But it showed that he did actually respect him in the end. I think it was just a professional thing rather than personal."

Stephen recalls that John had a good rapport with all the many Leeds managers he served under. "I always remember Brian Clough," Stephen begins. "Not long before he (Clough) died he had a function at Elland Road. There was a dinner and he did a question and answer thing about his time at Leeds. My Dad queued up to meet him, and he said to my Mum 'do you think he'll remember me after 30 years or so?' My Mum said 'of course he will'. Anyway, he met him and Clough said 'of course I remember you, John, you were the only friend I had at Leeds!' It got to him quite a bit did that. I think Clough mentioned it in a book too, that John Reynolds was the only friend he had at the club."

After he was moved up to Thorp Arch when George Graham was manager, the club employed Bill Butterworth as a short-lived groundsman in acrimonious circumstances connected to the recent takeover of the club. John always got on with George Graham as Graham was "a keen gardener, so I couldn't pull the wool over his eyes". Graham used to keep his ear to the ground and ensured John was kept informed of events at Elland Road, and as Stephen Reynolds says, "George Graham said he would make sure my Dad was looked after, and he did. The day Graham left the club he called my Dad over and asked him to sit in the car, he said he was in his scruffs, but Graham said 'don't worry about that' and they had a good chat. You don't often see that side of George Graham, but my Dad had that kind of connection with all sorts of people."

John developed cancer quite suddenly when still working for the club on a part-time basis in 2010, and within two years he had died. Stephen recalls how his dad made his final farewell to the Elland Road arena he had tended to for almost all his working life: "He had some quite specific requests for when he died. When he was at the hospital he said he'd been thinking and he was quite reluctant, but I made him tell me. He said he wanted to be taken around the ground at his funeral, by which he meant round the West Stand car park, back of the Kop and up Lowfields Road and off to the crematorium. But we spoke to a few people at Leeds and a lady set it up for us to go round the pitch. So on the day, after we'd been to the church we got dropped off at the players' entrance and they took my Dad down to the groundsman's tunnel and took him round the pitch. They stopped at the tunnel and some of the ground staff had put a marking machine, a tractor, a fork and some flowers saying 'John' on. It set us straight off. We didn't expect it, we just thought they were going to drive him round, but all the staff came out. It was

really nice and the club did well for us in that respect. It was standing room only at the church. Most of the Revie team were there and one was overheard speaking to another saying 'do you think there'll be this many here when we go' and the other said 'no way'." Maureen adds: "All the players from his original Juniors team from 1953 came to the funeral. He still used to meet them all on a Thursday, plus all the surviving Revie players."

"Funnily enough," Stephen interjects, "Eddie Gray was the last person to speak to my Dad. He didn't wake up very often towards the end, and we thought it was my Mum who he'd spoken to last, we didn't know Eddie had gone the following day and he actually woke up briefly for Eddie. I think that upset Eddie when we told him. There were people who had only met him once at the funeral. Two lads who he showed round the ground when they were nine turned up, they were in their forties and they said they had never forgotten what he did for them. It was amazing. There was a dustbin man that he got to know who turned up. I knew he was well thought of, but I didn't know how much until the funeral."

John Reynolds was a month short of 60 years' service at the club when he died on 5th April 2012, aged 75. Shortly before his death he received a Lifetime Achievement Award at the Leeds Sports Awards. However, after a request from the family for a minute's applause before the next Leeds United home game, to recognise the length of his service to the club, was turned down, a threatened mutiny from the current ground staff reversed the decision. It was clear that the well-received gesture relating to the funeral was not granted by the upper echelons of the club, whereas this decision was. Naturally the family were upset, albeit not necessarily surprised, by the decision even though it was eventually reversed. Howard Wilkinson puts it quite succinctly upon being told of the belated agreement to the gesture: "That's a shame, you should always look after people. That's part of being big, that's part of being great, that's part of being an institution. You look after those people that looked after you."

Eventually, a minute's applause before the Leicester City game on 28th April 2012 celebrated the lives of a number of the club's servants that had died during the course of the season, including title-winning midfielder Gary Speed, club president Lord Harewood and John Reynolds. Anybody that has visited Elland Road on a match day or during the week on any given day since 1952 will have crossed paths with John Reynolds. He befriended delivery drivers, business people, players, coaches, fans and officials, basically anybody in and around the ground. In short, he was always there, not taking the glory but doing the hard work that allowed others to take theirs and most importantly, Leeds United's.

JUVENTUS, MANCHESTER CITY AND...ERM...NELSON TOWN

Interspersed all too fleetingly amid plenty of dirge that we have tried to forget, Elland Road has been the staging arena for at least some occasions of exquisite theatre, heart-stopping tension and rousing, heroic victories. But the fact remains that in their 100-year existence Leeds United have only ever won three trophies on their own hallowed turf.

Of the three league titles the club has won, all of them were clinched away from Elland Road, two of them (1973/74 and 1991/92) technically without Leeds actually playing. Naturally our first ever major trophy, the 1968 League Cup, and our single FA Cup Final triumph both occurred at Wembley Stadium, as did our 1992 Charity Shield victory over Liverpool. Leeds United's first European trophy was won in 1967/68, but the final of the Inter-Cities Fairs Cup was a two-legged affair and the silverware was won following an epic performance in attaining a 0-0 draw in the hostile Nep Stadium in Budapest, as Leeds defeated Ferencvaros 1-0 on aggregate before 75,000 inhospitable fans. Furthermore, the previous season had seen Leeds offered the chance to win the trophy before their own fans, but a frustrating night couldn't see them overhaul a 2-0 first leg deficit to the winners Dinamo Zagreb.

Technically, for the first silverware the club ever won (discounting various regional cups and pre-season trophies) you have to go back to the season 1923/24. On the 26th April 1924 Leeds beat Nelson Town 1-0 in front of 20,000 fans at Elland Road to clinch the Second Division title with one game remaining. The home fans had finally seen tangible reward for their wavering but dogged support of the fledgling club, and even before that from the Leeds City days. Leeds finished three points ahead of second-placed Bury.

Other promotions came and went without Leeds being champions, and 40 years would pass before Elland Road had a sniff of seeing further silverware, as Leeds' young side steamed towards promotion from Division Two under Don Revie in 1964. With the coveted top-two finish already in the bag following a 3-0 win at Swansea Town the previous week, it was all set up for the title to be clinched at Elland Road on 18th April 1964, but Leeds stuttered unexpectedly and drew 1-1 with Plymouth. Results went their way fortunately, and Leeds were able to clinch the championship ahead of second-placed Sunderland in the last game of the season, with a 2-0 win away at Charlton Athletic. A similar scenario saw the bulk of the club's support denied a glorious moment again in 1989/90 when Leeds clinched the Second Division league title away at Bournemouth with a 1-0 win, and not the week before in front of a fervent and expectant crowd versus Leicester City.

It was 2nd August 1969 before Elland Road and its success-starved punters were again able to see silverware attained before their very eyes when the Charity Shield was won following a 2-1 defeat of

A rare sight at Elland Road: silverware paraded around the pitch by Norman Hunter, Paul Reaney and Billy Bremner after the Charity Shield win versus Manchester City in August 1969. The empty north west corner awaits its impending development behind.

Manchester City. As league champions, Leeds were given home advantage in the traditional season curtain-raiser which had yet to capture the public's imagination, and hence was not staged at Wembley. Goals from Jack Charlton and Eddie Gray saw the shield paraded around Elland Road before 39,835 fans.

Leeds' third and to date most recent trophy win at Elland Road was the final of the Inter-Cities Fairs Cup of 1970/71. Following a hard-fought 2-2 draw in Turin, Leeds faced Juventus at Elland Road on 3rd June 1971. Over a month had elapsed since the end of the league season and the shirt-sleeved 42,483 crowd watched on in balmy, summer evening temperatures as Leeds drew the tie 1-1 to win 3-3 on away goals, and paraded the trophy around the pitch afterwards with Elland Road still basking in the fading daylight.

Although you could count the much-appreciated 1992/93 FA Youth Cup triumph over Manchester United, which was achieved after a second-leg victory at Elland Road, since 1971 Elland Road has only been

Egged on and surrounded by his faithful disciples, a reluctant Marcelo Bielsa lifts the Championship trophy after the 4-0 defeat of Charlton Athletic on 22nd July 2020. But the trophy had been won the weekend before.

A joyous David Batty and a youthful Gary Speed lead the squad around the pitch with the Second Division championship trophy before the friendly with Genoa, and after the trophy had been won in Bournemouth the previous weekend.

the scene for episodes of plot-building leading to the consequent glory occurring elsewhere, or for fleeting fulfilment resulting only in ultimate failure. Save for the chaotic yet exhilarating promotion from League One, as runners-up, achieved with a 2-1 win over Bristol Rovers with ten men on 8th May 2010, most would agree that the many special moments that have been served up on our own blessed patch over the years, are scandalously under-represented in terms of actual, material achievement. In 1990, captain Gordon Strachan lifted the First Division trophy before a hastily arranged friendly versus Genoa at Elland Road, in the week after the 'lively' events in Bournemouth had secured promotion and the title. It was a similar story in 2020 after the final home game versus Charlton Athletic, when Liam Cooper was handed the Championship trophy which had been won without Leeds even playing, and of course, there were no fans there to see it due to the COVID-19 pandemic. And certainly there appears to be some weight behind theories that Leeds fans seem destined not to see glory unfold before them.

KAISER CHIEFS

Rarely have the words "I predict a riot" been so warmly received at Elland Road, or their uttering so foreseeable as on one sweet Saturday in May 2008. The football allegiances of the Kaiser Chiefs have never been a secret. Even when they first emerged from obscurity it was fairly clear that the band name was not a reference to their direct interest in a South African domestic football team. From the outset, with early publicity shots taken on the Elland Road pitch and others with a comically bemused Lucas Radebe, the band had nailed their colours to the amplifier, quite literally.

After a massively successful debut album and a string of rapturous appearances on the festival circuit, the band's rapid elevation into the nation's consciousness was cemented with a homecoming gig at, where else, Elland Road. It was to be a landmark occasion for the band and the tie-in with their beloved Leeds United was sprinkled with further fairy dust by the date falling the day before Leeds' League One Play-Off Final at Wembley against Doncaster Rovers. It was a weekend that dreams were made of.... well, half of it was.

Bassist Simon Rix remains a season ticket holder at Elland Road and explains how the idea of the gig evolved from a fanciful dream tossed around over a few pints in a tap room, to a genuine and quite natural prospect: "It was a joke ambition I guess, like Wembley. Our ambition at first was to sell out the (former Leeds live venue) Cockpit room 1, which we managed so I guess after that it was just a matter of time.........In the dim and distant past before the Leeds Arena was built and after the Town & Country Club had closed down, once you had played in the university dinner hall, there was nowhere bigger to play (in Leeds). People tried to be a bit creative, and we played Millennium Square, which was good, other than waking up all the patients at LGI, and we were looking for somewhere bigger and better to play. For the band, as soon as it became obvious that we could play pretty much anywhere, Elland Road was first choice. A gig at Elland Road would be a big deal for us, possibly the best place we could ever play and I think we all thought it would be a big deal to the city and an event for Leeds, more so, given Leeds United's position at that time, as we sunk to our lowest ebb in the third tier.

"So our folks got in touch with their folks," Simon continues. "The band didn't have to do much, other than insist it was the right place to play no matter what obstacles people came back with. I'm certain it will surprise people that we, the band, our management, etc. made zero pounds and zero pence out of a gig to 40,000 people. But that is just how difficult it was to put on and why no-one really plays the stadium on a regular basis. It also shows how much we wanted to make it happen."

Saturday 24th May 2008 soon came round, and stories were swapped on the day of the legions of fans amongst the 40,000 crowd, myself included, that were doing the 'double-header' of the Kaisers' gig and Wembley the next morning. Simon explains how the

date of the event was carefully planned: "The date was decided a long time before we knew how Leeds would do that season on the pitch. Obviously Leeds United were keen to do it as soon after the season as possible, to give the pitch time to recover, so it was always going to be on the first weekend after the season."

The build-up to the gig grew over many weeks and with Leeds United successfully navigating Carlisle in the Play-Off Semi-Finals the dream weekend scenario had been set-up, as Simon recalls: "Sitting in the Gelderd End on the Friday before soundcheck was my favourite moment. There's something special about empty football stadiums and it was great to see our stage, our lights, our guitars sitting on the pitch where so much history has taken place, and we were becoming part of it."

Inevitably the band placed their feet very firmly under the table, and in addition to having the whole of the South Stand executive box area for dressing rooms and general 'backstage activity', they also took advantage of the unique opportunity to have Elland Road pretty much to themselves: "We've played football on the Elland Road pitch a few times (in photo shoots). Obviously when we did the gig most of the grass was covered and the goals were gone but we still found a tiny patch so we could kick a ball. We had all access, pretty much everywhere. Again, we've been in the changing rooms, etc. a lot but obviously faked an interview in front of the advertising board, sat in the dugout, generally made ourselves at home. Luckily Ken (Bates, then chairman and owner) decided to stay in Monaco so it was a good time all round."

While the law of averages suggests that a fair percentage of the crowd that attended on the day were not actually Leeds United fans, or indeed, cared little for football at all, it didn't seem that way as the day inevitably became a Leeds United love-in from the off. Admittance gates for all the crowd were in the East Stand, whereupon you could then sit anywhere in the ground (other than the 'posh' seats in the East Stand Upper) or stand anywhere on the pitch, facing the stage that was erected in front of the South Stand. All the bars in the ground were open, allowing for the unique and much-abused concept of legally drinking beer in the middle of the Elland Road pitch. I even sat in my Kop season ticket seat with a pint for one of the support acts, Kate Nash, simply because for one joyous occasion, no steward could stop me.

The gig itself was a triumphant affair and was littered with Leeds United references. DJ Chris Moyles serenaded the crowd with a rendition of 'Marching On Together' during his introduction of the band, singer Ricky Wilson wore a blue suit jacket with a yellow and white shirt underneath, and drummer Nick Hodgson went one better by wearing a retro Leeds United 'Smiley' badge shirt from the late 1970s.

Leeds songs chanted by the crowd were liberally sprinkled throughout the set and it was all building up quite nicely to the next day's events. As the lights went

down and the crowd drifted away into the night wading through a sea of empty pint glasses, the stadium PA played 'Glory, Glory Leeds United'. It was a fitting end to the proceedings that left Leeds fans going to bed feeling unbeatable. The feeling 24 hours later was somewhat different.

Simon explains the logistics that took the band from their most triumphant gig to Wembley a few hours later: "It was pretty perfect really. We had the huge Leeds love-in, after the show we had a party inside Elland Road (in Billy's Bar) with our family and friends, then got on our tour bus down to London. We woke up in Wembley Arena, showered and had breakfast. We had another kick about/sing-along inside the Arena (where the staff allowed them to leave their bus and use the facilities as they had no event on that day) before heading over to disappointmentville."

Having lost 1-0 at Wembley in a striking example of how Leeds United have the inherent ability to ruin the most perfect of occasions, Simon explains the mix of emotions that weekend: "At the time it was awful, sort of ruined the whole thing, because the gig had become a combination of things. We'd lived up to our part but for whatever reason Leeds just didn't turn up. Elland Road is certainly in among the best gigs we've played, because it was more than just a gig. The whole build up and aftermath, it wasn't just about the 90 minutes on stage. It was a whole weekend of Leeds celebrating Leeds."

Since then, the Kaisers have played Elland Road twice more: a truncated set in May 2018 prior to Josh Warrington's triumphant world title fight against Lee Selby, and then being asked by the club to open their

Lucas Radebe, the original Chief, on stage with the Kaisers as they sound-check prior to playing the ringwalk music for Josh Warrington's world title fight at Elland Road in June 2018.

programme of centenary events with another mega-gig in June 2019.

Simon explains how the 'Leeds love-in' vibe from 2008 was in the air again: "When Josh announced his fight at Elland Road it seemed like it was going to be a very similar occasion. Everyone was going. Josh's agent got in touch to ask if we'd be available to play his ring walk 'I Predict a Riot' on the night. Obviously it's never as easy as people think with PA, lights and stage and everything, so I half expected that we would be asked to mime it in the ring. But as the night grew closer we were asked to play a short set and then 'I Predict a Riot' for the ring walk. Flanked by Lucas Radebe, it was hard to tell exactly what was going on (when Josh Warrington walked out) but the place went wild and I don't think it let up for the whole of the fight. I don't think we were prepared for quite how good the atmosphere would be. Despite the slightly unusual stage placement, it was every bit as good as any of our most raucous gigs. The stage was built over the top of the seats in the north east corner. Which meant we were right on the edge of the completely full and very loud Kop end."

Warrington took the world title in emphatic fashion but the euphoria of that occasion was possibly topped by the Kaisers' third gig in the famous old stadium, putting them two clear of Jean-Kevin Augustin for Elland Road appearances.

"When we got the offer to play the centenary gig, we were all obviously absolutely up for it," Simon explains. "I always say that I was never going to be a footballer so to somehow weave my way into the history of Leeds United is amazing. As it got close to the actual day, there was a slight feeling of disheartenment. Leeds hadn't got promoted and our album which was due to be released was also delayed. It felt like the right gig at the wrong time. But actually, it turned out to be exactly the right time. The hangover from the play-off game against Derby had dragged on, but on the day of the gig it suddenly all made sense. Here we all are, back in the stadium, with no pressure of football; a guaranteed home win. A great day out to celebrate being proud to be Leeds again and 100 years of our great club. It felt like us drawing a line under the old season and celebrating the start of the new one. Time to look forwards again."

Fans are on the pitch and the stage is set up in front of the South Stand for the Kaiser Chiefs gig in May 2008.

"In terms of comparing the two," Simon reflects when asked about the two mega-gigs 11 years apart, "I think the one in 2019 was better. There were actually fewer people in the stadium but, however it was set out this time, it felt full. I'm pretty sure Bielsa had signed up for another season by this stage so there was every reason to be confident going into the club's centenary season. Plus I think the extra 11 years of touring meant we were a better band and the set was better with more songs from more albums to choose from."

It was certainly a fitting occasion to launch the centenary and pretty cathartic in terms of people returning to the scene of the previous month's harrowing Play-Off Semi-Final collapse to Derby County. The after-party – again in Billy's Bar – certainly demonstrated that spirits had been raised, and the gig was another to go down in Elland Road's bounteous rock history. "I'm a bit upset we didn't film 2019," Simon concludes. Don't worry mate, I'm sure there'll be another opportunity.

KING'S SPEECH

Following hot on the heels of *The Damned United*, filmed in 2008, and scenes for the TV series *A Touch of Frost* in 2010, Elland Road was used once again later in 2010 as the backdrop for the atmospheric opening minutes of the Oscar-nominated film *The King's Speech*; a story of King George VI's struggle with a speech impediment, starring Colin Firth and Helena Bonham-Carter.

The opening scenes of the film depicted the then Duke of York's closing ceremony speech at the British Empire Exhibition at Wembley Stadium in 1925, when the future King's stammer was first ignominiously brought to the public's attention. As the old Wembley Stadium was long-since demolished and dressing the new one up was clearly illogical, what better framework in which to depict the unrefined simplicity of 1920s stadia than the 1950s-constructed West Stand at Elland Road?

Colin Firth earned wide acclaim for his portrayal of the King, and as he climbs the steps from beneath the stand, the white brick concourse areas of the West Stand, where many a pre-match pie and Bovril have been devoured, are comfortingly familiar. The close-up speech scenes of the King's first public address then follow, and were filmed in the directors' box of the West Stand. There is an ageing authenticity for the uninitiated observer, helped by the plumes of cigar smoke and smog in the background and the vintage steel rafters above. Perhaps less plausible were the following, longer-distance crowd scenes of Wembley, shot at nearby Odsal Stadium, home of Bradford Bulls, chosen simply for the curved ends to the stadium that vaguely resembled Wembley through tightly squinted eyes.

Behind the decision to use Elland Road was the influence of director Tom Hooper, who also directed *The Damned United*, and hence held prior knowledge of the ground. The day before shooting the crew could only gain access to the stadium from 10.00pm as Leeds United were staging a home game. Overnight they filled the stand with 1,200 surprisingly genuine-looking inflatable dummies dressed in period costume to create an authentic crowd scene. On the day of filming the weather was cold and accommodatingly misty with the threat of snow in the air, which added to the wistful evocativeness of the location, and fortunately in the most distant shot used, dense mist just about sufficiently obscures, to less keen observers at least, the electronic scoreboard in the corner between the South Stand and West Stand.

Nevertheless the director had specifically looked for a "smoggy and grungy"-looking location and knew the West Stand at Elland Road to be one of the "...few period stadiums that resembled the old Wembley". While the association with a BAFTA award-winning film is to be welcomed, the fact that the stand built in 1957 so closely resembled a construction from over 30 years prior to that, is something the powers that be at Elland Road may want to hurriedly gloss over.

A somewhat less successful movie, *The Penalty King*, also included some scenes shot at Elland Road. The 2006 film was billed as a black comedy and was a lesser cinematic experience that some critics might categorise as 'straight-to-video'. The story features a Leeds United-supporting blind footballer dreaming of making a comeback with a Sunday League team. A low budget film that few remember, it did have some redeeming features, notably some archive footage of Leeds United in action, some shots filmed at Elland Road, albeit largely outside around the Billy Bremner statue, a starring appearance from former Altered Images singer Claire Grogan and a cameo appearance from one Peter Lorimer.

KOP

Not the biggest and not the most recognisable, but feared and revered as one of the most menacing and formidable 'ends' in the country; that beast of acerbic wit, venomous hate, surging mayhem and stirring passions. The stand behind the goal on the northern boundary of Elland Road football ground has been known by a number of different names over the years: the Gelderd End, the North Stand, the North End, the Don Revie Stand or the Spion Kop. Some endure the test of time, others barely catch on, but the one that truly resonates after all these years is simply 'The Kop'.

It is the stand that, for many, distinctively characterises the reputation of Elland Road, mainly through its notoriety in the bad-tempered 1970s and 1980s, yet now and for several decades prior to 1968 it was 'just another stand'.

There is no definitive record as to when the original Kop was built; several sources refer only to the 1920s.

The original Gelderd End and its famously shallow rake, days before it was bulldozed and excavated in preparation for the construction of the new Kop in May 1968.

What is known is that as early as 1904 the ground consisted of cinder-banking on three sides, one of which, the 'north' side, also included a temporary stand originally erected by Holbeck Rugby Club, which was soon demolished when Leeds City took over the ground.

At that time the club was still dogged by frequent flooding and the atrocious, quagmire conditions that resulted hindered the team's progress as they experimented with moving the pitch orientation more than once. Shortly after achieving promotion in 1924, possibly guided by the building of Lowfields Road itself as a major thoroughfare in 1923, the club finally decided on a north/south orientation. With the first

West Stand by now in place, the club then disposed of the temporary barriers on the north and east sides of the ground, allowing them to finally develop the cinder banking into permanent stands: the original Kop and Lowfields terraces.

JP Pullans, the well-known Leeds building firm based on Sunnyview Gardens on the top of Beeston Hill overlooking Elland Road, were founded by Joseph Pullan, who had two sons, Ernest and Arthur, and the company was responsible for most of the housing construction on the streets of South Leeds. One employee of the building company was a lorry driver called Arthur Hopkinson who worked for Pullans in the early 1900s and was singularly instrumental, over a period of time, in building up the banking on the north side of Elland Road into which the terracing was eventually formed. Ross Pullan is the great-grandson of Ernest, and Ross takes up the story: "He started off with a horse and cart and ended up with a wagon. But Arthur remembered very well tipping any substantial waste that we got, brick waste and other stuff, to form what eventually became the Kop." The same somewhat rudimentary process was responsible for gradually building up the adjacent Lowfields banking and forming a terrace. It is believed that in the Leeds City era both the Kop and the

Building work continues as the sheer scale of the excavation in the north east corner is clearly visible.

Lowfields started as smaller mounds of dumped colliery waste unloaded onto the then empty land from nearby mines as they closed. Pullans later added to this with their own building waste and according to Ross's father, Neil Pullan, this process was undertaken, clearly with the club's blessing, over a period of about 20 years, roughly between the pre-war and post-war years, ie. mid-1920s to mid-1940s.

It transpires that Pullans had keys to the gates at Elland Road and were at liberty to dump waste as and when they chose to. Ross adds that "we stored a lot of building materials and stuff under the West Stand", so the company had a good relationship with Leeds United, and it was a relationship that was about to get much stronger when Ernest Pullan became the Leeds United chairman between 1937 and 1948. Ross explains: "He didn't go down there to get involved in Leeds United, he went to sort out the cricket ground over the road (Holbeck Cricket Ground on Lowfields Road where some building work was required) but Leeds United asked if he would get involved in them, and I think he just did his best to keep the club together during the war years basically."

This appears something of an understatement, and Ernest Pullan's stewardship during World War II was critical in the club still existing after it, as he steered Leeds United through a difficult period including relegation in the 1946/47 season. Therefore, nobody was likely to bat an eyelid at his family business

dumping waste materials with a view to making Elland Road a more imposing arena, which is gradually what happened. How games were safely staged whilst this work continued also offers an indication as to how high health and safety was on the agenda at the time.

"We did all sorts of work at the ground," Ross continues, "such as changing exit gates, etc. We had a joiners shop in the yard up the road, so we could make anything that needed making." One more significant aspect of improving the ground was beyond the powers of Pullans, however. Shortly after the war, and whilst Ernest Pullan was still chairman of the club, it was agreed that the ground needed some "sprucing up". The plan was to finally concrete the Spion Kop terracing to add some permanency to the structure, but these plans had to be postponed as the club were refused a licence by the Ministry of Works. With war-time rationing still enforced and several other austerity measures in place it was felt the works could not be approved as they were not seen as essential. It would be a number of years before the concreting would actually take place.

The original Spion Kop was completed to its eventual size and 17,000 capacity by the mid-1940s and was named after the famous hill from the Boer War in South Africa, where 322 British soldiers died in the Battle of Spion Kop; many other 'popular' ends in the country were similarly named at the time. Indeed, Elland Road's own Spion Kop was also referred to as "Heartbreak

Looking towards the BRS buildings and Fullerton Park, building work on the Kop starts in the summer of 1968, with the lower half built on the remaining mounds of waste from the previous Gelderd End.

Casual observers on bikes watch yards away from a major construction site. Note the temporary floodlight in the north east corner; these were eventually moved outside the ground when the twin corner stands were built, before being replaced permanently in 1973.

Hill" by its plentiful staunch foot soldiers during times of meagre pickings, which was the vast majority of its existence. The Elland Road version was a huge mound shaped into a rudimentary open terrace with a very gradual rise to it which meant the east side was slightly higher than the west. There was no roof and definitely no facilities. There were no steps leading up to the top of the terrace from behind, just a sheer mud bank, and access to the stand was via gates in the north west corner or, prior to a fence being fitted to separate the two stands, from the Lowfields Road terrace. Photos show the original Kop to have been stepped at a much shallower angle than the current stand; a further obstacle, in addition to the cramped capacity, to anyone of a shorter stature seeing much of the game.

In the post-war years the gates used to open from 12.30pm for a 3.00pm kick-off and it was common for fans to arrive up to two and a half hours before kick-off to grab their spot on the open terrace. But incongruously, despite having the freedom to watch the game from anywhere, fans were fiercely loyal and protective of their chosen spots. Younger fans in particular would arrive early to 'bag a spot', and for those even younger fans who were diverted to the Boys' Pen it was routine for adults to leave their children at a certain turnstile for a solo expedition to navigate the crowds and find their spot in the segregated pen, whilst the adult stood elsewhere, ideally but not necessarily, within eyeshot.

Open terraces of course were commonplace in most grounds right until the mass-construction brought about by the Taylor Report in 1989. Roofed stands were

something of a luxury and fans would gladly pay more for the privilege of being safe from the elements. No such luck for Leeds United's success-starved fans, or at least those who preferred to stand on the Kop, until 1968, when both a roofed terrace and trophies arrived together, like buses.

Prior to that, following a deluge it was not uncommon to see steam rising from the massed body of tightly-packed fans, equally saturated and swaying together on the overcrowded terraces, revelling in the black humour of communal discomfort. My Dad, Alan Howe, remembers a friend of his called Bob Marsh who decided to don a rather stylish new, blue trench coat to a midweek game against Walsall in March 1963. It rained solidly throughout the 90 minutes and as they finally escaped the sodden throng to walk home, Bob discovered his brand-spanking-new raincoat had shrunk several sizes. The cuffs were halfway up his arms and the back of his neck was indelibly marked with a disfiguring blue dye. Still, Leeds won 3-0 so all was not lost.

A Leeds fan from as far back as the early 1960s, Kevin Mulligan, also remembers the atrocious conditions fans were made to endure without a second thought: "There was one match at Elland Road one rain-drenched afternoon, it must have been the depths of winter as I remember it ending in the dark with the floodlights on. I was one of a handful of the few last faithful/stupid kids stood in a deserted Boys' Pen on the old Spion Kop. Leeds were getting hammered I think 4-1. It was absolutely belting down cats and dogs to the point I was so wet through my clothes couldn't have got any wetter. When the final whistle blew, I scampered my way to the New Peacock pub to meet my Dad and co. I was already disorientated as I had seen my beloved Leeds get trounced (something that hardly ever happened in those days, especially at home). When my Dad saw me, his first greeting was a clip round my ear for being so stupid to stand out in the rain for 90 minutes and get so soaked. He was under cover in the Paddocked West Stand, I was on an uncovered Kop in the Boys' Pen. He said he picked me out in the ground (not hard because there were only about six of us daft enough to stay and watch in the monsoon). I said 'where could I have gone?' to which my other ear was clipped; happy days!"

Former general manager of Leeds United Alan Roberts also stood on the original open Kop as a youngster. He recalls: "You used to get a lot of characters on the Kop, a lot of people making witty comments about players, referees, fellow supporters, etc. – but with an element of joviality and comradeship. It was like everyone was banded together, particularly on days when it was teeming down with rain – and the team was also not that good in those days. They were what you call the 'real' supporters."

Ray Fell also stood on the Kop from the late 1940s and remembers fans regularly climbing over the wall to gain entrance illegally, which was not too difficult in those days: "There was only one way in and one way out, there was a gate at the end of the West Stand in the corner. At the end of the game you only had to lift your feet up and you would be carried out by the masses. But there was only one entrance and one set of turnstiles for the whole stand. It was difficult if you came in late, and I remember people just climbing up the mud bank from the bottom to get up the terrace. At half time my Dad used to go up to the top of the stand where it sloped off down the back and he would say to my sister 'you can come with us but don't look', because that's where all the lads used to go to the toilet, down the back of the mud bank." As if transported into a brave new world toilet facilities did eventually arrive, although anybody complaining about the 'Gents' at Elland Road today might be interested to know that regular crowds of over 40,000 in the 1950s and '60s had to battle towards primitive corrugated iron sheds with a simple trough running through. And I've yet to meet anybody who actually recalls there being a 'Ladies' toilet at all. Just think about that for a minute.

Gary Edwards escapes the suffocating pack of the Kop in its seething, swaying heyday of the 1970s.

A sea of scarves and flags in the Kop hails Don Revie's champions in May 1974.

Long before restrictive health and safety regulations dictated safe capacities, the Kop itself held up to approximately 17,000 fans before it bent round and continued in the same shape along the Lowfields terrace, with just a fence at the far edge of the Kop to distinguish one stand from the other. To put that into context, that's a bigger capacity in a standing terrace behind one goal than now occupies the entire two tiers of the East Stand, which runs along the length of the pitch. In actual fact, at the time that it was demolished a Leeds United director let slip that they had entertained up to 19,000 on the Kop on more than one occasion. An aerial view of the original terrace shows how much land was made available when the new Kop was constructed in 1968, as Don Revie's team built on their initial success and the club made the brave move to push forward with an extensive re-modelling of the ground. The northern boundary of the ground was still the same, yet 60 feet/18 metres of spare land was created when the huge mounded terrace was stripped away in less than two weeks, and the pitch was moved nine metres northwards on two occasions. Ray Fell remembers: "Lorries were coming constantly moving the earth and I think they put it all in the quarry off Elland Road."

Certainly the original Kop had a much bigger footprint than the modern stand that replaced it in May 1968 despite them both having a 17,000 capacity, albeit officials somewhat worryingly claimed the new Kop was effectively 'full' when holding 14,000. Costing

£250,000 and constructed in just six weeks, the new Kop was the first ground improvement of the Revie era. As it was designed by Leeds-based architects Gillinson, Barnett & Partners, who also designed the city's famous Merrion Centre, Leeds fans can consider themselves fortunate that the new Kop did not resemble the universally despised 1970s relic of a shopping centre and further embellish Elland Road's already austere and solemn landscape with additional concrete decoration.

By the summer of 1968 the club's long-standing overdraft had been wiped away by European and domestic progression and the Kop was a monument to that new financial freedom. Leeds took on Liverpool in the last league game of the 1967/68 season with the Kop's capacity cut by 4,000 as the builders had already moved in. Eleven days later they played an Inter-Cities Fairs Cup Semi-Final against Dundee with no stand behind the north goal at all, and subsequently, the first game with the new stand in place was the first leg of the final against Ferencvaros, played in August of the following season.

Kevin Mulligan remembered thinking in 1968 that the new Kop was bringing Leeds United into a 'new age' and there can be no doubt that the construction was the first part of a significant change in Elland Road's physical appearance and natural aura. Kevin also recalls a hot summery evening in the close season of 1968 when, mid-construction, his dad decided to have a look at "what all the fuss was about" down at Elland Road.

The new stand was big news and tangible proof that Leeds United were finally moving up a gear. When the pair arrived at the ground it was almost deserted, with the construction workers having packed up for the day. Kevin recalls that "without anyone asking who we were, we walked straight into the building area and up on to the terraces of the Kop, which was only partially constructed. I remember my Dad holding on to me whilst I peered over the open-ended backdrop looking down on to the access road that is still there behind the stand. It seemed miles high back then, and looking back, the health and safety inspectors now would have a few things to say to such sightseers."

Between 1968 and 1994 the Kop forged itself a menacing notoriety as the more vocal fans transferred to the new stand from the old Scratching Shed, and Leeds' support took on new levels of fanaticism and, gradually, intimidation. Despite being far from the biggest 'end' in the country, something about the acoustics of the roof and the corner stands adjacent to it, in an unholy unity with the unerring venom and passion of its inhabitants, made the Kop a deeply uncomfortable backdrop for visitors to perform in front of. Fans also proclaimed the fact that the steeper angle to the stand meant that they could now see the match without straining for 90 minutes.

Among the many visual and structural changes that the construction brought upon the landscape, the new Kop would also see season tickets available for standing supporters for the first time, something that LUSC had argued long and hard about and were instrumental in bringing to fruition. It was a significant move in securing casual fans to a season-long commitment, an opportunity only previously available to 'them' in the West Stand; the perceived aristocracy of Elland Road.

Like most, Gary Edwards took a few years to graduate to being a Kop-ite, as he recalls: "It was around 1974 when I became a regular on the Gelderd End. My Dad had retired from watching the Whites and I was now free to roam among the elite on my own. The old Shed had been replaced with the brand new South Stand and there was a couple of month's transition period in which fans decided which end to watch their football from."

The new Kop was the backdrop to some of Revie's Leeds team's greatest performances, and a lasting legacy is the 'Champions' photo from 1974 with the first team squad bedecked in their individually named tracksuit tops saluting the Kop, which is a swarm of scarves and banners; a permanent reminder of the vibrant and colourful joy that Revie's team brought to Elland Road. In those halcyon days, the Kop had a reputation largely for unstinting support and fervent noise of a strictly positive nature. By the time of the 1973/74 season though, Revie's last as Leeds manager in which he guided his team to the league title, the general demographic of football supporters had changed. Tribalism and social discontent had manifested itself in a sinister movement of violence and aggression towards the opposition, where previously there had

More progress as the recognisable shape of the new Kop emerges.

Leeds United
Association Football Club Limited
INCORPORATED 1920

GROUND AND REGISTERED OFFICE
ELLAND ROAD · LEEDS LS11 0ES
TELEPHONE: 716037/9 LEEDS. TELEGRAMS: FOOTBALL LEEDS

WARNING

Unfortunately due to a small minority amongst you we are compelled to take the following action in an effort to stop objects from being thrown at matches.

Should any object whatsoever be found on the pitch at a match we shall automatically close the Kop for the following game. *NO PERSON WILL BE ADMITTED TO THIS SECTION OF THE GROUND.*

If the lesson has not been learned from this occasion then in the event of a repeat the Kop will be closed for the following *TWO* games and so on until normality is restored.

This action is found regrettable but necessary.

THE FUTURE OF THE KOP IS NOW IN YOUR HANDS.

By Order of the Board of Directors

Keith Archer
Secretary.

PRESIDENT: THE RIGHT HONOURABLE THE EARL OF HAREWOOD, LL.D.
Directors: MANNY CUSSINS, (CHAIRMAN), RAYNER BARKER, M.C.I.T., M.B.I.M., JACK MARJASON

The leaflet handed out to all fans and printed in the programme for the visit of Norwich in March 1979 following various incidents of crowd trouble and missiles being thrown from the Kop.

mainly been harmless sporting cut and thrust. At Elland Road it was largely a case of away fans trying to infiltrate the Kop, as it had now become the sole domain of Leeds' more vocal and openly passionate fans. This gradual movement of the hardcore Leeds support from the Scratching Shed had been ongoing since the Kop's construction five years earlier and it was undoubtedly now the place for them to do their worst in defending the name of Leeds United off the pitch.

At the same time, conscious of the prevailing shift in moods, the club promoted an initiative in the match day programme called 'Good Conduct Badges'. In the Wolves programme from 5th September 1973 a delightfully innocent and trusting feature titled simply 'Hooliganism' read as follows: "It's the word no one in football – and particularly Leeds United – wants to hear. Fortunately we are not severely troubled by crowd unrest at Elland Road...at least from our own supporters. But Leeds United abhor any acts, however small, of violence, wanton destruction or mob behaviour....we want the Leeds United fan to be able to hold his head up high...so we're introducing something

new in the field of club/supporter relationships. We are issuing 20,000 Good Conduct Badges to the fans who form the bulk of our behind-the-goals crowds. The wearing of a Leeds United Good Conduct Badge will stamp you out as a fan with a difference...an unpaid club official...a crowd control watchdog. The badge will be instantly recognisable as the sign of true support. The wearer will be expected to act as a crowd diplomat, a troubleshooting, highly responsible member of our supporting public. Leeds United feel this is a tangible way in which to tackle the current problem of crowd unrest – although we stress that we do not consider we have a serious problem at Elland Road."

Paris 1975 was the trigger for a marked decline in both the team's fortunes and the supporters' reputation. But amid the turbulence still there were rousing occasions. Many cite the Fifth Round FA Cup tie with Manchester City in February 1977 as an awe-inspiring tribute to the new Kop's wondrous and inspiring capacity. A late Trevor Cherry goal in front of 47,731 fans settled a classic end-to-end cup tie. The goal was heralded by the Kop's stirring eulogy to their fallen heroes who appeared to be achieving greatness again. Almost every fan in the stand held their scarf aloft and sang 'You'll Never Walk Alone' in a rousing defiance that made the hairs stand up and could be heard across the Pennines.

The *Daily Mirror* saw fit to reference the rapturous and impromptu display of heartfelt unity, with Derek Wallis writing: "...Elland Road has known some spectacular moments in the last decade but none I swear to match the colour and carnival of the last two minutes of this blood-and-thunder Cup-tie. Behind Joe Corrigan, Manchester City's goalkeeper, every scarf, every flag, every voice was raised in salute to Leeds. Nowhere, at home or abroad, have I seen such a memorable picture painted by a football crowd......it even put the Kop at Liverpool to shame."

On-pitch fortunes were nose-diving, but the seething Kop remained a swaying, animated and stimulating place to be in the mid- to late 1970s. Gary Edwards remembers the strange sense of joy and happiness to be found in losing all control of your whereabouts on a dangerously packed terrace: "It was in the Gelderd that I first witnessed being literally lifted from the floor as the crowd swayed forward. It was frightening yet strangely exhilarating not being in charge of where your body was being taken by the massive collection of people." At other times, the discomfort felt didn't just extend to being crushed, and highlights again how archaic the belief was that thousands of fans could just be herded together in a pen and left to fend for themselves, as Gary continues: "I also witnessed my first 'damp leg' in the confines of the Kop; the place would be so full that at half-time many people decided against going down to the toilet and instead just did it there and then. But people were so close together that it was only when the dreaded warm feeling seeped through your jeans that you knew

Having drawn the short straw an intrepid ball boy retrieves a stray ball from the building site of the new Kop during the Inter-Cities Fairs Cup Semi-Final versus Dundee in May 1968.

someone very close to you had done the deed. The thing was that you were crammed so close together, it was almost impossible to spot the culprit." Such was life.

As the late 1970s progressed so the Kop's reputation degenerated from rousing to acidic. Similarly, the regard in which the club's officials held its more vocal fans very quickly descended from staunch support, through withering tolerance to frequent and very public outbursts of despair, forewarning, admonishment and ultimately punishment.

While Manchester City goalkeeper Joe Corrigan had felt the breath of the Kop's thundering support on the back of his neck in 1977, a year later in 1978 a fan escaped from the Kop, confronted and struck that same player. Corrigan chased after the offender and rugby-tackled him, this sparking a pitch invasion which brought a temporary halt to a heated FA Cup tie. With Leeds losing 2-0 at the time, it was felt the fans were attempting to get the match postponed; after mounted police quelled the frustrated masses and herded them back into the Kop, that attempt failed. The club was subsequently banned from staging FA Cup games at home for three years, although this was later reduced and only actually affected one game, which was played 'away' at West Bromwich Albion in February 1979.

On top of the punishment, which the club accepted, space in the match day programme was put aside to appeal to the good natured fans amongst the Leeds crowd, but tellingly in an abrupt change in attitude from the message in 1973/74, when life was rosy, the club was now wanting to 'out' its own fans. 'It's Up To You' was the banner message below Jimmy Armfield's regular managerial column on page three. "Saturday

7th January 1978 was one of the blackest days in the history of Leeds United. The club in the past has had its share of ups and downs. Unless there is a dramatic improvement in the behaviour of some of our so-called supporters, the club may be banished to the lower divisions of the Football League, or as intimated by the secretary of the Football League, may eventually be banished from the League. Yes! THE SITUATION IS AS SERIOUS AS THAT.

"Once again, a mindless, childish minority have been responsible for crowd troubles of which you need no further reminder in this appeal. Because of their actions they have placed the club in the position where any of the above punishments could be put into operation.

"SUPPORTERS OF THIS TYPE WE COULD WELL DO WITHOUT. WE DO NOT WISH TO BE ASSOCIATED WITH THEM. THEIR PRESENCE IS NOT NEEDED. Their thoughtless actions may have resulted in permanent injury or even worse, loss of life to many innocent people. This type of person takes great delight in hiding amongst mass numbers, and no doubt are also the leaders of the obscene chanting which now reverberates around the ground.

"DO NOT TRY TO HIDE SUCH PERSONS."

The situation grew worse before it got better. Obscene chanting was now a given and conceded as almost impossible to control. A year later in March 1979, following various incidents of missile-throwing at opposing players and fighting amongst rival fans both inside and outside the ground, another stern message was posted in the programme for the Norwich City game. Manager Jimmy Adamson spoke of the club's threat to close the Kop for two matches and how it

could affect the team's good run in the league and pursuit of a European place. A leaflet was also handed out to fans entering the turnstiles.

Again, 12 months on, and the club finally enforced its punishment. The Kop was closed completely for two matches against Bolton Wanderers and Brighton & Hove Albion in 1980 following objects being thrown at Nottingham Forest players, including pieces of glass aimed at goalkeeper Peter Shilton. In the Bolton programme on 9th February 1980 a column headed 'Why the Kop is empty' read: "...this decision was taken because of the action of a mindless minority at the Nottingham Forest league game who threw items from the Kop onto the pitch...The club is determined to drive the small number of troublemakers away from Elland Road and make the ground a safe and trouble-free area for genuine supporters of all ages. In an effort to achieve this, the club is offering a £100 reward to anyone who can provide information that will lead to the arrest and conviction of any person throwing missiles."

No discernible improvement was seen in the general behaviour and the mood grew uglier as the club were relegated from the First Division, in the ultimate face-slap for anyone hoping for a positive upturn in the fans' general outlook. The Kop was closed again following missiles being thrown at Kevin Keegan, then of Newcastle United, in the first big game of Leeds' Second Division tenure in October 1982. In the affected games, against Queens Park Rangers and Shrewsbury Town, crowds dipped to 11,528 and 8,741 respectively.

For the first game after the incidents against Newcastle the club issued its most stark message yet. The front cover of the Charlton programme from November 1982 was dedicated to the club warning its fans that the "future of Leeds United Association Football Club hangs in the balance". The abrupt words were plain and simple, "in no way an exaggeration" and not "an idle threat". They talked of the "loathsome" actions of the "scab" element, which left the club's "very existence in jeopardy".

It seemed that the message finally got through, at least for the fans who attended home games at Elland Road. The atmosphere remained poisonous and tinged with hate and Leeds United's away following continued to run amok across the country for the remainder of the 1980s, creating enemies in every city and national headlines of outcry and dismay, but at Elland Road there were no further violent incidents of major significance. Indeed, the directors' attitude to the fans began to change also. In the summer of 1988 managing director Bill Fotherby worked with councillor John Trickett to refurbish the areas under the Kop for the fans, with artificial ceilings, seating in the bar areas and TV screens, all creating a more homely environment for the very fans that the rest of the world felt deserved nothing less than a ten-stretch. The

The new Kop nearing completion viewed from the Lowfields Road terrace; looking at the pitch markings it is clear to see how much space was created by the construction.

new facilities were officially opened by chairman Leslie Silver before the Manchester City game in September 1988, and the stand was renamed the 'Don Revie Kop', a first attempt at recognising the club's greatest ever manager, which in truth didn't stick.

Aside from incidents of racist chanting, which died out in the late 1980s, general behaviour improved. But it is true that many a visiting player visibly wilted in the face of the unforgiving taunting and incessant fervour of the Kop, and for sheer unrelenting hostility, few

stands shared the same reputation within the game. I personally recall Wimbledon striker John Fashanu enduring a torrid afternoon of unabated abuse in 1990. There was nothing race-related; it was purely triggered by the fact that his brother Justin had recently 'come out' in public as a homosexual. John had allegedly disowned his brother but nevertheless took the Kop's abuse with a generous good grace. When Fashanu hit the bar from fully 40 yards out with a spectacular effort in the second half, a rare and spontaneous moment of

mutual appreciation broke out. The Kop let its mask slip and applauded Fashanu with an unfamiliar concession to sportsmanship and humility and maybe even diversity, Fashanu waved back in return. It was like the end of a boxing match when two bloodied fighters finally drop their guard and embrace after being engaged in the ferocity of a 12-round bout.

Other past victims of the Kop's caustic witticisms in the 1970s, '80s and early '90s are too numerous to mention, with the Leeds fans' black book of ongoing

vendettas and pantomime villains reading like a who's who of British football. But take it as read that any player that left Leeds under a cloud, any player with a colourful reputation in the game, any player that has just 'got away with murder' from the referee, any player with longer than average hair and vaguely resembling the stereotypical image of a 'travelling' family member, and any opposing goalkeeper taking his position for the second half, will have received dog's abuse for their trouble. Alex Ferguson once called Elland Road "the most intimidating venue in Europe" and to be fair, he's seen a few.

At the height of the Kop's notoriety in the late 1970s and 1980s, the distinctive white exit blocks lined across the middle of the stand helped to break up the flowing surges of people at times of great excitement. From a distance you could marvel at the steady ripple of bodies that would flow forward as one and crash abruptly like waves against the white walls; fans with no cares in the world, high on the thrill of the exhausting human pinball machine they happily became part of every Saturday. The fence that ran vertically up the Kop steps to separate the stand into two sides, the 'right side' and the 'left side', performed a similar function. This created a healthy internal rivalry that was a staple part of Kop banter for many years, relating effectively to which was the more vocal side. A song referring to this rivalry is still sung at times today, with the barrier long gone and with younger fans somewhat perplexed as to the reference. Around the same time the Kop would reverberate to repetitive chants of 'Celtic' and 'Rangers' as fans butted against each other acclaiming the rivals in the Scottish Premier Division fiercely divided by politics and religion. You were either one or the other and you probably couldn't explain why.

Through those barren years on the pitch, most fans' enjoyment came from simply being part of a collective on the Kop, and the inherent wild abandon in which afternoons were passed. It was a treasured environment and Andy Peterson sums up many people's questionable cherishing of objects and features that elsewhere would draw curiosity to the point of sectioning, but in the context of an attachment to the Elland Road Kop seems perfectly understandable: "I'm sure there's something Freud would've had a field day with about forming a relationship with inanimate objects. OK, people regularly fall in love with cars, iPads, shoes, etc., but me? I'm still 'involved' with a 20 metre metal pole. The thing in question is the Kop's stanchion number 5, which throughout the first decade of my years at Elland Road not only fulfilled its purpose – keeping the roof over our heads – but was also a meeting place, surge protector and punch bag. Obviously, it was only the latter once."

Gary Edwards recalls one of the many characters from the late 1970s that used to single-handedly orchestrate the Kop into one of the most fearsome choirs in the country, the original 'King of the Kop': "A mate of mine for many years, Coller, was one of the early 'Kings of the Kop'. He used to divide the Kop into two halves whilst perched on a barrier. Poised like the conductor of a massive orchestra, he would signal to the 'Left Side' to begin a particular chant and then directed the 'Right Side' accordingly, who would wait patiently for their cue to join in. On occasion I would join Coller on the barrier and the sight of thousands of Leeds fans en masse hanging on your every instruction was unbelievable. My favourite of Coller's repertoire was when he would cup his hands round his mouth and shout, "Give us an ELLL! Give us an EEEE! Give us an EEEE! Give us a DEEE! Give us an ESSSS! The Kop would dote on his every word, joining in each time he asked them. It was pure magic."

Stephen Talbot also remembers Coller, real name Roy Coles, as a "big bloke who always tried to start the songs", but as he continues, "you had lots of people trying to get in on the act then, standing on the bars singing 'we are the right side, we are the left side' and then you'd get people singing 'we're from Bramley' or 'we're from Armley' or Seacroft or wherever, and you'd all start singing your own areas where you lived, everyone was just messing about pretending to be fighting and what not." This was as much a knock-on from the famously tribal Leeds following of the early 1970s when hooliganism was growing and Leeds fans would rarely stick together in any numbers. Though this seldom progressed beyond jocular jousting to serious violence at Elland Road, it created problems away from home due to a simple lack of numbers, as Stephen Talbot continues: "In the '70s especially they used to fight each other, from Harehills, from Seacroft, from Farnley and Wortley and Burley and wherever, they never used to stick together, and it was only certain travel set-ups like the Pioneer and the Kippax, they used to stick together but it still wasn't a lot to go away with, and Leeds used to end up on the wrong end of the stick many a time in the late 1970s. It all changed in the 1980s, everyone stuck together and travelled together and Leeds took great numbers everywhere."

Two smaller white exit blocks stood on their own towards the back of the Kop in each top corner until the seats were installed in 1994. These exits had towers of steps that circled downwards like a spiral staircase, with no rooms off them, to where the steps are now that lead up to the two Kop bars. That said, if you descended the stairs at the end of a match your feet would barely touch the floor, and you could quite easily traverse the winding steps all the way to the bottom expending no energy whatsoever, purely through the power of crowd force. Andy Peterson has fond memories of the steps at the back: "One of the sadder consequences of the Kop being made all-seater, probably only in my opinion, was the loss of the stairways that led directly to the back of the stand. Discovering them was something of a rite of passage that began with migrating from the Boys' Pen – no crueller stand existed in British football in terms of peer banter – and the easy access they afforded to the lawless frontier areas of the terrace was as much of a thrill as a convenience. The sense of loss was palpable when they were bricked up in the name of progress, paving the way for an all-seater stand, customers not supporters, and a better match day experience. Probably."

Another odd idiosyncrasy of the stand were the police sentry posts at the very top of the terracing under the roof. These were raised platforms where police could stand and survey the crowd from a heightened vantage point. "All the police were at the top in their walkway with the little turrets," remembers Stephen Talbot, "and they would stand on there and watch the crowd. I don't know how many times I got copped for swearing and they'd put you at the back and make you face the wall, it was like being at school. They took the young'uns because they could handle the young'uns, the big'uns they never bothered with." In later years when these were less-often used, the sentry posts became areas of prominence and prestige for fans and were highly sought after from 1.30pm onwards, particularly for younger fans fuelled by the excitement of making their faces known in the Kop. They also afforded a much better view of the pitch from their slightly elevated position.

Post-Hillsborough, the Kop saw its capacity reduced by the Taylor Report (capping standing capacity at just 7,866 from the previous 12,563, which in itself had already been reduced from the 17,000 it housed when first built in 1968) and immediately the atmosphere seemed to change. Nobody complained, as the unspeakable horror of the Hillsborough tragedy struck a chord with every football fan who had found themselves in similar situations. What seemed like endless fun on carefree afternoons suddenly held a chilling resonance that was too close to home. The subdued ambience and the extra space and comfort afforded by the reduced capacity popped the fizzing, youthful insouciance like a balloon overnight and the Kop, as we knew it, was gone forever.

With capacity duly reduced, the Kop was made an all-ticket stand during the 1989/90 season, as there were already 7,000 season ticket holders for it. Therefore, to prevent the lottery of thousands turning up en masse on a Saturday and not getting one of the 866 spaces left available, during a season of unprecedented demand, the club put these on sale during the week instead.

In the summer of 1994, after a final game on 3rd May, a 2-2 draw with Sheffield Wednesday, the closing act came when 7,000 seats were installed to make the Kop an all-seater stand. The game was billed as the 'Kop's Last Stand' and with a brass band accompaniment, a choir sang songs before kick-off and fans were handed souvenir song sheets so they could join in. In addition to the obvious Leeds United songs, the ensemble gave renditions of 'Ilkley Moor', 'Bless 'Em

All', 'We'll Meet Again', 'Auld Lang Syne' and 'Abide with Me'. Perhaps the most cherished moment was the appearance of the great John Charles, who ironically had never played before the modern Kop, singing a rousing version of his favourite '16 Tons', with the printed song sheet advising the crowd to repeat the chorus "only once, for John's sake".

With seating installed, partly funded to the tune of £400,000 by the Football Trust, and remaining so at present, the white exit blocks and the long-distance visage of the stand remains the same, but little else. Even the outside of the stand was cladded in grey and blue circles at the same time, to match the East Stand. Almost immediately back in 1994 the club re-christened it the North Stand, but a couple of months later, in October 1994, it officially became the Don Revie Stand, a name which this time has prevailed. Previously, beneath the stand the facilities were sparse, particularly before the small upgrade in 1988. Originally there was very little but small tea bars with just an open void looking up to the underside of the terracing, but when the seats were put in the twin Kop Bars were built to form a first floor, and the image and status of the stand took on a whole new life, as Bill Fotherby recalls: "I took that Kop and made it like Briggate. Under the Kop, I did it all out, I put carpet on the top floor and a bar. That was amazing for the Kop, for them, the supporters. They couldn't believe what I did there."

The Kop has always been the preferred end for Leeds to kick towards in the second half of games, and has generally been believed to act as a '12th Man', as the crowd always grows more animated and engaged in the proceedings when Leeds attack that end. Gradually, however, the atmosphere in the Kop degenerated as on-pitch fortunes flattered to deceive in the new Millennium, and fans hen-pecked by stewards, perhaps coupled with a changing demographic, largely struggled to raise the emotion to be vocal, and the title of the more vociferous end gravitated back to the South. Now, with fortunes raised again, it is a close call between the two ends. Its impact may be greatly reduced, but you suspect the Kop will forever be the 'popular' stand, and so it should be.

If you look at the Kop today from another stand or at pitch level, it barely resembles the throbbing, undulating, venomous snake pit of hate it once was. It looks half as big and tame in comparison, watered down by seats, steps and conspicuous stewarding. Maybe the swaying, surging mass of fans is gone, but the Kop at Elland Road remains one of the most iconic stands in English football and in full voice and aided by the acoustics within the stadium, can produce a shuddering and volcanic thunder from which many opponents have failed to recover. Advantage Leeds.

THE ONLY PLACE FOR US

LEEDS CITY

It is negligent to document the history of Elland Road without detailing the formation of Leeds City and indeed the cementing of interest in association football in the city of Leeds. Without this who knows what would be happening on Elland Road today? The 13th February 1905 edition of the *Leeds Mercury* printed an unobtrusive but hugely significant advert in its pages, for a 'Manager' of Leeds City Football Club. Such was the gathering pace of enthusiasm for professional association football in the city of Leeds and for finally building up an established club at Elland Road, that the formation of a management structure was considered the next step in delivering what the city so conspicuously lacked.

Two weeks later the *Mercury* printed an update on the situation, reporting that "...With regard to the position of manager, over a hundred applications have been received. These are at present in the hands of the sub-committee for consideration. It is recognised that it is essential that a man fully conversant with football, as well as the management of players, shall be engaged, and no efforts will be spared to obtain the best available applicant."

The words "fully conversant with football" offer a veritable ocean of ex-Leeds manager gags, but back in simpler times the serious nature of proceedings was now undeniable; Leeds City meant business. As the biggest city in England without a professional association football club the formation and promotion of Leeds City had become imperative to local businessmen, as the wave of interest in the 'dribbling code' took over the West Riding.

Prior to the turn of the 20th century the situation was much different. Rugby and cricket were the two sports of choice and association football was considered a 'soft southerners' sport. The wind of change began in 1895 when rugby was split into two codes by the formation of the Northern Union, an initiative by the Yorkshire and Lancashire rugby clubs to create their own league and adopt the first rules of what became rugby league. While it was still popular in Leeds, the fragmentation of the rugby world reignited local interest in association football, and by 1897 the already formed Hunslet FC were among the leading local clubs that formed the Yorkshire League. Hunslet went from strength to strength and were hell bent on becoming Leeds' first professional association football club.

By the turn of the century two of the most prominent local rugby league clubs were in dire financial positions. Manningham of Bradford and Holbeck of Leeds recognised the growing force of association football and both began ground-sharing partnerships to bring in much-needed cash. Soon enough Manningham decided to suspend their rugby team and formed Bradford City Football Club in 1903. Bradford City applied for and were elected to Football League status without playing

IMPROVING THE LEEDS CITY FOOTBALL GROUND

The work of extending and improving the Elland-road football ground, the home of the Leeds City club, for next season is already in progress, and on Wednesday the directors of the club witnessed the felling of a large chimney on the newly-acquired piece of land. The above snapshot shows the chimney in the act of falling, the 35 yards of heavy brickwork coming to the ground in almost one piece.
(Special "Mercury" Photos.)

A Leeds Mercury report from 1906 details ongoing work to develop Elland Road from a former mining site to the shell of a professional sports ground.

a single game, such was the game's hunger for growth in the untapped area of West Yorkshire. In Leeds this move was eyed with envy and consternation and, beaten to the post, moves were now afoot to ensure a professional club existed in Leeds without further delay.

In May 1904 Holbeck Rugby Club lost their play-off game with St Helens and stung by the financial implications of this devastating defeat Holbeck disbanded and their Elland Road ground was put on the market. At the time the ground stood with a pitch running east to west and a stand that the rugby club had built along the south touchline in 1897 when they first moved in, with a 'temporary' small wooden terraced stand on the north touchline.

Two years earlier Hunslet Football Club, eager for growth amid a nomadic existence, had lost the lease on their final home, the Nelson Ground, and unable to find an alternative in time they faced no option but to disband. The club's supporters and officials remained convinced that Leeds could sustain a Football League club, and further triggered by Bradford's election they made concerted efforts to force the issue.

The demise of Holbeck Rugby Club and the sudden availability of their Elland Road ground was just the opportunity that supporters of the football code in Leeds had been waiting for. On 30th August 1904 in a meeting at the Griffin Hotel in Boar Lane, the Leeds City Association Football Club was formed from the ashes of the disbanded Hunslet FC. Officials of the new club signed a lease on Elland Road, initially on 13th October 1904, for an annual rent of £75 with an option to buy for £5,000. This was finally reduced in November to £4,500, at which point Leeds City bought the freehold to the land.

Finally there were grounds for a football club in Leeds to challenge for election to the Football League. The game's governing body was extremely receptive to this, but the infrastructure of the organisation had to be sound and Leeds City were slow in creating the 'articles of association' and the club prospectus required to gain the necessary share capital from the Leeds public.

Nevertheless, a group of players was hastily assembled and the club joined the re-formed West Yorkshire League, despite holding much loftier ambitions. Their first competitive game was a 2-2 draw away at Morley's Scatcherd Lane ground on 1st September, a ground that is still in use today by Morley Rugby Club. The match was supposed to be a home game for Leeds City, but at the time they were waiting for Elland Road to be 'brought up to scratch'. They then played another 'home' game at the Wellington Ground, Low Road in Hunslet.

Two days after signing the lease Leeds City played their first game at Elland Road on 15th October 1904, a 2-0 friendly defeat to Hull City before 3,000 people. Whilst Leeds City were members of the West Yorkshire League they paid little attention to it, and preferred

Minutes of Meeting- 1919

Public Meeting held in Salem Central Hall Hunslet Lane, Leeds, Friday Oct: 17ʰ 1919.

By a unanimous vote, Mr Alf Masser was elected to take charge of the meeting.

It was proposed by Mr Smart, seconded by Mr Leggott that a Professional Football Club be formed in Leeds immediately which was carried unanimously.

Proposed by Mr Leggott. seconded by Mr R E H Ramsden that a Limited Liability Company be floated carried unanimously.

The meeting appointed the following gentlemen to act, pro tem, as a Committee to formulate a scheme & place before the next meeting a report of the progress made.

Committee
Messrs. Alf Masser, Joe Henry Jnr M. Barker C. Morgan, Dick Ray Chas Snape & R. E. H. Ramsden

Signed,
Joseph Henry jnr
Oct 31ˢᵗ 1919

The minutes from the meeting held at Salem Chapel to form Leeds United on October 17th 1919.

instead to play high profile friendlies against established Football League clubs such as Sheffield United, Preston and Derby. Indeed they postponed several league games or fielded a weakened 11, when an invitation to play a friendly came up.

On 7th March 1905 Leeds finally appointed their first manager, a Scotsman named Gilbert Gillies. As a working journalist, he was assigned the position as much for his administrative skills as for his latent football knowledge. He was previously a key figure in saving Chesterfield from extinction as they won re-election and remained in the Second Division of the Football League.

Buoyed by the encouragement of the Football League and its plans to increase its membership, Leeds finally fought through the restrictions of officialdom and floated the club as a limited company in April 1905, bringing in share capital to the tune of £10,000. The club were able to elect their first board of directors and now all barriers to possible election to the Football League had been removed.

Leeds' West Yorkshire League record was unimpressive in 1904/05. They finished 11th, winning just seven games out of 24. It was clear their priorities lay elsewhere and despite moderate success on the pitch, the financial stability of the club and promising crowds of around 3,000 led to an underlying confidence of the club gaining Football League election, via an application long-delayed by red tape and bureaucracy. On

29th May 1905 it finally happened. Gaining an impressive 25 votes, Leeds City were elected to the newly expanded Second Division of the Football League along with Chelsea, Clapton Orient, Hull City and Stockport County. Leeds became the fifth professional football club in Yorkshire, behind Sheffield United, Sheffield Wednesday, Barnsley and Bradford City and the rugby stranglehold in the city was about to be broken.

Summer 1905 was spent improving the facilities at Elland Road, although there was an initial plan to transport fully a stand from the West Riding Ground at Meanwood Road. Instead, the club demolished the two rugby club-built stands on the north and south sides and built a grandstand on Elland Road, then running along the length of the touchline. They also added to the ash, colliery waste and timber terraces around the other three sides, enabling a potential capacity of around 22,000.

By 28th August further development had taken place, as the *Leeds Mercury* reported: "The ground is now presenting a better appearance, and great progress has been made during the past week with the construction of the grandstand. When the first home match, against West Bromwich Albion, is played, on September 9th, the alterations to the ground will practically be completed." In addition, player recruitment of wholesale proportions confirmed everything was ready for the coming season; Year Dot of professional football in Leeds.

What followed over the next 14 years is what truly defined football in the city of Leeds, and most importantly, what led to the birth of Leeds United. Under Gilbert Gillies Leeds City initially fared well, finishing an encouraging sixth in that first ever season. Sadly despite decent crowds averaging 20,000, helped by the building of the first West Stand in 1906, the financial side of the club was always a problem and impacted severely on building a squad capable of challenging for top flight football. On two occasions the club was re-floated in an attempt to create new share capital, but responses were insubstantial.

In addition, the state of the Elland Road pitch and its surrounding banked stands continuously threatened the club's credibility, as many games ending up with fans engaging in 'mud-larking', with the referee and opposing players often the hapless victims. Several top-heavy results were seen at Elland Road as teams routinely failed to adjust to the conditions, and this was often Leeds City. The building of the West Stand enabled Leeds to experiment with moving the pitch orientation, but this barely improved the pitch condition.

Despite a promising start to life as the only Football League club in the area, Leeds City never capitalised on it. The club's second manager, Frank Scott-Walford, fared even worse, flirting with re-election on a number of occasions, the last of which in 1911/12 led to his resignation and the very real threat of a reluctant

expulsion from the league. Leeds City also fell into the hands of the receivers at this time, and there was even an unwelcome offer from the Leeds Cricket, Football and Athletic Club to take over City's affairs and move 'soccer' to Headingley.

Following a successful vote by other clubs in favour of Leeds City retaining league status at the end of the 1911/12 season, fortunes brightened somewhat, and Herbert Chapman was appointed as the club's third manager. He added an element of stability and even went about improving the image of the ground, investing in a new flag to fly from the masthead erected outside the, still new, West Stand. Despite Chapman steadying the ship in his early years, World War I intervened and the Football League programme was suspended.

During the war football was very much secondary. With many players and supporters joining the war effort, football only existed at all as a welcome means of distraction. Leeds City played in hastily arranged, regional friendly tournaments for four years and, like many other clubs, used 'guest' players who played for clubs based on the proximity of their war 'station'. It was this practice that was to be Leeds City's downfall.

Manager Herbert Chapman had been running a munitions factory in Leeds during the hostilities and returned to the club full-time in early 1918. In his absence there had been managerial issues festering behind the scenes as players and staff had become disgruntled with the running of the club. The re-negotiation of contracts after the war became a messy business as certain staff believed they should have been offered more as a reward for keeping the club alive during the war. One player, Charlie Copeland, was unhappy with the contract offered to him and was promptly sold to Coventry. His parting shot was a threat to divulge details to the FA of the 'excessive' payments Leeds City had made to guest players during the war.

Leeds called his bluff and carried on preparations for the first season back in professional football, and indeed played eight games of the 1919/20 season before they learned that Copeland had carried out his threat, and the FA had set up a commission to investigate the claims. Leeds never submitted their books to the commission and their 'silence' was deemed an admission of guilt. Despite strong rumours that most clubs carried out the same practice during the war, Leeds were made an example of and immediately expelled from the league.

On 17th October 1919 at Leeds Metropole Hotel, in a "melancholy spectacle", the entire first team squad, kit, nets, boots, goal posts and physio equipment was auctioned off in a humiliating exercise that raised £10,150. On the very same day a meeting at Salem Hall in Hunslet was attended by 1,000 dismayed Leeds City fans. In the meeting chairman Alf Masser passed an overwhelming motion to form a new club immediately. The name Leeds Trinity was discussed but the name

Leeds United was finally agreed, and ownership of Elland Road would eventually pass to the new club following the intervention of Huddersfield Town chairman Hilton Crowther.

Leeds City were a club of limited success, dogged by mismanagement and bad fortune, and have no recognised legacy in terms of achievement, other than the formation of Leeds United and, as a result, the continuation of association football at Elland Road. From this point on the life of Elland Road as a football stadium that we recognise and value, truly began.

LEEDS CITY COUNCIL

As with any football club in a major city there exists out of necessity a long-standing relationship between Leeds United and Leeds City Council. This particular relationship is unlikely to be unique in the ups and downs that have been experienced over the years, particularly given the impact that a club the size of Leeds United can have on the community and the very infrastructure of the city.

The club's links with the council can be seen in various areas of their activities. For many years Leeds United have won awards for their excellent partnership with 'Education Leeds' in working on community projects with local children. Numerous planning applications are submitted each season relating to licensing extensions and minor building developments. Finally, the council currently owns all the public car parks dotted around Elland Road including those on Fullerton Park and therefore, obligingly, there is dialogue and a relationship of sorts.

Council influence on Elland Road itself was evident as far back as the 1930s when the area was clearly designated as a dedicated sporting sector of the city, given the greyhound, speedway, football and cricket stadia that briefly operated concurrently within a quarter of a mile of each other. As Leeds United's crowds grew in size so in turn the council was largely co-operative in allowing the club to develop their stadium and transform the surrounding area, fortunately, and most significantly, in line with the development of the motorway network and the council's own plans.

However, it was in September 1985 that the most notable council intervention took place when the local authority actually purchased Elland Road from Leeds United for £2.5 million to help ease the club's dire financial troubles, and immediately leased it back to the club. Then chairman Leslie Silver addressed an extraordinary general meeting of the club's shareholders on Friday 13th September 1985, held in the 100 Club, in order to seek agreement on the proposed sale of the freehold of the Elland Road stadium. The proposal was agreed and the official seal was described by the club as "an exciting new era for both the club and the community". Anybody who

watched Leeds United at Elland Road, at least for the next five years, might question the accuracy of that forecast, but nevertheless the landmark agreement did wipe out much of what the club owed to the bank in one swift transaction. The club was steeling itself for a £250,000 loss in the financial year and Leslie Silver claimed the deal was like a "kiss of life" and "released the club from an intolerable burden of debt".

At the time of the sale the club's overdraft with the bank stood at £1.5 million, and even meeting the interest payments on that sum was a continual drain on the limited resources of the club. The sale was on the basis that the administrative block of the ground (ie. underneath the West Stand) was leased to the club for 125 years, and the club was given a licence to use the pitch (including Fullerton Park) and the stands, again for 125 years. Under the agreement the council took over the substantial burden of ground maintenance, including insurance, rates and electricity. A short term tenancy agreement was also agreed for the club to use the Souvenir Shop on Elland Road and the Kop Shop in the north east corner.

The council took one share in the club as part of the deal, which carried 'special rights' including the addition of four directors to the club's board. Ownership of Elland Road passed to Leeds City Council on 1st November 1985 and four representatives were duly appointed to the board of directors, one of which was Eric Carlile, the Leeds United Supporters' Club secretary, as the council wanted supporters' representation on the board.

Interestingly, the council was already talking in 1985 of building a new East Stand to replace the Lowfields Road Stand, though it would take seven years and a substantial about turn in on-pitch fortunes, for this to happen. But the council were not slow in making plans. Opposition came from MPs who claimed the council had been simply aiming to catch the "popular vote" with the Elland Road purchase, but very soon the council had received submissions from over 100 organisations wanting to develop shops and leisure facilities on the surrounding land. Within weeks of the sale the council was talking of borrowing £20 million to create an international sporting complex. By 1987, 14 developers had submitted plans ranging from demolishing Elland Road itself and building a futuristic 'Astrodome' stadium in its place, to an extensive leisure complex incorporating cinemas, restaurants and an indoor/outdoor "water fun palace". In Beeston.

By April 1988 one such scheme proposed by the Baltic Consortium had received outline approval, which also included building a second tier on the Lowfields Road Stand and upping its capacity to 7,500. Needless to say the plans never went ahead, but the council didn't stop there. They also considered a plastic pitch for Elland Road to open it up for more municipal use, and even sent delegates to QPR and Luton Town to view

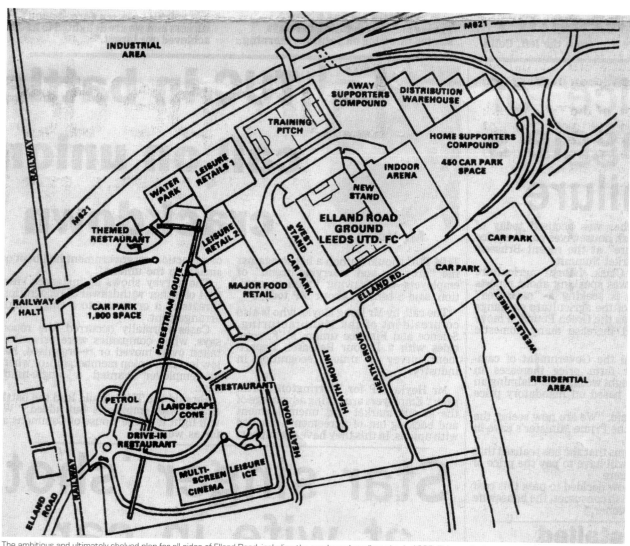

The ambitious and ultimately shelved plan for all sides of Elland Road, including the greyhound stadium site, in 1988. This reached planning stages and included a cinema, ice rink, railway station, water park, 'away supporters compound' and an indoor arena.

their versions of the much-derided feature of the game in the 1980s. A sample of artificial turf was flown over from Atlanta, USA, and laid out on Fullerton Park for a period of time.

Despite the relatively fluid, co-operative and trouble-free agreement over the sale of Elland Road, it was to be a sometimes fractured partnership with the council in terms of how, ideally, Leeds United wanted the stadium to be utilised. It is not by chance that the council's ownership of the ground coincided with rugby league, American Football, Jehovah's Witnesses, Gaelic football, cricket, boxing, U2 and the Happy Mondays all sharing residence with Leeds United for varying periods. It should be noted that the council did at least listen to the club's pleas, and most significantly those of Howard Wilkinson, with regards to the pitch and promptly withdrew Hunslet RL's tenancy agreement amid much acrimony and sanctioned a radical re-seeding programme in 1989.

Nevertheless, the partnership with the council will go down in history for many as the 1990 promotion and the 1992 title win were both achieved with the words 'Leeds City Council Welcomes You To Elland Road' emblazoned

boldly on the West Stand roof and above the tunnel in a disconcertingly coloured red banner; the unflattering backdrop to many images of a famous period.

The relationship by then was quite cosy, with chairman Leslie Silver enjoying an accommodating association at the top of the club. Howard Wilkinson remembers it the same: "The sooner we could get the ground back the better, but there was a price to pay for that because getting the ground back meant money being spent that we hadn't got. I personally thought the council were very good to Leeds United, I felt they took a very reasonable approach, and saw the club as a potentially huge advantage to the city. So I felt there were some enlightened people somewhere in the council who thought 'a good club and a good team is good for the city'. I know it's not the case in a lot of cities, but I always felt at Leeds there was a feeling of 'we need Leeds United to do well, and if we can help; terrific'. But in the proper way, not at the expense of the taxpayer."

As someone who perhaps was more involved on the ground floor level with the council, Bill Fotherby doesn't remember the relationship being quite so cordial: "Relations with the council, for me, and I had to deal

with the council, were not very good. Once they own it they dictate to you what you can do, you can't do what you want. Now I'm a builder, I want to do 'this', I want to do 'that'. I had problems. I built the Centreline Club (in 1987 in the West Stand) and in order to get to it I had to build outside, so I had a big glass tower made so you could go up and get in that way (the circular black tower that stood where the Radebe Entrance is now). I went ahead and I built this tower. They built a big hole in the West Stand car park and they put it in, and the chairman received a rollicking from the council for me doing this. I had to go in front of the council with the police and in the meeting they threatened to put me in prison for what I'd done without seeking the permission from the council. But they wouldn't go through with that and (after a few years' arguing) I had to take it down. Now I wasn't the easiest person to work with if anybody is dictating to me and telling me what to do, because I felt I was king of the castle at Leeds United. A year or so later the assistant manager, Mick Hennigan, came to me and said 'Mr Fotherby, we've got a bit of a problem.' I said 'why, what's your problem?' he said, 'Well coming up from the drains in the dressing room area is a terrible smell and Howard is complaining to me bitterly.' He said he'd tried everything. So we had a man who made himself a 'Mr Busy Busy' from the council who was in charge, on behalf of the council, for the Leeds United ground. We got on, but we didn't get on very well. We didn't care for each other. He was called in and they went with cameras down below the drains and they found that the foundations we'd done for this tower had pierced the main drain. Well, there was all hell let loose.....but we got over it. We got over it."

Bill dismisses what presumably was a messy ordeal for all parties with typical Fotherby bluster. By 1996 circumstances led to the club being sold to the Caspian Group, and Bill remembers the unsettling period in and around Elland Road when the ownership of the club was changing hands: "It's a shame but it's a fact, but if you get trouble upstairs it goes right through the club. There was the whole business of going public and who to sell to, and people falling out, arguments, and that was coupled with Leslie's very, very traumatic experience when he got burgled. The sense in his head (after that) was 'I've got enough problems without this'. He'd lost a bit of confidence. But fundamentally it was the unrest and lack of cohesion at the top that definitely has an effect; you've seen it at other places since. Things become in the public domain." The subsequent sale of the club to the Caspian Group enacted vast change around Elland Road, not least bringing Peter Ridsdale to the forefront of proceedings.

One of Caspian's first major acts upon purchasing Leeds United in 1996 was to negotiate the buy-back of Elland Road from the council, agreement of which was announced over a year later in December 1997, although the acquisition didn't go through until March

1998. At the time the Caspian Group announced that they had purchased a 50-acre site, at a cost of £11.3 million. It later transpired that this included the stadium site for £10 million and the Fullerton Park training pitches at a separate cost of £1.3 million, which by then had been vacated by the opening up of the Thorp Arch training complex. However, it is believed the club never actually bought back the Fullerton Park land and that remained in the ownership of the council, as it does today. The plan, again, was to build an ambitious sports, concert and exhibition arena on this area, and a 200-bedroom hotel, all adjoined to a redeveloped West Stand with 32 new executive boxes. At the same time Caspian changed their trading name to Leeds Sporting PLC to reflect the fact that they intended to introduce ice hockey and basketball teams to the Elland Road landscape and make the area a multi-sports leisure hub, just as it had been in the 1930s when as many as five different sports were regularly on offer to the masses. It sounded great...

All the plans were in place; Leeds United had even gone as far as negotiating a franchise for an ice hockey team in West Yorkshire, to be known as the Leeds Lasers, and externally Elland Road itself was to be narrowed and landscaped in a bold attempt to bring a cosmopolitan café culture to Beeston. In January 1998 Leeds Sporting chairman Chris Akers confidently predicted that building work would start between July and September that year and the Arena would be open for the year 2000. Delays followed delays and frequent updates in the match day programme became akin to 'the boy who cried wolf', with chairman Peter Ridsdale's assertions that "work will begin by the end of the year" eventually falling on deaf ears.

The complicated planning submission for the arena complex was never agreed and having dragged on for a couple of years it gradually drifted from the focus of Messrs Ridsdale and Leighton et al., as they nurtured far loftier plans to move to a whole new stadium altogether. Some theories suggest that the land on Fullerton Park that remained in council ownership eventually restricted Leeds United's ability to re-build the West Stand as they would have liked, and therefore they pressed fast-forward on Peter Ridsdale's plans to relocate from Elland Road and brushed the Arena proposals under the carpet.

Sadly, in terms of ownership of Elland Road, the club's feet were only back under the table for seven years until the main asset was sold again by chairman Gerald Krasner in November 2004, amid further financial gloom at the dog end of Peter Ridsdale's tenure. This sale was to Manchester businessman Jacob Adler and his Barnaway company for £8.5 million, and was believed to be for a 25-year lease with a specific buy-back clause. Elland Road then sunk into a period of murkiness during which little was known about its actual ownership, as then Leeds chairman Ken Bates

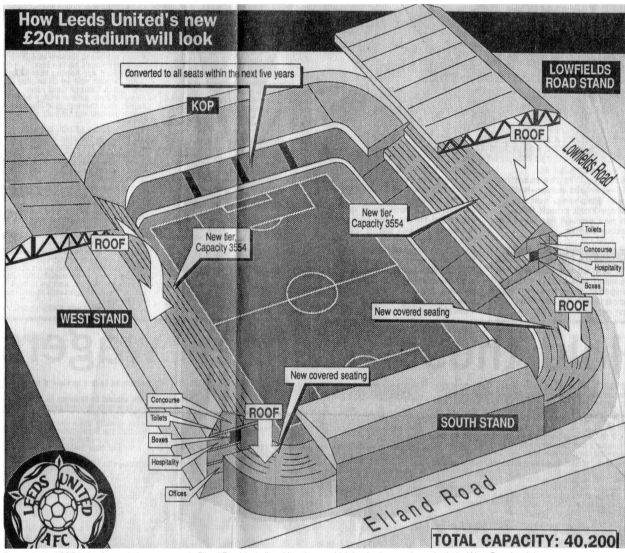

Promotion in 1990 led to fevered plans to upgrade Elland Road, including this scheme which involved a new tier on both the West Stand and the Lowfields Road Stand and a new South West Corner Stand.

extended his preferred method of operating, that being to leave everybody completely in the dark.

Very soon after his arrival at the club in January 2005, Bates announced his intention to buy back the 'crown jewels', ie. Elland Road and Thorp Arch. In his programme notes for the Luton Town game on 10th March 2007, Bates answered queries over who owned Elland Road, claiming that "the straight answer is that neither I nor anybody else at Leeds United knows who it is". The apparent nonchalance with which Leeds United were paying nearly £1 million a year, and rising, in rent to persons unknown, did not fool many. In the same match day programme a statement was printed by finance director Mark Taylor detailing the convoluted structure which made up the ownership of the club itself. This was a wearisomely complex tale of a string of opaque companies such as The Forward Sports Fund, Adulant Force, LUFC, LUAFC and Roman's Heavies which appeared to be designed to muddy the waters even further rather than clear it all up, and prompted more questions than answers.

Prior to this, in December 2006 Leeds fans thought they already had a straight answer, that Elland Road,

rather than being safe back in the soft bosom of its rightful owner, had been sold in September 2005 to Teak Trading Corporation Ltd, based in the British Virgin Islands, and fans were left to draw their own conclusions. Chief executive of the time, Shaun Harvey, was typically blasé as he dismissed Leeds fans' bemusement that the sale had gone through 15 months prior to the news being leaked. Harvey said: "The change of ownership has no material effect on Leeds United. We still have the same lease as originally entered into, albeit with a different company. More importantly, the buy-back provision has also been transferred." True, it was a case of 'nothing to see here' for Leeds fans and indeed the sale had been recorded, for anybody to see, at the Land Registry since September 2005, but the fact that something as significant as a change in the ground's ownership, albeit from one anonymous faceless owner to another, had only come to light accidently 15 months after the event, threw another six foot of distrust upon the soiled heap of the Bates regime.

For his part, Bates was keen to announce that he intended the club to take up the option of re-purchasing

Elland Road, as soon as the burden of players' wages had been eased, or as Mark Taylor called it "the last year of Peter Ridsdale's excesses". Still this never happened and in 2014 Leeds fans sat unmoved and understandably sceptical when new Italian owner Massimo Cellino became the latest protagonist to promise to buy Elland Road back.

Relations with the council hit a rocky patch in 2011 when Leeds United's option to buy back the Thorp Arch training complex at an agreed, fixed price ran out. The club had tried to agree a loan from the council to assist with the purchase but the council requested further information at the last minute and United's option expired, although they remain tenants.

Since the financial downfall of Leeds United in the mid-2000s, Leeds City Council has steadily purchased plots of land around Elland Road, including the Castle Brothers-owned plot between the Kop and the M621 and in 2011 the bus depot off Lowfields Road.

As the club ownership passes from one party to another it is always a key objective to build relations with Leeds City Council, as land remains undeveloped and inevitably their paths will cross. A convivial relationship will always make mutual plans come to fruition quicker and easier. Thankfully one owner who definitely grasped that concept very quickly was Andrea Radrizzani, who immediately recognised the benefit of having the council onside with plans for his 'Elland Road 2020' proposal. Planning documents and related discussions continue to evolve relating to the club's desires for a new training complex in Holbeck, and the council has been co-operative in the Park & Ride scheme being developed around Elland Road and the progress of the Parklife community sports hub scheme. The concept of mutual benefit has been taken on board and the council were vocally receptive when Radrizzani purchased Elland Road back for Leeds United in June 2017. A statement issued on 28th June read: "Leeds United Football Club is delighted to announce that Greenfield Investment Pte Ltd, the Aser Group Holding company and parent company of Leeds United Football Club, has completed the purchase of Elland Road Stadium. The agreement concludes a successful negotiation process with Teak Commercial Limited, the landlord, and achieves what owner Andrea Radrizzani had set out as a top priority in allowing the Championship club to buy back its stadium following the completion of Radrizzani's takeover of the club from Massimo Cellino."

In a statement development for his tenure as owner, Radrizzani was believed to have paid £20 million for the acquisition, and is now leasing Elland Road to the club until June 2032, but was initially charging no rent.

Leeds were paying whoever Teak Commercial Limited were close to £2 million annually by the time Radrizzani activated a buy-back clause in the contract, but Leeds United's accounts issued in April 2019 read:

"The company (Leeds United) entered into a lease agreement for the stadium until June 2032 with an entity which has control over the stadium. There was an initial rent-free period of 33 months", meaning Leeds started to pay rent during 2020.

Nevertheless, with the 'Elland Road 2020' masterplan very much in effect, and with promotion to the Premier League offering global exposure and commercial opportunities for the city on an unprecedented scale, relations between Leeds United and Leeds City Council are likely to be as closely aligned as they have ever been.

LEEDS WOODVILLE

A name that appears only very briefly in the history and significance of Elland Road is that of Leeds Woodville, as the very first association football team to call the ground their own, albeit only as paying tenants for two seasons.

Leeds Woodville were a local amateur side formed in 1898 and were founder members of the Leeds League. In 1902 they were based in the Belle Isle and Hunslet area of South Leeds. At that time South Leeds was the only area of the city that could be vaguely described as a 'hot bed' of association football, as it housed a number of amateur clubs. Having got wind of the FA's increasing desire to lay professional association football roots in the West Riding of Yorkshire, Leeds Woodville fancied their chances of becoming the team in the Leeds area. Given the opportunity therefore, they agreed a lease to share Elland Road with Holbeck Rugby Club for the 1902/03 season with its, even then, markedly superior facilities. Leeds Woodville's first game at Elland Road was on 13th September 1902, a 3-0 win over Hunslet Wesleyan Mission, and they also completed the 1903/04 season on the ground.

The very first association football team to play at Elland Road weren't Leeds Woodville, though. That honour was shared between Hunslet Football Club and Harrogate, who contested a West Yorkshire Cup Final on the ground in 1898, when it was still known as the Old Peacock Ground. Hunslet won the game 1-0 and six years later it was they who acted decisively in taking advantage of the need to form a professional club in the area, with Leeds Woodville crucially taking their eye off the ball. It was the board and supporters of Hunslet FC who combined with the interested parties within the newly disbanded Holbeck Rugby Club to form Leeds City in 1904.

Prior to this Leeds Woodville, being tenants of Holbeck Rugby Club, lost their lease on Elland Road and were also disbanded when Holbeck were defeated in the vital play-off with St Helens in 1904. Elland Road was put on the market and Leeds Woodville lost all advantage in claiming it for themselves. Leeds City was duly formed and association football and Elland Road became permanent bedfellows.

LOWFIELDS ROAD

Ever had a road built specifically to make life easier for you? Me neither, but one major LS11 thoroughfare owes its innately chequered past solely to Leeds United. When Lowfields Road was constructed in 1923 it was a perfectly straight road, roughly three quarters of a mile in length, linking Elland Road to Gelderd Road with a very gradual incline from south to north. Not only that, but the prior absence of the road meant the geography and character of the surrounding landscape was very different. Prior to its construction, as evidenced on a 1908 Ordnance Survey map, only a narrow pedestrian lane, almost a dirt track, separated the Holbeck Cricket Ground from the land that led up to the small terraced mound that lay on the eastern side of the football ground. It was only after Lowfields Road itself was built that Leeds United finally agreed on the north/south pitch orientation and gradually built a larger terrace on this side.

With Gelderd Road and Elland Road becoming quite major routes from the centre of Leeds westwards, it made sense from a town planning point of view to create a link road between them, particularly as the land that Lowfields Road was built upon was empty marshland ripe for development. In an example of their growing stature, however, Leeds United did have a large say in the road's construction, as football was developing into an increasingly popular pastime for the Leeds public. A major justification for the road was creating better access for trams to park at the ground, and also easing the considerable congestion after games by diverting traffic up to Gelderd Road and on to Whitehall Road into the city centre. Furthermore, Leeds United required a durable thoroughfare on which to transport the several tonnes of mining and building waste that was being used to build up their ever-expanding ground.

Burger vans and the 'northern' backdrop of the Nosters and Marleys. Welcome to Lowfields Road.

Local people with memories of the time prior to the road's construction recalled the 'low fields' around this area frequently flooding from the nearby Wortley Beck, which was often referred to as the 'River Twist' as it snaked around the fields behind the ground. Even after the construction of the road, which required significant civil work to manage the drainage issues, it was many years before anything was built on the land past the football ground and towards Gelderd Road.

A photo from 14th June 1923 of the just-completed Lowfields Road. The houses nearest the camera are on Elland Road and the houses on the horizon are the Nosters and Marleys on Beeston Town Street. The building rubble on the right hand side is the ongoing development of the early Kop and Lowfields stands by JP Pullans.

Of course, when the road was first built it was fitted immediately with tram lines and these served the Football Special trams that lined up bumper to bumper as far as the eye could see, upwards towards Gelderd Road on match days. Conveniently, between 1945 and 1957 a tram scrapyard was operating on Lowfields Road next to the cricket ground, and as the age of the tram began to conclude in 1955 the scrapyard ironically became the final resting place for many of the Football Specials. The scrapyard later became a hauliers' yard and for many years bordered the Petty's Field Sports Ground which stretched roughly to where the underpass is now.

Leeds fan Kevin Mulligan recalls the empty fields on the other, left hand side of Lowfields Road and partook of a ritual that is very different to that of most match-going fans today: "I lived in Wortley as a lad, I used to walk to the games. My walk led me through Lower Wortley, over the park known as the Recreation ground, over the railway bridge by the Dragon pub, and through a ginnel which is still there, which came out by Fletchers Motors on the junction of the top of Gelderd Road. Walking down Lowfields Road prior to reaching the Kop end, there used to be a large field. In this usually partially flooded field were always horses. I used to sneak out from home anything I thought the horses would like to eat, so I could feed them on my way to the match. If I walked to the game it became a superstition to do this. I was convinced that if I forgot to feed them Leeds would lose."

With the Castle Brothers haulage buildings appearing behind the Spion Kop in the early 1960s the area to the north of the football ground began to take on a more industrial feel. By the late 1960s the right hand side of Lowfields Road as you headed away from the ground already hosted a number of engineering workshops and warehouse units, such as 'Viceroy House' which still stands today, while the other side was still a wasteland of boggy marshes stretching up to the Co-operative Club at the corner of Gelderd Road and the LICS Sports Ground adjacent to it.

As with most aspects of the area around Elland Road, it was the construction of the M621 between 1971 and 1975 that had a considerable knock-on effect and completely changed the usage of Lowfields Road; not least because it literally sliced the road in two, with the underpass linking the two sections and a mini-roundabout constructed at the dead end of each segment. Side-roads were built such as Latchmore Road and Benyon Park Way. Gradually then, magnetised by Leeds United's success, industrial estates such as the 'Latchmore Road Industrial Estate', the 'United Business Park', 'Confederations Park', 'Maple Park' and the 'Gelderd Trading Estate' started to spring up as the easy access routes to the motorway network were exploited, and the 'low fields' of yesteryear were steadily covered over by the wheels of 20th century progression.

Structural and geographical developments were plenty on Lowfields Road in the 1970s, though sadly, an altogether less pleasant development during the decade was the proliferation of National Front newspaper sellers on the pavement outside the Lowfields Road Stand on match days. Many younger

From 3rd January 1922 the construction of Lowfields Road, looking up towards Gelderd Road. The frequently flooding fields on either side of the road were known locally as the 'low fields' because they were, you've guessed it, very low fields.

fans, including myself, were largely oblivious to them and the message they were peddling, but it was intimidating to others and looking back now was quite symbolic of the general mood around the ground in the post-Revie years. Leeds fan Chris Miller has vague memories of the National Front presence at Elland Road: "Unfortunately the late '70s and into the '80s saw the arrival of the NF and their *Bulldog* magazine at Elland Road. As a teenager, it was difficult for me to appreciate exactly what the National Front stood for, or what they were trying to achieve by utilising football as a vehicle for their views. Maybe I was a little naive, but looking back I simply wasn't interested in 'politics', I just wanted to see Leeds win and I didn't care what colour the players were, or for that matter the fans. It seems incredible now that they were allowed to sell their newsletter on the streets as openly as they did for many years, and more unbelievable that the club stood back and let them do so. Thankfully, we've just got the programme sellers competing with *The Square Ball* now."

Leeds-born striker Terry Connor had emerged as a promising youngster at the height of the racism problems at Elland Road in the late 1970s, and along with several visiting black players ran the gauntlet of the intimidating atmosphere that was already tinged with a violent bitterness at the club's plight, not to mention the right-wing element to it. This continued right throughout the 1980s when the National Front sellers actively targeted young Leeds fans in pubs in and around Elland Road and the city centre on match days, but most prominently on the open expanses of Lowfields Road as they approached the ground. The hatred, intimidation and violence was emblematic of the problem Elland Road had in general. A combination of the club and the police eventually tackling the issue, the signing of prominent black players by Leeds and an independent campaign by a Leeds-supporting anti-facism group meant the problem gradually faded away at the back end of the 1980s.

On the southern end of Lowfields Road past the M621, business premises were built on the site of the cricket ground in the early 1980s and the road network completely obliterated the housing in the area, whilst the bus depot was also built on the perimeter of the cricket ground. For many years a transport café also stood where the hauliers' yard was, and where the Centenary Pavilion and Leeds United Foundation offices now stand.

Lowfields Road on the north side of the M621 is a pedestrian route to and from the ground on match days and a huge car park for the travelling home fans, often with either brave, foolish or very creative methods of parking. After a game, for those on foot the walk home can be a slow trudge up a never-ending hill in defeat, or a buoyant, challenging stride in victory. But doubtless forever, Lowfields Road will remain a vital artery in the system that pumps fans and traffic to and from Elland Road, and imagine the scene had it never existed.

LOWFIELDS ROAD STAND

Modern, sponsorship-clad football grounds rarely trigger the imagination in the same way stands with names as evocative, daunting or dripping in narrative as the 'Lowfields Road Stand' do. Every fan at every club holds a unique fondness for street names that generate sometimes forgotten memories, like Platt Lane, Gwladys Street, John Street or Kemlyn Road. And 'Lowfields Road Stand' as three simple words seems to perfectly evoke reminiscences of a bygone age of primitive, uncomfortable but largely happy times; stranger perhaps, because the road itself still very much exists. But within the modern day development of Elland Road, one of the unrelenting succession of 'improvements' that hurt Leeds fans was the demolishing of the Lowfields Road Stand in 1992. Distressing photos show the roof collapsed forward over the terracing beneath it as if brutally wounded by a callous sniper. The diamond floodlights and the Lowfields going in one calculated swipe of progress was almost too much to bear, this being only months after the West Stand façade had also bitten the dust.

The Lowfields Road Stand, and in particular the terrace sections running the length of the pitch that survived to the death, had built up something of a cult reputation over the years. Whilst known at one stage as the 'Popular Side', 'popular' could also have meant 'smarter' or one that doesn't follow the crowds to the more obvious location. During the peak years of trouble and violence at Elland Road it was almost as if the more savvy Leeds fan stood on the Lowfields, to slip under the radar rather than be tarred with the same brush as the more notorious and widely demonised fans on the Kop, or in the South Stand. In truth, during the 1970s and '80s fans capable of blackening the Leeds United name were pretty much everywhere, but given the Lowfields' proximity to the away fans, it's fair to say the penned sections along the east side of Elland Road were an open interface on which home and away fans could exchange almost everything but goodwill. In short it was a lively place to watch your football, but throughout its almost 70-year existence few stands in the country can have been tweaked, ornamented and sapped of their former might, whilst maintaining their core structure, as much as the Lowfields Road Stand at Elland Road.

The Lowfields Road Stand following the storm damage of 1962; note the rows of seats did not extend down to the supporting pillars until the second installation of seats in 1967.

Leeds City in action in front of an early incarnation of the 'Popular Side' from 1907 before JP Pullans fully extended the terrace to twice this size. Behind the stand you can see the chimney stacks of the Leeds (Wortley) Fireclay Company.

from front to back, and for the remainder of its existence fans at the front of the Lowfields terrace would be cruelly exposed to the elements. The completion of the roofing of the terrace was the last structural change for over 20 years. The roofing work was again carried out by Pullans Builders, who also built the main stand at Oakwell, Barnsley, which survives to this day, and whilst smaller than the Lowfields is very similar in its crude and unsophisticated appearance, particularly where the roof only covers the back half of the stand.

Basic, mounded terraces always existed on the east side of the ground until the construction of Lowfields Road itself in 1923 determined a permanent orientation for the pitch. Built over a period of time from the mid-1920s, during the same time span as the huge open Spion Kop that it was joined with for more than four decades, the Lowfields terrace was built on top of the smaller, banked terrace that had survived from the Leeds City years. Exact dates don't exist, but soon after the opening of Lowfields Road the Lowfields terraces were built up by Pullans Builders in the same way as the Kop was built up, via dumped building waste. When the pitch orientation had been finally settled a solid, white concrete wall was built around all four sides of the ground, framing the pitch with a degree of certainty as if ensuring that nobody was able to change their minds again. The walls remained until each stand was gradually replaced over the next 70 years.

Pre-Leeds United, the stand on the east side was known simply as the 'Sixpenny entrances' with reference to the cost of admittance. In line with inflation the stand was also referred to as the 'Shilling Stand' in the 1920s and '30s, although this was more in relation to the shillings that fans had donated to help with building work. As the stand was now a more dominant terrace it became known as the 'Popular Side', and it is easy to see why as, pre-roofing, the stand was a vast sea of people stretching round to the Kop end. That name lasted until the early 1970s when the famed 'Lowfields' moniker took off.

It was the late 1920s before a roof was put on the stand, and curiously this was done in three stages from the south to the north, although the roof did not include the twin glass-screen ends at this time. The cost of roofing the stand was funded by the Leeds United Supporters' Club (LUSC) and by 1933 the work was completed, but this only covered half of the terrace

By wartime and the temporary cessation of professional football activities, the 'Popular Side' was regularly, and by definition, the most heavily populated area of the ground, and in the mid-1940s cost half a crown for admittance (12½ new pence). Post-war in 1948, manager Major Frank Buckley insisted that fencing was fitted onto the terrace in the north east corner as an early but primitive form of segregation. This was a move which also coincided with prices being raised, but most significantly made the Kop and the Lowfields two separate stands for the first time, and prevented fans from moving 'ends' at half-time. With footballing fortunes stagnant the club had little reason to develop or modernise the ground and the Lowfields remained all-standing and pretty much as it was, until promotion and the West Stand fire in 1956 kick-started a rush of progression.

The John Charles-led promotion of 1955/56 started a chain of events that, in stages, substantially reduced the capacity and the depth and magnitude of the Lowfields Road Stand. In the mid-1950s the Lowfields swept imposingly along the entire east side of the ground, continuing in an arc from the Kop and along to the Scratching Shed. But an initial installation saw 2,600 seats added in the upper section in the summer of 1956 in readiness for a return to Division One, with the stand becoming two constituents for the first time and the familiar glass screen ends also being added.

LUSC, according to Ray Fell, were again instrumental in raising the funds to pay for the significant improvement to the stand, which is an important point as shortly afterwards the club was stung by the West Stand fire and struggled to raise the funds to re-build the burnt down main stand. John Charles was of course sold to part-fund this with the LUSC funds now dry. Certainly, had the fire occurred a few months

An empty shelf in the Lowfields Road Stand during the opening weeks of the 1989/90 season, before the club found valuable extra space by installing 300 seats.

for the following season. The ferocity of the winds in that area must have been known to the club as Ross Pullan recalls a story whereby the club used to open a back exit gate during matches to create a through-draft and prevent the Lowfields roof from blowing off; evidently they didn't or couldn't take such precautions overnight.

Behind the stand a large bar was built around the same time as the seats were put in, in the late 1950s. This was a considerable, flat-roofed, two-storey brick building with the ground floor being a toilet block. Only accessible from the back of the Lowfields Stand, the bar area is remembered by Dave Cocker, who as a junior in the early 1960s used to retire to the bar for breaks when he and his colleagues were sweeping the terraces after a game: "They used to have a massive tea urn on the counter and Bovril, so we went in there for snacks to escape from the cold."

In January 1959 white retaining walls in front of the seated section and additional entrances were erected along with improvements to the steps leading on to the terrace, to alleviate the near-fatal crushing that would often occur on the terracing, most notably during the 1-0 home defeat to West Brom on 27th December 1958. And already, slowly the imposing mass of the

earlier the seating would never have been installed, but it is doubtful this would have prevented John Charles' inevitable sale. Only 300 of the seats were sold as season tickets, and for the first game in which the seats were used, a 5-1 opening day win over Everton, only 600 more seats were sold and it was reported that around 100 fans just climbed over the wall, without intervention, from the terracing to use the seats. It was perhaps just as well that more seats weren't sold as season tickets as, within a few weeks, the West Stand fire necessitated a mass migration of displaced season ticket holders from the West Stand to the Lowfields.

The new seats were wooden and remained so throughout the years, and the whole Lowfields construction was very soon looking dated compared to the more modern stands that sprung up around it when the Revie era really took off. Other unforeseen events saw the entire Lowfields Stand closed for the final two and a half months of the 1961/62 season, which involved several home matches, after overnight gales damaged the roof. Such was the strength of the gales the roof stanchions were ripped out of the concrete terraces all along the stand as the winds ravaged the 1930s-built roof. Robert R. Roberts builders were employed to install a new roof for the entire stand in time

The Lowfields Road Stand in 1969, still a solid mass of people and still the 'Popular Side'; compare this with the prodded and poked, broken up and downsized stand in the photo above.

A snowbound Lowfields Road Stand in 1978.

for months until the North East Corner Stand was built in 1972/73.

A narrow middle section, generally known as the 'shelf', also appeared above the terracing in the summer of 1971. The shelf was created when a long concrete wall was built which extended along the length of the stand at the back of the terraced section, up to the newly constructed section of terracing below what would become the North East Corner Stand. This 'shelf' used to pack fans, in affording a mixed vantage point, and the scheme was a curious oddity that became iconic but which few could explain. The top of the terraced section beneath it later gave way to advertising hoardings and was also the thoroughfare behind the back of the terracing section, which shouldn't be confused with what became the shelf above it. The alleyway was directly behind the back step of the terrace, which was raised to form a narrow passageway.

Kevin Mulligan recalls: "I do remember the alleyway being six to seven people deep with fans watching the game (which was virtually impossible from its sunken location). I remember being in this stand for the visit of Glasgow Celtic in the European Cup Semi-Final in 1970, when we were beaten 1-0. The Lowfields Stand was crushed with people, the alleyway was so full people had to be lifted up to see the action. That match was amazing, as the Lowfields was crammed with Celtic fans, and at half-time they attempted to 'switch' ends of the Lowfields stand. That alleyway was a death trap at half-time."

Another Leeds fan of many years, Dougie Wales, recalls the Lowfields alleyway as being a "death trap". "It was a right long, awkward narrow passageway," Dougie explains, "and it used to get snarled up in there something awful, it was a nightmare trying to get onto the terraces at the front. There were people coming out and going in, it was a free-for-all, and it was a nightmare."

Even with crowds generally reducing at Elland Road you would still see fans standing in the middle 'shelf' section until the early 1980s, and the alleyway below it existed right until the stand was demolished. Explanations for the creation of the shelf are mixed, but the general consensus appears to be that it was somehow by way of preparation for the extension of the stadium 'grand plan' development, which would eventually involve replacing the top of the Lowfields and linking it with the south east corner. The long wall along the back of the Lowfields terrace and into the north

Lowfields Road terrace was being diminished. Little else changed in the outward appearance of the Lowfields Stand until Revie's on-field success brought about significant change elsewhere in the ground, change that would inevitably force the Lowfields to fit in with it. This included a second installation of a few more rows of seats added to the upper tier in 1967, to bring the seating section down almost to the roof stanchions.

Development of the Lowfields was always on the agenda, right from when Don Revie and the Leeds United board combined to formulate a grand plan for an entire redevelopment of Elland Road in 1965. The board was always aware of disgruntlement at the conditions in the stand and indeed its somewhat veteran appearance. In April 1969 prior to a game against Manchester City, chairman Percy Woodward paid to get into the Popular Side for the first time in 30 years to see for himself why fans were complaining about queueing outside, poor viewing conditions and a lack of amenities. Entering at 2.15pm he experienced first-hand the diabolical view in some areas and the frequent crushing. He then left by an exit and paid again to enter the Kop to do the same. By kick-off he'd seen enough and whilst leaving to watch the game in the directors' box he claimed the complaints had been justified. Still, schemes came and went and never came to fruition. In June 1972 the next phase of the 'grand plan' was announced, which would start with the building of the North East Corner Stand later that year. The South Stand would follow, but the part of the five-year scheme that didn't go ahead was re-developing the Lowfields with an extra 1,500 seats and a "glazed internal concourse with bars and toilets".

In 1968 the terracing in the north east corner of the Lowfields was excavated away leaving a huge gap when the new Kop was built. It was 1971 before the lower terracing section of the Lowfields was extended back into the corner to meet the Kop, with nothing above it east corner which created the bottom of the shelf, was effectively the middle barrier between the two tiers that eventually would have met up neatly around most of the ground, had the proposed development continued. Therefore, the 'shelf' was never really intended to exist as a supporter vantage point long term.

In addition to creating the shelf, also in 1971, gangways were incorporated into the terracing, splitting the thronging crowd into sections, which was soon exacerbated by each section being separated into physical pens by fencing. Suddenly the heaving mass of bodies had been split into detached fragments and some of the stand's aura had been lost.

The summer of 1978, with the South Stand having been built, saw almost a third of the upper section of the Lowfields Stand being demolished and a new glass panel erected at the end of the stand, so you would actually never know it used to be longer. Sixteen-hundred seats were lost as foundations were built with the intention of completing the Elland Road 'bowl' effect. This plus the demolition cost was estimated at £1 million. But the building work never progressed and the Lowfields terracing in the southern third of the ground lay single-tiered and bleak, with the second grass bank standing above it, until the South East Corner Stand was finally built in 1991. Later, in March 1985, £7,000 was spent on lattice X-wires that were fitted to the stand's pitch-facing extremities to help with the roof stability, still a problem in high winds.

By the time the exposed foundations were built upon, the Taylor Report had also reduced the capacity of the Lowfields terracing yet further. The middle 'shelf' section of the stand was left unused as Leeds' fortunes dwindled in the 1980s, apart from as a useful vantage point for patrolling police, and that section of the stand was also taken up by more prominent advertising hoardings. However, in the season 1989/90, the onset of the Taylor Report and renewed success on the pitch meant Leeds had to find available spaces where they could. In time for the Newcastle match in December 1989, 300 precious and much-sought-after seats were re-installed in the shelf and remained there until the stand's demolition in 1992.

When the upper tier was shortened in 1978, the glass panels on the right hand side of the upper seating section became more visible to those at the ground and on television. Of course the glass panels had been there for years, but at both ends had banked terracing adjacent to them and in days of packed crowds, the glass panels became something of an obstruction, although some fans, such as Gary Edwards, seemed to take a liking to them: "I have watched the Whites from almost every vantage point possible at Elland Road: the Kop, the Shed, the Lowfields; I watched loads of games through the glass panels on the Elland Road end of the Lowfields stand. There was a small steep terrace which my Dad and I would stand on, with around a hundred others; this would be where we would head for when there was a big crowd (which was a regular occurrence back then) and we were unable to get to our usual spot at the front wall. We watched a few games through those dusty glass panels."

Gary also has other memories of comfortable times spent watching football on the Lowfields, which few others could share: "I think by far the most comfortable I have been when watching a game at Elland Road, was when a few of my mates and me would sit in the straw in front of the Lowfields Road wall. The straw was used to cover the pitch from frost and snow, before and after each game in the winter months. The police would periodically try to get us back over the wall, but eventually left us alone – most of the time."

The graffiti art partly created by Leeds midfielder Mateusz Klich following promotion in the summer of 2020 and painted onto the only remaining section of exterior wall from the original 1920s-built Lowfields Road Stand.

The back of the Lowfields Road Stand shortly before it was demolished in May 1992; note the white-painted ticket office on the left hand side of the picture.

Bill Fotherby faced the challenge of keeping Elland Road 'house proud' whilst money was in short supply in his position as ground director in the early 1980s. He recalls wanting to do something with the Lowfields Road Stand as soon as he arrived on the board in 1979, but he also recalls the problems that existed with the age and ramshackle nature of the stand: "Every year the council would not give permission for a safety certificate. That was a fight with the council all the time. It wasn't safe when it came to the highest winds, they were frightened of it blowing half the roof off." In fairness to the council this did actually happen again in 1983, the night prior to Leeds taking on Arsenal in the first replay of the epic FA Cup Fourth Round tie. As Leeds took the lead in the last minute of extra time only for Arsenal to equalise seconds later, the top tier of the Lowfields Road Stand was shut due to winds the previous night blowing a section off. Thankfully, the damage wasn't as severe as in 1962.

For much of the 1980s the upper section of seating often went unused as attendances dwindled, and it was also used by away fans on occasions when visiting numbers merited it. As with most parts of the ground in the 1980s, the Lowfields Road seating section carried a sense of brooding menace compounded by the numerous dark tunnels at the back of the stand that had to be navigated to access it. The terrace pens beneath the seats often demonstrated their adaptability in accommodating varying numbers of travelling fans, with pens opening and closing as required, but largely, the often-empty pens were an under-utilised reminder of how far the club had fallen. On the whole the Lowfields was looking tired and shabby, a reflection of the entire club, and a Vinnie Jones long-throw away from the intimidating sweep of faces that once made it the 'Popular Side'. Very soon though, as Leeds' fortunes

revived under Howard Wilkinson, the seats were never empty as every available vantage point was used to follow Leeds United's success.

Supporters' views on the Lowfields are mixed. The iconic, if not the most awe-inspiring, memory of the Lowfields was the twin grass banks on either side of the upper seating section, as much as it was the mountainous bank of terracing pre-1956, or the half and half stand that ran the length of the field and cast a backdrop of thousands of packed and awestruck faces onto the many classic images of Revie's all-conquering side.

When the stand eventually came down, as the flutter of 'League Champions' flags could still be heard dispersing from the epic celebrations against Norwich City in May 1992, long-standing groundsman John Reynolds was there to witness it. His son Stephen recalls: "They dropped the roof in two sections, he said they were waiting for ages to see it, they went for their break and came back to take a photo and they had dropped one section. So he waited ages for the second section, went off for another wander and they dropped it again. So he missed both, and he was a bit upset about that."

At a time in the late 1970s and '80s when re-building on and off the park was on hold, the Lowfields with its un-painted, corrugated roofing, oppressive blue fencing and prohibitive stanchions, was crying out for evolution as much as anything. But the crowd from that era embraced the Lowfields warts and all, and with deep affection they cherished the memories of those lesser years, where loyalty in persistence became a badge of honour, and they cherished them even after Wilkinson's success eventually brought change and the consequent destruction that everyone knew had to come. It was sad, it brought an era to an end, but it had to come.

The sensitive might want to avert their eyes: the roof collapses and the Lowfields Road Stand is expelled of all life and fight and about to disappear forever in May 1992.

A pale shadow of its former self: the plethora of fences, barriers and advertising hoardings that aged the Lowfields Road Stand dramatically and combined to ensure it had to go.

Another view of the gale damage that closed the Lowfields Road Stand for the last weeks of the 1961/62 season; see how the supporting pillars have been ripped out of the concrete by the winds.

M621

Not a shot, a save or an errant offside flag, but a stretch of road. While it is true that the success of Don Revie's Leeds United changed the Elland Road ground immeasurably, the single biggest factor in affecting the landscape of the surrounding area was the construction of the M621 motorway; interrupting the panorama with leaden brutality like a defender's outstretched boot as Sniffer shapes to round off a flowing move and bag the winner.

Official strategy for what was to become the M621 started in 1963 with the submission of planning documentation for public approval. But prior to that a 'slum clearance' had been undertaken in 1959, followed by further wholesale house demolition to eradicate several acres of housing around the east end of Elland Road towards Holbeck, in readiness for the proposed motorway network. Today aerial photos show the area is unrecognisable as green expanses, concentrated housing and heavy industry is replaced by the concrete myriad of complex carriageways snaking in and out of Leeds city centre.

Whilst it was mainly housing that made way for the roads leading off from the M621, the main section of motorway that passes the Elland Road ground itself was built on unused fields that included a short section of the Wortley Beck. Notably affected also were the former Holbeck cricket pitch and the New Peacock pub, which both bit the dust in the wake of development.

A Leeds fan from as far back as the 1940s, Reg French, remembers well the changing landscape

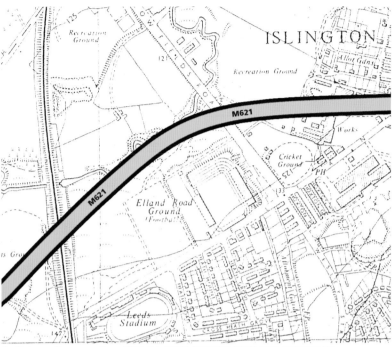

An Ordnance Survey map from 1952 showing the impending M621 route and hence the area of undeveloped land, sports fields and housing about to be obliterated by it.

that the M621 brought about: "It altered the whole character of the area. The trams would run up to Elland Road on flat roads, now the buses, coaches and all vehicles are having to travel up fairly steep inclines. The area is unrecognisable really. It was all just fields for miles with a through road called Lowfields Road, but the motorway changed the scene altogether."

Ray Fell was a local resident who was affected for years by the development, not just by having to move house to another home nearby, but also by having to subsequently live with the choking disruption of it being built: "I lived at number 3 Tilbury Terrace, which is now

A photo from 1975 that shows a freshness to the Elland Road panorama as the recently opened M621 combines with the green prosperity around it. Compare this radically changed landscape to the photo from the same angle on pages 46 and 47.

in the middle of the motorway, and that's how I came to live where I do now (on the nearby Heath estate). We moved out to allow them to build the motorway. The biggest thing I remember, and anybody living in the area then will be able to tell you, there was a swarm of crickets all over the place, in the houses and everything. All you could hear as you walked down the old Elland Road was this 'click, click, click' from these crickets. They even got in my airing cupboard. Never saw them before the motorway and never saw them afterwards, but they were dug up by all the earth being removed for the motorway. But the motorway was a godsend for Leeds United because it's the best motorway-served ground in the country, and people started coming in their cars more."

Construction of the M621 was done in three stages, beginning in 1971 and finally being completed in 1975. Section one was the three mile stretch moving eastwards from the M62 at Gildersome to Junction 1 which offers fantastic views of the city of Leeds, and travelling towards Elland Road is west of the ground and leads onto the A6110 Beeston Ring Road. Section two was the 1.66 mile stretch from Junction 1 to Junction 3 in Leeds city centre, which is the section that actually by-passes, and affords excellent views of, the football ground; this was completed last in 1975. Section three was originally just an extension of the M1, and didn't originally link with the other two sections. This two mile stretch took you from the junction for Leeds city centre where the M1 previously terminated, up to Rothwell. In 1999 this stretch was re-designated as junctions 3 to 7 of an extended M621, and the M1 now travels north to link with the A1. The whole original construction cost £21 million, of which nearly £5 million was spent on land acquisition and the complex issue of service diversions, including the Wortley Beck that ran past Elland Road.

While the original intention of the M621 was simply to take traffic in and out of Leeds city centre, the knock-on effect has completely changed the area in terms of the demographic and the size and scale of businesses that surround it. Accessibility is a key feature in business growth and certainly Elland Road has benefited as it is widely known to be one of the easiest football grounds to get to. This has definitely raised the profile of the ground and the value of the land surrounding it, and it has helped afford it the status of FA Cup Semi-Finals, England internationals, Euro 96, rugby internationals and World Cup bid nomination. Whilst it has become something of a moot point in recent years as perhaps more funds have been diverted to it than many fans would have liked, the M621 has also added prominence to the club's ability to host conference and hospitality events. Indeed, in terms of a single non-football factor that makes the ground as respected and desirable as it is today, the M621 construction is definitely the biggest.

MASCOTS

Mascots at Elland Road have traditionally come in two very distinct forms. There is the relatively recent emergence of an adult-sized cuddly version based on a fictitious Leeds-themed children's character, and there is the gathering of wide-eyed youngsters in over-sized kits who trot out onto the pitch with the captain, to take part in the pre-match build-up whilst sheltering from the arctic winds and lashing rain.

The former is a puzzling by-product of the Premier League era that we can surely blame a US sport for

encouraging. Such mascots usually carry a link to the club's nickname, badge or ground, and Leeds were a little sluggish in adopting the tenuously themed character of Ellie the Elephant as their first mascot in 1996. Ellie's flame did not burn brightly and by the beginning of the 1998/99 season had been erased from the junior sections of the match day programme, and more significantly, was not to be seen lurking with intent on the perimeter of the Elland Road pitch. In 2005, following the retirement of the loyal South

African defender Lucas Radebe, the club mascot was re-branded as Lucas the Kop Cat, an altogether more marketable character who remained omnipresent up to the beginning of the 2014/15 season.

Some club mascots are highly marketed but Lucas has kept a relatively low profile in comparison. He did have his own page in the match day programme, he appeared at all family events at Elland Road and for an 18-month period during Leeds' wretched sojourn in League One, his on-pitch antics with opposing

A grounded Vinnie Jones floors 5-year-old mascot Rob Kelly, prior to the game against Wolverhampton Wanderers in October 1989.

goalkeepers in front of the Kop provided much mirth amongst the embittered supporters. With astute comic timing and the slapstick presence of Eric Morecambe, Lucas played to the masses like a natural. Since this time it appears there was another body under the costume or else Lucas was severely reprimanded for unsporting conduct, but for a brief period he did lift the weighty gloom upon Elland Road.

Since the 1980s the team has run out of the tunnel headed by a gaggle of excitable youths. Not the Tommy Wright, Aidan White or Jamie Shackleton-type, but the official match day mascots enjoying a once in a lifetime experience. The role of the Leeds United match day mascot has been shared over the years by hundreds of stage-struck youngsters who we will never remember, but who themselves, will never forget their magical day. I often find myself wondering how thoroughly the Leeds United goalkeeper is actually preparing for the forthcoming, high-stakes 90 minutes of blood and thunder combat by saving tippy-tap shots from a six-year-old in his goalmouth. Nevertheless, the opportunity afforded to the mascots for the day is a mind-blowing one, and it is to football's eternal credit in the modern era that clubs still break down the barrier between professional footballers and the general public in this way. Although the unfortunate youngster

who took receipt of a merciless sliding tackle from Vinnie Jones before the Wolves game at Elland Road in October 1989 may disagree with that.

His name is Rob Kelly, and it might perturb you to discover that the knock-kneed five-year-old that was so savagely upended for the Kop's amusement, is now 36 and fully capable of dishing something physical back to Leeds' former arch-joker. Rob is aware of his cult status amongst Leeds fans, and while he doesn't exactly dine out on his notoriety he frequently finds himself talking about it. Certainly, save for a pantomime horse galloping across the 18-yard box in 1973, this was probably the most famously random incident to have occurred on the Elland Road turf.

"It was the only time I've ever been a mascot," Rob told me. "My Mum had applied for me to be a mascot only the week before, and was told I'd be put on a waiting list. However, on the Wednesday before the game she received a call and they said the kid who was due to be mascot was ill, so they asked if I'd be able to take their place. My Mum agreed and sent a cheque for £50."

So the most famous mascot in Elland Road's long history met his fate purely through the misfortune of another awestruck youngster. Having said that, is £50 a reasonable price to pay to feel the sharp end of one of Vinnie's infamous career-enders? I'm told it was a

The Kop and an on-duty policeman are enjoying the show as Vinnie pleads his innocence and a determined Rob Kelly gets up to have another go at goal (note the photo is signed by Vinnie Jones and was presented to Rob afterwards).

A rather more grown-up Rob Kelly is reunited with Vinnie Jones on Sky Sports' *Soccer AM* programme in 2016.

standard charge to become a mascot for the day back in 1989, and in return you received a full kit to keep, tickets in the West Stand, a couple of match day programmes, and in Rob's case a grazed knee and a lifetime of minor infamy.

Rob was well supported on the day by a network of family members there to watch his five minutes of exposure on the big stage, little knowing that he was about to take part in one of the most comical episodes ever to occur on the Elland Road turf, just nudging the entire Leeds United career of Roque Junior from the top spot. Rob continues: "My parents already had season tickets for the three of us and the club gave us two extra tickets. My Dad, his cousin, and my grandfather sat in our season ticket seats in the family stand, my Mum, her sister and myself were given tickets in the West Stand. My brother is also a lifelong Leeds fan and was going home and away at the time. He often tells me that this was the only game where he'd ever got into the ground in time for kick-off."

Prior to the infamous episode, of course, Rob's day was just like any other mascot's. He arrived at the ground at 1.30pm and was taken to a lounge bar where he was given his shirt, shorts and socks; his mum got her free programme and a team sheet. The Leeds

United official looking after him got his team sheet signed by all the first team players, though Rob can't actually recall going into the dressing room himself.

"My Mum tells me I was nervous before and had to be persuaded to go up the tunnel by Strachan, holding hands. When I got up the tunnel onto the pitch and saw the crowd, apparently I just froze completely. Vinnie Jones saw this, grabbed my hand and led me towards the Kop. He gave me a ball and said to take shots at Mervyn Day who was in goal. I took the first shot from what looked like a long way out but it was probably from about the edge of the six yard box. Day could easily have saved it but let it in and rolled the ball back. This was repeated, and as I was just about to take my third or fourth shot, Vinnie did the slide tackle."

Photos show Jones, the ultimate pantomime villain, expertly sizing up his infant victim on the blind-side, looming menacingly about to scythe his legs from under him with savage execution. Meanwhile Rob, tongue-clenched-between-teeth in earnest concentration, was focused fully on testing Day with another of his pea-rollers. Quite what prompted Jones to do it is something of a mystery, but he certainly employed a unique method of making a previously petrified youngster feel at home.

That said, it was nothing but an innocent prank that caught the mood of United's impassioned support at the time perfectly, albeit leaving the subject of its jollity somewhat bemused and shaken. Jones himself, with an early display of his soon-to-be-world-famous acting talents, was the picture of aghast innocence as he pleaded mockingly to the crowd that it was a fair tackle.

"It was completely out of the blue," Rob explains. "I thought the shots I was taking at Day were part of the actual game. The only involvement I'd had with Vinnie was when he led me towards the Kop. After the tackle, Vinnie helped me up and made sure I was OK, but I don't remember what he actually said. I didn't cry, but just got up and went for the ball again. The crowd started booing Vinnie jokingly, then when I got up they started singing 'sign him up'. Vinnie took me to the centre circle for the coin toss with Gordon Strachan and Wolves captain Gary Bellamy. After that, Strachan gave me the 50p they'd used, which my Mum's still got. I then lined up with the players for a photo.

"I had to leave the pitch," Rob continues, "but as I mentioned, I thought I was part of the game so couldn't understand why I had to go off. My Mum had to come onto the pitch to take me off." Presumably it was a coin toss that Strachan lost, as Leeds attacked the Kop in the first half and took an early lead from a Bobby Davison header, which proved to be the only goal of the game and was almost missed by Rob and his family as he was getting changed out of his kit underneath the West Stand.

The incident was captured for eternity by the club's official photographer, and from another angle by the *Yorkshire Evening Post* (*YEP*), whose images show an enduring depiction of the merriment the escapade created on the fans' faces in the Kop. The club's photos very quickly grabbed a lot of attention. Jones was big news in 1989 and the images perfectly encapsulated the jocular innocence of an incomparable period in Leeds United's history. Everyone was enjoying the times and laughing together, the mood was uplifting and infectious and swept Leeds along to promotion and two years later the Division One title.

Every fan that was at the game remembers the incident, plus thousands of Leeds fans worldwide. Even neutral football fans are aware of the classic photos, as Rob instantly became one of the most famous young mascots ever. Much like Vinnie's singularly incomparable man-marking methods on a young Paul Gascoigne a couple of years earlier, the photos became iconic and 31 years after the incident, it is still talked about.

"It wasn't until I got older that I realised that what had happened wasn't normal," Rob reflects. "Not long after the game we were invited to the opening of a shop in the St Johns Centre in Leeds. Vinnie

was opening the shop dressed as Santa Claus. The *YEP* were there and they took pictures of me pulling Vinnie's fake beard etc. Vinnie also signed all the pictures we'd been given by the club photographers."

Sadly Vinnie's Leeds career lasted only 15 months, but it was a period that defined and enchanted him, as much as his ubiquitous presence in the city charmed the locals. Since that day, hundreds of mascots have sprinted with wild abandon onto the Elland Road turf, no doubt fully believing they are playing for their ultimate heroes and about to change the course of history. They don't, but most will never get closer. However, there is still only one mascot that people recall even after the match has kicked off, never mind 31 years later.

"It comes up in conversation from time to time," says Rob, who has watched Leeds from the Kop for years now as a season ticket holder himself, and no doubt keeps an eye on the mascots to see if he will ever be upstaged. "Normally I'll be out with a group of friends and one of them will be talking to someone else and they'll mention it. People usually ask how it came about and whether or not it was planned, then I'm usually asked if it hurt or if anything happened to Vinnie for it. It's not something I tell people about myself too often unless a similar subject comes up in conversation. I wouldn't say I was famous among my mates, but all my mates know it was me who was the mascot. They'll always tell me whenever they've told the story to anyone else or anyone has mentioned it to them. It's surprising how often people still talk about it."

A year after I spoke to Rob about his brush with fame at just five years old, Sky Sports' Saturday morning programme *Soccer AM* got in touch with me wanting to trace Rob's whereabouts. Vinnie was due on the programme the next day and they wanted to surprise him with a visit from his grown up 'victim'. Less than 24 hours later the reunion took place in the studio and an iconic moment in football and Elland Road folklore was fondly remembered and given a suitably agreeable ending.

MONK'S BRIDGE IRON COMPANY

Elland Road's first burger stall originally cast from iron? Well, it's a nice image but the truth is a little less intriguing and goes a lot further back than pre-match burger sales. The Monk's Bridge Iron Company was founded in 1851 and under owner James Kitson became a famous manufacturer of "Best Yorkshire" Iron. The company's main works were a huge complex on either side of Whitehall Road on the western outskirts of Leeds city centre in Holbeck, which was so vast it had its own train system. Monk's Bridge took advantage of the cheap land and willing workforce to rapidly expand its business in the latter part of the 1800s to become a major employer in the area.

The Monk's Bridge Iron Company, however, also owned land on the "Gelderd Road and Churwell side" of the Elland Road ground, and several sources record that 3,961 square yards of this was purchased by Leeds City in 1906 for the princely sum of £420, at a time when they had just completed their inaugural season in the Football League. Such a large portion of land was purchased because Leeds City were wanting to change the orientation of the pitch from the east/west direction used by both the rugby club and Leeds City during their first season. Due to horrendous drainage issues causing diabolical, quagmire conditions (blamed on the rugby team, but actually as a result of past mining on the site and the nearby beck) the football club wanted to experiment in changing the pitch direction to the north/south, which remains today.

Purchasing the land allowed the club to spend £3,000 building a new 4,000-seater stand on the west side of the ground, the original West Stand which burnt down in 1956, although building work on the stand was delayed by several weeks when the council insisted the club built deeper foundations so as not to disturb the "rhubarb crops in a neighbouring field". Yes you read that correctly; rhubarb very nearly put the kibosh on the initial development of Elland Road.

In the late 1800s, the area around Beeston formed part of an extensive South Leeds region of rhubarb cultivation, which was known as the 'Rhubarb Triangle'. Frank Goddard of the Beeston Historical Society received, in the 1980s, part of a study carried out by the Leeds University Geography Department, which refers to the Beeston area and its rich rhubarb crops around the late 1800s. Many Leeds people of a certain age still refer to rhubarb as 'tusky', a name passed on from previous generations, and 'playing in the tusky fields' was a common pastime for youngsters in the 1800s.

When commenting on an Ordnance Survey map from 1894 the Leeds University report notes very little of rural significance in the Beeston area other than a series of "strange, large rectangular buildings" which stand isolated and sporadic, often in fields that can only be accessed via cart-roads. The report suggests these can only be rhubarb or tusky sheds, as the region had an unusual cash-crop of the plant at the time. Frank Goddard himself, a resident of Beeston for many years, has childhood memories from the 1950s of several 'rhubarb forcing sheds' in the locality, and indeed the area where White Rose Shopping Centre now stands was known to be all rhubarb fields at one time.

In addition to the land purchased by Leeds City, records show that Monk's Bridge Iron Company also owned the land where Fullerton Park later stood. A legal dispute erupted in 1927 when rival greyhound associations looked to set up competing tracks across from each other on Elland Road; this dispute referenced Monk's Bridge as owning the land on the north side of the road, ie. what was soon to become Fullerton Park Speedway Stadium. Therefore, the sale of land to Leeds City in 1906 only included a small portion of the land Monk's Bridge actually owned in the area. Indeed a report in *The Times* from 15th December 1911 references the 78 acres of freehold land that the Monk's Bridge Iron Company were advertising for sale on Elland Road (five years after they had sold a portion to Leeds City), and it also refers to the fact that the land is bounded along the whole of the western side by the Great Northern Railway. This is still the case today, and confirms that at one time Monk's Bridge owned all the land on the western side of the football ground.

Conspicuous in the middle of the 1894 Ordnance Survey map is a building that the Leeds University report calls "undeniably the prize specimen", which is located on what became the Fullerton Park training pitches, and therefore on the land owned by Monk's Bridge at the time. This was a building roughly 65 yards wide and 100 yards long, bigger than many factories of the time. The report then suggests that Beeston's otherwise backwater existence, boasting little of significance, may just, however, lay claim to the biggest rhubarb shed in the world; a proud boast indeed.

Nevertheless, with the unlikely diversion of rhubarb successfully navigated, building work recommenced and the opening of the first West Stand took place before a game versus Chelsea on 17th November 1906. At the time of the land purchase it is not known what Monk's Bridge Iron Company were doing with the land which is now the area upon which the Kop and the West Stand car park are built. There are no records of industrial activity and tithe maps of the time show only arable land in this area, so it is likely that the company merely owned the land and were not using it. It is possible there was an intention to use the land as a private company sports field, as many believe Bentley's Brewery were doing the same with the land originally bought by Holbeck Rugby Club as 'Elland Road'.

At any time up to the mid-2000s, any fans taking the roughly 35-minute walk from Leeds city station to Elland Road on match days would pass in between the two opposing halves of the mammoth Monk's Bridge site on Whitehall Road, with the walkway connecting the two above the road. The site was dark and imposing, and was sold to Doncasters of Sheffield in 1951, exactly 100 years after it was built. By 2005 Doncasters was sold to Dubai International and the site was closed and demolished. It is now one of the many plush office and residential complexes on the approach to the city centre, known as 'No. 1', which includes the new home of Yorkshire Post Newspapers.

NEW PEACOCK INN

Every Leeds United fan is aware of the Old Peacock pub and its statesmanlike position overlooking Elland Road, but many fans may be unaware of a second, and sadly long gone, pub further along Elland Road towards the city centre called the New Peacock Inn.

The New Peacock was originally built in the 1840s to serve the workers, housed locally, from the various brickworks in the area. Indeed the pub stood adjacent to the Leeds Fireclay Company and opposite Whitaker's Brickyard on the other side of Elland Road. Many workers lived in the Knowles Yard area effectively between the pub and the Leeds Fireclay Company. Such was the inherent link between the co-existing working and recreational establishments, that during the early years it was a regular occurrence for workers and New Peacock regulars to retire to sleep in the warm brick yard ovens after a heavy session, rather than face the wrath at home, and roll over ready for work the next morning.

Next to the Leeds Fireclay Company were empty fields and the New Peacock stood on the perimeter of what, around the turn of the century, informally became the New Peacock Cricket Ground. It was more widely known as the Holbeck Cricket Ground. The pub stood on the boundary edge and served as an unofficial pavilion for many years with access to the pub possible from the cricket ground behind it, and the pub itself afforded great views of the action.

When the Holbeck Cricket Club was disbanded in 1962 the pub remained, then under the stewardship of landlord Les Childs, and indeed the pub stood alone on the roadside when the adjacent housing of the former Islington area was demolished later that decade. This was all leading up to the building of the M621 and sure enough, with that work ongoing and the need for access feeder roads to be built, the New Peacock lasted only until the summer of 1974 when it was closed and soon demolished.

Stories exist suggesting the New Peacock, despite being appropriately painted white, was not a pub of any great significance, just an authentic local of its time with little glamour or atmosphere. Ray Fell, as a local resident, was fond of it though: "I used to go midweek when I lived on Tilbury Terrace, they held dances in the back room and you think about it now and wonder 'where the hell did we used to dance?' because it wasn't big."

Many local people suggest that the original Old Peacock was much the more lively and convivial pub of the two, at least prior to its re-build in 1963. Nevertheless the New Peacock had a reputation for fine ales and, in particular, how well its beer was kept, and the pub was also famous for the 'BYB' (Bentley's Yorkshire Bitter) logo painted on the side wall facing the cricket ground for many years. Bentley's Brewery owned the pub for most of its existence.

There are records of licensees of the New Peacock going back as far as 1842 when a William Bradley was

The New Peacock pictured in November 1963 with its vivid white exterior and BYB signage.

the landlord, 16 years later handing it over to his son Edward in 1858. This follows the logic that the 'New' Peacock appeared not long after the Old Peacock down the road, for which records of licensees exist as far back as 1826.

In 1963 a jocular contradiction was formed when the Old Peacock was re-built. The 'New' Peacock thus became the more senior building compared to the 'Old' Peacock, something which was immediately apparent in the external design of the two buildings. By this time the New Peacock's whitewashed walls had been weathered grey by over a century of industrial emissions.

The sad, final days of the New Peacock Inn were overseen by licensees Sammy and Betty Redmond, who had taken on the pub's tenancy in 1969 and instilled a new sense of life to it. The couple introduced bingo nights and Betty opened up a kitchen on the first floor to serve wholesome home cooked food for the workers in the nearby brickyards and factories. This was a time of course when serving food in a pub was almost unheard of.

Sammy Redmond hailed from Bathgate in Scotland and was an ex-miner who had moved to Yorkshire to work in the pits. Much of the New Peacock's trade would come from unemployed miners from Bathgate who had lost their jobs and stayed in one of the New Peacock's five bedrooms, at Sammy's invitation, whilst they sought work in Leeds. Once work was found they would often end up living in what remained of the nearby back-to-back terrace houses and an enclave of Scottish migrants and fiercely loyal New Peacock customers was created.

With the regrettable closure of the pub imminent, the Redmonds applied to become tenants of the New Inn on the Churwell stretch of Elland Road, and were expected to be successful. Unfortunately, just days before the couple were about to shut the doors on the New Peacock forever, the brewery instead awarded the tenancy to the now-retired Leeds United legend John Charles. Devastated, the couple were then offered the tenancy of the Old Peacock pub which they reluctantly accepted. It took the couple two days to move their belongings the 300 yards down the road between the two pubs, and they stayed at the Old Peacock until 1978 when Sammy died as a result of skull injuries sustained when he fell down the cellar steps. Betty also died a year later.

The exact location of the New Peacock pub is difficult to trace now given the dramatic alteration to the local landscape, but using estimative logic the precise spot is likely to be in the middle of the carriageway, as Elland Road bends around and becomes the A643/ Stadium Way that leads to the roundabout underneath the M621. The original Elland Road disappears at this point, and re-appears over the M621 carriageway. But again, there remains no palpable evidence that a rival to the Old Peacock, which many see as the everlasting epicentre of Elland Road, existed for over 130 years and in different circumstances may have outlasted it.

NEUTRAL GAMES

A picture from the 1956 invitation game between the Leeds & District FA and the Uganda FA with the newly seated Lowfields Road Stand in the background. Note the Ugandan player heading the ball is wearing boots but his two team-mates behind are playing with only bandaged feet.

Attempting to create a definitive list of neutral games that have taken place at Elland Road is a thankless task, particularly as criteria are pretty much open-ended in terms of what should and shouldn't be included. The only certainty is that there will be something missing, and as sure as a Sterland cross will meet a Chapman head, this section will not reference every single football game staged at Elland Road that has not involved Leeds City or Leeds United. What I have attempted to do is collate the information that is officially available, and much as we would like it to, that doesn't usually involve end of season games between the ground staff and coaching staff or the numerous schoolboy finals that Leeds City Council arranged during their ownership of the ground. Nor does it involve the more recent charity games where teams made up of mere mortals can pledge an amount of money to tread the hallowed turf. Hence, before anyone starts, I will not enter into any correspondence over the completeness of this section!

Whilst many might consider neutral games to begin and end with the high-profile FA Cup Semi-Finals, Euro 96 encounters and England internationals, these are dealt with elsewhere and don't actually do justice to the ground's civic importance in staging regional representative games, amateur finals and indeed FA Cup replays from earlier rounds. There are also the 'home' games staged by Huddersfield Town and Bradford City that have been documented in detail elsewhere.

Elland Road's first-ever recognised association football game was a regional final: the West Yorkshire Cup Final of 1898 when Hunslet defeated Harrogate 1-0. As the ground became more established as a venue capable of holding more sizeable crowds, it was awarded further and more varied games to stage. The

FA Amateur Cup was the premier cup competition for amateur clubs in England, as the name suggests. The first final took place in Richmond in 1894 and three finals were played in Leeds, at Headingley in 1895 and 1902, and in 1914 at Elland Road. Bishop Auckland triumphed over Northern Nomads 1-0 before a crowd of 5,294. The trophy was last played for in 1974 when the FA abolished its distinction between amateur and professional clubs and devised two knockout cups for non-league teams, the FA Trophy and the FA Vase.

The Leeds and District FA has always held strong links with Leeds United, particularly in the early years, and regularly played its Senior Cup Final at Elland Road during the Easter period. The gate receipts often provided a welcome financial boost to the association in the early years as the attendances were generally good. Games were played from the 1930s onwards, and in 1947 a gate in excess of 10,000 attended the final between Yorkshire Amateur and Leeds UYMI. The game actually went to two replays, both of which were also staged at Elland Road.

On Jubilee Day of 1935 a friendly match also took place between Leeds United and the Leeds and District FA for the King George Jubilee Trust Fund. One of the even more unusual games the Leeds and District FA played at Elland Road was when a representative side from several local Leeds clubs, including Farsley Celtic, East End Park and Yorkshire Amateur, played against a Uganda FA XI on 15th September 1956. This was the first time the Association had played a touring international team, and Leeds United actually postponed their reserves' game in order to accommodate the fixture. The most memorable feature of the game was that several of the Ugandan team played barefoot, and are surely the only team to do so at Elland Road. My Dad was present and recalls the referee having to stop the game on one occasion to count the players, and it was found the Ugandans had 12 or 13 players on the pitch. Another interesting footnote to this game is that it was the last to be played at Elland Road in front of the original West Stand, as three days later on 18th September, it burnt down.

Prior to the Uganda game the West Riding FA had faced what was quite loosely described as a 'South African Touring team' at Elland Road, on 31st October 1953, drawing 2-2. This was just one of many games that can only be described as 'miscellaneous' in nature and stature. On 9th October 1957 the Football League and the League of Ireland locked horns. The Football League side triumphed 3-1, partly due to the contribution of Jack Charlton and future Leeds manager Jimmy Armfield. The following month, on 20th November 1957, a team representing 'The Army' played a game against 'Ireland' at Elland Road, for what reason we simply don't know.

Elland Road has staged nine FA Cup Semi-Finals, details of which have been included in the 'FA Cup

Semi-Finals' section. But it has also staged the following replayed games where the ground was used as a neutral venue after an initial tie and first replay could not separate the sides. I have also included the aforementioned Farsley Celtic match here, which was played as a 'home' tie for Farsley:

FA Cup Sixth Round Second Replay
30th March 1912
Barnsley 0 Bradford 0 (AET)

FA Cup First Round Third Replay
9th December 1931
Doncaster Rovers 1 Barrow 0

FA Cup Third Round Second Replay
16th January 1939
Middlesbrough 1 Bolton 0

FA Cup Fourth Round Second Replay
4th February 1946
Middlesbrough 1 Blackpool 0

FA Cup Third Round Second Replay
16th January 1950
Middlesbrough 3 Aston Villa 0

FA Cup First Round Second Replay
3rd December 1951
Bradford Park Avenue 4 York City 0

FA Cup Second Round Second Replay
5th December 1960
Hull City 1 Darlington 1

FA Cup First Round Second Replay
5th December 1966
Darlington 4 Stockport 2

FA Cup First Round
23rd November 1974
Farsley Celtic 0 Tranmere 2

FA Cup Fifth Round Second Replay
23rd February 1976
Newcastle 2 Bolton 1

FA Cup Second Round Second Replay
22nd December 1980
Hull City 2 Blyth Spartans 1

FA Cup First Round Second Replay
30th November 1981
Hull City 1 Rochdale 0

The order and arrangement of professional football matches staged during wartime fall into the bracket best described as 'random', and while Leeds United played in regional leagues occasional representative games were staged at Elland Road, largely as a means of distracting the population with a form of entertainment; a bit like Gracie Fields for the great unwashed.

WARTIME REPRESENTATIVE GAMES

13th December 1941
FA XI 2 RAF XI 2
Attendance: 13,000

21st February 1942
Northern Command 1 Scottish Command 1
Attendance: 8,500

26th December 1942
Army 3 RAF 1
Attendance: 20,000

Finally, while major internationals at Elland Road are a relatively recent addition to the ground's proud heritage, more minor international levels have been represented at Elland Road as far back as the Leeds City days:

AMATEUR INTERNATIONALS

20th November 1909
England 4 Ireland 4
Attendance: 8,000

16th March 1929
England 3 Scotland 1
Attendance: 15,571

26th March 1958
England 1 France 1
Attendance: 6,000

ENGLAND TRIALS

22nd January 1906
The North 0 The South 2
Attendance: 7,000

21st January 1924
The North 5 The South 1
Attendance: 4,496

UNDER-23 INTERNATIONALS

9th November 1961
England 7 Israel 1
Attendance: 12,419

7th April 1965
England 0 Czechoslovakia 0
Attendance: 8,533

UNDER-21 INTERNATIONALS

7th October 2005
England 1 Austria 2
Attendance: 28,030

NORTH EAST CORNER STAND

A crowd of over 50,000 is packed into Elland Road for a 2-2 draw between Leeds and Manchester United in October 1970, but of course your eyes are drawn to the 'savage' excavation that chopped away the north east corner in order for the new Kop to be built in 1968.

The North East Corner Stand with the former Kop Shop and Programme Cabin buildings in the foreground before they were demolished in 2017.

A number of sources state that the two corner stands that flank the Kop were built at the same time in 1970. This is not the case, and the North West Corner Stand technically pre-dates the North East by two years. However, whilst a gaping hole existed between the West Stand and the Kop between 1968 and 1970, a similarly neglected gap existed between the Kop and the Lowfields Road Stand for the same time span. The difference being that the North East Corner Stand was developed in stages from 1970 onwards and was not fully completed until spring 1973.

When the North West Corner Stand was opened in February 1970, the north east corner remained as it was: a deep and savage-looking hollow in the previously towering corner terracing that linked the original Kop and the Lowfields. For a time the gap was an unseemly mess and was filled briefly by the temporary floodlight standing between the Kop and the sheer, steep edge to the Lowfields terracing that had been chopped away and abruptly appeared high into the sky. Gary Edwards also remembers the gap being a temporary vantage point for a select few: "The bus drivers and conductors from Leeds City Transport would congregate beneath the Kop/Lowfields Road floodlight pylon as they watched the game for free. They would be dressed in their dark green LCT uniforms, and most of them would be wearing their Leeds United woollen scarf. Unfortunately, despite what the score was at the time, they would have to leave the ground early to prepare the buses for the mass exodus of fans back into town."

On the eastern side of the cut away hill it was still possible to stand on a section of the upper Lowfields corner terracing for a couple of years before it was chopped away right up to the glass windows of the Lowfields upper seated section. Kevin Mulligan remembers standing there in the late 1960s and early 1970s when the huge gap appeared: "In those days I had progressed to standing high up to the side of the Lowfields corner where the North East Corner Stand is now, it overlooked the newly erected Kop. From my new viewing point I had a good view of the Kop end, but had to view through the glass-ended Lowfields stand towards the Scratching Shed end. It was a decent viewing spot up there all huddled together looking down onto the soil banking, that was until it was well into any given season's winter period when the winds could howl up there and any slight snow dusting that seemed to settle would be driven up onto the fans as a snowstorm. But in those days, at that age, I didn't seem to feel the cold."

It was not until during the 1970/71 season that the lower section of the Lowfields terracing was extended into the north east corner to join the Kop, and brought some order and permanency to the area. The remaining high banking of the Lowfields terracing above it was also cut away, creating the first of the infamous two grass banks either side of the Lowfields upper section. And it was not until well into the 1972/73 season that work started on the seating section above the terracing that curved round before

abruptly ending in line with the 18 yard box at the Kop end, as it awaited the further development of the east side of Elland Road. It would wait another 20 years and in the meantime fans in the North East Corner Stand and the Lowfields Road seats could wave at each other across the unfortunate gap that separated them.

When completed the £250,000 North East Corner Stand provided a welcome balance to the developing stadium, though while it looked modern and compact it had reduced the potential capacity of the stadium compared to the vast, open terracing it had replaced. The initial use for the terracing in the corner stand was the new location of the Boys' Pen, which had been without a home since the old Kop was demolished in 1968. But in later years it simply became general terracing, before becoming seated along with the other areas on the east side prior to the 1993/94 season.

At one stage this small terracing section in the north east corner gained huge significance. This was during the promotion season of 1989/90 when, as a result of the Taylor Report, Elland Road's standing capacities had been cut dramatically on the very eve of the season. This meant that a combination of increasing numbers of season ticket holders and a sudden improvement in on-pitch fortunes resulted in access to the Kop, South Stand and Lowfields terracing (ie. the cheapest options) becoming extremely difficult. Word soon spread that the north east corner terracing was a good available option as not many fans held season tickets in that section. Therefore, with the 'sold out' signs being shown around the ground it was not uncommon to see queues snaking outside the North East Corner Stand from about 2.00pm on a match day in 1989/90.

The seating section of the North East Corner Stand has always maintained a healthy population, and when full gives the ground an imposing uniformity from the northern end. The end gable of the original North East Corner Stand roof, which for so long was simply the emblem of an unfinished stadium, is still visible as it joins on to the East Stand, again adding to the untidy, visual confusion of the ground. However, the roof was shortened in 1993 when the East Stand was built, as the final two sections of the North East Corner Stand amalgamated, for once seamlessly, into the new East Stand and exits and facilities were re-designated accordingly when the East Stand was complete.

Alas, one feature that will always remain while ever there is a gable end roof to the North East Corner Stand is the unfortunate consequence of bad weather for those sat underneath. Leeds fan of many years Dougie Wales recalls: "The rain used to always drip off the guttering. That corner was always an open end and anyone stood in the Lowfields down there used to get soaked by the water dripping down." It's still the same today, although the luckless recipients are at least sat down.

NORTH WEST CORNER STAND

It's December 1969 and Allan Clarke scores one of two goals in a 2-0 win over Sheffield Wednesday with the West Stand extension and the North West Corner Stand being built in the background.

Unobtrusive, harmless and almost an afterthought in Elland Road's grand structure. While the building of the 'new' Kop in 1968 was undoubtedly the first move towards Don Revie's vision of a modern Elland Road, the construction of the North West Corner Stand in 1970 was also a significant factor in the masterplan. The humble stand was the first development towards creating the enclosed bowl effect that has done so much to enhance the atmospherics and create the intimidating character that a vibrant Elland Road is famous for.

The coupling of the new Kop to the West Stand was carried out after a huge gap had been left between the two stands in the north west corner for a year, during

which time you could quite clearly see a sizeable section of the pitch if, by chance, you happened to be taking a casual stroll around the perimeter of Elland Road on a Saturday afternoon.

In actual fact there had always been a gap there, but not so much at ground level, particularly as turnstile blocks had stood there until 1968. But that original incarnation of the 'north west corner' wasn't so much renowned for how you viewed the game, but for how you exited it. Like a railway embankment, the original Kop was a huge mound of soil and cinders and the left hand edge of it was steep banking that led out to the West Stand car park. For those not wishing to wait and queue to exit the huge terrace after games via the steps at the bottom, there was the option of hurdling the fence and taking the risk of sliding down the banking. Of

course today this wouldn't be an option and any access to 30 feet of sheer banking would be comprehensively fenced off, but pre-1968 hundreds of intrepid fans could be seen descending the banking in undignified fashion in a rush to head home. What many fans didn't realise, or those that did chose to ignore, was that the banking contained loose 'clinker', a brittle and sharp off-shoot from the brickworks around the area in the early 1900s, and its liberal scattering amongst the surface of the banking often resulted in grazes and cuts for those taking the perilous option of a hasty exit.

Gary Edwards recalls afternoons involving high danger of a slightly different kind, when he was a young fan in the West Stand and before the North West Corner Stand offered some protection: "We had season tickets in the West Stand in the seats close to the

The police tunnel in the north west corner showing the doors of the groundsman's storage room and the jail/Detention Room. The Perspex construction above the tunnel is where the match day DJ/announcer used to play his records. Note also one of the famous floodlight towers flashing a bit of leg; the little flirt.

north west corner – years before the present corner stand was built. We were on the end seats, almost at the back of the stand, and to our left it was a sheer 30 foot drop to the ground. Whenever we scored I would slide down the wooden shelf on top of the exterior wall. I was totally oblivious to the danger of falling over the edge. It is only now that I understand why Dad would run alongside me with outstretched arms – just in case. I always thought he was as excited as me that Leeds had scored. He was a busy man on those heady afternoons when we used to score five, six and seven regularly."

The building of the new Kop meant that a smaller banking was left in the north west corner for a year along with a wider, flatter area, leading up to the West Stand where the previous Kop had tapered away. The building of the North West Corner Stand began in the summer of 1969, just after Leeds had won their first league title, and also involved building a straight extension to the West Stand to allow for the extra yardage created by the new Kop.

Costing £200,000, fans expressed some financial concern at the time, particularly as the club had just spent £160,000 on striker Allan Clarke. Chairman Percy Woodward bluntly rebuffed such worry with the remark "one has nothing to do with the other". The construction was finally opened to the public on 7th February 1970 for a Fifth Round FA Cup tie versus Mansfield Town, which Leeds won 2-0, although at the time the stand was not fully completed, and just 1,500

seats from the new construction were able to be used. Regarding the cost, it is interesting to note that just less than two years earlier the entire Kop had been built for £250,000, clearly illustrating the crippling inflation of building work at the time, which would eventually derail the club's development plans completely.

Much of the money was spent on the aesthetics outside the North West Corner Stand. The red brickwork, concrete columns and windows that lined the back of the West Stand were continued on the back of the new corner stand. Matching the brickwork was no easy task and even today, 50 years later, you can see the very slight change in the colour of the brickwork which signals the point at which the original West Stand ended. An aerial view also shows where the roofs of the West Stand and the North West Corner Stand were joined. From inside the stadium the West Stand roof appears continuous until it meets the Kop, albeit, unfortunately, it is a few feet lower and as such does not offer the artistic contours that more modern football grounds possess. Instead we have the clumsy irregularity that gives Elland Road the more traditional, unpolished edge that most Leeds fans prefer, although the symmetry provided by the North East Corner Stand's roof also not meeting the Kop enhances the graceful effect very slightly, if unintentionally.

Having housed the Family Stand for a few years, in 1990, Bill Fotherby split the North West Corner in two and spent £80,000 creating the Captains' Lounge; yet another of his 'exclusive' corporate ventures. It lasted less than five years but somehow the name has stuck. For a seasonal membership fee fans were offered bar and food facilities, televisions and a carpet. The area was later utilised by LUSC for a number of years before Ken Bates returned it to a normal stand. The facilities were immediately ripped out, as heaven forbid the average fan would be allowed a carpet to walk on at no extra cost, rather than bare concrete.

In terms of capacity, the North West Corner Stand is slightly lower than its twin, the North East Corner, due mainly to the police control box in the centre of the stand between the upper and lower sections. This was opened in October 1991 at a cost of £150,000, and utilising 18 cameras was claimed to be the most advanced in Europe at the time. The police/groundsman's tunnel next to the West Stand, and the barrier that bisects the stand separating the 'Captains' Lounge' from the other, regular half of the North West Corner, also serve to reduce the capacity of the stand. The police tunnel effectively takes up half of what would be the lower tier and this is now just an extension to the Kop, and as such was also previously terracing until 1994.

Currently the disabled fans situated in front of the Kop and West Stand are able to use the facilities behind the North West Corner Stand known as the Eddie Gray Suite. Indeed Gary Edwards recalls the north west corner being one of the first shelters for disabled Leeds fans back in the 1970s when such facilities were not obligatory by law: "...at that time light blue three-wheeler invalid cars would be parked in front of the Kop wall as their occupants watched the game from the comfort of their cosy little cars with heaters on full blast and wipers on fast (mostly)."

Also built into the external wall outside the stand are the premises of the St John's Ambulance, whose First Aid room is the old manager's office, first used by Don Revie in 1970. This area was also briefly the premises for the souvenir shop of Hunslet RL when they played on the ground in the 1980s, and the home of their dedicated bar, the 'Pheonix Bar'. When the North West Corner Stand was built in 1970, the players' lounge, manager's and secretary's offices were relocated down there, and these areas still exist today as the rooms mentioned above. Dave Cocker recalls the office move, its new location and the somewhat flexible workforce in Revie's era: "As you walked down that tunnel next to the North West Corner Stand, Don's office was on the immediate left and next door was his secretary, Jean, and then there was the players' lounge. Until then the manager's office was roughly where the ticket office was in the middle of the West Stand behind the blue facade; they were just glass-panelled offices. The only non-football staff they had then was Sue Williamson the general secretary, Peter Crowther the assistant secretary,

A 1978 view of the completed North West Corner Stand when the bottom half was terracing.

the ticket office manager, a girl in the ticket office, a typist, a nightwatchman, the two laundry girls and two groundsmen. That was it." Today, in comparison, the who's who of Leeds United Football Club reads like the directory of Exxon Mobil.

The North West Corner Stand location of the manager's office was inherited for the first time by Brian Clough, who held an infamously frosty relationship with his predecessor Revie. Legend has it, and confirmed by Duncan McKenzie, Clough's first signing for Leeds, that Clough arrived on his first day and was shown into his office by his new secretary. As McKenzie tells it, "Cloughie had said 'whose is this desk?' and the secretary said 'well, it's yours Mr Clough'. So he said 'whose was this desk?' and she said 'well, it was Mr Revie's', so he said 'I want it burnt.'" Peter Lorimer tells the same story, elaborating slightly with the addition of Clough's justification for his actions, that being "he wouldn't sit on anything that Don had sat on". Alas, the manager's office didn't stay in the North West Corner for long, and by the mid- to late 1970s it was back in the central area of the West Stand behind the reception area.

Another long-standing 'facility' beneath the North West Corner Stand is the 'jail' on the left hand side of the police tunnel as you exit the ground. This was adapted from a spare room in August 1970 as Leeds' hooligan problems began to develop, and still includes a charge room, office, briefing room and detention cell. It allows for fans to be detained and questioned during the match as necessary and also enables radio communication with officers outside. Subsequently the police tunnel also serves as a convenient route through which to expel fans from the ground completely should no further action be required. The jail now goes by the more formal name of the 'Detention Room'. Like many small and unassuming rooms dotted around the stadium, the Detention Room will have many stories to tell and will have been privy to some very colourful exchanges over the years, not least with a pantomime horse.

OLD PEACOCK PUB

Not a listed building yet but also not just a simple pub, but a monument to a lifetime of match-going protocol for generations of football fans, and a symbol of the once very fine divide between the fan and the football club. The Old Peacock pub stands proudly on Elland Road to this day, an example of the fabric of everyday life blending in with the affection and rituals of a football fan, and much like the ravens in the Tower of London you sense that if it disappeared, the very essence of Leeds United would go with it.

Despite its indelible link with the football club, the link is not a congenital one, as the Old Peacock pub actually existed long before Leeds United and even Leeds City were formed. Evidence of the pub goes back to 1826 when a pub simply listed in the Leeds Directory as 'Peacock' existed in 'Beeston', and its proprietor was a William Pike. By 1830 a 'Peacock Inn' is listed as residing in the small borough of Islington, with licensee William Bradley described as a "victualler and maltster".

Despite the names there is some conjecture regarding which pub appeared first, the Old Peacock or the New Peacock. Certainly, prior to the 1842 Leeds Directory there is only one pub named: the Peacock Inn. By 1842 there was a 'New Peacock' and another pub also in Islington named quite plainly 'Peacock'. You

have to assume this was the same pub as referenced identically in the 1826 directory, and slightly differently in 1830. The boundaries of the borough of Islington have always been open to question, but it would appear logical that sometime after 1842 the 'Peacock' pub changed its name to the 'Old Peacock' to reflect and distinguish itself from its newer acquaintance, and life went on from there. Confirmation of this is found listed in the 1870 directory where both pubs are recorded with their most commonly remembered names.

With William Bradley listed in 1830 as the proprietor of the 'Peacock Inn', it would appear he was quite a prominent part of the local public house trade. The 1817 and 1826 Leeds Directories list him as proprietor of the Old White Hart, which is on Town Street at the top of Beeston Hill. It remains a popular pre-match pub today and proudly pre-dates both the Old Peacock and the Drysalters. By 1842 William Bradley had pitched up as the first listed proprietor of the New Peacock, and Samuel Blackburn had taken over the 'Peacock'.

Samuel Blackburn was followed in the Old Peacock hot seat by a licensee simply known as 'Crowther' in 1854 (also listed as a cattle dealer), Samuel Sanderson in 1858, John Barraclough in 1866 (also listed as a cattle dealer), Elizabeth Barraclough in 1888 and

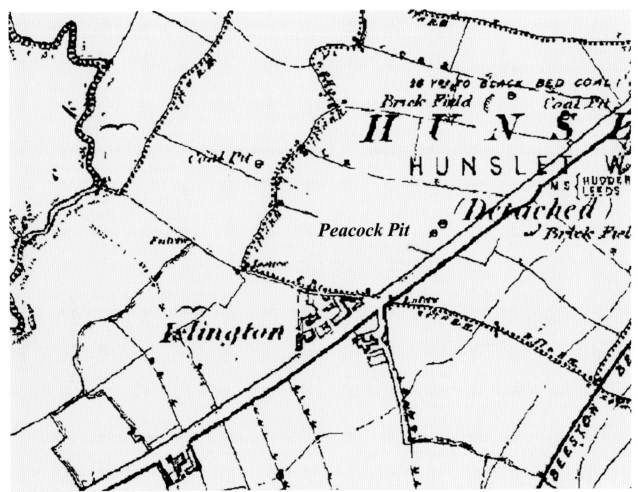

An 1852 Ordnance Survey map showing the location of the Peacock Pit. The small collection of buildings on the south side of Elland Road in the bottom left hand corner of the map is the Old Peacock pub, hence at this time there was nothing at all standing opposite on the land that became Elland Road football ground.

Joshua Rhodes in 1894, by which time the pub was now curiously listed as standing in Holbeck. The three boroughs that the pub had already been listed in (Beeston, Islington and Holbeck) clearly demonstrates the evolving nature of the geographical landscape, with residential and mining developments already in place and sporting developments also starting to appear.

Conjecture also exists over where the 'Peacock' name originates from. It is true that there was a 'Peacock Pit' in the borough of Islington near the site of the cricket ground in the 19th century, and although that was actually nearer to the site of the New Peacock it is thought by some to be the origin of the name for both pubs, and initially what became the Old Peacock. But then where did the name of the pit originate from? Many of the pits around that time took their name from the family name of a prominent owner or businessman, such as the nearby Lee Pit and Hall Pit in the Beeston area. 'Peacock' was a popular surname in Leeds at the time, as listed in many 19th century directories, and it is certainly possible that a pit owner lent his name to the colliery. Then again, many people believe that the pubs existed before the pit did, and this is actually more feasible. There are no available records to evidence when the Peacock Pit was created, but given the Old Peacock pub was in place in 1826 and coal mining in the area was most prominent in the second half of the 19th century, it is certainly possible that the pub arrived first. Therefore the question becomes, was the 'Peacock' name derived from an early owner, land owner or licensed victualler of the pub? And did this name unwittingly create a huge and ongoing legacy? It certainly appears likely.

The Old Peacock was re-built in 1963. The original pub was a much grander, more prominent building rising high above the Scratching Shed roof if viewed from the Kop end. It also stood much closer to the road than the current one; a car could just about park front end on as the pub opened out almost directly onto the pavement of Elland Road.

This original pub was demolished after the current building was constructed in the space behind it, creating the vast front car park that exists today, and thus was better equipped to deal with the increasing crowds and general interest in the area of LS11 that Don Revie's impending success would create. The licensees of the time, Bill and Ann Fox, simply moved from one pub to the other behind it. It is not known why the pub was re-built, as in 1963 the degree of Revie's success could not possibly have been predicted, but there is no doubt it then looked much more modern than the 'New Peacock' that now pre-dated it by over 120 years. Locals of the time also speak about the re-built Old Peacock somehow lacking the ambience and joviality of its predecessor from this point onwards, despite retaining the same management and clientele.

One of the regular and perhaps more questionable match day activities for visitors to Elland Road, and more specifically to the Old Peacock pub, right up to the early 1960s was the indulgence in tripe provided free in the pub's tap room. Tripe, for our younger readers, is a type of edible offal made from the stomach of various farm animals, usually cows. That's right, edible. Every Saturday lunchtime on match days and non-match days a huge plate of tripe would be brought into the Old Peacock by an operator after his shift at the nearby 'Sausage Factory' and Tripeworks at the foot of Crow Nest Lane next to the Drysalters pub. The landlady would dress the tripe and set it out onto the long bar with the essential accompaniment of vinegar.

Despite the obvious attraction of the pub on match days it has always served as a community focal point in the meantime, albeit with varying degrees of success. The pub had always been a Bentley's pub with a distinct local flavour, until Whitbread's bought the brewery in 1968, at which point it became a Whitbread's pub and perhaps this was a trigger for the downturn in mood experienced by locals who were fiercely loyal to their brand, at a time of limited options. In addition, during the week the pub had always been regularly frequented by Leeds United staff and players after training, right up until the opening of Thorp Arch in 1996 dragged the thriving custom and disposable income of the typical first team footballer away.

In simple terms though, to most Leeds fans the Old Peacock is as convenient as match day pubs can possibly get, assuming of course that you can sufficiently indent the vacuum-packed body of people that are somehow housed in the building prior to kick-off. On several occasions I have walked in to be greeted, with a heavy heart, by a solid and seemingly impenetrable massed throng of people around nine deep at the bar, which requires stern elbows and much motivation to make any headway in.

Thankfully the beer garden at the back, cited as one of the biggest in Leeds and for many years dating back to the early 1900s the site of a proud and distinguished bowling green, is able to ease the pressure of people inside. Even on a cold winter's day you will find many fans preferring to stand outside rather than tackle the constant flow of people in the bar. Prior to being filled with picnic benches and the recent addition of the marquee, on a day of more favourable weather the beer garden has been the scene of some ferociously contested football matches between teams of up to 20-a-side. The children of beer-supping fans did battle and served up entertainment often far more intense and invigorating than the official 90 minutes that would follow.

The bowling green was most regularly used as such between the two World Wars and was the home of Holbeck Ltd Bowling Club, who played at the Old Peacock from their formation in 1914. At this time the pub was owned by Bentley's Brewery and the green

Old Peacock regulars boarding for a bus trip to Bridlington in the summer of 1962, just a year before this original pub was demolished and replaced by the current one behind it.

was kept in good condition and also used for county matches as it grew in prominence. Alas, a dispute with the brewery over the costs of maintenance led to the 'Holbeck' club moving to a new venue just off Town Street in Beeston, where they remain in good health today, whilst stoically persisting with their original Holbeck name.

In the days of Elland Road's Scratching Shed it was also common for fans to stay behind in the Old Peacock beer garden to scale the trees at the back and get a decent, unhindered view of the action in the Kop half of the pitch. Some games even saw fans sit on top of the pub roof. The building of the South Stand in 1974 soon put paid to that practice.

Fans assemble on the roof of the Old Peacock for a dubious view over the Scratching Shed of the FA Cup Fourth Round Replay versus Liverpool in February 1972.

The front car park to the Old Peacock has long since been a hive of entrepreneurial activity. For years numerous vendors have opened stalls of varying description, including merchandising, framed photos and the current location for Phil Beeton's Programme Cabin. Food vans have also lined the front of the car park for many years. The car park itself is also open for general use, at a price, and provides a decent income for the pub. Car parking spaces are limited and the convenience of the proximity to the ground is perhaps not quite justified by the risk you take in actually leaving your car there. Quite apart from it being a pub with hundreds of thirsty Leeds fans in it, the car park has also been a frequent battleground when away fans enter and exit, although this has somewhat subsided now that away fans are largely herded in and out of the West Stand area.

In April 2007, with Leeds United's fortunes about to hit an all-time low as relegation to the third tier of English football for the very first time was followed swiftly by an orchestrated fall into administration, the incumbent tenants of the Old Peacock, the Teesside-based Local Heroes Pub Company, advertised the leasehold of the pub at a price of £90,000. This threw the pub into possibly the most challenging and uncertain period of its – at the time – near 180-year existence.

Having spent nine years looking for a permanent home since losing the social club buildings on Fullerton Park, the Leeds United Supporters' Club (LUSC) purchased the leasehold of the pub in October 2007. At a time when the faith and commitment of Leeds United fans was being sorely tested, it was a bold move by LUSC to copper-up the £90,000 required to purchase the lease, let alone the annual rent then required to be paid to owners Greene King. Having scraped together the money from ring-fenced membership subscriptions, the one benefit of having had no permanent home on which to pay rent for the last nine years, LUSC took the step into what Ray Fell willingly admits was "the unknown".

LUSC held meetings in the pub on non-match days and ran it with relative success for nearly five years, despite the existing and direct competition from Leeds United and Ken Bates in the form of Billy's Bar across the road. But with the pub trade dying a slow death generally LUSC were fighting a losing battle. The generally muted and disenchanted mood around Elland

Road did not help, even though many fans were boycotting club venues such as the Pavilion, Billy's Bar and the concourse bars inside the ground as a protest aimed at preventing Ken Bates profiting from their money. While this should have meant 'independent' drinking establishments such as the Old Peacock prospered, it simply resulted in fans not attending matches at all, and contributed to LUSC biting the bullet in the face of an uncertain future and finances that had "run into a black hole".

In June 2012 LUSC announced they were calling time on their foray into the pub trade and Greene King took on the lease themselves. Many Leeds fans feared the worst; with a number of other pubs in the area also having closed in recent years it no longer seemed inconceivable that the Old Peacock may disappear with them. After all, the pub's demise was commensurate with the financial strife and barren, ambitionless landscape at Leeds United, so the connection was unavoidable.

By August 2012 Greene King had managed to re-open the pub again in time for the new season, which was ironically greeted by the news that Ken Bates was heading out of the exit door, albeit with a very long and overbearing goodbye. With a further, unforeseen twist Bates appeared to cool his strangely fractured relationship with LUSC at the same time, a move that, had it happened earlier, may have prompted LUSC to have held out a little longer with their unlikely pub venture.

The summer of 2013 saw unexpected developments that once again drew inescapable parallels between the destinies of both the pub and the football club ingrained in its history. As GFH Capital ousted Ken Bates from Leeds United and introduced a raft of crowd-pleasing ventures, so the independent and hugely successful Ossett Brewery took on the lease of the Old Peacock. With a £300,000 refurbishment and a rebranding as a real ale pub with good food and good service, it was clear that the pub was starting afresh just as the football club was, with both now taking a different, more considered, but ultimately very positive approach and deserving of the appropriate support. While the ownership struggles at Leeds United very quickly took a dark turn for the worse, before Andrea Radrizzani took 100% control in 2017, the Old Peacock continued to prosper under Ossett's canny management and grew into a formidable and well-drilled match day operation, which maximises the space available with a marquee and numerous outside bars to at least attempt to satiate the ever-thirsty Leeds United hordes.

And so for years to come match days will continue to follow the trusted structure; like a pie, a bet and unrealistic expectations for the game ahead, the Old Peacock prevails like an old friend.

THE OLD PEACOCK GROUND

It can only be the space and opportunities offered by the acres and acres of open fields, that tempted somebody to build a sports ground on the flat land at the foot of Beeston Hill in the Holbeck Valley, sometime in the 1870s. Tithe maps from 1856 show the land to be flattened, but they show little else that would prompt you to imagine, in a million years, what it would later become.

The land on the current location of Elland Road was flat in 1878 and had been extensively mined with numerous coal mines existing in the vicinity. It is also known that a rugby football team called Leeds Athletic were the first team to play a competitive game there. By this time the land was under the ownership of Bentley's Brewery and sure enough it had been decided that the flat land would make an ideal sports ground, to be named the 'Old Peacock Ground', after the pub that they also owned. Leeds Athletic became permanent residents, albeit only leasing the ground off Bentley's. A pitch was laid out and the nearby colliery waste was found to be suitable in making embankments around the pitch and producing a venue capable of holding "around 23,000". These embankments lasted a number of years, but they weren't permanent structural stands and, with the pitch running in the opposite direction to what it is now, the development of the ground was limited because Bentley's Brewery didn't own the land behind the pitch on the north and west sides of the ground. This wasn't purchased until 1906, by Leeds City, allowing the permanent stands and terracing to be built on those sides, thus creating the recognisable origins of the ground that Leeds United later developed.

In 1880 the pitch was drained and levelled further, but Leeds Athletic had pretensions of becoming Leeds' premier rugby club despite facing very stiff competition. After two seasons of leasing the Old Peacock Ground they moved back to their 'Royal Park' ground near Woodhouse Moor in 1881, because they deemed the Old Peacock Ground to be 'too isolated' in south west Leeds in terms of attracting support. That Leeds itself was saturated by competitive rugby teams gave the comments of Leeds Athletic a rather arrogant tone. Under their new name 'Yorkshire Wanderers' the club returned to the Old Peacock Ground for one more season in 1882/83, before their sorry demise.

It was to be another 14 years, involving little activity, before Holbeck Rugby Club bought the ground off Bentley's Brewery, and during Holbeck's tenure the sparse and relatively featureless patch of land gradually became commonly known as 'Elland Road'. Hunslet Association Football Club, technically the forerunners of Leeds City, were the first team to play the 'round ball' game on the ground in the West Yorkshire Cup Final versus Harrogate on 23rd April 1898, winning the game 1-0 before 3,400 people. Therefore, under its original guise as the Old Peacock Ground, this is believed to be the only association football game played competitively.

P

COUPON
NUMBER

ENTRANCE TO PEN 4 ONLY

Enter at your peril: the turnstiles to Elland Road's notorious Pen 4.

PEN 4

Whether gasping for breath after manic goal celebrations or cascading down the terracing with no control over your eventual whereabouts, there was fun to be had in Pen 4; the end pen on Lowfields Road, a playground of high-stakes games and an abrupt introduction to young adulthood.

Gradually throughout the early 1970s the Lowfields terrace was split up from one collective, seething mass, into a number of dissociated pens with fencing and gangways and the peculiar narrow shelf in between the terracing and the seats. But whilst this may have reduced the visual impact of the imposing assemblage, the atmosphere created was just as fierce, if not more so. The location of the away fans and the Leeds hooligan element was replicated from the earlier years when attendances dropped dramatically towards the end of the decade. Away fans were housed in the far corner of the Lowfields terrace, uncovered, with Leeds fans of a certain intent choosing to stand in the Lowfields Pen 4 or on the seats in the half-empty South Stand, which gave them the freedom of movement which the penned terraces didn't. Fans in the Kop and South Stand would then regularly instruct their fellow fans to carry out their duty, with the refrain "Lowfields, Lowfields do your job".

As attendances fluctuated the installation of the pens allowed the Lowfields terrace to be adapted accordingly match-by-match in terms of how many pens were allocated to Leeds fans and/or away fans. Eventually in 1987 away fans were given the South Stand when it was returned to terracing, if their numbers warranted it. But generally speaking the away fans stood isolated and exposed on the Lowfields terrace, and naturally,

the end pen on Lowfields Road housing Leeds' fans became an environment not for the faint-hearted, and fans seeking entertainment of the off-pitch variety soon gravitated there. Only a section of fencing and a few yards of empty terracing, which became known as 'no-man's land', separated you from the enemy and this became a caged battleground of missiles, insults and bubbling antagonism. There were no pipes of peace and Christmas-time cease fire.

"It used to get naughty in there," comments Stephen Talbot, who recalls the impossible conundrum the police faced in the days before all-ticket games could regulate how many away fans turned up: "I remember when Liverpool came once and the police let them in and they ran straight up to us, they had the segregation part but there were that many Liverpool fans they had to open it up and they all came in and ran up to the fence (next to Pen 4) and climbed up on the fence, it all went mad then. They had to put them in no-man's land because there was nowhere else to put them."

"I also remember," Stephen continues, "when we played QPR once. There had been no trouble in the ground at all, but something happened with two Leeds lads in Pen 4, and these coppers went in and got a hiding. I saw it myself, this lad absolutely leathered this copper and he got away. I'll never forget it, he hit him so hard the copper's helmet flew off and he had him over the barrier right at the front hitting him and hitting him, and he got away, he got out of that."

For some time a sign outside the turnstiles on Lowfields Road quite clearly stated 'Entrance to Pen 4 only' as if this was a disclaimer of sorts, ie. enter

through these turnstiles and you should know exactly what to expect. In reality the sign was less sinister, as Pen 4 was so popular that it merited an entrance all of its own, which was particularly valid for big games when there was no apparent 'safe' capacity.

Entering and embracing Pen 4 was like taking on a different identity, a 90 minute exercise in trying to stay on your feet, a breathless joy-ride in goading the opposition fans and players, a hair-raising challenge in trying to remain in contact with your mates, and god help you if Leeds scored, or you lost a shoe. In Pen 4, or similarly on the Kop in its pre-1989 heyday, a goal induced ritual uproar like an earthquake off the Richter scale and could quite easily see you end up in a different postcode. Yet the bruises or knocks or broken spectacles emanating from such riotous disorder were just laughed off between strangers as occupational hazards.

The nonchalance with which fans were squeezed into the pens in almost any numbers was accepted by both fans and authorities alike; for years safety was a mere afterthought. In 1973/74 a football ground didn't even need a safety certificate, though that was one of the recommendations of the Wheatley report that followed the Ibrox Disaster in 1972 when 66 people were crushed to death and 200 more injured. That said, in 1973 the Leeds United match day programme ran a feature entitled 'Just How Safe Is Elland Road?' for the game against Everton on 25th August. The summer had seen "extensive" health and safety checks on the crush barriers at Elland Road, possibly the first tests of their kind, following the Ibrox Disaster. The reformist backlash only went so far, however. Yes, Elland Road came out of the tests as "one of the safest grounds in the country", but several hazards still remained unchecked.

All the 168 crush barriers on the Kop and Lowfields Road terraces were impact tested in the 1973 checks, and "only" 15% of them failed, which was deemed a success. The indifference in the report is alarming given the overcrowding that regularly occurred in some areas of Elland Road. No regard was given to the fact that fans were shoehorned into the pens until it was physically impossible to fit any more in. The report did indeed conclude that the safety levels at Elland Road were high, and the 15% failure rate was "the smallest number on any ground we have tested so far". Everyone was very proud and 15% of failures was evidently acceptable.

Looking back now, post-Hillsborough, it is shuddering to think of the archaic mentality of all football clubs and authorities, and the deeply perilous conditions we just accepted as the norm. In a way we were all guilty of passive acceptance and whilst the danger was there we didn't complain; we were simply engrossed in it. There were many occasions where I was in danger of being crushed in the Lowfields Pen 4; it was impossible to create room for yourself and there appeared to be no limit to the amount of bodies that were squeezed into the throng. After 20 minutes of this your chest would feel tight and you would start to sweat.

Of course the Kop was just as bad in the halcyon days of terracing. But you never feared for your safety and were joyously oblivious to the potential consequences. You had to make an early decision as to whether to put your hands in your pocket or not because you couldn't change your mind. You could spend a large proportion of the afternoon with your arms clasped upwards to your chest, feeling the uncomfortable heat and often unholy stench from the body of the person in front of you. Regularly your feet wouldn't even touch the floor for minutes on end; you were just carried along by the roll of the wave. When it rained you could see the steam rising from the thermal mass of bodies, and you certainly never felt the cold. The football on the pitch was almost incidental, a sideshow to the absorbing ride you were on. It was all fun and the atmosphere was menacing but within the pen itself, amongst Leeds fans, it was convivial. If someone fell over there would be hundreds of people offering to pick you up. There was a wonderful dichotomy of the externally perceived mentality of the Leeds fans and the cosy kinship of the brothers in arms community deep within it.

Post-match you were literally shattered from the experience; physically from the struggle to maintain your very being in a state of functional order, and mentally from the exhilaration of the game, the spectacle, the crowd, the noise and simply growing up in such an environment. Truly, this was a place where boys became men.

From 1989 onwards the reduced capacity of terraces throughout the country meant that the physical struggle involved in watching football was gone, and with it, much of that element of combat that contributed towards the crowd trouble that was so prevalent in the game. Finally, even at big games you could pick a spot, stand still and watch the game in a civilised manner; you could even bring the wife and kids. Pen 4's days were numbered.

Indeed for the beginning of the 1990/91 season, in a bid to improve the club's image in the wake of over a decade of hooligan problems, culminating in a chaotic weekend in Bournemouth, Pen 4 was re-allocated as a 'Dads and Lads' paddock. The move didn't work out, however, largely as a bigger Family Stand had also been created in the South Stand, and after only five games of the season, and amid critical supply and demand issues for tickets, the venture was scrapped. The administration manager at the time, Alan Roberts, said: "There was room for 933 people, but we were getting only around 150 at some games. The club has been subjected to constant criticism from our supporters because of the lack of use of this area, at a time when all other standing areas are sold out."

The final three years of the Lowfields Road terrace's existence were a far cry from what had gone before; it was now a tame beast compared to the roaring ogre that used to sweep Leeds United past their opponents. Slowly Elland Road was losing its aura, but in some ways it had to. It was not alone in that as the football landscape was changing dramatically, and forever.

PETTY'S FIELD SPORTS GROUND

An aerial shot from 1964 showing not just the open expanses of the Petty's Field Sports Ground, but also the extensive flooding in the fields behind the Wortley Beck, the cars shoehorned into the car parks of the West Stand, United Garage and Old Peacock pub, and the fans shoehorned into the sweeping terraces of Elland Road.

The area around Elland Road is so rich in history and diversity that in every direction the most inanimate objects and most uninspiring panoramas that we bypass every fortnight have a story to tell. This is particularly so when gazing at the utterly unrecognisable scene to the north east of the ground.

In the 1840s John Petty was an apprentice printer at the local newspaper the *Leeds Times*, and having subsequently worked in two other printing firms in Leeds, John set up his own company in 1865 called Petty & Sons, with original premises on Albion Street in the city centre. Having moved premises several times the company settled on a location on Whitehall Road and became known as 'Whitehall Printeries', at the time well-renowned as being the 'largest printing works in Leeds'. The family business was handed over to John's son Wesley Petty who held the position of chairman for several years until his death in 1928.

It was in the later years of Wesley Petty's life that the company bought land on Lowfields Road and built a sports ground for its employees in the mid-1920s, pretty much as soon as Lowfields Road itself was built in 1923 and the land around it became accessible. Wesley Petty was famous for his interests in public improvement and he was an active member of several societies, councils and associations which in particular fostered a concern for the welfare of the working classes. It was this principle that led to the provision of a sports ground for his staff.

Whitehall Printeries formed an amateur football team in the early 1920s which became a very successful club, and the sports ground on Lowfields Road became their home pitch. In 1927, shortly after they had won the Leeds FA Senior Cup, they even sold a player to nearby Leeds United. Alan Fowler was a young striker transferred across the road to become a professional player, though in a full seven years at Leeds United, competing with the likes of stellar names such as Tom Jennings, Charlie Keetley, Russell Wainscoat, Arthur Hydes and Billy Furness, he managed the somewhat lopsided statistics of only 15 appearances, but which yielded eight goals. Despite a very decent goals return given his sparse usage over such a period of time, in 1934 he left for Swindon Town. Fowler was actually loaned back to Leeds briefly upon the outbreak of World War II, but in 1944 he died in northern France when he was called up to join the hostilities.

Another notable success for Whitehall Printeries was a run in the FA Amateur Cup in 1933 which saw them beat Whitby Town, Badsey Rangers and Clapton before losing to eventual winners Kingstonian in the Semi-Final held at West Ham before 20,000 fans.

The most significant connection between Whitehall Printeries Sports Ground and Leeds United, however, was the unfortunate circumstances in September 1956 when the West Stand at Elland Road burnt down, taking the dressing rooms with it. For several games Leeds United, the visiting club and the officials had to get

changed in the dressing rooms at Whitehall Printeries, before boarding a coach to take them round the corner to Elland Road. For this generous intervention, Whitehall Printeries will forever hold a place in the history of Elland Road, although after a few games Leeds United erected a dressing room block on Fullerton Park, which was meant to be temporary but still stands, unused, today.

Dominating the north east side past Elland Road, the Whitehall Printeries Sports Ground itself covered a huge area and was effectively just football fields and cricket pitches, albeit pitches of a very good quality. On the right hand side the sports ground bordered the 'tram knackers yard' where scrap trams were laid to rest, and the back of the ground bordered the playing fields of Matthew Murray High School, which was located on Brown Lane and was demolished amid much controversy in 2007. On the northern side of the ground industrial units began to spring up during the 1950s and 1960s as the land around Lowfields Road started to change dramatically in character.

The company's name was changed to 'Petty's Printeries' sometime in the 1960s, and likewise the ground became more popularly known as Petty's Field Sports Ground. As Don Revie adopted more progressive training techniques Leeds United did occasionally use it to train on when they needed to replicate the turf conditions at certain specific away grounds, as the pitches at Fullerton Park were often barren and relatively grassless.

Inevitably as the M621 was built in the early 1970s the sports ground was closed and covered up forever in the name of progress, obliterated as a mass expanse of sporting activity. The site, as was, is now bisected by the motorway and on either side is engulfed with industrial units, showrooms and the council-owned bus depot. Such is the confusion of different buildings and the motorway, to stand and imagine it now as vast open fields is enough to give you a headache.

The huge multi-building site on Whitehall Road covered several acres as it headed into town, and in its heyday the buildings extended almost to the famous Monk's Bridge Iron Company further down the road. The business became known as Polestar Petty's but the Leeds site permanently closed down in December 2014 with the loss of 250 jobs and the transfer of work to Sheffield and Wakefield. In October 2016 the now-abandoned site burnt to the ground in a fire and has since been re-built as "world class" TV and film studios.

In the 1960s another sports ground was created by the Leeds Industrial Co-operative Society, and was known as the 'LICS' Sports Ground. This was an offshoot just behind what many locals referred to as the 'Co-op Club', which was a big building on the corner of Gelderd Road and Lowfields Road. The building was flattened in 2005 and lay empty and derelict for several years before becoming yet another car showroom for the area in 2018.

PITCH INVASIONS

DJ Bear, the Panda of Peace, blends seamlessly into the 1991/92 league title celebrations in front of the Kop. Sadly he didn't qualify for a winners' medal.

There is something confusing about a pitch invasion during a football match. Your eyes are transfixed on the game and you are focused, you are 'in the zone' and see only the players and the referee on the pitch and any foreign body that enters the field of play is instantly conspicuous. Elsewhere I have discussed some of the more infamous pitch invasions that have taken place at Elland Road over the years, such as the pantomime horse that galloped onto the pitch against Liverpool in 1973. Others, however, are plentiful.

Such alien invasions include the fan from the Kop that struck Manchester City goalkeeper Joe Corrigan in the 1978 FA Cup tie. On this occasion there then followed a more significant pitch invasion as hundreds of fans spilled out of the Kop following the altercation and police horses had to enter the arena to restore order, though fans were mainly restricted to the track behind the pitch. The incident which sparked the mass pitch invasion was the culmination of an afternoon of bitter antagonism between the fans of both teams and the players. This wasn't helped by a first half spat between Leeds' centre-half Gordon McQueen and his own goalkeeper David Harvey in front of the Kop end.

In what proved to be his last game for Leeds before a controversial transfer to Manchester United, the mountainous McQueen swung a punch at Harvey, curiously wearing a red Scotland goalkeeper's jersey, as they argued whilst lining up for a corner. The tension never subsided and having survived a first half onslaught Leeds deservedly fell two goals behind midway through the second half, and another trophy-less season was looking likely for Leeds' fading side.

Different stories exist as to who actually ran on the pitch and hit the Manchester City goalkeeper on that folkloric day. One story involves a fan called Micky James who was part of the Teesside Whites, another sees a South Yorkshire White called 'Tusk' as the main protagonist, whilst a third version simply centres around a "lad from Dewsbury". Leeds fan Stephen Talbot was stood on the Kop that day and takes up what he sees as the definitive story, which is backed up by several other fans: "It was a lad called Marshall who ran on and hit Joe Corrigan. Marshall was his surname but I can't remember his first name, we just knew him as Marshall, he was from Wakefield. I always remember a Leeds fan who ran out and jumped into

the Man City fans before this, and that was a lad called 'Ashy'. Obviously he got ten bells kicked out of him and it was kicking off that much all over the place because City brought thousands, they came right across halfway down the Lowfields.

"It had been a right day," Stephen continues. "Corrigan was having a blinder, I don't know, we just couldn't score and Corrigan was always giving signs to Leeds fans in the Kop all game, and when they scored their second goal he turned round and he stuck two fingers up. Now I was stood on the left of the goal and Marshall was stood on the right hand side. I knew 'of' him, I didn't know him, but I knew a lot of his mates and as 'legend' has it, one of the lads said to Marshall 'he's sticking two fingers up at you!' just as a laugh, and that was it. He just ran straight on, slotted Corrigan and they were both literally brawling in the net, and I think he got three years for that. The police all piled in because you didn't have stewards in them days, all the police piled in and it was chaos."

Directly after that hundreds of Leeds fans swarmed onto the pitch and the game was stopped for several minutes whilst police horses were called for and everyone was gradually herded back into the stand. The game re-started in a poisonous atmosphere and while Leeds pulled a late goal back through a Frank Gray penalty, the off-pitch, or rather on-pitch-non-football, incidents had taken the edge off the game itself and everyone was pretty pleased when the final whistle went. Except the police who then had to contend with swathes of pitched battles outside the ground and long into the night. In all there were 32 arrests at the game, 21 Leeds fans and 11 from Manchester City.

Leeds United legend Jack Charlton prompted a pitch invasion of sorts from the police in February 1966, during a particularly heated Inter-Cities Fairs Cup tie with Valencia. In their first ever season of European football Leeds had forged a fierce reputation for their somewhat robust style of football, but they more than met their match in a Valencia side who were hotly tipped as one of the tournament favourites. In a constantly antagonistic first leg at Elland Road tension was bubbling throughout and an overspill was never far away, with both teams hurtling into savage tackles with reckless abandon. Valencia took a first half lead but Peter Lorimer equalised in the 64th minute. Leeds were hell bent on winning the tie and, as he often did, Jack Charlton added his considerable presence to Leeds' increasingly desperate attacks.

If a violent undercurrent had been simmering near the surface all game, it erupted with 15 minutes left. Charlton's tendency at the time was to stand right on top of the goalkeeper at corners. As most teams soon adopted the same tactic it became a staple part of an attacking team's armoury, but at this time it was considered ungentlemanly foul play by Leeds, and Charlton's jagged elbows protruded once too often for

Unfortunately TV astrologer Russell Grant failed to predict that the club shop wouldn't have a
kit big enough for him to wear for this alien invasion on the Elland Road pitch in 1983.

Valencia's liking on this occasion. Goalkeeper Rivero Nito landed a right hook square on Charlton's jaw as they wrestled brusquely at the corner. Charlton, not for the first or last time, saw red and, enraged, chased after the Valencia keeper seeking revenge.

There then followed a comical episode, where observers recall the Spanish keeper heading towards the corner of the pitch at the Scratching Shed end appearing to look for a way out of the ground to the perceived safety of the streets of LS11. With no exit visible he was hemmed in by the corner flag and faced with the unenviable choice of jumping into the crowd, heading for the tunnel or facing up to Big Jack. He perhaps unwisely chose the third option and he and Charlton traded blows in the south west corner of the pitch whilst team-mates intervened. Eventually the police waded onto the field of play to call order to the chaos, and a bristling melee ensued. Dutch referee Leo Horn ordered the teams off the pitch for a cooling off period, during which Charlton was officially advised he was not required to return to the pitch with his colleagues. The game ended 1-1 and Leeds triumphed 2-1 on aggregate to progress.

Another notable pitch invasion from the Revie era saw a number of suited gentlemen provide the rather bizarre spectacle of a more mature intrusion, after referee

Ray Tinkler had awarded a controversial offside goal for West Brom against title-chasing Leeds in 1971. One of the most notorious refereeing decisions ever to have taken place on a football pitch was greeted with blanket astonishment at Elland Road, and around a dozen respectable-looking fans could not contain themselves and took to the pitch in pursuit of the referee, before the police intervened. The goal itself is familiar to every Leeds fan, but as Dougie Wales explains: "(West Brom striker Jeff) Astle tapped it in and the next thing you see is a man running from the Kop, but he wasn't a young lad he was about 50-odd years old, making a beeline for the referee, and then maybe another dozen followed, grown blokes you know. The decision was that bad, well, it cost them the title and people just couldn't understand it."

Clearly this was an invasion in defiance of a perceived effrontery to justice, rather than an out-and-out act of hooliganism, demonstrated by the otherwise reputable manner in which these particular invaders appeared to carry themselves. However, the club were punished and had to play four 'home' games away from Elland Road at the beginning of the next season as a result.

In 1983 a more unexpected but equally unsavoury pitch invasion took place when TV astrologer, and every 1980s housewife's favourite rotund celebrity,

Russell Grant squeezed into a Leeds United kit to present a segment of the BBC *Breakfast Time* show live from the Elland Road pitch. Later Russell admitted: "Football's not really my game, but I'll be following United's results closely in the future, and my prediction is that there's plenty of success coming up for the club." Cannily, no time limit was put on quite when this "success" would be achieved, but readers and astronomy-sceptics may like to be reminded that this comment was made in 1983......

An unorthodox pitch invasion, almost akin to the pantomime horse, was made by a giant panda which gatecrashed Leeds' title celebrations on the Elland Road pitch in May 1992. Photos show the likes of Strachan, McAllister, Cantona, and Chapman holding the Football League trophy aloft in celebration, with a life-size panda incongruously stood next to them soaking up the goodwill. The unlikely invader was known as DJ Bear, dreamed up for a promotion in *Match* magazine by artist, PR supremo and all-round visionary Paul Trevillion. Yes, he of the sock tags, pre-match training drills and individually named tracksuit tops of Revie's Leeds in 1972; indeed, he even contacted Les Reed, on Revie's behalf, to instigate the writing of the 'Marching On Together' Leeds United anthem. Somehow it seemed appropriate that 'The Beaver' had a hand in Leeds' on-pitch celebrations for their last major triumph.

DJ Bear, the 'Panda of Peace,' was Trevillion's brain-child, designed to work with the Football League to promote harmony on the terraces in the late 1980s as hooliganism threatened to shut the football industry down. In the early days Trevillion, never one to avoid getting his hands dirty, would don the DJ Bear suit himself and run the gauntlet of the perplexed masses. Sadly, though it would have been a perfect denouement for Trevillion himself to have been on the pitch in May 1992, it was not he who donned the DJ Bear suit on that particular day as Wallace and Fairclough jigged in front of the Kop.

A female pitch invader was welcomed much more warmly in May 1997 during a game against Middlesbrough, if only because the 1996/97 season had officially erased the word 'entertainment'. George Graham's Leeds stuck rigidly to a 'they shalt not pass' philosophy, which was frequently in desperate need of such frivolous distraction. Middlesbrough needed to win the game to save themselves from relegation and certainly the streaker broke the tension, as midway through the first half she raced down the middle of the pitch sporting only a pair of trainers, sunglasses and a pair of light blue shorts. It later transpired that the stunt was part of a collective show of flesh organised by men's magazine *Loaded*, whereby a number of Premiership games on the same day were interrupted in similar fashion. If the 'Boro players felt somewhat more relaxed afterwards it didn't do the trick, as the game was drawn 1-1 and Middlesbrough were relegated.

Celebratory pitch invasions have taken place upon promotion being achieved, most recently in May 2010 when Leeds finally escaped the suffocating clutches of League One by beating Bristol Rovers 2-1. As thousands ran on the pitch and celebrated with the players the enduring image was of the scoreboard sheepishly requesting fans to "Please Keep Off The Pitch". Prior to that, the club's previous promotion in 1990 was achieved in Bournemouth, but not before a premature pitch invasion had followed a dramatic 2-1 victory over Leicester City in the final home game of the season. Believing Leeds had been promoted, prompted by Vinnie Jones mishearing a scoreline from Newcastle, thousands again took to the pitch to the backdrop of ITV commentator John Helm repeatedly asking "is that confirmed?" Alas, the celebrations were cruelly cut short and replaced by a further seven days of nail-biting.

In stark contrast, the day Leeds were relegated to League One in May 2007 was punctuated by a pitch invasion of a different sort. When Ipswich Town crucially equalised an early Richard Cresswell goal to condemn Leeds to relegation, a few hundred Leeds fans promptly took to the pitch with the ill-advised intention of holding up play and getting the game abandoned. Tellingly, and demonstrating how the crowd's mentality had changed in the modern era, the Kop's chant to the pitch invaders was not one of encouragement but a contemptuous "you're the scum of Elland Road". Several minutes later the pitch was cleared and the players acted out the last rites of a wretched season amid a solemn atmosphere.

Other oddities on or beside the Elland Road pitch involve star striker Duncan McKenzie vaulting over a Mini before 19,376 stunned fans ahead of Paul Reaney's testimonial game versus Newcastle in 1976. McKenzie had fashioned the trick as an apprentice at previous club Nottingham Forest, and his eccentric capacity for performing feats requiring abnormal ability but that had little or no use in everyday life, never mind football, did not end there. He was also famous for throwing golf balls particularly long distances, and on one occasion while standing in front of the Kop, at a time in 1974 when the South Stand was being built in place of the demolished Scratching Shed, McKenzie threw a golf ball the length of the pitch. With ease it passed the building site that was the stand and travelled clear onto Elland Road where it bounced off, no doubt for some puzzled schoolboy to one day find.

Goal celebrations have often extended into an over-exuberant pitch invasion for strikes of major significance or timing. Fans in the North East Corner Stand are prone to spilling forth onto the pitch if a player runs that way in the act of taking the crowd's acclaim. Odd goals have resulted in a lone raid on to the pitch in celebration by a spectator, prompted by a rush of blood to the head or, more likely, several pints in the bloodstream and which, today, while encouraged joyfully by the crowd, will certainly end in arrest.

PLAYERS' ENTRANCE

Different managers have different protocol for pre-match routines and currently Leeds players arrive at Elland Road together on a coach and enter the stadium via the original players' entrance, albeit it is no longer called that. The away team coach is usually parked at the north end of the car park and those players enter via the tunnel in the north west corner. The players then walk down the pitch side along the West Stand and up the tunnel to the dressing rooms, usually wearing massive headphones because, well, that's what footballers do.

An official players' entrance no longer exists at Elland Road but did until the mid-2000s. Back in the 1960s there were two ways into the dressing room area on a match day for the players. Originally this was through the directors' entrance in the West Stand underneath the facade, but later the club added a specific players' entrance further down, where the entrance to the LUTV studios has been until the summer of 2020, underneath the Banqueting Suite, although the actual original entrance has been bricked over by the work that contributed to the Banqueting Suite extension. This players' entrance was also used by visiting teams and the match officials.

Inside the dressing room area Dave Cocker explains the layout as you walked in through the players' entrance in the 1960s and '70s: "At the end of the corridor that housed all the dressing rooms were a pair of double doors that opened up into the West Stand Paddock bar area and led to the gym. These were locked obviously on match days, but they built a walkway up to these double doors so that the players could walk up to the players' entrance and not be bothered by fans on the way in."

It appears that for a short time until this walkway was built, you had potential for the likes of Bremner and Clarke to be walking through the players' entrance and effectively mingling with the crowds underneath the West Stand, before being let through the double doors into the dressing room area by a security guard. Not surprisingly, the walkway tunnel was built to prevent unnecessary confrontations, and that walkway still exists, but having led to the LUTV studios for a number of years, now leads to the left to the newly constructed media suite, and to the right through those same double doors into the dressing room area.

That players' entrance was also used by several generations of Leeds United players up to 1996, as the exit and well-trodden thoroughfare from the dressing rooms and on to the Fullerton Park training pitches across the car park. So whilst it was a routine feature of their place of work during the week, doubtless laden with stud-marked deposits of Fullerton Park mud that the likes of Batty and Jones would throw at each other, it took on a much different and more official stature on a match day.

PLAYERS' LOUNGE

It is not an exaggeration to suggest that every square inch of Elland Road carried some significance during the Don Revie era. The players' lounge at most grounds is simply a room with a bar where players mingle post-match with sponsors and guests, and wind down after the exertions of the afternoon before heading home. At Elland Road the players' lounge is most famous for its integral role in fostering team and competitive spirit amongst Don Revie's squad.

In the early 1970s certain footballers such as George Best, Peter Osgood, Stan Bowles and Charlie George, amongst others, were just beginning to achieve superstar status, and the trappings of such fame led them into a glamorous and well-rewarded lifestyle, including the introduction of nightclubs, celebrity girlfriends, shop openings and other endorsements into their daily routines. They were happy to embrace it and happy to talk about it. Up in Yorkshire, the Leeds players spoke of extra-curricular activities such as fiercely contested games of carpet bowls and bingo. It sounded like a bad weekend at Pontins and the quaint and rather simplistic nature of such pursuits was widely derided by the media and the Leeds players' contemporaries alike. But what they all missed was that the unorthodox methods that Revie had instilled clearly worked.

It may not seem befitting to imagine Norman Hunter rolling balls along the carpet, or the twin midfield terrorists of Bremner and Giles totting up the scores for a gaggle of on-looking international footballers on tenterhooks, but it is what forged them as an unbreakable clan. Throughout the Revie era what was often cited as the team's most formidable quality was their 'togetherness'; their unquenchable spirit and professionalism that would extend to watching each other's backs on the pitch and fighting, often literally, for the collective cause. It was not about celebrating individuals at Leeds United, there was no 'star' player, and that quality of teamwork is what carried them further than most other teams of the time, and that was largely forged in the players' lounge at Elland Road as they all grew up together.

That said, the 'carpet bowls' scenario was somewhat overblown. The players' lounge was mainly only used on match days during the successful years, but it was integral to the match preparation. Even then, often the carpet bowls and pre-match team talks were done at the Craiglands Hotel in Ilkley, where the team sometimes stayed before big games. During the week the players would finish training, hop over to Sheila's Café and then off on to the Mecca in town for the rest of the day or to the Burton Arcade to play snooker, much like most other professional footballers. What the media picked up on were the relaxation methods used on match days, which were unfairly mythologised to paint Revie's players as remote and faintly peculiar, dispassionate robots; 'Daddy's boys' who barely socialised outside their rigid inner circle.

When Revie arrived at the club as a player in 1958 the situation was rather different and, as you would imagine, somewhat less professional. Dave Cocker takes up the tale of what Les Cocker and Revie found when they took over the management of the club in 1961, but particularly when Les Cocker arrived at the club as a coach before Revie took charge: "At the end of the tunnel you would turn right towards the dressing rooms, but on the left at the end of the corridor was a door that led into a room which had a full-size snooker table in it. That was the players' lounge then. They used to cover the snooker table over on match days with boards and that's where they would serve the tea and sandwiches from.

"But my Dad used to play absolutely holy hell about it," continues Dave, "because when Jack Taylor was there (as the manager prior to Don Revie) it was impossible. The guy had no control and my old man was going berserk about it, because the players just wouldn't do anything. Don was a player then and he saw it. My Dad used to go above Jack Taylor's head and see Harry Reynolds about it and say 'look this is bloody stupid, they're just not doing anything.' Big Jack (Charlton) was the biggest culprit and all they wanted to do was piss around and go and play snooker for money after training. My Dad always thought Don wouldn't be hard enough, but when Don came into the job he just got rid of them all, and as you know now they gave Jack another chance. The team talks used to take place in that room because it was quite a big room, no windows at all, and I don't even know what it is now."

The snooker room has now been taken over by the many alterations within the West Stand, and although the corridor that led to it is now blocked off by a plain wall, the original room is now known as the 'Jack Charlton Suite', with no suggestion that is because he used to spend all his time and money in there. It is a sizeable and well-equipped room available for banquets and conferences during the week, but, wouldn't you know it, used as a players' lounge on match days, albeit the players' match day schedule is much different today. Opposition players rarely mingle with the home players after a game and even many of the home players head straight off as soon as they can. Indeed, in the post-COVID-19 restructuring of the West Stand operations, there is talk of turning this players' lounge into an exclusive 'tunnel club' hospitality suite, which would be quite easy given it is directly adjacent to the tunnel and only needs a brick wall replacing with one-way glass.

The snooker room remained a players' lounge until around 1964 under Revie's watchful eye, but in 1970 when the North West Corner Stand was built the players' lounge was moved down there. In keeping with his position as the figurehead of the 'family', Revie moved his office down there too. As you face the beginning of the groundsman's tunnel at the back of

the stand there is one door in on the left, and then on the left hand side was Revie's office with his secretary's next door. Indeed the manager's office door opened up into the open-plan lounge where the players relaxed before and after games. "They used to congregate in there before a match," recalls Dave. "They would have their team talks and play carpet bowls and putting comps or whatever, and then they would walk down the groundsman's tunnel by the North West Corner there and down the track by the side of the pitch towards the tunnel. I can still visualise the chairs, they were like armchairs with wooden arms, but that room was everything at the time. That's where Don and me Dad would go through the dossiers. But they never went in it during the week, after training they were off, because at the time they were playing so many games a season from 1965 onwards they would only be training for a couple of hours in the week between matches. When you're playing Saturday and Wednesday, Saturday and Wednesday, there's no need.

"But they used to meet their families in the players' lounge after matches," Dave continues. "There was a bar with Tetley's, just a keg of Tetley Bitter, that was it, and tea and coffee. It had a television too because you'd get the football results at five o'clock and everybody would crowd round to watch that. The opposition would always go in there after games too, every time, even midweek, the players would have a drink together after the game, both teams talking away and mingling away, they don't do that anymore. The refs weren't allowed in. Referees went to the game and went home, that was it, there was no chit chat."

That famous players' lounge was converted into a learning area for the Leeds United Foundation, the charity arm of the club that delivers educational programmes to the younger fanbase and the wider community. It is only occasionally used now, and on match days the room is also used as the disabled lounge pre- and post-match for the LUDO disabled spectators.

The players' lounge in the North West Corner didn't last for long after Revie had left, and by the time Alan Sutton joined the club in 1986 it was back in the central area of the West Stand, just to the left as you entered through the players' entrance. In 1989 Howard Wilkinson had part of that room converted into a 'video lounge'. Here re-runs of previous matches could be viewed by the whole squad, and also top European matches could be watched via a, then very advanced, satellite system for Wilkinson and his colleagues to scout players or teams, or just to keep abreast of the football world. Alan Sutton recalls: "Where the players' lounge was, we used to play carpet bowls in there in Billy's time as manager and John Sheridan was always top man at that. But what Wilko did was he took part of that players' lounge off and made it into a video lounge."

Whilst Leeds remained based at Elland Road until 1996, the players' lounge continued to act as the works

canteen, the sixth form common room or the recording studio or rehearsal room; the place where work isn't work, where players would rather be with their mates than go home. Where gangs forged bonds, where spirit was formed, where idle time brought inconsequential, everyday things that would develop into friendships. A place where the laughter and competitive spirit of carpet bowls, or putting competitions or bingo would be translated into running your heart out for your team-mates week after week, to keep fighting; and going the extra mile on the pitch simply because you wanted to.

POSTPONEMENTS

A postponed game: a black mark against the groundsman or the disobedient fallout from an act of God? Either way the weather can be a groundsman's worst enemy, even when a postponement is inevitable. John Reynolds lived at West Ardsley, about four miles from Elland Road, for much of his time spent tending to the Elland Road pitch. Stephen Reynolds recalls his often burdensome dedication to duty: "We had a really bad winter in 1978/79 with lots of snow. Leeds had a match and he knew the match was going to be off, but he had to go down, meet the referee and let him in. My Dad managed to walk to the main road and get on a bus. The bus driver said he couldn't stop the bus but he could get on, so he jumped on. He got so far to the ground then he walked the rest of the way. Met the referee, went in, opened the tunnel doors, 'yep, game's off', straight back home again. Even though you know full well the game's going to be off you've got to do the job."

Leeds United hold a proud record of not having postponed a first team fixture for 26 years, a far cry from the 1964 embarrassment when a scheduled England youth international versus Wales had to be switched to East End Park WMC at Skelton Road, when Elland Road became waterlogged. Sadly, little information exists on matches that were postponed before the World War II, at least not enough to confidently produce a definitive list. Therefore, the following is as complete a record as is currently possible on the post-war first team fixtures that have been postponed at Elland Road due to weather (ie. not due to cup games or replays).

- 08/03/1947 – Portsmouth
- 27/11/1948 – Blackburn Rovers
- 22/12/1956 – Tottenham Hotspur
- 08/02/1958 – Arsenal
- 20/02/1960 – Birmingham City
- 26/11/1960 – Luton Town
- 04/04/1961 – Scunthorpe United
- 09/12/1961 – Newcastle United
- 18/12/1961 – Rotherham United (League Cup)
- 29/12/1962 – Scunthorpe United

- 05/01/1963 – Stoke City FA Cup
  (this was the first of 12 postponements of this tie)
- 12/01/1963 – Huddersfield Town
- 19/01/1963 – Swansea Town
- 09/02/1963 – Luton Town
- 27/11/1965 – Manchester United
- 02/04/1968 – Bradford City (Grenville Hair Testimonial)
- 15/03/1969 – Nottingham Forest
- 01/01/1977 – Everton
- 15/01/1977 – Birmingham City
- 11/02/1978 – Derby County
- 01/01/1979 – Nottingham Forest
- 17/02/1979 – Bolton Wanderers
- 17/03/1979 – Liverpool
- 25/04/1981 – West Bromwich Albion
- 25/11/1981 – Manchester City
- 26/12/1981 – Birmingham City
- 05/02/1983 – Sheffield Wednesday
- 10/12/1983 – Swansea City
- 05/01/1992 – Manchester United FA Cup
- 03/01/1994 – Aston Villa
- 11/02/1995 – Ipswich Town

In addition to the games that were postponed before a ball was kicked, the following is a list of games at Elland Road that were abandoned after kick-off, due to inclement weather.

- 16th of February 1935 v Portsmouth (League). Abandoned after 53 minutes due to a waterlogged pitch with Leeds leading 1-0. The game was replayed on the 2nd of March 1935 and Leeds won 3-1.

- 25th of January 1936 v Bury (FA Cup). Abandoned after 76 minutes due to fog with Leeds leading 2-1. The game was replayed on the 28th of January and Leeds won 3-2.

- 12th of December 1936 v Wolverhampton Wanderers (League). Abandoned after 83 minutes due to fog with Wolves leading 1-0. The game was replayed on the 21st of April 1937 and Wolves won 1-0.

- 25th of January 1939 v Huddersfield Town (League). Abandoned after 63 minutes due to snow with Huddersfield leading 1-0. The game was replayed on the 19th of April 1939 and Leeds won 2-1.

- 15th of November 1952 v Nottingham Forest (League). Abandoned after 10 minutes due to fog with the score at 0-0. The game was replayed on the 22nd of April 1953 and Leeds won 2-1.

PRESS BOX

Commentating on, photographing and reporting on the arbitrary and wildly fluctuating fortunes of Leeds United can be as taxing an occupation as supporting them, and even playing for them. Elland Road is certainly accommodating in providing the drama and absorbing narrative required; that is beyond question.

A regular match day at Elland Road will see a generous array of familiar faces within the press areas, and despite the club's most recent standing outside the top division, the media interest is always fervent, incorporating both local and national reporters, plus away club and agency reporters. The cosy press lounge beneath the stand, used for many years until recently, was a cramped and antiquated yet vibrant environment pre-match and at half-time, and was certainly a room where you were frequently privy to some interesting tit-bits of information, as you ducked beneath the low beams of the slanted roof.

The old press lounge was situated next to the Radebe Suite and across the corridor from the Chairman's Suite, and was accessed via the glass-doored Radebe Entrance in the West Stand car park. The press lounge is in the process of being moved to the ground floor of the West Stand in the area next to the tunnel and dressing rooms and most recently occupied by the LUTV studios. This should be completed and in use by the end of 2020. And it is hoped hot food will permanently replace the lonely tray of curled up sandwiches usually offered to the country's finest journalistic and broadcasting talent, as Leeds start to rub shoulders more frequently with Premier League staff and officials and the impressionable entourage that comes with them.

Paul Dews, former head of media at Leeds United, explained the long-standing facilities at Elland Road: "From memory, the previous press lounge had been in use since 2001. The lounge was so used because of its easy access to the press seating area. Pre-match food was served, there was tea and coffee at half-time, and post-match it was set up for a press conference."

I am fortunate to have watched many games from the press area of Elland Road. It is a very different experience where two worlds collide, and it is very easy to forget you are actually in a place of work. A typical match day experience therefore diverts measurably from that of a normal fan. The first thing that strikes you is actually receiving pleasantries from a doorman and treading the plush carpets leading up to the press lounge, where all press personnel must sign in. You then scan the room for familiar faces from the local or national press and ex-pros working for Sky Sports or other agencies. You also see visiting staff from other clubs carrying out scouting missions. Everyone watches the telly at the far end of the room and chats until roughly 15 minutes before kick-off before heading up to watch the game.

Back in Don Revie's era the press areas were in a similar location but much more basic. Steve Parker was a teenage, fledgling press photographer working for Photopress Leeds Ltd in 1971, and he describes the facilities and the ground itself during that magical time: "At Elland Road the press room was nothing but a dimly lit room with a couple of old tables against the wall, and a big old table in the middle of the floor with a few chairs around it. When I first attended Elland Road the buzz was fantastic and the boss, Jimmy, used to have me cover the Kop end while he would take the Shed end. It wasn't for the advantage of who was going to get the best pictures or anything, it was because I could run faster than Jimmy and grab us both a cup of tea, sandwich, and pork pie each. On the days of the big games there was never enough cups of tea, and you had to be fast to get anything at all in the way of nibbles. Leeds United were a massive club with a full multi-international team. But they were tight with the spread, unlike the little clubs such as Huddersfield Town who used to lay out a banquet."

Whatever the era, in the relative confines of the press box or the gantry at least there is cover from the elements for the media hordes, not so much for the pitch-side photographers, as Steven continues: "Lots of people used to think that my job was all glitz and bling, but far from it. At the back end of the season the good weather would be coming back and you knew that you would miss the Saturday afternoons at Elland Road. The seat wasn't very comfortable but it was, more times than not, the best view of all the goalmouth action. And when the new season kicked off on the end of a warm summer's afternoon you could be forgiven for forgetting about the coming winter. When the frost came the pitch would be covered in straw and if it snowed they would heap all the straw around the edge of the pitch and that is where the press photographers sit. I came back from Elland Road to the office frozen, drenched, and covered in snow on many occasions over the years. I remember Jimmy saying to me once that he had puddles in his pockets. Sometimes it would rain or snow all through the game and the ink would run on my caption sheet and my notes would be unreadable, the match programme soggy wet and the pages sticking together. My hands would be so cold that I could not work my fingers. Half-time couldn't come soon enough so I could thaw out over a cup of tea and have a decent fag."

In the early 1970s of course there were no such luxuries via which photos could be emailed or tweeted across the world in seconds, and Steven had to leave the match 20 minutes before the end, pray he had the winning shot, develop the photos in an office in central Leeds, then run like mad to Leeds train station to get the prints on the 5.55pm train to Manchester. Then it was a case of waiting to

see which of the Sunday papers carried his photos, assuming they even got there.

Still, there were some more glamorous moments, as Steven describes: "I suppose it was only a matter of time before I got my moments of fame. At the shed end of the pitch in front of a large home crowd and broadcasted highlights on television later that evening, I was left with egg on my face, or should I say Hunter on my face.

"As the ball was going out of play about level with the six yard box markings, Norman Hunter leapt over the top of my head as I sat on my little canvas seated fishing stool. He managed to head the ball back in to the goalmouth but the linesman signalled that the ball had gone out of play. Like a true sports journalist I never wanted to miss anything and I followed Hunter's leap as he jumped upwards but he came crashing down on me and bust my lower lip with his boot. He rubbed my head and said 'sorry 'r kid' and ran off back downfield. Luckily in them days they didn't have as many television cameras as in this day and age, but it did get a couple of replays.

"Big Jack Charlton was always going to be my hero," Steven continues, "so one afternoon on my return from Elland Road, Jimmy's first question was 'did you get the Charlton goal?' 'No,' I replied, 'he scored from way outside the box and he was on my blindside, but I got the celebration shots after the goal.' 'Good,' he replied. That Sunday the game was televised and I watched the game thinking that I might have got away with my excuse, but when it came to the Charlton goal it was like I was spotlighted in front of the camera. Big Jack volleys the ball straight into the net from 20 odd yards, a dream of a goal. Unfortunately from the three different camera angles all I could see was a very clear image of me, with my almost waist-length hair, leaping up with my right fist clenched punching the air."

Council planning documents show an application from Leeds United in 2011 to build an extension to the press lounge, which would have come out into the West Stand car park as a first floor level above a turnstile block for entrance 4. The move would have been to accommodate Premier League requirements, but never happened, much like the Premier League never happened. Instead Leeds decided to 'wing it' until the Premier League did happen, in 2020.

What represents the press box itself is a now-expanded area of 30-plus seats at the back of the West Stand in the Kop half of the pitch. The new facilities – fitted out in the summer of 2020 – have better benches and electrical ports, and each have small monitors to see replays of the match action, a Premier League requirement. In years gone by the desks will have been fitted with telephones for stories and match reports to be relayed back to the office. To the right is the directors' box, and seats reserved for corporate guests plus officials and guests from the visiting club. To the left there is nothing separating the gentlemen of the press from the regular West Stand fans, who are not slow to offer their advice on what should be written.

Press box etiquette is such that football colours can't be worn and the protocol extends to having to refrain from shouting at players or becoming too over-excited when goals go in. This was a challenge for me in any circumstances, but particularly so when you are yards away from the visiting directors who are not quite following the same protocol.

Post-match all the media reporters for the written press and local and national radio retire back to the press lounge to await the managers' interviews. Over the years the incumbent Leeds manager has been required to speak to LUTV, Sky Sports and/or BBC Sports before heading up to the press lounge. It can be half an hour after the final whistle before the written press get an opportunity to ask questions, although this does offer an opportunity to make a start on their match reports, or for match facts to be exchanged or for conspiracy theories over dubious decisions to develop. At least the new media suite built and opened in 2020 will raise standards to the appropriate level and enable quicker access to the written press for the players and coaching staff.

Paul Dews explains how the Elland Road press facilities, including the radio and TV gantry, are fondly thought of among press circles: "The gantry is pretty unique, and offers one of the best media viewing areas at any ground in the country. It's very popular with the media too. The press area is well equipped considering the age of the ground, but with the amount of new stadiums and the improvement to media facilities, there are many that are far better, certainly in terms of viewing and access to the tunnel area, etc. Sadly Elland Road is limited with the space, and they make the most of it. Canvassing the media who do visit, they certainly enjoy coming to Leeds and are happy with the facilities."

Spending a day in the press area at Elland Road is certainly a departure from the normal routine and it offers a fascinating insight into the media world, and how this is approached as a normal day's work rather than a simple football match. Any emotion or lenience has to be left outside. Observing the post-match press conference reminds you of the pressure a Leeds United manager is under. Inevitably the imagination wanders to what visible spectacles have taken place in the press lounge post-match over the years when the likes of Revie, Clough, Wilkinson or O'Leary have addressed the very people that have the tools to enhance or destroy them.

PROGRAMME CABIN

The Programme Cabin began life as the 'Programme Centre', effectively a next-door extension to the much-loved and much-missed Sports & Souvenir Shop on Elland Road, and was established at the start of the 1981/82 relegation season. The centre was run by Richard Bennett who, at the time was employed by the club in accounts.

Walking through the door was like opening Pandora's Box to impressionable Leeds United-obsessed teenagers, often still reeling from the sensory overload experienced next door in the souvenir shop. The niche pursuit of programme collecting does seem to attract youngsters drunk on the first flush of an LUFC neurosis, and at the other end of the scale, the mature scholars, like acid veterans, visibly frazzled by a lifetime of over-exposure to the emotional sewer that is Leeds United. Andy Peterson was not alone as an early devotee of the original Programme Centre: "There's a certain age at which, just before girls become interesting, football memorabilia is the last thing standing in terms of adolescent obsessions. My first season watching Leeds, punctuated as you would expect by mediocrity, had left my early teenage self somehow crazy for more, and thus a city-spanning trip on the number 1 bus took me to the place where all my dreams were fulfilled: the club's programme cabin, located on Elland Road next to the original club shop. There you could bag a cherished souvenir of the home game against Oldham, or perhaps even something as collectable as an edition for the illustrious Shrewsbury Town. I spent many an afternoon satisfying myself with glossy mementoes of the 1982/83 season's glories, which I guess you can put down almost solely to late development."

Very soon, by the mid-1980s, the Programme Centre was moved because it is believed the club intended to break the Sports & Souvenir Shop up into four retail units, although this never happened. The 'Kop Shop' was opened in March 1974 as an accompaniment to the main shop on Elland Road, which was proving to be a very shrewd investment. The purpose of the Kop Shop was to serve the many thousands of fans wanting souvenirs and memorabilia on match days, but who never approached the ground from the Elland Road side. It was smaller than the main shop on Elland Road but stocked pretty much the same range of products.

The Kop Shop was situated within the fencing of the Elland Road compound but as a stand-alone building behind the North East Corner Stand. Attached to the back of the Kop Shop was a small office which eventually became the 'Programme Cabin'. This was run by Phil Beeton, programme-collecting enthusiast, current treasurer of the Leeds United Supporters' Club (LUSC), chairman of the Griffin Branch of the Supporters' Club and 2,000 successive Leeds United match-attending superfan/medical phenomenon. Phil was not directly involved in the running of the previous incarnation on Elland Road, but gave advice on rarity and prices. Now it

was his show and he was later joined by Simon Sargent and stocked a treasure trove of items from Leeds United games home and abroad.

Whilst only tiny, the shop used its space well and was crammed to the rafters with monuments to Leeds United's history, from all the famous games to the obscure friendlies that appealed only to the 'complete-ists'. Unfortunately it was difficult to fit more than three people in the shop at any one time and doubtless passing trade was somewhat put off by this. Nevertheless, the Programme Cabin was a vital source for fans looking for that rarity or just wanting to pick up a copy from last week's away game. Operations such as this inevitably attract characters, and certainly the regular enthusiasts that crossed the threshold of the Programme Cabin were die-hard Leeds fans of stubborn stock.

The programme business moved into the Kop Shop itself in 2003 as the shop had stopped selling souvenirs some years earlier, as Phil explains: "I was involved when the shop moved to the north east corner, firstly using the rear of the shop, whilst the front sold souvenirs, and then negotiated in 2003 to take over the shop fully for programmes. We ran our business 'Kick off Programmes' from there on a licence agreement with Leeds United."

In early 2006, with a Machiavellian twist, Phil Beeton was given three months' notice by the club to find new premises as the site was earmarked for development as part of the East Stand expansion. Phil said: "The reasons were that they were desperately short of space and needed the area for possible offices/storage." Sadly the Programme Cabin was no more, and despite being flatly denied a stay of execution until the end of the season as there were only three games left, Phil gave up the lease with no ill-feeling as he didn't want to hold up progression of the club's plans. The Kop Shop became a lottery office and there was talk of it becoming the HQ for Ken Bates' Members Club. This never happened and the building evolved into a signing-in office for the many temporary security and catering staff on a match day, before becoming disused and eventually being demolished to make way for the Fosters' Fan Zone in the summer of 2017.

Now Phil Beeton runs his Programme Cabin from a temporary stall in the Old Peacock car park. This agreement was clearly not an issue in the years after Phil had been ejected from the shop within the ground, as LUSC also ran the Old Peacock. Thankfully, the current leaseholders of the Old Peacock, Ossett Brewery, have proved more co-operative and accommodating than others, as Phil explains: "We have a very good relationship with the owners of the Old Peacock from where we currently trade. In the summer of 2013 when the pub had a huge refurbishment we approached a representative of Ossett Brewery to ask if our 'pitch' would still be available. They were very keen to help us and agreed to allow us to trade once the work had been completed."

THE ONLY PLACE FOR US

WEST STAND

to pitch

CAR PARKS

R. F. WINDER STAND

ELLAND ROAD

LEEDS

HALIFAX/HUDDERSFIELD → GELDERD ROAD → LEEDS

SOUTH STAND

B D

A C E F

M

L

pitch

G

M

Q

K K

H

J I

M

LOWFIELD ROAD STAND

2257

QUEEN

Is that 'Queen' or 'the Queen'? Well, both actually, and not many football grounds can say that. Queen Elizabeth II visited Elland Road as part of her Silver Jubilee celebrations on 12th July 1977. With the ground packed with 40,000 excitable schoolchildren chanting "we want the Queen", Her Royal Highness, accompanied by the Duke of Edinburgh, was driven around the perimeter of the pitch in an open-top Range Rover and carried out a short walkabout amongst the crowd before heading off to meet other dignitaries at Leeds Town Hall. Reports that the Duke of Edinburgh had to be retrieved from the queue at United Fisheries cannot be substantiated.

As ever, Gary Edwards was there, and he recalls: "I've even cheered Her Majesty the Queen from the Gelderd End – when she visited Elland Road during her Silver Jubilee celebrations in 1977. She walked along the front of the West Stand and part of the way across the front of the Kop."

Maureen Reynolds, widow of groundsman John, recalls that the club had to build a special toilet because, naturally, the Queen couldn't possibly use one that was already there. It was never used. After a quick lap of the pitch in a car via the groundsman's tunnel and a brief walkabout she was gone, as Maureen comments: "All these kids had practised their singing and dancing on the pitch for weeks and she was gone within about a minute." A sense of crushing disappointment and anti-climax at Elland Road? It's in the brickwork I'm afraid. Later that year, 22nd November 1977, Leeds United played a friendly against Ajax at Elland Road as a special game in further celebration of the Silver Jubilee.

Moving five years on and Elland Road was rocking with a vibrancy not seen since Lash was rippling the onion bag week-in week-out, as a crowd officially recorded as 40,200 witnessed a celebrated performance from rock

"Got a photo of an Ajax player I can use?", "How about Peter Lorimer playing for Scotland against England? You can just draw a red stripe down the England shirt, nobody will ever know", "That'll do!" The official programme for the Jubilee Friendly match between Leeds United and Ajax in 1977.

royalty in the shape of Queen, on the European leg of their 'Hot Space' tour. The gig was originally arranged for Old Trafford, Manchester but was switched to Elland Road and took place on Saturday 29th May 1982.

It was a baking hot day in the middle of a bank holiday weekend and various local residents had raised concerns about their safety amid the notorious 'rock fans' that were converging on their neighbourhood, oblivious to the fact that they faced much more immediate threat from the football fans that visited every other week of the year. However, demonstrating due caution Leeds City Council rented a local property to install noise-monitoring equipment and a 10.30pm curfew was implemented, although this was later extended by the local police. Consideration was also given to the condition of the pitch and only 7,000 fans were allowed to stand on it, so as to avoid too much damage.

In the event the show was a triumph and was hailed by guitarist Brian May as being among Queen's best ever shows; "...one of those one-offs" he commented, somewhat illogically. The stage effects and lighting were rumoured to have cost over £1 million and fans of Leeds United, who weeks earlier had been relegated to the Second Division, could only look on and marvel at such extravagance as they stared ruefully at tear-stained photos of Peter Barnes.

The West Stand entrance bedecked in flowers as the Queen arrives for her Silver Jubilee visit in 1977.

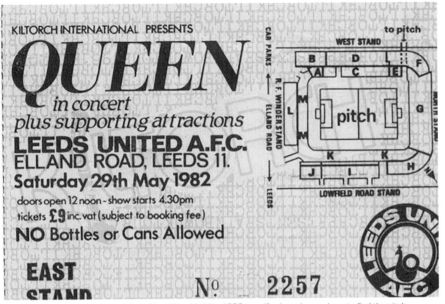

A ticket for the legendary Queen gig at Elland Road in May 1982; now if only we knew where to find the pitch...

KILTORCH INTERNATIONAL PRESENTS

QUEEN

in concert
plus supporting attractions

LEEDS UNITED A.F.C.
ELLAND ROAD, LEEDS 11.
Saturday 29th May 1982

doors open 12 noon - show starts 4.30pm

tickets £9 inc. vat (subject to booking fee)

NO Bottles or Cans Allowed

EAST STAND   N⁰ 2257

there is no doubt that having hosted other landmark gigs by U2, Happy Mondays and Kaiser Chiefs, Elland Road's unlikely status as a legendary rock venue is assured.

Leeds' chairman at the time, Leslie Silver, was particularly keen to pursue other such ventures, more than likely motivated by the income streams rather than maintaining Elland Road's decadent, leather-clad, drum-kit-smashing rock legacy. In his programme notes from the following season Silver wrote: "The Queen concert in May went very well and I am sure we will repeat the exercise, especially as we lack a major arena in the area around Leeds."

The city of Leeds would lack an arena for another 31 years, but sadly the exorbitant costs and logistical complexities of staging concerts on the Elland Road pitch, as confirmed by the Kaiser Chiefs, have limited such ventures since 1982 to just a handful of special occasions. In the same notes, Silver also mentioned that the club had considered introducing greyhound racing as a possible source of income, though this was quickly dismissed on the grounds of expenditure. However, intriguingly he added: "but concerts and the possibility of staging lawn tennis would suit us, as we can offer 20,000 seats".

Support acts on the day were American rock band Heart, English alternative band The Teardrop Explodes, whose singer Julian Cope was showered with bottles, burgers and other less-palatable missiles during their set which clearly didn't translate to Queen's steadfast fans, and finally Joan Jett & the Black Hearts.

One person not overly ecstatic about the occasion was groundsman John Reynolds. His son Stephen recalls: "He said he was sat on the stage after the gig had finished with his head in his hands, looking at the pitch and nearly in tears. He said there were nails all over the place, and it was a really hot day so they had been hosing the fans down in the crowd, it was a horrendous mess. He couldn't believe it. He did have full 'access all areas' though and he said he remembered Brian May used to love himself. He used to just stand on the stage and play guitar to an empty stadium while my Dad walked about working. But the pitch was only partly covered, South Stand to halfway line if memory serves. Back then technology wasn't what we have now and the covers weren't great and because of the hot day and the sheer weight of people packed in and jumping up and down the pitch had no chance, especially when wet. The covers for the Kaiser Chiefs gig years later weren't as heavy in weight, and they were made to help the pitch breathe while at the same time protecting the grass. The ones put down for Queen in 1982 were steel and very heavy. A lot of damage was also done by vehicles carrying all the stage gear across from the groundsman's tunnel in the north west corner down to the stage area in front of the South Stand."

Queen's set was recorded for posterity, and much like the Happy Mondays' Elland Road gig nine years later, is renowned amongst hardcore fans as an 'I was there' moment in the band's career, and bootleg recordings are highly sought-after. Having just scored mega-success with their soundtrack to the film *Flash Gordon* and the recent hit single 'Under Pressure', Queen were on the crest of a huge wave at the time of this gig and

QUEUES

A British characteristic just ahead of talking about the weather, drinking an awful lot and donning shorts the minute the clouds part, queuing is also a particular trait of the hard-nosed football fan. Having been able to order match tickets online and over the phone for many years now, it seems hard to believe that we used to drag ourselves out of bed or camp out overnight, to physically queue for stupid amounts of time in horrendous conditions for tickets. But this was just another outdated aspect of football-supporting that we simply used to accept, and to be fair, until the technological advancements of the computer age and the internet, there was little alternative.

When Leeds' stock grew dramatically in the mid-1960s it was perfectly normal to see huge queues of fans snaking around the West Stand car park and out onto Elland Road, and regular sufferance in all weathers, in the name of Leeds United, was the norm. Modern society would be aghast at having to demonstrate any commitment beyond raising a finger to an iPad, but such was the draw of Leeds United at the time.

Fans queue to get into the opening game of the 1924/25 season.

Leeds fan Dougie Wales spent many hours queuing for tickets for Cup Final, Semi-Final and European ties in the 1960s and '70s, as he recalls: "We used to go across on a Sunday, it was always a Sunday when they went on sale. You had to save tokens printed in the programme, you would cut them out and put them on a tokens sheet, and then the club would say how many tokens you needed to have to qualify for a ticket. So you had to go across and stand and queue."

Bill Fotherby admits that he was not averse to employing 'creative' tactics to drum up interest in certain fixtures, with the art of generating publicity central to most activities our larger-than-life ex-director and chairman engaged in. "It was non-stop," he begins, "doing things commercially to get people involved. I stood in that car park and we had a fella called Jack Williamson, they called him 'Fotherby's Rottweiler'. He was voluntary this man, for Leeds United, and I got him a big cap and a uniform, made him feel he was somebody important. I was stood there in the car park and we had Radio Leeds doing an interview about a cup tie, and I had Jack saying 'they're queuing out of the ground, you can't get in, you can't move for tickets'. There were nobody in the car park, there were nobody there buying tickets, but I was making it out as though the car park was full, 'oh the excitement here today, people here for the cup tie tickets', just trying to generate enthusiasm. The club was dead, but we brought it back to life: 'zoom, we're going places'."

Since the early 1990s tickets have been available for sale over the telephones and therefore transactions can take place away from the frontline. Furthermore, with online sales it is now rare for queues to form other than on match days, or when big game match tickets go on general sale with very short notice.

In recent years, however, the club's two Play-Off Final appearances have seen disorderly scenes as panicked fans have frantically pursued tickets, not helped by some administrative clangers dropped by club officials. In 2006 for the Championship Play-Off Final against Watford in Cardiff, ticket information from the club was poorly communicated. In addition, all applications, for some reason, had to be on a paper application form handed in at Elland Road in person. This created hysterical scenes amid mass migration to Elland Road. Exaggerated internet reports spread like wildfire of huge queues circling three-fold, as thousands descended on the ground on an otherwise quiet Tuesday afternoon. In the event it appeared that several fans had to be treated for sunstroke and dehydration, having stood motionless in baking heat for more than eight hours not knowing what was happening.

Chaotic scenes of a more serious nature were created two years later when Leeds reached the League One Play-Off Final against Doncaster Rovers at the new Wembley. Having handled the allocation of tickets much better than in 2006, the club were left with a few thousand tickets for 'general sale' to non-members. Queues promptly formed overnight and there was a general feeling of good-natured camaraderie, as fans drank together and played football in the car park and later on Fullerton Park as the queue spread further back. The now-empty and derelict BRS Haulage buildings were ransacked and huge, wooden doors were pilfered and smashed up to make firewood, despite which, the mood was communal and peaceful.

There was little communication from the club as to the ticketing arrangements or security in place to control the expected crowds, and the scene very quickly turned nasty as dawn broke. Hundreds of fans arrived from nowhere and started to push into the queue as it snaked around Fullerton Park. This lead to huge surges of people, some frantically gathering up food, sleeping bags and clothes in order to keep their place and their Wembley dream alive. Stories then describe fans stood crammed against fences, motionless for hours, with no communication and no idea if they were likely to get tickets.

Of course queues don't just form at Elland Road for the purpose of buying tickets. You can queue outside the fish 'n chip shop, queue at the bar of any of the many ale establishments in and around the ground, you can even queue to get in the megastore on a busy day. The scrum to access the toilets at half-time is also a thing to behold, which, not having experienced any other set of football fans to any great extent, is something Leeds fans have a particular urgency to do.

The lawless melee attempting to access the Kop toilets at half-time would astound any free-thinking person in any other walk of life. I often marvel at the difference in behaviour between Leeds United fans and those of rugby league, for example, where orderly and patient queues are as normal as toast. At Elland Road it seems fans are given licence to push and shove in a 'dog eat dog' scenario where no concessions to life's basic rules of courtesy and etiquette are allowed.

Official Souvenir Programme

NORTHERN RUGBY LEAGUE CHAMPIONSHIP

FINAL GAME

HUNSLET
v LEEDS

Played at ELLAND ROAD

(Ground of LEEDS UNITED A.F.C.)

Saturday, April 30th, 1938

Kick-off 3-30 p.m.

Price . . . . Threepence

RECORDS

ELLAND ROAD ATTENDANCES (LEEDS UNITED)

Lowest League attendance: 3,950
v Sheffield Wednesday, 9th April 1930

Lowest FA Cup attendance: 9,531
v Northampton Town, 7th November 2008
A crowd of 1,500 was recorded for a 5-2 win over
Boothtown on 11th September 1920, but this was
classed as a First Qualifying Round and also as a reserve
team fixture as the first team also played a league game
at Leicester City on the same day.

Lowest League Cup attendance: 4,517
v Brentford, 13th September 1961

Lowest Full Members Cup attendance: 2,274
v Sheffield United, 16th October 1985

Lowest FL Trophy attendance: 8,429
v Darlington, 6th October 2009

Lowest European attendance: 13,682
v Valletta (UEFA Cup), 3rd October 1979

Highest League attendance: 56,796
v Arsenal, 27th December 1932

Highest FA Cup attendance: 57,892
v Sunderland, 15th March 1967

Highest League Cup attendance: 43,222
v Nottingham Forest, 8th February 1978

Highest Full Members Cup attendance:
(then known as the Zenith Data Systems Cup): 13,387
v Everton, 19th March 1992

Highest FL Trophy attendance: 20,128
v Bradford City, 2nd September 2008

Highest European attendance: 50,498
v Glasgow Rangers (Inter-Cities Fairs Cup),
9th April 1968

- The lowest recorded number of away fans for a league
  fixture at Elland Road was for the visit of Swansea in
  February 1984, when just 24 fans travelled up from
  South Wales for a re-arranged midweek fixture, to
  boost a crowd of 10,031. Leeds won the game 1-0
  with a Peter Lorimer goal. It is likely that teams have
  brought less fans than this in the past, before the days
  of segregation and specific, known areas for away
  fans. Also, some sources claim that Cambridge United
  only brought 14 fans for a Friday night fixture in the
  same season (14th October 1983) to supplement a
  crowd of 9,923, though this is not officially recorded.

- For the first game of the 2005/06 season
  Millwall actually brought zero fans to the game, at
  least officially. In protest at the draconian travel
  arrangements imposed on them, involving picking up
  tickets at a motorway service station on the M1 and
  being subject to a police escort from there, no Millwall
  fans made the visit. Leeds won the game 2-1.

ELLAND ROAD ATTENDANCES (LEEDS CITY)

Lowest League attendance: 2,000
v Chesterfield, 27th February 1906
v Leicester Fosse, 30th April 1910

Highest League attendance: 35,000
v Bradford City, 1st February 1908

ELLAND ROAD WINS (LEEDS UNITED)

Most wins in a league season: 18 in 1968/69

Fewest wins in a league season: 5 in 2003/04

Most successive league wins: 15 from 24th January
2009 to 19th September 2009

Most successive league wins in one season:
12 in 1968/69

Longest run without a league win:
10 games between 6th February 1982 and 12th May
1982. The run was ended with a dramatic 2-1 win over
Brighton & Hove Albion.

Biggest win: 10-0 v Lyn Oslo (European Cup),
17th September 1969

Biggest league win: 8-0 v Leicester City, 7th April 1934

Biggest FA Cup win: 8-1 v Crystal Palace,
11th January 1930 (Leeds also won 7-0 v Leeds
Steelworks on 25th September 1920, but this was
classed as the Second Qualifying Round)

Most league wins against a single team: 36 v Everton

ELLAND ROAD DRAWS (LEEDS UNITED)

Most league draws in a season:
11 in 1981/82 and 1982/83

Fewest league draws in a season: 2 in 1927/28,
1929/30, 1962/63, 1970/71, 1999/00, 2008/09

Most successive league draws: 4 in 1926/27,
1958/59, 1974/75, 1986/87, 1991/92, 1996/97

Longest run without a league draw: 23 games between
19th November 1977 and 25th November 1978

ELLAND ROAD DEFEATS (LEEDS UNITED)

Most league defeats in a season: 11 in 2011/12

Fewest league defeats in a season: 0 in 1963/64, 1968/69, 1971/72 and 1991/92

Most successive league defeats: 5 in 2002/03

Longest run without a league defeat: 39 games between 14th August 1968 and 28th February 1970

Biggest defeat: 1-6 v Watford, 10th November 2012

Most goals conceded at home: 7 v Nottingham Forest, 20th March 2012

Most league defeats to a single team: 19 v Liverpool

- Leeds were drawn at home to Cardiff City in the FA Cup Third Round for three seasons running, between 1955/56 and 1957/58. Leeds lost all three games 2-1. Not surprisingly, the attendances reduced from 40,000 for the first game, to 34,237 for the second and then 30,374 for the third inevitable defeat.

ELLAND ROAD GOALS (LEEDS UNITED)

Most league goals scored in a season: 63 in 1927/28

Fewest league goals scored in a season: 15 in 1996/97

Failed to score most in a league season: 10 times in 1996/97

Failed to score least in a league season: 0 in 1955/56 and 1967/68

Most goals conceded in a league season: 46 in 1959/60

Fewest goals conceded in a league season: 9 in 1968/69 and 1998/99

Most clean sheets in a league season: 14 in 1923/24 and 1980/81

Fewest clean sheets in a league season: 2 in 2003/04

- Len Armitage scored Leeds United's first Football League goal at Elland Road, in a 2-1 defeat to South Shields on 1st September 1920

- Ernie Goldthorpe was the first Leeds United player to score a penalty in a league game at Elland Road in a 3-1 win v Leicester City on 8th September 1920

- Harry Roberts was the first Leeds United player to score two penalties in one game at Elland Road v Aston Villa on 7th September 1929

- The quickest Leeds United goal at Elland Road is thought to be the one scored by Jermaine Wright against Burnley on 3rd November 2004 after only 12 seconds. Leeds lost the game 2-1

- The first Leeds United hat-trick at Elland Road was scored by Eugene O'Doherty in a 5-2 FA Cup First Qualifying Round win over Boothtown on 11th September 1920

- Tom Jennings scored hat-tricks in consecutive home games in the 1926/27 season. He scored three against Arsenal at Elland Road and then four against Blackburn 14 days later. In the game in between, he scored four away at Liverpool

- John Charles scored 11 hat-tricks for Leeds, eight of them came at Elland Road

- Charlie Keetley scored nine hat-tricks for Leeds, eight of them came at Elland Road

- Carl Shutt is the last player to score a league hat-trick on his Leeds debut at Elland Road vs Bournemouth, 1st April 1989

- Samuel Saiz scored a hat-trick on his full debut on 9th August 2017 in a 4-1 League Cup defeat of Port Vale

- Phil Masinga's hat-trick in the 5-2 FA Cup Replay win over Walsall on 17th January 1995 at Elland Road was unique at the time for two reasons. It was the first Leeds United hat-trick by a substitute, and remains the only Leeds United hat-trick scored solely in extra time

- The only five-goal haul at Elland Road was by Gordon Hodgson v Leicester City, 1st October 1938

4-goal hauls at Elland Road (Leeds City & Leeds United):
Fred Hargraves v Morley (FA Cup) 1905
Dickie Morris v Morley (FA Cup) 1905
David Wilson v Clapton Orient 1906
Billy McLeod v Nottingham Forest 1913
Tom Jennings v Blackburn 1926 & Chelsea 1927
Russell Wainscoat v West Ham 1927
Arthur Hydes v Middlesbrough 1933
Gordon Hodgson v Everton 1938
John Charles v Notts County 1953
John McCole v Brentford (League Cup) 1961
Allan Clarke v Burnley 1971
Mark Viduka v Liverpool 2000
Brian Deane v QPR 2004

Highest aggregate of goals in a single game: 10
v Leicester in 1938 (8-2)
v Lyn Oslo in 1969 (10-0)
v Preston North End in 2010 (4-6)
v Nottingham Forest in 2012 (3-7)

ELLAND ROAD POINTS

Most in a season (3 points for a win): 54 – 1989/90

Most in a season (2 points for a win): 39 – 1968/69

Fewest in a season (3 points for a win): 22 – 2003/04

Fewest in a season (2 points for a win): 17 – 1946/47

MISCELLANEOUS

- The first Leeds United player to be sent off at Elland Road was Archie Gibson on 27th December 1958. This was only the club's second ever sending off, the first being Billy Poyntz on 11th February 1922, 36 years and 1,259 league games earlier, in a game away at Bury.

- Leeds United played in all-white at Elland Road for the first time in a 4-4 draw with Middlesbrough on 17th September 1960, a full six months before Don Revie took over as manager, and in the summer of 1961 changed the kit permanently from blue and gold.

All facts correct as of the end of the 2019/20 season.

REFEREE'S ROOM

Most people love a fly-on-the-wall documentary that takes you beneath the surface of professional football. It is only usually in this type of situation that you have access to the inner sanctum of a football club and can gain precious insight into the match day routine behind the scenes. Such revelation would take in the no doubt priceless conversations that take place in the referee's room; the small dressing room reserved for the Man in Black and his three other officials. At Elland Road this is a relatively plush and well-appointed room bang next door to the away dressing room, which itself is right opposite the home dressing room. Clearly the referee's room is supposed to be an area of solace and rest away from the madness of the game, but they must often sit in silence dreading the rap of knuckles on the door wanting 'a quiet word'.

In the early 1960s, however, the ref's room was on the opposite side of the corridor and the first room on the right hand side as you turned the corner from the tunnel. Then it was simply a room for the officials to get changed in, and during the week was actually the 'coaches' room' where Don Revie, Les Cocker and Syd Owen spent most of their time. Dave Cocker recalls it well: "It was a really small room, maybe ten foot by nine foot, and at the back there was a bathroom with two domestic baths in. But it was the coaches' room during the week, that's where they'd be getting stripped and putting tracksuits on every day. Cyril (Partridge) and Bob (English) used to use the referee's room in the dressing rooms on Fullerton Park, where the juniors changed."

But the match day etiquette was very different in the 1960s, particularly when you hear stories today of managers knocking on a ref's door to discuss certain incidents. There was no 'open door' policy back then. "The ref used to close his door and lock it, that was it," says Dave emphatically. "You never saw the ref. The next thing you knew, you'd hear his buzzer at 2.55pm and he'd come out once both sets of players were out on the pitch."

Given the pressure that officials are now under through endless televisual dissection of their decisions, it is somewhat surprising that they have become more conspicuous around the grounds on match days. Back in Revie's day the ref was seen and not heard, except for his whistle, and by common consent was at the very least respected.

By the mid-1980s the referee's room had been moved to the far end of the open area adjacent to the dressing rooms that was used as a gymnasium, which meant that the officials had a slightly longer walk into the tunnel area than they do now. Physio Alan Sutton particularly remembers the location of the old referee's room because "David Batty locked me in there one day, tied the door up and left me there for hours".

As with most of the rooms in the central dressing room area, the referee's room was moved to its current location as part of the Euro 96 refurbishment, and much as fans might like to read that it is fitted with a set of stocks for potential post-match tomato pelting, in reality it is unassuming and consists of most home comforts; the Neil Warnock dartboard being optional.

RELOCATION

'The only place for us'? Not if Peter Ridsdale had had his way. Under his chairmanship many weird, wonderful and frankly inexplicable things happened to Leeds United and its fans. Following a dramatic and tantalising season dining at the very top table of football's lavish and gift-laden peer structure many heads were turned including, most importantly, the faceless suits on the board of Leeds United PLC. Before we knew it a Leeds United Formula One team, a travel agency, a publishing arm and more international strikers than a pack of Top Trumps were on our agenda.

During the following season Leeds were no longer in the Champions League and were faltering in the Premier League. Behind the scenes we now know that Ridsdale had mortgaged the future of the club based on continual Champions League qualification, which in the precarious world of football, ignoring for a moment the cataclysmic 'shoot-yourself-in-the-foot' ability that Leeds United itself inherently possesses, was an extremely risky policy.

That said, in August 2001 all was relatively rosy on the surface and Leeds fans were still coming down from the Champions League thrill-ride. These were good

ELLAND ROAD WILL HOLD 70,000 IF BIG PLAN GOES AHEAD

ALL-ROUND STANDS, 17,000 SEATS FOR LEEDS FANS

A headline from the 11th August 1965 edition of the *Yorkshire Evening Post* detailing the exciting proposals for the first 'grand plan' for Elland Road dreamed up by Don Revie and his ambitious board. This involved moving the pitch orientation back to east/west but a year later the plan had changed.

times. We had, and were still acquiring, quality players that we could never have dreamed of and we had no reason to question Ridsdale's judgement because he was 'one of us', and so far he had delivered.

So Ridsdale's plans to relocate Leeds United from Elland Road to a brand new purpose-built stadium in an area of Skelton, just to the south east of Leeds by the M1/A1 link road, were met with merely a raised eyebrow and much discussion, rather than the standard reaction of abject horror. The plans, which had allegedly been passed by Leeds City Council, were for a 50,000-seat stadium with the obligatory naming-rights partly funding the move, in conjunction with the sale of Elland Road. The idea indeed did horrify the majority of Leeds fans, who would simply not consider a move from their beloved Elland Road, but the very fact that Ridsdale had suggested it, at the time gave it some credence and meant it warranted consideration.

Voting postcards were sent to all 18,500 season ticket holders on 16th August 2001 and impassioned pleas were made by Ridsdale in a letter containing a step-by-step dissection of the situation. This all led to the assertion that Leeds United simply had to move in order to compete, as they currently were, with the best. We were told that the prospect of renovating Elland Road to create a 50,000-seat stadium was simply not an option from a cost point of view, due to the 'piecemeal' nature of the work and the loss of income in the meantime. Ridsdale also argued that naming rights on an existing stadium were "not a practical option" and hence the funding to redevelop Elland Road would have to be found elsewhere. Before and since, numerous other clubs have re-named existing grounds lucratively, but who were we to argue with Peter Ridsdale?

Concerns were raised over the ashes of deceased fans that had been spread on Elland Road, not to mention those of Billy Bremner and Don Revie, but Ridsdale even countered that, with the promise of a Garden of Remembrance at the new stadium with turf from Elland Road and plaques commemorating those that had their ashes spread on the pitch. It was also promised that the Billy Bremner statue would be

relocated and roads leading up to the new stadium would be named after Christopher Loftus and Kevin Speight, the two fans killed in Istanbul in April 2000.

The argument was effectively: if we didn't vote 'yes' to the stadium move the very future of the club was in doubt. Highly emotive and bordering on undue coercion, and while two options were available for the vote, the accompanying letter was hugely biased in favour of the move. Ridsdale put it bluntly: "On the one hand there is the history and the memories that we all share, and on the other hand is the need to ensure that we offer future generations a world-class team and a world-class stadium."

In the event I don't know anyone who actually voted 'yes' to the proposal, and it was the first sign that Ridsdale's halo was slipping in the eyes of the fans. Yet it was amid some consternation that Ridsdale announced, some weeks later on 7th September 2001, that 87.6% of fans had voted 'yes' to the proposed move. Seemingly, despite no concrete plans of the stadium to consider and a raft of unanswered questions as long as the queue outside United Fisheries, most had been indoctrinated in Ridsdale's scheme. Apparently 16,276 had voted for it and 2,301 had voted against. Ridsdale, clearly euphoric, continually used the term 'consultation' as if there had been an open dialogue over the process instead of the prejudiced rhetoric of his heavily slanted letter.

At a Supporters' Club function the day after the result was announced, Elsie Revie, widow of Don Revie, expressed some concern. Turning to Peter Ridsdale, who was also at the function, she said: "I hope, Peter, your dream comes true and we have the fantastic stadium. It will be tinged with a little bit of sadness because my husband's ashes and Billy Bremner's ashes are scattered in front of where the old Scratching Shed used to be."

Ridsdale replied by talking up the emotional commitment of the fans' vote, saying: "Yesterday was very special – not because we are to have a magnificent stadium for magnificent supporters, but because those supporters decided we should build a magnificent stadium for magnificent supporters."

With unfortunate prophesy, Ridsdale added: "The decision, while very difficult, recognises what we have to do to build and have longevity of success. Here we have a lady (Elsie Revie) whose husband had a great team and then we went into the wilderness. I don't want to spend Tuesday nights at places like Plymouth Argyle ever again," said the future Plymouth Argyle chairman.......

This was a strange, strange time and the vote results were met with some scepticism as many fans suggested the vote was rigged purely to give the result that Ridsdale and his PLC cronies required; after all, what do businessmen care about where Leeds United play? Suddenly there was confusion and factions breaking away, and the first cracks were appearing in the 'dream'. As the 2001/02 season unfolded Leeds' fortunes nose-dived on the pitch amongst a myriad of conspiring circumstances, and any plans for Ridsdale's dream move to Skelton pretty much went with them. Ridsdale resigned from his position in 2003 and disappeared into the sunset, and despite relegation from the Premier League, Leeds United fans at least had their feet back firmly under the table, forever in LS11.

It may surprise some to learn that this wasn't the first time the club had considered moving lock, stock and barrel to another site within the city. Don Revie's frustrations with the Leeds public in the 1960s and 1970s are well documented, although at the time he kept his feelings and the assertion that his team never truly got the support that they deserved, largely private. It is true that while Leeds enjoyed healthy 40,000 plus crowds in the good times, the gates would soon dip in holiday periods, or for meaningless European or league games, and the average gates weren't as high as the likes of Liverpool or Manchester United enjoyed.

Dave Cocker remembers discussions taking place with a view to moving Leeds United's home to a more densely populated area, containing a demographic more associated with attending football, rather than the staunch rugby and cricket areas dotted around Leeds: "Don disliked the fact that we couldn't pull many fans. That stadium there in the early 1960s had a capacity of around 55,000 and we were only pulling 35,000 regularly, and he could never understand that. He would say 'look, we played like that and there's only 32,000?' The club actually talked about moving when they demolished Quarry Hill flats. They were looking at building a new stadium down there because Don thought Elland Road was too far out of town this side, and he wanted to pull people in from the more working class areas like Seacroft and Cross Gates where a lot of the fans came from. So Don always wanted to move to that side of town and there were talks going on to move to Quarry Hill flats, because you'd have everything then, it was central, it was right by the bus station. But obviously it never happened, it was too central and it would have caused planning problems."

Quarry Hill is an area to the east of the city centre which in Victorian times was almost a lawless slum area, notorious for anti-Semitic and anti-Irish riots, overcrowded back-to-back housing and frequent cholera outbreaks. In 1938 it became the site for the largest social housing complex in the UK, a sprawling development of high rise flats famed at the time for its modernist architecture. But by the early 1970s talks were already underway, amid social issues and poor maintenance, to re-locate the inhabitants, presumably

the same point at which Leeds United entered into discussions. The flats were demolished in 1978, by which time Leeds United's fortunes had taken a similarly earthbound trajectory and the plan to move predictably floundered.

Moving further forward, Howard Wilkinson confirmed there were no such relocation discussions during the club's more recent 'glory' period. He said: "If you took an aerial photo of the ground, looking at where it is, unless you moved it outside the city like they do in Germany or France and having a park surrounding it, for an urban ground it was amazingly blessed with space and access off the motorway, etc. I would argue in terms of location, access and space it was on a par with Old Trafford (in the early 1990s) at a similar stage in its development. When you look at what they've done there, it's unbelievable."

A curiosity to the Elland Road grand plan that Leeds United had at the onset of their 'glory years' can be found in August 1965, and refers to plans for a relocation of sorts that are wildly inconsistent with what actually happened soon after. Fastened by the unprecedented success of the club's first season in the top flight, and with a debut European campaign on the horizon, the club were not slow in looking forward.

It was very much felt that a new era had arrived and in the Sunderland programme for the first game of the 1965/66 season and in the local press, chairman Harry Reynolds announced a plan to revert the pitch back to the east/west pre-1906 direction and completely redevelop the ground. This would have resulted in a near 70,000 capacity, with the board proudly boasting that this would include an 'impressive' 17,000 seats. Reynolds was deadly serious. In the programme he described the plan as "no pipe dream" as planning approval had already been granted in principle and architects' plans were being submitted, and in 12 months' time they expected to have the full plans approved and ready to present. The scheme would create a 'modern' stadium with seating and standing all-covered, plus the best recreational, social and catering facilities to make "...all of Leeds, let alone all our fans, sit up smartly". Reynolds continued: "Do believe us. A new era has already started at Elland Road. Our past is not all that interesting, or it wasn't until last season! But our future will be something to watch indeed if everything goes to plan."

The plan involved leaving the West Stand as it was and building a new Lowfields Road Stand behind the existing one and a new Gelderd Road Stand that extended much longer at the ends as this would now be the longer stand along the length of the pitch. Turning the pitch around would allow better use of the Elland Road side of the ground, as that was always the limiting factor with the Scratching Shed being so close to the road. Initial estimates of a then staggering £500,000 were soon revised to around £1 million.

Set into the wall outside the south west corner is the Revie/Bremner tribute paid for and donated to the club by the Leeds United Supporters' Club.

Dave Cocker remembers the plan well: "They were talking then to the Castle Brothers, to buy that land behind the Kop, the board wanted it because it was a no-brainer, it was a big chunk of land. If they had turned the pitch round they would have had more space. The problem has always been Elland Road, you can't build above Elland Road, unless you do what Atletico Madrid did and build over the road." So Elland Road itself was always the major constraint to development.

Clearly everything did go to plan on the field, at least those things under the club's control, but in terms of this particular grand plan there must have been a fairly swift re-think, possibly because of a lack of cash to buy the Castle Brothers land. A year later in May 1966 a new "slightly less ambitious" scheme was proposed which was to carry out the full development in stages, still costing around £1 million, but keeping the pitch in the same orientation.

Not two years later a new Kop was already in place putting a pretty bold full stop to any plans to turn the pitch around. It appears safe to assume that the abandoned pitch move was the first grand plan and the alternative involved simply redeveloping the ground in situ and in piecemeal fashion, which they did successfully between 1968 and 1974, but didn't quite complete. It seems unlikely that a pitch switched 90 degrees in the mid-1960s would have been able to cost-effectively produce a stadium to match the modern Elland Road any quicker. But the very clear vision and ambition that Reynolds and Revie shared right from the very first seeds of 'success', were there for all to see.

REVIE/BREMNER TRIBUTE

Sometimes football touches you in a way you can't describe and you feel a gripping urge to lavish praise on someone or something and you just don't know how. At the end of the 1990/91 season, Leeds United's first back in the top flight after eight years away, I was genuinely affected by the club's startling and unforeseeable progression and the impressionable me was moved to send a letter of appreciation to manager Howard Wilkinson. It was the only method I could think of to demonstrate how I felt and it was not something I was prone to doing. I didn't know what I hoped to achieve but I just had gushing praise inside me I wanted to get out; and Howard replied to say 'thanks'. I dare say a number of effusive youngsters have sent similar missives to Marcelo Bielsa in the wake of 2020's long-overdue promotion.

I am reminded of this when I see the Revie/Bremner plaque built into the wall at the southern end of the West Stand. It is a simple, brass plaque with an artists' impression of the two legends holding the FA Cup at Wembley following the win against Arsenal in 1972.

The plaque reads:

"In commemoration of Don Revie and Billy Bremner, with eternal thanks from the members of Leeds United Supporters Club."

Clearly this was an idea that came to mind following the untimely death of Bremner in December 1997, and along with Revie (who had died eight years earlier) it was felt that the passing of two such significant figures in the club's history should be recognised by the fans' group. Given this was a time when the Bremner statue had already been commissioned but not completed, it is to the club's credit that Leeds United Supporters' Club (LUSC) were still allowed to do it.

The plaque was paid for by LUSC branch donations, as Ray Fell explains: "It was shortly after Billy's death and we wanted to commemorate Billy somewhere, and we were also a bit peeved that Revie had never been commemorated, so we had this plaque done. It was done with the club's blessing and we had a reception which Elsie Revie and Vicky Bremner came to, Ridsdale was there too, which we held in the Goal Line Restaurant."

Since this time, of course, both Revie and Bremner have received a statue to grace the external perimeter of Elland Road, Revie's in particular being long overdue. But prior to this the plaque was the only official recognition. The wording doesn't thank the two of them for anything in particular. It doesn't list the achievements or heap praise on either, it doesn't list the qualities or the legacy they left. How could it? It simply says "thanks". And that's enough.

ROD STEWART

On a Saturday afternoon, the Dragon Hotel on Whitehall Road would usually have punters spilling out onto the front patio area, resplendent in replica shirts, scarves or designer menswear and throwing as much lager down their necks as possible before the ten minute walk down the road to catch kick-off. On such frequent occasions the demographic is pretty one-dimensional: male, mid-twenties to mid-forties, the odd party has females in it, and there are usually some small children about too.

The evening of 3rd June 2011 saw me drive past and the scene was very similar with jovial crowds mingling outside the front of the pub, but I had to do a double take because the population structure was markedly different. This was a mixed-sex crowd of largely 60-somethings, with wine and Pimms appearing to be the drink of choice. Yes, Rod Stewart was in town.

This gig saw the veteran Scottish rocker returning to the city for the first time since a 1973 show at the since-demolished Queen's Hall with The Faces. In contrast to the other legendary gigs held at the stadium in modern times, Rod Stewart didn't sell out, far from it, but an estimated 15,000 crowd enjoyed a spectacular concert all the same. Nine thousand seats were installed on temporary flooring on the pitch itself, while other fans sat in the West Stand, Kop and East Stand Lower facing the stage set up in front of the South Stand, as with all previous gigs on the hallowed turf.

Given the nature of the artist, Stewart was himself in his mid-sizties, and the expected crowd there was a distinct lack of protests from local residents, which had been a thorny feature of preparations for other such events at Elland Road. On the night, despite the attendance, the gig was a resounding success for those who attended but also for Rod Stewart, a well-known football fan who particularly loves to perform at famous football grounds, and who pre-match was able to meet his Scottish heroes Peter Lorimer and Eddie Gray.

RUGBY LEAGUE

Love it, loathe it or just simply tolerate it, the influence of the sport of rugby league on Elland Road is far reaching. With Leeds sitting plum in the middle of the 'M62 Corridor' that cradles the majority of the major forces within the game in this country, it is inevitable that the city would have a central role in rugby league's development. From Hull on the east coast to St Helens almost on the west coast, the intensity of the rivalry between so many clubs in such close proximity is what gives the game its unrivalled competitive edge.

Leeds and the West Riding in general was a rugby stronghold long before football had any prominence in the area. South Yorkshire, and Sheffield in particular, was much quicker off the mark to embrace the round ball game. As Leeds City and the early formation of Leeds United struggled to achieve a tangible progression in stature, they struggled to compete for public interest with the more traditional success story of Leeds RL, plus rival rugby union and cricket attentions. It was not until the Revie era that Leeds United truly became the major sporting institution in the city; prior to that it was very much a second class citizen.

While Headingley has always been the home of Leeds RL/Rhinos, the traditional element of the stadium has limited their expansion plans. Since the early 1980s many major rugby league games have therefore been held in Leeds, but at Elland Road rather than Headingley, due to the facilities and access, plus the ability and capacity to deal with larger crowds. This may be to the chagrin of the famously proud and stoical rugby league fans who look down their noses somewhat at whatever football has to offer, but retaining the major games in the city, within the game's heartland, is seen by the Leeds-based Rugby Football League as the main objective. That said, most recently in 2012 and 2013, the big games such as the World Club Challenge and World Cup fixtures have returned to Headingley.

In truth, rugby league is intrinsically linked to Elland Road and was so before the stadium was linked to football, with the ground having hosted the game even when it was called the Old Peacock Ground. The formative ground was purchased and used for seven years, of course, by Holbeck Rugby Club between 1897 and 1904; the early years of the Northern Union. Prior to that Leeds Athletic used the ground briefly on two occasions, the second when they had changed their name to the Yorkshire Wanderers.

Elland Road also has a rich history of hosting major games going back as far as 1938, when some argue the Championship Final between Hunslet and Leeds RL on 30th April drew Elland Road's biggest ever attendance. It is officially recorded as 54,112. But as ever with high profile games held at Elland Road, and indeed elsewhere around that time, this doesn't account for the chaotic scenes that such occasions descended into and the 'unofficial' entry by scores of opportunist fans.

The game was initially scheduled to be played at Belle Vue, Wakefield. However, at the semi-final stage before the competing teams had even been decided, Leeds and Hunslet each voiced their concerns over the choice of Belle Vue for the potential 'All Leeds Final'. A little presumptuous maybe, but fears over unprecedented demand for tickets raised Elland Road as the only suitable venue, and both clubs agreed despite their intense local rivalry. To set up the 'All Leeds Final' Hunslet beat Barrow and two days later Leeds beat Swinton in their semi-final.

Initially the rugby league committee rejected the Elland Road proposal, but amid outcry from fans and clubs alike, they relented and common sense prevailed. The furore had naturally triggered a frenzy of interest and with the date and venue set, rugby posts were borrowed from Hunslet's Parkside ground and erected on Elland Road for the first time since Leeds City took over the ground in 1904.

Advance ticket sales were good and the official crowd on the day of 54,112 was a record attendance for a British rugby league game, perfectly vindicating the strength of feeling in the two clubs insisting the game was moved to Elland Road. The fans also paid record receipts of £3,572 18s 6d, which helped to finance both the competing clubs for the foreseeable future. Newspaper reports claim that the crowd could indeed have been bigger, even though the gates were locked and many fans gave up trying to get in some 20 minutes before kick-off. Many resorted to the now oft-attempted vantage point of the Old Peacock roof. It was claimed in newspaper reports that "bad packing, particularly behind the sticks at the Gelderd Road end", could have led to more fans being accommodated. This is likely to be due to the fact that no fences existed to separate the Lowfields and Kop stands at the time, and with most public transport terminating and disembarking on Lowfields Road, it will be unlikely that sufficient fans would walk around to the Kop turnstiles in the north west corner. Instead, they would enter in the Lowfields turnstiles, resulting in some areas being tightly packed and others further westwards on the Kop, sparsely packed. This does also throw doubt on the rugby league enthusiasts' claims that the unofficial crowd was much higher than any Leeds United crowd, as there were certainly no cases of 'bad packing' anywhere in the ground at the Sunderland game in 1967.

In the event the game was no classic with Hunslet running out 8-2 winners, but the huge crowd made the occasion a truly historic event which is still talked about by fans of both clubs. The first floodlit rugby league game in the city of Leeds also took place at Elland Road, when in 1958 Hunslet again took on Leeds beneath the ground's recently acquired lights and in the absence of similar facilities at Headingley or Parkside.

During Leeds United's peak years of success under Don Revie rugby league rarely encroached on the Elland Road arena. But in the 1980s, particularly when the ground was sold to Leeds City Council who were anxious to explore additional revenue opportunities, Elland Road became the venue for John Player Special Cup Finals, Challenge Cup Semi-Finals and Challenge Cup Final Replays as well as tri-nation international matches between Great Britain, Australia and New Zealand.

Of course, Hunslet RL also took permanent residency on the pitch for the beginning of their 1982/83 season when they had to leave the nearby greyhound stadium, and when Leeds United were still the owners of Elland Road. With Leeds United having just been relegated and in need of financial support, and with Hunslet homeless and with some history at the ground, it was thought to be a reciprocal arrangement all-round despite concerns over the pitch. With Leeds United reserves to consider, Elland Road would be regularly hosting three games a week.

The official programme for the famous 'All Leeds Final' of 1938.

A photo taken by John Reynolds in 1982 to commemorate the first time rugby posts had been erected on the Elland Road pitch since 1958. This was prior to Hunslet's first game as official tenants and hence whether Hunslet played 'ace' was yet to be fully established.

Football League approval was required for the ground-share but it was granted. Hunslet were charged £1,000 per game on a lease arrangement with there being 16 games a season at the time. In addition there were bar and catering takings to consider for crowds of around 2–3,000, so it was a profitable arrangement for the football club that were about to lose £2 million in the financial year. Hunslet were afforded their own souvenir shop and their own bar called the 'Phoenix Bar', both built into a small unit in the back of the North West Corner Stand, and they also had some external identity visible to passers-by, as a black 'Hunslet R.L.F.C.' sign was stuck to the end wall of the West Stand for the term of their residency up to the end of the 1988/89 season.

Rugby league's growing influence at Elland Road in the 1980s had already been evident, as the ground had hosted the Challenge Cup Final replay the previous May before a crowd of 41,171, when Hull and Widnes met. At the time Elland Road accommodated 19,626 seated fans, more than five times the number any traditional rugby league ground could seat. As Hunslet kicked off their Elland Road tenure with a season opener against Salford on 22nd August 1982, before 3,150 fans, rugby league firmly had its feet back under the table at Elland Road. Sadly for Hunslet, only 2,000 of those were paying customers as the others were either Leeds United season ticket holders, who were admitted free

to all Hunslet games, or complimentary ticket holders through other means.

Looking back, while it is not a celebrated era for either Hunslet or Leeds United, there are some fond memories and most Hunslet players loved playing at Elland Road. It became a factor in attracting a number of players to the club, particularly as the facilities were much improved and the Fullerton Park training pitch was also convenient. Many cited the improved atmosphere, despite the low crowds and generally only the West Stand and Kop being open. The record crowd Hunslet attracted to Elland Road was the 14,004 who attended the Challenge Cup Quarter-Final tie against Castleford in 1983.

The relationship soon became rocky though, and despite Hunslet having negotiated a 20-year lease with the council when they took on ownership of the ground in 1985, they were soon having to gather their belongings and up sticks once more. Following discussions with their main tenants, Leeds United, the council showed their compassionate side and gave in to the club's desire to re-surface and re-seed a pitch that was seen to be hindering their progress in regaining top flight status. Hunslet RL were promptly evicted in 1989 when Howard Wilkinson was looking for 'quick wins' in improving the barren fortunes of Leeds United. This is despite the fact that the poor state of the pitch was said to be down to bad drainage, rather than the damage created by rugby league games. Howard Wilkinson was particularly forceful in Hunslet's eventual ejection, however, saying: "I put my foot down on that. It was a source of revenue and the council owned the ground, but no, it was non-conducive so that went quickly."

Stephen Reynolds recalls particular issues with the club holding rugby league games on the Elland Road pitch and the problems it would present his dad John in preparing it, with two sets of pitch markings clearly visible in all games: "The rugby posts were roughly on the six yard line, and there was a foot square of turf that they had to dig up, put the posts and the footings in and then afterwards take the posts out and replace the square of turf."

Continually changing the posts around to accommodate each sport became a taxing occupation for John Reynolds: "When the rugby was there," continues Stephen, "he used to have to change the pitch over for the rugby the next day, change the pitch markings and put the goals away and put the rugby posts up. The rugby team didn't have their own groundsman, my Dad did it all. They did employ Brian Cartwright from Batley Rugby Club to help out, because at first nobody had ever marked out a rugby pitch before. But they became friends and eventually they took Brian on." It would take six men working flat out for two and a half hours to change the pitch around, which often had to be done three or more times a week.

Leeds City Council were duty-bound to assist Hunslet in finding a new home within the Leeds city boundary, and hence the club played games at both Batley and Bramley before settling at the South Leeds Stadium in 1995. When Hunslet vacated Elland Road it was on the understanding that they could play the occasional big match at the ground if the desired capacity demanded it. One such occasion, and indeed the last time Hunslet have played at Elland Road, was in February 1997 when they played Bradford Bulls in a Challenge Cup tie. A crowd of 6,102 watched the game, more than double the capacity of the South Leeds Stadium. Needless to say, Leeds United general manager of the time, Alan Roberts, was moved to placate worried fans that the gesture was strictly a one-off.

Prior to this, Elland Road staged its first rugby union game. On Tuesday 10th November 1992 a representative match between England North and the touring South Africans was staged to the backdrop of the emerging East Stand, with a crowd of 14,471 in attendance. South Africa won it 19-3. In September 2015 Elland Road hosted the colour and carnival of the Rugby Union World Cup, with two games staged in LS11. Scotland beat USA 39-16 before a crowd of 33,521 and then Italy beat Canada 23-18 before a crowd of 33,120.

Since the mid-1990s rugby league has undergone fundamental change in the development of the Super League and 'summer' rugby. On 29th October 1996 Paul Caddick and Gary Hetherington were revealed as the new board of Leeds CF&A Co Ltd and the new owners of Headingley and Leeds RLFC. Prior to this, both Leeds Rugby League and Yorkshire CCC were in dire straits. Speculation at the time suggested that the rugby league team could leave Headingley for Elland Road, as Yorkshire CCC had announced plans to move to a new site at Durkar near Wakefield and Leeds Rugby Union, who had only just moved into Headingley, were in National Division Three.

Rugby League Internationals

Date		Teams		Crowd
9th November 1985	6	Great Britain New Zealand	6	22,209
8th November 1986	11	Great Britain Australia	34	30,808
10th November 1990	0	Great Britain Australia	14	32,500
20th November 1994	4	Great Britain Australia	23	39,468
16th November 1997	20	Great Britain Australia	37	39,337
27th November 2004	4	Great Britain Australia	44	39,120
26th November 2005	0	Australia New Zealand	24	26,534
14th November 2009	16	Great Britain Australia	46	31,042
19th November 2011	8	England Australia	30	34,174
11th November 2018	0	England New Zealand	34	32,186

Super League Fixtures

Date		Teams		Crowd
8th February 2018	20	Leeds Rhinos Hull Kingston Rovers	11	16,149
23rd March 2018	24	Leeds Rhinos Castleford Tigers	25	23,246

Yorkshire Cup Final

Date		Teams		Crowd
15th October 1983	13	Hull FC Castleford	2	-
31st October 1987*	11	Bradford Northern Castleford	2	-
16th October 1988	33	Leeds RL Castleford	12	22,968
23rd September 1990	11	Castleford Wakefield Trinity	8	-
20th October 1991	28	Castleford Bradford Northern	6	-
18th October 1992	28	Wakefield Trinity Sheffield Eagles	16	-

*Replay, original game at Headingley

World Club Challenge

Date		Teams		Crowd
4th February 2005	39	Leeds Rhinos Canterbury Bulldogs	32	37,028
29th February 2008	11	Leeds Rhinos Melbourne Storm	4	33,204
1st March 2009	20	Leeds Rhinos Manly Sea Eagles	28	32,569
28th February 2010	10	Leeds Rhinos Melbourne Storm	18	27,697

Summer rugby transformed the game dramatically, as Leeds Rhinos grew to become one of the most successful operations in world rugby and are part of the world's first dual code partnership with Leeds Rugby encompassing both the Rhinos and Leeds Tykes in one business. The partnership also helped Yorkshire cricket and 2006 saw the historic announcement that Yorkshire CCC had purchased the freehold of Headingley cricket ground from the parent company of the rugby club, and owned the ground for the first time in their history.

Modern grounds such as the DW Stadium at Wigan, KC Stadium at Hull and McAlpine/Galpharm/John Smiths Stadium at Huddersfield have ensured that many big games are accommodated there rather than at Elland Road, and Old Trafford with its 75,000 capacity is usually seen as the focal point of the rugby league game in the modern era, more so than Wembley. In recent years Elland Road has most regularly been used for World Club Challenge games where, on four occasions, Leeds Rhinos as English champions have faced their Australian counterparts before 30,000 plus crowds. In 2018 Leeds Rhinos played two 'home' fixtures at Elland Road whilst their Headingley ground underwent significant re-development, facing both Hull Kingston Rovers and Castleford Tigers in front of healthy crowds on both occasions, whilst England lost 34-0 to New Zealand in a Baskerville Shield game, also in 2018. Elland Road was also due to host the second of three Ashes tests between England and Australia in November 2020, but the series was postponed due to the Coronavirus pandemic, whilst the stadium is at present due to host a semi-final in the 2021 Rugby League World Cup.

As far as is officially recorded, the full list of rugby league 'one-off' games, ie. excluding the permanent and long-term tenures of Leeds Athletic, Holbeck Rugby Club and Hunslet RL, is:

Challenge Cup Semi-Finals

Date		Teams		Attendance
2nd April 1983	11	Hull Castleford	7	26,031
24th March 1984	14	Wigan York	8	17,156
23rd March 1985	18	Wigan Hull KR	11	19,275
29th March 1986	24	Hull KR Leeds	24	23,866
3rd April 1986*	17	Hull KR Leeds	0	32,485
30th March 1988*	4	Halifax Hull FC	3	25,117
27th March 1993	15	Wigan Bradford Northern	6	20,085
1st April 1995	39	Leeds Featherstone	22	21,485

*Replay

Challenge Cup Final Replay

Date		Teams		Attendance
19th May 1982	13	Hull Widnes	9	41,171

Challenge Cup Fourth Round

Date		Teams		Attendance
9th February 1997	10	Hunslet Hawks Bradford Bulls	62	6,102

Premiership Final

Date		Teams		Attendance
11th May 1985	36	St Helens Hull KR	16	15,518
18th May 1986	38	Warrington Halifax	0	13,683

Championship Final

Date		Teams		Attendance
30th April 1938	8	Hunslet Leeds	2	54,112

John Player/John Player Special/Regal Trophy Final

Date		Teams		Attendance
22nd January 1983	5	Leeds Wigan	15	19,553
11th January 1986	11	Wigan Hull KR	8	17,573
23rd January 1993	15	Wigan Bradford	8	13,221

S

SCOREBOARD

Elland Road's electronic scoreboard pictured shortly after its installation in 1979.

'GOAL', 'GOAL', 'GOAL'; who can forget the flashing black and amber backdrop to the dizzying jubilance of a George McCluskey screamer against Carlisle? Few images stir the passions of my generation of Leeds United fans more than a picture of a packed Kop with the electronic scoreboard above it. Whimsical memories still strongly resonate of joyously celebrating goals and being thrust around the Kop in a riotous melee of bodies, a world cast off its axis as you fleetingly catch a glimpse of the scoreboard flashing 'GOAL' in huge letters, interjected with the square and rudimentary-pixelated dancing men.

You would never have the opportunity to stand still and watch the scoreboard announce a 'GOAL' in all its bursting ceremony. After all, when the opposition scored you never looked at the scoreboard because the pain was unnecessary, and I always considered that our scoreboard shouldn't really be getting quite

so excited about Leeds conceding a goal anyway. A more apologetic, strictly non-flashing and lower-case 'goal' would suffice, with the dancing men replaced by a weeping peacock trudging off stage mournfully, like the animated duck that Australian TV brilliantly used to adopt when a batsman scored 0 in an Ashes series.

No, seeing the scoreboard in all its glory was only ever a chaotic experience, and the combined flashing images and violent noise produced an occurrence something akin to strobe lighting at a Chemical Brothers gig, as you leapt around the Kop in manic celebration, your head spinning in exuberant glee for 30 arresting seconds, maybe 40 if Ian Baird had scored.

It is easy now to look back to the electronic scoreboard with nostalgia at its primitive graphics and basic functionality, but when it was installed in 1979 it was widely proclaimed as state-of-the-art, and Leeds United were once again pioneers of a sort, as if I recall, only Norwich City and one or two others had a similar one at the time. Even the widely used name itself, the 'electronic scoreboard', is a sentimental throwback to a more plain and uncomplicated time, via the requirement to qualify that a scoreboard could indeed be 'electronic'. The scoreboard was a rectangular construction measuring 89 feet by 5 feet and was hung underneath the roof and also attached to the stanchions towards the back of the Kop. It was used for the first time on 8th August 1979 when Leeds entertained Dutch side NEC Nijmegen in a friendly, and the dancing men embarked on their inaugural celebratory jig when Trevor Cherry scored the only goal in a 1-0 win. However, the scoreboard was officially revealed for the Everton game a few weeks later on 22nd August, when the first home game of the season saw Kevin Hird and Carl Harris score in a 2-0 win.

Batty and Baird celebrate the latter's diving header versus Bournemouth in November 1989; sadly the photographer clicked during the split second between the scoreboard's flashing 'GOAL' climax.

The dancing men in all their glory, pictured in May 1994
before the last game with the Kop as a standing terrace.

On the left hand side of the board you had the panels for the score, above which the home panel was headed with 'LEEDS' or sometimes 'LEEDS U' or 'LEEDS UTD'. The other panel was sometimes headed with the opposition's actual name, but mostly with 'VISITORS' or more accurately for much of its existence, 'VISITORS'. The main section of the board in the middle most memorably displayed the flashing 'GOAL' and dancing men symbols when someone scored, but for 99.95% of its life this section showed rolling adverts, compromised by a dozen or more missing bulbs that nobody could be bothered to replace. Pre-match saw the team line-ups flash up as everyone craned 180 degrees around, owl-like, to see if Davison was finally being preferred to Pearson. This main section also made futile attempts to restore order on occasions with police messages to "Please Keep Off The Pitch" or just the hopelessly vague "Please Behave", which flashed up in 1982 as Newcastle's Kevin Keegan nursed a head wound having been struck by a ball bearing and rival fans threw seats at each other from adjacent stands. On the right hand side of the board were singular sections showing the shirt number of the last goal scorer and the shirt number of the last substitute, and finally a bigger square with no header to display the minutes on the clock from one to ninety.

There is no doubt that the electronic scoreboard was a welcome fixture at Elland Road and provided an iconic background to many images of the time. What many people who never stood to the rear of the Kop might not be aware of is that at the back of the scoreboard were two much smaller versions attached at right angle facing inwards with a display on either side, so that fans stood behind the main scoreboard could see the score and the minutes. After just ten years' sterling service, the scoreboard malfunctioned during the 1988/89 season and was left unused for a number of games. But after a "major overhaul" during the summer, the dancing men were back and ready to celebrate with additional frequency during the 1989/90 promotion campaign.

A combination of the seating of the Kop prior to the 1994/95 season and the installation of a bigger, square scoreboard in the south west corner led to the electronic scoreboard's sad and lamentable demise.

For one season there was a scoreboard at either end of the ground, but the superior location of the south west corner in terms of the eventual progression to a bigger screen and the technology that comes with it, meant the Kop scoreboard's days were numbered by the end of the 1994/95 season. Although similar scoreboards still exist across the country today it was with a reluctant sigh that you had to acknowledge the electronic scoreboard was by then somewhat outdated. Simply being 'electronic' was no longer an exceptional virtue by 1994.

It is with both shame and guilt that I didn't mourn the passing of the electronic scoreboard more at the time, as with the Kop already seated the fun element of supporting from there had largely passed already. With another scoreboard having been in place for 27 years now at a polar opposite position, I no longer find myself turning backwards to check out the minutes played automatically like I used to. And also gone is the homely feeling in winter exuded by the glow of the bulbs on the scoreboard amid the darkness of the Kop roof structure.

Before Leeds United embraced the technological age in 1979, communication methods adopted were somewhat more basic. A source of fascination to Gary Edwards was the crude method employed to communicate the half-time scores to fans: "At half-time in the early 1970s two people, usually nice looking ladies in hot pants and boots, would walk around the pitch holding aloft a white board with the 'golden goal' or 'lucky number' on it which was in your match programme. There were no electronic all-singing-and-dancing scoreboards in those days of course; instead results from all over the country would be displayed on the wall in front of the Kop and the Scratching Shed. Using large white squares with numbers on, the scores were then displayed thus: A – 0-1 B – 2-1 C – 1-1 D - 1-1 and so on. The identities of each letter and the respective teams would be printed in the match programme under the ingenious headline – 'Half-Time Scores'."

John Cave, a Leeds fan since the 1950s, doesn't remember the purveyors of such information being quite so glamorous. He recalls: "One character was a quite sinister figure – the half-time score man. This flat capped hobbit-like figure would trudge around the ground at half-time, piece of paper in hand, to the two half-time scoreboards behind the goals where he would post the interval scores from our league. He was a real miserable sod; if at a reserve team game we wanted to know how United's first team were doing, he refused to say a word, keeping an inane grin on his face until he had posted the score on the board against the pre-set letters where the fixtures were listed in the match day programme – just a one page effort for reserve games. No amount of cajoling from us kids would keep him from his moment of glory of announcing how our first team were getting on. At least he had the grace to put up our score first with us desperately looking to see which numbers he was pulling out of his box! The other feature of reserve games was waiting for the tannoy announcement in the West Stand Paddock at the end of the reserve match giving the final result of the first team's away game. No details or scorers, just something along the lines of 'The result for the game at Derby is (pause) Derby County 2, Leeds United 3'. And that was it!"

Progress has undoubtedly been made and the modern fan now wants for nothing in terms of scores, line-ups and pre-match and half-time entertainment. Perhaps I should be more grateful that my early Elland Road years in the late 1970s and early 1980s were enriched by the discovery of electricity, and amid high definition action replays and giant-sized close-ups of Lucas the Kop Cat, I can pretend that somewhere and somehow the dancing men haven't quite danced their last dance.

SCRATCHING SHED

The 'old lady' of Elland Road, the one physical structure that almost links the modern stadium with the Leeds City era, is the Scratching Shed. Much-missed by some, but in reality born from a more unsophisticated time and reflective of when Leeds United were a struggling local club with limited ambition.

There is some conjecture over the date of the Scratching Shed's original construction, but the critical factor is that it was originally an uncovered terrace that was roofed in the early 1920s. A stand was running along the length of Elland Road in the days of Leeds City and even prior to that when Holbeck Rugby Club were resident. Holbeck built a stand on Elland Road in 1897 as soon as they took residence of the 'Old Peacock Ground' and it is likely that it was just a terraced stand. However, this is not the stand that later became the Scratching Shed.

During the 1904/05 season Leeds City employed the services of a consultant to give them advice on how to develop their new ground. This was Archibald Leitch, already a well-known Scottish architect who would become famous for designing 'classic' stands in a distinctive style at Highbury, White Hart Lane, Bramall Lane, Villa Park, Goodison Park and Ibrox Stadium, amongst many others. If he influenced the construction of Elland Road at all, however, his designs were more modest, and certainly short-lived.

By July 1905, the *Yorkshire Post* had reported some ground improvements after the first full season of Leeds City's existence and prior to their bow in the Football League: "The ground at Elland Road is now undergoing great improvement all round. To commence with, arrangements are going forward with a view to improving the condition of the surface. When the Holbeck Northern Union club used to play on the enclosure there was rarely much grass on the ground. In this direction it is expected there will be a decided improvement.

"During the present week some important alterations have been decided upon to afford increased accommodation to spectators. It has been decided to erect a new covered stand which will be 75 yards in length and 35 feet in breadth. On it 4,000 or 5,000 persons will be, if necessary, accommodated. In the centre a commodious Press box will be constructed. The tender for this work has been given to Messrs H Barrett and Sons of Bradford, and the price to be paid for it will, it is stated, reach four figures. The stand has to be completed within a couple of months.

"In addition, the old stand at the north side of the ground has been pulled down, and it is proposed to erect a wind shelter right along the west end. The present stand is in a dilapidated condition, and its demolition is already in progress. On the terraces new 'treads' will be constructed, and each terrace will be faced with creosoted battens. There will, when the work is finished, be about 30 terraces extending right round the ground, and accommodation for spectators will be largely increased. It is also proposed to place posts inside the railings for a short length down each side, but the rails at each end will be brought back a few feet, and this will lengthen the playing area to 115 yards and its width will also be increased to 72 yards, with a clear space of 10 to 11 feet between the touchlines and the rails. The ground will then be quite large enough for the playing of any matches governed by the rules of the Football Association."

Whilst the wording of the newspaper report is quite confusing, the new stand being built in 1905 replaced

The only known photo in existence of the short-lived stand built on the south side of the ground in 1905. This photo is believed to be from a game against Stockport County in April 1924. It must have been shortly after this that the pitch orientation was switched one last time and the north, east and south sides further developed, including the construction of the terrace that became the Scratching Shed.

A good photo showing the distinctive barrel-shaped roof of the Scratching Shed in 1957 during construction of the West Stand, which included joining the two stands together via terracing in the south west corner.

have been replaced due to the settling of the pitch orientation. This was dictated by the construction of Lowfields Road in 1923, and therefore going forward didn't require as big a stand on the south end. Leeds took this opportunity to also build up the embankment on the east side (the 'Popular' side and what would become the Lowfields Road Stand) to accommodate 20,000 fans alone, and the total stadium capacity would be around 40,000.

What we also know is that the Scratching Shed was a much-loved stand; a cosy terrace that housed the more staunch and dyed-in-the-wool supporters in the days when Leeds United were yet to establish themselves as a significant football club of any stature. As time went on and visiting fans became more prominent at Elland Road in the 1960s, accordingly, the Scratching Shed became the home for those Leeds fans seeking to retain, in their eyes at least, the club's honour off the field.

Due to its small capacity the stand was nearly always full, but aesthetically, whilst it gave the ground an authentic and traditional warmth, it was tiny compared to the other stands that later developed. It gave a lop-sided appearance to the ground that by the onset of the 1970s the club were keen to upgrade, as if embarrassed by their past as the provincial non-achievers they had almost always been.

the small stand built by Holbeck Rugby Club on Elland Road, which may well have been demolished some time before. The 1905 stand also, therefore, preceded the Scratching Shed. The report states that the stand – which cost £1,050 to build – was at least intended to be covered, therefore we must assume that it was. The 1905 stand described above also had a press box and was a much grander construction than the primitive, uncovered terrace that followed it, and this original 'South' Stand ran along the side of the pitch for the season 1905/06. The 'wind shelter' referenced above was presumably just a temporary measure during demolition and re-construction. The stand on the north side being pulled down was the very rudimentary wooden structure also built by Holbeck Rugby Club, and terracing on mounds of earth was also beginning to be constructed on the north and east sides of the ground at this time.

In the early 1920s it is known that a 'barrel-shaped roof' of 'Belfast' design was added to a terrace on the south side of the ground, to match the roof of the 1906-constructed West Stand. This means that the stand built in 1905, as reported by the Yorkshire Post, remained until the early 1920s when it was demolished and replaced by a smaller terrace to accommodate 5,000 fans, which was later roofed to complete the 'South Stand' as it was officially known, but the 'Scratching Shed' as it became more popularly known. The 1905 'South' Stand, of which very few photographs exist and the Yorkshire Post passage above is one of very few pieces of written evidence, is most likely to

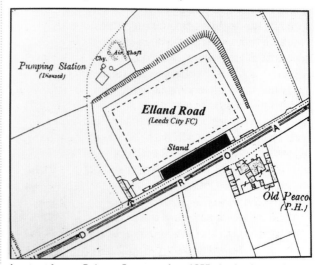

An extract from an Ordnance Survey map from 1905, showing the east/west orientation of the pitch and the stand built on the south side of the ground in the same year. This would later be replaced by the terrace that became the Scratching Shed. The 1906-built West Stand is yet to appear.

Leeds fan Reg French spent only a small part of his several decades supporting Leeds United in the Scratching Shed. He remembers it as the original home of the more vocal supporters. "That's where they used to chant 'Leeds, Leeds, Leeds', 'Bread of Heaven' and 'Come All Ye Faithful'," Reg recalls. "They were the first songs I can ever remember the crowd actually singing in unison." Ray Fell also remembers the Scratching Shed, but less warmly. He only ever went in once in the early 1960s and "didn't like it at all" due to the cramped conditions and the more vociferous and partisan nature of the fans that had already started to accumulate there.

Dougie Wales also recalls the Scratching Shed as housing the more passionate fans: "All the vocal support used to come out of there in the early days, there was no Kop as it is now, and all the singing came out of that Scratching Shed. They were a loyal lot in there. There were no airs and graces. It was just a basic stand, very basic, but all the atmosphere used to come out of there."

The move of the more vocal and hardcore fans from the Shed to the new Kop was already being mooted in May 1968 when concrete plans for the impending development were first announced. A loyal Shedender spoke to the *Yorkshire Evening Post* about the momentous moving of camps: "We think we will be able to make more din and get more people to join the clan under the bigger stand." Sure enough it slowly happened.

Popular opinion is that the Scratching Shed earned its name purely through informal use of the phrase that described the stand's resemblance to a barn. The barrel-shaped roof and rudimentary brick rear wall always reminded fans of a farmyard building housing livestock scratching around for food, rather than a football terrace, and the suitably agricultural name was adopted. The stand's design, such that it was, with the barrel roof was almost identical to a stand at Huddersfield Town's Leeds Road End, which their fans sentimentally dubbed the 'Cowshed' in a similarly earthy put-down that appears perhaps meaner than it was intended.

It is true that there was little glamour to the Scratching Shed with its low roof creating a dark void beneath it, and the shallow terrace never afforded a great view of the action, particularly from 1970 until its demise when the pitch was moved northwards away from the Scratching Shed towards the Kop.

Adding to the crude characteristics was the fact that the turnstiles opened directly onto the terraced steps of the stand, so you walked literally off the street into the back of the stand in one movement; there was nothing in the way of facilities or a tiered introduction to the basic realities of life in the Scratching Shed. Whilst this was typical of many football grounds of the day, it adds logic to the fact that, in 1974, Leeds United were very keen to progress away from this rather over-simplified existence with the more gentrified construction of the new South Stand.

The low wall to the right of the back of the Scratching Shed, where the shallow terracing curved round towards the Lowfields Road terrace before sweeping upwards, was a haven for those who wanted to risk shinning over to gain an unlawful entrance, and certainly until the authorities became a little more professional in managing such things, this easily identifiable weak spot was easy prey for the opportunists.

Ray Fell also remembers the western corner next to the Scratching Shed stand hosting the first of a very modern football stadium phenomenon: "The first eating place ever at Elland Road was in the south west corner next to the Scratching Shed. I know that because the Supporters' Club put it there, it was a little shed that sold coffees, biscuits and sandwiches. It will have been there pre-war but I remember it after the war."

Doubtless much to the relief of the Leeds United board the last rites were served on the Scratching Shed when it was finally demolished on 29th April 1974, more than a week after the final home game of the title-winning season. With the league title won and Don Revie leaving for the England job it seemed an appropriate time to be waving goodbye to the past, but little did Leeds fans know what stability and fruitfulness they were also confining to history.

SEASON TICKET HOLDERS

The bedrock of many a football club is the loyal supporters that turn up week-in week-out and provide one constant amongst the ever-changing landscape of the football industry. This is particularly true at Leeds United where, in recurring times of trouble, the club can rely on a solid supporter base paying money up front while other loyal fans attend match-by-match when they can.

Given the known income from the season ticket holders the club can budget accordingly for the season ahead and hence the season ticket revenue becomes central to forward planning. Accordingly, often the season ticket holders' status affords them certain privileges. For one magical season at Elland Road in 1995/96 this involved vouchers for free pies (OK, they were food and non-alcoholic drink vouchers, but for most fans that simply meant 'free pies'). Other privileges have stretched to free entry to reserves games, discounted

A much sought-after season ticket for the 1989/90 season.

offers in the megastore and for a short period, an exclusive 'season ticket holders only' bar in the Kop.

On 15th July 1905 Leeds City were preparing Elland Road for the start of its very first season of professional football in the Football League Second Division, and as the *Yorkshire Post* reported on that day, season ticket income was vital for the fledgling club: "The prices of the season tickets have been fixed at 10s and a guinea, and shareholders will be entitled to the higher priced tickets for the sum of 15s. The lesser priced tickets will admit holders to the ground only, while the others will pass to the ground and stand. In all 36 league matches will be played within the enclosure, 19 being Second League games and the remainder Midland League games played by the Reserve team. The season tickets, however, will not admit to any English Cup engagement that may be played at Elland Road. Applications for season tickets, which will be ready in the course of a week or so, should be made to the club secretary, Mr G Gillies, of 28, Cross Flatts Place, Beeston, Leeds, up to August 10. After that date they should be made at the offices on the ground." Incidentally, the club secretary Mr Gilbert Gillies, referred to in this extract, was also generally known as the first team manager; the mind boggles at the thought of someone being asked to juggle these two tasks in the modern game.

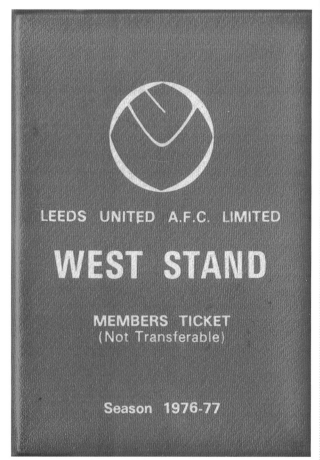

A season ticket book from the 1976/77 season, and no, you are not colour blind.

Even as recently as 1991/92, ie. prior to the introduction of the Premier League, the relative cost of a season ticket at Elland Road was dramatically less than it is now, and it is no surprise to learn that the loyal supporter has funded much of the odorous wealth that surrounds the game today via inflated ticket prices. On the flip side, it could be argued that those season ticket holders that have stuck behind Leeds United from their pursuit of the Champions League 'dream' right down to League One and back again, have kept the club afloat during very uncertain times.

For a long time though, season tickets were really only something associated with the more affluent supporters, and season ticket holders held a status almost akin to a shareholder. In fact, at Leeds United's outset, that was literally the case. In the summer of 1920 a *Leeds Mercury* report explains how season tickets would only be made available to shareholders for Leeds United's inaugural season in the Football League. 'Pavilion season tickets' at £3 3s were only available to '£19 shareholders'. 'Ground season tickets' at £1 1s were made available to '£5 shareholders'. Naturally, there was some opposition to this from rank and file supporters, and hence such exclusivity was short-lived.

At this time, season tickets were only designated to the seats and terracing sections of the original West Stand from Leeds City's days, until the turn of the 1960s when Don Revie's management changed the whole club. In the lean and barren pre- and post-war years the vast majority of fans would not entertain such a long term investment, even in the team they loved, and for many years match-by-match attendance was a strictly cash-on-the-day affair; even match tickets were not common and season tickets were purely a commitment for the elite.

This is confirmed by Reg French, who first attended with his dad, aged seven, in the mid-1930s. "In those days," he recalls, "not many people had season tickets. My Dad certainly couldn't afford one, and we went together for many years."

Such was the general scarcity of season ticket holders among the overall support in the 1930s that the club would personally write to each season ticket holder during the summer to establish whether they intended to renew their ticket. Gary Edwards picked up a letter at an obscure flea market one day which is dated 24th July 1939, and is written from Leeds United's club secretary C. A. Crowther to a Mr. S. Webster. In the letter the ticket holder is asked whether he wishes to renew his ticket in the West Stand for the forthcoming season for £3 19s 10d, which at a decimalised cost of just under £4 was becoming a more serious consideration, and at the time was definitely an investment only contemplated by a select portion of Leeds society. The holder was also offered a car park season ticket for 10/6.

In later, more successful years, Leeds fan Kevin

Mulligan recalls the southern section of the West Stand Paddock that extended from the tunnel to the Scratching Shed as being a designated season ticket holders' section for many years in the 1960s and 1970s. He adds that season tickets were "budgeted for and never an essential household purchase", and the paddock was therefore always an elite part of the ground, with the rest of the standing crowd paying their money and taking their choice wherever and whenever they could. As an aside Kevin adds that "this was an area instrumental in creating the repetitive and simplistic chant of 'Leeds....Leeds....Leeds' which was sung gruffly and deeply voiced, interspersed between each 'Leeds' with a breath pause".

Still, regardless of the status of the team or the volume of crowds they are attracting the club has always had season ticket holders. It became more regular and accepted for 'normal' supporters as time went on. Season ticket holders still represented a smaller percentage of the crowd though, and even in the 1973/74 season Leeds proudly boasted an "all-time record" of 10,727 season ticket holders from an average crowd approaching 40,000.

Seated season tickets to watch the league champions in the following season, 1974/75, cost only £25.50 in the West Stand and just £19.40 in the Lowfields Road Stand. In the 1978/79 season, by which time Kop and Lowfields standing season tickets had become available after much Supporters' Club lobbying, a Kop season ticket was £19 for 21 league matches. With match day admission only £1 anyway, a season ticket was only saving the investor £2 per season, but relatively speaking that was still an acceptable justification for the investment.

As the prices of season tickets gradually increased, of course the club broke records for season ticket income. This was a fact regularly announced with some pride despite it being somewhat predestined. In the opening weeks of the 1988/89 season, which was not a happy period given manager Billy Bremner was about to be sacked, managing director Bill Fotherby, never shy of overstating a fact, described the season ticket sales as "staggering". Income had risen to over £500,000 from the previous season's record of £450,000. Fotherby was the master of putting a positive spin on things and fostering the belief that the club was on an upwards curve, and he commented at the time: "Until last season we were never a club that generated too much in season ticket sales. This season however we have over 6,000 season ticket holders."

Season ticket holders have never had their own stand at Elland Road, though when the terracing capacities were reduced following the Hillsborough Disaster in 1989 the Kop and Lowfields terracing became almost 100% season ticket holders. Sales went through the roof after an extensive summer outlay on players, which was just as well given that the reduced capacity impacted on the money the club could recoup for that outlay. Indeed it was fortunate that these areas were not over-subscribed, as season tickets had been sold before the Taylor Report restrictions were announced and hence a major issue could have ensued had the club sold more season tickets for a stand than could then be accommodated. As it was, the restrictions caused severe headaches in accommodating the more casual fans.

Leeds United's popularity in the Howard Wilkinson period saw season tickets become more valuable than ever before, in monetary and loyalty terms. During the 1989/90 season Leeds ended the campaign with 16,000 season ticket holders in a capacity just over 32,000, and doubled the season ticket income to over £1 million for the first time. Two years later when Leeds won the First Division title they had 20,000 season ticket holders, and by the height of the Peter Ridsdale era this had crept up to 22,000. In 2020/21 the club had around 23,000 season ticket holders, the maximum they could have, and a waiting list of about 20,000-more hopeful and patient applicants.

Still, whether you renew out of blind faith, genuine optimism or just to escape once a fortnight for a few beers with your mates, season ticket holders have their loyalty frequently tested and as such, have a right to feel a central part of their club. Nevertheless, feeling undervalued and taken for granted is something of a character trait for any football fan and certainly for the typical season ticket holder. While recent years have shown that their unquestioning dedication does sometimes get rewarded at Leeds United, the club should need no reminding that it would be struggling without them.

SOUTH EAST CORNER STAND

Another Wilkinson legacy or Revie's bold plan finally kick-started after laying idle for 13 years? Given the club's rising fortunes in finally escaping the clutches of the old Second Division in 1990 and then completing a very successful first season back in the top flight, the time at last seemed right, in the summer of 1991, to build on the exposed foundations in the south east corner that

A pre-season photo from 1994 showing yellow seats in the South East Corner Stand and the South Stand.

An aerial photo from 1980 which clearly shows the foundations left exposed in the south east corner between 1978 and 1991. This photo also shows quite well how the white wall built all along the east side in 1971 to create the shelf, was intended as the first stage of developing the Lowfields upper section, ie. the shelf was only meant to be temporary.

had been left in place since 1978. At last, two years after his death and 17 years after he had left the club, the final components of Revie's vision for a modern, alluring and well-appointed Elland Road began to take shape.

With a third of the Lowfields Road Stand roof and upper tier cut away at the southern end in the summer of 1978, everything appeared to be in place to complete the re-development of the Elland Road 'styled in success', by extending the south east corner around to meet the Lowfields Road Stand. The club eventually intended to replace the Lowfields Road upper tier completely, to build something similar to what exists now, although not on such a grand scale as the current East Stand, hence they left a gap between the North East Corner Stand and the Lowfields and didn't build flush up to the side of the existing stand.

Sobering news came in May 1978 though, when Leeds United's secretary, Keith Archer, announced that the building of the South East Corner Stand was approved, but that the club "didn't know how soon the scheme could go ahead". This depended on "commercial and playing success". Regardless, 1,600 seats were lost when part of the Lowfields Road upper stand was demolished and 25,000 tonnes of earth was removed from the area in order to flatten it and build the foundations for the new stand.

If the plans had gone ahead in 1978 the South East Corner Stand would have been built exactly how it

eventually was in 1991, and for a short time would have left the two grass banks, before a re-developed 'Lowfields/ East Stand' was built snugly between the two corners. It appeared that Leeds United were proceeding with their plan with gusto in 1978 when they demolished part of the upper section of the Lowfields Road Stand, and finally gone was the banking sweeping around the south east corner, which had housed many a fan peering through the glass panels towards the Kop when the crowds were huge.

Not so. As it was, despite the significant cost of preparation work and the installation of foundations, said to be approximately £1 million, the plan was shelved and the south east corner, and indeed the Lowfields Road Stand, was left as an incomplete relic and a lasting testament to the sharp decline in Leeds United's fortunes. As a further indication of this, the fourth diamond floodlight (which had not been erected in 1973 with the other three because it was waiting for the building work on the east side to take place) was finally erected as the building work was evidently not going to happen.

Dave Cocker recalls the era very well: "What happened was they got thrown out of Europe in 1975 (after the crowd trouble following the European Cup Final defeat in Paris) and suddenly there's no money. It was the European games that would generate it, because in Europe you kept all your gate money. In the league, what happened then was you split the money 40/40/20 between the two clubs and the Football League, so you made your money in Europe. Although they weren't taking a fortune because it was five shillings into the Scratching Shed in 1966, 25 pence; it wasn't a fortune, but Europe really paid for everything that was done to the ground."

Irrespective of the ban, Leeds wouldn't have qualified for Europe until 1979 anyway, by which time the expulsion had been overturned. Nevertheless, with ten consecutive seasons of European football coming to an abrupt and controversial halt after that crazy night in Paris, it is not surprising that the board's plans became less ambitious. This is particularly so with Revie, his focused and stabilising zeal and many of his players long gone, and with the smell of 'transition' hanging dull and heavy in the air. It is certainly telling that even in the mid-1970s, ten years of domestic and European success were not sufficient to offer a club as big as Leeds United the stability to carry forward their long term plans to fruition. From the building of the West Stand in 1956 to that point in 1978 when the grand plan was swiftly halted, Leeds United had spent nearly £2.5 million developing Elland Road. With the escalating cost of building work far outstripping inflation, it would have possibly cost at least all that total again to continue with and complete the ambitious Elland Road scheme. Having come so far, finally and exasperatingly it had become the quixotic and fanciful dream that many sceptics had derided it as in the excitable mid-1960s, when Revie's team were mere unproven fledglings champing at the bit.

Amid the uncertainty of 1978, nerve was lost and the collective thinking was to leave a lopsided and unfinished carbuncle, a visual and conspicuous depiction of how everything had very clearly not gone to plan. This fenced-in faux pas of unsheltered bare concrete would create its own mystique for its austere and uncompromising hostility, as it perfectly exemplified the changing image of the club: from a glorious and thriving past to a wounded animal struggling for breath, surrounded by half-arsed ideas and a following hell bent on destruction. The view then of the shallow and uncovered Lowfields corner terrace with the overshadowing melancholy of the hills and houses in the background, will forever capture that debilitating period of a good thing gone very quickly amiss.

The fourth diamond floodlight that had been missing from the south east corner was hastily erected in the summer of 1978, at the same time as the top section of the Lowfields Stand was demolished. The explanation was that the building work not going ahead could allow the floodlight to complete the ground's wanting symmetry.

Those of a suspicious nature may question why the club would go to the trouble and expense of demolishing the Lowfields upper section and putting in the foundations, and yet at the same time, finally install the fourth floodlight and admit defeat on their development plans. Dave Cocker, who still had an ear on the ground at Elland Road even in 1978, has an explanation: "I know the reason for that. I remember talking about it at the time. If you've got the footings in already then there was a tax exemption on the building. So if they had some cash to get rid of they could start the footings and make a down-payment. So they might have spent however much on the footings but given the builder the rest of the money, which would have been Bob Roberts. I'll never forget it, because they knocked the wall down and you could see it round the corner there, they just put up a steel-posted fence, and you could look in and see this building site with concrete and strengthening bars sticking out. It was like that for years. It was a tax situation. They got the money for McQueen and Jordan (both sold to Manchester United during the 1977/78 season for a total of just under £1 million) and they've got to spend it otherwise it just gets taken in tax. So the builder gets his money and the club will avoid paying tax on the players they have sold. I know for a fact that's what happened because I was talking to Don and my Dad about it. There was a guy that Don wanted to get onto the board called Gabby Harris. He died suddenly and his wife Sheila later married Leslie Silver. Gabby came out to Dubai when I was out there with Don and my Dad, he was Leeds United mad and a multi-millionaire but they wouldn't have him on the board. At that time Bob Roberts was controlling that club. So that's what happened, they had to get rid of some money or it will have all gone in tax."

A tall steel fence at the back of the often empty terrace hid the foundations from view as if concealing a tawdry secret. The club was aware, it should be said, that the foundations would never suffer from exposure and could be built on at any time, and in the summer of 1991, like an unstoppable force, that time finally came.

Howard Wilkinson had arrived and with Leslie Silver and Bill Fotherby had instilled not only some guts and ambition to the club, but also a semblance of thinking beyond the meddling constraints of the short term. It was a far more positive time and finally the 1,395 capacity South East Corner Stand was built with additional terracing capacity below it. Work was taking place during the infamous Happy Mondays gig at Elland Road in June 1991 and took just 12 weeks to complete at a cost of £1 million, partly self-funded by the council's rent profits from Leeds United and partly with money from the Football Trust. The stand was complete by the start of the title-winning 1991/92 season.

For the first two seasons following the completion of the building work, the lower section of the south east corner remained as the terracing from the old Lowfields, and this was finally seated when the rest of the Lowfields terrace bit the dust in the summer of 1993. Indeed the only original construction was the addition of the upper yellow-seated section to the existing Lowfields terrace. However, the seats in the South East Corner lower tier were initially blue. This was to correspond with the South Stand, which at the time also had yellow seats in the upper tier and blue seats in the lower. Later in the mid-1990s the seats were swapped round, and the South Stand became all blue, and the South East Corner Stand became all yellow. The 'Cheese Wedge' was born.

In the area behind the stand the Leeds United Crèche was built in 1994 but currently, with it not being run by the club, it is possibly one facility on the Elland Road site that many fans don't even know exists. The crèche, now known officially as the ABC Nursery, has been privately owned since September 2004.

Until 2011 the South East Corner Stand had predominantly housed away fans but since then has combined itself with the adaptable South Stand in accommodating home fans as and when required, a sort of buffer zone with little identity. When away fans were moved permanently into the West Stand in 2011, for the first season the South East Corner Stand remained closed virtually all season, as ticket demand failed to raise sufficient justification for opening it; a somewhat ironic comparison with the very lean years which caused the delay in the stand being built in the first place.

SOUTH STAND

added a character to the ground that nobody would want to forget, you do feel that there must have been a sense of irritation that the South Stand could not have been built earlier.

The Scratching Shed's position on the very edge of the pavement on Elland Road meant there was no scope for a bigger stand to be built, even if there was a prior ambition to do so, until the pitch and North Stand were moved northwards to accommodate it. There was land behind the Gelderd End of course, plenty of it, but the construction of the new Kop in 1968, with a smaller footprint, enabled the template for a bigger stand at the south end to be formed without extending the boundaries of the club's property. But frustratingly, it was not until the coupling of the Kop with the two corner stands was completed that the South Stand could finally be built and Elland Road be granted the balanced sheen of a fully re-developed stadium.

Perhaps explaining the rather grand inclusion of a line of flagpoles along the back of it, Leeds United had

The original South Stand exterior before it was cladded in 2006. Visible here are the 'windows' of the Goal Line Restaurant and the slightly grandiose procession of flagpoles.

To those too young to have witnessed the Revie years at Elland Road it is perhaps a sobering revelation to learn that the entire era of dominance was played out before the Lilliputian, austere and uninspiring Scratching Shed at the south end of the ground. While the other three sides of the stadium had created a formidable arena, having been re-developed in line with the club's progression and stature, the southern end was left untouched until 1974, indeed, just weeks after Revie had departed for the England job. Leeds had forged an intimidating aura at Elland Road during the late 1960s and whilst the Scratching Shed was loved by many and

just been crowned league champions for a second time when the construction of the South Stand commenced in May 1974, although preliminary work for the demolition of the Scratching Shed began two months earlier in March. Architects for the development were Braithwaite and Jackman of Leeds and the building work was undertaken by Robert R. Roberts, also of Leeds, and a family business synonymous with Leeds United.

Bob Roberts was, of course, also a director of Leeds United with the somewhat superfluous title of 'ground development director', awarded presumably on the basis that he built most of it. Bob Roberts was a local

The South Stand in all its glory pictured in 1979, before the installation of executive boxes impacted upon what was a decent-sized upper tier.

man who was born and lived in Wortley just a mile or so from Elland Road, and he was integral to much of what we look at and sit in whilst watching Leeds United today. He had been on the board of directors since 1958 and served the club right up until 1975, when his son Brian joined the board and took on the role of ground director from him.

The building company Robert R. Roberts started off in a joiners shop on Lower Wortley Road where Bob Roberts was an apprentice. He arrived at work one day to find his boss had hung himself and he slowly took hold of the business himself, finally taking a loan out to buy the business from his old boss's widow. From there the business flourished, building hundreds of houses in the Wortley area and later developing to building the West Stand, Kop, corner stands and finally the South Stand at Elland Road, by which point Bob Roberts was firmly ensconced as a Leeds United board member. Bob Roberts died in 1980, though the building business remained in the family until they were bought out in 1996. By this time the family had also established a successful Ford car dealership in Leeds and Doncaster called 'Ringways', which to this day has close links to the club in terms of sponsorship. However, as soon as Brian Roberts left the board in 1980 when his father died, any building work undertaken by the club was awarded to GMI, the company owned by Peter Gilman, an associate of new board member Bill Fotherby, and a future board member himself.

Robert R. Roberts were omnipresent around the Elland Road ground from the late-1950s and for the ensuing two decades, and undertook all the significant building work of the golden period under Don Revie's leadership. This even extended to carrying out the annual safety load testing on the terracing crash barriers and erecting the fences on all four sides of the ground in the late 1970s. Guy Roberts, the son of Brian and grandson of Bob Roberts, was working for Ringways in 2015 and told me how well thought of Bob Roberts was at Elland Road: "When my grandfather died, and I think this was one of the tipping points for my father resigning, he had done so much for the club over the years in terms of development, I remember I was in the car park with my father and Manny Cussins came out and said, 'We're going to do something to recognise your father [Bob Roberts] because he's done so much, we're going to name one of the stands after him.' It never happened, we got a silver salver."

In the Burnley match day programme from 23rd March 1974, in which plans for the South Stand were first revealed, Bob Roberts was quoted as saying: "It has always been our intention to bring Elland Road up to international standards, and this latest development will again enhance what we already consider to be some of the finest football facilities in the country."

The plans for the South Stand were indeed impressive for the time and Roberts' comments suggested a Nostradamus-like foresight in terms of how the South

Stand would be developed for corporate fans in the 1980s. He continued: "The football fan of the future is likely to be more demanding in his requirements, and the stand has been built with this in mind. Our ultimate aim is to make the stadium a complete bowl with each stand inter-linked. To that end, the Lowfields Road stand has been earmarked for the next phase of development as soon as finance is available." Ah yes, finance.

It took a number of months to complete the South Stand and several games of the 1974/75 season were played with the stand incomplete, although the terracing was practically ready for the start of Leeds' ill-fated title defence under manager Brian Clough in August 1974. Bob Roberts had been fundamental in bringing Clough to Elland Road and Guy Roberts also tells me how his grandfather was on holiday when Clough was sacked in October 1974; maybe history would have been very different had that not been the case?

The first game where both tiers of the stand were operational was against Manchester City on 1st March 1975, a 2-2 draw where the 47,489 crowd was significantly up on the 32,346 that had watched the stuttering league champions in the previous home game. The first game to host a fully complete South Stand was the FA Cup Sixth Round Replay against Ipswich on 11th March 1975, when, during a season of generally disappointing attendances, 50,074 crammed into Elland Road, 7,500 of which were in the brand new stand.

Originally the stand had a 4,500 capacity standing paddock in the lower section and a 3,000 capacity seated section above. At the same time as the South Stand construction, seating was also provided to link the South Stand lower tier to the West Stand. While this is technically the 'South West Corner', the area has never been known as that in terms of it being an actual stand. It is really just an extension to the South Stand, and in most recent years has been left unused as segregation. It has also housed disabled fans at various times.

For the first couple of years the standing section of the South Stand was segregated and partially or completely used for away supporters when demand required it. However, in the summer of 1977 seats were installed in the lower section for the first time and it became an all-seater stand. In 1987 it was decided to take the seats out and for three seasons the South Stand lower section became terracing again. This predominantly housed away fans for the 1987/88 and 1988/89 seasons, but became particularly significant during the promotion campaign of 1989/90 in creating what Elland Road became famous for in that season. Home fans were re-admitted to the South Stand via the section being reserved for Supporters' Club members only. It was a venture that took a few games to take off and due to a lack of publicity 3,000 fans were locked out of the first game versus Middlesbrough even though capacity was far from being reached. Violent clashes ensued outside Elland Road because none of the 3,000

fans were Supporters' Club members. But organisation was restored and the South Stand slowly evolved to become one of the 'three Kops' that contributed to the inspiring and highly-charged atmosphere that intimidated visiting teams, and swept Leeds to a long-overdue promotion.

Attending Elland Road in 1989/90 was like following THE band of your teenage years on every date of a sell-out tour: euphoria was guaranteed. It was the season that perhaps saw the South Stand makes its most direct and noteworthy contribution to the fortunes of the team, and the 'three Kops' idea (ie. the Kop itself, the Lowfields and the South Stand) was all by design, as Howard Wilkinson explains: "That was the idea. The things we looked at during the first half a season I was at the club (1988/89) were 'in how many places next season can we claim an advantage?' and one of them was that (moving away fans from behind the South Stand goal). 'Why?', 'well it's tradition', 'well let's have home fans behind both goals'. I enquired about, and we did it to a degree, amplifying the sound in the ground by getting microphones in the stands, in the roof, to give this greater impression of intimidation. So it was all part of trying to make sure our own patch had a lot of things going for it. Everyone prefers to play at home, so make home as nice as possible.

"Basically," continues Howard, "in the middle of it all is winning football matches, so that's the reality, what's going on on the pitch. In this country at that time, and less so increasingly now, the manager was able to influence all sorts of other things as well. But the actual bread and butter is there on the pitch. But you look to maximise your advantage, you look at everything you can try and improve. So we had a discussion about the away team bus coming in the car park (amongst the crowds) before the game; there was the danger factor with health and safety and all this, and I was saying 'no, no, we want the bus having to crawl through crowds", and having the police there, as long as the fans aren't misbehaving we want the sense of intimidation and 'Christ, it's only half past one'."

Having exerted its sizeable influence, somewhat strangely seats were re-installed for the following 1990/91 season and the South Stand was re-branded the 'Family Stand'. The supercharged aura of menace was gone. Many thought this was influenced by the trouble at Bournemouth that marred the promotion celebration and the ongoing battle with the club's public image. In reality the Taylor Report dictated that standing capacity was reduced by 20% each season until a ground was all-seater. This meant that either the Kop was seated in 1990 or the South Stand was.

Back in 1974 when the £500,000 construction was complete, the South Stand, as another propped cantilever construction with a deep over-hanging roof, gave Elland Road a more polished and complete appearance, albeit the final piece of the jigsaw adjacent to it had to be put on hold. Still the South Stand was viewed as a state-of-the-art construction and the club boasted of its facilities underneath the stand which included a restaurant and office space. Certainly it changed the landscape quite significantly, and while allowing the club to finally move the pitch right up to the front of the Kop at the north end, that move did create some restricted views in other areas. Those fans sat in the very southern end of the West Stand upper section (known then as 'Wing Stand B') now had a better view of the traffic on Elland Road than of the game itself, directly facing, as they were, the side of the South Stand, where previously they had at least faced the side of the goal.

Another issue that the new stand created was that of its shadow on the pitch. The more domineering profile of the stand compared to the unassuming Scratching Shed meant that less sunlight was getting on the pitch, a problem also attributed, to be fair, to the shadow from the West Stand. Different groundsmen across the years will attest to the fact that the grass on the West Stand side of the ground is far less healthy than on the east side, and the building of the South Stand was no doubt greeted with a bulk order of grass seed in this respect. Translucent sheets were eventually installed into the South Stand roof to allow sunlight through on to the pitch to appease the situation, although it should be noted that there are three metres of the South Stand end of the pitch that never get sunlight, no matter what time of day or year it is.

Current groundsman Kiel Barrett confirms that the translucent sheets help "a little bit" but the ground suffers from an 'L-shape' shadow from the South Stand and West Stand, whereby sun can't dry the pitch out and what is called a 'black layer' develops where water can't move through the soil fast enough. The age of the West Stand roof means a similar translucent sheets experiment can't be carried out there, because the roof would probably crumble into a million pieces if anyone so much as got a pair of ladders out.

Up until the re-branding as the Family Stand in 1990, the South Stand had grown a notoriety for housing the sections of Leeds' support that were intent on confronting the opposing fans. Indeed the stand itself was closed for the Ipswich Town game in October 1979 following missiles, including darts, being thrown at visiting fans from the standing paddock section during a game against Manchester City. With increasingly empty spaces in the stands in the late 1970s and early '80s fans were penned into certain sections of the Lowfields terrace, but the South Stand seats allowed fans the freedom to run at the away fans and it soon became the stand of choice for Leeds' disreputable and casually attired element. Leeds fans at this time were viewed with curiosity as the first fans to permanently stand en-masse in a seated section; indeed at some stages they all chose to stand on the seats themselves,

a phenomenon that I recall completely bemusing BBC commentator John Motson during the Friday night FA Cup tie with Everton in 1985.

For much of the South Stand's existence, however, and particularly since the East Stand was built in 1993, it has suffered from something of an identity crisis, as different seasons have brought different purposes for the stand. Where the West Stand, Kop and Lowfields/ East Stand have always housed roughly the same sections of Leeds' support, the South Stand has gone through a series of changes, often match-to-match, which have seen the club take advantage of its dual purpose nature.

Adding complexity to the identity crisis has been the series of sponsors' names that have been emblazoned on the stand. 'Systime' even had the stand re-named the 'Systime South Stand'. But right from the start of shirt sponsorship in 1981 with 'RF Winder' and carried on by 'WGK', 'Lion Cabinets' and 'Burtons', the benefactor's name has usually been added to the facia of the South Stand as part of the sponsorship package. In 1991 the *Yorkshire Evening Post* leant their name via sponsorship of the 'Yorkshire Evening Post Family Stand'. More recently the South Stand has been sponsored by Hesco Bastion in 2006, before they sponsored the East Stand, and solicitors Neil Hudgell in 2010. Ultimately though, and as is the case with the similarly-sponsored East Stand, few fans will refer to it as anything other than the South Stand, though that may change following the 2020 re-naming of the stand in honour of Norman Hunter, when the Revie legend sadly and unexpectedly died.

The installation of executive boxes, initially in 1983, has reduced the capacity significantly, and where the stand once housed 7,500 the current capacity is just 5,000. The boxes have halved the capacity of what was originally a decent-sized upper tier and the seats in the lower tier have further reduced the capacity.

Major work was undertaken in 1998 to redevelop the areas underneath the South Stand, and £2 million was spent on creating the 'Community United' educational classrooms all along the full length of the stand. Also, in the summer of 2006 building work was carried out to modernise the then 32-year-old stand, which carried on into the 2006/07 season when the whole stand was closed for the first couple of games. This delay was mainly due to asbestos being found when the Goal Line Restaurant underneath the stand was refurbished to become Billy's Bar, a common feature of anything built in the 1970s or before. The 2006 work also included the boxing-in of the concrete columns and flag poles on the back of the stand, to create a more modern exterior that matched the East Stand. This was further decorated in 2017 by the addition of a pictorial historic timeline of the club's achievements along the back of the stand.

There has been recent talk of removing the executive boxes from the upper tier of the South Stand as the

East Stand development created all the boxes that were required, and the South Stand boxes were now considered outdated and inferior, and indeed for a period of time were unoccupied. This would subsequently create an increased seating capacity in the South Stand. However, recent successes on the pitch have seen the boxes fully occupied and they will soon be undergoing a major refurbishment, to further disguise the 'Portakabin' chic Bill Fotherby hoodwinked the Leeds business community with back in 1983. This suggests the boxes will stay, at least until a new West Stand offers Leeds all the corporate entertainment capacity they will need.

During the 2013/14 season a fans' movement known as 'South Stand SS5', which referred to a specific section of the stand, found like-minded fans congregating in the SS5 area with a view to improving the atmosphere, and reigniting the passions of yesteryear. Amid a sterile and floundering ambience throughout the ground the movement largely worked, and in response aroused the fading passions of the Kop also. As Leeds found success under Marcelo Bielsa from 2018, the South Stand's renewed buoyancy became central to the match day atmosphere and a series of club-permitted flags and banners added to the vibrancy and sense of theatre. Older fans made sage observations that the movement and southern-based atmosphere was akin to the old Scratching Shed pre-1968, when that was the area where the more vocal fans congregated and the Kop was altogether more sedate. It's a bold leap, but maybe that is the next stage of the South Stand's evolving identity?

SPEEDWAY

It is not hard to find Leeds United fans with memories of the thriving greyhound stadium further down Elland Road, as events are still fresh for many who passed the dog track on the way to the match or even went to the meetings themselves. The bowling green survived behind the Old Peacock pub for some of those within living memory, and stories of cricket being played across the road from the football ground for many years can still be told by some of those who were there.

However, finding any Leeds United fan who recalls speedway meetings also taking place on Elland Road, and completing the sporting metropolis the area quite briefly was, definitely proves a little more challenging. For a brief ten-year period between 1928 and 1938 Elland Road was the go-to place for sporting entertainment, a bustling quarter offering thrills of varying description including the intriguing glamour of speedway. The incessant roar of motorbike engines, the rousing attachment sparked by the smell of fuel and the clouds of dust that enveloped the watching crowds; it was all there as a Saturday night spectacle that magnetised the public from miles around, with crowds ranging from

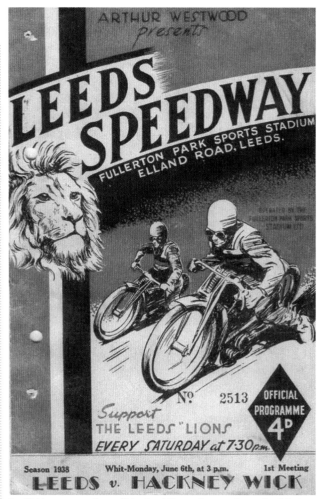

An official programme from a Saturday night speedway meeting on the Fullerton Park track in June 1938. This was during the brief and unsuccessful attempt to resurrect speedway on Elland Road and hence was one of the last ever meetings.

10,000 to 12,000 attending the meetings. But while the other sports spanned many decades, speedway had an all-too-brief flirtation with the Elland Road landscape.

Located on Fullerton Park between the railway line and the football ground, the track had hosted greyhound racing very briefly the year before speedway took over. A first greyhound meeting was held on 4th October 1927, attended by 6,000 people, but when a legal wrangle between two rival associations erupted amid a battle to establish greyhound racing in the area, the track on the south side of Elland Road evidently won it and Fullerton Park took its attentions elsewhere. The first speedway meeting at Elland Road was a practice session on 8th October 1928, with the first official meeting held on 13th October.

The speedway track itself was built at a diagonal to the road, with the track made up of a solid clay base followed by a mixture of hard-rolled clinkers, cinders and coarse yellow sand on top. While the speedway stadium was locally referred to as simply the 'dirt track' it was a stadium of some prominence, at one stage, and perhaps rather ambitiously, estimated at being able to host 50,000 people. There was space for people to stand around the entire perimeter of the track and there were three small covered stands situated at equidistant points on the Elland Road side.

Admission was 6d in 1928, roughly 2.5 pence, and programmes were 3d. Meetings were generally held on a Saturday night and the Leeds Lions team was formed to compete in the northern section of the Provincial League against giants of the sport in Belle Vue, New Cross and Sheffield. Leeds attracted some high quality riders such as the Langton brothers, Oliver and Eric, who later opened a motorbike shop on Call Lane in central Leeds, Jack Brett, George Greenwood, Ray Barraclough and Max Grosskreutz; all genuine national stars in the halcyon days of speedway's most prominent era between the two wars.

Leeds Lions' most successful season came in 1931 when they finished runners-up to Belle Vue, despite the clear handicap of racing in a red and black uniform, colours more associated with their Manchester-based rivals. Sadly, in the meantime the club had run into financial difficulties and struggled to operate a team on a professional basis in the national league. The promoting company (Leeds Stadium Ltd) had fallen into liquidation after the first season of meetings and the creditors decided to run the track themselves, but it never really worked out. Open invitation meetings were regularly held at the track in place of league meetings. Also 'Pirate' meetings were held on Sundays, devoid of association governing, with several riders wearing masks and using assumed names to avoid identification. But it was a risky process rife with hazards in a sport where health and safety was never a prominent factor, and indeed one rider, John Hastings, died after crashing at the track in 1930. Alas, in 1932 after only four seasons

the track was closed for five years before re-opening in preparation for just one further season of league racing in 1938. During the intervening years the track was barely used, except for the rather charming spectacle of pony racing and occasional open-air exhibition boxing meetings. One of these, in March 1932, involved the Italian heavyweight boxer Primo Carnera, nicknamed the 'Ambling Alp'. He was to become world heavyweight champion the following June, but back in Leeds in 1932 he boxed two rounds on a Sunday afternoon with each of three opponents – Bert Ikin, Jack Holland and Bill Hudson, the former Wakefield Trinity rugby league player.

Promoter Arthur Westwood made a final attempt to give speedway momentum in the area in 1938, and during that final season periphery facilities were opened to attract crowds and their income. Fans were invited to attend a ballroom that had been opened under the grandstand and entertained 500 race-goers who wanted to "dance to a really first-class band" until 11.45pm. There was also an American Milk Bar which professed to be the only one in the country. It served the "most delightful milk shakes in many varieties and flavours" and was in the '2/6 Enclosure' and also stayed open until 11.45pm.

The Leeds track was also instrumental in introducing 'Doodle dicing' to the nation's sporting appetite, which was fundamentally car racing, but the cars were little more than a chassis, a seat and a streamlined body. With the hope that it would catch on, draw the crowds and generate a national competition, it once again failed to do so.

A photo from 1930 showing the Fullerton Park speedway track looking towards the Gelderd End of Elland Road and the distinguishing "Dewar's White Label Whiskey" advert carried on the back of the old West Stand.

In a programme for the 22nd August 1938 meeting, Arthur Westwood made a very frank admission that the sport of speedway would be no more in the city if there wasn't sufficient support, and that meant the very meeting the fans were attending could well have been the last. As it was, the sport limped along for a few more weeks.

The final league meeting was on 13th October 1938, exactly ten years to the day after the first. Fittingly Leeds lost it, a Northern Cup Challenge against Newcastle, by four points. For a short period greyhound racing took place on the track as a rival association again attempted to compete with the well-established greyhound track on the opposite side of Elland Road. Predictably this did not last long and soon the site was left derelict, as many buildings were during World War II. The stadium was demolished in 1946 and Fullerton Park was now flat and empty and became an unsightly rubbish dump. The land was levelled and used as a car park for some time before Leeds United purchased roughly half of the land in 1951 and built two training pitches. The other part of the land was eventually bought and used for various industrial purposes, the most well-known being Jackson Boilers.

While the speedway meetings attracted race-goers from miles around, some of the most prominent memories of the track are those of the local children transfixed by the aural din of bikes with no silencers poisoning the air long into the night. Some may have been lucky enough to watch the actual races, but others living in the many streets that then surrounded the track said they could hear the bikes racing at night when they were trying to get to sleep. You then appreciate that the unrelenting buzzing of the engines may have been a comforting sound to those tucked up in bed. Other local children recall helping out on the track the day after meetings, and having a great time on Sunday mornings helping to push bikes on the dirt track. To some schoolchildren the speedway track was just another place to play during holidays; hours could be spent climbing all over the walls and getting covered in cinders from the track, and nobody would bat an eyelid.

In Victorian times legislation was passed that cut short Saturday working and many of the working classes were left with spare time to pursue sports that were previously derided as the preserve of 'toffs', such as football, rugby and cricket; hence the abundance of pitches and grounds all around Leeds. In the days long before 'Saturday Night TV' took over many people's lives, and between the austerity of the war years, getting out on a Saturday night to watch sport was the normal thing to do. So when scanning the sporting landscape of Leeds over the years it is easy to dismiss speedway as having no impact in the city, but for a brief period it was part of a thriving sector around Elland Road and ensured this little district of LS11 produced many varied and vivid memories that deserve to be remembered in the tapestry of the city's recreational culture.

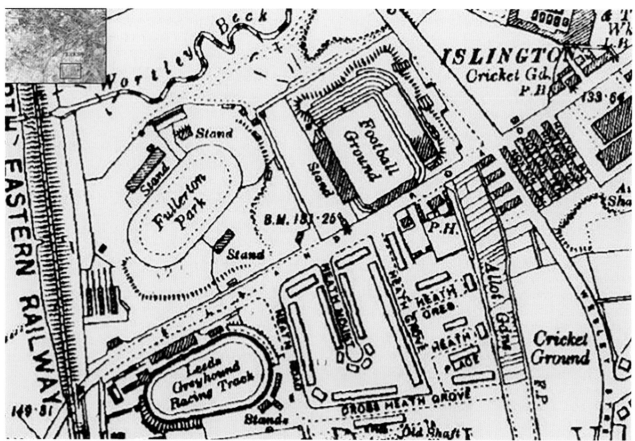

An Ordnance Survey map from the 1930s perfectly illustrating how the area of LS11 was designated as a dedicated sporting district, with the greyhound, football and cricket grounds sharing the landscape, at least for a short time, with speedway.

SPORTS & SOUVENIR SHOP

With the bumper-selling colossus that is the Elland Road megastore now in the south east corner of the ground, some might forget how exciting the 'Sports & Souvenir Shop' was when it opened on 30th September 1972. Exciting not just because of the intrigue surrounding the shop's title – not merely a Souvenir Shop, but a Sports and Souvenir Shop – but also because Leeds United were in the midst of their most glorious era, and having just won the FA Cup, anything seemed possible. Who can blame the club for cashing in on this and opening up commercial opportunities to fly the club's flag and allow fans to show their colours at home, in the streets and at the match? Even if it was in the form of a gonk.

The souvenir industry of the 1970s was a burgeoning market of enterprising splendour, albeit quite often ill-judged in terms of design and concept, with many items dating very quickly and rigidly synonymous with the times. The Elland Road shop was to sell many items never before available to fans officially through the club, though the most popular items were very different to today. It was also a far cry from the cavernous megastore now on Elland Road; in fact, until recently you could still see it – like a disused scout hut it stood as a rather sad and neglected empty building facing onto Elland Road, back-to-back with the West Stand ticket office. As something of a derelict and prominent eyesore next to the main access gates to the ground, it is something of a surprise that the club have only recently clad it with a fresh and fancy 'wrap-around' exterior and amalgamated it into the Ticket Office operation it backs onto. The building is now an Elland Road-facing ticket office facility, whilst the back offices house the new LUTV studios.

A quite narrow but long pre-fab building, the shop was as exciting a place as a young boy of my age in the 1970s was ever likely to visit, particularly when you couldn't afford to go to many games and a visit to the shop was the first thing you did on a match day or at any other time you passed the ground during the week. The shop was literally an explosion of 'Leeds United' as you entered through the door on the right hand side. In the days before the internet, full colour magazines and programmes and wall-to-wall accessibility to photos of the players, the shop was a rare physical connection with the club. It was a public visage for the players and the club's image that was rarely on television and only replicable at matches. There was an almost overwhelming surge of exhilaration as you came face to face with the replica kits, the bobble hats, the gloves, the huge, round lapel badges, the t-shirts, the silk scarves, the woollen scarves, the team photos, the pennants, the rosettes, the underwear, the sweat bands, the tea towels, the mugs. Just ten minutes in the shop was mentally exhausting.

Every Leeds United-related item imaginable was on display, drawing-pinned attractively to a felt board behind the counter for you to gawp at, but tantalisingly

We're here to help you

We're the Leeds United Sports and Souvenir Shop why not call and see us sometime.

We've got over 150 items for you to have a look at from anoraks to swimwear — cuff links to tee shirts.

We're open from 10 to 5.30 every day — 7.30 on Wednesdays and Fridays — and from 10 to 3 on Saturdays. After the match too on first team days.

As we said before . . . . why not call and see us

© Published by : Leeds United Association Football Club Limited.

A match day programme from 1973 promotes the Souvenir Shop. Here are the shop counters that we used to line up against and peer over at the Leeds United treats positioned tantalisingly out of reach.

out of reach. There was nowhere to casually wander and browse or to hold an item up for consideration, or feel the material or the fit. You simply stared slack-jawed at the items on the wall and shuffled silently around on the gritty vinyl flooring, while the omnipresent Shirley and Barbara (plus Tracey on match days, don't forget) behind the counter busied themselves, or at least pretended to.

Whatever size or colour of item you wanted it seemed to be available in the sets of three Tardis-like drawers underneath the display boards; a continually impressive stock control system despite its back street gift shop appearance. There is no doubt that this was a fairly small operation even back in the club's most successful days, but it was homely and personal and as a first step into the progressively lucrative business of merchandise and souvenirs, it was to prove a very successful one.

The shop grew into having a mail order operation, vastly expanding its potential sales. During the week the shop would largely deal with mail order items with requirements being received from all over the world, particularly when the club was regularly in Europe and spreading the name of 'Leeds United' far and wide.

After having only been open for two years a second shop, 'the Kop Shop', was opened in the north east corner in 1974. The Burnley match day programme from March 23rd 1974 has a feature heralding the

Pennants, rosettes, sew-on patches, err, what looks like a crucifix; "Replica shirts? Don't sell 'em love".

new shop, which was "...for the thousands who never go on the Elland Road side of the ground where the club's original shop is situated". The Kop Shop was only open on match days but stocked all the club's souvenirs, which amounted to "...well over 100 different lines".

In the same programme feature, to celebrate the opening of the Kop Shop fans were drawn towards a grandly presented item: "This month's brand new winner – a beautifully made vacuum flask in the club's colours of Yellow, White and Blue, complete with a cup type screw top. Just the thing for cold match days at £1.10. This exciting new item, really has to be seen to be appreciated." One can imagine the ripple of excitement as the flasks were unveiled, drawing gasps from the masses camped overnight outside the shop and exuding the reflective glow of the Ark of the Covenant.

A browse through other match day programmes of this time gives a wonderfully evocative insight into what was fashionable in the late 1970s: "Specially in stock for Christmas are large and small 'cuddly' Teddy Bears (£1.10 and £2.15) with safety eyes and, of course, in the club colours. They're smashing.........a wonderful gift for a youngster – and maybe a grown up too! Also available among soft toys are Gonks (£1.15), Leeds Lambs (85p) and Fluffy Mascots (50p)."

In 1978 the souvenir shops were selling 'distinctive pin badges' with messages so excruciatingly dripping in cheese you could use them at a fondue party. 'A Stein means a big Cup' presumably had a short shelf-life, but others were classics of their time: 'Hot Currie', 'Look on the Gray side', 'Hankin; Our Ray of Light', 'We've got it

MADEley', 'You ain't seen nothing like the Mighty Flynn' and 'The team with Hart'. At 20p each there were ten in a set, plus half a kilo of Edam.

By 1981 you could get a Leeds United Bowler Hat for £1, a Leeds United Quartered Cap for £1.95 and a set of five sew-on patches for £1. The Sports & Souvenir Shop at Elland Road also held an impressive collection of programmes, which were on display behind the counter but were soon moved to a separate section of the shop through a door on the left hand side, which opened for the 1981/82 season.

After years of fallow in the 1980s, Leeds' fortunes briskly improved on the pitch and with that came more commercial vision and enterprise. It soon became apparent that the Sports & Souvenir Shop had outgrown itself. Merchandise and particularly replica shirts was now big business and Leeds United had to step up to the next level. This they did with the opening of the 8,000 square foot megastore behind the South East Corner Stand on 1st June 1996 to coincide with Elland Road's hosting of three Euro 96 games. Suddenly here were brand names like 'Ellanique' and the 'Leeds United Collection'. The megastore allowed the club to rapidly expand its business in terms of replica kit, particularly as it coincided with the most lucrative kit deal the club had ever signed, with Puma. In addition to the full range of home, away, third, training and retro kits, the megastore stocked books, videos and leisurewear, but perhaps less predictably, mouse mats, cuddly toys, chocolate bars, pencils, lunch boxes and even garden gnomes. Put simply, if there was room to put a Leeds United badge on it, the megastore sold it. In 2020, merchandise and replica kits are of course big business, and on match days the club have moved to site pop-up souvenir stalls in exterior locations around the stadium, to fully tap into those beer-fuelled impulse buys prior to kick-off or when your extremities are frozen solid on the way out.

The Sports & Souvenir Shop remained open for a time as an operation solely printing names and shirt numbers on replica shirts, but it was like Marks & Spencer keeping its Kirkgate Market stall open when there was a 5,000 square foot signature store over the road on Briggate. Sadly the days when you would stop off during the week to chat with the ladies in the shop and pick up a 'Leeds United: Ace of Clubs' sew-on patch for your denim jacket had now passed. Amid the hunger for big business, the personal touch had gone. But thankfully the building itself remains, and if you squint your eyes slightly you can be transported back to the early 1980s when your youthful urges were very easily satisfied

STREET ART

For most of the 16 years Leeds United spent outside the Premier League, the grey landscape surrounding Elland Road matched the mood. It felt like the circus had left town, the sun never shone and acres of featureless, undeveloped land, much like Leeds United, sat waiting for investment and for the right person to seize the opportunity. A succession of owners routinely failed to lift the dour and heavy-hanging air of Elland Road, and also failed to appreciate the status Leeds United holds in the community of LS11. Outside of 23 match days a year, there was little evidence that a football club existed in the vicinity, bar a few famous street names and numerous pubs that had seen better days. Whilst nobody really had much to shout about at the time, there is a balance to be found between forcing 'identity' down the throat of the local community and almost being ashamed of it.

In fairness, the absence of the players training at Elland Road during the week doesn't help in pretending that the stadium is anything other than just a regular workplace that only comes alive on a match day. But there was a distinct sense that the football club had no pride in itself, didn't understand and didn't exploit its potential and, in effect, had no visibility or personality in its own surroundings. That sounds stupid when there is a 40,000-seater stadium hiding in plain sight, but in the streets leading up to it, a new visitor to the city would have no idea that the behemoth of Leeds United was just around the corner, and indeed you could be in any other faceless suburban enclave in Leeds.

So the explosion of street art in and around Elland Road in recent years has been a welcome addition to a barren landscape and has grown to become a vital

element of the vista to greet fans on a match day. Perhaps recognising this, the club swiftly acted to 'dress' Elland Road with a more recognisable exterior theme depicting players, colours and a historic timeline on external stand facades. However, whilst the club has been receptive to all the creative schemes that have mushroomed around the streets surrounding the stadium, the actual street art projects have been exclusively and independently fan-led.

Andy McVeigh is an artist who was previously well known for painting otherwise drab and anonymous electrical junction boxes in his local area of Burley. He expanded this to the Elland Road vicinity and his works have germinated rapidly and now adorn boxes on the ring road, Gelderd Road, Lowfields Road, Brown Lane, Domestic Road and of course Elland Road.

"I felt the area was tatty and uninspiring," Andy explains. "You're going to the match, which is always great, but I just felt if I could maybe add an 'art pathway' towards the stadium it'd make that walk just a little more enjoyable, add to the anticipation a touch maybe, a bit more 'Leeds'. It was mainly for kids really and their parents; a little history lesson, especially for primary-age kids, with the older badges, shirts, chants, player references, etc. But a nostalgia trip for the dads too!"

Andy's work, as he originally hoped, has become a staple feature of people's match day routine and he feels their gratitude. "I'm genuinely overwhelmed by the reaction," Andy continues, "in the nicest possible way. It seems to mean a lot to people, gives them pride in the city and the club that I've sort of celebrated Leeds United on the streets. People constantly beep their horns and give the Leeds salute when I'm out painting; it's lovely really. I never expected it would mean that much to people, I really didn't."

Spending so many unsociable hours dedicated to his art – and in all weathers – has also exposed Andy to the more 'colourful' side of the LS11 populace, as he explains: "I've met hundreds of genuinely lovely people, which gives you a bit of hope for the future in difficult times. One guy I remember stopped to chat and said how much he loved the art; he was perfectly normal then said 'and remember, the Earth is flat. Don't believe 'em when they say it's round. You're being brainwashed!' Another time, a bloke stopped me outside the East Stand and asked if he could bless me. He was riding a bike and dressed as a lion. He then put on a blue lady's wig and boxing gloves and said 'may God bless the Burley Banksy, his art and relieve him of his stresses'. Then cycled off. I thought I must have been spiked with LSD. And I'm an atheist."

Around the same time Andy was starting to decorate the area around Elland Road, the Leeds United Supporters' Trust commissioned artist Jameson Rogan to paint a mural to cover the corrugated stone wall of the underpass beneath the M621 on Lowfields Road. Fans voted for a design depicting the four midfield

Andy McVeigh's artful interpretation of Eddie Gray's solo goal versus Burnley in 1970, as depicted on the exterior brick wall of a basketball court on the Holbeck end of Elland Road.

Jameson Rogan's 1992 title-winning mural by the Lowfields Road underpass, as commissioned by the Leeds United Supporters' Trust in 2017.

The Leeds United badge depicted on an end terrace on Tilbury Road, Holbeck, by resident Shane Green.

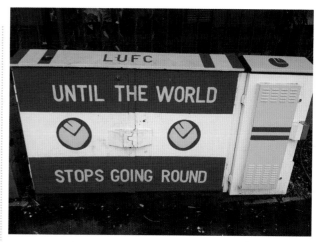

A selection of Andy McVeigh's now famous painted electrical junction boxes dotted around the Elland Road locality.

maestros of the 1992 league title win, Gary Speed, David Batty, Gary McAllister and Gordon Strachan, with an image of Howard Wilkinson in the middle. The mural was completed in September 2017 and has since become a ubiquitous landmark and photo opportunity, albeit some fans lamented the loss of an opportunity to daub graffiti on that section of wall, as it had famously carried the words 'BATES OUT' for several years. A later adaptation to 'CELLINO OUT' was amended overnight to read 'CELLINO IN', but in fact, like a kind of drunken hokey-cokey, became incoherent and indecipherable, and therefore lost any impact.

Since the Trust gave the street art movement some visible thrust, Andy's plentiful contributions have been complemented by a local resident, Shane Green, painting the entire gable end of his house on Tilbury Road in Holbeck with the Leeds United badge. As the end terrace, this was strategically located as it can be seen by passing traffic on the M621 and by the pedestrian crowds as they cross the footbridge over the motorway to and from Elland Road, like a Lowry painting for the 2020s. Just around the corner, on the 'old' section of Elland Road, Andy depicted Eddie Gray's famous goal v Burnley in some more wall art.

The most recent example of street art appeared quite covertly on a Sunday afternoon not long after promotion to the Premier League was secured in the summer of 2020. Street artist Adam Duffield was joined by title-winning midfielder and Polish international Mateusz Klich to paint a 'Champions 2020' graffiti mural on a brick wall on Lowfields Road. Such a vivid statement so close to the stadium raised a few eyebrows – not least because it was painted on a particular brick wall that is the only standing remains from the original 1920s-built Lowfields Road Stand and should therefore be listed and protected in some way – but the club had approved it and the work cemented Klich's burgeoning reputation as "not your average footballer".

Other Marcelo Bielsa-themed murals have appeared in Wortley and Hyde Park since promotion in 2020, with the promise of more to come, whilst Andy also adds "I've got loads more ideas for boxes and also big murals and hopefully some in the stadium concourses."

It appears the creative juices of the Leeds United faithful have been fully uncorked by success on the field. But in truth, the proliferation of street art is a fine example of spontaneous fan power and a movement born out of frustration that the club itself, at the time, didn't share the fan's inherent pride in Elland Road, Leeds United's deeply entrenched heritage and its distinctive visual character.

TICKET OFFICE

In Leeds City's formative years large crowds brought frequent chaos. As the potential volume of fans could not be predicted by pre-sales, fans simply turned up and paid cash on the day. As the game evolved into the 1930s and crowds grew bigger, some bright spark recognised the need to have a regulated system for predicting and controlling the expected crowd volumes and hence match day tickets became more popular.

The first ever all-ticket game at Elland Road wasn't until 28th January 1950, when Leeds entertained Bolton in the FA Cup Fourth Round before 51,488. Some of the attendances in that particular year do highlight what a variable crowd Leeds United attracted at the time, and therefore how difficult it was for club officials to cope with staging games, way before mass purchase of season tickets ensured a core crowd. The first home game of 1950 was against Tottenham Hotspur on 14th January which attracted a crowd of 50,476. However, by the final curtain of the season in April, the last two home games saw 12,538 come to watch Blackburn, before the season ended with just a paltry 8,913 watching the visit of Bury. The lakes of unsold Bovril do not bear thinking about.

Leeds fan John Cave remembers the very basic ticketing systems operated at the turnstiles in those pre-Revie and pre-West Stand ticket office days, when success was scarce but large crowds were still frequent: "Only cup-ties were ever all-ticket, so much was the power of the FA Cup in those days, and these tickets were usually bought by the expedient method of buying the ticket as you paid your entrance fee at one of the previous games – including Central League – before the cup fixture itself. This certainly happened against Chelsea and Spurs in 1952 and 1954 respectively. These tickets themselves were works of art, akin to a wedding invitation, being on heavy card with match details printed in copper plate handwriting, far grander than the computer printed efforts issued today."

Following its re-build after the fire in 1956 the first permanent ticket office was created in the current West Stand, with a tiny window looking out onto the car park and utilising only two permanent staff. This same ticket office served the crowds of Elland Road right through the 1960s when fixture congestion was commonplace and Cup Finals and Cup Semi-Finals at home and abroad were a regular occurrence.

Another fan from that early Revie era, John Jackson, recalled the hotly anticipated return of John Charles to Elland Road from his sojourns in Italy in 1962. Upon Charles' return Leeds increased ticket prices with the ruse that "the public of Leeds could contribute to the cost of bringing John back to Elland Road" bordering on emotional blackmail. John Jackson recalls: "As I remember there were no half price tickets for children (I was 12 at the time), so my Dad had to fork out 7s 6d (just over 35 pence) each for Kop tickets for the match

£2.50 for an adult to sit in the West Stand in 1982.

against Rotherham. We lost, but Charles scored with a powerful shot from the edge of the area at the Kop end. It cost ten shillings (50 pence) on the Lowfields Road terrace to see us beat Sunderland 1-0 with a goal by Billy Bremner. When the prices returned to normal for the rest of the season, I think it cost 3s 6d (15 pence) for adults and 1s 9d (5 pence) for children to stand on the Kop."

In 1970 with the need to expand and professionalise the ticketing operation, the familiar landmark of the hexagonal ticket office was built which was merely an extension to the existing office and another focal point of the West Stand frontage, underneath the blue 'LEEDS UNITED' façade. The ticketing operation in the 1970s, when Leeds United were one of the biggest clubs in Europe never mind England, was primitive and almost quaint. A section of the match day programme running throughout the 1973/74 season alluded to a "limited number of reserved seats available on a matchly basis". These could be obtained by sending a stamped addressed envelope addressed to the Ticket Office Manager, not more than 12 days before a particular game. You could also turn up in person at the ticket office, but either way "all seat tickets are priced £1.50".

The information is wonderfully vague, yet it worked. Even the vouchers printed in every copy of the programme, which had to be collected over the season and exchanged for Semi-Final or Final tickets, worked. At the same time standing admission was 75p on the Lowfields Road terracing and £1.00 on the Kop.

Of course Elland Road was regularly packed out with no fuss. Life was much simpler in the black and white world of the early 1970s but even Leeds United, with their supremely efficient ticketing empire run with the modest and submissive humility of a corner shop, could not ignore the lurking behemoth of IT. In 1978 'Albert'

was introduced to Elland Road. Albert was the name given to the GEC 'computer' installed in the ticket office, and given the techno-fear that still exists in society to some extent today, it is amusing to consider how this 'computer' will have impacted upon the somewhat unrefined operation in 1978. The blanket reference to a generic 'computer' in itself demonstrates the dread and incomprehension that was naturally prevalent in most people who were quite content with how a pen worked. In the match day programme for the game against Birmingham on 30th September 1978, a photo shows ticket office manager Don Toulson and his assistant Marion Booth staring blankly at the 'computer', their manifest perplexity half-masked by an uncomfortable grin. Albert was huge, like a butcher's chest freezer, and named after the GEC engineer that installed the 'computer' and carried out maintenance work.

ALBERT

You are unlikely to find Albert's name normally featured in the United match programme but he is proving to be one of the best signings the club has made in recent years!

Albert is the name that has been given to the GEC computer that was installed in the Elland Road Ticket Office last year to make life easier for supporters wanting season tickets and individual match tickets.

United's Ticket Office Manager Don Toulson says: "The computer has made our job more straight forward and we are now able to offer supporters tickets for any match at Elland Road instantly. This can obviously save a lot of time queuing on match days. Before the computer, we could only deal with match tickets twelve or fourteen days before a specific game."

At the press of a button the computer will come up with the seats available in any part of the ground and for any match over a season. When a sale has been made, the seats will be logged in the computer's memory bank as sold and the tickets will be printed.

"We can now have tickets for a Cup game here on sale within half an hour of the draw being made," says Don. "Previously, it used to take several days to get the tickets printed. And when we were dealing with season tickets during the last close season, the computer saved us a lot of time having to check back through cards to see which seats were available."

Don and his assistant Marion Booth, pictured in the Elland Road Ticket Office, advise all United fans wanting tickets to make use of Albert and book as early as possible.

Name note . . . "Albert" was named after the GEC engineer who installed the computer and carries out maintenance work.

"It's doing it again, Don!", "smile Marion, just smile"; IT arrives in the Elland Road ticket office in 1978 via Albert the 'computer'.

"The computer has made our job more straightforward," Don Toulson explained, possibly through gritted teeth, "and we are now able to offer supporters tickets for any match at Elland Road instantly. This can obviously save a lot of time queuing on match days. Before the computer we could only deal with match tickets twelve or fourteen days before a specific game." The programme goes on to explain how the 'computer' shows available seats in any part of the ground, and when a sale is made the seats "will be logged in the computer's memory bank as sold". Quite what Marion made of the technology, sadly, we are not privy to, but life went on as the ticketing system evolved.

It was not until Leeds' fortunes saw a recovery in the late 1980s that bigger premises were sought away from the West Stand itself, and at the end of the 1989/90 season the current two-storey headquarters of the ticket office was built at the south end of the West Stand car park, backing on to the old Sports & Souvenir Shop. This, for a couple of years, had previously been a much smaller ticket office. Facing unprecedented demand as the team steamrolled towards promotion, and balancing this with the unforeseen capacity restrictions of the Taylor Report and a computer system not updated since the mid-1980s, the club were heavily criticised by fans during the 1989/90 season.

The new, bigger ticket office, which was soon christened the 'Synchro Ticket Office' after the computer system installed within it, was another brainchild dreamed up by the Fotherby/Gilman partnership, as Bill Fotherby explains: "One of the things you've got to give Mr Gilman a bit of credit for was that we had a meeting where he stated that 'we are losing money at Leeds United because of the ticketing situation', ie. going through turnstiles. If you remember in them days what used to happen was that you were escorted with a policeman to take your money (from turnstile takings) into the main office, and the gate receipts were all put out onto a big, long table, all the 50p pieces and god knows what, it was a hell of a task and it had to be counted. Well, give an honest man an opportunity and he becomes a thief. It was wide open. So the ticket office (ie. a bigger, more professional and secure system with less cash turnstiles and more pre-booked tickets) was the idea of Mr Peter Gilman, and I implemented that in there for him, which made such a big difference for people getting their tickets."

Dave Cocker describes the current site of the ticket office in the West Stand car park from when he first started spending time at the club in June 1960: "There was nothing at the end where it is now; they eventually built the ticket office at the end of the West Stand car park but initially, in the early 1960s, that was just a big, concrete slab wall. There was a goal marked out on it because when it was snowing they used to play five-a-side in the car park. The wall must have been about 15 feet high."

In the early years of the main West Stand ticket office, the rise in Leeds' fortunes frequently led to ticket chaos or at best some uncertainty as to whether you could actually get in for any given match. Pre-match announcements over the tannoy system in a monotone female voice that, by the very nature of the information it was conveying, became quite irritating, would regularly announce to the unlucky hordes snaking around the West Stand car park that "there are now no tickets remaining for today's game". It was a period of extraordinary growth, at extraordinary speed, and the ticket office bore the brunt of that more than anyone. From a sleepy existence for much of the 1980s where the ticket office had three members of staff, two terminals and was dealing with crowds of around 14,000, suddenly the operation had new technology and a new office altogether, with 12 terminals, eight staff, six enquiry windows and two girls manning the phones permanently, dealing with crowds of 30,000 plus every week. The situation has been pretty much the same ever since, with advances in technology, the efficiency of transactions and also online bookings making the system faster for people who often seem to have less patience and common courtesy than in any other walk of life.

Since the 1970s the ticket office has seen various other temporary and permanent off-shoots to its operations. There was a small ticket office outside the back of the Lowfields Road Stand for a few years until the stand was demolished in 1992, with the less-than-impressive frontage being a grimly painted white brick wall. Another temporary ticket office was built at the north end of the West Stand car park also during the late 1980s, which was a prefabricated building used only for match day sales. There has also been a short-lived move to the East Stand concourse for the whole ticketing operation when the stand was fully opened in 1993/94. Finally a new, additional ticket office was built behind the North East Corner Stand shortly after the East Stand was opened, which still exists today and was built on the site of one of the old Lowfields Road Stand's toilet blocks.

In 2011 a small ticket office was created to cater for away fans when they were moved to the south end of the West Stand. For the romantics, it should be noted that this does resemble the original hexagonal ticket office that was built in 1970; perhaps the work of a local designer with a nostalgic eye for the image of the lost West Stand façade?

It is true that over the years the ticket office staff have been at the forefront of club activities, often the only face-to-face contact with the club that supporters have, and consequently they have probably had more direct fury vented at them than the players and management. Thick skin is required to play for Leeds United, perhaps even thicker for those who might have to tell a fan that he or she cannot watch them.

TRAMS

Nothing that documents the history of an early 20th century football ground can legitimately ignore the role played by the humble tram. Various bus services had run along Elland Road in the late 1800s but these were independently operated, unreliable and often didn't run for more than a couple of months. Altogether more frequent, convenient and unfailing was the tram, and in the first half of the 20th century the vast majority of spectators attending Elland Road, not to mention most of the first team squad and officials, will have done so via this sadly departed transport medium.

The first regular mode of public transport directly to Elland Road for the sole purpose of transporting football fans was the tram, and at the time, bar walking, or for those exclusive enough to own a car, the tram was the essential means by which to attend the game. The first trams in Leeds ran from 1871 and as football gained in popularity in the early 1900s three separate services were used to transport fans across the city to LS11.

The most established service was the 'No.8' from Meanwood to Elland Road via the city centre. There was also a route which dropped passengers off at the top of Beeston Hill for the walk down Wesley Street, and

A tram travels along Elland Road in September 1952 with the southern end of the Lowfields Road Stand just visible.

A photo from April 1930 showing the tramlines on Elland Road travelling past the greyhound stadium, which is on the right, up towards Elland Road in the distance. The two stone gateposts visible on the right are still there, despite the recent construction of the new police headquarters on this site.

Football Special trams lined up on Lowfields Road in 1952 as far as the eye can see, back towards Elland Road. Fans who approach the ground down Lowfields Road might notice that the building on the left still stands today and is known as Viceroy House.

eventually there was a 'Football Special' route laid on specifically for football fans. At first these ran from the Corn Exchange but due to problems with overcrowding in the city centre they were soon switched. For the beginning of the 1921/22 season they set off from Swinegate and Sovereign Street; ironically, the same place underneath the Dark Arches that the overcrowded R2 buses still depart from today and frequently take 'dangerous driving' to a new level.

It is well known that the 'Football Specials' were run on a different, more expensive tariff to other comparable routes. It is perhaps heartening for the modern fan, stung by extortionate ticket prices and Sky Sports subscriptions, to know that even in the early 20th century football fans were being openly deceived of their hard-earned money simply for watching the game they loved.

The No.8 service continued along Elland Road itself and also transported attendees of the greyhound stadium before heading off up to Churwell, whereas the Football Specials turned right into Lowfields Road, which was built in 1923 specifically to make access to the ground easier and to link with Gelderd Road to make transporting fans away from Elland Road easier after games. On Lowfields Road fans would disembark and the vehicles waited en masse along the protracted stretch of straight road heading away from the ground, now bisected by the M621. Most of the drivers went in to watch the game until 15 minutes before the end when they returned to their vehicles to await the wholesale scramble of fans making the return journey.

Having attended Elland Road from 1934 onwards Reg French remembers the 'Football Special' trams

The popular 'No. 8' trams lined up on Lowfields Road next to the sports ground at that time known as Petty's Whitehall Recreation Ground.

fondly: "They used to go from near where the buses go from now on Swinegate. They were all lined up there. The trams were very popular because they could move a lot of people very quickly. You were dropped off on Lowfields Road and then the trams would just wait there in a long queue to take you back."

Ray Fell also remembers the trams with affection: "The line of trams on Lowfields Road was a sight to behold and they probably cleared the ground quicker than what they do now. The first one would come up, inspectors would put you on, 'right, move', then the next one would come up, same again. It was just a succession of trams, god knows how many."

With Leeds United's promotion to the First Division in 1924 crowds immediately increased. This created acute congestion and a chaotic scramble to fill up the trams and led to planning being sought to build a single track siding on Lowfields Road. This was directly opposite the ground on the same side as the Holbeck Cricket

The huge adverts on the back of the West Stand are again visible as this tram travels along Elland Road in October 1952.

Ground, and indeed some of the land used to build it was rented off the cricket club. This new siding opened on 31st August 1925 and greatly eased the problems immediately. The sense of order and increased efficiency also led to the fares for the Football Specials being halved to 11/2d, to bring them in line with regular trams for a similar journey. In 1932 additional track was laid from the Lowfields Road siding to land adjoining the cricket pitch to create a yard. From February 1939 this yard became used for burning old tramcars, with locals referring to it as the 'Tram Knackers Yard'.

Sadly the future for trams was already looking uncertain between the two wars. Special corporation buses began to run from City Square to Elland Road in 1926 to supplement the trams, and gradually began to replace them. Bus services increased in prominence from the 1930s with routes directly to Elland Road opening from Cardigan Road and Burley Road near Headingley, and the Leeds United Supporters' Club also requested services from West Park, New Farnley and the Wyther Estate, which were all granted. To accommodate the increase in buses a bus park was constructed on Lowfields Road in 1937 roughly where the current one is, although at that time, of course, the bus park was surrounded by open grass fields.

Football Special trams ran to Elland Road until June 1955, although cynics and opponents of progress were delighted only 12 months later when the Suez Crisis led to fuel shortages and trams were again used to transport football fans. On Saturdays from December 1956 to March 1957, the Football Special buses were the first victim of the fuel rationing. When

that dispute was resolved, however, and the buses returned to the streets, the tram tracks remained in place as, conveniently, the Tram Knackers Yard on Lowfields Road had become one of the main tramcar scrap yards in Leeds. Although the Football Specials had now ceased, the same route was unwittingly used to take trams to their disconsolate, final resting place.

Leeds was one of the last cities in the country to have active trams, the remaining services finally terminating in 1959, with Sheffield being the final city to stop trams in 1960. Certainly the vast majority of the tracks from the original tram network are still in situ across the city beneath a few inches of tarmac, and it is true that a small portion of tram track was visible on Lowfields Road during the early 1990s prior to some much required re-surfacing work.

Buses and cars have now replaced this emblem of a bygone era with the purpose-built Football Specials bus depot on Lowfields Road, opened in 1972, now catering for the majority of bulk travellers to Elland Road. It has long been discussed that a rail station could be justified at Elland Road with the Doncaster line running just a few yards from the ground on the western side, and indeed in 1974 a concrete proposal was put forward, but again this has never happened. And whilst Leeds City Council has spoken previously of implementing a new 'Supertram' system, similar to Sheffield and Manchester's, this currently seems a distant prospect. Even if it happened, the experience in terms of noise, comfort and speed would be strikingly different to the trams of the early 20th century, and you would be unlikely to find Leeds United first team players sharing your seat as they regularly did up to 60 years ago.

TROPHY ROOM

A standing joke applied to about 95% of all professional football clubs is why there is a need for a trophy room. Leeds United teeter on the edge of falling into that category. But one visit to Elland Road to view the array of 'trophies' that qualify to be shown in a trophy room demonstrates that with some imagination most clubs can put together a concentrated area to show off their achievements, however varied and humble they are. And while trophies for winning the 'Second Division' might not be classed as 'major', they hold treasured memories for many and should rightly be shown off.

Until the Revie era brought tangible achievement and European adventure, a collection of local and friendly tournament awards are all that will have adorned a modest treasury in the West Stand. Revie's success saw the beginning of the rich harvest of exchanged pennants, silver salvers, tankards, shirts, medals and miscellaneous artefacts from the club's European travels, and so the history that is so widely celebrated today had begun.

In the 1960s and '70s, however, there was none of the grand corporate extravagance we see today. The West Stand was the functional hubbub of all club activity. Therefore, despite this being the most celebrated era the club had yet experienced, the trophy room was little more than a few centrally located unpretentious glass cabinets stacked against the walls outside of what is now the Revie Room Suite, but at the time was the 100 Club lounge.

Howard Wilkinson famously removed many of the memories of the Revie era upon arriving at the club. However, somewhat ironically, in November 1988, shortly after Wilkinson's appointment and with the walls freshly shorn of Revie's photos, Bill Fotherby purchased two smart, dark wooden trophy cabinets "complete with internal lighting" to show off the many minor trophies and souvenirs the club had been awarded over the years.

With the task of creating modern history duly achieved the 'trophy room' expanded once the Banqueting Suite was built on the back of the West Stand in 1992. Having more than one era to celebrate, the prize collection was spread around the foyer upstairs entering into the Banqueting Suite, and into the other suites used for corporate purposes on match days. Whilst some of the collection has been removed from public view following an internal refurbishment, and is held in storage, that is still largely the case. In essence there is no longer a single room that houses Leeds United's trophies, although that is not necessarily as impressive as it sounds; the collection is merely spread over several cabinets dotted around the internal West Stand areas.

Leeds' rich history now adorns some of the areas open to the public via the stadium tours and provides a fascinating insight into the achievements of the club, its players and its managers. What the club still doesn't have though is a museum that would make the majority of this wealth of treasures a central feature. This is despite much talk of a museum being created by the Bates regime in 2012. A full-time curator was employed at the time and much work was done in creating a catalogued archive of objects and artefacts, but alas the project ran on stony ground and still today the club remains strangely inhibited by its successful past.

TUNNEL

The point from which there is no hiding place and where every Leeds United player holds the baying crowd's full glare. The players' tunnel at Elland Road has seen hundreds of famous faces trot up and down it over the years and has been the backdrop for many of the best images chronicling the history of the club. Be it 'The Wombles' providing a guard of honour when Leeds entertained Wimbledon in an FA Cup Replay in 1975 or Paul Reaney striding out with the Smiley badge on his tracksuit top sewn on upside down, they all tell a story before the action even begins.

Prior to the construction of the current Kop in 1968 the players' tunnel was, naturally, bang on the halfway line of the pitch. As mentioned previously, the building of the Kop enabled the pitch to be moved northwards and consequently with the tunnel itself remaining static it is now approximately 18 metres south of the halfway line.

Still, the tunnel, regardless of its position, has always been the focal point of the expectant crowd in the tense minutes leading up to kick-off. Even up to the mid-1990s fans in certain seats in the West Stand were able to lean downwards and sneak an early glimpse of the players lining up in the tunnel, with Vinnie's war cries bouncing off the bare brick walls. The modern trend, regrettably, is for the spoilsport fun-prevention of a retractable plastic horning that guards the players and officials for security reasons, and ensures they are not visible or touchable until they actually set foot on the pitch. This was first installed in November 1994 and was done with a view to requirements for Euro 96, as such types of tunnel were commonplace in Europe at the time. Several Premier League clubs followed Leeds' example as they appeared to blaze a trail in this regard.

The tunnel area itself is now a relatively wide corridor approximately two metres wide, in recent years decorated with large wall panelling depicting the images of current players, which naturally, need updating quite often. The tunnel is carpeted externally as the players enter the pitch, with vinyl flooring in the area under the stand where they line up; an area which in Revie's day and certainly prior to that, was simply rough concrete under foot. From the external part of the tunnel, the corridor under the stand leads

Paul Reaney and the rest of the Leeds team exit the Elland Road tunnel, whilst someone awaits a chastising for not reading the 'sewing on badges the right way round' memo.

at the end on the right to the dressing rooms and referee's room. On the left, just before the old medical room, was the recently created sponsored backdrop for the post-match interviews, which was little more than an alcove off from the tunnel and on appearance could just as easily have been a parking spot for the half-time tea trolley. A much bigger post-match interview area has now been created in the old medical rooms, again at the behest of the Premier League, with several adjacent areas allowing various national and international press crews to set up and await their turn to interview players and staff.

Also on the left past this new area is the manager's office. Today this is just an area in which the manager can relax on a match day – if indeed Marcelo Bielsa EVER relaxes on a match day – but in years gone by it was the 24/7 hub of the manager's existence. Howard

Wilkinson has few fond memories of his original office in this exact location, before the building of the Banqueting Suite necessitated a change: "Yeah, it was in a horrible place, no windows, at the end of the corridor as you came through reception. You went to go into the changing room corridor and it was at the end of that corridor. It was oak-panelled, it had no windows, it was stuffy. I was pleased when it was moved. But it was low-priority for me."

The players' tunnel is equipped with ports for setting up radio mic equipment for LUTV and other post-match interviews and has static doors which are closed and locked for security reasons when the ground is not open on match days or for stadium tours.

Security now of course is very tight, but Dave Cocker recalls that "almost anybody" could get access to the fabled tunnel area in the 1960s and 1970s. Although

he was afforded unique access around the club at that time anyway, Dave recalls the infamous West Brom game in 1971 when Ray Tinkler's astonishing decision to allow a Jeff Astle goal robbed Leeds of vital points in pursuit of the league title they eventually lost out on by one point. "I was there and managed to confront him (Tinkler)," Dave says, though the police soon intervened and the under-pressure ref, who had already been challenged by fans on the pitch, was whisked away. "There was one guy on the players' entrance," Dave continues, referring to the security on the double doors leading into the dressing room area, "to stop fans already in the West Stand concourse getting in, although they eventually built a separate walkway to prevent that, and there was a commissionaire just to salute everybody as they came in through the directors' entrance, but you could go anywhere. I remember going to Anfield when we won the championship in 1969, and I'm stood outside thinking 'come on Dad where's me ticket?' He didn't come out so I thought 'sod it' and walked straight in. I was in a suit and I just said 'hiya, you alright?' 'yeah, fine' and I just walked straight into the dressing rooms. I asked my Dad 'where's me ticket?', 'I haven't got one', so I ended up watching the game in the dugout for that one, and it was brilliant. But you just used to walk into the grounds and you could at Elland Road too. If you got used to it and had the confidence to do it, you could walk in anywhere. They were more embarrassed to stop somebody if they looked right."

Dave continues to describe the routines immediately pre-match in the Revie era, but the empowering sense of energy and adrenalin as the players are about to come out does, for once, transfer to other eras too. However, when Revie's pumped and highly primed combatants were about to do battle it must have been quite a sight to witness. "At five to three I'd stand and watch the players walk out," begins Dave, "and then I'd run down the tunnel and jump into the (West Stand) paddock, as we all did. After a while Leeds would be out early doing the old psychological dancing bit, but for European games they both walked out together. Other than that they just came out when they were ready. The referee had a bell which was wired into the dressing rooms, and he just hit the bell which meant 'right, get on the pitch!' Leeds might come out first and the opposition two or three minutes later."

There was no parade or ceremony like there is now, as the announcer tries desperately to build up an atmosphere that often isn't there and the players come out side-by-side to organised music and line up to shake hands. Revie was the master of psychology and with Paul Trevillion in 1972 he orchestrated a pitch entrance that became a much grander affair than simply a casual saunter out of the tunnel in twos and threes like a Sunday League game. Revie's troops now walked to the centre circle to wave to all four sides of the ground before embarking on a specially designed formation warm-up, which the crowd lapped up and cheered. It worked to a tee in terms of intimidating the opposition further, as Dave recalls: "I remember the Spurs game in the FA Cup (in 1972), the first time that they'd done the 'ole's out on the pitch in the warm-up, and Pat Jennings (Spurs goalkeeper) said that was the first time they'd been sat in the dressing room knowing they didn't have a chance. They were sat in there absolutely shitting it. There were players like Gilzean, Greavesy and everybody, and he said 'we just sat there looking at each other and they're all cheering outside'. You could see it when they came out, they absolutely bricked it."

Dave goes on to describe the general tunnel area in the 1960s: "Halfway down the tunnel as you head towards the pitch on the right hand side was a medical room. When they got Doc Adams in they went 'right, we want the best medical facilities', because obviously, the team then was playing 70 games a season, so they got all this fantastic medical equipment in and Bob English was trained on all that. There was a couple of hospital beds in there, pulleys for players with broken legs and other things, and all this electronic gadgetry. It was very early on for that standard of equipment and the room is still there, but I don't know what it is now."

Alan Sutton, physio since 1986, confirms that this particular room was pretty much exactly as it always was until the summer of 2020 and promotion to the Premier League. The old medical room was still split into three consecutive rooms, although the lack of day-to-day use meant the rooms were less critical than they used to be in '60s, '70s and '80s. "The treatment room was the first room you went into," Alan explains. "The middle room was a rehab room, it had wall bars on the wall and the same cupboards that were always there, and the back room was a doctor's office, which is now a toilet. At one time the manager's office, which is at the other side of the old physio's room, had a door leading directly into the physio's room, but it's blocked off now." Before being refurbished as the new post-match interview area in the summer of 2020, the old medical rooms were under-used for many years, particularly as the home dressing room also had a physio's room. In fact a quick scan suggested they were used more for storage than anything else, and upon my own investigation back in 2014, the back room, the old doctor's office, was evidently being used as Lucas the Kop Cat's changing room when I poked my head around the door. Not exactly what the pioneering Doctor Adams had in mind in the 1960s, I suspect.

A frequent visitor to the tunnel area is Thom Kirwin, who offers his take on the bustle of activity that the now heavily guarded central tunnel area is party to: "Next to the dressing rooms, the tunnel is the next sanctuary. You're only there if you definitely need to be there. For radio commentary, at first I was reporting from the tunnel after games so I'm telling fans what's going on in the tunnel, you know if the opposition manager had stormed out in a bad mood or what was being said, within reason, because obviously there's some stuff you wouldn't be reporting down there. It's very strange straight after a game because it's all sealed off and as soon as every player is in the dressing rooms, everyone else is allowed to descend on it. It's a busy place after a game, all the TV interviews, radio interviews, both managers. You get players coming back out to warm down and I use it quite a lot to gauge what the feeling is about the performance from the players so you can get a bit of reaction before the manager comes out. See what the general mood is like. You've got families and then the players coming out when they're leaving, because of where it is in the West Stand the tunnel is actually a route out of the place, so everyone comes through it from the players' lounge, down the side of the pitch and to their cars, so it ends up being quite a busy thoroughfare.

"For a lot of managers post-match interviews are a bit of a game," Thom continues. "You might not say what you actually think. They have a bit of time to actually compose themselves. Neil Warnock took ages, so we were in the tunnel a long time; he used to have a bath after every game. So we were waiting ages, whereas Brian McDermott was literally out, quick chat with the team then straight out and done, it's not really a drawn out process.

"I've worked here for a lot of years now and been in and around the ground, almost every bit of it. Sometimes I take it for granted, sometimes you're in a part of the stadium and you think 'bloody hell the fans would love to be here'. It's like a lot of things in the job, you have to pinch yourself and even when you're a bit depressed after results, you just have to think that people would give their right arm to be here. It's a privilege without a doubt."

As Thom says, the tunnel area is second only to the dressing rooms in terms of the place any fan would kill to be, and the otherwise unassuming stretch of a few yards has been privy to countless exchanges and altercations over the years that the public has never seen. But when people like Gianni Alioski are about, it's no surprise that the modern phenomenon of Tunnel-cam now affords us priceless access we could only previously dream about. Whether it's a pumped-up Batty repeatedly bouncing a ball off the wall as he lines up, as much to annoy the opposition with the reverberating thud as anything else, or Lee Bowyer and Spurs' Tim Sherwood continuing the verbal debate they embarked on for several seasons, the tunnel area used to keep its counsel. Football's protocol saw to that. But now the tunnel is fair game, and as a key part of the match day spectacle and our hunger for every forensic detail, it is as captivating as anything else.

TURNSTILES

I was once dragged through the Kop turnstiles at Elland Road by a complete stranger. First Division Queens Park Rangers were in town, it was February 1987, it was the FA Cup. Leeds United were re-born and the gates were closed at 2.20pm. I escaped the anarchic melee outside the turnstiles completely by chance, somehow finding myself at the front after a frantic surge. As the gateman tried to shut the gate, a hand reached through from inside and grabbed me at random, and thus began one of my finest Leeds United experiences; Baird, Ormsby and all.

The creaking, the clicking, the awkward shuffling; the turnstiles are not just the conduit through which you enter the ground, but the first solid contact with Elland Road, the point where tension and excitement builds, the gateway to dreams and nightmares. It may be hard to believe but the design of the simple turnstile has evolved over the years, and like most inanimate objects in the modern world, has not escaped influence from the dual demons of the computer age and health and safety laws.

When Elland Road was in its infancy during Leeds City's years turnstiles still existed, despite crowds being largely estimated and uncontrollable in terms of numbers. As football gained popularity and Leeds City, and then Leeds United, drew bigger crowds and developed the various stands, so came the need to keep a tighter rein on the financial income from gate receipts and to regulate the inflow of spectators into the ground. Technical advancements had come so far as to enable a 'clicker' on the turnstile to count how many rotations it had made, thus aggregating the number of fans passing through each individual gate.

A single rotating turnstile at torso level was commonplace at all football grounds until the 1960s. By that time the demographic of the average football fan was changing and wise to the opportunity of gaining illicit entry, most clubs extended the turnstiles to over seven feet in height, thus ensuring there was no method of climbing over them and disappearing into the throng inside. Furthermore the turnstile operator was completely caged in for his own safety. A computerised turnstile system was not installed at Elland Road until 1968 and only then could the club control sections that were becoming full, and only then could they see that fans were entering the ground at approximately 1,000 per minute in the frantic run-up to kick-off. A newspaper story documented the installation of the new system at Elland Road "Trials of the system at Elland Road have shown that small boys get through the turnstiles twice as fast as adults. At the special boys' gates, they tend to turn up with the right change and are quicker off the mark than adult spectators. The ratio in a recent test showed that 4.2 boys got in during the time it took 1.9 adults." Those pesky adults with their fully-grown bodies, or just a downtrodden Leeds fan not in a great rush to get in whilst also wrestling with a burger, perhaps?

Health and safety warning: a policeman minds his own business as the overcoated hordes cram into a single turnstile, while clambering over the casually stacked building materials for the ongoing West Stand construction in 1957. Note also the 1953-installed floodlights built into the mud bank of the Gelderd End.

During a period when I couldn't afford a season ticket in 1993 I required an enterprising venture through which I could feed my obsession, and so I spent two seasons as a turnstile operator for Leeds United, during which time I was astonished at the prospect of being paid for effectively watching home games.

My first game was against West Ham in August 1993, which was the first official use of the completed East Stand, and I had the honour of working on the East Stand turnstiles. When the gates opened you took a ticket stub or a season ticket coupon from each approaching fan and activated the turnstile via a foot pedal; simple. The key was ensuring the number of tickets you had exactly matched the number of rotations the turnstile had made, which became increasingly difficult as kick-off approached and beery fans, sloshing trays of mushy peas on your counter as they restlessly barged the immovable turnstile before realising they needed to produce a ticket, became more frequent.

The weather was a constant source of irritation, stood as you were in a bleak and amenity-free brick cubby hole with the wind and rain whistling in from outside and within five minutes of opening for most matches, I was physically unable to write as the freezing conditions sent my digits an ugly shade of blue and purple.

Gates were closed at approximately five minutes after kick-off unless you had drawn the short straw of having the half-time gate, which, as it says on the tin, was one gate from each section in the ground which remained open to allow for the stragglers. On the occasions where I had the half-time gate I was frequently presented with cash bribes to allow ticketless people in. I recall a Christmas game against QPR in 1993 when I worked on the Kop gates and had to endure a barrage of people offering me cash to expedite their entry, including many a sob story as to why certain fans couldn't afford full-price tickets. There was never a steward or policeman within eyesight when I needed one and while I was sympathetic to every plight put forward to me, the financial gain was not worth the risk. With the Kop being all-standing at the time there were no allocated seats to prompt their detection and lead the sorry tale back to me. Therefore potentially there were no repercussions had I let those fans in. However, being a morally upstanding individual and quite partial to the privilege of being paid to watch Leeds United thanks very much, I never succumbed despite much temptation and provocation.

This does though bring to mind the generations of my predecessors who had no doubt not held such honourable principles and had regularly swelled the crowd and taken an illicit income into the bargain. This might explain how inexplicably and dangerously packed the Kop and Lowfields were in some games, and there is every chance many fans were regulars in the art of going to a particular turnstile and taking advantage of an ongoing arrangement with an obliging gateman.

On busy days where the queue at the turnstile was constant, there was a certain rhythm to the practice which I very soon mastered: ticket – write number – say "thanks" – operate turnstile – ticket – write number – say "thanks"..... and at a time when Leeds were getting 40,000 crowds most weeks, the ceaseless flow of people through the turnstile up to and after kick-off began to evolve from a chaotic undertaking to a perfectly smooth and measured operation.

When gates were closed, whether at 3.05pm or at half-time, I dashed, ticket stubs in hand, to a small office beneath the South Stand where the stubs were tallied up against the system. I was never privy to the tallying process but it took a matter of minutes before someone poked their head through a window, gave you some cash and said you could go. If okay, you arrived breathless in a spare seat in the West Stand to watch the game at around 3.15pm, and at the time, a massive £13 richer.

From nervy beginnings I began to feel at home and found myself allocated the same gate on the West Stand most matches, which was pretty steady. I began

to get onside with the wily individuals, the 1970s-attired gatemen, the Revie-era veterans, who had made a lifelong career out of being a turnstile operator and who had possibly found it much more 'lucrative' than I had. I was able to casually watch from the safety of my caged dwelling one day as Newcastle fans fought a running battle with Leeds fans in the West Stand car park. I began to know which gates had a dodgy pedal and skilfully managed to swap with more wet-behind-the-ears colleagues. I avoided the gates where the wooden desk wasn't screwed down properly so you couldn't write on your tickets. I even brought my own money bags so the ticket stubs didn't get blown all over at 2.55pm and I'd have to start counting them again, thus missing Gary McAllister's inevitable third minute 25-yarder. I was the young buck of the turnstile operating crew; the self-assured hipster with his foot, quite literally, on the pedal.

Alas by the end of the 1994/95 season I could afford to get a season ticket, and I have ever since. My turnstile operating career was over; I was a fan again. Just a regular fan back on the outside, back with my usual pre-match rituals, back to seeing the lads walk out of the tunnel. Back to not missing goals in the first 15 minutes of games and experiencing the strange paradox of obviously wanting Leeds to score, but cursing at the thunderous sound of the celebrations under the stand because I had missed the goal.

Now we have charmless 'season cards' that are activated for cup games and bar codes on paper tickets which trigger the unmanned turnstile; a hassle-free advancement, but sadly, a backward step for those who like to collect tickets as souvenirs, and a mortal blow to the humble turnstile operator.

An early version of the computerised counting system for the turnstiles at Elland Road.

U2

Regular events at Elland Road are more likely to prompt a refrain of 'Saturday, Bloody Saturday' but on one hot and steamy day in 1987 the call was quite different. The ground has appeared to drop lucky with its staging of major rock concerts and the U2 gig on Wednesday 1st July 1987 is possibly the most high profile of the lot.

In that surly and bad tempered summer, Leeds United fans were still coming to terms with the twin hammerhead blows of the shattering Play-Off Final Replay capitulation to Charlton and the FA Cup Semi-Final defeat to Coventry weeks prior to that. Contemplating another season in the Second Division was something that required a welcome and sizeable distraction, and for some that came along in the form of the country's biggest band of the time.

U2's album *The Joshua Tree* had finally propelled the Irish group to a global level and while they had been a 'stadium' band for some time, it was after the world tour supporting this album that even venues such as Elland Road were too small for them. Indeed their next two visits to Leeds in 1993 and 1997 were to 90,000 crowds across the city at Roundhay Park. The Elland Road gig came during the second leg of three of their 'Joshua Tree' world tour. The band mesmerised the 30,000 fans with a typically triumphant performance during which Bono, somewhat sycophantically, declared himself a Leeds United fan.

With the stage again erected in front of the South Stand the gates to the stadium opened at 2.00pm, with the first support act starting at 4.00pm. Given their frequent public spats with U2, The Fall were a curious choice as the opening support act and were not well-received by the famously loyal U2 fans.

Andy Peterson has a particularly vivid memory of the hostility shown towards the exalted but famously cantankerous Manchester band: "The tap on my shoulder was purposeful enough to be in shove territory; my attention gained I turned round to find a posse of red faced, beery Lancastrians, dumbstruck by my appreciation for The Fall. The Mancunian pugilists were a late addition to the supporting bill for U2 at Elland Road after The Chameleons pulled out, a decision which, going by the dozens of plastic bottles filled with piss being thrown stage-ward, the crowd were disappointed with.

"Do yew laaak these?' I was asked by a lad who looked like he boxed draymen for a living. 'Yes,' I responded holding, with reservations, to an honesty is the best policy erm..policy. 'Ah think they're shiiite' came the response. I decided I'd catch the rest of the show from the back of the Kop."

Following The Fall were Leeds goth band The Mission, who couldn't fail in the circumstances. Leeds fan Darren Clark also took in the U2 gig and remembers the day fondly: "This pre-dated the health and safety jackboot, so was probably far more enjoyable and raucous than perhaps the recent concerts at the ground. The atmosphere was tremendous, this was my first stadium gig and I soaked it up. Support acts The Fall (bottled off) and the Pretenders were good but in between them were The Mission, what a fantastic surprise for me personally. I'd bought a Joshua Tree Tour 87 t-shirt and slipped it on over my Mission t-shirt, but soon whipped it off again when Wayne and the lads came on. (The Mission singer) Wayne Hussey always wore a wide brimmed hat but had dispensed with it due to it being a bit breezy outdoors. He made reference to it as he came on (I have a bootleg recording of The Mission's set) and here's the best bit – he also said, and I quote verbatim: 'Elland Road has never seen so many people, and it never will again.' He also sang 'With a S and a U and a P,E,R, with an L and an E and an E,D,S. U,N,I and a T,E,D. Super Leeds United FC lalalalalalalalala....' which was picked up by a large section of the crowd; a top moment, and he's a Liverpool fan!"

The Pretenders were the final act before U2 hit the stage at approximately 8.30pm. U2's set comprised numerous snippets of cover versions, such as 'Stand By Me', 'C'mon Everybody', 'Exodus', 'Gloria', 'Break On Through', 'Norwegian Wood', 'Walk On The Wild Side', 'Ruby Tuesday', 'Sympathy For The Devil', 'Shine Like Stars' and 'Love Will Tear Us Apart'. These were cleverly interspersed at the end of classic U2 tracks such as 'Sunday, Bloody Sunday', 'New Year's Day', 'Pride (in the name of love)', 'I Still Haven't Found What I'm Looking For', 'With Or Without You' and '40'.

Like other bands that have played at the ground the identity and context of the setting couldn't be ignored and inevitably it was referenced in the set. Clearly it was not 'just another gig'. Sadly history records that U2 did not fully embrace the nature of their surroundings as Darren also recalls: "As much as I'd have loved Bono to have brought Shez, Baird and Batts on to harmonise on 'Where The Streets Have No Name', my memory doesn't recollect it."

Despite the gig's classic status among U2 aficionados and in contrast to the other gigs at Elland Road, there are no official or even bootleg recordings of the show and very little footage. It has been discussed on U2 fan websites that the concert was recorded for future broadcast, but no evidence of this appears to exist.

UNDERPASS

Win, lose or draw, for many fans the match day experience is as much about the journey to and from the ground; the anticipation, the buzz of conversation and the pre-match rituals. The 90 minutes itself is often incidental and long forgotten. But the sense of routine is the one constant that evolves into a precious thing that a fan is loath to disrupt.

For any supporter walking down Lowfields Road from the direction of Gelderd Road it is a physical necessity for you to access Elland Road via the underpass

A gateway to the stars or a road to nowhere? The underpass beneath the M621 leading to Elland Road.

beneath the M621. Many football grounds carry an aspect or feature that adds to the atmosphere or the aura of intimidation as you approach them, and for Elland Road the short subway that traverses the divorced segments of Lowfields Road must be it. Of course, prior to 1973 fans had been able to walk the long stretch of Lowfields Road uninterrupted, but the construction of the M621 led to the complete alteration of the characteristics surrounding the football ground. This included the accommodating provision of an underpass to allow fans to walk underneath the motorway and continue towards their place of worship.

The underpass is about six metres wide and only 20 metres in length. Austere, grey, dark and threatening, it is a concrete letterbox lined with political propaganda, septic water leaks and graffiti, another brutalist postcard from 1970s Leeds. Fetid and unsightly, but it's ours. The walls are tiled in a welcoming mosaic of gold, blue and white, and the staggered design creates a striking image and acts as a reminder that the underpass exists for one reason and one reason only.

Over the years the underpass has become a focal point for merchandise sellers. As you approach there are stalls selling scarves, t-shirts and badges, and more recently art prints of hand-drawn player caricatures. On the external end as you head towards the ground is usually Michael or Rob, the cheerful but weathered

The Square Ball fanzine sellers, now enjoying new landscaped surroundings after the Park & Ride extension in the summer of 2020.

What is most notable about the underpass, and what gives it an unlikely but comforting warmth on a match day, is the echoed hubbub it generates when you walk under it, along with the other fans hurriedly approaching the ground. It is the head-in-a-fish-tank moment. Whatever your pre-match routine, the moment you head beneath the underpass you are hit with the deep, busy murmur of conversation. It is impossible to pick out one discourse from another, even the one you were involved in a few seconds ago, and you are thrust headlong into the pre-match atmosphere for the first time that afternoon. From then on you are in the zone, you emerge energised, you are at the ground and anything can happen.

Whatever your age, whatever the weather, whatever the team's fortunes, after the match the vibration of chatter that reverberates around the underpass is cranked up ten-fold as everyone scuttles away from the ground together; quick pint, home for tea then maybe off out. Lots to discuss regardless of the result, the hum of dialogue, rage to dissipate, a force, if harnessed, to propel Leeds United skywards. You catch snippets of a thousand post-match dissections, but the event becomes an afterthought as we disperse into the night.

UNDERSOIL HEATING

In recent seasons the Elland Road pitch has come full circle in receiving much praise for its durable condition in testing circumstances. Apparently the pitch is about 20 years overdue being replaced, and the drainage problems on the West Stand side render its consistently immaculate state – at least to the layman – something of a miracle. Back in the Leeds City days complaints about the state of the pitch were frequent and threatened to compromise the credibility of the club as a professional outfit. Even during the Revie era the pitch never received a huge amount of care and attention, but had at least evolved from being described as a 'pudding' of a pitch in the early 1900s to some sort of dry flan by the 1960s.

Things did improve, but council ownership and multiple usage in the 1980s, added to drainage issues and a minimal maintenance outlay, meant the pitch gradually deteriorated from being one of the best in the league in the late 1970s to one of the worst ten years later.

It is true that mind-blowing techniques in drainage and grass cultivation have developed to assist the club in recent years; indeed experts from Bingley Sports Turf Research Institute were drafted in to advise as early as the late 1960s. But the greatest single factor that assists the club in staging matches throughout the year is the undersoil heating system.

Never one to undervalue the key details throughout the club that contributed to success, the undersoil heating system was first installed in 1971, at the behest of Don Revie, and effectively the same system is still in place in 2021. The system consisted of 59 miles of piping, but this was upgraded in 1988 and it now consists of only 22 miles of piping. Naturally the system is very expensive to run, but it has paid for itself many times over in terms of the club staging games when others couldn't. Though it does cause the detriment of drying out the pitch, which contributes to the often dusty and lifeless pitch condition you get in spring, before the grass really starts growing again.

For the initial installation in 1971 electricity cables were planted just 14 inches below the surface of the pitch, which afterwards also received a major facelift. These 14 inches of soil were taken away and replaced by new drains covered with six inches of graded clinker, an inch of fine ash covered by two inches of sand, and finally five inches of new soil. Doesn't sound very seductive or desirable but soon after, Elland Road was regarded as having one of the finest surfaces in the country.

About the concept of undersoil heating, Dave Cocker recalls the absolute necessity of installing it: "That had

This and the image above may look like John Reynolds' "roll it flat and get on with it" mantra gone badly wrong, but are in fact pre-season maintenance work on the undersoil heating system.

In the mid-1960s before undersoil heating, more primitive methods were used to ensure a game went on; here braziers, straw and as many pairs of hands as possible worked through the night.

to happen," he says. "You couldn't risk a situation, with the amount of games we were playing, of having half a dozen league games called off. You saw what we were doing, we used to go down there on a Saturday and Don would be down there on a morning. The pitch would be covered in straw but the straw's then got to come off for the referee to inspect the entire pitch. So the problem then is, if the ref wants to inspect the pitch at say ten o'clock then the pitch is left exposed for another five hours before kick-off, so we used oil drums and coke braziers to heat the pitch. All the players would be down there, me Dad, Don, everybody would be helping to get that game on. It was important because we knew we could win it, we'd gain points on everyone else because all the other games were off and also we're not going to get fixture backlogs at the end of the season. So it was always imperative to get the games on."

The same kind of hands-on approach is prevalent today, but more to the streets approaching the ground and clearing snow from the 'public areas'. In the 1960s the club and society in general cared very little for how fans would get to the game and indeed for the conditions in which they watched it. The health of the pitch was the sole concern. In the modern era it has been known for a game to be postponed when the pitch is perfectly playable but it is not safe for fans to get to the game. That has yet to happen at Elland Road, however.

Of course today most professional clubs have an undersoil heating facility, but the timing of using it in terms of being aware of forthcoming inclement

conditions is key to ensuring a match can go ahead. An undersoil heating system can't, for example, shift thick ice a couple of hours before kick-off, nor can it tackle five inches of snowfall. But if a groundsman is anticipating a cold snap he is well-advised to stick the system on overnight for two or three days before a fixture, making use of programmable timers to adjust the settings at key times and praying for no malfunctions. Groundsmen at many clubs can now operate modern undersoil heating systems from their front room, using a laptop and a timer system. Current groundsman Kiel Barrett informs me that his counterpart at Old Trafford has a camera fixed on the pitch that he can monitor from home, and operate the sprinklers and undersoil heating accordingly while he watches *EastEnders*; not so at Elland Road.

The now nearly 50-year-old undersoil heating system is operated simply by a manual switch underneath the South Stand. So the onus is very much on Kiel Barrett to keep an eye on the weather and remember to switch the system on before he goes home at night, pushing all thoughts of his impending sausage and mash to one side.

Soon after the undersoil heating was first installed in 1971 sprinkler systems were also implemented to help water the pitch. At first they were just on the sides of the pitch along the touchlines, but eventually sprinkler heads were laid across the middle of the pitch. Stephen Reynolds remembers the sprinkler systems that his dad helped install: "I remember the original sprinklers being put in on the sides, but they never had them on the pitch and my Dad used to have to drag these massive triangular things

A new sprinkler system is installed in the early 1970s.

on to the pitch to water it. It was a massive construction like a snake and every so often it used to get away and you couldn't control it, it was dangerous really flapping about, and you had to run on and wrestle it. It was really hard work, but I know when they re-did the pitch quite recently they put pop-up sprinklers in the middle of the pitch. They've had them round the outside for a long time, but now they're in the middle too.

"There have been a couple of problems with the sprinkler systems that I remember," Stephen continues. "There was that time in 1996 (during an icy cold evening game against Southampton) when the sprinkler system went off in the middle of a game. All the crowd's wondering what the hell's gone off and one of the coaching staff had to sit on it with a bucket. My Dad was up at Thorp Arch by then, but there was another incident a few years earlier when he was still on duty down at Elland Road. The sprinkler went off during the game and my Dad jumped up and rushed off to the South Stand where the water system was to turn it off."

UNITED FISHERIES

Obviously we were put on this earth to eat fish 'n chips; not just Yorkshire folk or Leeds fans: all of us. As a fan that has been attending Elland Road since 1978 I have only ever known there to be a fish 'n chip shop in the last unit of the parade next to the Heath Estate, opposite the gates to the West Stand car park. As far back as I can remember this was called 'United Fisheries' but in 2006 it was bought by the chain 'Graveley's' that still run it today.

Fish 'n chip shops in modern times might well be fighting off the inescapable demon of takeaway emporiums of variable repute, but as an aspect of post-war Leeds the tradition of fish 'n chips on a Saturday followed by football at Elland Road was as familiar as rationing and TB jabs. There is evidence of the United Fisheries site being a fish 'n chip shop as far back as the 1940s as a local resident of the time, Edna Newton, recalls that the Price family owned and ran it after the war. This was still the case in 1956 as then owner, Arthur Price, was the startled neighbour who raised the alarm from his flat above the shop when the West Stand caught fire in the middle of the night. For the record, Edna also recalls that the Johnson family had the newsagent which still exists on the corner of the parade, then a Mrs Moorhouse ran a grocers shop and the Sellars family ran a barbers.

Ray Fell, a local resident since 1933, believes the unit on the end has always been a fish 'n chip shop, and he can't recall it being named anything other than United Fisheries until recently. Ray says: "I remember a guy called George ran it for many years from the 1960s, he always used to come into the Supporters' Club (the Social Club over the road from United Fisheries)

Forever a fish 'n chip shop: here in its current guise as Graveley's, with the omnipresent café next door.

because the shop was closed on a Saturday night, but he'd nip back over and fry us some fish and chips and we'd eat them on the way home."

It goes without saying that United Fisheries, as I will forever remember it, did a roaring trade on a match day and still does in its present guise. My main memory will always be the huge queues snaking out of the shop and along the pavement until they could just about catch a wayward Kevin Hird shot. Yet fans waited, with a patience that was difficult to fathom, for the pre-match ritual that they dared not forsake.

Inside United Fisheries, the décor not surprisingly had a Leeds United feel to it with white tiling with blue and yellow trim, and famous photos of Elland Road on the walls along with the current season's fixture list and results. Even the pickled eggs on the counter complemented the 'LUFC' colour scheme.

What is undeniable is that an Elland Road match day and the smell of fish 'n chips saturated in vinegar, how nature intended, is an intoxicating marriage that will stand the test of time, and while ever there are fans attending with fierce local roots you would think there is a value to having a fish 'n chip shop so close to the ground you could shout an order across from Wing Stand B.

UNITED GARAGE

While on the outside it may appear to be a modest and unobtrusive building of little history or significance, the property that once housed the 'United Garage' is linked to and has overseen many changes to the landscape of the Elland Road area.

Today the building, which stands opposite the entrance to Billy's Bar in the South Stand of the football ground, is home on the ground floor to Subway, the American chain of takeaway sandwiches. From February 1999 the building was utilised by Leeds United for their ill-fated and ill-advised financial services and travel agents operations, which closed in 2003. The building has also been a tanning salon in recent years.

However, the building itself was constructed in 1947 by the three brothers who later owned Castle Brothers Haulage. The upstairs windows in the building still follow the same pattern as they did in the original building, and the shape of the roof and the profile of the building are quite striking and visible on many photos as a backdrop to Leeds United match action from the Scratching Shed end, although the original building had huge chimney stacks on either side, which are no longer there.

The Castle brothers opened the business in 1947 as 'United Garage' and two of the brothers, Jack and Joe, lived in accommodation above the garage, while the third brother Sid owned and lived in the bungalow adjacent to the property, on land that now stands empty between Subway and the Old Peacock pub. The petrol pumps stood on a forecourt in front of the building which served as the shop, reception area and offices.

United Garage was a thriving independent enterprise and long before the giant oil companies built their own filling stations, the business had separate pumps dispensing a choice of 'Shell', 'National Benzole', 'BP' and 'Power'.

The business later became a major Vauxhall dealer, yet the Castle brothers sold the garage in 1960 and

The United Garage opposite the main gates of Elland Road open for business in the 1950s. The Castle brothers built and owned the business and two of them lived in the flat upstairs. The area where the pumps are is now the forecourt of Subway. And no, that isn't Ken Bates peering out of the top right window...

The short-lived travel agents and financial services organisations set up by Leeds United in the former United Garage premises in 1999.

built other premises, also called United Garage, on nearby Dewsbury Road and transferred the garage and Vauxhall dealer business there. At the same time they also opened a haulage business on land behind the old Spion Kop. The original garage building on Elland Road remained as a petrol station into the early 1990s when it was a Shell garage, though to many it was still referred to as 'United Garage'.

Before the bungalow was demolished between the United Garage and the Old Peacock pub, and at least until the mid-1970s, that land housed a company called 'AJC Fallas'. This was a coach company that ran coaches to Leeds United away games, among other things. The coaches were a distinctive pale blue and on some aerial photos they can be seen parked at all angles around the bungalow that stood quite isolated in the middle of what was effectively a coach park, and not a particularly big one either. Later, when the bungalow was gone, a transport company operated a bus and lorry depot on the site for many years but the land has been empty and unused now at least since the early 2000s.

Interestingly, in 2016 Jacob Adler, the Manchester-based businessman and recent owner of Elland Road stadium until selling it to Teak Commercial Limited, put forward a proposal for a mixed-use retail development on the vacant plot of land. This was a two-storey development which would include a children's nursery. Leeds United, along with other nearby businesses, objected to the proposal. And though the planning application was eventually granted council approval in March 2017, Andrea Radrizzani's company Greenfield

Investments PTE Ltd buying Elland Road in June of the same year, seemed to end any interest Adler held in any LS11-based development.

Programme Cabin proprietor Phil Beeton does recall a rather different operation that often took place on that patch of land adjacent to the United Garage: "I do remember in the '60s or '70s the local paper having a truck parked by the side of the Old Peacock car park. Inside was a very basic printing press. At the end of the game, 4.45-ish, the local *Green Sport* paper was sold from there but with a 'stop press' section where the football results were printed within minutes of the final whistle."

The United Garage building had gradually faded into inconspicuousness in recent years, until a deeply curious twist in November 2013, when former Leeds United owner and chairman Ken Bates opened a media company in the offices above Subway. This became, in February 2014, the offices and studios of 'Radio Yorkshire', an inelegantly conceived project to raise Yorkshire Radio from the ashes. Quite why he executed this in a small office above a takeaway bang opposite a football ground, when there was ample affordable office space in central Leeds begging for tenants, can only be eyed with intrigue by onlookers. Nevertheless it wasn't a huge success and Bates abruptly pulled the plug in 2017, with the station going online-only for a while before morphing into Proper Sport. 'Radio Yorkshire' signage still adorned the exterior of the building above Subway whilst it was empty, until late 2020 when it became occupied by an insurance brokers.

VOLKSWAGEN

The Volkswagen showroom on Elland Road is the centrepiece of the VW business in Leeds and is possibly the shiniest and most stylish new building in the area, the finest example of how the re-developed sector around the stadium was supposed to look when the motorway network began to change the landscape forever.

Situated next to the McDonalds drive-thru, the Volkswagen showroom is on the site of the old Beggars Hill Farm, which itself was situated behind the housing on the Hoxtons on one side and the Hartleys and Dobsons on the other. Prior to Volkswagen acquiring the land in 2004, the site had been the home to a series of different industrial units since the 1960s. Just adjacent to Volkswagen is Revie Road and the Revie Road Industrial Estate, which until the Kop was re-named and a statue erected on Lowfields Road was the singular and somewhat underwhelming permanent recognition for the club's greatest ever manager.

The fields behind the Volkswagen garage are still known to some as Beggars Hill and lead up to Holbeck Cemetery on Beeston Town Street, and to the roads known as the Nosters and Marleys which offer a spectacular view over Elland Road's expanses. In between them there is still a football pitch which is used for local Sunday League football and is roughly on the site of the old Beggars Hill Colliery, which was disused from the early 1900s.

Robert Endeacott, a local resident from the mid-1960s onwards, remembers the area as a haven for local kids playing during the holidays and refers to it by a local name derived from its mining past: "It was always known as the 'Quarry' that area," says Robert. "St Anthony's Church had a team that played on that pitch for quite some time, they were in the Red Triangle League. They were the inspiration for the amateur team in my *Dirty Leeds* novel, funnily enough. St Anthony's Church is at the top of Wesley Street on the corner of Old Lane.

"They filmed some of the *The Damned United* film on that pitch too, probably the more believable parts of it as well, thinking about it!"

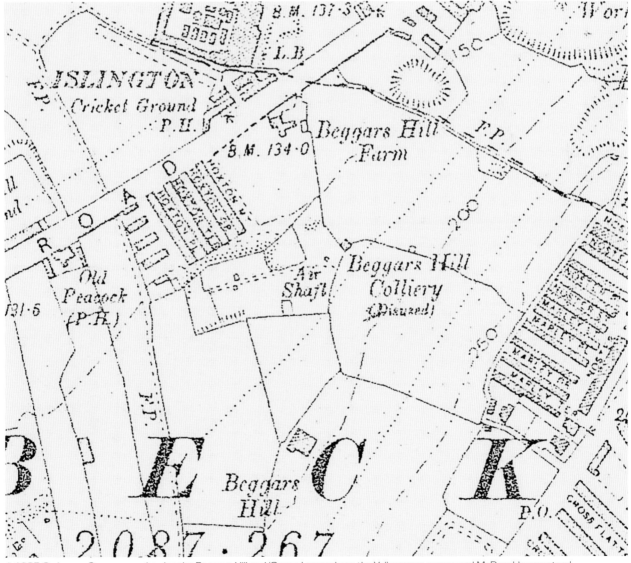

A 1905 Ordnance Survey map showing the Beggars Hill and 'Quarry' area where the Volkswagen garage and McDonalds now stand.

W

WAGGON & HORSES

Of all the pubs that surround or have surrounded Elland Road, the Waggon & Horses is probably the least celebrated and the least notable in terms of being attached to the identity of Leeds United. In fact to a visiting Leeds fan not necessarily familiar with the city or the wider area beyond the immediate vicinity of the ground, it is also the most inconspicuous pub, despite the fact that it has an 'Elland Road' address and until recently went by a completely different name with inherent football links: the United Bar.

With the pub perched on the ostracised length of the 'old' Elland Road that was savagely cut adrift by the M621, the Waggon & Horses undoubtedly suffered in its later years through disassociation, even though the ground itself remained only five minutes' walk away.

The Waggon & Horses appears in Leeds Directories as existing at 111 Elland Road as far back as 1866 when its licensee was a Mrs Ann Hartley. At this time of course Elland Road ran uninterrupted from the football ground, through Islington and Holbeck and towards Leeds city centre. The Waggon & Horses therefore formed part of a lively and convivial community in the early 20th century, with a barbers next door and a grocers, newsagents and chemist all within 15 yards serving a local population that packed into the rows and rows of terraced housing in all directions.

The estranged section of Elland Road hosts the current incarnation of the Waggon & Horses, known as the United Bar, but currently closed. Apart from the sign above the door, not much has changed.

Behind the Waggon & Horses in 1866 was the Recreation Ground, the original home of Holbeck Cricket and Rugby Club. This was developed for housing in the 1890s when Holbeck's teams moved along Elland Road to inherit the New Peacock Cricket Ground and the Old Peacock Ground respectively. While the Waggon & Horses may have lost some trade from this move in the short term, on balance they will have ultimately gained plenty as the Recreation Ground was immediately built upon with yet more housing and the developing Holbeck community expanded, including many flourishing businesses. Also immediately behind the pub in the early 1900s was a successful haulage business belonging to Thomas Spence, who had a fleet of vehicles serving the Joshua Tetley's Brewery in Leeds.

Throughout the 20th century, the Waggon & Horses became a popular pub for fans en route to Elland Road and right up until its eventual closure in 2009 it was a stop-off for fans coming from town or living locally, despite its somewhat bleak external appearance, which didn't improve greatly once inside the doors.

Robert Endeacott remembers visiting the pub but not necessarily on match days: "I went to school round there in the late 1970s and early '80s so it was one of my first ever pubs – doesn't say much for my dedication to academia, does it? It was a match day pub, but virtually all the pubs in Holbeck were stop-off points on a match day, the Spotted Cow, Bull's Head, Britannia, Peter Lorimer's pub The Commercial, even the Cambrian and the Crystal Palace on Sweet Street. They were all regular haunts on the route from town to Elland Road. Obviously then you're not far away from town with the Scarbrough, Spencers and the Prince of Wales."

Sadly many of these pubs are no longer with us. That is true of a number of other pubs in the vicinity of Elland Road and that is not just a consequence of the recent dire drop off in the pub trade. The Punch Bowl, Unicorn, General Abercrombie and Duke of York were all booming pubs in the Beeston area in the mid-1800s but disappeared at various stages of the early-to-mid-20th century. The same is true of the Old Dusty Miller and the Butcher's Inn, both on Elland Road. The Coach and Horses is also long gone and was a huge pub situated at the eastern extreme of the original Elland Road as it met Beeston Road, close to where the John Charles Centre for Sport (formerly South Leeds Sports Stadium) is today.

In later years the Waggon & Horses did gain a reputation for housing members of Leeds' infamous organised firm before and after matches, as did many pubs in the Holbeck area, serving as it did as a useful vantage point a safe distance from the ground, but near enough to monitor the comings and goings of away fans. Many running battles took place on Holbeck Moor just yards along from the pub, as fans headed back into town after the game, and inevitably the Waggon & Horses, and before they closed the Britannia, the Bull's

Head and the Spotted Cow, became convenient havens for those wishing to keep a low profile.

As with many pubs struggling in the 21st century the Waggon & Horses eventually bit the dust as Leeds United's fortunes took a similar nosedive, but it was only closed for around 12 months, emerging triumphantly in 2010 as the 'United Bar' after the building and business was bought outright privately. The pub remained much the same as it was, however, but with the short stretch of the 'old' Elland Road very different to how it used to be, somewhat choked of life, the pub only opened on match days and eventually closed altogether in 2018. The pub and its signage remains in place in the event that any plucky publican fancies having another go.

WELL

For years Leeds United conspiracy theorists have felt that something dark and sinister resides below Elland Road. Don Revie may have exorcised a gypsy's curse in 1971 but did he consider there may be demonological beings lurking beneath the sacred turf drawing all energy and positive vibes from the 11 men in white? My first knowledge of there being a well underneath the Elland Road pitch was during a stadium tour in the summer of 1981 when I was just ten years old. I recall walking down the side of the gloriously green pitch and noticing a dark square in the middle of the turf. Somebody must have asked the question and we were given an insight into the rare and extremely convenient water source that the club had inherited.

The well, situated in the north west corner of the pitch just outside the penalty area, is 70 feet deep and is left over from the pumping station that serviced the various mines in the area in the mid-1800s. An old chimney had remained on the site from the pumping station and this was demolished soon after the land became a sports venue in around 1878. The well is what used to be a water-filled shaft and was first capped at the end of the 1905/06 season by Leeds City staff when the pitch was switched around and the north end terraces, ie. what became the original Spion Kop, were being extended. It was then covered by progress and it was nigh on 60 years before anybody realised either that the well was there at all, or that it could be used to nourish the turf.

Building staff from Robert R. Roberts uncovered the well in 1968 when they were excavating in preparation for building the new Kop. Such was the vast area uncovered when removing the original Kop, with the new stand being built almost directly behind the old one, that the well was undetectable until the earth had been dug away. Among the hundreds of glass bottles, mining debris and other miscellaneous waste they found amongst the huge mound that the Kop had stood on, the builders discovered a direct link to the area's mining past and a useful free water source for the club. The

Paul Reaney peers down the well in the Elland Road pitch during some essential pre-season maintenance work in the early 1970s.

discovery caused a short delay in building the new Kop as Roberts were then employed to make the well safe, and upon the necessary water testing it was also made usable for the ground staff.

The pitch has been tended around the well ever since and it has been retained and used regularly, although in the last decade or so it has only been used in emergencies during the summer months upon a water shortage, when the well has been used to serve the pitch sprinklers. Kiel Barrett confirms that the club no longer use the well at all, although it is still operational and an available source: "When we were pumping the water out into the tanks it was too cold to go on the grass, and so the grass wouldn't grow and the seed wouldn't germinate. Also I'm told they used to get mushrooms coming through on the pitch using that water. We've still got four storage tanks under the South Stand where they used to keep it, but we don't use it now."

As a natural water source the club requires an abstraction licence from the Environment Agency in order to use the water. When it was being used most regularly in the 1970s and 1980s the well used to be accessed via a manhole cover which was barely detectable on the pitch itself. The head of the well had a ladder attached to the wall enabling access if required, though in general, all that happened on the occasions that an additional water source was required, was that a section of pipework was attached to the pumps which fed the water out from the bottom of the well. Now there is no manhole cover and the well head is not accessible, but the pumps are, as Kiel Barrett explains: "You would have to dig a square of the pitch away to get to it. But just at the side of the pitch is a cover where you can just turn the pump on."

The first time the well was used to water the pitch in the early 1970s, the grass actually turned black because the water was too cold. After that, when the water was to be used, it was treated via a pump filtration system before it touched the pitch. Stephen Reynolds also confirms that his dad John had the water from the well tested at one point and it was actually drinkable.

John Reynolds' widow, Maureen, recalls some occasions when the well was used: "During the very hot summer of 1976 John worked nights for ten weeks watering the pitch, because there was a hosepipe ban. He said 'we've got our own well, I can use the water from that'. Which he did, but it was also supplemented, shall we say, by town water. So if you flew over Leeds in 1976, every bit of grass was parched except one bit of green at Elland Road. He used to sleep down in his store until the morning."

There is a second well underneath the South Stand in the eastern corner, also left over from the old pumping station in the 1800s, but this has never been used and certainly can't be now. Stephen Reynolds recalls: "There is a well under the South Stand but they never found it. It was on the pitch originally, but when they demolished the Scratching Shed and built the South Stand it was covered up. It's down in the south east corner somewhere, but nobody has ever found it. They never used it and probably years ago they didn't even know it was there. It must be near the front somewhere because it was on the pitch originally, but then they moved the pitch when the South Stand was built."

BEHIND THE SCENES

15

United have had a new automatic sprinkler system installed at Elland Road which will help the pitch become the equal of any in the country.

The system, put in by Leeds City Council during July, is the second major development in quick succession following the new undersoil heating scheme of 12 months ago.

It consists of 14 sprinkler heads — 10 along the verges of the touchlines and four down the centre of the pitch.

Head groundsman John Reynolds said: "It is a case of Elland Road coming up to date and we will be able to water throughout the summer if required and keep the playing surface lush and healthy.

"It was not installed until the second week of July and took 10 days so we will have to wait a little to get the benefits as our preparations for this season were already well advanced.

"But by the third match of the season I would say things will be looking A1 from a playing surface point of view.

"We have seen setbacks with the main pitch with the weather being so hot and temperatures in the 80s for three-quarters of the summer.

"And with local Cup Finals played here until the middle of May and Anderlecht the visitors before the end of July we have been under pressure to get the pitches going and you cannot always work miracles.

"There is little time for good grass growth but all things considered the pitch is in good condition.

"And with the lads hoping for promotion and needing a reasonable pitch to play on, the ground staff are willing to sacrifice a little for the sake of the club."

Reynolds added: "Because it has been so hot during the day we have been watering in the evenings so the moisture is kept on the pitch at night.

"And there is also an automatic clock on the sprinklers set for approximately 2am so you could say that while the rest of the city sleeps, work continues at Elland Road.

"Even if there is a water shortage there will be no problem because of the well on the ground which can be utilised for the sprinklers.

"It is part of a pumping system

from the Beeston mine going back to the late 1800s and early 1900s before Elland Road was ever heard of as a football area.

"The main sufferers this summer have been the adjoining training pitches which had a tremendous baking in the sun.

"Howard Wilkinson did us a favour by training at Leeds University and we are confident that by the autumn the training area will be back in good nick."

The pitch will again double up as a Rugby League ground for Hunslet and in October will be the venue for the Second Test match between England and New Zealand.

The undersoil heating system has been a great success with the 22 miles of pipes ensuring matches can go ahead even at temperatures of minus five degrees.

John Reynolds Leeds United groundsman

An article in the match day programme from the 1989/90 season showing groundsman John Reynolds stood in the head of the well situated in the north west corner of the pitch.

WEST STAND

Dizzied but stubborn and unflinching, the West Stand has been a constant amid an ever-changing landscape at Elland Road, not just physically but also in terms of the size and ambitions of the club itself. Almost acting as a bridge between the old and the new, the West Stand is like Yoda: the wise and trusted senior figure that the club will forever turn to in uncertain times. While the rest of the ground and the club has dalliances with progression, modernist design, and philosophies based on extending its boundaries, the West Stand remains as a dogged and unwavering emblem of leaner times, when the club expected, and had literally won, nothing and in football terms barely registered on the map.

Still, believe it or not, there was a time when it wasn't there. And something else was. The original West Stand was a grand construction at the time of its opening in November 1906. With a 4,000 seated capacity and some standing capacity in front, it was much shorter in length than its 1957-built replacement, despite having a running track underneath it, which, prior to buying and developing the Fullerton Park land, was the club's only training facility. Opened officially before a game against Chelsea on 17th November 1906, the stand was considered a significant landmark in the club's formative history and was heralded as a signal of intent. In that day's edition, the *Yorkshire Evening Post* reported that the stand "...was opened this afternoon by the Lord Mayor of Leeds (Mr Joseph Hepworth), in the presence of a large company. A handsome gold key, bearing the arms of the city in enamel, with which to open the stand, was presented to his Lordship by Mr Sam Kirk. Mr Norris Hepworth, the chairman of the directors, presided."

On the following Monday, 19th November 1906, the *Leeds Mercury* stated that the stand was "... 93 yards long and six yards wide. Over half a mile of steel has been used in the formation of the girders, and there are over 2,000 yards of corrugated sheeting in the roof. Running underneath the stand its entire length is a training track for the use of the players in wet weather. There are also dressing rooms and officials' rooms,

Leeds City players training behind the original West Stand in 1914.

A distant shot of the first West Stand from 1930, showing the double-barrelled roof which matched that of the Scratching Shed.

while at the Elland Road end of the stand a motor garage has been provided, so that the management are quite up to date."

The West Stand's construction allowed Leeds to switch the pitch orientation, with the new stand becoming the focal point of the club, taking over from the stand built a year earlier on the Elland Road side. As time went on, the West Stand stood as a significant monument, and as now, the stand attracted the more genteel and affluent sections of the Leeds United crowd. You could even buy a cushion for your seat for just 2d (roughly 1 new pence).

A distinctive double-barrel-shaped roof was a feature of the original West Stand, which was later mimicked by the installation of the Scratching Shed roof on the south side. In 1906, upon its initial construction, only the top half of the stand was roofed by one barrel, with the second barrel being added to cover the bottom half of the stand in the 1920s, most likely at the same time as the identical Scratching Shed roof was built. However, numerous pillars supporting the wooden construction of the original West Stand created a claustrophobic atmosphere within the cramped facility. Another stark feature of this first West Stand were the advertisements emblazoned on the back of its long exterior, presumably for the benefit of the passing trains. One of the most famous bore the words "Dewar's White Label Whiskey" in huge white letters which covered half the stand for many years.

Time passed with little change and Leeds fan John Cave has distinctive memories of the early-to-mid-1950s when John Charles was just emerging and Leeds United, as a club, were stuck in a rut of seemingly no outward ambition: "As small boys we never noticed the generally decrepit state that Elland Road was in in the 1950s – the place had an almost cathedral-like place in our minds, to the extent that the rusted corrugated iron fences, old brickwork and a lack of paint anywhere totally passed us by. The reality being, however, that no development or updating of facilities had been undertaken since the 1920s."

That sense of stasis and lack of forward thinking was typical of many similar football clubs around World War II when basic priorities lay elsewhere. The regressive and neglected state of Elland Road was due to no real post-war aspirations; there was no figurehead

A shot from the car park of the early stages of construction of the new West Stand in 1957.

An early construction shot of the 1957-built West Stand, showing the Fullerton Park training pitches and the greyhound stadium in the distance.

with vision and lofty ambition and no confidence that the club could sustain itself to merit spending money on Elland Road, other than the innovative but largely unsuccessful Major Frank Buckley purchasing the land for the Fullerton Park training pitches. Even when John Charles arrived on the scene it took unforeseen circumstances to trigger a shift in ground development out of sheer necessity.

The fire of 1956 signalled the end of the original West Stand and unwittingly kick-started a spluttering surge of progress. Only a skeleton of the old stand was left after the fire, showing how little of it was constructed out of steel. It was very clear from an early point that little could be salvaged, including none of the club's records and memorabilia of the time.

A public appeal launched by the Lord Mayor of Leeds, Alderman T. A. Jessop, raised £60,000 towards the £180,000 cost of the new West Stand and while construction went ahead, the shortfall in payment wasn't raised until the end of that season when the club could no longer resist the advances of other clubs towards their prized asset, John Charles. It was therefore with a hint of sadness and little fanfare that the new West Stand was eventually unveiled in time for the beginning of the next season, 1957/58. While a new stand was great, Leeds, tentative and unwitting, were starting life without John Charles, their pivotal, exemplar force, and the stand will forever be synonymous with that epoch-defining transfer.

The design of the new West Stand was carried out by Leeds architects Braithwaite and Jackman, and was specifically based on a reinforced concrete and steel-framed structure to prevent further risk of fire. It was a propped cantilever stand, similar in design to the Main Stand at Birmingham City's St Andrew's, which also still exists today. The Elland Road version had a roof that extended out further, however, adding more weight

to the opinion that this was a barrier-breaking design for its time, particularly given that someone saw fit to add a resplendent and dignified façade that perhaps aggrandised the club's status at the time. Various local contractors were employed to build the stand, the main builders being Robert R. Roberts Ltd (the company owned by soon-to-be Leeds United director, Bob Roberts). The concreting was done by Holst & Co Ltd, the steelwork by Dunlop & Rankin and the painting and guttering by Marsh, Jones and Cribb Ltd, who had premises on nearby Beeston Road.

Painting contractors from Marsh, Jones & Cribb smile for the cameras during the 1957 West Stand construction. Also visible here is the top right hand corner of the fenced-off Boys' Pen behind the goal and the much shallower angle of the old Gelderd End Kop.

Like a weathered old actress staring wistfully at photos of her
electrifying heyday, this 1957 architect's illustration is the West Stand
in its Mary Quant pencil skirt and Vidal Sassoon pixie bob pomp.

When it officially opened, before a 2-1 victory over
Leicester City on 31st August 1957, the stand had a
capacity of 4,000 seats along the length of the back of
the stand, with room for 6,000 standing fans in what
became known as the 'Paddock' along the front of the
stand. There were also media facilities on the gantry
and of course the directors' box, dressing rooms, a
gymnasium and offices. Externally, various annex store
rooms and turnstile blocks were added on to the back
of the stand that extended out into the car park. There
was even a car port built into the stand to the left of
the façade with two car spaces, from which various
managers would later conspicuously appear before
facing a frenzy of reporters.

In a bid to raise income to cover the expenditure on
the stand, at least the shortfall from the John Charles
transfer and the public appeal that the club had to
cover, admission prices to the new stand were raised
accordingly, to 7/6 for seating and 5/6 for standing.
The West Stand was still seen as the domain of the
more wealthy supporters, particularly so as it was
now a much more palatial and imposing structure, and
therefore not much fuss was made by the general fan
as ticket prices were unaltered elsewhere.

Over time the West Stand has developed a more
stately reputation as, for many years, it housed the
administrative core of the club and was the epicentre
of all club activity. With it being a simple steel structure
with supporting girders, the brick walls beneath can
be knocked through and adapted at will. Certainly the
club has never been shy of converting and re-shaping
the areas beneath the stand for their changing needs,
which have been many.

For several years all the corporate entertaining
done by the club, in the 100 Club and other suites that
came and went, was in the West Stand. Bill Fotherby
recalls the club's first tentative steps into corporate
entertaining, which naturally he instigated, in the area

that recently housed 'Howard's Way' and 'Howard's
Restaurant': "One of the first projects I did was in
the West Stand as you walked in the car park on the
right hand side, called the 'Executive Suite'. A season
ticket at that time (the suite opened in April 1982) was
£65, and I took this area, which I called the 'yuppies'
area, where people are wanting to make a bet, etc,
and under the stand I had this area and I got Peter
Gilman from GMI in to build it, and to the chairman I
suggested I could get season tickets for this area for
£250 for a member. He said, 'You're joking, you're
joking, you'll never get that'. I said, 'Listen, I know the
layout of a football ground and I know the supporters.
I know what we can do.' Cart blanche, I had: 'OK Bill,
off you go.' I got the builder in January and it cost me
£64,000 to do it all out and I had to pay in September.
The seating was behind the 100 Club, so they had
special seats there. I made the membership £250
and I filled it... filled it. Paid for it, and that was the first
job where the board said to me 'Mr Fotherby, you go
ahead and do what you feel is the right thing for Leeds
United.' That was the beginning."

With rapid progression around it the stand soon
dated as Leeds United's post-Revie fortunes dipped.
A rather feeble attempt to add some much-needed
identity to the stand came in 1989 when the club spelt
out the words 'LEEDS UNITED AFC' in white seats, as
was the emerging fashion at several other clubs at
the time. Unfortunately, the design of the upper and
lower sections was such that only the few upper rows
of seats could be used, and rather than creating an
impressive backdrop to the annual team photo we

Builders dig out the concrete terracing of the 1906-built West Stand
in an attempt to clear the site for the new construction in 1957.

were left with an uninspiring and ham-fisted insignia that from a position only a couple of yards left or right of square-on, was barely legible. The moving of the directors' box and press areas soon signalled the end of a fairly graceless attempt at club identity, and it was gone by the mid-2000s.

Today the part-brick walls at the back of the stand, the painted drainpipes, the tarnished steel rafters and the dull, grey corroding roof all combine to frame the West Stand as a relic of a past age. It has stood still whilst the ground has developed around it, save for the straight extension added to it when the North West Corner Stand was built in 1970. Elsewhere, all sides and corners of the ground have changed and, furthermore, the building of the South Stand has meant that part of it doesn't even face the pitch anymore. For this reason, the south end of the West Stand has been somewhat 'out on a limb' since 1974. Now it is a discarded area with little real identity, like an overflow car park that is always dark, usually empty and largely to be avoided. An appropriate spot for away fans you might say.

Numerous plans have been submitted to re-build the West Stand over the years, but evidently none have progressed to a realised stage. Bill Fotherby was central to one of these plans just after the 1992 title win but the team's fortunes dictated that it was at least one Wilko-era plan that never went ahead: "My plan was to put another tier of 10,000 on top," Bill begins. "Now the idea was, while the season was ongoing we would build the outside frame, which was in the West Stand car park, and put some of the

An aerial view of the 1957 West Stand construction.

floor in, during the close season put the roof on, so I've got the frame all done. The close season we do the infrastructure, bringing the floor out from the West Stand across to the new outside wall and so on. That was all ready to take the capacity up towards 60,000."

Another plan was submitted following the Caspian Group takeover of 1996 and incorporated the long-discussed Leeds Arena. The most recent plan was to accommodate the city's 'supercasino' within the West Stand, with a re-build and an extra tier being part of the very appealing package. Sadly, in May 2013 the licence was awarded to the Eastgate development in Leeds city centre.

The West Stand takes shape in 1957, but the concrete terraces of the Paddock are yet to be laid.

Clean brickwork, spotless windows and
soon to be structurally sound. The West
Stand as you've probably never seen it
before during its 1957 construction.

The familiar silhouette on the Elland Road landscape is almost complete in 1957.

In recent years the club has done much to cosmetically modernise the stand and its infrastructure without really altering the external perception of it, which by now is nigh on impossible. New executive suites have been installed, the LUTV studios were modernised but have now been moved out completely, the directors' box has been moved and the away fans' enclosure has been created. Facilities for fans below the stand have also been improved, but only a complete re-build will hide the fact that it is a stand from the 1950s, albeit given all the internal changes, there won't be much of that original structure left. In 2010 safety netting was erected underneath the roof after reports of small fragments of the construction falling on fans below during a game, a quite disturbing development and a more accurate reflection of the stand's status than the surface polish of adding a few new facilities. Consequently, in the summer of 2017 50% of the roof was re-cladded as part of an asbestos removal programme.

The West Stand has long since been the refuge of the more 'mature' Leeds supporters, and as such is not known for a particularly rousing atmosphere. That said, when it is full it reverberates like any other stand and the age of the construction, the confined space and the undecorated facilities offer a traditional feel to Elland Road that endear it to many fans, but is perhaps lost on the younger generation.

Reg French was a regular occupant of the West Stand from the time it was opened in 1957, and he recalls the friendly atmosphere which by and large has remained while the rest of Elland Road has undergone mood changes not necessarily for the better: "We stayed in the West Stand for a considerable number of years, and I've met people there I've known for all my working life. There was quite a rapport between people and you got to know them."

The fondness of fans for the West Stand is possibly best illustrated by the fact that fans still refer to it as the 'West Stand' rather than the 'John Charles Stand' as it was re-named in 2004. Still, every era of the modern game has seen Leeds players scoring iconic goals and celebrating famous wins with the same backdrop of faces. The shadow cast against the pitch by the sunlight has always been the same, and amongst vast transformation all around it, the West Stand remains as a reminder of humble beginnings, before Bielsa, before Wilkinson and before even Revie.

If the club ever gets carried away with ideas beyond its station, the West Stand is always there as a reminder that a glorious past is just that. Despite two relatively successful periods since the Revie era the club has still failed to improve upon the West Stand, as if rooted to a history it can't escape. Something tells you that, whatever fond memories we have of the West Stand and the series of eras it has provided a backdrop to, only its replacement with a stand of a more 21st century outlook will arrest the club from a seemingly terminal inferiority complex. Perhaps sensing that, the incumbent regime at Elland Road were quick to announce plans to build a new West Stand to cash in on bigger expectancy upon promotion to the Premier League in 2020, but not until they had consolidated their place in the top flight and the extra demand for capacity could be substantiated. So for the next few years, the inferiority complex remains.

That is simplistic of course, but few other clubs who have seen success of the calibre Leeds United are desperate to emulate still have stands built in or before 1957, and while nobody wants a flat-pack, plastic ground with no character, there will be little argument from most Leeds United fans if the West Stand does make way for a construction more befitting of the status we consider our club to hold.

WEST STAND PADDOCK

For the first ten years of its existence the West Stand was segregated into two clearly distinct sections of seating and terracing. The terracing became known as the 'paddock' and was a very popular part of the ground. It was the first and for many years the only area offering standing season tickets, afforded great views of the action and, unlike the pre-1968 Kop and the Lowfields terrace opposite, was completely under cover.

It was not until the summer of 1967 that the first section of the West Stand Paddock that extended from the Kop end to the tunnel was seated. One of the first games where the 'paddock seats' were available was the Inter-Cities Fairs Cup Final Second Leg against Dinamo Zagreb on 6th September, which despite drawing 0-0 Leeds lost the tie 2-0 on aggregate. The final had been held over from the previous season and Leeds felt this may affect the attendance, coming at the tail end of the traditional summer holiday season. Yet this didn't stop the board hiking ticket prices for the final and with an eventual crowd of 35,604, Leeds achieved their record gate receipts for the fixture of £20,177.

The increase in ticket prices was understandably not well-received by the Leeds fans, who were not used to having to partly fund their club's ambitions. Of particular concern was the admission cost for the remaining terraced section of the West Stand Paddock, as Phil Brown of the *Yorkshire Evening Post* commented: "One increased Elland Road price jarred me – the 10s (50p) for the paddock. Ten shillings to stand seems a bit grim even these days." This was justified by then chairman Harry Reynolds with the retort: "We trust the public will accept the normality of us putting up our prices this time, and will realise that any profit we make will go back into the club to help pay for not only its costly running as a leading side, but for the very large scale ground improvements we have been and are undertaking."

From 1967, therefore, the West Stand Paddock remained as only the short section of terracing from the tunnel to the Scratching Shed. A small area of terracing just next to the tunnel was sectioned off

by the club and this became an area housing an assortment of well-known faces and illustrious guests. As Dave Cocker recalls: "As you came down the tunnel there was a fenced off pen on the right. There's a photograph of me with Paul Reaney with a broken leg, and there's Gary Sprake and Terry Yorath stood with us, it was known as the 'Players' Pen', so any players that weren't playing actually stood in that pen. Some of the families stood in there too. You could only access it from the tunnel and there was a little wooden ladder that dropped down into the paddock and you were stood at almost pitch level."

In the summer of 1974 this final section of paddock terracing went, as explained in a match day programme for the game against Derby in April of the 1973/74 title-winning season: "More alterations will see the disappearance of the Standing Paddock in the West Stand. This area of the ground currently accommodates some 3,000-plus spectators, most of whom have standing season tickets. During the summer a thousand seats will be installed in the paddock, so making the whole of the West Stand seating only." Anyone with a basic grasp of mathematics could see that 2,000 season ticket holders would be uprooted by the move, and predictably a petition was arranged by disgruntled fans, albeit with no resulting impact whatsoever.

A year after the area was seated Leeds entertained Barcelona in the European Cup Semi-Final and Dave Cocker recalls watching the game in the 'Paddock seats', an area of which was still reserved for families, friends and guests of the players and coaches, basically in the same area as the previous 'Players' Pen'.

Dave remembers this occasion vividly as he had been stood in the dressing room area a few minutes earlier with Jimmy Johnstone (Celtic) and Mike Summerbee (Manchester City) as news broke that Leeds manager Jimmy Armfield had dropped Norman Hunter for the crucial game: "We were stood outside the laundry room," Dave begins, "outside the home dressing room. Billy (Bremner) came out of the dressing room going fucking berserk, he was fuming. Summerbee and Jimmy Johnstone were stood in there giving Jimmy Armfield dog's abuse for dropping Norman Hunter, because he didn't think Norman could handle the pace of Cruyff. But all the players were friendly then, Jinky (Jimmy Johnstone) was good mates with Billy and all the Scottish lads so they just came along to watch."

Forty-six years later and the West Stand remains the same. However, the lower section of seats is often still referred to as the 'paddock' seating by more long-in-the-tooth fans, perhaps triggering a quizzical raised eyebrow from a younger fan unaware that it used to be a standing terrace.

A paddock regular from the 1960s onwards was this man. Affectionately known by all as 'Scarf Man' for obvious reasons, it is to be hoped that someone knew his real name.

A 10,000 crowd gathers at Elland Road on 5th July 1941 to watch a military parade and a public address from foreign secretary Anthony Eden, the tallest of the four men stood on the platform.

WORLD WARS I AND II

World War I coincided with Leeds City's formative years as a football club, and by the time of World War II in 1939 Leeds United had still made little impact on the football world. Therefore Elland Road like most prominent buildings remained untouched, unloved and of little significance during the period of both wars, when words like 'building', 'development' and 'progress' were very much on the back burner country-wide.

Leeds City had successfully won re-election to the Football League at the end of the season 1911/12, and under new manager Herbert Chapman had seen their fortunes change dramatically for the better in the subsequent two seasons. But any ambitions of a promotion spot in the 1914/15 campaign were rendered futile upon the outbreak of World War I in August 1914.

While military service was not compulsory in the UK, the media put moral pressure on professional footballers to join the army, which many senior players did. However, with arrangements in place already for the new season and no precedent to work against, the Football League proceeded with the campaign in the face of public opinion. *The Yorkshire Evening Post* reported on 1st September 1914: "While many people think it would be a disgrace to this country to have thousands of able bodied players devoting themselves to the game, and hundreds of thousands of men watching them, when there is an urgent need for volunteers, others declare that, like other amusements, football will provide a much needed release for the large

numbers who must be left at home and serve to divert their attention."

Jimmy Speirs and Evelyn Lintott were perhaps the most high profile of the six players with Leeds City connections that died in the hostilities, with Lintott ultimately losing his life in the Battle of the Somme in 1916. The immediate effect of the war was that attendances plummeted to an average of 6,000 at Elland Road and the majority of the season was played out in meaningless fashion. There was very little enthusiasm for football as devastating numbers of war casualties were reported.

After the first game of the season at Elland Road, a 1-0 defeat to Fulham, local MPs and the Lord Mayor addressed the crowd on a recruitment drive. During the week the Leeds players underwent military drills at the ground by way of preparing for all eventualities, also submitting 5% of their wage to the War Fund. Local regiments also used the Elland Road pitch for army drilling and shooting practice.

In the event, Leeds lost their first four games of the season and struggled for any kind of form. Nobody could really blame the war effort because it affected each club equally, but the season petered out with no incentive of promotion as there was little prospect of competitive football the following season. Leeds finished 15th, with Billy McLeod topping the scoring charts for the ninth consecutive season with 18 league goals.

For football clubs the outlook was bleak in the face of the continuing hostilities. *The Yorkshire Evening*

Post reported on 20th April 1915: "The end of a very unsatisfactory football season will find practically every league club in the Football Association and the Northern Rugby League much worse off financially than it was at the beginning of the season."

Football was rightly lower on the agenda and the next four seasons were simply played out as regional leagues of little competitive nature, although, ironically, Leeds City fared very well. The players effectively became amateurs at this time as no wages were paid in the summer between May and July and during the new regional tournaments the players would only receive legitimate expenses, the practice which eventually proved to be the root cause of Leeds City's demise. Many players joined their manager, Herbert Chapman, in the munitions industry and appeared as 'guest' players for the teams local to where they lived, in order to avoid unnecessary travel and use of fuel.

As the war raged on, football continued to provide superfluous entertainment only. Leeds City actually won the Regional League in 1917/18, beating Stoke City 2-1 over two legs in a Play-Off Final to become the unofficial champions of England, though this achievement brought little fanfare and is barely recognised anywhere. From the two games Leeds were awarded a whopping £913 in gate receipts, something that would not have been budgeted for pre-season. Rather than spending the money on improving Elland Road's sparse facilities or their impoverished finances, in a gesture typical of the time, Leeds City donated the money to the National Footballers' War Fund. Thankfully, by May 1918 an end to the war was in sight.

World War I didn't end officially until November 1918, but by the start of the 1918/19 season Herbert Chapman was back in place as manager to re-build a fractured club. Circumstances intervened though and Leeds City's demise led to the brief absence of football of any kind at Elland Road.

In contrast to the 'Great War' of 1914–1918 the outbreak of the hostilities of World War II, officially on 1st September 1939, led to the almost immediate abandonment of the competitive Football League programme, something the League were criticised for not doing the first time around. This was perhaps just as well for Leeds United as they lay bottom of Division One at the time, having gained one point from three games, and had yet to score a goal. The last game of the abandoned league programme was a 1-0 defeat to Sheffield United at Elland Road in front of just 9,779 supporters; a clear indication that most people's minds were already elsewhere.

The same scenario then took hold as non-competitive regional leagues and knockout tournaments kept the players fit and entertained sparse crowds for six years. Leeds' crowds averaged around the 4,000 mark, although the last home game of the first season during the war, 1939/40, against Newcastle United drew a crowd to Elland Road officially recognised as just 200. Leeds United employed 'guest' players as City had before, but with more formal guidelines in place the club were thankfully more thorough in following procedure.

During World War II Elland Road itself was actually requisitioned by the British Army and the offices within the West Stand were used for administrative purposes, with it being an under-utilised local building of some stature. During this period of the war, therefore, Leeds United were effectively only allowed access to the stadium for two or three hours on a match day. This military use of Elland Road also led to a famous visit to the ground by foreign secretary Anthony Eden on 5th July 1941, to address a 10,000-strong crowd and watch a military parade. On the day only the Kop wasn't used for the visit which did much to boost flagging local morale.

Reg French was in his teens during the war and can remember his dad taking him to some of the regional league games. He recalls: "I can't remember specific games because a lot of them were effectively friendlies, they were meaningless. The crowds were much reduced and it was a strange atmosphere because I can remember the raids, and Leeds certainly got a couple, which meant people were a bit more reluctant to travel about unless they had to. It was a period of austerity and considerable anxiety, and people didn't have any routine so nobody went to Elland Road regularly. It was nice when you could go without that kind of threat, but if you could go it was a break from the tensions and made you forget it a little bit."

This time around the war had robbed Leeds United of several key players and the return of competitive football for the 1946/47 season did the club no favours. They had laboured alarmingly during the war years and sure enough, under manager Billy Hampson, were relegated in the first season of professional football after the war, having slumped to a dismal bottom-placed finish with just 18 points, which stood as a record low until Stoke City beat it in 1984/85.

Shortly after the end of World War II the Festival of Britain was organised by the Government, which was a national exhibition held throughout the UK in the summer of 1951. The main aim was to give Britons a feeling of recovery in the aftermath of the war and to promote the British contribution to science, technology, industrial design, architecture and the arts. In terms of revitalising Elland Road it was perfect timing. The dormant arena hosted two exhibition matches where Leeds played out a 2-2 draw with Rapid Vienna of Austria on 9th May 1951 before 18,000 fans, and five days later on the 14th May, they beat FC Haarlem of Holland 2-0 in front of 9,362 fans. 'Recovery' was the key word and there is no doubt that Elland Road post-war, after a period of convalescence, was about to finally arrive.

X

X-RATED

The Kop informing opposition fans or players that they were "going home in a St John's Ambulance" was perhaps as close to a concern over their welfare that a visitor to Elland Road was likely to get in the 1970s and '80s. For many years, particularly since the 1960s, Elland Road has held something of a fearsome reputation for visitors and been the scene of a series of gruesome and bloodthirsty encounters both on and off the pitch. In recent years, however, the atmosphere at games has been diluted by all-seater stadia, stewarding, family areas, ownership issues and the general standard of football, and so Elland Road has lost much of its venom and in many respects is no different to any other modern stadium. But while Leeds fans were robbed of the opportunity to roar home their heroes to promotion in 2020 due to the COVID-19 pandemic, the general consensus was that prior to games being played behind closed doors, much of the natural buoyancy and uplifting acoustics were back.

And in the media and with many older neutral fans, Elland Road still retains a gnarled status that it will never shake off regardless of the flat sterility that enveloped it through much of the 2010s. This reputation sees Elland Road and its occupants bearing devil's horns and a forked tail and is born from decades of incendiary football and non-football encounters, and with steam rising from a collective boiling kettle the lead was wilfully taken from the self-styled aura of Revie's great team.

While it is generally accepted that football was a sport fashioned in crude aesthetics in the 1960s and '70s, and tackling of a decidedly agricultural description was commonplace and acknowledged in jovial fashion as part and parcel of the game, when Leeds United used those tactics to their advantage they were widely condemned as cynical and calculating. Intimidation became an art form, of which Leeds were the vilified pioneers that everybody consciously imitated but wouldn't dare acknowledge. Perhaps it was the success that it helped to achieve, perhaps it was the railroading gang-mentality that was positively encouraged by Revie, or perhaps it was just the perceived arrogance with which Revie attempted to justify it? But while the likes of Ron 'Chopper' Harris, Tommy Smith and Dave Mackay are revered as endearing 'characters', honourable rogues who 'loved their mums', the unforgiven Leeds United remain despised and condemned.

There is no doubt that the outlawed stigma that Revie's side had gained was seized upon by the Elland Road faithful, and this was fostered to form a psychological bond that had many visiting teams beaten before they left the dressing room. But again, like Revie's players, was Elland Road any more intimidating than any other football arena in the 1960s and '70s? At a time when thousands of young men across the country found escape in squeezing onto crumbling and dangerously packed terraces week-in week-out,

when social and political unrest was rife across the nation, and when popular culture was challenging and confrontational, what made Elland Road a more unnerving, hate-filled amphitheatre than any other ground in the country?

The truth is it probably wasn't, but embedded in the Revie era there was an air of tribal kinship smothering Leeds United's unwelcoming abode that revelled in creating an uncomfortable experience for anybody daring to visit. The accompaniment to that was a Tetley's and Woodbine-infused period framed by mud, raised studs, sly grins and sliding tackles, yet glorious football; the antithesis to the music of the time, the fascinating glitz and showmanship of Bowie and T-Rex. Leeds United were anti-glamour, anti-popular and loving it, revelling more in the laddish pub rock and then the disorderly chaos and ungovernable mobocracy of punk and new wave that came later. Numerous incidents on the pitch during the Revie era captured the imagination of a crowd seemingly anxious to embrace a football culture of aggravation, altercation and devious, guileful combat. That spirit remains with many fans today, but was garnered from watching the tenacious duels fought by terriers such as Bobby Collins, Billy Bremner and Johnny Giles, not to mention Norman and Big Jack; one-on-one conflict where the ball was almost secondary and strong-arm tactics were a key psychological weapon. Once Leeds had earned the right to play they certainly played, but the skilful grace and audacious domination of the team is not remembered vividly in wider football circles. At Elland Road, the Leeds fans demanded the same fearsome spirit in the 1970s and 1980s and beyond, when sadly they didn't always have the personnel to deliver it. It is often mentioned that Leeds fans will accept a battler and an honest 100% breadwinner quicker than any other kind of player. Elegance and sheen doesn't sit well in LS11. We will put up with the limitations of a Vinnie Jones, a Robert Molenaar or an Andy Hughes, because they represent the attitude we would show on the pitch ourselves, if we had the chance. The cult hero, whatever that means because we can interpret it how we want, always has a 'welcome' mat at Elland Road.

Off the pitch, the Revie era also coincided with the nurturing of a more fearsome pack-mentality amongst football fans. Maybe the layout of the stands at Elland Road contributed to the daunting acoustics, with the South, Lowfields and Kop stands all in unison during the 1970s and '80s; three sides of the ground fused in vocal, hate-filled harmony. Whatever you think about the causes of the rise in football hooliganism, the facts are that Leeds fans revelled in that hostile prestige more than most, and the Elland Road atmosphere prickled with underlying malice that never needed much excuse to surface.

Crowd trouble at Elland Road wasn't necessarily a 1970s phenomenon, however, and incidents of crowd

MARCHING ALTOGETHER
NUMBER 3 april '89

THE NAZIS ARE STILL AMONG US

TIME TO GO....

An April 1989 edition of the *Marching Altogether* fanzine produced by the group Leeds Fans United Against Racism and Fascism, which did so much to educate and raise awareness in reducing racism at Elland Road in the late 1980s.

disorder can be traced back even to the Leeds City days when 'mud larking' was frequent, ie. the act of fans throwing mud from the desperately basic terraces and surrounding areas, at the referee and opposing players. Some hostilities went further than the more 'considerate' missile of mud, however. In the final game of Leeds City's first season in the Football League, 1905/06, they entertained who else but Manchester United. A 3-1 defeat didn't go down well with the 10,000-strong Elland Road faithful, although the trigger for the violence was thought to be the selection of a referee who had previously officiated a recent hot-tempered game between Bradford City and Manchester United. It was considered that the trouble was instigated by a mixture of Bradford fans with long memories and some Leeds sympathisers.

The *Leeds Mercury* of 23rd April 1906 reported: "The fact that Leeds were handsomely beaten on the play had the reverse of a soothing influence on the crowd, but it seemed at the close that hooting would be the extent of the trouble, for the referee had only a few yards to go to reach his dressing room, and there were a number of policemen, officials and players around him. However, some person who was not detected put in a well-directed shot with a sharp piece of cement, and struck the referee on the nose, inflicting a slight wound.

"One or two more missiles were thrown without damage, and for a time a crowd of lads and young

men hung about outside the ground. The police were nearly as strong numerically as the knot of hangers on, and the latter were cleared away from the vicinity of the club premises. So the incident ended. More will be heard of it, no doubt, when the referee makes his report. It is unfortunate that the Leeds club should have to suffer for the misdeeds of a few larrikins, for if a large section of the crowd amused itself by hooting, the dangerous hostility to the referee was the work of only two or three."

Without doubt any such incident at Elland Road in the early 1900s could be described as 'isolated', which was far from the case in the desolate post-Revie years. The 1980s were generally regarded as the epitome of the anti-football era at Leeds United, where dismal attendances, wretched entertainment and low self-esteem contributed to an eight-year malaise on the pitch and a rapid rise in widespread thuggery off it. Physically dominant players like Kenny Burns, Ian Baird, Neil Aspin, Brendan Ormsby, David Batty, Noel Blake, Mark Aizlewood, John Sheridan and Ian Snodin were heralded by the fans as their minders on the pitch and games often took on a brutal edge which Elland Road lapped up salaciously.

During Leeds' decline from the Revie era the positive buoyancy of the Elland Road crowd became not only hostile but decidedly sour, particularly with regards to open and frequent outbreaks of racism. The street campaign adopted by the National Front saw representatives selling the *Bulldog* newspaper on Lowfields Road before games, and many known figures within Leeds' hooligan firm were targeted and recruited. There were many verbal attacks on visiting black players at Elland Road, including Manchester City goalkeeper Alex Williams in September 1983, Portsmouth's Noel Blake in September 1984, several Aston Villa players in October 1985 and Crystal Palace's Andy Gray in October 1986. Gray would later publicly condemn his treatment at Elland Road, which he declared as probably the worst ground in the country for racial hatred, and this finally prompted some action. The FA had repeatedly threatened Leeds United with the closure of Elland Road for certain games, but the club failed to decisively act on the racism problem or even condemn it and were accused of gross complacency.

The matter was brought to a head by local newspapers, and following further public condemnation of a lack of action by the club a group of supporters, in conjunction with the Leeds Trades Council, set up a leafleting campaign called, 'Leeds Fans United Against Racism and Fascism' in October 1987. The Leeds Trade Council and Leeds Anti-Fascist Action Group called for a ban on National Front literature being sold at Elland Road, and also issued a report entitled 'Terror on the Terraces' in April 1988. In it Leeds United were left in no doubt as to their central role in proceedings. One quote in the report read: "For much of the last

LEEDS
UNITED

LEEDS UNITED AFC

OFFICIAL MATCHDAY
PROGRAMME No. 8
PRICE 35p

The future of Leeds United Association Football Club hangs in the balance.

This in no way exaggerates the position and must not be taken as an idle threat.

Despite repeated pleas and warnings, the mindless actions of a minority of the club's so-called followers last Saturday have placed an enormous degree of uncertainty over this great club.

We know from comments received in the last few days that many true supporters deplore what took place at the Newcastle game.

And we would ask for the help and co-operation of everyone who have Leeds United at heart — and we appreciate that this is the majority of our supporters — to help rid the club of the 'scab' element who, although small in numbers, have caused the club so many problems and whose loathsome actions now place the very existence of Leeds United in jeopardy.

LEAGUE DIVISION TWO
Saturday 6th November 1982

TODAY'S MATCH SPONSORS:

CHARLTON ATHLETIC

Carson Hadfields

In terms of impact, the strongest message Leeds United ever made in attempting to stamp out hooliganism at Elland Road. The match day programme cover, a historical document and at the time the only visual output from the club, is given over to a stark command that change must come.

fifteen years Elland Road football ground has been an important cog in the Leeds fascist machine."

This was swiftly followed by a fanzine called *Marching Altogether* which was launched just as the nationwide supporters' fanzine movement was beginning to give fans an independent voice. It didn't succeed straight away as initially Leeds United objected to the group's unauthorised use of the club badge, which it said inferred that the movement had official standing. The club distanced itself from the movement, but at last behind the scenes had begun to act itself. Eighteen thousand leaflets condemning racism were inserted into match day programmes and the Elland Road ground regulations were amended. Later, a similar statement signed by all the first team squad was issued. Black players Noel Blake and Vince Hilaire, both previously targets of Elland Road abuse, were signed for Leeds and became popular players, and in March 1989 Chris Fairclough also joined the club. In the background West Yorkshire Police had initiated 'Operation Wild Boar', which was an undercover operation that saw officers infiltrate the organised firms orchestrating violence and right-wing hatred at Leeds games. A combination of all the above initiatives from the police, the club and Leeds United fans' groups, and not least a successful football team, saw the racism and violence gradually disappear from Elland Road. The atmosphere was still intimidating and fiercely passionate, but channelled at least a little more positively.

Unfortunately, as ever in times of lean pickings, the crowd could still turn on individuals irrespective of race, and one of the most unsavoury on-pitch acts involved Mark Aizlewood, then the club captain, during a game against Walsall in 1989 at the tail end of Howard Wilkinson's first season in charge. Leeds were heading towards another glum mid-table finish and a disgruntled crowd was making the muscular Aizlewood its scapegoat for the club's ills. When the Elland Road populace 'breaks' it is rarely pleasant and the general long-term optimism resulting from the initial months of Howard Wilkinson's tenure had yet to truly kick-in. At 0-0 against the already relegated Walsall, Aizlewood missed a second half sitter in front of the Kop and received the rough end of the crowd's gathering vexation. A couple of minutes later Aizlewood was presented with another opportunity which he promptly buried for the game's only goal. The celebrating crowd was immediately silenced as Aizlewood approached the Kop and with vivid sincerity stuck two fingers up to them, with both hands, for several seconds, before blowing sarcastic kisses. Like a flicked switch the cheers turned to boos and Aizlewood's team-mates hastily pulled him away, and before the game kicked off again Wilkinson reacted by hauling his captain off the pitch and replacing him with David Batty. Alan Sutton recalls the incident: "I remember in the dressing room afterwards Gordon Strachan said to me privately 'listen, he's doing that, but he's also doing it to young

kids in the crowd as well'. The crowd were into him (Aizlewood) big time and that was his reaction. So Howard took him straight off and he bombed him off to Bradford, it was a black or white situation with anything like that."

Howard Wilkinson offers his thoughts on the incident and reveals the substitution was far from a kneejerk reaction and, more in keeping with his managerial style, was part of a more considered long term plan: "Mark scored a goal, he'd had a bad time from the fans and that resulted in him giving the V-sign. I obviously, by then, had my thoughts on the coming season and about recruits and Mark wasn't included in those plans, not in any first team sense anyway. So in the circumstances, given it was the end of the season, from his point of view, from the club's point of view, from everybody's point of view it was better that I ended it then, rather than let it fester on. I had my reasons for making changes for next season and the fact that Mark wasn't in those plans had nothing to do with that day, my mind was made up before then." Nothing too much was said in the dressing room afterwards as maybe Aizlewood sensed himself that his Leeds career was coming to an end regardless of his actions, and the incident was something of a flamboyant finale for him. "I think I addressed them all," continues Howard. "I said, 'The nature of football is such that frustrations like that are best kept with yourself, you can't win. The best way to win is to go out, play well and score goals. I wouldn't say I had sympathy (for what he did) but on the other hand I wouldn't say that I couldn't understand it. These things happen, it's a very emotional game and sometimes fans vent their feelings, you might say, sometimes unreasonably, but if you play the game, if you're in the game, if you're earning your money out of the game then you know that these are the sort of things that you have to deal with, and there are ways of dealing with them." In the aftermath of the incident Aizlewood was stripped of the captaincy two days later and suspended for two weeks. This involved missing the last two games of the season, and indeed Aizlewood never played for the club again as he was sold to Bradford City in the summer.

As with the many on-pitch battles between combative players over the years, individual incidents of violence on the terraces are too numerous to summarise, but certainly games against Manchester United and other notable opposition had a crackling intensity that often boiled over into raging hatred. I remember Lee Sharpe scoring a last minute winner in a League Cup Semi-Final in 1991, and wheeling away to perform his trademark 'dance' in front of the small band of Manchester United fans in the Lowfields terrace amid a shower of coins, spittle and unbridled rage. Most games against Manchester United were like that in the early 1990s; acidic and brimming with so much wanton venom that CS gas would have been dismissed for its sweet-smelling bouquet.

The epic promotion tussle between Leeds and Sheffield United in 1990 also boiled over during the climactic Easter Monday clash at Elland Road, which Leeds won 4-0. Guests

Mark Aizlewood's parting shot as a Leeds United player, as he salutes the Kop following his winning goal versus Walsall in May 1989. The ref, sensing the rising wrath of the Elland Road crowd, beats a hasty retreat, whilst even Ian Baird is thinking "ooh, I think that's a touch aggressive Skipper".

of the directors from Sheffield United were verbally abused and terrorised in the West Stand directors' box, and the club were admonished from all angles. The directors' box was universally presumed to be a safe haven, an impregnable retreat away from the great unwashed. But not at Elland Road where, if the situation arose, such a hierarchy didn't exist and an 'anything goes' mentality appeared to prevail among some supporters, which further fuelled the perception that the ground was a tinderbox of danger and malignity.

As Leeds' fortunes improved and the game generally cleaned up its act, Leeds fans still retained an appetite for a ruck at Elland Road, even if it became more of a watching brief. It was in the early '00s when a famous on-pitch brawl took place that had been simmering for a number of years. Leeds played Tottenham Hotspur on 12th February 2000 and a healthy rivalry that had been bubbling between the two clubs, sparked initially by George Graham's controversial defection to Spurs in 1998, spilled over into a spectacular public melee. An ongoing feud had also been smouldering between Leeds midfielder Lee Bowyer and Spurs' Tim Sherwood, which had involved a number of altercations going back two or three years. As Leeds led 1-0, a mass brawl involving every player on the pitch erupted when Bowyer and Sherwood clashed in midfield, and as Elland Road echoed to the sound of the baying masses, it took several minutes to restore order. Both clubs were fined and threatened with a points deduction.

The acoustics of Elland Road appear to create a boiling cauldron that mentally disorientates opponents at its best/worst. Leeds fans have seen many a visiting defender or goalkeeper visibly capitulate, such as Sheffield United's Simon Tracey in the gladiatorial atmosphere of that Easter Monday promotion clash

in 1990. The bear-pit quality of the united crowd has often led to players being taunted with a ceaseless and remorseless antipathy until, quite often, they have cracked. I recall two AS Roma players literally seeing red in the closing stages of Leeds' 1-0 UEFA Cup win in 2000, as the crowd riled them into submission while Alan Smith harried them around Elland Road. Many goals have been scored as a result of direct mockery and derision, and on one occasion in 2001 Bradford City duo Stuart McCall and Andy Myers fought amongst themselves amid a humiliating 6-1 defeat. Leeds-born McCall was left with blood gushing from a facial wound received from his team-mate in a bizarre altercation that Elland Road met with rapturous applause and zero sympathy.

Despite today's era of corporate hospitality, copious cotton-wool safety measures and the clear absence of any such intimidatory sparks, Elland Road will forever hold an ambience of cold, unwelcoming hostility for some. Home fans are wisened and softened to it. But for visitors there will always be a gritty realism to attending Elland Road and an undercurrent of discomfort and apprehension, however much Lucas the Kop Cat larks around on the pitch, a plush away-fan-only bar is provided or the visitors are gifted a 2-0 half-time lead.

Leeds United are still the last truly unreconstructed major football club, and success might bring a smile to the faces, but the snarl is never far away. Whether it is the mismatched inelegance of the stands, the inhospitable cloistered vim of the nearby pubs, the derelict land and industrial estates that surround the ground or simply the Leeds fans' persecuted and rancorous mentality, Elland Road harbours a mistrust that visitors are seldom at ease with, and as such remains a traditional football ground that we wouldn't change for the world.

ND FULL D

LEEDS CITY GROUND LET TO AMATEURS.

LEASE TILL AUGUST, 1921.

Y

OLD SUPPORTERS' HOPES OF NEW PROFESSIONAL TEAM.

The future of the Leeds City football ground at Elland Road has been definitely settled to-day. Mr. W. H. Platts, who has taken over the liabilities and the winding-up generally of the Leeds City club, has decided to let the ground for the remainder of the season to the Yorkshire Amateurs Association Club. The Amateurs, who only came into existence as a club towards the close of last season, have their headquarters at present on the Redcote Farm ground, Haddon Place, Leeds, which used to be the playing field of the now defunct Northern Forces club.

With the winding up of the Leeds City club, the Amateurs have a chance such as is vouchsafed to very few amateur bodies. They realised this full well when, at a meeting of the mem-

at at
read
this
as to
pro-
An
n the
hint
this
with
al.
sure
tion,
posi-
sidy
e at

R

All
Labo
will b
says :
" I
nego
way
Staff.
addit
they
natio
" A
Labo
whole
tion c
negot
this
' Gen
" I
Labo
ponsi
have
not as
" I
mach

YORKSHIRE AMATEUR A.F.C.

A minor local football team they may be, but Yorkshire Amateur played an integral role in Leeds United becoming resident at Elland Road, and indeed in preventing the ground being sold and turned into a brickworks. The club was formed in November 1918 by a gentleman called Kolin Robertson. It was a time when Leeds City were emerging from their uncertain existence during World War I and were beginning to make preparations for their return to competitive league football. What happened to Leeds City after that is documented elsewhere, and Yorkshire Amateur were quick to seize upon an opportunity amid the confusion and uncertainty following the professional club's sudden and untimely demise.

During the first half of 1919, Yorkshire Amateur had been playing only friendlies as they sought to establish themselves as a major amateur club in the north of England. The club's headquarters was at Redcote Farm, Haddon Place in Leeds, but in a unanimous vote, club members agreed to apply for the tenancy of the newly vacated Elland Road ground. Mr W. H. Platts, who had taken over the liabilities and the winding up of Leeds City, agreed to let it to the club with the players making themselves responsible for the rent. This move thwarted the plans of many local developers looking at Elland Road's clay deposits with a view to opening a brickworks on the land. As the *Yorkshire Evening Post* reported in October 1919 "...Mr Platts entered into a contract to let the Elland Road ground to the Yorkshire Amateur Club for the remaining period of the lease, which expires in August 1921, with the option of renewal for another five years. The rent agreed upon was £250 per annum."

Elland Road was seen as the perfect platform from which Yorkshire Amateur could satisfy their ambitions. The honourable secretary of the club, Kolin Robertson, spoke to the *Yorkshire Evening Post* on the day of the lease agreement and declared: "...that the Yorkshire Amateurs, with the splendid opportunity now afforded to them, hope to establish amateur football in Leeds on a very high plane."

But they hadn't counted on the force of public will behind the unfortunate Leeds City, and the strength of local desire for that club to re-emerge and carry the 'Leeds' name in the professional Football League. It took only a matter of weeks for Leeds City to officially morph into Leeds United, and with many of the same personnel involved behind the scenes, naturally, the club wanted Elland Road back.

The auction to sell off the assets of Leeds City was held on 17th October, and on the same day a meeting took place to agree to form 'Leeds United'. It was not until 31st October that this was officially ratified and Leeds United took the place vacated by Leeds City Reserves in the Midland League for the remainder of the 1920/21 season, but almost immediately the move to take back Elland Road was also agreed.

Yorkshire Amateur had been tenants of Elland Road for less than a month and had played only a handful of friendly games on the ground, yet they offered to stand aside and give up the lease to Leeds United for the sum of £250, the amount they had already paid for a year's rent. This was not before they became Leeds United's first ever opponents, playing a friendly at Elland Road on 15th November 1919. Immediately laying the first brick of Fortress Elland Road, Leeds United won 5-2 and a week later began their professional life in the Midland League.

Yorkshire Amateur became founder members of the Yorkshire League in 1922. The club went on to share Harrogate Town's ground for a short time before finally establishing their own home at Bracken Edge in Harehills, also in 1922. Today Yorkshire Amateur remain at the same ground, and with a proud history behind them blotted only by inviting Peter Ridsdale to be the club's president in 2001. Over the years the club has produced a number of players that have gone on to play for Leeds United, such as Albert Saxton, a useful outside left who represented Leeds during World War II, and others who earned professional contracts, most notably Brian Deane, who played with distinction for Doncaster Rovers, Sheffield United, Leeds United, Benfica and, indeed, England.

A story in an October 1919 edition of the *Yorkshire Evening Post* detailing the short-lived letting of Elland Road to Yorkshire Amateur Football Club after Leeds City disbanded.

Z

ZENITH DATA SYSTEMS CUP

While Row Z and its evading occupants is perhaps the most common feature of Elland Road to have routinely participated in the ground's history, the Zenith Data Systems Cup merits recognition under the letter 'Z' for the sheer ignominy of much of the 'entertainment' it produced. Although the tournament was originally known as the Full Members Cup, and subsequently the Simod Cup, it is the Zenith Data Systems Cup name that is most strongly remembered as the competition that, in truth, never caught the imagination and, indeed, led to the lowest ever attendance at Elland Road for a competitive game involving Leeds United.

The tournament came about as a result of the banning of English clubs from European competition following the Heysel Disaster in 1985. While this only affected three or four clubs each season it was decided to form a new competition to fill the 'gap' left by the removal of the European Cup, UEFA Cup and European Cup Winners' Cup from the English football calendar.

Reaching the Full Members Cup Final itself pledged to provide a visit to the Twin Towers of Wembley. However, the meagre crowds the competition attracted suggests most fans expected the small print to include a clause which removed that dangling carrot should anyone still be interested at the Final stage.

Perhaps wise to this, in the first four years of the competition Leeds United never progressed further than the second round, playing just two games in each season. Indeed, Leeds exited the competition ingloriously by losing 2-0 away at Millwall two years running in 1987 and 1988; happy days. And while some of the away attendances were moderate, the Elland Road attendances were a fair reflection of the level of interest among Leeds United fans, who given the team's general fortunes were clearly in a sizeable huff with football.

Leeds' first home game was a 1-1 draw with Sheffield United on 16th October 1985, which attracted just 2,274 fans. There has never been a lower attendance for a competitive home game involving Leeds United before or since. A year later Leeds lost a local derby at Elland Road to Bradford City 1-0 after extra time, before 3,960 fans. 1987 saw a change in fortunes and a 3-0 win over Sheffield United was watched by 4,425 fans, by which time the competition had become known as the Simod Cup. But in 1988 only 3,220 fans watched a 3-1 win over Shrewsbury.

As Leeds' fortunes rose rapidly with the appointment of Howard Wilkinson, so in turn did their performances in the now Zenith Data Systems Cup. 1989/90 saw Leeds reach the Fourth Round, losing 2-0 to Aston Villa away. In that run they only played one game at Elland Road, a 1-0 win over Blackburn Rovers before 5,070 fans.

The next season was the one and only time that the competition truly stirred the club and its supporters. Wins over Wolves, Derby and Manchester City took Leeds to the Northern Area Final. In a two-legged affair, played amid a punishing glut of backlogged fixtures

for the club, Leeds eventually lost 6-4 on aggregate to Everton. The home leg was played on 19th March 1991 and a see-saw game ended 3-3 before a crowd of 13,387, easily the highest gate attracted to Elland Road for the competition. The second leg was played just two days later, both games were in midweek, and Leeds lost 3-1 after extra time. Another epic defeat with glory beckoning and Leeds fans cursed the knock-out format again for titillating them with false hope. The physical effect on the team amid a draining season was notable though, and it is perhaps telling that the following season, during which Leeds eventually won the League title, a Second Round exit at home to Nottingham Forest before 6,145 fans provoked only an indifferent reaction.

With the advent of the Premier League in 1992 and the reduction of the Football League to just three divisions, the Zenith Data Systems Cup was scrapped, amid almost universal approval.

ZERO

Teams that have played but never won at Elland Road in domestic league and cup games:

Accrington Stanley (Played 2 – lost 2)
Barnet (Played 1 – lost 1)
Boothtown (Played 1 – lost 1)
Bournemouth (Played 6 – lost 6)
Bradford Park Avenue (Played 7 – drew 1, lost 6)
Bristol Rovers (Played 9 – drew 4, lost 5)
Cambridge United (Played 2 – lost 2)
Chesterfield (Played 6 – drew 2, lost 4)
Darlington (Played 2 – drew 1, lost 1)
Exeter City (Played 2 – lost 2)
Gillingham (Played 5 – drew 1, lost 4)
Hartlepool United (Played 5 – lost 5)
Kettering Town (Played 1 – lost 1)
Leeds Steelworks (Played 1 – lost 1)
Milton Keynes Dons (Played 3 – drew 1, lost 2)
Nelson (Played 1 – lost 1)
Northampton Town (Played 5 – drew 2, lost 3)
Peterborough United (Played 4 – drew 1, lost 3)
Rushden & Diamonds (Played 1 – lost 1)
Southport (Played 1 – lost 1)
Torquay United (Played 1 – drew 1)
Wimbledon (Played 13 – drew 5, lost 8)
Wycombe Wanderers (Played 1 – drew 1)
Yeovil Town (Played 4 – lost 4)
York City (Played 1 – drew 1)

Teams that have played but never lost at Elland Road in domestic league and cup games:

Torquay United (Played 1 – drew 1)
Wycombe Wanderers (Played 1 – drew 1)
York City (Played 1 – drew 1)

- Billy Bremner scored six goals in the FA Cup for Leeds United, but none of them were at Elland Road. All were away or on neutral grounds.

- Arsenal have played seven cup games at Elland Road against Leeds United and never lost. In the FA Cup they have played six games, drawing two and winning four, and in the League Cup they have played one which was a 1-1 draw.

- Leeds United have never lost to an Italian, German or English team at Elland Road in European competition.

- Leeds United never lost in the European Cup Winners' Cup at Elland Road.

- In total, Leeds have only lost 11 out of 74 Elland Road games in European competition (to Real Madrid, Celtic and Rangers in the European Cup/Champions League, to Real Zaragoza and Ujpest Dosza in the Inter-Cities Fairs Cup, and to SK Lierse, Malaga, AS Monaco, PSV Eindhoven (twice) and Universitatea Craiova in the UEFA Cup).

- Matt Le Tissier was the first midfielder to score 100 Premier League goals, and he ended his career with 209 goals for Southampton in all competitions. But in 17 appearances against Leeds United, eight of which were at Elland Road, he never scored.

- Gary Kelly made 430 league appearances for Leeds United, but never scored a league goal at Elland Road. He scored four goals in his career, three away from home, and his only Elland Road goal came in the FA Cup against Wigan on 17th January 2006, his 478th out of 531 appearances for the club.

- In more modern times, Andy Hughes made 139 appearances for the club between 2007 and 2010, but never scored at Elland Road. His only goal came away at Millwall.

- Robert Snodgrass scored seven goals during the 2010/11 season, but none of them were scored at Elland Road.

- In the 2019/20 season Leeds United played five home games at the end of the season versus Fulham, Luton Town, Stoke City, Barnsley and Charlton Athletic with ZERO spectators attending due to the COVID-19 pandemic. At the time of writing they had also played five home games during their 2020/21 Premier League season with zero spectators present.

All facts correct as of the end of the 2019/20 season.

#ELLANDROADMEMORIES

Brought up in Birmingham but long told Elland Road was where my Grandad's ashes were buried (under the Gelderd End penalty spot), first match there Carlton Palmer scored a last minute winner, hooked

@gigsinparis

The Kop being orchestrated by Coller in the 70s/80s. A sight & sound to behold. Waccoes at the proper speed

@royceylufc

Stood on the fence that divided the Kop when we beat Sheff Utd in the promotion-winning season after Gary Speed's goal

@davidfirth11

I managed to climb through the West Stand toilets with 2 or 3 others & saw the last 20 minutes, after being locked out of the QPR FA Cup tie in 1987

@boothsj

In with West Ham fans on Lowfields Road for FA Cup Semi-Final v Everton - they'd never seen a scoreboard before and read every scrolling word out loud

@daverowson

The European nights were something special, the noise of MOT being sung round the ground

@kennybrown1964

Hearing Marching on Together from the M621 whilst running down to the ground after being stuck in traffic. Millwall PO Semis

@LeedsUnitedLiam

Leeds fans spontaneously bursting into song amid the graffitied walls of the Lowfields tunnel, before the giant East Stand appears

@steve_creek

1st game at Elland Road aged 15. November '95. 1-0 win against Chelsea. I felt like I'd entered a coliseum in ancient Rome

@Jase0909

The only time I was in the old Lowfields was to watch Man Utd fans wearing bike helmets cross the pitch from the Scratching Shed to the Kop and being repulsed

@AdrianTeakdesk

Boys' Pen: 50p to get in, once inside, in through one toilet door, out the other into Lowfields. Saving of 75p I think

@PeteWardPonte

My 1st game on 14/4/83. Tommy Wright's debut. Entered the Kop and the crowd were singing "You Are My Sunshine". Hairs stood up on the back of my neck

@SimonHelliwell

Leeds v Spurs at ER, my brother was in the toilet when we equalised, grown men jumping around mid-pee not knowing what to do with themselves

@danellis1993

Early memories of the Football Special bus from town, 50p Boys' Pen, then jump over into Kop for cup of Bovril and Chipmunk crisps, those were the days

@Distanttexan

Playing football in the West Stand Car Park at 2am before joining the queue to buy our Cup Final tickets in 1965

@mikexile

Elland Rd memories? Happy Mondays' Shaun Ryder: 'Brave Raver Brave Raver come down' as man climbs Europe's tallest floodlights

@OurLocalExpert

First game v Colchester League Cup '77 age 8 - smell of cigar smoke & Dad's sheepskin coat, 4-0 (Graham, Hankin, Jordan, Lorimer) #90milesanhour

@cadallacjukebox

Picking a spot on the Kop at start of 91/92 and not moving until we lost. Became known as "the appointed spot" #Undefeated

@LCSEd_Clarkyboy

I will always remember the floor of the East Stand Upper bouncing up and down beneath my feet during the Bristol Rovers promotion winning match

@BeenWilson

Running out of the Boys' Pen when the gates opened and watching the last 10 mins on the Kop, part of a fan's evolution

@MarkrReynard

When 'Underworld - Born Slippy' was on the loud speakers at 14:55 #lufc #goodtimes

@chanLUFC

Free bus from city centre to ER during Revie era. Bouncing along the road with both decks spamping feet and chanting. Poor drivers

@sbpjh

Sight of the diamond lights, smell of cigars, feel of a Kop surge, taste of a Balti Pie & sound of MOT being belted out. Every sense has a memory of ER

@MickHowe1969

Brooding, bristling, brilliant. Floodlights, fog, football. Menacing, mysterious, magnificent. #lufc

@andylimb

My first game as a young child. Utd v Forest. Dad got good seats so a five year old could see but with little money couldn't afford prog etc on top. Guy next to us noticed and showered this ardent Leeds fan with every goodie available...it was Matt Busby on a scouting exercise! And we won 1 - 0!!

Mike Abbott

Trying to engineer trips to Leeds with my Mum for Saturday afternoons so I could sit on the top of the 54 bus and keep my fingers crossed for heavy traffic so I could watch a glimpse of the action through the gap in the stands

@cavievoltaire

When Trackers (the peanut bar) were given out for free outside the ground, I remember when the away team's Keeper approached the Kop at the start of the 2nd half he got pelted with them. They had to clear them from the 18 yard box

@simmy1975

Most emotional... the video montage & Oasis song played on the screen after Gary Speed died. Nearly choked on my adam's apple

@royceylufc

One highlight was when I DIDN'T watch a match inside ER. FA Cup v QPR in '87. From the despair of not getting in to the utter joy on ER outside the south stand as first Bairdy scored and then the thrill of seeing Ormsby's winner from on the hill overlooking the ground. Pre cheese wedge days obviously!

@super_leeds70

First game us V Bradford. Jan 88. Can't forget climbing the stairs and seeing the crowd, the pitch, first time. My Dad watching my reaction closely. He told me later in life he wanted to capture the moment Leeds "got" me. It did and he did

@thetravellingb

Over 25 years going to Elland Road, lots of ups and downs: Best atmosphere Stuttgart at home. Best memory Strachan vs Leicester. Most painful moment being knocked out by a Gary McAllister shot stood on the Gelderd in the warm up

@FooWhiter

ACKNOWLEDGEMENTS

MANY THANKS TO ALL.

FOR THEIR EFFORT AND CO-OPERATION IN DESIGNING, PRODUCING AND PUBLISHING THE BOOK:
- Paul Camillin and Jane Camillin at Pitch Publishing and Duncan Olner and Matt Gilbey at Olner Pro Sport Media.

FOR INTERVIEWS AND CONTRIBUTIONS TO THE BOOK:
- Dave Cocker, Rob Kelly, Gary Edwards, John Cave, Reg French, Robert Endeacott, Ray Fell, Stephen Reynolds, Maureen Reynolds, Howard Wilkinson, Ross Pullan, Neil Pullan, Kiel Barrett, Bill Fotherby, Dougie Wales, Thom Kirwin, Stephen Talbot, Phil Beeton, Simon Rix, Andy Peterson, Darren Clark, Howard Mais, Alan Ryan, Kevin Mulligan, Gary Barrass, Chris Mabbott, Anne Booth, Paul Dews, Eddie Taylor, Karl Skirrow, Alan Sutton, Guy Roberts, Alan Howe, Chris Miller, Dave Kirby, Nick Hammond, Frances Segelman, Steven Dennis Parker – Sports Photographer formerly of Photopress (Leeds) Limited, Jason Stevens, Julian Barker, Adam Pope, Phil Hay, Andy McVeigh.

FOR HELP WITH RESEARCH, GENERAL ASSISTANCE, LEADING ME AWAY FROM BLIND ALLEYS AND PIECING TOGETHER INFORMATION:
- Graham Schofield, Frank Goddard, Edna Newton, Graham Edward MCIAT, Christopher Otter, Marc Bracha, Mark Raynor, Secret Leeds posters – Drapesy, LoinerPete, geoffb, Johnny39, The Parksider, buffaloskinner, Leodian, UncleMick, ChrisM, Bridget Howlett of LMA Enquiries, Helen Skilbeck and Louise-Ann Hand of Leeds Central Library and Information Service, Kenny Sharpe of www.LeedsUnitedprogrammeguide.com, Nick Roberts for help with research and support, Paul Gregson of www.WAFLL.com, Rose Gibson, James Hoyle of Pathe Images, Martina Oliver of Getty Images, Jane Chippindale of Johnstone Press, Jamie Guest of Leeds Transport Historical Society, Paul Kent, Dan Moylan, Sarah Collins at the League Managers' Association, David Peel, Martin Jarred, James Willoughby, Andy Pye, Andrew Varley, Alan Howe, Gary Edwards, Stephen Reynolds, Maureen Reynolds, Eddie Taylor, Phil Beeton, Charlotte Taylor, Matt Diamond, Paul Dews, Neil Jeffries, Alan Sutton, Johnny Lord, Lynn Whitbread, Brian Sanderson, James Sandom and Nadia Shukri at Red Light Management, Ross Pullan, Dave Cocker, John Chaplin, John Somerville, Graham Deacon of Aerofilms Archive Service, and finally the staff at Leeds Central Library local history section for their patience in repeatedly assisting me with the microfiche machine, Hayden Evans, Ernest Lundy, Thom Kirwin and Mark Broadley at Leeds United Football Club, Andy Shaw and Daniel Chapman.

SPECIAL THANKS TO:
- Laura Collins, David Clay, Paul Robinson and Nicola Furbisher at Yorkshire Evening Post Newspapers for their co-operation in assisting with research, allowing access to archive resources and authorising use of material
- Joe Gamble (www.joegamble.co.uk) for his dedication, skill, extreme patience and attention to detail with the Elland Road timeline graphics
- Daniel Chapman and Hayden Evans for help in arranging the foreword and of course David Batty for agreeing to support the book
- Chris Miller and Dave Kirby for contacting me at a vital time, allowing me to pool resources with them, bounce theories and wild assumptions around and steal their title for the introduction
- My parents Alan and Audrey Howe, my brothers Michael and Andrew Howe and especially my wife Elizabeth and daughter Ruby for their unwavering tolerance, understanding and support

PHOTO CREDITS
- Yorkshire Cricket Archives: page 137
- Andy Starmore: pages 91, 98, 142, 208, 247, 257, 264, back cover
- Gary Barrass: page 93
- William Dobson: pages 22, 34, 80, 81, 87, 253
- Guy Roberts/Ringways Group: 46/47, 57, 92, 99, 100, 162, 163, 164, 167, 170/171, 185, 191, 219, 250, 278, 279, 294, 295, 296, 297, 298/299, 300, back cover
- Ross Pullan: inside front cover, page 125, back cover
- Chris Robertshaw: page 63
- Tim Whelan: page 105
- David Dobson: page 82
- Nick Roberts: pages 46/47, 57
- Keith Fuller: pages 13, 33, 60, 69, 97, 118, 187, 240, 247, 282, 301
- John Grogan www.flickr.com/photos/johnnyg1955/: page 63
- Jari Ojanen: pages 109, 188, 209
- Gary Edwards: pages 26, 165, 193, 252
- Chris Miller/Dave Kirby: pages 36, 147
- Kenny Sharpe: pages 89, 143, 231
- www.ordnancesurvey.co.uk: pages 58, 146, 147, 250, 262, 289
- www.Old-Maps.com: page 211
- Yorkshire Evening Post Newspapers: pages 27, 59, 179, 181, 214, 238, 309, 311
- Alan Howe: pages 44, 74
- Tony Lazenby: page 202
- Stephen Reynolds/Maureen Reynolds: pages 85, 86, 103, 152, 231, 243, 285
- Steve Elsworth: pages 79, 102, 104, 190, 191, 217
- Andrew Varley from the Varley Picture Agency: pages 16, 18/19, 25, 27, 41, 52, 54, 56, 68, 72, 76, 98, 107, 108, 110, 123, 139, 149, 151, 154, 156, 157, 166, 169, 187, 194/195, 206/207, 220/221, 222, 248, 254, 274/275, 287
- Stuart Clarke Photography: pages 314/315
- Andrew Howe (www.andrew-howe.com): pages 111, 141, 183, 205, 291
- David Moylan: pages 121, 122, 123
- Nick Crebbin: page 160
- Tapani Olkku: page 256
- John Somerville: page 261
- Leeds Transport Historical Society: pages 271, 272, 273
- Leeds United A.F.C: pages 119, 168, 263, 270, 293, 307
- Leeds Library and Information Service, www.leodis.net: pages 145, 183, 184, 271, 286, 295, 297, 302
- West Yorkshire Archives Service: pages 149, 201
- Michael Barber: page 67
- Artemis Collection, Leeds City Council: page 272
- Arthur Waller and Graham A. Schofield: page 213
- Rob Kelly: pages 196, 197
- @leedsfanzines: page 306
- Steve Lawrence: pages 251, 269
- Press Association: pages 15, 133, 204
- Getty Images: front cover, pages 20, 77
- Alamy: pages 48/49, 101
- Jon Howe: pages 37, 42, 55, 93, 102, 103, 112, 127, 128, 135, 186, 189, 232, 233, 242, 249, 260, 266, 267, 285
- Andy Shaw: pages 28, 51, 175
- Thom Kirwin: page 73
- Paul Kent: page 82
- Simon Rix: page 160
- Clair Hufton: inside back cover
- Unknown: page 176

BIBLIOGRAPHY

BOOKS/PUBLICATIONS

The Origin and Development of Football in Leeds
Mike Green
[published by Mike Green]

Hunslet and Beeston in 1890 – Coal and Industry
C. G. Dickinson
[published by the University of Leeds]

Remembering How It Was: Mining in the Leeds Area
Granville Williams
[published by Leeds City Council]

Aspects of Leeds: Discovering Local History
[published by Barnsley Wharncliffe]

Beeston near Leeds
Keith Richards
[published by Beeston Local History Society]

Focus on Holbeck in 1881: With Reference to Holbeck Cemetery
Eve S. Tidswell
[published [Leeds]: Friends of Holbeck Cemetery]

"Swaps": Holbeck
editor Steve Truelove, various authors
[published Castleford: Yorkshire Arts Circus]

'Tis Thirty Years Since: Or, the History of an Industry
James Brodie
[published by Leeds: Beck & Inchbold, 1894]

Twisting my Melon
Shaun Ryder
[published by Transworld Publishers]

Hard Man, Hard Knocks
Terry Yorath
[published by Celluloid]

Marching On Together: My Life with Leeds United
Eddie Gray
[published by Hodder & Stoughton]

Leeds Transport (Volumes 1–5)
J. Soper
[published by Leeds Transport Historical Society]

100 Years of Leeds League Cricket
R. E. Wheatley
[published by Pannells Leeds & District Cricket League]

The Essential History of Leeds United
Andrew Mourant
[published by Headline]

Leeds United 1919–1996
Andrew Mourant
[published by Hamlyn]

Hamlyn Official Illustrated History of Leeds United
Andrew Mourant
[published by Hamlyn]

Leeds United: The Official History of the Club
Don Waters
[published by Wensum Books (Norwich) Limited]

The Ultimate Directory of English & Scottish Football Grounds 2nd edition 1888–2005
Paul and Shirley Smith
[published by Yore Publications]

The Leeds United Story
Martin Jarred & Malcolm MacDonald
[published by Breedon Books]

The Leeds United Cup Book 1920–1991
Martin Jarred & Malcolm MacDonald
[published by Breedon Books]

Leeds United The Complete Record
Martin Jarred & Malcolm MacDonald
[published by DB Publishing]

Leeds United The Complete European Record
Martin Jarred & Malcolm MacDonald
[published by Breedon Books]

Images of Sport: Leeds United Football Club
David Saffer & Howard Dapin
[published by Tempus Publishing Limited]

Elland Road Encyclopedia: An A-Z of Leeds United
Paul Harrison
[published by Mainstream Publishing]

The Football Grounds of England & Wales
Simon Inglis
[published by Collins Willow]

The Football Grounds of Great Britain
Simon Inglis
[published by Collins Willow]

The Leeds Rugby League Story
Dave Callaghan
[published by Breedon Books]

Leeds, Leeds, Leeds Magazine (1998–2011)
[published by Leeds United Publishing, IFG, Green Park Publications and Ignition]

100 Years of Leeds United
Daniel Chapman
[published by Icon Books]

Twelve at the Top: The Story in Words and Pictures of Leeds United's Great Years
Colin S. Jeffrey
[published by Colin S. Jeffrey, 1977]

NEWSPAPER ARCHIVES

Yorkshire Evening Post
Leeds Mercury
Yorkshire Post

WEBSITES

Leeds United Websites

www.ozwhitelufc.net.au
www.leedsunited.com
www.WAFLL.com
www.mightyleeds.co.uk
www.thesquareball.net
www.ludo1992.com
www.lufctalk.com
www.motforum.com
www.luscfullerton.co.uk
www.onemickjones.com
www.thebeatengeneration.co.uk
www.leedsunitedprogrammeguide.co.uk
www.network54.com
www.WACCOE.com
www.sheridan-dictates.com

Local Interest Sites

www.leodis.net
www.secretleeds.com
www.yorkshirepost.co.uk
www.yorkshireeveningpost.co.uk
www.stmarysbeeston.org.uk
www.tithemaps.leeds.gov.uk
www.southleedslife.wordpress.com
www.publicaccess.leeds.gov.uk

General Interest Sites

www.sabre-roads.org.uk
www.geograph.org.uk
www.mylearning.org
www.cricketarchive.co.uk
www.motorwayarchive.intservices.co.uk
www.defunctspeedway.co.uk
www.national-speedway-museum.co.uk
www.blackcountrybiker.blogspot.co.uk
www.lighting.phillips.com
www.igg.org.uk
www.boxrec.com
www.iMDb.com
www.VSLeeds.co.uk
www.addyourlocalhistory.WetPaint.com
www.LevelPlayingField.org.uk
www.englandfc.com
www.englandfootballonline.com
www.wsc.co.uk
www.footballgroundsinfocus.com
www.safetyatsportsgrounds.org.uk
www.stevesfootballstats.co.uk
www.nonleaguefootballhistory.co.uk
www.yorkshireamateur.co.uk
www.farsleyafc.co.uk
www.whitbytown.com
www.leedscougars.co.uk
www.wikipedia.org
www.greyhoundderby.com
www.telegraph.co.uk
www.guardian.co.uk
www.thetimes.co.uk
www.thebritishnewspaperarchive.co.uk
www.thefreelibrary.com
www.specialcollections.le.ac.uk
(Leeds Directories from 1800 to 1894)
www.old-maps.co.uk
www.ordnancesurvey.co.uk
www.gettyimages.co.uk
www.skyscrapercity.com
www.thisislondon.co.uk
www.untoldstories.co.uk
www.metro.co.uk
www.jehovahs-witness.net
www.freepages.genealogy.rootsweb.ancestory.com
www.queenconcerts.com
www.queenzone.com
www.songkick.com
www.pitchcare.com
www.rleague.com
www.rugbyleagueproject.org
www.hunslet.org
www.yorkshirefilmarchive.com
www.britishpathe.com
www.greyhoundracingtimes.co.uk

PROGRAMMES

Official match day programmes of Leeds United (published by Leeds United AFC, Leeds United Publishing, Greenpark Publishing, Ignition Publishing) have been used from the following seasons/games:

1965/66 v Sunderland

1973/74 v Derby County, Tottenham Hotspur

1974/75 v Luton Town, Manchester City

1979/80 v Everton

1980/81 v Tottenham Hotspur, Aston Villa, Crystal Palace

1981/82 v Wolverhampton Wanderers, Nottingham Forest, Coventry City, Stoke City

1983/84 v Newcastle United, Cardiff City, Manchester City

1984/85 v Grimsby Town

1985/86 v Bradford City, Sheffield United, Norwich City, Crystal Palace

1986/87 v Stoke City

1987/88 v Plymouth Argyle, Sheffield United, Aston Villa, Reading, Swindon Town, Bradford City

1988/89 v Chelsea, Plymouth Argyle, Manchester City, Watford

1989/90 v Middlesbrough, Blackburn Rovers, Bournemouth, Oldham Athletic, Hull City, Ipswich Town (FA Cup), Swindon Town

1990/91 v Crystal Palace, Manchester United, Tottenham Hotspur, Arsenal (FA Cup), Oldham Athletic (League Cup)

1991/92 v Nottingham Forest, Arsenal, Luton Town, Coventry City, Notts County, West Ham United, Tranmere Rovers (League Cup), Sheffield Wednesday, Queens Park Rangers

1992/93 v Middlesbrough, Sheffield Wednesday

1993/94 v West Ham United, Swindon Town, Arsenal, Southampton, Crewe Alexandra (FA Cup)

1994/95 v Newcastle United, Manchester United, Wimbledon, Coventry City, Ipswich Town, Mansfield Town (League Cup)

1995/96 v Tottenham Hotspur, Arsenal, Newcastle United

1996/97 v Portsmouth (FA Cup), Derby County, Newcastle United, Sheffield Wednesday, Nottingham Forest, Chelsea, Crystal Palace (FA Cup), West Ham United

1997/98 v Everton, Barnsley, Birmingham City (FA Cup), Aston Villa, Wimbledon, Coventry City, Crystal Palace, Grimsby Town (FA Cup)

1998/99 v Aston Villa, Blackburn Rovers, CS Maritimo (UEFA Cup), Wimbledon, Newcastle United, AS Roma (UEFA Cup), Charlton Athletic, Leicester City, Tottenham Hotspur

1999/00 v Newcastle United, Aston Villa, Middlesbrough, Sunderland, Watford

2000/01 v AC Milan (Champions League), Aston Villa

2001/02 v Southampton, Bolton Wanderers, Derby County

2002/03 v Newcastle United

2003/04 v Arsenal (FA Cup), Manchester City, Leicester City

2004/05 v Nottingham Forest

2005/06 v Cardiff City, Reading

2006/07 v Luton Town

2008/09 v Millwall, Peterborough United

2009/10 v Carlisle United, Southampton

2010/11 v Derby County, Hull City, Queens Park Rangers, Portsmouth, Norwich City